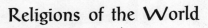

Religions of the World

D1562306

RELIGIONS

of the WORLD

S. Vernon McCasland
Professor Emeritus, University of Virginia

Grace E. Cairns
Florida State University

David C. Yu
Temple Buell College

RANDOM HOUSE   NEW YORK

FIRST PRINTING

Copyright © 1969 by Random House, Inc.
All rights reserved under International and Pan-American Copyright Conventions.
Published in the United States by Random House, Inc., New York, and simultaneously
in Canada by Random House of Canada Limited, Toronto.
Library of Congress Catalog Card Number: 69-10524
Manufactured in the United States of America by
The Haddon Craftsmen, Inc., Scranton, Pa.
Designed by Richard-Gabriel Rummonds.

To all the great persons, past and present,
known and unknown, who have given the world its religions.

Preface

The aim of this book is to present the major living religions of the world—the faiths by which the major peoples of the world live at the present time. However, in order to provide an understanding of the living religions, we have found it necessary to consider some of the religions of the past.

The order in which we have presented these religions has been chosen primarily on the basis of two principles: the first is phenomenological and has to do with the obvious similarities among some religions; the second is geographical. These two principles are often complementary. For example, the religions of Mesopotamia, Egypt, Greece, and Rome all developed in the Mediterranean area and are thus bound by the principle of geography; as contemporary polytheisms they also constitute, phenomenologically, a natural family. The main line of kinship runs from Mesopotamia to Egypt, from Egypt to Greece, and from Greece to Rome, although there are also minor lines that run directly from Mesopotamia to Greece and from Egypt to Rome.

Zoroastrianism, Judaism, Christianity, and Islam, the four great monotheisms, together make up one of the most definite families of religions; they are linked with one another by worship of one God, as well as by possession of high moral codes and similar eschatologies. The geographical bond between them lies in the fact that they all originated in the Middle East. The kinship of the religions of India stems from the fact that Jains, Buddhists, and Sikhs look back to Hinduism as their common mother. But one must go far beyond the frontiers of India to follow the story of Buddhism, so we have also been compelled by geography to consider Buddhism as one of the great religions of East Asia, the others being Confucianism, Taoism, and Shinto. The pervasive influence of Confucianism and Buddhism is indeed the bond that unites the diverse cultures of East Asia.

In using this book the order of the parts as well as of the chapters within each part may be varied in accordance with the interests of particular instructors and classes.

We believe that the religion of any people is closely related to its culture, and that it can therefore be best understood against the background of its geography, social life, and history. For that reason, we have introduced Parts II, III, IV, and V with chapters on the geography, history, and sociocultural life in those lands in which the religions under discussion are found or originated. Although dates and other forms of statistical information have been included, our main concern is, of course, with ideas and general concepts.

We have worked on this book as a team, primarily because we believe that the field is too vast and too complex for any one scholar to undertake alone. Although each of us has taught survey courses covering the entire field for many years, in this book we have limited our specific contributions to those areas in which each has the greatest competence. While the problems we faced were by no means minimal, we feel that our collaboration has enabled us to present all the religions we have dealt with in greater depth than would have been possible otherwise.

Because of the availability of inexpensive paperback translations and in order to conserve space, we have limited the extent of our quotations from source materials. In the bibliography for each part, we have marked with asterisks the titles of those paperbacks that we think are suitable for class use; where no paperback is available, we have indicated hardbound books.

In order to vitalize the presentation, we have made use of pictures; we also recommend the use of slides and filmstrips as well as moving pictures. The slides on Hinduism prepared by Professor Kenneth W. Morgan, of Colgate University, and the *Life* filmstrips on the religions of the world are among the excellent materials of this type. Films on the various religions are available from the McGraw-Hill Book Company, the Encyclopaedia Britannica, and some of the foreign embassies. Good wall maps showing the areas of the world in which the different religions are practiced should also be found helpful.

In addition to what I have written myself, I have also been responsible to the publisher for editorial supervision of the entire book; and I want to record my gratitude to Dr. Cairns and Dr. Yu for their competent collaboration. I am also indebted to Father E. Paul Doyle, School for Catholic Studies, Charlottesville, for reading the section on the Roman Catholic Church and giving me helpful suggestions; Rabbi Raymond Krinsky, Charlottesville, who read the chapter on Judaism and permitted me to benefit from his accurate knowledge; Professor Joseph M. Kitagawa, of the University of Chicago, for reading the sections on Buddhism in China and Japan and the chapter on Shinto; and the following professors and colleagues of the University of Virginia: Richard J. Coughlin, who read the section on primitive peoples; Harry J. Dell, the chapters on Mesopotamia and Egypt; James S. Constantine, the chapter on Greece; and Eugene N. Lane, the chapter on Rome.

It is a pleasure to thank Martha Obenshain, Jerrie Parmley, Ruth Ritchie, and Ann Wood for their expert typing; Peninah M. Blaustein, manuscript editor, Random House College Department, for her selfless devotion to this work; and my wife, Louise, for encouragement and assistance beyond measure.

S. Vernon McCasland
University of Virginia

June 21, 1968

Contents

Illustrations

Maps

PART I INTRODUCTION

1 The Elements of Religion

THE PHENOMENOLOGY OF RELIGION

The phenomenological approach to religion seeks to define religion, to isolate its essential elements, to discern its general pattern; to do so requires extensive observation and analysis, and above all the willingness to understand religious phenomena on their own terms. Essentially, the phenomenological approach brings within its purview the characteristic and dominant interests of entire cultures, and may therefore concern itself as much with secular life as with religious practices and beliefs. The phenomenology of religion is based on the work of anthropologists, philosophers, theologians, historians, and other students of culture. A phenomenologist studies music, painting, sculpture, architecture, dramatic arts, general literature, economic life, labor, government, and interprets symbols of many kinds. No human concern or activity is regarded by him as irrelevant to his study of religion. Further, he is committed to the proposition that all religions, despite their diversity and complexity, are similar in essence, and for that reason exhibit a profound kinship.

Rudolf Otto, whose book *The Idea of the Holy* (published in German in 1917 as *Das Heilige*) has become a classic, was one of the pioneers in this field. He saw the essence of all religion in the phenomenon of the *holy* viewed as a bipolar mystery, which combines the fascinating—the *mysterium fascinans*—with the terrifying—*mysterium tremendum*. As mystery, the holy can never be brought fully into the range of comprehension and in this sense it has its roots in irrationality. Nevertheless, it does play a creative role in human existence, in that it brings to man a sense of fullness of being. It is this phenomenon of the holy, Otto holds, that is the unique factor of all religions, adding that we never truly under-

stand any religion until we have uncovered in it the hidden depths
where the holy dwells.

Following in Otto's footsteps, but expanding his concept so as to
include the rational as well as the irrational element of the holy,
Mircea Eliade stresses the ideas of the *sacred* and the *profane,* which
he sees as the real substance of religion, pervading all its structures
and forms. The goal of the interpreter, he states, must be to bring
to light the sacred and the profane in all the varied expressions of
a culture. As he sees it, the sacred is the dynamic element in *hierophanies*—experiences in which one becomes aware that the holy
has manifested itself. Certain places, objects, times, persons, elements of personality, and the like may become sacred, causing the
area of the sacred to grow and that of the profane to be diminished.
It is also true that this process may be reversed: with cultural
changes, the sacred area may be eroded and eventually, under the
impact of the profane, vanish altogether. A culture may neglect and
later even reject the hierophanies by which it once lived, so that
what was at one time a religious culture may become a secular
culture in which the sacred is replaced by the profane.

Martin Buber approaches the problem of the essence of religion
through analysis of human personality in the concepts of *I-Thou*
and *I-It.* The world is twofold, he asserts, in accordance with our
two ways of viewing the world and the two primary words we
speak. The first of these primary words is I-Thou, in which the I
confronts another being as Thou. Such a relation is a creative
event. The I is created by its recognition of the Thou, just as the
Thou, on its part, is created by its recognition of the I. The other
primary word is I-It, in which the It is grasped by the I as a thing
to be known, used, experienced. A human being may be reduced
to the status of an It when he is deprived of his freedom, dominated,
or exploited; conversely, an inanimate object may take on the character of a Thou when the holy manifests itself through it. Buber
developed his philosophy in an effort to show man how to retain
his freedom and autonomy in the face of the increasing mechaniza-
tion of life. He holds that the self is free only in the I-Thou relationship, in which one enters into true spiritual life. In every such
relationship man touches the fringe of the Eternal Thou, which
truly creates man and makes him a real person.

According to Paul Tillich, religion is best understood as faith,
which is an ultimate concern and implies an ultimate reality.
Faith is not the same as a creed that one subscribes to as part of

belonging to a religious society or a church. While faith may be reflected in such creeds, it is not to be equated with any of them. Faith confronts man with a demand, a threat, and a promise. It demands submission of the will to what one regards as ultimate; it threatens nonbeing to one who rejects its demand; and it promises fulfillment to all who accept it. Religion has to do with true being: the fulfillment promised by faith is realization of the fullness of being.

We discern a similar pattern running through the thought of all these men, Otto, Eliade, Buber, and Tillich, who are representatives of the phenomenologists of religion. There is a close relationship between the holy of Otto, the sacred of Eliade, the I-Thou of Buber, and the ultimate as presented by Paul Tillich. On the basis of their analyses of the world's religions, these scholars have pointed out the common elements that bind all religions together: awareness of the holy, the idea of the sacred, the I-Thou relation, and the response of faith. In showing us how to find our way through the maze of religious phenomena of different cultures they have indicated the basic kinship of different religions.[1]

Religious man celebrates his participation in the creative life of the world; but religion also reflects man's frustrations and failures, his illnesses, old age, and death. Man is beset with fear and anxiety, being aware as he is of his unholiness, his profanity, his doubt, his guilt. Nevertheless in his religions we observe man searching for light, for truth, for hope—and finding them. It is with such things as these that all religions are concerned.

Applications of the Phenomenological Approach

The phenomenological approach provides us with criteria for analyzing a culture and recognizing its religious elements. The advantage of this method of study is that the criteria are such as to enable us to do justice to all cultures, from the lowest to the highest, recognizing the genius and originality of each culture without attempting to evaluate it in terms of religious ideas derived from our own culture.

The analyses of those mythologies that are present in most cultures serve as illustrations of the phenomenological approach. A myth is a story about a supernatural figure who plays a role in human history as if he himself were indeed a human being. Creation stories are examples of this; so too are stories that detect the

presence of gods in the inanimate phenomena of the natural world
or in those of the human personality. The best-known mythologies
in the Western world are those of the Babylonians, Egyptians,
Greeks, and Romans, along with those that are found in the religions of India and in Japanese Shinto.

It is not unusual for Western readers to minimize these myths
by regarding them as no more than interesting creations of the
imaginative fancies of early peoples. As literature became more
sophisticated—as it did among the Greeks and Romans—the early
myths came to be embellished by gifted writers and to be used, at
least in part, simply for purposes of entertainment. But even in
such predominantly literary forms, the religious overtones of the
myths still remained. Myths are never, of course, literal presenta-
tions of historical events, and to judge them in that light is to
misconstrue them.

In man's primary religious experience he usually apprehends the
holy in a personal way, and myths present the powers of either
nature or man in this personal way. For example, spirits and gods
appear in myths as persons. This personal view of the holy is found
in all religions ranging from those of preliterate peoples to those
of the most sophisticated. We can therefore refuse to study myths
as sources of knowledge of religion only if we reject the idea that
religions are generally based on belief in revelation, and that it is
the myth that most clearly demonstrates this revelatory character.
As a people grows in philosophical and scientific knowledge its
myths come to be accepted as symbols, rather than as statements of
historical facts, but they continue to express something of the sense
of mystery that they had when they first took shape.

The myths of the Greeks may be considered an example of this.
Initially, Zeus was the shining sky; in time, however, he acquired
many other attributes. He then reflected not only the fascination
and awe that the Greeks felt when they contemplated the night
sky, but also the terror inspired in them by the bolt of lightning
or the clap of thunder. Similarly, Poseidon represented the ever-
changing moods and the power of the sea, with which the Greeks,
and particularly those in the coastal areas, were familiar. Aphrodite
symbolized the natural tendencies of human beings to love—surely
one of the most mysterious, unpredictable, and often uncontrollable
experiences in the life of man. Ares, as the god of war, represented
its fury, its ruthlessness, its devastation.

From our point of view, mythology could be dismissed as fiction. But this is fiction with a purpose. The gods are presented in the myths with many of the characteristics of human beings, the chief difference being that they also possess superhuman powers. In their moral relations, however, the Greek gods, for all their superhuman powers, often behaved exactly as human beings would. The writers of the Greek myths did not hesitate to deal with the parts played by the gods in both the joys and sorrows of men. The basic religious character of much of Greek literature is exhibited with striking clarity in Greek theater; both their tragedies and their comedies were rooted in religious festivals.

The animal sacrifices that were characteristic of many peoples of antiquity take on new meaning when they are seen in the light of the phenomenology of religion. These sacrifices consisted mainly of animals that the peoples used for food; blood sacrifices were frequently accompanied by loaves of bread, vegetables, and wine. The worshiper placed on the table of the god—that is, on his altar—the food and drink that he himself ate. Thus laid on the altar with the proper words of consecration, the food was made sacred. A fire, representing the god, usually burned on the altar and, in most cases, consumed only the fat of the animal. Other parts of the sacrifices, which were suitable for food, were returned to the worshiper and his family, who then ate the food as a holy communion. These sacred meals were a means of participating in the holy, a form of spiritual renewal.

The ethical life as an expression of religion is also illuminated by this phenomenological approach. The culture of China may be taken as one illustration. Confucianism has been so concerned with the moral life that some scholars have held it to be only a system of ethics, not a religion. It is true that Confucianism did not develop either an elaborate mythology on the order of that of the Greeks, or a theology like that of the Judeo-Christian tradition, but it did develop remarkable insight into the moral life. If we take Martin Buber's approach to religion, from the standpoint of I-Thou and I-It relations, we gain a new appreciation of the religious element in Chinese culture, where strong emphasis is laid on the five cardinal relationships of society: sovereign and subject; man and wife; father and child; elder and younger brother; senior and junior friend. There is a specific attitude that is appropriate to each of these relationships, but all of them are marked by reciprocity; each member recognizes the dignity, the freedom, the integrity of the other. This is what Buber means by I-Thou; in each of these relationships, as Buber would say, the Chinese touches the fringe of the Eternal.

The relationship between philosophy and religion is also clarified by phenomenology. The kinship between them becomes apparent whenever philosophy inquires into reality—that is, speculates on the nature of being. That quest is called "ontology." Since the fourth century B.C. most philosophers of the Platonic tradition have interested themselves in this question. Plato's philosophy, idealism, held that the visible world is not the real world: it is temporal and evanescent. Because all its manifestations have a fleeting character, the idealists hold that these must be only temporary expressions of an invisible, eternal reality. Plato himself taught that only eternal ideas were truly real and all earthly forms merely their reflections or shadows. All his successors have held ontological views of a somewhat similar character. This preoccupation with the ultimate as real is close to the concern of the theologian, who also focuses on the true nature of the ultimate.

Indian culture has also produced notable schools of philosophy that have had an idealistic character. Vedanta is the best known of the Indian philosophical schools. Advaita (nondual) Vedanta regards the visible world as illusory (maya). It sees beyond the evanescent forms of the visible world an ultimate reality, which it calls Brahman; this is the universal self. The self or soul of an individual person is the Atman. Salvation, or deliverance from the cycle of reincarnation, is attained when one realizes that the Atman is Brahman. The Atman itself therefore is not temporary or individual, but identical with the universal Brahman, which is impersonal and eternal.

Buddhism holds to the concept of Nirvana, which is impersonal and eternal; liberation here means being swallowed up in Nirvana. Chinese Taoism, with its concept of the Tao, has arrived at a similar view: Tao is the eternal and impersonal, and yet the truly real. Complete realization of one's identification with the Tao is the true goal of life.

These examples of ontological thought show a profound interest in the ultimate, which is the fundamental concern of religion. Nor have philosophically based cultures, with their views of an impersonal ultimate, created an impassable gulf between themselves and religion. They have been impelled in their quest by a passion that is not entirely unlike that which has inspired the theologians. We are justified, therefore, in concluding that, in their effort to grasp the ultimate, these philosophers have caught a vision of the holy.

Mysticism approaches the holy through the intuitive, in contrast to the rational and volitional, elements of human personality. This approach has been most prominent in Hinduism, Buddhism, and Taoism, but has had some importance in Christianity and Islam and has on occasion appeared in Judaism, notably in the Hasidic movement of the late Middle Ages. The presupposition of mysticism is that man is able to experience a real participation in the holy. There are different degrees of mysticism in the various religions. It may be the same thing as the fullness of being that is experienced in the complete commitment of faith; or it may manifest itself as only a mild ecstasy, a warm glow of personality, an ineffable sense of security, of value, of meaning.

Mysticism does not necessarily repudiate reason, good works, or sacraments; it does transcend them. In its milder forms it may serve as an accompaniment to these other approaches to the holy. In extreme forms of mysticism, however, the mystic develops a unique procedure, a technique, a discipline of his own. Beginning with physical, moral, and intellectual achievements, which may require years to master, the mystic is then in a position to devote himself to meditation, concentration of the mind, and contemplation. His goal is to attain a vision, a hierophany, which may culminate in complete union with the holy.

The holy has to do with sacred inanimate objects; sacred animals, birds, persons; sacred places, times, rituals, words, books, music. It also has to do with other sacred phenomena—terrestrial, celestial, and cosmic. All these sacred things have been at times, and may continue to be, the occasion of hierophanies. It is these hierophanies that give both the myths and the sacred phenomena their meaning.

THE RELIGION OF PRIMITIVE PEOPLES

The word *primitive* is derived from the Latin *primitus,* which means "first of its kind," "for the first time," "firstly," "originally." As applied to individuals, *primitive* could be used to describe the Hebrew Adam, the Hindu Manu, the Chinese P'an-ku, or the Japanese Jimmu Tennō—each of whom was, in his own sphere, the first man, the absolute primitive. But this, of course, is not what is meant when one speaks of primitive peoples. Very few people today consider any one of them to be the absolutely first person on earth. As it is now used, (the word *primitive* is a cultural term.) It is meant to indicate that the individual or group so designated is part of a culture that, in comparison with our own culture, is (undeveloped, retarded, or backward,) and has few, if any, of those features of life which we call modern or civilized.

A truly primitive culture is (preliterate) whatever culture exists among such peoples is carried by oral tradition and handed down in that way from generation to generation. It has no libraries to collect, preserve, and pass along its growing knowledge and wisdom. Except for simple matters of custom, (each new generation of a primitive people has to start at the beginning.) One result is that a primitive society is essentially (a static society;) it has not found the means to achieve cultural progress. Whatever instruments and tools a member of such a society possesses are things that he finds ready at hand in nature: stones, pieces of wood, leaves, horns, shells, and so on. He has (no science, no engineering, no technology; no agriculture beyond the gathering of the fruits of nature; no means of communication or transportation aside from those with which every human being is equipped by nature.)

Few entirely primitive peoples exist in our time. Many peoples who are still relatively primitive have already taken a few steps in the direction of the tools, instruments, weapons, and technology that are characteristic of civilization. In varying degrees they have learned to use fire, to domesticate such animals as the dog and horse, to make clothing, build houses, and practice agriculture.

Every part of the earth that has been inhabited by man has at some time witnessed a development of aspects of culture, including religion, from lower to higher forms. Not that the same religious rites and ceremonies have occurred everywhere; but those that have occurred have exhibited a primitive character—that is, in terms of what we now regard as primitive. A thorough study of primitive religions, past and present, would cover the entire world. Even in our own time a complete survey of existing primitive religions would touch on every part of the globe, from the hot belts of the tropics to the frozen regions of both the Arctic and the Antarctic. While (most of the primitives of our time are of Negroid and Mongoloid racial stocks, some of them are Caucasoid)—for example, the

Ainu of the Japanese islands of Hokkaido and Sakhalin and the Lapps of Arctic Europe.

Social Organization and Government

Tribal organization is characteristic of primitive life, although any one people may include several affiliated tribes. Each tribe may in turn be subdivided into clans, and each clan into families. The organizational structure of a tribe will generally include outstanding persons (chieftains), each with his particular function, such as presiding over matters of war, the pursuits of peaceful life, or the performance of the religious rituals) Together these leaders constitute a council, in which important questions of tribal policy are decided upon.

The Iroquois of North America, at the time of the discovery of America, comprised five affiliated tribes: Mohawks, Oneidas, Onondagas, Cayugas, and Senecas. Some 200 years later, after the Tuscaroras had been expelled from North Carolina, they were admitted as a sixth tribe into the Iroquois league. Each of the six tribes was subdivided into clans, but the number of clans was not the same in all of them. The Mohawks and Oneidas had only three clans each; the other four tribes had seven each. The Wyandot tribe of Kansas was divided into twelve clans; the Delawares, in the region north of Delaware Bay, had three.[2]

Some such pattern of social organization was found among most of the Indian tribes of North America, the type of organization in each case being suited to the requirements of the particular group. In general, this holds true for primitive societies throughout the world. For example, Le Roy's study of the primitives of Africa shows a rather similar social structure. The Ba-vili tribe of Loango is based on the family. A village is simply an enlarged family, all of whose members reside together, with the head of the great family being at the same time the head of the village. All the people— including men, women, children, and slaves—are his people and recognize his authority. The villages in a certain area constitute a province; seven of these make up the Ba-vili people, who at that time recognized Maluango as their king.[3]

Nowhere among the primitives does one come upon any such complicated governmental organization as that of a modern state or nation, primarily because the very nature of primitive life does not require such complex organization. Indeed, an elaborate form of government could not be supported by a primitive society, which lacks the means of production, communication, transportation, and distribution that are characteristic of a modern society. For its own people, however, the primitive organization is probably adequate.

The Primitive and Nature

One of the most common ways of defining a primitive is to say that he is a (man who lives close to nature) A primitive does live close to nature, in a literal sense. His clothing, his house, his weapons, his tools, his food—all these may be limited almost exclusively to articles that he finds in the natural world about him and which he can use more or less in the state in which he finds them. Whatever garments he has are made from the bark of trees or the skins of animals. His home may be a tree or a clump of trees or it may be a cave; his weapons, clubs or stones; and his food, wild fruit, fish, animals, and birds, secured with little effort and often eaten without further preparation.

In addition to this, however, the primitive feels a kinship, a rapport with nature; he feels himself to be a part of nature. The life that he sees in nature he feels also exists in himself; like himself, nature is a living being. This is especially true of anything that moves: the animals, birds, trees, springs, rivers, winds, storms, lightning, rain, hail, sleet, snow. He deals with these phenomena as if they were beings that are able to understand and respond to him. His own reactions, whether they be of confidence or joy, fright or terror, are in response to the moods that he senses in nature itself.

One of the chief differences between a primitive and a civilized man is that the former still sees himself as a part of the visible, tangible world of nature, never having become separated from it. He still understands, responds to, communicates with nature. He belongs to its world and speaks its language; he deals with it face to face, on a personal basis. Civilized man, on the other hand, approaches nature essentially as a scientist does. Natural phenomena, whether inorganic or organic, are impersonal to the civilized man. He refers to any one of them as "it," not as "thou," not as a person. One of the most telling evidences of civilization is that civilized man has become separated from nature and no longer feels a kinship with it or sees himself as belonging to it. He has lost the primitive's ability to draw support, a sense of comradeship, from the strange yet not unfriendly life that resides in nature's inexhaustible wonders.

(Animism)

The view of the world that is held by most primitive peoples today is animism. For them, (most of the phenomena of the world, certainly the really important ones, are animated by spirits or souls that reside within them.) This is not to say that, in the mind of the primitive, all natural phenomena are absolutely equal in their significance for him. The blacks of Africa, for example, see the world about them as a structural social organization parallel to that of the human world. The spirit beings themselves are organized into families and tribes, each of which has its own style of functioning—indeed, its own sex, male or female.[4]

These spirit beings are not confined to the physical bodies that they customarily inhabit, but are able, even more than human beings are, to move about free of physical limitations, and invisible to the human eye. The world of primitive man is thus not composed of passive, inactive, inanimate objects, such as are seen by scientifically trained people, but is instead (inhabited by spirits that are thoroughly alive and active, expressive, responsive, and capable of doing things of their own volition) From the human point of view, this is of great importance, for these invisible spirits may interest themselves in the lives and destinies of human beings. They may turn out to be either (friends or foes) and as such may determine the whole course of human life. (They may bring prosperity, health, and happiness or else cause adversity, failure, and tragedy. The main concern of primitive man may therefore be to cultivate the good will and secure the assistance of the spirits that inhabit the same world in which he lives, but are ordinarily concealed from him by their invisibility. This explains many of the strange rites and ceremonies of primitive life.)

Ancestor Cults

Equally important among many primitive peoples is the belief that the spirits of the dead linger about the abodes of the living, continuing their interest and participation in, if not actual control of, all the affairs of the living) (That is why we often come upon elaborate rites intended to cultivate the souls of the dead and gain their assistance. Ordinarily it is the souls of the family ancestors—the parents, the grandparents, and other close relatives—that are involved most. In Confucianism, for example, side by side with a highly developed culture, an ancestor cult survives. Underneath all Chinese religions there is a substratum of animism, involving two classes of spirits: those of natural objects and the souls of ancestors. The ancestor cult in China can become important enough to be an economic burden on the poor, who may find themselves unable to provide the accepted kind of funerals for their dead, as well as the subsequent rites required by popular belief.

Mana and Taboo

While the primitive believes in a pervasive invisible power that controls his world, this is not a physical power, in the ordinary sense of the term. We are not justified in saying that the primitive has any conception of the supernatural—which is a philosophical concept and has meaning only in contrast with its opposite, the natural; to say that he has would be to impose our categories of thought on his. Yet there is no English word that is better than "supernatural" to designate the power that a primitive senses all about him. It is not his own physical strength, nor any skill he has learned, but a force that transcends his own powers.

Anthropologists use the word *mana*—a word found among Melanesians and Polynesians—for this uncanny power.[5] Words that are used by other groups for the same concept include *orenda* by the Iroquois, *manitou* by the Algonquins, *wakanda* by the Sioux, *mulunga* in East Africa, *hasina* in Madagascar. In general usage, *mana* now replaces all other terms to mean a potency apprehended by primitives in many aspects of their life. Exceptional persons possess mana: a ruler, a chief, a medicine man, a corpse, a woman during menstruation or in childbirth. It is also possessed by great warriors or hunters and by all persons who manifest exceptional skill. Moreover, the personal belongings of these mana-filled persons are also charged with this potency. The chief's clothing may not be worn by another, nor may his food be eaten by another—not even the left-over portions. To do so might bring instant death. Robertson's journal recording the discovery of Tahiti tells of a queen on that island who could not feed herself with her own hands—the hands were too full of the dangerous power—but had to be fed by two young women, who sat on either side of her.[6]

All the objects that are used in tribal rituals possess mana and must therefore be handled with care.

Everyone is aware of this powerful potency and desires to possess it or to control some of it in his own interest. Hence he will attempt to obtain articles that possess mana. Such articles serve as his charms, talismans, fetishes, amulets. He may carry them on his person or attached to his bow or spear; he takes them with him on the hunt or in battle, where he expects the mana to bring him success. This is probably the basis of the American Indian's practice of scalping his victims: the scalp was believed to carry the victim's power, so that the warrior who took the scalp secured additional mana for himself. Other primitive tribes cut off the victim's head and preserve the skull, while still others eat human beings, especially those that have been captured in war. In these ways they acquire or augment their mana supply. Such objects are like storage batteries charged with electricity, which one carries about to use whenever necessary; the more batteries one has, the greater one's power.

Taboo is closely related to mana, except that its meaning is negative. It is intended as a protection against unnecessary or sudden exposure to mana; the word itself means *beware, be careful.* Every mana-filled object will normally be surrounded by taboos. One must come into contact with mana only under carefully controlled conditions; otherwise such contact may be fatal. If we represent mana by the current of electricity carried on a high-powered cable, taboo would be represented by the insulation surrounding the cable, which is for the protection of persons who might otherwise make contact with the dangerous charge of electricity. The two concepts together are very important in the lives of primitive peoples. They may both seem irrational, perhaps even amusingly so, to us; to a primitive, however, they carry real meanings and, granting his presuppositions, they are perfectly logical.

Animatism

R. R. Marett, an eminent anthropologist, developed the view that animism, as we see it today among primitive peoples, was preceded by a preanimistic stage that he called *animatism,* in which the whole world was thought to be alive, and especially certain objects in it. In their present sense, the terms mana and taboo do not necessarily imply that spirits reside in the objects to which they are applied. They simply indicate that a mana object possesses a vital potency that is neither friendly nor unfriendly; like electricity, it is without any moral character and therefore capable of being either useful or destructive. There is much evidence to support this view, especially with regard to the mana objects such as charms and amulets that a man collects and carries on his person, or stores in his house or other place of abode. There is no need to assume that these objects obtain their power from the spirits that reside in them. All that is necessary is to believe that the object itself possesses a mysterious, powerful energy. Animism is therefore not the only theory that can account for this potency; in fact, one can attribute potency to an object without having any particular theory to account for it.

It would probably be accurate to conclude, therefore, that even among the primitives of our own time animism and animatism exist side by side, that some mana objects have spirits residing in them, while others do not. Yet both may possess an equal measure of mana.

At the same time, the theory of animism, once adopted, did constitute a tremendous step forward in primitive man's experience. What a change came over his view of the world when he began to believe that the mana potency was not a fixed quality that always remained in its object, but was instead a living being with feelings like his own, able to leave its object and move about in an invisible form! This was a real milestone in man's voyage of penetration into the mysteries surrounding him; it brought to that voyage not only greater possibilities for hope, but also fear or terror.

Totemism

The word *totem* is derived from the Algonquin word *ototeman,* meaning "his brother-sister kin," which refers to brothers and sisters born of the same mother. It was first introduced into English in 1791 by J. Long, who had discovered it during his travels among the Indians of North America.[8] The practice of totemism has been found to be most widespread in North America and Australia, but it also exists in Central America, Africa, and India. In parts of Asia,

FIGURE 1.1   Totemic magpie dance, Australia. (*Richard A. Gould: The American Museum of Natural History*)

South America, Polynesia, northern Africa, and arctic North America, however, totemism is unknown.

Totemism is a system of tribal divisions of primitive society based on the belief by a clan or tribe of people that it is united, in some mysterious way, by blood kinship with an animal clan, a bird clan, or that of an insect, or even one or another of the heavenly objects, such as rain or a star. Each member of the totem group is regarded as a member of its allied human clan, and all its members are bound together by a powerful covenant to support and protect it. The totem object or animal is highly revered by the human clan as well as protected by certain taboos. The members of a human clan will generally not kill the animals of its totem clan except for ceremonial purposes or in self-defense, although these animals may

be provided as food for another human clan. At certain times they slaughter totem animals and eat them in covenant rites, seeking thereby to strengthen or recover the blood kinship between the human and animal clans. At other times, they not only protect the totem animal but consider themselves safe in its presence.

Totemism was at one time believed to be the basis of exogamy, the practice of marrying outside of one's totem. But Frazer has shown that exogamy is practiced by clans that are unfamiliar with totemism.[9] Often a human tribe will believe itself to be descended from totemic ancestors. Some tribes in central Africa believe that at death each person is changed back into a totem animal. Even while they are alive, it is believed, members of the human clan tend to acquire the personality traits of the totem animal: one will become as skillful as a lion, as greedy as a hyena, as cowardly as a crow, as thievish as a hawk.

Many tribal rituals are based on myths about totemic ancestors (see Figure 1.1). When scholars first discovered these totemic ceremonies, some—Herbert Spencer in particular—believed that here at last they had found the origin of religion.[10] While it is probable that totemism has had an important influence on many religious ceremonials, the fact that some tribes in various parts of the earth do not practice totemism suggests that it cannot properly be considered the origin of all religion.

The Manitou

Another form of relationship between human beings and animals or other creatures to whom possession of supernatural powers is attributed is often designated by the Algonquin word *manitou*. Here (the animal becomes the guardian of his human comrade for life.) This phenomenon, which is best known in North, Central and South America, occurs in a variety of forms in different parts of the world. It is similar to the clan totem, but is not identical with it, nor can it with certainty be regarded as a deviation from it. It does not always occur where clan totemism is found, and sometimes appears where the clan totem is unknown. The animal guardian is not inherited from ancestors, as is the case with the clan totem, but is chosen by each individual for himself at puberty.

The usual procedure is for the pubertal boy to retire into the solitude of a forest or to some other retreat, where he engages in stern ascetic practices, denying himself food and sleep and even sometimes lacerating his body. By doing so, he eventually succeeds in inducing ecstatic dreams, trances, or visions. The first creature to appear to him in his ecstasy becomes his protector for life. It is believed that the animal possesses mana potency, which is now placed at the service of his protégé. In this way the boy acquires the mana power of his manitou and at the same time assumes its personality attributes. A friendly covenant relationship has been brought into existence, which is expected to endure until death. The man's life is in the keeping of his manitou: so long as the manitou lives, the man lives; when the manitou dies, they die together.[11]

The Nagual

The word *nagual* which is closely related to the word *manitou*, was used by Central American Indians to designate their own personal guardians—usually a bird, a snake, an alligator, or a wolf—in whom the mana potency or spirit is believed to reside. The phenomenon was first encountered by Spanish invaders when they came into contact with the tribes of Central America. The main difference from the manitou was that ordinarily the man carried the nagual with him for life; it was supposed to keep his human friend in good health and prosperous as long as he lived.[12] Frazer relates a legend preserved by the Spaniards about a battle with an Indian tribe, in which the naguals of the Indians fought in the form of serpents. The nagual of the first chief, however, was especially conspicuous because it was a large, beautiful, green bird. When the Spanish general killed this bird, the chief fell dead with it. Ideas such as these still appear in some parts of Africa and Asia, where the soul of man is on deposit, as it were, in an animal of the forest.

The natives of Central America believed that a man could change himself at will into the form of his nagual and in this disguise commit acts of violence, even murder, without being discovered. This belief has its parallel in the lamia of ancient Greece, the werewolf of medieval Europe, the man-tiger, man-lion, or man-leopard of other lands, and the bloodsucking vampires of European folklore.

The Indians of Central America also believed that a nagual could assume human form, either male or female, and as succubus or incubus engage in sexual orgies with either men or women. The story in the apocryphal Book of Tobit of the demon Asmodeus, who was in love with the girl Sarah and killed seven of her bridegrooms, shows that beliefs of this sort had already found their way into the Jewish religion by the end of the Old Testament period.

Ceremonials

The religion of primitive peoples is made up largely of ceremonials of one kind or another. Major tribal ceremonies are under the direction of a shaman, or medicine man, who is a specialist in such matters (see Figure 1.2). These rites have to do with affairs of general interest to the tribal group—among them, hunting, fishing, war, the care of flocks and herds, the planting and growing of crops —depending on the cultural advancement of the tribe. The ceremonials are intended to obtain the necessary mana, or the assistance of presiding spirits, in order to ensure success in all these undertakings. Other ceremonials, which have to do with the seasons, are related to the welfare of the tribe; still another cycle of ceremonials

centers in the family, dealing with conception, birth, growth, puberty, marriage, death and burial, and, in some cases, with reverence for the spirits of ancestors. The individual may also engage in his own private ceremonies: he knows certain rituals and possesses certain mana objects that are supposed to bring him personal skill, courage for the hunt and war, and protection against enemies, whether animal or human, as well as against illness of every sort.

There has been considerable debate over whether these ceremonials should be regarded as religion or as magic, but there is probably no final answer to that question, for it depends too much on how the terms "religion" and "magic" are defined. [We are accustomed to say that religion includes all those rites that allow autonomy to both man himself and the mana, spirit, or god with which he deals, while magic appears whenever man performs a ritual in order to compel his mana, spirit, or god to do his bidding.] But it is doubtful whether this set of categories would be understood by the primitive, who simply performs the rituals he believes will accomplish his purpose, with no thought of whether they are religion or magic. The very terms "religion" and "magic" are probably foreign to his way of thinking. From our point of view, it would be more correct to say that the primitive's science, art, drama, play, magic, and religion are bound together within the same complex of symbolic actions and rudimentary ideas. They express his sense of mystery, his hopes and fears, his joys and sorrows, his certainty and uncertainty, his philosophy and his faith.

Morality

It is difficult for us to form sound appraisals of the morality of primitive peoples, if only because of our tendency to judge them by our own way of life, to assume that our own customs, our mores, our moral insights are the standards by which all others must be judged. The importance of the family in primitive morality is shown by the widespread prevalence of totemism, which is itself rooted in the family and holds a fundamental place in primitive life. Yet there are various types of family organization. Both patriarchal types—where lineage is through the father—and matriarchal —where it is through the mother—are well known. So are monog-

FIGURE 1.2   A Tibetan nukhwa or shaman. (*Harrison Forman*)

amy, polygyny (a plurality of wives) and polyandry (a plurality of husbands). Polygyny is not so shocking to us, perhaps because of its place in the Judeo-Christian heritage, but polyandry is little known in Western culture. While it is generally rare, polyandry is practiced among a few peoples—for example, the Todas of India, the Tibetans, and the Sakanais, an Indian tribe of the Rocky Mountains. There are also reports of it among ancient Arabs, Britons, and Picts. But the scarcity of this form of marriage indicates that, where it does exist, it must have resulted from unusual circumstances, as is true of polygyny. The latter developed in cultures in which the men had been decimated by the dangers of hunting and war; it served not only to provide care for widows and orphans but also to provide more children with which to build up tribal strength. Polyandry, on the other hand, probably resulted from a scarcity of food, leading to the destruction of female infants and thereafter to a family in which several men share one woman. Usually the husbands are brothers, which also serves to keep property together.

One comes upon strange customs, as with the Eskimos, among whom wives are shared with guests; there are even instances of marital communism. Robertson's journal about the discovery of Tahiti leaves the impression at first that the women of that island were promiscuous. Yet careful reading of the journal shows that, once married, Tahitian women were expected to be faithful to their husbands—which appears, in fact, to be the general rule among primitive peoples. In passing judgment on primitive morality, it is necessary for us to keep our sense of perspective. These matters are closely related to the position of the woman in any given society. Her morality cannot be judged without reference to her social position, or her economic, legal, and political status—which, in turn, are dependent on the nature and structure of the society in which she lives. If these considerations are kept in mind, we shall probably have to conclude that the sex morality of primitive peoples is not very unlike our own.

Do Primitives Believe in God?

Our concept of God is based on a number of things, including: our biblical heritage, the theology of both Jews and Christians; Western philosophy from the Greeks to the present, now enriched by the thought of the Middle and Far East; the discoveries of modern science, including both the atom and space travel; and our economic, social, and political life. We cannot think of God as we do except in terms of that background of knowledge. But what equivalent does the primitive have? It would be unfair and unrealistic to expect him to hold any idea of a Supreme Being that would be comparable to Western man's.

On the other hand, such a competent scholar as Alexander Le Roy has produced much evidence in support of his conclusion that the African tribes among whom he worked do hold an idea of a God who is both transcendent and spiritual.[13] This is not an unreasonable conclusion. While he does not argue that these tribes have an advanced theology, of the kind that is now possible for civilized man, he does hold that these primitives believe in a Supreme Being who is appropriate to their knowledge of themselves and their world. It is probable that careful investigation would lead to a similar conclusion with regard to the faith of most primitive peoples.

NOTES

1. For a further discussion of Buber, see pp. 221 f. For a further discussion of Tillich, see pp. 221 f.
2. J. G. Frazer, *Totemism and Exogamy* (London, 1910), III, 4–7, 30, 39.
3. Alexander Le Roy, *The Religion of the Primitives* (New York: Macmillan, 1922), pp. 64–65.
4. *Ibid.*, p. 55.
5. R. H. Codrington, *The Melanesians* (Oxford: Clarendon Press, 1891).
6. George Robertson, *The Discovery of Tahiti* (London: Hakluyt Society, 1948), p. 204.
7. R. R. Marett, *The Threshold of Religion* (London: Methuen, 1909).
8. J. Long, *Voyages and Travels of an Indian Interpreter and Trader* (London, 1791).
9. Frazer, *op. cit.*, IV, 10 f.
10. Herbert L. Spencer, *The Principles of Sociology* (New York, 1896).
11. Frazer, *op. cit.*, III, 436 ff.
12. *Ibid.*, pp. 439 ff.
13. Le Roy, *op. cit.*, pp. 20–131.

Bibliography

GENERAL REFERENCE BOOKS

Archer, John Clark. *Faiths Men Live By*, rev. by Carl E. Purinton. New York: Ronald Press, 1958.

Buttrick, George A., ed. *The Interpreter's Dictionary of the Bible*, 4 vols. Nashville: Abingdon, 1962.

Hastings, James, ed. *Encyclopedia of Religion and Ethics*, 13 vols., New York: Scribner, 1908–1927.

————. *A Dictionary of the Bible*, 4th ed. rev. by F. C. Grant and H. H. Rowley. New York: Scribner, 1927.

Long, Charles A., ed. *Alpha: The Myths of Creation*. New York: Braziller, 1963.

Moore, George Foote, *History of Religions*, 2 vols. New York: Scribner, 1920, 1932.

Müller, F. Max, ed. *Sacred Books of the East*, 50 vols. Varanesi, India: Motilal Banarsidass, 1963.

La Saussaye, Chantepie de, ed. *Lehrbuch der Religionsgeschichte*, 2 vols., 4th ed. rev. by A. Bertholet and E. Lehmann. Tübingen: J. C. B. Mohr, 1926.

PHENOMENOLOGY OF RELIGION

*Buber, Martin. *I and Thou*. New York: Scribner, 1958.

Burtt, Edwin A. *Man Seeks the Divine*, 2nd ed. New York: Harper and Row, 1964.

*Eliade, Mircea. *Patterns in Comparative Religion*. Cleveland: Meridian Books, 1963.

* Indicates paperback.

*————. *The Sacred and the Profane.* New York: Harper Torchbooks, 1961.

————. *Birth and Rebirth: The Religious Meaning of Rebirth in Human Culture.* New York: Harper and Row, 1967.

King, Winston L. *Introduction to Religion.* New York: Harper and Row, 1954.

*Leeuw, Gerardus van der. *Religion in Essence and Manifestation,* 2 vols. New York: Harper Torchbooks, 1963.

Lessa, William A., and Evon Z. Vogt. *Reader in Comparative Religion.* New York: Harper and Row, 1965.

*Otto, Rudolf. *The Idea of the Holy.* New York: Galaxy, 1929.

*Smith, Wilfred Cantwell. *The Faith of Other Men.* New York: New American Library, 1962.

————. *The Meaning and End of Religion.* New York: Macmillan, 1963.

*Tillich, Paul. *Biblical Religion and the Search for Ultimate Reality.* Chicago: Phoenix, 1955.

*————. *The Dynamics of Faith.* New York: Harper Torchbooks, 1957.

*Wach, Joachim. *Sociology of Religion.* Chicago: Phoenix, 1944.

*————. *The Comparative Study of Religion.* New York: Columbia University Press, 1961.

RELIGION OF PRIMITIVE PEOPLES

Boas, Franz. *The Mind of Primitive Man.* New York: Macmillan, 1911.

Bowers, A. W. *Mandan Social and Ceremonial Organization.* Chicago: University of Chicago Press, 1950.

Burkett, M. C. *The Old Stone Age.* New York: Macmillan, 1933.

Codrington, R. H. *The Melanesians.* Oxford: Clarendon Press, 1891.

*Dubois, Cora. *The People of Alor.* New York: Harper Torchbooks, 1961.

*Durkheim, Emile. *The Elementary Forms of the Religious Life.* Glencoe: Free Press, 1954.

*Eliade, Mircea. *The Sacred and the Profane.* New York: Harper Torchbooks, 1961.

*————. *Shamanism.* New York: Pantheon, 1964.

Frazer, James G. *Totemism and Exogamy,* 4 vols. London, 1910.

————. *The Golden Bough: A Study in Magic and Religion,* 12 vols. London: Macmillan, 1911–1915.

————. *The Fear of the Dead in Primitive Religion,* 3 vols. London: Macmillan, 1933–1936.

Goode, William J. *Religion among the Primitives*. Glencoe: Free Press, 1951.

Jensen, Adolf E. *Myth and Cult among Primitives*. Chicago: University of Chicago Press, 1963.

Le Roy, Alexander. *The Religion of the Primitives*. New York: Macmillan, 1922.

Lowie, Robert H. *Primitive Religion*. New York: Liveright, 1924.

*Malinowski, Bronislaw. *Magic, Science and Religion, and Other Essays*. Garden City: Doubleday Anchor Books, 1954.

Marett, R. R. *The Threshold of Religion*. London: Methuen, 1909.

*Mead, Margaret. *Sex and Temperament*. New York: Mentor, 1950.

Norbeck, Edward. *Religion in Primitive Society*. New York: Harper and Row, 1961.

Parsons, E. C. *Pueblo Indian Religion*. Chicago: University of Chicago Press, 1939.

Reichard, G. A. *Navaho Religion*, 2 vols. New York: Pantheon, 1950.

Rivers, W. H. R. *The Todas*. London: Macmillan, 1906.

Schmidt, Wilhelm. *The Origin and Growth of Religion*. London: Methuen, 1931.

Wallis, Wilson D. *Religion in Primitive Cultures*. New York: Crofts, 1931.

Weyer, Edward, Jr. *The Eskimos*. New Haven: Yale University Press, 1932.

―――. *Primitive Peoples Today*. New York: Doubleday, 1960.

PART II POLYTHEISMS OF MESOPOTAMIA AND THE ANCIENT MEDITERRANEAN WORLD

2 Mesopotamia
and the Ancient Mediterranean World

MESOPOTAMIA

Mesopotamia ("between the rivers") is the picturesque name the ancient Greeks gave to the strip of land lying between the Tigris and the Euphrates. These rivers have their source in the towering mountains of Armenia. The Euphrates is a sluggish stream that follows a meandering course of about 1,700 miles. After leaving the mountains of Armenia, it goes southwestward as if to empty into the Mediterranean, but then turns south through Turkey and Syria, and finally southeastward, making its way across northern Arabia before reaching the Persian Gulf. Only two tributaries reinforce it after it leaves the mountains. The Tigris flows more swiftly, fed by numerous strong tributaries from the Kurdistan highlands and the Zagros Mountains.

During the course of their long journeys, the waters of both these rivers collect loads of silt, which they finally deposit in the Persian Gulf. As a result, the shoreline of this gulf is pushed back into the sea about seventy-two feet each year, or a mile and a half each century. Since the time of Herodotus, the shoreline has retreated some thirty-five miles, and, according to some scholars, at one time the Persian Gulf reached inland as far as the present city of Baghdad. The entire area from Baghdad southward consists of alluvial soil, deposited there by the two great rivers during the course of some 20,000 years.

It was this land, made fertile by the intelligence and energy of men who knew how to get water to the otherwise dusty, worthless soil by means of canals between the two rivers, that made possible the extraordinary civilizations which arose in Mesopotamia in ancient times. The area has a desertlike climate, with only six inches of rain a year; the desert sun brings either life or death to all that it touches; hot winds blow out of the Arabian Desert; and the land is sometimes swept by storms that rush down out of the eastern and northern highlands. But in ancient days the whole area from Baghdad to the gulf was filled with gardens, orchards, and fields. The region was a paradise, the envy of the ancient world, and it produced the richest and most powerful nations of that part of the world for some 2,000 years.

Historical Background

When the peoples of Mesopotamia were not at war among themselves, they were nevertheless not free from dangers from beyond their borders, for the area had no natural barriers: mountain tribesmen from beyond the Tigris were always seeking to raid the settled areas across the river, Arabs came out of the deserts to the west, and still other mighty peoples pressed in from the northern mountains and beyond. The result was that, in order to prosper in Mesopotamia, the peoples that lived there had to be vigorous and brave. It is not surprising, therefore, that some of the fiercest peoples, some of the most powerful armies, and some of the most ambitious rulers of antiquity came from the "land between the rivers."

Little is known about the prehistoric tribes that presumably roamed the arid region of northern Mesopotamia, or else constructed huts by the marshes that had formed where the two great rivers emptied into the gulf. Whatever was left around the marshes by such inhabitants was soon buried by the mud of the growing delta. But in the region beyond the most ancient shoreline, just above the present city of Baghdad, archaeologists have uncovered neolithic villages that stood there not later than 5000 B.C. One of these is Tell Hasunna, not far below Mosul; a second is the lowest stratum of the mound of ancient Nineveh, across the Tigris from Mosul. A third neolithic village has been found at Tepe Gawra, some twelve miles northwest of Nineveh. Artifacts left behind show tools and weapons of stone and other natural materials, similar to those used today by primitive and semiprimitive peoples.

The discovery of the use of copper about 4500 B.C. ushered in the first important culture of Mesopotamia, which emerged in the northern area. Tell Halaf on the Khabur River was the first site of this stage of Mesopotamian culture to be uncovered.

Another 500 years passed before the shoreline of the Persian

Gulf receded sufficiently to allow a settled culture to develop in the southern part of Mesopotamia—that is, in Babylonia. From about 4000 B.C. on, however, we have a continuous record of civilizations in the southern area. The construction of irrigation canals was one of the greatest attainments of that period; indeed, they made the new culture possible and the cultivation of the rich alluvial delta brought wealth and power to Babylonia. The first evidence of Babylonian culture was found at Tell el-Obeid, a mound about four and a half miles northwest of Ur, the city from which the biblical Abraham migrated. During the biblical period both these cities were located on the west bank of the Euphrates; but since then the river has changed its course and left them standing some miles back in the desert. Evidence of the Obeidian culture has also been found in the lower strata of other cities of the area, such as Ur, Uruk, Lagash, and Eridu, as well as in the corresponding stratum of the mound of Tepe Gawra near the site of Nineveh, across the Tigris. The earliest houses of this Obeidian period were built of reeds from the marshes; these were soon followed by those built of mud-brick, neither stone nor wood being available. Weapons and tools were made of copper. During the Obeidian period Babylonian culture assumed the forms it was to manifest for some 3,000 years.

The Sumerians were a non-Semitic, agricultural people of uncertain origin who began to occupy southern Mesopotamia around 4000 B.C. They irrigated the land, formed city-states for political protection, and imposed their language—Sumerian—upon the area.

The next great stage in Mesopotamian culture is reflected in discoveries at Uruk, about thirty-five miles north of Obeid but east of the river. The most important development here was the invention by the Sumerians of the cylinder seal—a stone cylinder, engraved in intaglio with symbols of identification, which left an impression when rolled across wax or soft clay that could be affixed to an object or document. The cylinder seal, in turn, led to the invention of writing, which occurred, also at Uruk, shortly thereafter. This not only facilitated long-range communications but also made it possible to record legal transactions and make other records of many kinds, including those of religious rituals and theology. The creation of libraries now became possible and contributed enormously to the growth of knowledge and the development of civilization. The writing materials used for this purpose

THE ROMAN EMPIRE (c. 117 A.D.)

0   100   200   300 miles

BRITAIN

Lutetia

Rhine R.

Danube R.

G A U L

Po R.

I T A L Y

ADRIATIC SEA

ATLANTIC OCEAN

S P A I N

Rome

Capua

Naples

Dyrrhachium

Appolloni

Appian Way

Brundisium

SARDINIA

M E D I T E R R A N E A N

Hippo Regius

Caesarea

Carthage

SICILY

Syracuse

MALTA

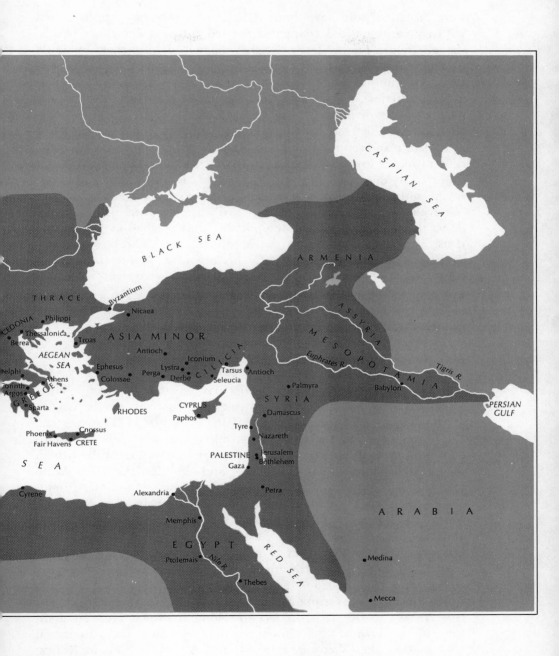

were tablets of soft clay, about the size of a cake of soap, inscribed with conventionalized characters pressed into the clay by a wedge-shaped stylus. The tablets were then baked, making them virtually indestructible. Vast quantities of these tablets have been recovered from the mounds of Mesopotamia. Many have also been found in other countries, such as Syria and Egypt, with which Mesopotamia had commercial, political, and cultural contacts.

As early as 2600 B.C. Semitic peoples, probably from Arabia, began to infiltrate and soon to dominate Mesopotamia. The earliest Semitic center that is known was Mari, on the north Euphrates; this was followed by the better known Akkad and Babylon, on the Euphrates in the south, and Nineveh, on the Tigris to the east. Babylon and Nineveh conquered each other in turn, at times establishing kingdoms that included all of Mesopotamia and reached as far beyond it as Syria and Palestine on the Mediterranean. The power of the Semitic kingdoms was not finally broken until Cyrus the Persian conquered Babylon in 539 B.C.[1] The Persians were overthrown, in turn, by Alexander the Great in 331 B.C.

EGYPT

The culture of ancient Egypt, which rivaled that of Mesopotamia in importance and surpassed it in splendor, owed its very existence to the Nile, itself more magnificent than either the Tigris or the Euphrates, or even the two of them taken together. The Egyptians were undoubtedly quite well aware of the deserts that walled them in on either side, the almost rainless and cloudless sky, the blazing sun, the brilliant stars that hung large and low in the desert night, the cooling breeze that came most of the time from the sea on the north, the hot wind that occasionally rushed in out of the south-west with its stifling load of dust. But it was the Nile that they knew best and loved as they loved a father or a mother. They were indeed children of the Nile for it was their source of life, bringing them water and food and giving them work.

Next to the Mississippi-Missouri system, the Nile is the longest river in the world; it is, in fact, the longest single river. Its main branch, the White Nile, rises three degrees below the equator in Africa—the lakes Victoria, Edward, and Albert, located in Kenya,

Tanzania, Uganda, and the Congo, supply its headwaters—and it flows almost 4,000 miles as it meanders to the Mediterranean. Six times during this long course, the free movement of the river is slowed down by great cataracts, where the stream has had to cut through upturned strata of hard rock. The last of these, which is called the "first" cataract and is only 570 miles from the sea, is where Egypt as it was known in antiquity actually began.

The cataracts made it impossible for boats from Lower Egypt to get beyond them, and they protected Egypt against invaders from Africa. The Nile was Egypt's only highway, there being virtually no other means of transportation. Aswan, just below the first cataract, became an important marketplace; indeed, that is what the name means. Here Egyptian merchants and African traders met to exchange their wares.

At Khartoum, above the sixth cataract, the White Nile is reinforced by a strong tributary which comes down from Ethiopia on the east. It rises in Lake Tana and is called the Blue Nile, deriving its name from the cast of the silt it brings down every spring when rains fall in the highlands. The Atbara, another stream from Ethiopia, enters the Nile about 140 miles farther down. The immense volumes of water that these two streams pour into the Nile cause the annual inundations which begin in June and crest in October or November, overflowing the river banks and irrigating and enriching the valley all the way to the sea. At its crest below Aswan, the water rises about twenty-six feet; it also rises about twenty-three feet in Cairo some 400 miles north. Then it enters the delta, where in antiquity it broke up into seven outlets (now only two) before disappearing into the Mediterranean.

The delta is a triangular area of fertile soil of great depth, deposited there through the centuries by the flooding Nile. It filled up and replaced a bay that, in some prehistoric time, extended up from the sea almost to the point where the great pyramids now stand, just across the Nile west from Cairo. Thus the area lost what could have become a good seaport, and it has never had one since. But in its place the river's long, patient labor has created Egypt's best farming region.

The very nature of the Nile was such as to arouse a sense of wonder, of awe, in the hearts of those ancient people, who from a time before recorded history began watched its actions and observed its steady character, its inexhaustible energy, as well as its changing moods, year after year, as the seasons themselves repeated their cycle. Here was a vast stream of water coming from some mysterious source beyond the people's knowledge: they did not know its headwaters. In spite of the almost complete absence of rainfall, the river never failed to irrigate their land and thus to support their life. The annual overflow was the greatest miracle; each year, with the spring season, the water returned to its high level, bringing new life to the valley. How could a primitive people, with no information about lakes deep in Africa or the floods of Ethiopia, understand this annual wonder? The river appeared to be charged with mana; it was moved by a spirit, a god, who generously provided for the inhabitants of the valley. Thus the Nile became enshrined not only in their hearts, but also in their legends and myths, their religion. It became perhaps the most significant single element in the production of the arts, sciences, and philosophy that arose to adorn the long green paradise—so narrow that you can stand with one foot in a desert and the other in a cultivated garden on the east, while easily seeing the line where another desert meets the fields on the west.

Historical Background

Remains of neolithic villages that are still being uncovered from time to time along the borders of the Nile prove that man had begun to settle in this fertile area as early as 5000 B.C.; the village type of life itself shows that the men who lived there had already made considerable progress beyond the nomads who must have preceded them in the Nile Valley.

The use of copper and beautiful pottery attests to the rapid advances of the Nile culture by 4000 B.C. Boats made of papyrus plants tied together were already converting the river into a highway, and hunting and fishing along the Nile were thus facilitated; the exchange of produce developed between different regions; villages became more subject to attacks by marauders from other districts; and the foundation was laid for extensive conquests. Widely separated communities could now be welded together by military power, and small states with orderly governments became possible for the first time.

Two powerful states eventually arose, one in Upper Egypt and the other in Lower Egypt. The former included all communities between the first cataract and the delta; the latter was the delta itself. The kings of Upper Egypt wore tall, white, pointed crowns and used the lotus as their symbol; the rulers of Lower Egypt wore a diadem of red wickerwork, and the papyrus plant was their symbol. The capital of Upper Egypt was Ombos, some 440 miles from the sea; the capital of Lower Egypt was Behdet, close to modern Alexandria.

Menes, a king of Upper Egypt, is credited with conquering Lower Egypt, thereby founding the United Kingdom about 3110 B.C. He showed his political astuteness by combining his own white crown with the red diadem of the north to form a new crown appropriate for the United Kingdom, as well as building a new capital at Memphis, located at the head of the delta, where the borders of the two kingdoms came together. Memphis remained the capital of the United Kingdom for about a thousand years, a period usually designated as the Old Kingdom. It witnessed a phenomenal development of Egyptian culture, leaving as monumental evidence the great pyramids at Giza, the cemetery of the kings of the Old Kingdom.

About 2100 B.C., with the decline and fall of the Old Kingdom, which had been centered at Memphis, power shifted back to the south. Thebes, about 125 miles below the first cataract, became the new capital, and it remained dominant until around 1000 B.C., when the Pharaohs moved their headquarters back to the delta, a move made necessary not only by important new commercial developments in that area but also by increasing dangers of military invasions by peoples of Syria and Mesopotamia as well as by the Mediterranean nations. The capital remained in the delta area during the period of decadence, when Egypt was conquered first by Assyria, then in turn by Persia and Alexander the Great, and was finally absorbed by Rome in 30 B.C.

GREECE

While Greece can boast of no great river, it is cut by towering mountains and bounded on the west, south, and east by the sea. Most of its rivers are short: they rise in the mountains and their waters rush down swiftly when it rains; otherwise they are dry.

The mainland of Greece is the southern end of the Balkan
Peninsula, which extends southward out of Europe into the Mediterranean. The Pindus Mountains form its sharp, rough backbone.
Mount Olympus, the mythical abode of the Greek gods, rises to a
height of 9,793 feet on the border between Thessaly and Macedonia, and its snow-capped peaks look down on the Aegean below
Thessalonica. Mount Parnassus, near the shrine of Apollo in Phocis,
attains a height of 8,061 feet, and is pictured in Greek mythology
as a favorite haunt of Apollo and his retinue.

Greece is cut almost in half by the Corinthian and Saronic Gulfs.
Only the Isthmus of Corinth, some twenty miles long, and at one
point only four miles wide, remains to connect northern Greece
with the Peloponnesus to the south. The irregular coastline of
Greece is rough, broken by gulfs and bays, and provides numerous
harbors, so that the Greeks quite naturally became sailors and
merchants, their chief rivals being the Phoenicians. But their proximity to the sea also brought dangers: hostile peoples could attack
them by sea from every side except the north.

Southern Greece was the location of Mycenae, Pylos, Tiryns,
Corinth, Epidaurus, Sparta, and other historic places, including
Olympia, the site of the Olympic Games. Its main provinces in ancient
times were Elis, Achaia, Argolis, Arcadia, Messenia, and Laconia.
The most important political divisions of northern Greece were
Macedonia, Thessaly, Epirus, Aetolia, Phocis, Boeotia, and Attica.

Historical Background

The earliest inhabitants of both the mainland of Greece and the
adjacent islands were the Pelasgians, a non-Indo-European people,
who were overrun by invasions of Indo-Europeans, beginning about
1900 B.C. From earliest times Greece had ties with the adjacent
islands, especially Crete, which lies some sixty miles to the southeast. Its civilization is called Minoan, from Minos, a legendary
king of Crete. Under Mesopotamian and Egyptian influence, the
culture of Crete developed earlier than did that of the Greek mainland. Elaborate palaces were built at Knossos and Mallia by 2000
B.C. Cretans learned to write a script similar to Egyptian hieroglyphs, using clay tablets like those used in Mesopotamia. They
became so powerful that they were able to extend their influence
even to the Greek mainland. Mycenae, located in Argolis, which

was at that time the chief cultural center of Greece, itself took on a Minoan character. But by 1400 B.C. the Greeks, under the leadership of Mycenae, conquered Crete along with some other Aegean islands.

Greece was strong in matters of intellectual creativity: it was outstanding in the arts and sciences, and poets, painters, sculptors, architects, philosophers, scientists, and historians were its glory, excelling those of all other nations of antiquity. All the peoples around the Mediterranean admired Greek culture, and for about five centuries after Alexander—the period that is known as the Hellenistic Age—Greek culture continued to be imitated and adopted by other peoples. But the Greeks were weak in things practical—especially in matters of government. True, they were outstanding in the development of city-states: no other nation of antiquity excelled the Greeks in the attainments of individual cities; Athens, Thebes, Sparta, and Corinth were famous throughout the world of their time. The high attainments of individual Greeks were without parallel in antiquity, and, on an individual basis, the Greeks were good soldiers.

However, the Greek cities were characterized by intense pride, and there was bitter rivalry between them. Patriotism meant loyalty to the particular city in which one was born, lived, and was a citizen. For the most part, there was no sense of a nation that included all the Greek cities, lands, and persons of Greek blood. The most bitter wars of Greek history were between such cities as Athens and Sparta. At times of danger, when the Greeks were threatened by invaders, such as the Persians, the otherwise hostile cities would join forces to repel them; but once the danger was past the local rivalries revived, no less sharp than before, and sometimes even more so.

Alexander the Great of Macedon (who ruled from 336–323 B.C.) succeeded both in conquering the states of the Greek mainland and in uniting them for a brief thirteen years into a powerful kingdom. During his short reign, he was able to conquer all of the Middle East, as far as India. But when Alexander died, the kingdom fell apart, and, in antiquity, Greece was never again able to attain a unity that transcended the local states. It remained for the Romans to become the real successors of Alexander. They encountered little difficulty, during the second century B.C., in conquering the Greek states and absorbing them into the Roman Empire.

ROME

Rome means, first, the city by that name standing picturesquely on seven hills on the south bank of the Tiber, which empties into the Mediterranean nearby. The city is close to the middle of the western coast of Italy—a peninsula extending southward out of Europe, somewhat parallel to the Balkan Peninsula on which Greece is located. But Rome is also synonymous with all Italy, of which it became the capital. Once Italy had come under Roman power, this vigorous people began to expand far outside the Italian Peninsula, reaching westward beyond the islands of Corsica, Sardinia, and Sicily to destroy the powerful Phoenician colony of Carthage in North Africa and to absorb all its territories. Thus the Romans created a political bridge, indeed almost a land bridge, from Europe to Africa. Their ambition for conquest next turned eastward. Greece, Asia Minor, Syria, Palestine, and Egypt were easily conquered and annexed to the rising empire of Rome. Still unsatisfied, the Romans then expanded northward and westward, until finally most of Europe, including the British Isles, came under their dominion.

Italy is cut off from Europe by the spectacular Alps, which rise to great heights across its northern frontier. The peninsula is shaped like a boot, the toe pointing toward Sicily, the heel toward Greece, and its backbone is formed by the Apennines. The most important rivers of northern Italy, the Po and Adige, are streams of moderate size fed by snows from the Alps and flow southeastward into the Adriatic. The Arno and the Tiber are small streams, rising in the Apennines and flowing west and southwest into the Mediterranean, which on that side of Italy is called the Tyrrhenian Sea. This is a name derived from the Greek word for Etruscans, a people who are thought to have migrated to north central Italy from Asia Minor around 800 B.C.

The Lombardy Valley, below the foothills of the Alps, and the Campanian Plain, below Rome and east of Naples, are good farming regions. Otherwise, much of Italy is rough, suitable only for fruits and small animals. While olives, grapes, sheep, and goats abound, the peninsula is unable to produce enough food for its population. Even in ancient times, Rome had to import large quantities of food, especially grain from Egypt.

Three active volcanoes have at one time or another dominated the Italian landscape: Vesuvius, at Naples; Mount Etna, across the strait in Sicily; and Stromboli, which rises out of the sea on a small island just north of Sicily. Vesuvius has erupted at least fifty times in recorded history; in A.D. 79, it destroyed the cities of Pompeii and Herculaneum.

Although Italy is surrounded by the sea on the west, south, and east, the city of Rome has always been handicapped by the lack of a convenient harbor. The only good ports on the west coast of Italy are Genoa and La Spezia, to the north of Rome, and Naples to the south. Lack of a good harbor of its own may explain why Rome was slow in becoming a sea power. But once the Romans realized the importance of controlling the sea, they soon made themselves masters of the entire Mediterranean and grew rich from the use of ports in the lands they had conquered. They regarded the Mediterranean Sea as a Roman lake, and in fact it was.

Historical Background

The Romans were the last of the great peoples of antiquity to come to maturity. They were the heirs of the civilizations of Greece, Egypt, and Mesopotamia, as well as of all the other earlier nations in the Mediterranean basin, and finally of the continent of Europe. The Romans came to maturity as the Hellenistic Age was reaching its culmination; they were, in fact, the most Hellenistic nation of all, and they profited more than any other people from the treasures of culture the Greeks bequeathed them. Learning also from the military and political conquests of Alexander the Great, they brought into existence the world empire of which the young Alexander had dreamed. Not so brilliant in architecture as Egypt, nor in art and philosophy as Greece, the Romans nevertheless surpassed all their predecessors in the practical arts, in the development of natural resources, in military power, and in practical political wisdom.

The history of Rome began with the founding of the city by the legendary Romulus in 753 B.C. The Roman Empire survived in the west until Rome was overwhelmed by the barbarians of Europe in A.D. 476, and in the east until Constantinople was taken by the Muslim Turks in 1453. No other nation of the west could compare with Rome in its capacity to survive; it is only in the east, perhaps in India and China, that we encounter peoples with such a long history.

When the Romans first made their appearance in history, they were only one of several minor peoples inhabiting the peninsula of Italy. At that time, they were Latins and occupied the tiny state of Latium, just south of the Tiber and adjacent to the Mediterranean, with a territory no more than twenty miles wide and eighty-five long. The sea provided its southwestern boundary; by land, beginning on the south and going northward, Latium was bounded by Campania, Samnium, and Etruria.

The city of Rome began as a military outpost against the Etruscans on the northern frontier of Latium. This outpost was protected first by the Tiber on the north, then by the hills on which the city stood. Rome controlled both sides of the river down to the sea. The fortress was strategically located for defense, as well as for offense, when the Romans were finally ready to undertake the conquest of the Etruscans, along with other peoples to the north. As late as 500 B.C., however, the entire peninsula of Italy was still divided into small independent states. Among these the Etruscans were the most highly civilized, as well as, for a time, the strongest; but being divided among themselves into small city-states, they were unable to withstand the rising power of Rome.

This disjointed condition of the Italian Peninsula left it open to invasion and colonization by ambitious foreign powers. Gauls from beyond the Alps managed to penetrate into northern Italy and establish two states, one above the Po, another below it. Etruscans came in from Asia Minor—according to Virgil, they were exiles from Troy after that city had been destroyed by the Greeks —and colonized a large area across the Tiber north from Rome, later to be known as Etruria. Varro, a learned Roman antiquarian (116–28 B.C.), states that the Sabines, bitter foes of the Romans on the northeastern frontier of Latium, were native Pelasgians from Greece. After about 800 B.C., numerous Greek cities established colonies in southern Italy, Sicily, Sardinia, Corsica, and on the southern coast of France and Spain. Several Greek colonies were established even on the western coast of Italy, the most northern being Cumae, above Naples, from which the Romans were later to acquire the Sibylline Books. This process of exploitation of Italy by foreigners did not come to an end until 270 B.C., when Rome was at last able to extend its authority over all of southern Italy.

All these foreign colonies left their influence on the developing Roman culture, especially on religion. The Romans were remarkably free of prejudice against foreign cultures. For the Greeks in particular they had great admiration: a majority of Romans gladly recognized the superiority of Greek literature, arts, philosophy, and religion, and in time it even became difficult to distinguish the original Roman religion from the Greek religion, which had been superimposed on it.

NOTE

1. Herodotus, *The Histories* (Baltimore: Penguin, 1954), I, 178 ff., gives a vivid description of Babylon as it appeared about 450 B.C., when this famous Greek traveler and historian visited it.

3 The Religion of Ancient Mesopotamia

The religion of Mesopotamia derived its early structure from the fact that the social and political life of that area was centered in individual states, each of which had its own king and was independent of all the others. Associated with each capital city were the surrounding villages and farms, the area extending as far as military and political control could be maintained.

The organization of religion was similar to that of the political state. In each capital city there was a chief deity who had a goddess wife. The two were assisted by other deities, both male and female, each of whom had a specific function, such as watching over the personal and business affairs of the royal household (including the harem), the political subdivisions of the capital city, irrigation canals and fields, and on whatever else the life of the people depended. At first the king himself served as high priest; in time, however, an elaborate professional priesthood arose. In each city, the chief deity had his own shrine, and the subordinate deities usually had theirs; but often the latter were merely assigned space in the main temple.

There was little difference between the religions of the different cities of Mesopotamia. This was especially true of the delta region in the south, where the cities were close together, and the close cultural kinship between them was the result of their constant social, commercial, and political contacts.

Above the gods worshiped by each city there was also a triad of deities who, from an early period, appear to have been accepted by all the cities. This triad included: Anu, god of the sky; Enlil,

FIGURE 3.1 The 4,000-year-old Hammurabi Stone, bearing the Code of Laws of King Hammurabi of Babylon. (*Keystone*)

who ruled the affairs of men on earth; and Ea, god of waters. In one way or another, and sometimes under different names, these three appear in the theologies of almost every Mesopotamian city. The reason is not difficult to find. The life of these peoples was supremely dependent on the actions and influences of sun, moon, and stars, heat, wind, storm, and water—especially the rivers and irrigation canals—and on military and political power, and these were the areas watched over by the great gods of this triad.

When a city like Babylon or Nineveh became powerful enough to conquer all the other Mesopotamian cities and rule over them as one kingdom, that event was paralleled in the theology of the cities: the gods of the conqueror either replaced or absorbed those of the conquered cities. Thus, such great gods as Marduk and Ishtar of Babylon came to achieve supreme status. It now became possible to conceive of a pantheon that included the deities of all the Mesopotamian cities living harmoniously together with Marduk, or some other god, as their divine king. In a general sense, this was similar to the later development in Greek religion.

Moreover, there is some evidence of a tendency toward monotheism as Mesopotamian culture came to its maturity. In some documents one finds the same deity referred to as both male and female. This shows that the author of the lines in question did not limit himself purely to anthropomorphism; in a real sense, the category of sex could not be applied to a deity—the divine must transcend the ordinary things of human life. One also comes upon texts in which the names of deities are used interchangeably; this demonstrates that the divine names are thought of as no more than different ways of designating the same spiritual being. While Mesopotamia did not achieve the level of abstract philosophical thought that was still some centuries away, such passages indicate that for some Mesopotamians a monotheistic conception of the divine was not far away.

MAGIC

One of the most characteristic features of Mesopotamian religion was its development along the lines of magic. Divination of the intention and will of the gods was undertaken in many ways. One of the most popular was inspection of the vital organs of animals that had been slaughtered as sacrifices in the temples. Another was observation of the heavenly bodies, which were believed to be gods themselves or at least the abodes of divine spirits. From movements of the sun, moon, stars, and planets it was believed to be possible to discover what was to happen in human affairs, for it was the heavenly bodies that shaped the destinies of men. Studies of the heavens for this purpose constituted the beginning of the science of astronomy. Elaborate rituals for the control and expulsion of evil spirits, which were regarded as the causes of illnesses and other misfortunes, produced a flourishing practice of exorcism by the exorcists, who were believed to be experts in these matters. Determination of the guilt or innocence of a person who had been accused of crime, by casting him into a river to see if he survived, was another manifestation of magical thinking. Here, apparently, the idea was to allow the spirit of the water to pronounce judgment. These various practices show that, alongside development of some higher insights, a primitive animism continued to be a vigorous component of Mesopotamian religion.

RITES AND MYTHS

Fertility Rites

Fertility cults in the various religions revolve about the concept of sexual generation at all levels of life, ranging from vegetative to human. One of the oldest myths based on this idea is the Sumerian story of Enki, also known as Ea, the water god, and Ninhursag, a variant for Ishtar, the earth mother.[1] This divine pair, like Adam and Eve, live in a paradise called Dilmun, in which all is pure and clean; there is no pain or sorrow, and no one grows old. While the chief protagonists are Enki and Ninhursag, in the background stand Anu, god of the heavens, and the Annunaki, the multitude of other deities. Only one thing is lacking in paradise: there is no sweet water. In response to the request of his wife, Enki gets the sun god Utu to supply water in abundance. The bitter (salt?) waters are transformed into sweet, and fields bear grain.

But now, under the impact of sexual motivation and imagery, tragedy strikes. Enki waters the dikes with his phallus until the reeds are submerged; this is the creation of the marshland. Taking an oath before Anu, Enki reserves this marshland for himself, as a private retreat in which he can indulge in his amours. In the secrecy of the marshes, he first cohabits with Ninhursag, who bears a fair daughter Ninmu. Then he cohabits with Ninmu, who gives birth to a granddaughter Ninkurra. Next Enki impregnates the granddaughter, and she bears a great-granddaughter, the fair lady Uttu.

This time Ninhursag intervenes, with the result that when Enki impregnates Uttu, she gives birth not to another divine child, but to a series of eight plants. Enki is so surprised at this that he orders a servant to cut down the plants and then eats them one by one. His wife Ninhursag, however, is angered and pronounces a curse on Enki. As long as he lives, she swears, she will never look upon him again. Sorrow then enters paradise: all the gods sit in mourning, for Enki has become ill. Now a clever fox gets Ninhursag to return; but even though she ministers to Enki, the primordial perfection of paradise is never restored.

The exaltation of sex in this story of the gods reflects that type of ancient thought which lies behind the sexual rites that were often included in temple worship. Religious prostitution was a well-recognized practice among the Mesopotamians. Temple brothels are mentioned in the law codes, and we may learn something about how they operated from the various statutes recorded. Statute 14 of the Middle Assyrian Code deals with the case of a man who may have unwittingly lain with the wife of another in a temple brothel. In such a case he is guiltless, although if he knew that she was another man's wife, he is guilty.[2]

The status of temple prostitutes is clearly recognized in the codes, especially in the Code of Hammurabi in which about a dozen statutes relate to them.[3] Such a hierodule or sacred slave retained her property rights in her father's estate, and she was not regarded as being in any sense inferior or degraded. Since several statutes in the Code deal with cases in which men have married hierodules, it is evident that their profession did not make them ineligible or undesirable for marriage. It is also clear that this profession was regarded as one form of high religious devotion, a form of priesthood; it must have been considered as an honor for a family to have a daughter enter this type of temple service. The fathers themselves dedicated their daughters to temples for this purpose. Statute 181 of the Code of Hammurabi defines the case of such a girl; and Statute 182 deals with hierodules of Marduk of Babylon.

The fertility rites apparently had a sacramental meaning. In his sexual ecstasy a devotee believed that he attained a mystical union with his deity that was not otherwise attainable. He participated in the experience of generation, as it was used by the gods themselves in creating all forms of life. As often as he repeated the sacrament, therefore, he renewed the realistic union with his god. Moreover, the sacrament he performed at the temple was believed to arouse the divine pair of deities, male and female, to whom the shrine was dedicated, so that they would continue to make fertile the fields, flocks and herds, and human beings. Thus creation was a continuous process: life was always being reborn.

Out of this form of apprehension of the divine has come also the concept of religious experience as a divine marriage, a courtship between God and the human soul. Both Jews and Christians have used this symbolism to interpret the Song of Songs; and it was Paul, for example, who pictured the Church as the bride of Christ.[4]

Creation

Mesopotamia produced different stories of creation, a reflection of the fact that in the early period various city-states stood side by side, each with its own institutions and traditions. As greater political and cultural unity came to be attained, some of the earlier myths were preserved, apparently in competition with one another. Others were reinterpreted as a way of expressing the faith of later times. As has already been noted, the Sumerian myth of Enki and Ninhursag relates that Uttu, the great-granddaughter, gave birth to plants.[5] Another old Sumerian myth ascribes creation, in a more comprehensive sense, to Anu, Enlil, Enki, and Ninhursag.[6] These gods gave shape to the "black-headed people," to vegetation, and to animals, after which they brought kingship from heaven and founded five great cult centers, assigning each to its patron deity.

A third and later myth, associated with Akkad of Babylonia, ascribes creation to Marduk, patron deity of Babylon, which had by that time become supreme. This myth begins with Apsu, god of the fresh waters of rain and rivers, and his wife Tiamat, goddess of the salt-water sea, who lived before anything else had come into existence. The brood of gods they have for offspring are so rude and boisterous that Apsu cannot bear them. With the support of Tiamat, he determines to destroy them; but the plot becomes known to the young gods, and Ea kills his father. The younger generation then becomes even more obnoxious to Tiamat, who decides to destroy them herself, a task in which she is aided by a host of monsters. The young gods cower in terror; only Marduk, son of Ea and Domkina, has the courage to challenge Tiamat, whom he slays in hand-to-hand combat.[7]

Then follow Marduk's acts of creation, assisted now by the other gods, whose courage has returned. First he cuts Tiamat's body in half, as if he were slicing a shellfish; one half he fixes in position as the sky. The other half, apparently, he establishes as the flat earth resting on a subterranean sea. He places in the sky astral constellations, three for each month of the year, as stations for the gods, adding the moon to illuminate the night and mark the months, by indicating the seven-day quarters of each month by means of the shape of its crown. Finally he creates mankind from the blood of the slaughtered Kingu, the evil deity whom Tiamat had chosen to be her consort and to assist in destroying her children.

Tammuz, the Dying and Rising God

The myth of the descent of Ishtar, the earth mother, to the underworld in quest of her child or lover Tammuz is a poetic account of the spirit of vegetation, which dies every autumn and rises from the dead every spring;[8] its death and resurrection, however, are also symbolic of the continuing life-death-life cycle throughout the biological world. With great courage Ishtar makes her way down into the dark and filthy region from which no one returns, save for a few heroes who are temporarily brought back by magic. She successfully faces Ereshkigal, her sister, the cruel queen of this domain without hope, and brings her lover back from it. When he rises from the dead, life and joy return to the world. In an earlier Sumerian version of this myth, Inanna is the heroine, Dumuzi the hero.[9]

The Great Flood

The story of a great flood in Mesopotamia is worthy of note, not only because it shows how religion is related to geography, but also because this story was taken over by the Hebrews and, in a revised form, incorporated into their own Bible.[10] In southern Mesopotamia, where the narrow land was dominated by the two great rivers, floods were not unusual. One in particular was so destructive that a record of it, with a theological interpretation, was preserved in Mesopotamian literature.

The oldest version of this story is Sumerian. While it is fragmentary, it nevertheless does retain the essentials. When the gods had decided to destroy mankind with a flood, a friendly deity warned the saintly Ziusudra to build himself a ship. In that way he survived and also saved the seed of mankind, as well as other forms of life. Ziusudra thereupon offered sacrifices to the gods, who then permitted him to dwell in the paradise land of Dilmun, the land where the sun rises.[11]

A later and fuller version of this story occurs in the Akkadian form of the epic of Gilgamesh.[12] Here the hero is Utnapishtim, and the friendly god who aids him is Ea, who presides over waters. This time the flood is produced by a black cloud that rises above the horizon. Its thunder and lightning are so fearful that even the gods cower in terror, like dogs crouching against a wall. But Utnapishtim's ship, with its precious cargo, survives; and as the waters begin to subside he sends forth first a dove, next a swallow, then a raven. The hero and his wife, who were originally fully human, now become like gods and are granted an abode far away at the mouth of the rivers, where the sun shines; and they never die.

The Hereafter

The general view in Mesopotamian religion is that death is the end; there is no hope beyond. While the soul does survive, its destiny is the dark dominion of Ereshkigal inside the earth, where all are accepted and from which none are allowed to depart. Here the function of religion is to provide for the present life; it has nothing to offer after death. The assumption is that all men, good and bad, get their just deserts in this life, so that neither rewards nor punishments are expected in the hereafter. Yet this abode of the dead is a place of gloom, of dread.

There were thoughtful persons, however, who had already begun to question the view that every man attains justice in this life and who were depressed by the finality of death. They wished for light on the hereafter, and yearned for something to strike a balance between the equities and inequities of life. Proof of this is evident in the myth of Gilgamesh, who is the prototype of epic giants like the Greek Hercules and Ulysses and the Hebrew Samson.

Gilgamesh left the throne of Uruk to go in search of the faraway semidivine Utnapishtim in an effort to remove his uncertainty about the hereafter.[13] He had to overcome ferocious beasts and dangers that none had ever been able to survive. When at last he reached the abode of Utnapishtim, the fabled sage received him kindly, but explained that the plant of immortality grows only at the bottom of the sea. Undeterred, the hero weighted his feet with stones and went to the sea bed, where he secured the magical shrub. But on his way home, while he was refreshing himself by a well, a serpent stole the fragrant herb and made off with it, before he was even able to taste the food that could make old men young again. So the hero returned alive to his home at Uruk disconsolate, the besetting dread still with him.

Several times in this moving story, Gilgamesh is assured by one speaker or another that his quest is in vain; that it is man's destiny to be mortal; that he must adjust himself to this destiny and find his consolation in the simple joys of life; that only the gods live forever. This was the perennial philosophy of the Mesopotamians, who did not ordinarily concern themselves very much about the hereafter. They believed in the possibility of a happy life here and now, and they accepted death. Ereshkigal and her underworld dominion appear to have had little reality, and few persons acknowledged the anxiety of a Gilgamesh.

Royal Tombs of Ur

Further light on Mesopotamian faith about the hereafter can be derived from their burial rites, about which there were intimate and sentimental feelings. The dead seem to have been thought of as continuing members of the family, for it was customary to bury them under the house in which the remaining members of the family lived. In time such graves became so numerous that it was necessary to leave one house to the dead and build another. Gifts of many kinds were placed in the graves, their value and kind depending on the wealth and social position of the family. A drinking cup and pitcher were usual, as well as food, various items of clothing, jewelry, furniture, weapons, tools, and so on. The custom appears to assume that life after death, in some invisible realm, continues to be much like the life of the still living.

Remarkable evidence along these lines came to light with the excavation of the royal tombs of the kings of Ur from about 2600 B.C. These mausoleums contained fabulous treasures of gold, silver, precious stones, and fine examples of art of the period. Most remarkable was the fact that, in some of these tombs, which were referred to by the excavators as "death pits," there were found from twenty-five to as many as seventy-six bodies of both men and women, who apparently had died willingly, as companions of the royal person in whose grave they were found. The arrangement and location of the bodies indicated that they first assumed their positions

FIGURE 3.2   A model of the Tower (Ziggurat) of Babylon (model by Robert Koldeway). (*Keystone*)

and then either took their own lives or allowed others to dispatch them. Perhaps they used poison or sleeping potions before the tomb was covered and sealed. If scholars are correct in this interpretation, we should probably understand it in the light of a view that is occasionally found in the literature—namely, that kings were deified at death. If so, their status in the hereafter might be conceived as similar to that of the gods themselves, each of whom had his own family, court, and retinue of servants. It may be, therefore, that the court and friends of a king gladly joined him in death in anticipation of a glorious life in the beyond. Such a view appears to be supported by a text on the death of Gilgamesh.[14] More light may be thrown on this interpretation by further excavation and by the study of texts that have not yet been translated.

LAW

Mesopotamian law always had a religious basis. The Code of Hammurabi,[15] best known of all legal formulations of that ancient culture, represents King Hammurabi as receiving his code from the sun god Shamash, who presided over justice, just as Moses in the biblical story received the Law from Yahweh (see Figure 3.1).

The Code of Hammurabi deals with both civil and criminal law. The different social classes that are recognized in it include royalty, nobility, commoners, priests (both male and female), temple hierodules, and slaves.

Much of the code has to do with sex. Polygamy is expected and common. Rape, incest, and adultery are subject to the death penalty. Otherwise, the general penalty for assault is an eye for an eye, a bone for a bone, a tooth for a tooth.

A surgeon's fees are set: ten shekels for saving a noble's life by an operation; five for a commoner; two for a slave. If a noble dies or loses an eye from an operation, the surgeon's hand is cut off. In a similar case for a slave, the surgeon must replace him. He gets five shekels for setting a bone or healing a sprained tendon.

The economy appears to have been stabilized by statute. The prices of many articles of commerce are specified, and wages are fixed. Generally speaking, penalties are harsh, but there is a clear perception of individual rights, as well as the responsibility of an individual for his actions.

TEMPLES

The earliest evidence of temple construction in Mesopotamia was found in the north at Tell Halaf. These circular structures, some with rectangular antechambers, are believed to have been shrines, possibly the oldest temples so far known. Large numbers of plaster female figurines, both human and animal, would seem to indicate that a fertility cult flourished there. This culture dates from around 4500 B.C.

The next evidence of temple construction was found at Tepe Gawra, near the site of Nineveh. Remains of a temple on this site, dating from around 4000 B.C., show that formal religion had already attained considerable development.

Excavation of the Sumerian city of Uruk, whose culture dates from around 3500 B.C., made possible the spectacular discovery of the first known example of a new type of temple construction, called a *ziggurat*—a word meaning "mound" or "mountaintop." This Uruk ziggurat, built of mud-brick and layers of asphalt, was some 65 feet long, 50 feet wide, and 30 feet high, the temple itself being located at the top. Apparently the idea was to build an artificial mountain to please a deity who had been accustomed to a mountain shrine in some other region. This ziggurat apparently set the pattern of temple construction in Sumerian Babylonia, for more than two dozen such structures have been found there. The ziggurat must have been as characteristic of Sumerian religion as is the pagoda of Buddhism or the minaret of Islam. The Greek historian and traveler Herodotus, who visited Babylon about 450 B.C., described the great ziggurat of his time dedicated to Bel. Its base was 660 feet square; then, rising like a pyramid in a series of seven additional towers to its summit, it reached a total height of close to 100 feet[16] (see Figure 3.2).

NOTES

1. See J. B. Pritchard, ed., *Ancient Near Eastern Texts*, 2d ed. (Princeton: Princeton University Press, 1955). This reference work is an authoritative collection of translations of the most significant texts of the ancient Near East.
2. *Ibid.*, p. 181.

3. *Ibid.*, pp. 163–180.
4. Ephesians 5:21–33; I Corinthians 6:12–20.
5. Pritchard, *op. cit.*, pp. 39–40.
6. *Ibid.*, pp. 42–44.
7. *Ibid.*, pp. 60–72.
8. *Ibid.*, pp. 106–109.
9. *Ibid.*, pp. 52–57.
10. Genesis 6:1–8:22.
11. Pritchard, *op. cit.*, pp. 42–44.
12. *Ibid.*, pp. 93–95.
13. *Ibid.*, pp. 73–100.
14. *Ibid.*, pp. 50–52.
15. *Ibid.*, pp. 163–180.
16. Herodotus, *The Histories* (Baltimore: Penguin, 1954), I, 178 ff.

in Egypt as early as the Middle Kingdom. The justly famous Book
of the Dead (texts relative to the hereafter written on sheets of
papyrus and enclosed in caskets which have been collected and
put together in the form of a book by modern scholars) makes it
clear that what a person faces in the hereafter is based largely on
his moral character: whether he has been honest, generous toward
the poor, and the like. The destiny of the king, in particular, was
related to this idea. The king was thought of as being divine during life. He was Horus, the son of Re, or Aton, the sun, that is,
he was the son of Osiris. In death, if he passed the final judgment
successfully, he became Osiris, a mystical identity which apparently
raised no metaphysical problem.

The coffin papyri preserve pictures of the judgment which took
place (see Figure 4.2), although with a considerable variation as
to the divine beings who participated in the proceedings. Usually
Anubis, the jackal-headed god, leads the deceased by the hand into
the judgment hall, where a pair of balanced scales is waiting. He
then places the heart of the dead in one pan of the balance and
Maat, justice, represented by a feather, in the other pan. Standing
by may be Thoth, the ibis-headed god, with a tablet and stylus

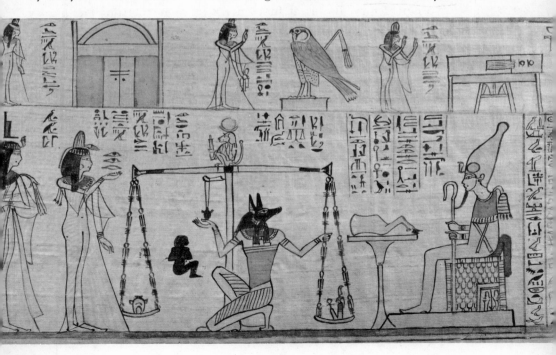

ready to record how the judgment goes. Also nearby may appear
Amemit, a composite creature with the head of a crocodile, the fore-
quarters of a lion, and the hindquarters of a hippopotamus, ready
to devour the deceased if he fails to pass the test. Standing by also
may be Horus ready to lead those who pass the test into the eternal
kingdom of Osiris.

The power that this faith came to hold over the Egyptians is
shown by the enormous amount of energy and wealth they devoted
to the construction of their temples and tombs, all of which are
oriented toward life beyond the grave. One comes upon no such
remains of Egyptian royal palaces, state houses, banks, or other
commercial establishments, and there are certainly no private homes
that compare in elegance with Egyptian temples and tombs.

The Isis Cult

(The Egyptian quest for immortality came to its ultimate expression in the cult of Isis, which flourished during the Hellenistic
period)—that is, four or five centuries after Alexander the Great
(336–323 B.C.). Although Isis had been known in earlier periods of
Egyptian history, it was at first only as a vague personality, hardly
more than a name, with no cult of her own. But (her role in the
myth of Osiris, who met a violent death yet was raised from the
dead by Isis, caused her to become the center of the interest in
immortality.) The cult was popular not only in Egypt; it also
spread far beyond, especially to Greece and Rome. While the doors
of its temples were open to all, its mysteries were revealed only
to those who were initiated and were therefore permitted to have
a part in the reenactment of the divine drama in which Osiris died
and rose again (see Figure 4.1). The initiates were assured that
they too, like Osiris, might gain a victory over death and become
immortal. This hunger for immortality was characteristic of the
Hellenistic Age.

TOMBS AND RELIGIOUS STRUCTURES

The Pyramids

The great pyramid builders flourished about 2600 B.C. Solidly built,
the tombs they reared were apparently expected to last forever and

the embalmed bodies to remain there as long as the stones did. No other undertakers have ever equaled the Egyptians in the art of embalming.

Located on the desert sand just across the Nile west from Cairo, the pyramids were built of limestone blocks cut from quarries on the Cairo side and floated across the river while the water was high. Each block weighed on an average two and a half tons. Khufu's pyramid, the largest of the group, required no less than 2,300,000 such blocks. It has a square base of 746 feet on each side and is 481 feet high. The burial chamber in which the king's body was placed, together with appropriate treasures of gold, precious stones, and other works of art, including many objects of a religious character, is approached by a steeply inclined passage that reaches far into the heart of the great structure. Once the burial had been completed, the passage was closed by huge monoliths. Though access to it was very difficult, it was apparently not difficult enough to keep out thieves, who later robbed the tomb. Nearby are two other pyramids of nearly the same size and several smaller ones. It is said that 100,000 men labored twenty years to build Khufu's pyramid. The construction of this giant tomb was the chief enterprise of the nation during the reign of Khufu. Its cost must have been the major item in the national budget every year for twenty years; this applies also to the other large pyramids. Both the king and the nation were in this extraordinary way reaching out for immortality.

Underground Mansions for the Dead

The Theban kings of the south did not engage in pyramid construction; instead, they built ornate underground tombs for themselves. The best examples of this type of royal burial are those that have been uncovered in the Valley of the Kings, west across the Nile from the modern town of Luxor. Thebes, capital of the Middle Kingdom, stood nearby. These underground mansions, laid out in long corridors and suites of rooms, their walls exquisitely inscribed with texts relative to the dead, are more beautiful than the massive pyramids; but they too have been robbed, with one exception: that of the little-known and for centuries forgotten tomb of Tutankhamen, which was found in 1922 with all its treasures intact. Apparently, the only reason why it escaped the robbers was that the very memory of this quite unimportant monarch had been lost. (The treasures from his tomb, as well as vast quantities of other similar antiquities, may be seen today in the Egyptian Museum at Cairo.) But thieves were not interested in the inscribed walls of these underground tombs, which remain well preserved to this day; the information contained in their inscriptions reveals to us the life and faith of the ancient Egyptians, as well as the delicate beauty of their colors and symbols, which are still able to delight and amaze us.

Temples

The first great Egyptian temples were the pyramids that were erected for their kings, who were worshiped as gods after they died. A chapel for this purpose was always provided either as part of the pyramid itself or nearby. The original idea of pyramid construction, even its shape, appears to have been borrowed from Mesopotamia, where Egyptian travelers had seen the ziggurats, the temple towers built of mud-brick. A decisive difference between the Babylonian and Egyptian constructions was that, while Egypt had a generous supply of both limestone and granite as well as of other hard stones, Mesopotamia had almost none. The early influence of Mesopotamia on Egypt is also shown by the fact that the Egyptians first cut their stone into small sizes, like the mud-brick. But it was not long before the Egyptian architects learned how to exploit their superior building materials and cut out massive slabs, blocks, and columns. This enabled them not only to build the mammoth pyramids but also, during the Middle Kingdom, to abandon that unimaginative type of construction and to produce instead magnificent temples.

The Theban kings of the south moved in two directions: on the one hand, they built exquisite underground tombs for themselves; on the other, however, they grasped the importance of building suitable houses for their gods. Hence theirs was the age of great temples. No other nation of remote antiquity has left behind comparable architectural monuments of its faith; many of their columns still stand in their original positions—after 3,000 years. These impressive, aboveground monuments are reminders of the high civilization of the ancient people who lived along the Nile.

AN ATTEMPT AT MONOTHEISM

Belief in a great number of gods was deeply imbedded in the religion of Egypt. Theirs was one of the most elaborate and complicated polytheisms in the history of religion. This not only brought preoccupation with temples and tombs but also permitted the emergence of powerful priesthoods which virtually controlled the life of Egypt, including the policies of the king. The Pharaoh was little more than a puppet in the hands of the priests. Some of the kings, however, must have considered the possibility of breaking the priestly power and freeing themselves from their domination. Moreover, there were some persons of philosophical bent who began to realize that beyond the multitude of gods there was only one ultimate reality.

Little evidence of philosophical speculation among the Egyptians has survived. About 1375 B.C., however, a young Pharaoh by the name of Amenhotep IV came to the throne. Combining a desire to break the power of the priesthoods with deep piety and a philosophical interest; he zealously repudiated the authority of the priests along with the gods of the old polytheism and devoted himself solely to the worship of Aton, the sun, proclaiming himself the son of Aton. In order to dramatize the faith, he dropped his inherited name and adopted the name Aken-en-Aton, or, as he is better known, Ikhnaton. By royal decree he imposed the worship of Aton and abolished the worship of all other gods. With profound insight he proclaimed the existence of only one God, not only as king of Egypt but also as king of the entire world, embodying in his character and essence all the attributes that all the other gods together had stood for. Insofar as he was able, Ikhnaton had the very names of the old deities erased from the monuments and substituted for them the name of Aton.

However, the old order was too strong. By 1350 B.C., after the passage of a quarter of a century, Ikhnaton had disappeared from history, and one of his successors had already restored the old priests to their former power and greatly enriched their temples. Thus the religion of Egypt remained polytheistic to the end.

5 The Religion of Ancient Greece

EARLY GREEK RELIGION

Herodotus, in the second book of his *Histories,* devotes several paragraphs to the aborigines of Greece. He calls them Pelasgians and states that Greece was at that time called Pelasgia. According to the *Histories,* Herodotus was informed by the priestesses of Dodona, an ancient oracle of Epirus, that the Pelasgians had offered sacrifices of many kinds and prayed to gods, but without any distinction between them as to name or title, because they had never heard the divine names. They had called the gods *theoi* on the ground that it was the gods who had arranged everything in order. Long afterward, according to the priestesses, the Pelasgians learned the names of the gods from the Egyptians. These traditions are probably correct in their reflection of primitive animism and of the early influence of Egypt on Greek culture.

There is archaeological evidence of the existence of the neolithic Pelasgians, but little can be said with certainty about their religion. Several caves originally used by the Pelasgians as dwellings and later as cult sites, after other types of dwellings came to be adopted, have been discovered in Crete. Among the objects that have been found in these caves are bell-shaped images—female figurines with a snake held in the hands or wrapped around the bodies—and double axes which appear to have some cult significance. Similar items have also been found in the ruins of Mycenae on the mainland.

Although no records of old Mycenaean myths and rituals have yet been discovered, recent decipherment of Minoan inscriptions

FIGURE 5.1 Zeus, king of gods, abducting young Ganymede. (*Museum of Olympia*)

has thrown new light on the Minoan-Mycenaean religion. This is limited, of course, by the brevity of the texts, which are book-keepers' records inscribed on clay tablets that were found in the archives of the ruined palaces of such places as Knossos in Crete and Pylos and Mycenae in southern Greece. One of the Knossos tablets documents an issue of oil to the shrine of Zeus on Mount Dicte; the same tablet records oil issued to the shrine of Daedalus, a name previously known only as that of an ancient craftsman. A goddess called "the Lady" is associated with several shrines. The worship of Eileithyia, the goddess of childbirth, whose shrine was at Amniosos and who was already known from the Odyssey, is confirmed by a tablet.

Poseidon was the main deity of Crete. The Pylos tablets show that he also headed the pantheon in southern Greece, and thus demonstrates his preeminence in all Minoan-Mycenaean religion in addition to indicating the influence of the sea. Two queens—that is, mother goddesses—are associated with Poseidon; besides inscriptional evidence of this, there are numerous terra-cotta figurines of two women joined together like Siamese twins and holding an infant, suggesting the divine mother and child motif familiar in a number of later Mediterranean cults. Other deities include the Horse God, the Dove God, and the Handmaidens, who accompany the mother goddesses. Zeus and Hera appear, but only in a minor role; apparently Zeus did not become supreme until the classical period. Athena also appears in the Minoan inscriptions and is associated there with a serpent, which survives as one of her symbols, along with the owl, in her better-known subsequent history.

Among gifts given to the shrines, the Pylos tablets mention gold vessels and men and women, presumably to be used as temple slaves. Olive oil was issued, along with perfumed oil, which was delivered in stirrup jars that were made in Crete and shipped as far as Eleusis in Attica. All supplies at both Knossos and Pylos were delivered from the palace warehouses, which shows that the government controlled the economy.

Of the religious festivals mentioned, one was a spring celebration that included a marriage between a mother goddess and her resurrected son, thus symbolizing the renewal of life every spring. At another festival, celebrating the first new wine each year, the dead were provided with drink offerings.[1]

CLASSICAL GREEK POLYTHEISM

Here archaeology continues to provide information; but in addition we now have the literary classics themselves on which to rely. Homer's *Iliad* and *Odyssey,* both epic poems that tell about the Trojan War and about the gods and men who participated in it, are important sources of information about Greek religion. Archaeology has confirmed our confidence in the authenticity of Homer's accounts by uncovering the sites of Troy, where the war was fought; Mycenae, whose King Agamemnon was leader of the Greek forces; Pylos, from which Nestor came; Knossos in Crete, from which King Idomeneus came with his men and his ships; Phthiotis, homeland of Achilles; Mount Olympus, headquarters of the great gods during the war; Mount Ida, near Troy, from whose summit Zeus watched the battles; Mount Ida in Crete, another sanctuary of Zeus; Athens; and many other places mentioned by Homer.

The story Homer tells has its setting near the end of the Minoan-Mycenaean Age, possibly 1200–1100 B.C.; its characters include gods as well as men. While archaeology has confirmed Homer's story insofar as the human beings in it are concerned, it does not confirm to the same extent what Homer says about the gods. According to Homer, Zeus has become king of the gods, and reigns from his palace on Mount Olympus. Poseidon is there, too, although his position has been reversed from what it was in the Minoan-Mycenaean Age; Zeus is now his chief. Homer's gods reflect Greek religion at around 800 B.C., the time when Homer is thought to have lived. By then Greek polytheism had become mature; it had a pantheon, a development that apparently did not take place in Minoan times.

The *Theogony* of Hesiod, another poet, who lived somewhat later than Homer, is another of our best sources. Here one finds the most exhaustive list of the gods, goddesses, and spirits of the sky, air, earth, sea, mountains, forests, rivers, springs, trees, and underworld, together with the servants, ministers, messengers, monsters and related creatures, both angelic and demonic, who constitute the cast of invisible divine actors in the drama of Greek religion.

The Sacred and the Profane

As presented in the mythology of Homer and Hesiod, the Greeks are no longer a primitive people, having already attained a well-articulated polytheism organized into a pantheon with Zeus, king of gods, on the throne. Yet there remain numerous survivals of an animistic, and even preanimistic, culture, which were retained and reinterpreted as they were absorbed into the more sophisticated religion. These primitive survivals are best understood as forms of mana and taboo. Greek religion exhibits a continuity in development from the lower to the higher forms, with no sharp breaks, no prophetic reformations. Although the Greeks showed keen awareness of the sacred and the profane throughout their history, they usually maintained their composure in regard to these matters, and never lost their sense of being at home in the midst of all the mysterious powers through which the holy manifested itself to them.

Greek hierophanies were associated with temples and statues of the gods, such as those found on the Acropolis of Athens, at Olympia, or Delphi, but the original sites of hierophanies were springs, trees, mountains, the sea, awe-inspiring phenomena of earth, air, sky, and human life, all of which came earlier than temples and statues. But the temples, the priests, the sacred precincts, the sacrifices, both animal and agricultural, were also expressions of the sacred and the profane. Even the leftover fragments of the sacrifices, including the ashes, were sacred. Once offered, minor portions of the sacrifices were given to the gods, but the major, edible portions were eaten in the holy precincts as sacred meals by the worshipers. Something of this sanctity belonged even to the home, where fires sacred to Hestia, goddess of domestic life, always burned on the hearth.

The most extreme example of sacrificial communion was the *omophagia,* the Dionysiac rite in which the devotees tore a living animal to pieces and devoured the warm, bleeding parts, believing that Dionysus himself was incarnated in the animal. In this way they participated in what amounted to orgiastic communion with the deity. But this act of emotional frenzy was not characteristic of Greek religion as a whole.

The Greeks never lost sight of the terrifying, destructive character that the holy often manifests. Their myths abound in monsters of many kinds: Pan, satyrs, dragons, giants, Titans, sileni, sphinxes, Cyclops, Hydra, centaurs, Minotaur, Gorgons, Cerberus, Fates, Furies, and an unlimited number of other demonic beings. Often the gods themselves had an amoral, if not immoral, character; but the holy also manifested a friendly, creative face, and it was this friendly hierophany that gave the Greeks the faith by which they lived.

The healthy optimism of Greek culture is nowhere more evident than in their interpretation of the arts. Hephaestus, the divine artist and architect, was one of the gods of Olympus; the nine Muses were the goddesses who inspired the poets and presided over the arts and sciences. The most famous example of Greek architecture was the Parthenon, with its surrounding temples, on the Acropolis at Athens. Phidias, the sculptor who supervised the construction of these buildings, and then himself created the statue of Athena that adorned the Parthenon, as well as the Zeus of Olympia, was inspired by religious themes as he executed all these works.

The hierophanies that inspired the Greek philosophers were their visions of the rational, the beautiful, and the good.

THE GODS OF OLYMPUS

The deities most often referred to as residing on Mount Olympus are Zeus, Apollo, Ares, Hermes, Hephaestus, and Poseidon, along with the goddesses Aphrodite, Artemis, Athena, Demeter, Hera, and Hestia. Others were found there from time to time; some were used as entertainers, servants, and messengers by those who lived there. Nor were any deities confined exclusively to Olympus: each of them had temples, shrines, and haunts elsewhere or might be found pursuing his interests and discharging his responsibilities anywhere on earth, or in the sea or sky.

Zeus

Zeus was the most important deity; his authority was in theory absolute, controlling all other deities (see Figure 5.1). He usually had his way—but not always without opposition. His subordinates were jealous of his power; they protested his decisions; at times they even attempted a rebellion. In a general sense, every god had his particular sphere and function, with certain rights pertaining to it, which the other gods, including Zeus, respected. The particular function of Zeus, so far as the world of nature was concerned, lay in the phenomena of the air and sky. He was the shining sky itself, as well as the god of lightning, thunder, storm, and rain, and his personality was best expressed, his will implemented, by resort to these dreadful forces.

Zeus had not always enjoyed this august position among the gods. Indeed, he had secured it by acts of violence, like an ambitious man who seizes a throne by agitation, subversion, rebellion, or revolution. Zeus was not the first of the immortals, being the son of Cronus and Rhea, who were themselves children of Uranus and Gaea (that is, Heaven and Earth), who in turn sprang from Chaos. Beginning with Chaos, according to Hesiod, all the gods had a genealogical relationship to one another; they all belonged to the same immortal family. In this way, Greek intuition expressed its sense of the unity, the kinship, underlying all the forms and phenomena of the world.

The violence that Zeus had used to reach the throne was inherited from the jealous and suspicious natures of his divine father Cronus and his grandfather Uranus. When Uranus' sister-wife Gaea gave birth to three monstrous creatures, each with fifty heads and a hundred hands, so terrifying were they to Uranus that he thereafter began to neglect his wife and took Night as his mistress. The outraged Gaea, in order to get revenge for her husband's infidelity, devised a stratagem with the aid of Cronus, her youngest son. After ambushing his father, Cronus emasculated him with a sickle his mother had made for that purpose, and then cast the amputated genitals into the sea. Drops falling from the virile organs, however, impregnated Gaea, Earth, who then proceeded to give birth to the Furies, terrifying female spirits that punished persons who had committed unavenged crimes. Gaea also bore the Titans, who were mighty giants with gleaming arms and long spears. Moreover, according to Hesiod, the genitals of Uranus impregnated the sea, so that from its foam there sprang Aphrodite, goddess of love, who was born in Crete.

Having seized his father's throne and married his own sister, Rhea, Cronus, who was also a jealous being, swallowed his first five children as soon as they were born. But when the sixth child, Zeus, was due, Rhea fled in desperation to Crete and gave birth to the infant there, and then concealed it in a cave at Dicte. Instead of turning the child over to Cronus, she wrapped a stone in swaddling clothes and gave that to Cronus upon his arrival. And he swallowed it confidently. However, the child soon reached maturity, bested the father in combat, and took the throne from him. At the same time, Zeus compelled Cronus to disgorge the five earlier children. These were Hestia, goddess of hearth and home; Demeter, goddess of the fields; Hera, goddess of marriage and childbirth; Poseidon, god of the sea; and Hades, god of the underworld. His grateful brothers and sisters then gave Zeus the thunderbolt, the basis of his rule over both gods and men.

Rebellions against Zeus

There were two rebellions against the reign of Zeus, both by the demonic progeny of Uranus and Gaea. The first was that of the Giants, who seized Zagreus, the son of Zeus and Persephone, dismembered his body, and devoured its parts. Zeus put down this rebellion with a blast of his thunderbolt, which burned the Giants to ashes. Out of these ashes mankind arose, thus combining in man's nature both divine and demonic elements: the divine from Zagreus, the demonic from the Giants. This view of man, which was prominent in the Orphic cult, is somewhat similar to the biblical idea of original sin.

The second rebellion against Zeus was called the Titanomachy, the war of the Titans, the dispossessed children of Uranus and Gaea. It lasted for ten years, but finally the Titans were conquered and cast into Tartarus in the underworld, where the wicked dead are punished. The gateway into Tartarus rose just across the River Styx and was guarded by Cerberus, a hundred-headed (some say three-headed) dog. The palace of Hades and Persephone, king and queen of the dead, also stood just outside the gate. Later writers add that Charon, the boatman, ferried the dead across the Styx and that Greeks placed an obol in the mouth of the dead to pay the boatman's fare.

According to the myths, however, most of the dead went to Asphodel, a neutral, colorless region in Hades, there to pass a shadowy existence without either reward or punishment. The poets also say that a few fortunate dead went to Elysium, a lovely paradise.

The myths of the rise of Zeus to power should probably be interpreted as the religious counterpart of the military and cultural conquest of Crete and Greece by the Indo-Europeans, a long struggle in which the indigenous culture of the Pelasgians was either de-

stroyed or absorbed into that of the conquerors. Zeus is the Greek
version of the older Dyaus, the sky god of the Indo-Europeans; but
the pantheon of Zeus included some Pelasgian deities as well, of
whom Poseidon is an example. The Indo-Europeans were not a
sea people and therefore had no god of the sea.

The Other Olympians

Six of the major Classical Greek deities, as we have seen, were children of the deposed Cronus—namely, Zeus and his five brothers
and sisters: Poseidon, Demeter, Hera, Hades, and Hestia. Hades
reigned over the dead in the nether world and was not an Olympian.
The other seven major deities were sons and daughters of Zeus
himself. Thus the gods of Olympus were a close-knit family, all of
the same blood.

Aphrodite, goddess of love, was, according to Homer, a daughter
of Zeus by Dione, one of the Titans. However, this view is in conflict with Hesiod's mythical account of Aphrodite being born of
seafoam. The beautiful Aphrodite, whose lovely form is best known
in the sculpture from the island of Melos popularly called the
Venus de Milo, was the expression of romance, desire, passion. She
was subject to no law, no moral code, no restraint beyond that of
love itself. She set the pattern that was followed routinely by the
gods themselves, as for example, by Zeus. Of his seven children
among the Olympians, only two were begotten of his wife, Hera;
the other five were the children of mistresses. Nor did the gods limit
their romantic adventures to divine beings; they often fell in love
with mortal men and women. Homer relates that Zeus begot Heracles of Alcmene, the wife of Amphitryon, king of Thebes. Achilles
was the son of Peleus, a mortal, who was married to Thetis, a
goddess. Aeneas was the son of Aphrodite and Anchises. Homer's
Odyssey tells of the goddesses Calypso and Circe, who were impregnated by Odysseus while they held him prisoner on their islands.

Apollo, son of Zeus and Leto, was god of music and poetry; he
was also the archer-king and the patron of bowmen. In a sense, he
was the angel of death, especially the sudden death of men, which

FIGURE 5.2 A model of the sacred precincts of Delphi, showing the Temple of
Apollo and the theater. (*The Metropolitan Museum of Art, Dodge Fund, 1930*)

was generally attributed to his darts. He loved war, and participated with enthusiasm on the Trojan side in the Trojan War against the Greeks; one of his shrines was located on Pergamus, a mountain near Troy. This versatile deity was also the god of prophecy, and his shrine at Delphi (see Figure 5.2) was famous all over the Mediterranean world. It was constructed over a cavern in the earth, which was inhabited by a spirit of revelation named Python. This was, in fact, an epithet of Apollo, who, according to the myth, slew the serpent of that name which dwelt in the cave. The priestess who sat on a tripod over this cavern and inhaled the rising vapors came under the intoxicating influence of the Python; in the resulting ecstasy she would utter inspired answers to those who came with questions. Finally, Apollo was identified with the sun and worshiped in that role.

Hephaestus, son of Zeus and Hera and husband of Aphrodite, was the lame god of fire and the forge, the great divine architect

and artisan. He constructed palaces for all the gods of Olympus and decorated them with ornaments that were in keeping with the taste of such a society. He also made arms for the gods.

Ares, son of Zeus and Hera, was the god of war—to which he was savagely devoted. Ares and Aphrodite had much in common: each was restrained only by his own passion, but followed that with abandon. Hence they were well suited to each other as violent lovers.

Artemis, daughter of Zeus and Leto, was the sister of Apollo and in many ways similar to him. She loved the hunt, the bow, and wild animals, whom she protected. Like Apollo she caused death, especially to women, by firing darts. Artemis was apparently a virgin goddess; she was never married.

Athena, a daughter of Zeus, was a strange case of a deity without a mother. Zeus had taken Metis, a goddess destined to have brilliant children, as his first wife; but on the advice of Gaea and Uranus, his grandparents, and fearing that one of the children of Metis might rise up and drive him from the throne, Zeus swallowed her when she was at the point of bearing her first child. He thought that with Metis thus inside him he might still be able to benefit from her advice. Nevertheless, the bright-eyed and intelligent Athena, the child with whom Metis was pregnant, sprang fully grown and completely armed from the head of Zeus, and in this way was born without a mother. Athena, the goddess of wisdom and of the arts and crafts, was also a fighting goddess, a lover of war, and at times Zeus even permitted her to wield his own thunderbolts. Athens was her favorite city. The Parthenon, her temple that stands on the Acropolis in Athens, was not only a supreme example of Greek art but also one of the most beautiful buildings ever constructed; its name is derived from *parthenos,* the Greek word for virgin. Athena was known as the virgin goddess, for, like Artemis, she never married. Neither of these goddesses showed any aversion or hostility toward sex or marriage as such, but they never yielded to the passions of Aphrodite, finding full expression of their personalities along intellectual, moral, and artistic lines. This showed that Greek culture recognized the full range of human emotions—including the enjoyment of romance, passion, and love—and at the same time attached great importance to the pursuit of intellectual and artistic ideals. This was true especially at Athens, where Athena enjoyed the highest honor. Neither Aphrodite nor Ares nor any other deity—not even Zeus—could displace her in the hearts of the Athenians.

Hermes, one of the minor Greek gods, but not the least picturesque among them, was the son of Zeus and Maia. His chief function was to serve as messenger or ambassador of the gods, Zeus in particular; he was a specialist in communications and gave the different races of mankind their languages. Homer often refers to him also as "slayer of the giant"—the monster Argus, who was also called Panoptes because he had eyes all over his body. According to the myth, Zeus changed Io, one of his mistresses, into a heifer in order to conceal her from the jealous Hera. But Hera saw through the stratagem and detailed Panoptes to watch the heifer, whereupon Hermes, as the agent of Zeus, beguiled Panoptes to sleep and killed him. By the time of the *Iliad,* however, all this had become part of the past, and in that epic Hermes is merely the courier.

Olympian Anthropomorphism

The Olympian gods were represented by the Greeks as having intensely human characteristics. They manifested desire, passion, jealousy, hatred, vengeance, cruelty, compassion. While their powers exceeded those of men, they were usually neither omnipotent nor omniscient; they were certainly not always good. They differed from men, however, in their possession of immortality; they never grew old, never died—at least not permanently, as mortals did. On occasion, one of them could even be described as receiving a wound. They carried weapons and wore armor in battle. But they could also appear and disappear at will. They could conceal their identity from human beings by appearing in human, as well as animal, forms.

Nereus, god of the Aegean and known as the Old Man of the Sea, lived in a palace at the bottom of the sea with his wife, Doris, and their fifty Nereid daughters. Against her will, Thetis, one of the Nereids, had been forced by Zeus and Hera to become the wife of Peleus, king of Phthiotis in Thessaly. By Peleus she became the mother of Achilles, and she watched proudly, but with a sad heart, as her son grew to manhood, for she knew that he was fated to die young. She was also grieved by her marriage to the mortal Peleus, because he became senile and decrepit, while she, a goddess, remained eternally young.

JUSTICE

The question of justice was of great concern to the Greeks. In the religious sense, justice is the idea that God is the righteous sovereign of the universe and that, therefore, everything which happens both to nations and to men is an expression of justice. This means that in this life a man gets what his conduct deserves: a just man prospers; a wicked man suffers. Nevertheless, the facts of life do not support this theory; from early times Greeks saw that misfortune often strikes upright men.

This paradox between what the Greeks thought the world ought to be and the way it is fascinated some of their great dramatists. Sophocles dealt with this theme in three of his plays: *Antigone, Oedipus Rex,* and *Oedipus at Colonus.* All are efforts to penetrate the mystery of the tragedy of Oedipus, son of Laius, king of Thebes, who in infancy was cast out to die by his parents because of an oracular prediction that a son of theirs would grow up to murder his father.

The child was rescued by a shepherd and given to the king and queen of Corinth, who adopted him and brought him up as their son, so that Oedipus believed that he was their own child. On coming of age, Oedipus went on a journey through nearby Greek states. As he approached Thebes, he met King Laius, his own father, approaching with bodyguards in chariots. They pushed Oedipus out of the road and his father struck him with a staff, each of them unaware of the other's identity. A brawl resulted in which Oedipus killed his father and all his father's servants but one, who escaped and lived to remember what had happened.

In the meantime, Oedipus had also slain a sphinx, a monster with the head and breasts of a woman and the body of a lion, which had been destroying all travelers passing that way who could not solve a riddle she propounded. Oedipus therefore entered Thebes as a hero. Since their king was now dead, the Thebans crowned Oedipus king, and he married Jocasta, his own mother, the widow of King Laius. They, in turn, being unaware of each other's true identity, became parents of a new family of children. Thus Oedipus was guilty of both parricide and incest. But the truth at last became known, whereupon Jocasta committed suicide, and Oedipus put out his own eyes. Driven from his throne into exile, he carried to his death the conviction that his horrible deeds, even though he had committed them in all innocence, merited the fate which had come upon him.

In *Prometheus Bound,* Aeschylus dealt with a similar theme. This time the protagonist was Prometheus, a demigod, and Zeus, ruler of both gods and men, replaced the Fates and Destiny. The story therefore has to do with gods, not men. Yet it also concerns the destiny of man, and most particularly the final step in his creation. Up to that point man had no culture, no civilization, indeed no intelligence beyond that of other animals. As a result his life depended on the uncultivated fruits of nature.

Zeus intended man to remain in this natural state; anything beyond was reserved for the gods. But Prometheus, sensing man's possibilities, had compassion for him. First he stole fire and gave it to man. Then he taught him how to use it in developing the tools and arts of civilization—whereupon a new world opened to man. But Zeus reacted ruthlessly to crush this rebellion against his rule: he decreed that Prometheus, the rebel, must be chained hand and foot to the rock face of a mountain, with a spike driven through his breast into the stone. The victim hung there day and night. By day an eagle tore out his liver and ate it; each night it grew back. This grisly cycle was repeated endlessly. Friends pleaded with Prometheus to relent and beg for mercy, but this he would not do. Down to the end of the play, he still protests the savage decree; he affirms his compassion for man and his own innocence of wrong; he defiantly challenges the injustice of the divine tyranny. This protest against the irrationality of tragedy in the world, whether in the life of gods or in that of men, is precisely the point that Aeschylus seems to have wished to make; yet he too, like Sophocles and the Hebrew Job, who wrestled with the same problem, left the mystery in the end still unresolved.

FESTIVALS, RITES, AND CULTS

No presentation of Greek religion would be complete without reference to its joy. The festivals of Dionysus (also called Bacchus), god of wine and of the intoxicating and productive powers of nature, exemplify this aspect of Greek culture. As the spirit of vegetation, Dionysus was believed to die in the fall and to rise again from the dead in the spring. His resurrection was celebrated in vineyards and fields, while the grapes were being cultivated, harvested, and processed, and reached its culmination with the opening of the first barrels of the new wine, in a festival called the *Pithoigia*. Processions of intoxicated persons, believed to have been inspired by the spirit of Dionysus, went dancing through the fields in frenzied revels. Particularly noteworthy among them were the women, known as bacchants or maenads, who, according to the myths, were accompanied by an assortment of wild animals and spirit creatures, such as sileni and satyrs.

It was out of the festivals of Dionysus that the Greek theater was born. The comedies were intended to brighten the gloom of winter; the solemn themes of tragedy accompanied the rituals of spring.

Every Greek state had its own festivals representing its particular interests and devotion to its own deities. Athens celebrated the Panathenaea every year (with special brilliance every fourth year) in honor of Athena, its protecting goddess. This festival, which included games and contests, began with processions from different parts of the state converging on the capital, and came to a culmination at the Parthenon on the Acropolis.

The best-known festivals were those for citizens of all the states, which brought the Greeks together in a spirit of unity. The Olympic Games, the most famous of these celebrations, were held every four years at Olympia in Elis and included competitions in athletics, music, and poetry in honor of Zeus. The victors were treated as heroes throughout the Greek lands. Another festival in honor of Zeus was held at Nemea in Argolis every second year. Poseidon, god of the sea, was celebrated in a similar festival on the Isthmus of Corinth. The Pythian Games at Delphi, in honor of Apollo, were held every fourth year.

Even funeral rites sometimes included athletic contests. The twenty-third book of the *Iliad* describes the sports that Achilles staged as part of the funeral rites of Patroclus. These included a chariot race, boxing, wrestling, foot races, and archery. Such sports events were always celebrated in honor of one or another of the gods and constituted a real part of Greek religion, for Greeks understood the function of celebration and play or recreation as a relief from tensions and sorrows.

The Eleusinian Mysteries

The Eleusinian Mysteries were celebrated in the shrine of Demeter at Eleusis, some twelve miles northwest of Athens, where the Cephisus River reaches the Eleusinian Gulf. This ancient cult, which went back to prehistoric times, was for many centuries related only to agriculture. It involved three deities: Demeter, goddess of the fields, especially of grain, and earth; her daughter Persephone, representing the spirit of vegetation which dies in the fall and rises from the dead in the spring; and Hades, god of the underworld. According to the myth, Persephone was stolen and carried to the nether world by Hades. Demeter, the distressed mother, frantically sought her missing daughter, and finally discovered that, with the connivance of Zeus, Persephone had become the wife of Hades. In her grief, Demeter refused to give life to vegetation, and all Attica was caught in famine. The famine brought Zeus and Hades to terms, and a reconciliation was effected. It was agreed that Persephone would spend half of the year with her husband in the underworld and half with her mother on earth, thus reflecting the cycle of the agricultural seasons. The rituals performed at Eleusis were believed to contribute to the fertility of the fields and to the growth of grain.

In later times the rites of Eleusis became a mystery cult, offering initiation to those who were morally pure, and promising them a divine rebirth in this life and immortality in the hereafter. The initiation was at first open only to Greeks, but in time it became internationalized. Men, women, even slaves, were eligible, and came from all over the world to be initiated.

The Cult of Asclepius, the God of Healing

By Hellenistic times, Asclepius, who was said to be the son of Apollo, had attained eminence among the Greeks as god of healing. While his best-known temple was located at Epidaurus in Argolis, he had numerous other shrines in Greece proper, the islands, and even at Rome, Carthage, and in Phoenicia.

The cult of Asclepius was introduced into Rome in 293 B.C. when, in order to avert a pestilence, a temple to Asclepius was built on an island in the Tiber. Testimonial inscriptions set up by persons healed at this temple have been recovered, and we now also have some from the more famous shrine at Epidaurus. The healing procedure at these shrines was for patients to sleep in them; the healing god could then reveal to them in dreams the remedies they were to follow.[2] Palestine itself felt the influence of this cult during the first century A.D. A coin celebrating the hot springs near Tiberias on the Sea of Galilee, struck in A.D. 99, shows Hygeia, daughter of Asclepius, seated on a rock by the bubbling springs holding a serpent in her hands. Snakes were regarded as sacred in this cult and were kept in the temples. Presumably, they had something to do with the healings.

Yet the Greeks were one of the earliest peoples to develop a rational view of disease, as is shown by the Hippocratic corpus, a collection of medical writings ascribed to Hippocrates. In an essay on epilepsy, which he refers to as the Sacred Disease, Hippocrates states that this ailment has natural causes, not supernatural ones, and that it should therefore have rational treatments.

PHILOSOPHY

The Greek philosophers deserve to be mentioned in this study of religion, because their thought was so closely associated with religion both during their lives and in subsequent centuries. But we have space to mention only three.

Socrates (469–399 B.C.) left no writings. We are dependent almost entirely on what Plato and Xenophon, his two most famous pupils, wrote about him. He was born near Athens and spent his entire life there. He studied sculpture first and attained eminence in that art. But his real interest lay in teaching; he devoted the latter part of his life to this profession, although practicing it in a very informal way and not in any school. He lived simply, in actual poverty, disdaining shoes and wearing only a minimum of clothing.

His method of teaching was to engage interested persons, especially the young, in conversation. His concern was to show his listeners how to think clearly and how to arrive at sound conclusions. He was gifted in the use of questions and answers—the dialogue type of instruction. One of his chief principles was "Know thyself." This means having a realistic opinion and judgment of one's inner motives, being under no illusion as to one's true desires and intentions. Logic and ethics were therefore his basic concerns. He knew how to lay bare, with a few bold strokes, every form of pretense, sham, hypocrisy.

As a result of his ruthless penetration into the motives of persons, Socrates made enemies. He was brought to trial ostensibly on the charges of destroying faith in the gods and corrupting the youth;

but political considerations had much to do with his trial. It is true that Socrates was critical of the myths and legends of the Greek gods; yet he was a religious man. Nevertheless, he was put to death, forced to drink the cup of hemlock.

Plato (427–347 B.C.) continued where Socrates left off, but his interests led him into the field of metaphysics. The nature of being, itself, was for him the most important of all questions. He was driven to this by his observation of the transitory character of the phenomenal world. Feeling that there must be something more nearly ultimate than the things we know by the senses, he concluded that the tangible world is only a shadow of eternal patterns or ideas that exist in a higher dimension, a metaphysical realm. True knowledge consists not merely in knowing the visible world but in pressing on in a rational manner. He would have us grasp the ideas of which the visible world is but a shadow, a veiled expression. The highest of all ideas is that of the Good, in which all lesser ideas participate.

Plato's system gave rise to idealism, one of the best-known schools of philosophy, a type of thought that had a strong influence on early Christian theology. Yet Plato's thought tended toward dualism. He became so engrossed in eternal ideas that he depreciated the phenomenal world, regarding it as a handicap, a barrier to knowledge of the ultimate reality. He even went so far as to say that the phenomenal world had been created by a sort of evil god, a demiurge. Christian Gnostics later took up this view, regarding the human body as evil; this led them to the practice of asceticism.

Aristotle (384–322 B.C.) was the greatest of Plato's students; his interests were wider than those of his teacher. To begin with, he was a scientist, and based his learning on firsthand observation of the phenomena of nature. He developed the empirical method, which was to be used by the sciences in modern times. But he too went beyond the visible phenomena and raised the question of ultimate reality. Differing somewhat from Plato on this, he developed the concept of substance as the ultimate basis of all the forms and species of being. Every kind of life, he held, is a combination of substance, or essence, with form. The visible character or attributes of a tree, for example, are its leaves, the texture of its wood, the configuration of its branches, and so on; these constitute the form of the tree; they are, in short, its "accidents." What determines the kind, the species of the tree, even its accidents, is its substance or essence, which is invisible, metaphysical. This is true of all classes of beings in the world. Substance, which replaces Plato's concept of idea, is therefore the cause of everything. Yet substance, like the idea, is intelligible; it is a rational concept.

Aristotle was far more interested in theology than Plato had been. As one product of his scientific thought, he showed that the simplest motion requires, for its ultimate explanation, a prime mover. So too, any chain of causality points to an initial cause. Intelligibility itself presupposes an eternal reason or rationality, which is independent and self-sufficient, and therefore perfect, infinite, the basis of all knowledge. This infinite Reason is God, the perfect actualization of intelligence or mind, the ultimate cause of all that is. This exaltation of reason was to have an enormous influence on both Christian and Jewish theology, beginning with the scholasticism that preceded the Renaissance and continuing down to the present day.

NOTES

1. Leonard R. Palmer, *Mycenaeans and Minoans* (New York: Knopf, 1962), pp. 119–131.
2. S. V. McCasland, "Religious Healing in First-Century Palestine," in McNeill, Spinka, and Willoughby, eds., *Environmental Factors in Christian History* (Chicago: University of Chicago Press, 1939), pp. 18–34; also, *By the Finger of God* (New York: Macmillan, 1951), pp. 28–29.

EARLY ROMAN RELIGION

The earliest form of religion in Italy was a primitive animism. Every important phenomenon of nature was endowed with its *numen;* the world was full of numina, to which men reacted with a sense of mystery and awe, sometimes in terror. The Latin word for this feeling about the numen was *religio,* which is similar to mana, a term used in animistic cultures in our own time. *Religio* is probably the word from which our word *religion* was derived; and *numen* has given us *numinous,* which is used to designate an object or experience that has a spiritual quality or atmosphere.

When Latium emerged into the period of recorded history, the people were still living on the land, cultivating their cereals, small fruits and vegetables, and caring for their flocks. Each family owned and occupied its own piece of land. The family was not, however, based strictly on blood kinship; slaves might be included in it, and even animals were thought of as belonging to it, since a place connected to the family home was provided for them. Moreover, the family might include three or possibly four generations, all of them living together; the oldest man, the *paterfamilias,* was its head and exercised supreme control—even over life and death. The earliest Italian house, possibly located on a hilltop, was built of earth and poles thatched with grass; in historical times, however, this primitive hut was replaced by a rectangular atrium adequate for the family and slaves, with a fireplace, a dining and living area, a storage room, and a roof opening into a central court. The ancient families of

FIGURE 6.1   A Roman haruspex examining the entrails of a bull. (*Alinari–Art Reference Bureau*)

Italy lived separately, not grouped together in villages as they were in some other parts of Europe.

The religious life of such a family revolved about the spirits who were concerned with its welfare. Perhaps most important was Vesta, spirit of the fire on the family hearth, on which so much of the life of the family depended. After the noon meal a period of silence was observed; then a fragment of the loaf of bread cooked for the family was broken off and tossed into the fire for Vesta. The penates were spirits which guarded the storeroom, *penus,* where the food supplies were kept. The lares, at first revered as spirits that ensured the productivity of the fields and guarded its boundaries, later became associated with protection of the house; they too were important in the family rites. The manes, spirits of the family dead, were the objects of special concern, as was the burial ground. When honored with proper burial ceremonies, these spirits departed in peace to the underworld and were ordinarily heard from no more. But spirits of the dead who had not received the burial rites to which they were entitled were believed to be unable to secure entrance into Hades. Instead, they lingered about as angry ghosts, *lemures,* sources of misfortune, to haunt the living. Janus, guardian of the doorway, was also prominent in family rituals. The genius of the paterfamilias—a term that is derived from *gens* (clan), and testifies to the membership of the family in that larger social unit—was devoted to the welfare and perpetuation of the family, and therefore of great importance in family religion. Accompanying the paterfamilias from birth to death and surviving him after his death, the genius was a sort of oversoul or second soul, an expression of the Romans' belief in immortality.

The religion of the family was simple and practical, being related entirely to the concerns of the family. Little equipment was necessary for its rites: the only altar in the home was the hearth with its fire, sacred to Vesta, always burning; the paterfamilias, the only priest. The family was also careful of the rites of Terminus, the guardian of the boundaries of their land; each family, led by its paterfamilias, took part in the community ceremonials involving the common interests of adjacent farms, as the annual seasons returned.

The simplicity that was so characteristic of the early Latin families continued to be evident in the early Roman state, which was formed by a group of closely related tribes with similar cultures and common interests. The state was conceived of as a great family, with the king assuming the role of the paterfamilias. All military, political, and economic power was vested in the king, as well as the responsibility for religion. He was the chief priest, but religion continued to be practical and unadorned. There were sacred places, all rites related to the welfare of the people were faithfully performed, and plain altars were necessary; but there were no images or statues to represent the gods, nor any elaborate temples. Houses for the gods were little more pretentious than the thatched dwellings of families. The deities were nature spirits, without definite personalities, and thus without elaborate mythologies. They were conceived of along the same lines as spirits in primitive religions the world over.

The adornment that was to be characteristic of Roman religion appears to have begun about the sixth century B.C., under the influence of the more advanced cultures of the Etruscans and Greeks. From the Etruscans, Romans learned to make images and statues of their gods, as well as beautiful temples. The Greeks taught them to endow their gods with the personalities of human beings, and with morality like that of men and women—no better, no worse. In this way, both Greek and Roman gods came to be like human beings. In later centuries, the Romans slavishly identified their gods with similar Greek deities, ascribing the same personalities and functions to them, and often telling the same stories about them. The process of identification reached its culmination with the Romans taking over Greek Mount Olympus as the abode of the Roman gods—a view that had become quite commonplace by the time of Virgil's *Aeneid*. The theory behind this was that, all along, the Greek and Roman gods had been the same gods, only called by different names.

It was characteristic of Romans of the later period, notably of Varro the antiquarian, to divide Roman gods into two groups; the native, or indigenous gods, the *di indigetes,* and the gods imported and adopted from other people, the *di novensides.* The real genius of Roman religion is to be seen in the original gods, the *di indigetes.* Yet the *di novensides,* the foreign gods adopted during the periods of the Republic and the Empire, reflect the hospitality of the Roman mind to new and strange ideas, reverence for gods wherever encountered and desire for their favor (as well as political wisdom).

The *Di Indigetes*

Careful inventory of the gods in the Calendar of Numa, the deities associated with various festivals, and the names of gods in Roman literature or recovered from inscriptions has yielded a list of thirty-three gods from the ancient period. Most of these *di indigetes,* however, are no more than names; if they once did have real meaning, that meaning can no longer be recovered. Out of the list of thirty-three, only five are of any importance: Janus, Jupiter, Mars, Quirinus, and Vesta. And even these retain the essential character of nature gods, designating spirits little higher than the numina of primitive religions.

Janus is the least important of the five major *di indigetes.* Long before the end of Roman history he had lost whatever status he had had as an intelligible deity. The Romans themselves had forgotten his significance: some speculated that he was the sun or the sky or the wind, but they had no convincing evidence for any of these. It seems that Janus was the guardian of the city gates, in addition to being the guardian spirit of the family doorway. A symbolic gateway to the Roman Forum was dedicated to Janus, although he never was a god of major proportions. The meaning of the double-headed Janus on some old Roman coins is of uncertain origin. After Rome had become a city, the chief priest, *rex sacrorum,* sacrificed to Janus on the Calends, the first day of every month. In January, the month named for Janus and the first month of the natural year—that is, the month that followed the winter solstice—Janus was worshiped on the Calends and on the fifteenth. But he was not important enough to have a temple of his own until 260 B.C.

Jupiter, however, was a truly great god, even in the ancient period, and his priest, the *flamen Dialis,* ranked next to the *rex sacrorum.* He was the awesome potency of the sky, with all the phenomena related to it: light, lightning, thunder, storm, rain. These wonders, as well as the etymology of his name, associate Jupiter with Zeus Pater (Father Zeus) of the Greeks, with similar gods of other ancient European cultures, and ultimately with Dyaus-pitar, the father sky of the ancient Aryans, thus pointing to Aryan influence on cultures throughout Europe, in addition to those in India and Persia.

Jupiter had attained a secure position in Latium—he was worshiped at Alba Longa—long before Rome was founded. When his cult first reached Rome, he was worshiped there in a small temple, only fifteen feet wide and with the simplest equipment. This modest

FIGURE 6.2 Ruins of the Temple of Mars, in the Forum of Augustus. (*Italian State Tourist Office*)

worship continued for a considerable time before the late Etruscan kings became the kings of Rome. It was these kings who established Jupiter on the Capitoline Hill and built for him a great temple. There he acquired the title of Optimus Maximus and attained the position of chief protector of the Roman people.

On the basis of his religious character and his name, it may be possible to lodge against Jupiter a suspicion that, during some pre-historic period, he had been imported into Italy from abroad; such a charge, however, could hardly be brought against Mars, his chief rival for the affections of the Romans. It appears quite certain that Mars was an indigenous god. Originally belonging to forests and mountains, where wild beasts (notably packs of Italian wolves) roamed, Mars was like them—wild, ferocious, implacable. He ap-

pears to have been domesticated first by shepherds and farmers, who sought his protection against marauding animals. But Mars was also to gain his greatest role as protector of the Roman people against hostile human beings. Above all else he was the god of war, popular among soldiers. Surrounded as they were by unfriendly tribes from the beginning, Romans had to be good soldiers. The military virtues were among the chief characteristics of the Roman people and were the discipline of Romans from childhood; Mars was the god of these virtues. Roman armies of the early days were made up of citizens, who fought until they won or died; they never surrendered.

During the ancient period Mars never had a temple inside the walls of Rome. The Romans built his temple outside the walls, possibly because they believed that his wildness made him unwilling to live behind walls, or they may have feared that his combative nature might arouse strife among the people. It was not until the reign of Augustus, who became the first emperor of Rome in 30 B.C., that Mars came inside the city. A temple was built for him in the Forum of Augustus (see Figure 6.2). The early Romans honored him by naming the first month of the year Martius or March. At that time, the calendar year contained only ten months and began in the spring, because it was then that all life seemed to start again, and it was the season when war preparations were made. (Romans later added the months of January and February, making a year of twelve months, and in 46 B.C. Julius Caesar, when he was Pontifex Maximus, adopted the Egyptian method of reckoning the length of the year from movements of the sun.) Priests of Mars, the *Salii*, celebrated the opening of the military season by their leaping dances in the streets of Rome. In October, when the campaigns closed, after rituals of purification, weapons and standards were replaced in the armory, ready for use again the following spring.

Of Quirinus, fourth of the important gods at the time the Calendar of Numa was compiled, we have few solid facts. He was the only one of the early great gods to reside in Rome from the beginning. His temple was located on one of the seven hills of Rome, the Quirinal Hill—a name which itself testifies to the importance of this deity. As this hill was assigned to a colony of Sabines, it may be that Quirinus was originally a Sabine god, brought along by the Sabines as their protector when they settled in Rome. On February 17 of each year, a festival was celebrated in his honor, but the nature of this festival is today unknown, and even the Romans of later centuries did not know its nature. The *flamen Quirinalis,* priest of Quirinus, along with the priests of Jupiter and Mars, constituted a triad that ranked above all other flamens. There is some evidence that Quirinus was the god of citizens of a town in public assembly; citizens themselves were sometimes called Quirites. Another view is that Quirinus, like Mars, was originally a war god, but that he was devoted to peace rather than to war itself. He therefore preferred to live inside the city, whereas Mars, who was wilder by nature, remained outside the walls.

Vesta, the last of the five important gods of the early period but, as we have seen, not the least in the affections of the Roman people, was central in the life of every ancient Roman family. Further, the Roman state was conceived of on the order of a family to which all the people belonged, with the king in the role of the paterfamilias and a hearth fire of Vesta as the center of national life. Vesta had her own small house in Rome, a round structure, which was technically not a temple, since it had the simplicity of a family home. The holy fire was tended by six priestesses, the vestal virgins, who had been chosen from patrician families. They took a vow of chastity, any violation of which was punishable by death. The accused vestal was not executed outright—she was too holy for that—but locked in an underground chamber and allowed to die of either suffocation or starvation; her partner in guilt was executed.

A vestal served thirty years. Her training was rigid, the rules by which she lived exacting. Her duties had to do with tending the fire and preparing the cakes offered to Vesta. For this purpose, on the days of May 7–14 the vestals gathered the first ears of the ripening grain. On June 7 the doors of the shrine were opened to the women of Rome, who came barefoot to make their offerings. Bakers and millers also celebrated a holiday at this time. The shrine of Vesta had a storehouse like that which every Roman home contained. On June 7 the vestals cleaned it thoroughly, as if in preparation for the approaching harvest. Then they closed the room again, and it remained so until the next June 7. The storehouse was said to contain certain sacred objects which no one but the vestals and the Pontifex Maximus ever saw. On March 1, the early Roman New Year's Day, the vestals rekindled the holy fire by the primitive method of rubbing sticks together.

Vesta represented the true nature of the old Roman religion, and her cult remained relatively simple and pure to the very end. No cult image of her was ever made. Even as late as imperial times she was still worshiped as the potency of the flames: Vesta was the fire itself.

Although our discussion has already covered the most important early gods, the Roman polytheism included numerous others, some of them of considerable significance. One of these was Saturn, the god of sowing and harvest. As a primitive numen, he was probably thought of as the potency of the seed grain, which causes it to sprout and grow. His chief festival was the Saturnalia which was celebrated on December 17, after fall plowing was finished. The festival was later extended for several days as a time of rejoicing, play, and relaxation of social customs, when masters and slaves forgot their relative positions and mingled together freely in licentious indulgence. The celebration coincided with the winter solstice, the turning point in the sun's southward movement and the point when days begin to grow longer again. No doubt the Saturnalia was also related to the fertility of the earth and the new life of fields and pastures, animals and men.

Saturn's wife, according to the myth, was Ops, later identified with Ceres, goddess of fields and grain, and eventually with the Greek Demeter. Saturn was made the father of Jupiter, Neptune, Pluto, and Juno and, with little apparent reason, equated with the Greek Cronus, who was father of Zeus, Poseidon, Hades, and Hera, among others. He was also credited with bringing to Italy the knowledge of agriculture and the arts of civilization; while he reigned as king the land enjoyed a golden age. His temple stood at the foot of the Capitoline Hill.

The extensive influence of Greek religion on Roman religion becomes evident if we consider the following pairs of deities, as they were equated or adopted in the poetic mythology of the late Roman Republic: Cronus with Saturn; Zeus with Jupiter; Hera with Juno; Poseidon with Neptune; Hephaestus with Vulcan; Ares with Mars; Hades with Pluto; Aphrodite with Venus; Athena with Minerva; Hestia with Vesta; Asclepius with Aesculapius; Demeter with Ceres; Persephone with Proserpine; Helios with Sol. The Greek god Apollo, so versatile that Romans had no deity with which to equate him, was brought into the Roman pantheon under his own name. Along with this process of equation, many features of the Greek mythology were transferred to their Roman counterparts. Virgil's *Aeneid*, written at the very end of the Republic, is an excellent source of information of this nature.

PRIESTS AND DIVINERS

From early times the Romans were a deeply religious people. They believed that the health and welfare of their families, as well as the safety and prosperity of the state, depended on the good will and protection of the gods. It was only natural, therefore, for the state itself to assume full responsibility for the performance of rituals of various kinds that had to do with the nation and for all religious worship. The performance of religious rites was considered as important as, if not more important than, the other functions of government. The king himself was vested with priestly power, as well as with all other powers of government, and in time associated himself with a *rex sacrorum* who assisted in the religious rites. When the kingship was replaced by a republic, at about 500 B.C., general administrative responsibility for state religious affairs was assigned to the Pontifex Maximus, who had the power to appoint high-level priests, even the *rex sacrorum*.

Far more than Greek religion, the Roman religion witnessed a development of priests, who were organized into colleges or guilds according to their functions. The *pontifex* was a priestly official with administrative duties. The *sacerdos* was a priest who was active in sacrificial rites, especially animal sacrifices, which were central in the worship at public temples. Each important deity usually had his own priest or flamen, who lit the altar fires. The *augur*—of whom there was a board, first of three, four, or five, but increased to fifteen by Sulla and finally to sixteen by Julius Caesar—was a specialist in interpreting unusual phenomena of animals, birds, earth, and sky. Such phenomena were regarded as signs, wonders, omens, portents, that brought messages from the gods. The Romans were strong believers in divination. Decisions about important matters of state were often delayed until a propitious augury could be obtained.

The Romans even went beyond their own borders in quest of divine messages. Early in their history they began to send to the Etruscan cities on their north, where an official called a *haruspex* was an expert in divination by inspecting the vital organs, especially the liver, of sacrificed animals. But in time the Etruscan haruspices were imported into Rome itself, where they would always be available, thus supplementing the native Roman augurs (see Figure 6.1).

The Romans also learned to consult the oracle of Apollo in the Greek colony of Cumae, north of Naples, where the Sibyl, a priestess of Apollo, practiced her art of divination by interpreting sacred writings known as the Sibylline Books. These too were finally brought to Rome itself by the Romans. In certain emergencies, the Romans even sent messengers to the renowned temple of Apollo at Delphi in Greece.

NEW GODS

The multiplication of gods at Rome during the late centuries of the Republic and the proliferation of rites of divination and incantation suggest the profound attachment of the Roman people to super-natural powers. On the other hand, this elaboration of rites also indicates that the old religion had begun to lose its power. In this loss of faith, which was certainly far advanced by the end of the Republic, several factors played a contributory role. One was that the vast number of deities which had been recognized led to con-fusion, in that they tended to neutralize one another. Gradually the strength of all of them ebbed away. The expansion of Roman frontiers, which now included so many peoples, each with its own gods, was another factor, for to these peoples the old Roman gods had little meaning.

Greek philosophy, which by the Republican period had become familiar to all educated Romans, had also brought its own skepticism of everything that was based on the intervention of supernatural beings in the natural world. The best known of these philosophies were Stoicism, Epicureanism, and Neoplatonism. Common to them all was belief in the idea of a universe and the orderly character of the natural world. These philosophies taught that by scientific ob-servation one could discover the order which is manifested in the world, in history, and in human personality.

The Stoics regarded the old mythologies as, at worst, outright fabrications, and at best, only symbols of natural phenomena. Zeus or Jupiter meant the powers seen in the sky; Poseidon or Neptune, the energy and power in the sea. Ares or Mars was the combative character of man; Aphrodite or Venus, the love passion. Thus they continued to see meanings in all the gods, but only as symbols of things found in nature which they could point out without recourse to symbols.

Epicureanism was even more devastating in its effect on the ancient religious traditions. One of the best examples of this philosophy in that age is the poem *On the Nature of the Universe,* an exposition of the Epicurean philosophy in readable poetic form written about 55 B.C. by Lucretius. Lucretius scoffs at the belief in supernatural beings, doubting that man has any power to turn to besides himself and his fellow-man. Further, he is doubtful about immortality, with all its promises of a hereafter. Instead he advocates a life of temperance, prudence, fortitude, and justice—virtues that the Greek philosophers had advocated for centuries.

At the same time, the Roman masses, even in their disillusionment with the old religion, still apparently carried in their hearts a deep spiritual hunger, and as a result they began to turn to new types of religion. These last centuries of the Republic belonged to the Hellenistic Age, one of the most characteristic features of which was the collapse of the old nations and cultures and their absorption into the emerging empire of Rome. The gods, formerly supposed to be protectors of the old kingdoms, had now been discredited. Individual men found themselves with no protectors, no faith, no hope. Men therefore became absorbed in their own predicaments. There was a general craving for a sense of personal meaning, personal security—something beyond the uncertainties of this present life.

In response to this new quest new religions were emerging that devoted themselves not to the protection of states or nations but rather to the redemption of individual men. The new cults were called "mystery religions." One of the oldest was the Eleusinian Mysteries of Greece (see pp. 84–85), which for centuries had been concerned solely with the cycle of agriculture, but during the Hellenistic Age was converted into a mystery society into whose secrets individuals had to be initiated. Initiation carried with it promise of mystical security, certainty in this life, and hope of immortality, all based on analogy with the death and resurrection of the vegetation spirit in the fall and spring. Devout persons from all over that world went to Eleusis for initiation. The Roman emperors Augustus, Marcus Aurelius, and Commodus became *mystae.* Nero, it is said, also wished to be initiated, but was afraid to apply, for fear his reputation would cause him to be rejected. Other cults of somewhat similar character and promises that found devotees in Italy were those of Cybele and her consort Attis of Asia Minor; the religion of the Persian god Mithras (see pp. 139–145), popular with soldiers; the cult of the Greek god Dionysus; and the Egyptian cult of Isis.

These mysteries of redemption brought values to their initiates, but not one of them had sufficient substance to endure for long. In time they were replaced by Christianity, a new religion, which appeared in Palestine during the reign of Augustus and quickly spread throughout the Empire. Christianity, which had its source in a historical founder, not a nature myth, made its appeal to individual persons, not to states as such, and therefore satisfied the same essential hopes as the mysteries but offered more in real substance. It brought into being a great literature and a mature theology, and was ready to accept the best of Greek and Roman philosophy and art in the development and exposition of its faith.

EMPEROR WORSHIP

One of the last manifestations of vitality on the part of the Roman religion was the deification of the emperors, which took place as the Republic was coming to an end and being replaced by the Empire. When many of the gods had been forgotten outright and their temples deserted, the magnificent rituals decadent if not altogether dead, some of the patriotic statesmen of Rome and the admiring poets, notably Virgil and Horace, began to endow the emperors themselves with divine qualities and to set them up alongside the old gods as objects of worship. Here one can see clearly the phenomenon of euhemerism. If not during their lives, certainly upon their deaths, the emperors were elevated to the status of deities. This tendency was shown first in regard to Julius Caesar, and was then encouraged, especially by Augustus, his adopted son and successor, who was interested in doing what he could to capture for the emerging Empire the splendor that had once belonged to the Republic. Emperors were not ordinarily worshiped as gods in Rome during their lifetimes, but in the outlying eastern provinces they did receive that honor. In Rome, from the time of Julius Caesar, it became a custom to add the divine epithet *divus* to an emperor's name after he died. Deification of the emperor was rooted in the ancient Roman view that all one's ancestors became *di manes,* divine ancestors, at death; the view also had roots in the genius of the gens, that is, the divine spirit of the clan.

Aside from its importance as an expression of patriotism, emperor worship had little significance for the common people. Their desire for spiritual satisfaction required something more substantial. In the hands of emperors like Nero, Domitian, and Trajan, the emperor cult became a source of danger to Jews and Christians, who, while not unpatriotic, did refuse to compromise their faith by worshiping man.

Bibliography

MESOPOTAMIA

Albright, William F. *From the Stone Age to Christianity,* 2d ed. Baltimore: Johns Hopkins Press, 1946.

Finegan, Jack. *Light from the Ancient Past.* Princeton: Princeton University Press, 1946.

*Frankfort, Henri. *Birth of Civilization in the Near East.* Garden City, N. Y.: Doubleday Anchor Books, 1951.

*Herodotus. *The Histories,* trans. by Aubrey De Selincourt. Baltimore: Penguin, 1954. Cf. esp. I, 129–140, 178 ff.; V, 52; VI, 119.

*Kramer, Samuel N. *Sumerian Mythology.* New York: Harper Torchbooks, 1944.

*———. *History Begins at Sumer.* New York: Doubleday Anchor Books, 1959.

*Moscati, Sabatino. *Ancient Semitic Civilizations.* New York: Capricorn, 1951.

Pritchard, James B. *The Ancient Near East in Pictures.* Princeton: Princeton University Press, 1954.

———, ed. *Ancient Near Eastern Texts,* 2d ed. Princeton: Princeton University Press, 1955.

Wooley, Leonard. *The Sumerians.* Oxford: Clarendon Press, 1928.

———. *Spade Work.* London: Lutterworth, 1953.

EGYPT

*Breasted, James H. *Development of Religion and Thought in Ancient Egypt.* 1912. New York: Harper Torchbooks, 1957.

———. *A History of Egypt.* New York: Scribner, 1912.

* Indicates paperback.

Finegan, Jack. *Light from the Ancient Past.* Princeton: Princeton University Press, 1946.

Mertz, Barbara. *Temples, Tombs and Hieroglyphs.* New York: Coward-McCann, 1964.

Pritchard, James B. *The Ancient Near East in Pictures.* Princeton: Princeton University Press, 1954.

————, ed. *Ancient Near Eastern Texts,* 2d ed. Princeton: Princeton University Press, 1955.

Waddell, W. G. *Manetho.* Loeb Classical Library. Cambridge: Harvard University Press, 1940.

*Wilson, John A. *Culture of Ancient Egypt.* Chicago: Phoenix, 1951.

GREECE

Albright, William F. *From the Stone Age to Christianity,* 2d ed. Baltimore: Johns Hopkins Press, 1946.

Bevan, Edwyn. *Later Greek Religion.* New York: Dutton, 1927.

*Blakeney, E. H. *A Smaller Classical Dictionary.* New York: Dutton, 1952.

Cornford, F. M. *Greek Religious Thought from Homer to the Age of Alexander.* New York: Dutton, 1923.

Evelyn-White, G. *Hesiod, the Homeric Hymns, and Homerica.* Loeb Classical Library. Cambridge, Harvard, 1914.

*Grene, David, and Lattimore, Richmond, eds. *Greek Tragedies,* 3 vols. Chicago: Phoenix, 1960.

Harrison, Jane Ellen. *Themis: A Study of the Social Origins of Greek Religion.* New York: Meridian Books, 1962.

Hesiod. *The Poems and Fragments,* trans. by A. W. Mair. Oxford: Clarendon Press, 1908.

————. *The Works and Days. Theogony. The Shield of Heracles,* trans. by Richmond Lattimore. Ann Arbor: University of Michigan Press, 1959.

Hesiod, Callimachus, and Theognis. *The Works of Hesiod, Callimachus and Theognis,* trans. by J. Banks. London: George Bell, 1897.

*Homer. *The Iliad,* trans. by E. V. Rieu. Baltimore: Penguin, 1963.

*————. *The Odyssey,* trans. by E. V. Rieu. Baltimore: Penguin, 1964.

Kerenyi, C. *The Religion of the Greeks and Romans.* New York: Dutton, 1962.

Murray, Gilbert. *Five States of Greek Religion.* New York: Columbia University Press, 1930.

Mylonas, George E. *Ancient Mycenae*. Princeton: Princeton University Press, 1957.

Nilson, Martin P. *A History of Greek Religion*. Oxford: Clarendon Press, 1925.

Palmer, Leonard R. *Mycenaeans and Minoans*. New York: Knopf, 1962.

Rose, H. J. *Ancient Greek Religion*. London: Hutchinson's University Library, 1948.

ROME

Altheim, Franz. *A History of Roman Religion*. London: Methuen, 1938.

*Blakeney, E. H. *A Smaller Classical Dictionary*. New York: Dutton, 1952.

Cumont, Franz. *The Oriental Religions in Roman Paganism*. Chicago: Open Court, 1911.

Fowler, W. Warde. *The Religious Experience of the Roman People*. London: Macmillan, 1922.

————. *Social Life at Rome*. New York: Macmillan, 1927.

Holliday, William Reginald. *Lectures on the History of Roman Religion*. London: Hodder and Stoughton, 1922.

Kerenyi, C. *The Religion of the Greeks and Romans*. New York: Dutton, 1962.

*Lucretius. *The Nature of the Universe*, trans. by R. E. Lathum. Baltimore: Penguin, 1958.

Richardson, Emeline. *The Etruscans*. Chicago: University of Chicago Press, 1964.

Rose, H. J. *Ancient Roman Religion*. London: Hutchinson's University Library, 1948.

Varro, Marcus Terentius. *On Agriculture*, trans. by William Davis Hooper, rev. by Harrison Boyd Ash. Loeb Classical Library. Cambridge: Harvard University Press, 1934.

————. *On the Latin Language*, I, trans. by Roland G. Kent. Loeb Classical Library. Cambridge: Harvard University Press, 1938.

*Virgil. *The Aeneid*, trans. by E. Fairfax Taylor. Everyman's Library. New York: Dutton, 1963.

PART III RELIGIONS OF MIDDLE EASTERN ORIGIN

PERSIA

The name "Persia" is derived from Fars (Old Persian *pārsa*), a small province in the Zagros Mountains of southwest Iran whose capital was Pasargadae (Persepolis in Greek). After Persia became a great power its kings transformed Persepolis into one of the most beautiful cities of the ancient world. The current name of the country, "Iran," is derived from the Avestan *airyāna*, meaning Aryan. The Aryans were a people who penetrated into Persia either by military invasions or peaceful migrations between 1400 and 1000 B.C.

The Aryans are thought to have come from southern Turkestan through passes in the Khorasan and Elburz mountains which form the northeastern border of Iran. Some of the Aryan tribes turned eastward through the Khyber Pass into India, some of them occupied Iran, and others continued westward into Asia Minor and Europe. Evidence of these Aryan migrations is found in the common elements of language and religion that occur in different cultures all the way from India to Europe. The Aryans who settled in Iran are the Indo-Iranians; those who went into Europe are the Indo-Europeans. In Iran itself they settled first in Bactria, a region in northern Afghanistan along the Oxus River. Its capital was Bactra, probably located at the site of the modern town of Balkh. Next the Aryans took territories in north central Iran around the cities of Rhagae and Ecbatana, which were to become the nucleus of Media. To the south the Aryans occupied Fars, which was to be the homeland of the Persians. Turning northwestward from Media, the Aryans occupied Urartu, the mountainous area around Lake Van, where they fortified themselves so well that even the Assyrians failed in efforts to conquer them. Aryans also ruled Mitanni in northern Mesopotamia and the Hittite Empire in central Asia Minor.

Bactria is now believed to have been the land that produced Zoroaster. Little is known of its history; even King Vishtaspa, who was Zoroaster's patron, has not been placed with certainty in Iranian history. We do know that the region depended on agriculture because remains of irrigation channels are still extant. The fact that the camel with two humps bears the name "Bactrian" suggests that the Bactrians also took advantage of their strategic location to participate in the caravan trade between India, Turkestan, Persia, Mesopotamia, and the Mediterranean lands.

Although the exact political boundaries of Iran (or Persia) have been modified through the centuries, its geographical borders have remained fixed. The northeastern frontier is determined by the Khorasan Mountains, which run westward from the Himalayas to merge with the Elburz range south of the Caspian Sea. This range then turns northward to connect with the Caucasus Mountains, which form a towering stockade running from the Caspian to the Black Sea. The Caucasus Mountains are the natural boundary of Iran on the northwest, but at the present time Russia rules Transcaucasia, a small region south of these mountains. The western geographical boundary of Iran is formed by the Kurdistan Highlands and the Zagros Mountains. Turning eastward from the Persian Gulf, the Kurdistan Highlands form the southern boundary of Iran and intersect the Hindu Kush range, which comes down from the Himalayas on the east. In addition, Iran is bordered on the north by the Caspian Sea and on the southwest and south by the Persian Gulf and the Gulf of Oman. At the present time Iran is separated from India by the states of Afghanistan and Pakistan.

The mountains are also significant because of their effect on the climate of Iran. The enormous ranges on the north, the south, and the west catch so much of the rainfall that large interior areas of Iran have been converted into deserts. Mount Demavend of the Elburz range reaches 18,000 feet, and the fertile belt along the southern slopes of the Elburz Mountains supports about one-fifth of the population of Iran, which today is around 15 million.

Adjacent to ancient Persia on the northwest and to Media on the southwest was the small non-Indo-Iranian kingdom of Elam whose capital was Susa. From the point of view of climate and rainfall Elam had a fortunate location, but it was cramped by the Zagros Mountains on the east and by the Tigris River on the west, and it was exposed to invasions by the successive kingdoms of Mesopotamia.

The economic life of Persia was also based on its commerce. Although the southern mountains almost completely isolated it from the sea, Persia was strategically located for caravan trade with most of southwest Asia. One of the caravan trails led from India through the Khyber Pass to Kabul, the capital of Afghanistan, and then turned northward through Bactria into Turkestan to Bukhara and Samarkand. Another highway went westward from Kabul to Rhagae and Ecbatana. From these cities of Media, routes went south to Isfahan, Persepolis, and Susa; north to Lake Urmia, Lake Van, and the cities of Urartu; and west to the land of the Hittites, from which point caravans could go north to the Black Sea ports or east to the Greek cities on the Aegean. From Ecbatana a route went westward through the mountains to Nineveh on the Tigris; another turned southwestward to Babylon on the Euphrates. Caravans made their way from both Nineveh and Babylon to Mitanni in northern Mesopotamia. Westward from Mesopotamia, the caravan routes led to the Syrian cities of Palmyra, Antioch, and Damascus; to the Phoenician cities of Tyre and Sidon; to the Hebrew cities of Samaria and Jerusalem; and to the metropolises of Egypt. There was also a great highway that connected Smyrna and Ephesus on the Aegean with Susa and Persepolis of Persia by way of the Cilician Gates and Antioch.

These caravan routes served military as well as economic purposes. From Ecbatana and Rhagae on the caravan routes, the Median armies had good mobility in all directions. First they conquered Urartu on the north, and thereby extended the northern frontier of Media to the Caucasus Mountains. From Urartu the Medes pressed westward to conquer the Hittite Empire in Asia Minor. Then, in league with the Babylonians, the Medes in 612 B.C. captured Nineveh, thus bringing the Assyrian kingdom to its end. The Medes, the first of the Indo-Iranian peoples to rise to power, had become the greatest power of the Middle East, but they were to enjoy their triumph for little more than half a century.

According to legend, the state of Fars was established in about 700 B.C. by an Indo-Iranian king named Achaemenes and his followers. About 550 B.C., Cyrus (Cyrus the Great), an ambitious young prince of Fars who was descended from the legendary Achaemenes, seized Anshan, a district of Elam, and proclaimed himself as its king. His next move was to conquer all of Elam and establish himself in Susa, which was to be his capital. He was then ready to challenge Media, which he did successfully by defeating Astyages,

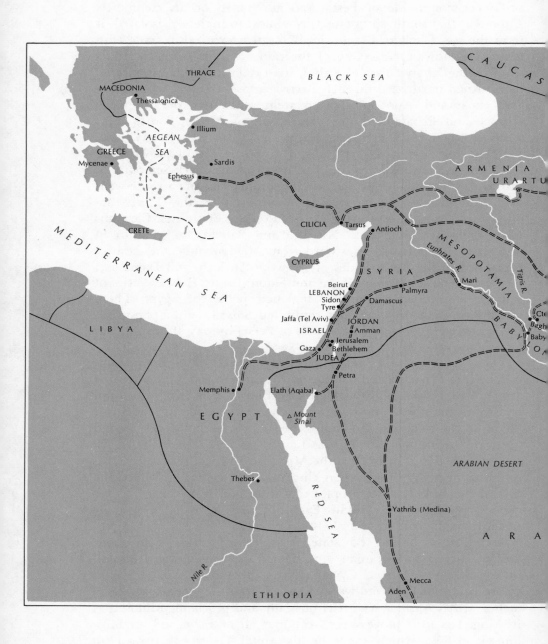

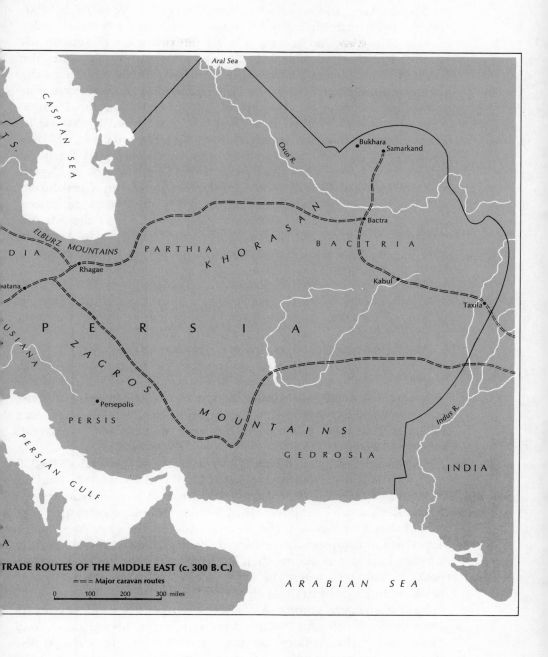

CASPIAN SEA

Aral Sea

Oxus R.

Bukhara
Samarkand

ELBURZ MOUNTAINS

PARTHIA

KHORASAN

BACTRIA

Bactra

DIA

Rhagae

atana

Kabul

Taxila

P   E   R   S   I   A

ZAGROS

USIANA

Persepolis

PERSIS

MOUNTAINS

GEDROSIA

Indus R.

INDIA

PERSIAN GULF

A

TRADE ROUTES OF THE MIDDLE EAST (c. 300 B.C.)

=== Major caravan routes

0   100   200   300 miles

ARABIAN   SEA

the Median king, and he thereby became master of the entire Median empire. With little difficulty he was able to conquer the remainder of Asia Minor to the Aegean, add all the provinces of Iran to his empire, and then advance into Mesopotamia in 539 B.C. and take Babylon. This victory added the entire Babylonian empire to the already vast kingdom of Cyrus, which extended to the Mediterranean and as far south as the borders of Egypt, including the Hebrew lands of Israel and Judah. Israel had been conquered by Assyria in 721 B.C., and Judah had been taken by the Babylonians in 587 B.C.

Cambyses, the son and successor of Cyrus, conquered Egypt in 525 B.C. and at the same time secured the Greek islands of Cyprus and Samos. Darius I (521–486 B.C.) had to put down a revolution at home, but when that was accomplished he undertook ambitious campaigns to extend the Persian frontiers. He added the African territory of Libya, but failed to capture the Scythian territory around the Black and Caspian Seas or to defeat the Greeks in a battle at Marathon. Continuing Cyrus' generous policy of allowing exiled peoples who had settled in his lands under earlier Assyrian and Babylonian rulers to return home, Darius permitted Jews to return to Jerusalem to rebuild the Hebrew temple during the years 520–516 B.C.

Darius was succeeded by his son Xerxes (486–465 B.C.), who is best known for the defeats he suffered at the hands of the Greeks at Salamis in 480 B.C. and Plataea in 479 B.C. Successive kings of the Achaemenian dynasty continued to rule Persia, the largest and most enlightened major power in the Middle East to that time, but Persia had become decadent by the time of Alexander the Great, king of Macedonia (336–323 B.C.).

Alexander had little difficulty in defeating Darius III (336–330 B.C.), last of the Achaemenian kings, at Granicus in 334, Issus in 333, and Arbela in 331. Making good use of the caravan routes, Alexander's armies subdued all of Persia, including every province from Libya and Egypt in the west to India in the east. Alexander's appetite for conquest drove him to continue through the historic Khyber Pass into India; he then led his troops both by land and sea back to Babylon, where he died. Alexander's campaigns were a brilliant but brief interlude in the history of Persia.

In the struggle among Alexander's generals for his territories after he died, Seleucus Nicator acquired Persia, Mesopotamia, and Syria, and built Antioch on the coast of Syria to serve as the capital of his new empire. Assuming the crown, he established the

Seleucid dynasty, which survived until the Romans incorporated Syria into their empire in 65 B.C. The Seleucid kings had been unable to weld the different ethnic groups of their lands into a single people, and the kings themselves exhibited singular ineptitude. Seleucus Nicator, for example, bartered the province of Afghanistan to the king of India for a corps of war elephants, and Antiochus IV (175–164 B.C.) undertook to impose Greek religion on the Jews by military force.

When the Romans acquired Syria, however, they did not get all of what had once been the Seleucid empire. Even before 200 B.C., Bactria and Parthia rebelled against the Seleucid kings and formed independent kingdoms. The Parthians made themselves masters of most of Persia, including Mesopotamia, and their capital was Ctesiphon on the Tigris near Baghdad. The Romans coveted those rich lands but were unable to dislodge the Parthians.

The Parthian empire flourished for more than four centuries (c. 250 B.C.–A.D. 225) but was finally overthrown by the Sassanians, a new Persian dynasty which, like the Achaemenians, emerged from Fars. This was also a strong dynasty; it ruled most of Persia proper and even regained Armenia when King Shapur I defeated the Romans and captured Valerian, the Roman emperor, at Edessa in A.D. 260. Persian culture reached a high point during this period, stimulated by contacts with India, China, and the Roman Empire. But the brilliant Sassanian era came to an end in 651 when Yazdegerd III was assassinated in the province of Merv while fleeing from advancing Muslim armies, which had already gained decisive victories at Bowaib in 634, Kadisiya in 637, and Nehavend in 642.

The Muslim conquest of Persia was neither as swift nor as spectacular as Alexander's had been, but it was more profound. Alexander had overthrown the government of Persia but had left its culture intact. The Muslims brought the Persians a new government but also brought about a radical transformation of the Persian culture. With the exception of a few Zoroastrians, the entire population of Persia accepted the Muslim faith and law; and, in fact, Iran continues to be a stronghold of Islam to this day.

Persia was still to suffer from other invaders who came by the old caravan trails: Genghis Khan (1162–1227), who conquered much of Asia and eastern Europe to the Dnieper River, included Persia in his dominions; Tamerlane (1336–1405), another of the great Mongol conquerors, came down from Samarkand to add Persia to his kingdom.

During some 1,300 years since the Muslim conquest, the government of Persia has often exhibited instability, yet Persian culture has been remarkably stable. The Persians have been satisfied to live as their forefathers lived, devoted to their faith and customs, with little interest in the outside world. But the past half century has brought some real changes, and the caravan trails and camels are finally being replaced by modern forms of communication and transportation. The discovery of one of the richest oil fields in the world in southwestern Iran has had much to do with this awakening. A railway now connects the Persian Gulf with the Caspian Sea. A new highway which runs 10,000 feet above sea level crosses the Elburz Mountains and reaches from Teheran to the Caspian Sea. The city of Tabriz, located in the mountains east of Lake Urmia, has become the industrial center of Iran.

SYRIA AND PALESTINE

The western border of Syria and Palestine was the Mediterranean Sea. On the east they were bounded by the Arabian desert. Syria was (and still is) bounded on the northeast by the Euphrates River and on the north by the Taurus Mountains. The natural boundary of Palestine on the south and southwest was the Red Sea and the Gulf of Suez, which separated it from Egypt. Syria and Palestine therefore constituted a belt of land which begins with the Taurus Mountains in the north, runs the full width of the Mediterranean Sea, and terminates in the Sinai Peninsula on the Red Sea.

A chain of highlands, which in its central portion is the Lebanon Mountains, extends through this belt of land approximately parallel to the Mediterranean coast. The Anti-Lebanons, another chain, facing the Lebanons, runs north approximately parallel with this western range until it reaches Damascus, where it turns northeastward toward Mesopotamia. The Lebanons rise to a height of 6,000 feet. Mount Hermon of the Anti-Lebanons, near the border between Syria and Palestine, rises to 9,100 feet and is snow-capped the year round.

Syria is more fortunate with respect to rainfall than the Palestine area. There is more rainfall on the western side than on the eastern side of the Anti-Lebanons. Damascus has abundant water from the Abana and Pharpar rivers which come down from the foothills of

Mount Hermon. Palmyra, 120 miles northeast of Damascus on the caravan trail from Mesopotamia, also has plentiful water. Antioch, the Seleucid capital of Syria, was built beside the Orantes River and is also near the sea. The Jordan River, which has its source in springs in the Lebanons and Anti-Lebanons, is an important water supply for the Middle East. The Jordan first passes through Lake Huleh, a small fresh water lake 270 feet above sea level, then rushes only twelve miles to the Sea of Galilee, a body of fresh water 650 feet below sea level. From the Sea of Galilee the Jordan flows swiftly on a meandering course for another sixty-five miles and empties into the Dead Sea which is fifty-three miles long, nine miles wide, 1,274 feet below sea level and 1,300 feet deep. The bottom of the Dead Sea is therefore almost a half mile below sea level. As the Dead Sea has no outlet it depends upon evaporation and has gradually acquired a concentration of salt and other chemicals five times as great as that of the ocean. No fish or other animals can live in its water, and few evidences of vegetation appear on its shores or on the surrounding cliffs.

The Yarmuk and Jabbok rivers are small streams which flow into the Jordan on the eastern side; and the Arnon and Zered rivers flow into the Dead Sea from the east. There are numerous wadis on both sides which flow into the Jordan and the Dead Sea during rainy seasons. There are also a considerable number of springs, some of them hot. The Arabah is a dry valley between the Dead Sea and the Gulf of Aqaba.

At the present time, much of the land of Israel and Jordan is bare and badly eroded. The denuded hillsides reveal rocks and sandstone or bright colors of clay. In most places the forests have been cut away. We may conjecture that in ancient times these hills were once covered by a topsoil which supported vegetation.

The inhabitants of the area, which today includes Syria, Lebanon, Jordan, and Israel, have been devoted to animal husbandry, especially to sheep and goats, but they have also produced some cattle, camels, and asses. Farming has been difficult except on the seacoast, in river valleys, where some irrigation is possible, and in cities such as Palmyra, Damascus, and Jericho, which are built on oases. The Plain of Esdraelon, which extends from Haifa to the Jordan River, is also a farming region. Numerous cities on the coast, including Antioch, Beirut, Sidon, Tyre, Haifa, Tel Aviv, Jaffa, and Gaza, have profited from farming on the coastal plain as well as from commerce by the sea. The coastal plain of Israel and

Lebanon and the oasis at Jericho produce an abundance of vegetables and fruits, especially citrus fruits. The highlands produce grain, grapes, and olives. The Syrian oases also produce a variety of vegetables, fruits, and grains.

During the period of the ancient Hebrew occupation the boundary between Palestine and Syria was located in the southern foothills of Mount Hermon. It was customary to say that Palestine extended from Dan to Beer-Sheba. This statement is true in the sense that the majority of the Hebrew population lived between these points, although at times the Hebrew territory reached as far south as Aqaba.

Syrians and Palestinians profited greatly from the caravan trade. Palmyra, Damascus, and Antioch were on the main trade routes which came out of Mesopotamia, Persia, India, and Turkestan, and the same routes found their way both east and west to the cities of Palestine. Caravans also came out of the Arabian desert, and from such distant places as Yemen and Aden. During the ancient period, Phoenicia grew rich from the trade of the caravans that transported wares from the entire Middle East and exchanged them for goods which Phoenician ships brought from every Mediterranean port. Syrians and Hebrews got along well with the Phoenicians, for they were mutually dependent on one another.

The great Phoenician city of Tyre was built on a rock far enough from the shore to make it impregnable to all invaders from Mesopotamia. But the Greeks, who were also great seamen, were rivals of Tyre. When Alexander came through Palestine on his way to Egypt his engineers built a causeway from the land to the rock on which the city was built because Tyre defied him. Then the Greeks battered its walls down and destroyed the city. Tyre never regained its greatness. When Seleucus Nicator built Antioch on the northern coast of Syria, he further sealed the doom of Tyre because Antioch became the most prominent metropolis of the eastern Mediterranean. With greater resources than Tyre ever had, Antioch soon grew rich from the commerce of both land and sea.

When the Hebrews entered Palestine, even as early as the time of Abraham, they found the land already occupied. Some cities, like Damascus, Jericho, Beth-Shan, Gezer, and Hazor, had been there for as long as 3,000 years when Abraham arrived. When the Hebrews made their penetration under the leadership of Moses and Joshua around 1200 b.c., the land was so strongly occupied that no less than two centuries passed before the Hebrews succeeded in establishing themselves as an independent nation in the land.

The land at the time was called Canaan, and its inhabitants were known as "Canaanites" or "Amorites." This population included some Hittites from Asia Minor, Hurians from Mitanni, as well as Egyptians, Babylonians, Philistines, and other minority groups. The Hebrew kingdom was surrounded by Syrians on the north, Ammonites and Moabites on the east, Edomites on the south, and Philistines and Phoenicians on the west. All of these groups except the Philistines were Semites and spoke languages that the Hebrews could understand. David, Solomon, and some of the later Hebrew kings conquered all of the surrounding kingdoms except those of the Philistines and Phoenicians. Bitter struggles took place with the Philistines, but the wars were indecisive. The Hebrews were never at war with the Phoenicians. The Hebrews had no seaports of consequence, but since the Phoenicians lived on the seacoast the Hebrews sold their cattle and agricultural products to the Phoenicians and received imports from all the lands around the Mediterranean in exchange.

The Syrians, Hebrews, and their neighbors from smaller kingdoms had the misfortune of being located in a land which lacked the necessary resources to become a strong military power. At the same time, some of the major highways which connected the great powers passed through Syria and Palestine, and they were the bridge between Egypt, Mesopotamia, and more remote lands on the north and east. As each of the great nations embarked on its effort to achieve world domination, it was therefore necessary to conquer Syria and Palestine in order to control the highways. Whether the invaders were Egyptians, Assyrians, Babylonians, Persians, Greeks, Romans, or Muslims, each case was essentially the same. If one of the small powers defied the invader, the small power was either reduced to the position of vassal and exploited or destroyed. For example, the Assyrians destroyed Damascus in 732 B.C. and Samaria in 721 B.C., and the Babylonians destroyed Jerusalem in 587 B.C.

It was possible for small kingdoms to be independent and prosperous only during the interludes between the periods of prosperity and strength of the major powers. The Hebrews enjoyed a second period of independence from 165–63 B.C., when the Maccabees rebelled against oppressions of the decadent Seleucid kingdom of Syria. But the Romans, who had in the meantime risen to power, invaded Judea and captured Jerusalem in 63 B.C., bringing the Maccabean period to an end. When the Jews rebelled against the Romans in A.D. 66–70, the Romans destroyed Jerusalem. A second

Jewish rebellion against Rome occurred in A.D. 132–135, when
Jerusalem was again destroyed. The Muslims conquered both Syria
and Palestine in A.D. 638 in the course of campaigns which made
them dominant over Egypt and all the Middle East.

ARABIA

Arabia is located on the southwestern corner of the continent of
Asia. On the east and northeast it is bounded by the Persian Gulf
and the Euphrates River; on the north and northwest, by Syria and
Palestine; on the west, by the Red Sea; and on the south, by the
Gulf of Aden and the Arabian Sea. Ancient Mesopotamia (today
Iraq) lay just across the Euphrates from Arabia. Across the Red Sea,
to the west of Arabia, is Africa, with Egypt on the north and
Ethiopia on the south. Much of central Arabia, like North Africa
and the interior of Iran, is desert and thereby unfavorable to human
settlement. Most of the population, which today is estimated at 10
million, is found along the western, southern, and eastern borders,
where there is more rainfall and better access to the sea. The chief
cities are Riyadh, the capital; Mecca, the holy city of Islam; and
Aden, the chief seaport. The principal ports on the Red Sea are
Jidda, which brings both pilgrims and commerce to Mecca and its
hinterlands, and Yanbu, which serves Medina, another holy city of
Islam.

The parallel chains of mountains, which extend from the Taurus
Mountains southward through Syria and Palestine, continue on both
sides of the Gulf of Aqaba and the Red Sea, turning eastward from
Yemen across Arabia to Oman. These ranges, which attain heights
of 6,000 to 10,000 feet, prevent rain from falling on the Arabian
deserts. But during rainy seasons vegetation does appear in the foothills of the mountains and around the edges of the deserts.

The inhabitants of Arabia have for centuries been Bedouins—
nomadic Arabs—who graze their flocks of sheep and goats and herds
of camels around the fringes of the deserts, wherever they can find
water and pasture. The Bedouins lead an uncertain existence, deriving their food, clothing, and shelter almost exclusively from their
animals. They dress in flowing garments, with scarves which are
held in place on their heads by goat-hair cords. Their garments are
well suited to protect them against the desert heat, the wind, the

sand, the cold of winter, and the night chill which arrives soon after sunset. The Bedouins lead a very meager existence, having few garments, almost no furniture, and tents which look as if they might easily blow away. Yet the desert Arabs are the only people who have ever been able to survive in this forbidding land, and the very inhospitality of the desert has protected the Arabs against foreign invaders.

The social life of the Bedouins is tribal. Each tribe has its own sheik, and through the centuries they have not recognized any other authority for very long. Muhammad was the first leader to succeed in uniting the Arabs. The unity he gave them was based on a new religious faith and, to a considerable extent, transcended the tribal loyalties. Yet even under Islam, the tribes in Arabia have retained their essential independence to this day. The tribes are often hostile to one another and spend much of their time raiding the flocks and herds of their neighbors.

Until recent times, the only important form of passenger and freight transportation in Arabia was the camel. Arabs who acquired sufficient property to set themselves up as merchants founded cities and operated caravans. Slaves from Africa were brought across the Red Sea by ship to Mecca and sold to wealthy Arabs.

Mecca, an oasis with an abundant year-round water supply, has been both a commercial and a religious center since ancient times. It was this combination of factors that enabled Mecca to develop a large population and to become the foremost city of Arabia. Caravans came from Yemen with south Arabian wares; from Damascus and Jerusalem with Syrian, Mesopotamian, Persian, Phoenician, and Palestinian goods; and from Cairo with North African products. Ships also docked at Red Sea ports with imports from east and central Africa and even from India. The caravan trade thus brought Arabs into contact with the Jews and Christians of Palestine and with the Zoroastrians from across the northeastern frontier in Mesopotamia and Persia.

Bedouin life was especially characteristic of central and northern Arabia. Early in the second millennium B.C. these northern tribesmen had penetrated into Mesopotamia, where they eventually founded the Assyrian and Babylonian dynasties. Similar Arab migrations also took them into Syria and Palestine. The Ammonites, Moabites, and Edomites were descendants of Arabian tribes which had forged their way from the desert. The last of these Arab migrations was that of the Nabateans who, as early as 500 B.C., conquered the Edomite stronghold south of the Dead Sea. There they built the city of Petra which continued to serve as their capital until the rise of Christianity. Under Aratus IV (9 B.C.–A.D. 40), the border of this Nabatean kingdom extended as far north as Damascus.

There were considerable differences between the roving Bedouins of central and north Arabia and the Arabs who occupied the settled regions of south Arabia, and each viewed the other with suspicion. The Arabs of the south built cities, engaged in both agriculture and commerce, and developed a high civilization. The strategic location of their ports made it a natural center for the transportation of not only its own products, but also the rich and exotic wares of lands from Africa to India. The south Arabian commerce by sea was matched by its caravan trade. Sana in Yemen was the focal point of trade routes that reached all the cities of Arabia and extended to Egypt, Palestine, Syria, Mesopotamia, and beyond. The merchants of south Arabia enjoyed a virtual monopoly on commerce by both sea and land.

The remains of well built homes, fortresses and temples from pre-Christian times are conspicuous in Yemen, Aden, and the Hadraumat, and a dam which served as the center of a system of irrigation, which was discovered at Marib, would be a credit even to modern engineering. Another reason for the prosperity of south Arabia was the frankincense and myrrh produced there, which found extensive use in unguents and perfumes in both religious and secular life throughout the Middle East. In addition, some gold was also produced in this region.

The next powerful movement to come out of Arabia was led by Muhammad in the seventh century A.D. It originated in Mecca and did not end until the Arabs were masters of most of the rich lands of both the Near and Middle East and had even penetrated into East Asia. The Muslim conquests were inspired by religious faith, but the religious element was supplemented by political, military, and commercial factors.

As the enthusiasm generated by the Muslim conquests subsided, the life of Arabia gradually returned to the quiet pattern which it had followed for centuries. No significant new development occurred until the early eighteenth century, when Sheik Muhammad ibn Abd al-Wahhab began a religious reformation, which was called the Wahhabi movement. Like the earlier movement led by the Prophet Muhammad, this religious movement also acquired political and military overtones. The result was the rise of what we know today as the kingdom of Saudi Arabia, which was mainly the creation of King Abd al-Aziz al-Saud who died in 1953. This kingdom includes all Arabia except the small states on the south. At the time of the emergence of Saudi Arabia, a rich oil field was discovered on the Persian Gulf, and this new wealth has resulted in the development of the cities of that region and is bringing profound changes to the life of all Arabia. A railway has been constructed from the Persian Gulf to Riyadh, the capital, and airports now connect cities in the oil field with Jidda on the Red Sea, as well as with other cities of Asia, Europe, and North and South America.

THE OLD PERSIAN BACKGROUND

Although the early Persians did not leave behind either a history or a description of their religion, the inscriptions of Persian kings and the scriptures which the followers of Zoroaster wrote provide much information concerning the ideas, beliefs, and practices the prophet set himself against and undertook to eradicate. A third source of information on early Persian religion is the Greek writer Herodotus, who visited Babylon about 450 B.C., and then went on to Susa, a Persian city that stood on the plain between the Tigris River and the Zagros Mountains.

Herodotus pictures the Persians as a religious people, with a social system suggestive of the caste system of India, but not so extreme.[1] At the top was a caste of priests called *magi*, who interpreted dreams, portents, and wonders, and presided at sacrificial rites. The magus had much in common with the *rishi*, who chanted the hymns of the Rig-Veda, and the *shaman*, who was known under various names among the different primitive peoples the world over.

According to Herodotus, the Persians had no temples, no altars, no fires (he could be in error in this), no flute music, no garlands. When making a sacrifice, a worshiper inserted a spray of leaves, usually myrtle, into his headdress and then selected an open place and slaughtered his victim; invoking the deity he was sacrificing to by name, he cut up the sacrificial animal and cooked it, then placed it on a mound of green stuff, preferably clover. At this point

FIGURE 8.1   Mithra the bull slayer. A Mithraic rite, possibly the taurobolium. (*Alinari: Vatican Museum*)

the magus delivered his chants, which recounted the birth of the gods. When the magus was finished, the worshiper was free to take away the meat, presumably eating it as a holy meal with his family and friends, a practice common in other religions of antiquity in which blood sacrifices were offered.

The Persians worshiped Zeus, Herodotus informs us, as the dome of the sky;[2] they sacrificed to him on the tops of mountains. They also worshiped sun, moon, earth, fire, water, and winds. Herodotus says that these were their original deities, and that it was only later that they learned to worship Aphrodite.

The reliability of the essentials of this report is confirmed and illuminated by the Rig-Veda of India, which reveals a strikingly similar picture of the religion of those Aryan tribes (Indo-Iranians) who went down through the Khyber Pass and conquered the northwestern plains of India. The nature deities worshiped by these people were almost identical with those revered by the Persians, according to Herodotus.[3] Herodotus, of course, imposed the names of Zeus and Aphrodite on Persian deities. Zeus was no doubt substituted for Ahura Mazda, and Aphrodite for the Persian goddess Anahita.

The nomadic ancient Aryans, living close to nature, worshiped Mithras as a god of light. The stars were his eyes as he looked down on the world. Mithras was also associated with the sun, but not always identified with it. He was an active, vigorous god, and stood for morality, truth, loyalty—virtues that appeal to soldiers. He appears in the Rig-Veda of India, but not as a major deity.

ZOROASTER

The exact place of origin of the prophet Zarathustra—Zoroaster, as the Greeks called him and as he is known in the Western world today—has long been a matter of debate. Until recent years his homeland was generally thought to have been Media in northwestern Iran, but opinion has shifted to Bactria, which is located in what is now called Afghanistan.

Persian tradition gives the date of Zoroaster's birth as 660 B.C. and of his death as around 583 B.C.; these dates are now accepted by most scholars. His full name was Zarathustra Spitama: Zarathustra his personal name, Spitama his family name. A man of high social position with friends in the royal court, Zoroaster married a woman named Hvovi, who was the daughter of Frashaoshtra, a noble attached to the court of Vishtaspa, the king. Zoroaster is said to have had a son named Spitama and a youngest daughter Parucista. Jamaspa, who was Vishtaspa's minister and a powerful noble, was Zoroaster's friend.

By profession Zoroaster was a priest—that is, presumably, a magus, a member of the priestly caste referred to by Herodotus. However, Zoroaster was a magus with a difference. While he knew the rituals practiced by the magi generally, and recognized and practiced the veneration of fire, as shown by Yasna 43:9, he turned away in horror from all blood sacrifices, regarding the slaughter of cattle for that purpose as the most heinous sin (Yasna 31:10, 15; 32:8, 10, 12, 15). In Yasna 33, Zoroaster's priestly hymn of dedication, he proposes by his prayers to repel discord from the family, evil from village life, and enemies from the tribe and the herds (33:4).

At the same time, in Yasna 33:6 Zoroaster shows that in his vocabulary the care of animals has a symbolical meaning. Here he expresses the wish to learn how to practice true husbandry, presumably to care for the souls of men—the Wise Lord's cattle and sheep in the spiritual sense. He pleads for the privilege of seeing Ahura Mazda himself and taking counsel with him. Like many of the great prophets of the Bible, he yearns to see his God face to face. In the same vein, the prophet refers to himself as Ahura Mazda's friend, pleading with the Wise Lord to reveal his secrets to "a friend such as I am" (44:1),[4] thus reminding us of the biblical Abraham, the friend of God (James 2:23), as well as of Moses, with whom God spoke as friend to friend (Exodus 33:11).

It would be a mistake, however, to think of Zoroaster as an ascetic who deprived himself of the joys of the present world. He was neither monk, nor hermit, nor, on the other hand, was he an emotional ecstatic or dervish, whose bliss is induced by spiritual intoxication. He was not even an Indian-type yogi, devoting himself to solitary meditation in an effort to escape from the present life and lose himself in the infinite. Throughout the Gathas, the poems that he himself wrote, Zoroaster shows that he is a vigorous, active, and optimistic man who looks to a future in which all evils will be eliminated and the happiness of the righteous will be complete and endless.

From time to time in Zoroaster's poems, we come upon evidence of the hardships he had to endure in his efforts to reform the religion of his time. At first he was unpopular; he met with no success, and had to suffer isolation. At times he felt that his cause might be hopeless. He encountered rejection on every hand and was forced to flee. Scorned in his village, hated by the rulers, thrust out by family and tribe, he lamented the poverty that made him a weak man (Yasna 46:1–2). In this he reminds us somewhat of the Hebrew prophet Jeremiah, who was probably his contemporary. Yet he feels that God has chosen him to make known the divine will for his time (Yasna 46:3), indeed that he was chosen for this mission from the beginning (Yasna 44:11). He is like Jeremiah, the Second Isaiah, and Paul, who were also convinced that God had determined their prophetic destinies even before they were born.

Eventually both Frashaoshtra and Jamaspa became Zoroaster's converts, as did also King Vishtaspa himself. Although Zoroaster had tried for several years, without success, to spread his faith before he reached this pinnacle of success, once the king's favor had been gained, Zoroaster's position became secure, and he appears to have become a trusted counselor in the small kingdom of Vishtaspa.

ZOROASTRIAN SCRIPTURES

The general name for the sacred writings of the Zoroastrians is the Avesta. There are four main parts: the Yasna, the Vispered, the Yasts, and the Vendidad. The Yasna is a collection of seventy-two hymns, which are chanted in connection with the preparation and offering of the Haoma, a sacred drink. Seventeen of these, thought to be by Zoroaster himself and the oldest part of the Avesta, are called the Gathas. The Vispered, also a liturgical work, is a supplement to the Yasna. The Yasts comprise twenty-one hymns addressed to the angels and the heroes of ancient Iran. The Vendidad, known as the law against demons, contains priestly regulations concerning purifications, penalties, and expiations. Also included in the Avesta are several important works of a more popular and theological character. The sacred texts are written in old Iranian, an Aryan dialect related to the Sanskrit of the Rig-Veda, the earliest literature of India. (Later Zoroastrian writings are in Pahlavi, a Middle Persian dialect.)

The Avesta, believed by Zoroastrians to be revelations to Zoroaster by Ahura Mazda, the infinite God, is accepted by them as authoritative in all matters of faith and practice. Zoroastrianism is thus based on a concept of revelation: it holds that Ahura Mazda, who made himself known to Zoroaster, the great prophet, still continues to make himself known to Zoroaster's followers through the Holy Scriptures.

ZOROASTER'S THEOLOGY

Zoroaster's faith embodies monotheism, dualism, and eschatology, ethics being the dominant element in each of these categories. But such a brief characterization has a deceptive simplicity, for Zoroaster's vocabulary is, in fact, very complicated. Much of the time he speaks an apparently naïve pre-philosophical language, as though he were unaware of critical problems, unconcerned about the clarity of his monotheistic concepts, and unconscious of having compromised the purity of his thought by the use of anthropomorphism. However, if one reads and ponders the Gathas, it becomes clear that while we may be looking for philosophical expressions, Zoroaster did not write with philosophy in mind. His utterances are poems chanted in a worship liturgy and by their nature could not take the form of philosophical exposition. Their character is rather like that of the Psalms of the Bible.

The basic theme that runs through all of Zoroaster's poems is the struggle to overthrow the nature polytheism of ancient Iran. Zoroaster seeks to supplant the nature spirits, which he calls Daevas, and the life they represent with one God, Ahura Mazda (also called Ormazd or Ormuzd). The conflict between Ahura Mazda and the Daevas therefore forms the continuing subject of his verses. The poet often represents this struggle for truth and for a new way of life as Spenta Mainyu and Angra Mainyu (also called Ahriman), two primordial spirits that are eternally hostile to each other, the Good against the Bad. Ahura Mazda, the Wise Lord, is often identified with Spenta Mainyu, the Holy Spirit; Angra Mainyu, the Evil Spirit, is also called the Druj—that is, the Lie.

As for the origin of these two spirits, the Good and the Evil, Zoroaster never attempts any explanation. Apparently he assumes them to be eternal—an idea that is reflected in Yasna 45:2. Since the beginning of time, he informs us, a struggle has been going on between these opposing spirits. In every essential expression of their personalities, they have found themselves in opposition to each other, their positions absolutely irreconcilable. This dualism of Zoroaster's thought is ethical rather than metaphysical. It has to do with thoughts, principles of conduct, moral choices, words, deeds, consciences. Zoroaster would have us understand that all life, human and divine, is like that: man has the capacity to discern good and evil, and he must choose between them. There is no middle ground; either man chooses to be on the side of Ahura Mazda or else he is a supporter of Angra Mainyu—that is, of Ahriman, the Druj, the Lie. This is the very heart of Zoroaster's theology. Its simplicity is its strength; it is picturesquely stated, easily comprehended.

But such clarity is by no means always characteristic of Zoroaster's language. In order to implement his will in the world, we are informed, Ahura Mazda has associated with himself the six Amesha Spentas—entities, divine spirits, or angels—which are moral attitudes or principles and, at the same time, are spirits controlling natural realms or functions. They are attributes of God, as well as qualities of men. Asha (also called Arta) signifies right or order, but he is also the spirit or genius of fire. Vohu Manah (good or best mind) is the genius or guardian of cattle. Armaiti (piety or devotion) is the spirit of earth. Kshathra (kingdom, both heavenly and earthly) is the genius of metal. Haurvatat (integrity or health) is the genius of plants. Ameretat (immortality) is the spirit of water. To these six, which are constantly on the tongue of Zoroaster, we should add Sraosha, a later addition to the Amesha Spentas, signifying obedience as well as the spirit of dawn.

Dualism

Although the Hebrews had arrived at a monotheistic theology not less than two centuries before Zoroaster's time, this fact does not discredit Zoroaster's achievement, for he appears to have attained quite independently his concept of the one God, whose major attribute is justice. The unique and creative element in Zoroaster's theology, however, was his dualism. Zoroaster's chief claim to uniqueness lies in his understanding of evil. Here, for the first time in the history of religion, we encounter this view of one being, Angra Mainyu (Ahriman), who is the source of all evil. Evil spirits, dragons, monsters of many sorts, had been common in the faiths of peoples since primitive times, and some of these myths appear to have been anticipations in some dim way of the mature principle of dualism which Zoroaster apprehended with such clarity.

Ahura Mazda

The strength of Zoroaster's prophetic message lay in his concept of God. Ahura Mazda, Zoroaster affirms, is the only God, a God of goodness, justice, morality. This was a radical view for Aryan peoples at that time. In the past their religion had involved many gods, most of whom were spirits of natural phenomena, and natural forces in themselves cannot be moral in the ordinary sense, for they are destructive as well as creative. The uniqueness of Ahura Mazda is that he is only good: he creates only good things; he does only good things; he gives only blessings to his worshipers. In terms of this conception the world is divided in half. There are two kingdoms standing side by side, the kingdom of the good against the kingdom of evil; a good God reigns over one, an evil God rules the other. Zoroaster places Angra Mainyu over the kingdom of evil just as he places Ahura Mazda over the realm of the good.

This reform of Aryan faith required Indo-Iranians to repudiate the ancient gods, even the highest, who were called "asuras." Zoroaster takes just one asura and recognizes him as the one and only good God, whom he calls Ahura Mazda, the Wise Lord. Apparently Ahura Mazda is actually derived from Varuna, an old Aryan god of the sky who, as is indicated in the Rig-Veda, had also developed in the direction of moral character. As we have seen, Zoroaster retains the most important functions of the old nature deities and assigns these to the Amesha Spentas, which in his system are no longer thought of as gods in themselves, but rather as functions or angels of the Wise Lord. It is in this picturesque way that Zoroaster presents the attributes of the one God. Ahura Mazda expresses himself through justice and order, intelligence and good government, piety and devotion, good health and integrity, and eternal life.

Zoroaster's message had certain weaknesses, however. From the beginning of time, for example, Ahura Mazda has shared control of the world with Ahriman, the Evil Spirit. Each has created and maintained his portion of the world as his own kingdom. Ahura is therefore not omnipotent. A second handicap was that Zoroaster had to deprive his followers of old sacrifices and rituals which were dear to their hearts. He repudiated blood sacrifices entirely, as well as the cult of Haoma, intoxicating liquor. The only sacrifice he preserved from the old religion was the cult of fire (Yasna 34:4; 43:9).

Another difficulty Zoroaster's new gospel had to encounter was the complexity of its theological concept. While Zoroaster proclaims one God, he also proclaims the Amesha Spentas, each of which had a meaning in the daily life of the people. Even in the rituals, Ahura Mazda tends to recede into the background and to become just one of the seven holy beings.

Eschatology

Eschatology, which means a theory or doctrine of last things, is a concept based on the belief that God will eventually bring history to an end. In its primary and natural sense, it is a chronological idea and refers to time, to history, although it is sometimes interpreted philosophically to mean ultimate, in the sense of an ultimate reality. But, by and large, people of this world have little philosophical training and, therefore, take words in a simple, elementary sense, which is probably the way we should interpret this concept in the religion of Zoroaster.

Zoroastrianism teaches the importance of good *deeds*, as well as of good thoughts and good words. Implicit in Zoroaster's dualism is the idea that religion is not what it ought to be until faith is expressed in action. Zoroaster's intention is to call men into the service of God as if they were joining an army; this is to be an active service throughout a man's life. Since the forces of a righteous God are in continuous combat with the hosts of the Evil Spirit, the way a man acquits himself in his personal struggle with evil determines his destiny.

Eschatology implies a belief that death is not the end of life; that it is in fact a doorway into another world, in which there are rewards for the righteous and punishment for the wicked. The concept of immortality, with the implication of a life of happiness in the hereafter, is one of the constant elements in the theology of Zoroaster.

The sovereignty of God over history is another idea that is implicit in eschatology. God reigns as king over history; he has a plan for mankind that he is trying to work out, and men are called upon to assist him. The doctrine implies that God is just; in the hereafter, therefore, a man will be rewarded according to the life he has lived. At the same time, it assumes that an upright man does not necessarily receive his reward in the present life.

Eschatology also includes the idea of a final judgment. There has to be a great assize, when each individual will have his day in court, where his eternal destiny will be made known by an omniscient and just judge. This is an optimistic faith; there is no doubt that the forces of good in the world are more powerful than the forces of evil.

Details of Zoroaster's view of the end of time are often visible, but they are sometimes not consistent with one another. Mazda himself appears to serve as judge. But his means of determining whether a man is innocent or guilty may be fire (Yasna 51:9) or a wave of molten metal through which everyone must pass (Yasna 32:7). In other hymns, one has to cross the Bridge of Judgment, the Chinvat Bridge, which spans the awful abyss of Hell. As a good man approaches, the bridge expands in width and he crosses it without difficulty (Yasna 46:10–11) to enter into the House of Song (Yasna 28:8; 45:8). But the evil man finds that the bridge is as narrow as the edge of a razor and he plunges downward from it to become an inmate of Hell.

In other parts of the Avesta, more details of the eschatology are provided. Mazda no longer serves as judge; now it is Mithras, assisted by Rashnu and Sraosha, who weighs souls on a pair of scales. We also learn that on his journey to Chinvat Bridge, which is guarded by dogs (Vendidad 13:9), the upright man enjoys a sweet-smelling scent from the gardens of paradise. As he approaches the bridge, he meets a beautiful maiden with the dogs at her side. "Who are you?" he asks. "I am your conscience," she replies. Then she leads him across the bridge and on to the House of Song, where he joins Mazda and his righteous company (Vendidad 19:29–30; Yast 22:1–14).

By contrast, the soul of an evil man is forced to inhale a sickening odor as he approaches the bridge. He is met by his conscience in the shape of a profligate woman, naked, filthy, obnoxious, who promptly shoves him from the razor-edge bridge into the pit below.

There, in darkness, as wages for his life of evil thoughts, evil words, evil deeds, he is compelled to eat poisonous food with a horrible stench.

The varying degrees of goodness and evil in men became a problem for later Zoroastrian thinkers. Ardai Viraf, who, like the biblical Enoch or Dante in his *Inferno,* was granted a tour through the world of the dead, found people placed in different stations, where they received reward and punishment in exact proportion to the moral character of the lives they had lived on earth. One region was inhabited by the Hamistagan—people in whose lives there had been an exact balance of good and evil, not bad enough to go to Hell, not good enough to go to Heaven. Viraf found Hell so dark that one spirit could not see another. The road led through "snow, ice, storms, intense cold, mephitic exhalations." There was bitter wailing. The region was filled with pits, and the spirit confined in each was being stung, pierced, and torn by serpents, scorpions, and other noxious creatures.[5]

The concepts of a coming savior and a future resurrection of the dead also found their place in late Zoroastrian thought. The Zamyad Yast[6] is devoted to the Hvareno, the awe-inspiring kingly glory, and to the characters and deeds of those who possess it. The first of those who possess Hvareno is Ahura Mazda himself. Then follows a series of gods and heroes, concluding with Saoshyant, the coming savior, who, with the aid of his helpers, brings a restoration of the world and a resurrection of the dead to immortality. Aeshma Daeva and the Druj (Angra Mainyu), conquered by the divine warriors, either perish or, stripped of their power, bow and flee away. The world will never again decay, never again grow old, never die. The victory of the Good Spirit over the Evil Spirit is complete and permanent.

CLEAN AND UNCLEAN

The religion of Zoroaster has much to do with clean and unclean things, an idea that grows out of the concept of dualism itself. All of Mazda's world is clean; that of Ahriman is unclean. The struggle between these two primordial spirits may be interpreted as the conflict between Mazda's attempt to purify the world and Ahriman's desire to contaminate it. Worship of Mazda is therefore concerned with ways to become pure, to remain pure, to spread purity in the world, as well as with ways to purge oneself of impurity once it has been acquired.

There are two parallel kinds of purity in Zoroastrianism: moral purity and ceremonial purity. The worshiper of Mazda considers good, pure, clean rituals as the basis of the spiritual life, the concepts of the moral and ceremonial being found side by side throughout Zoroastrianism. Zoroaster's dictum, "Good thoughts, good words, and good deeds," might also be expressed as "pure thoughts, pure words, and pure deeds," or "clean thoughts, clean words, and clean deeds."

The contrast between clean and unclean in its sharpest form is seen in the difference between the life and death of Mazda's creatures, and those of Ahriman. The death of the noxious creatures of Ahriman represents a triumph of Mazda over Ahriman; Mazda brings purity and the carcasses of Ahriman's creatures are not unclean. But the life of Mazda's creatures, primarily men, is clean, while their death is unclean; a human corpse is the most impure, the most contaminating object, and represents Ahriman's greatest victory over Mazda. Burial of the dead is therefore surrounded with a great panoply of ritual designed to protect all other clean things from contamination. Water, fire, and earth are pure and holy, they too must be protected. Thus a corpse may not be buried in the earth or cast into a stream, a pool, or the sea; nor may it be destroyed by fire. The feeling here is close to that of mana and taboo in primitive cultures.

The Vendidad, one of the most important sections of the Avesta, is devoted almost exclusively to rituals of purification. Here one finds spells and incantations, which must be uttered on all sorts of occasions as protection against invading demons, since impurity, uncleanness, is caused by demons. A large portion of the rituals described in the Vendidad have to do with death and burial of the dead. Hair and nails cut from the human body are thought of as dead, and therefore unclean; they must be scrupulously disposed of because they have come under demonic power.

The type of impurity ranking next to that of the corpse is that of the menstruating woman and the woman in labor (Vendidad 5:45 ff.). During these times a woman must be isolated in a special room in the home in order to avoid contaminating other persons. Like a woman under taboo in a primitive tribe, no one may touch her. Food must be passed to her from a distance of three

steps; she must be fifteen paces from the fire and in such a position that her gaze will not even fall on it. She must be kept at
the same distance from consecrated items intended for sacrifice. If
a child touches her, it too must be purified. If a menstruating
woman has not recovered in nine days, she must be bathed in cow's
urine, and 200 corn-carrying ants must be killed if it is summer,
or 200 ants of any other sort if it is winter. Ants are agents of
Ahriman (Vendidad 16:1–12).

Funeral Customs

Zoroastrians believe that the soul of the dead lingers about the
corpse for three days before departing, hoping all the while to reenter the body. At the present time, Zoroastrians in both Persia
and India dispose of the dead by placing the corpse in a *dakhma*,
a Tower of Silence, located in an isolated place, where the flesh is
consumed by vultures.[7] The dakhma is a round tower, some twenty
feet high, built of stone in the shape of an open cone, with one
door near the base, through which the body is carried in. In the
center of the tower there is a pit about six feet deep, which is lined
with concentric shelves paved with stones, one course above the
other, like an amphitheater. Two *nasa-salars*, official pallbearers,
deposit the corpse on its proper resting place (some areas of the
stone paving being designated for men, some for women, some for
children), remove its clothing, which is cast into the pit, and then
depart, leaving the corpse naked. Within two hours vultures have
stripped all flesh from the bones. At least twice each year the nasa-
salars cast the bones onto the floor of the pit, where they lie until
air, rain, and sun change them into dust, thereby making them
pure again.[8]

　　The impurity of a corpse is explained by the theory that death
is caused not by fire or water or any other such thing that Mazda
has created, but by an attack of Nasu, the unclean spirit of death
sent out by Ahriman. When Nasu has killed a man he takes possession of the body, making the corpse so unclean, so dangerous,
that no man is permitted to carry it without the protection of at
least one other person.[9] A person who has committed the great sin
of carrying a corpse alone is condemned to live as a hermit in a
wilderness area that is rarely frequented by flocks and herds. He is
required to keep himself thirty paces from fire, water, and bundles

of *baresma* (a shrub used in sacrifice) and three paces from faithful persons, who provide him with food and worn-out clothing. When he grows old a strong young man is ordered to go to his isolated hut and decapitate him. In this way the criminal atones for his sin.[10]

In earlier days in Persia the corpse was deposited on a mountain to be devoured by dogs and vultures. To make sure that it was not carried into any water, or brought into contact with trees, it was made fast by brass, stones, or clay. Not to make the corpse fast was a crime.[11] The Nasu will flee from a corpse when a yellow dog with four eyes (two spots above the eyes) or a white dog with yellow ears is made to pass by it three times and look upon it.[12] But ordinarily the Nasu remains with the corpse until all flesh has been stripped away by beasts and birds. Then, in the form of a bee, it flies back to Hell. Because of its contact with dead bodies, the dakhma is considered to be one of the most unclean spots on earth.[13] Therefore, although the faithful are urged to build dakhmas for the protection of earth, fire, and water, they are also instructed to tear them down at least every fifty years in order to let that place become pure again.[14]

ZOROASTRIAN POLYTHEISM

Zoroaster had hardly passed from the scene before a reaction in the nature of a counterreformation restored the old gods with their ancient cults. They were welcomed with enthusiasm by persons who had long found satisfactions in them. The magi priests, who spearheaded the restoration, celebrated their return to the ancient altars. Zoroaster's faith, which had bravely set forth as a monotheism, now found itself submerged in a reinstated polytheism.

The Zoroastrian Pantheon

Mithras

Mithras was the most notable of the old gods to be brought back. At times he was virtually equal with Ahura Mazda and stood by his side; they were the lofty, eternal, and holy two (Yasna 2:11). Mithras was one of the Yasatas; that is, one of the popular gods, subject to Ahura Mazda, yet worthy of worship, for when Ahura created Mithras, according to the Mihir Yast,[15] he created him to be as worthy of prayer as himself. The remarkable Mithras liturgy, some thirty pages long, is one of the finest literary pieces in the Avesta. Here Mithras is presented as the Lord of wide pastures, with 1,000 ears and 10,000 eyes, reminiscent of the Aryan period when he was god of the sky, and with the gleaming stars, which were his eyes, watched over all the world; nothing was able to escape his eyes, his ears, his knowledge.

In the religion of Zoroaster, however, Mithras emerges primarily as a divine warrior who never sleeps and is swift and strong. He is closely associated with the sun, but not yet identified with it, although on his way to that consummation (Yast 10:13). When the dawn begins to appear over Mount Demavend, Mithras is first of the gods to reach its summit. As a warrior he flashes across the sky, his golden chariot drawn by four stallions, their forefeet shod with gold, their hind feet with silver; his chariot is equipped on one side with a thousand bows, on the other with a thousand feathered arrows tipped with gold, a horned shaft, a brass tail. These arrows fall through heavenly space on the skulls of the Daevas. At his disposal are also a thousand two-edged swords, a thousand iron maces, and a great knotted club of brass with which he crushes Daeva skulls. Mithras was therefore the idol of the warriors and was popular among the Persian nobility, especially in Armenia and eastern Asia Minor, where the frequently occurring name Mithridates testifies to his popularity.

The description of Mithras in this Yast surpasses the attention given to any other deity in the Avesta. It shows that in some circles, at any rate, he was the equal, if not the superior, of Ahura Mazda himself. Zoroaster placed Mithras in the company of the nature spirits whom he repudiated; he was one of the Daevas, in alliance with Ahriman. But Mithras was so popular that he could not be kept in this state of bondage. After Zoroaster's time, Mithras returned with more vigor than ever, side by side with Ahura Mazda. His return to power is clearly attested in the inscriptions of Artaxerxes Mnemon (404–359 B.C.), where he appears along with the goddess Anahita. Zoroaster's reform had not destroyed the Mithras cult. The concept of Kshathra, which means power and dominion, was pale alongside the colorful warrior god. Mithras had been in exile, not dead; when he returned to his people, he was more powerful than before.

Ashi Vanuhi

Ashi Vanuhi, the picturesque goddess of plenty, is another of the old Iranian deities to return to the Zoroastrian pantheon. An entire Yast is devoted to her cult.[16] Tall, shining, full of intelligence and power, she rides in a strong chariot, dispensing welfare and healing. She joins the fellowship of those who drink the holy Haoma, all other drinks being associated with Aeshma, the fiend. Ashi is a happy goddess, radiant with joy. The house where she is revered is full of perfumes. She brings kingdoms rich in horses, chariots, weapons, food, home and family life.

Lords devoted to Ashi have beautiful wives at home waiting for their return, as well as lovely daughters; their wealth is counted in caravans of large-humped camels, which bring silver and gold, beautiful garments, and other precious wares from faraway lands.

Ashi is a daughter of Ahura Mazda; her mother is Armaiti; her brothers and sisters include the Amesha Spentas as well as Sraosha, Rashnu (genius of truth), and Mithras. She has loved Zoroaster and taken him under her protection, as she has done also for other demon-smiting heroes of the Iranian past.

As goddess of wealth and plenty, it is characteristic of Ashi Vanuhi to refuse the sacrifices of aged men whose virility is lost, of prostitutes who waste their strength in abortions, of boys not yet arrived at manhood, and of girls who have not yet known a man. She is typical of the Persian ideal of life—enjoyment of the good things of the world: family, the home, sex, material possessions, good food, and drink. Nothing good is to be rejected in ascetic piety. All things of beauty and loveliness are blessings with which the gods have surrounded the life of man.

Anahita

Another goddess of considerable importance in the late Zoroastrian pantheon is Anahita, worshiped under the name of Ardvi Sura Anahita, goddess of the waters and of women, as well as of soldiers and great heroes. Her worship was popularized by Artaxerxes Mnemon (404–359 B.C.), who set up statues to her, and presumably temples, in Babylon, Susa, Ecbatana, Bactria, Damascus, and Sardis. This appears to be the first time that the Persians had accepted the use of images of gods in human shape. Prior to this, they had sacrificed under the open sky, regarding fire and water as the only symbols of the gods.[17] The cult of Anahita is syncretistic; it combines

the simple elements of Aryan nature deities with a Semitic cult
that has a sensual, orgiastic character.

The worship of Anahita was widely diffused in the Persian Empire, but especially powerful in Armenia and Asia Minor, the
provinces of Cilicia, Asia, Cappadocia, and Pontus.[18] The Greek
geographer Strabo notes that daughters of noble families in Armenia were accustomed to go to the temple of Anahita and prostitute themselves to strangers before they were married. He also reports that Anahita's temples in Pontus, Cappadocia, and Cilicia
were attended by sacred slaves of both sexes.[19] Such sexual rites had
been well known among Assyrians and Babylonians, in the cults
of Asherah of ancient Palestine and Astarte of Phoenicia, as well
as in the temples of Aphrodite and Venus of the Greeks and Romans, but among Persians they were not characteristic; they constituted a deviation from the rites of Zoroastrians.

Sraosha

Sraosha, one of the great angels in Zoroastrianism, was apparently
unknown in the thought of Zoroaster himself, as is reflected in the
Gathas; certainly he was not one of the Amesha Spentas, of whom
there were only six, unless we add Spenta Mainyu or Ahura Mazda
himself, as was sometimes done, to complete the Holy Seven. But
in later parts of the Avesta, Sraosha, whose name means "obedience," gradually becomes so important that he is added to the
other six to complete the seven Amesha Spentas. A Yast is devoted
to his worship.[20]

Ahura Mazda created Sraosha for the specific purpose of withstanding the fiend Aeshma Daeva and of protecting the faithful
against him. The struggle between Sraosha and Aeshma Daeva is
another variation of the dualistic principle we have already noted
in Zoroastrianism.

All the faithful joined in the protection of good and friendly animals and the annihilation of destructive beasts, animals, and insects—especially lizards, frogs, and poisonous insects. The role of
Sraosha, who fought against the world of invisible demons, was
parallel to that of Mithras, who protected faithful soldiers on the
battlefield. Sraosha and Mithras are so similar in character that they
are often mentioned together in the Avesta. Sraosha was one of the
most colorful figures in the pantheon of Mazda worshipers, at the
popular level, and probably outstripped all but Ahura Mazda himself.

Mithraism and the Cult of Anahita

Mithras and Anahita were both popular deities in the Persian communities of Armenia, as well as in the later Roman provinces of Cappadocia, Asia, and Cilicia. The cults of Mithras and Anahita did not merge, but remained natural allies, mutually complementary. Mithras was a god of men; Anahita, a goddess of women whose worship merged easily with other cults for women. In Asia Minor Anahita was gradually absorbed into the cult of Cybele, Great Mother of the gods, the most popular goddess of that area, who was known best at Ephesus under the name Artemis, although she was more Asiatic than Greek.

Cybele, the Great Mother, was best known as Mother Earth, goddess of fertility. She was associated with a consort named Attis, the spirit of vegetation, who died in the fall and arose from the dead in the spring. Cybele became so popular that in 204 B.C., when Rome was threatened with destruction by Hannibal the Carthaginian, on advice of the Sibylline Oracle the Romans brought her cult to Rome. When Hannibal was defeated and destroyed, Cybele became strongly entrenched in Rome, where she had a temple on the Palatine Hill.

The history of Mithras in Armenia and Asia is not so well known, although his popularity there is attested in the names of their kings. The Romans appear to have come into contact with Mithras first through pirates who operated out of strongholds in the Taurus Mountains and preyed on Roman ships in the eastern Mediterranean. They became such a problem that Pompey the Great was sent to destroy them in 67 B.C. Many of the prisoners he captured and carried to Rome were worshipers of Mithras; it was from them that the cult spread to Roman prison guards and soldiers, and soon became popular in the Roman armies throughout the Empire. Remains of their shrines in the form of underground chapels have been located at the sites of army camps from Armenia across Europe to Britain and from the Black Sea into North Africa.

Many evidences indicate that the alliance between Mithras and Anahita continued in the Roman Empire, although this was through the fusion of Anahita with Cybele, which brought Mithras and Cybele close together, and gave to Mithras a semiofficial acceptance in Rome, where the cult of Cybele had been recognized since 204 B.C. The complementary character of these two cults created a natural bond between them. As men adopted the worship of

Mithras, their wives and daughters were being accepted into the cult of the Great Mother.[21] Cybele

The cult of Mithras acquired new dimensions in the Roman world, without losing those that had long characterized it. Mithras was still the smiter of evil, god of light and god of soldiers. Now, however, he became more closely associated with the sun. At last he was identified with it as Sol invictus Mithras. But the cult of Mithras now also became a religion of redemption and took the form of a mystery cult, thus reflecting the mood of the Hellenistic Age, when men had come to crave eternal life, not merely temporal rewards and pleasures. Mithras offered them the hope of immortality, a legacy from Zoroaster, but now to be obtained through initiation into secret mysteries. Initiates were assured that they were reborn for eternity. Over a period of time, and no doubt after much instruction and discipline, a mystic advanced through seven stages or degrees, each represented by a name that he assumed: Raven, Occult, Soldier, Lion, Persian, Runner of the Sun, and Father. Monuments picture the celebrants wearing masks and impersonating the characters of the names they bore.[22] Each role evidently symbolized some element of the Mithraic faith.

In each of the underground shrines of Mithras there was an altar with the holy fire burning; on the wall beyond was a bas-relief in stone portraying symbols of the faith of Mithraists. It showed Mithras the Bull Slayer in the act of driving a sword into the heart of the divine bull (the bull was sacred to both Anahita and Cybele). Two acolytes stood by holding torches, one upright, one inverted. Helios, the sun god, and Selene, goddess of the moon, drove their chariots across the sky. As symbols of Ahriman the relief included a serpent and a scorpion trying to defeat the purpose of the sacrifice, and it portrayed a dog seeking to drink the divine blood (see Figure 8.1). It may be that this relief was intended to represent the sacrament of the taurobolium, a rite certainly characteristic of the Cybele cult, probably also of that of Mithras. The sacrifice could be performed with either a bull or a ram; hence the words *taurobolium* and *criobolium,* which had the same meaning. A neophyte knelt under an altar which had a grated cover. As the bull or ram was sacrificed above him, he was drenched by its blood. In this way, he believed, he was sacramentally reborn.[23]

At first Mithraism was popular only among lower-class Romans and foreigners, especially Asiatics. But before the end of the second century A.D., the Emperor Commodus (180–192) is said to have become an initiate; for the next hundred years emperors were friendly to the cult. At that time Mithraism was a strong rival of Christianity, but by the end of the third century the latter had begun to win the struggle. When Constantine, after A.D. 312, gave his support to the Christian faith, Mithraism in the Roman Empire was doomed.

Yet Christianity inherited at least one important symbol from Mithraism. It took over December 25 as the date for its celebration of the birth of Christ. That was the day when Mithraists had observed the birth of Mithras. The day comes at the culmination of the Roman Saturnalia, following the winter solstice, when days begin to grow longer and the sun seems to be born again. As Mithraists had identified Mithras with the sun, they transferred the old ritual to him. But for hundreds of years the Saturnalia had been popular among the Romans, and Christians found no way to eradicate it. In order to Christianize the old pagan festival, they reinterpreted December 25, to celebrate it as the birthday of the Son of God.[24]

CONTEMPORARY ZOROASTRIANISM

The Muslim conquest of the Persian Empire in A.D. 651 was of momentous importance to the followers of Zoroaster, who suddenly found it necessary to make a major decision about the future of their faith. Should they seek to preserve their own religious identity and ancient culture at all costs, or should they come to terms with the Muslim conquerors? Most of them appear to have taken the latter course. They simply transferred their allegiance to Islam and continued to live in Persia under the new Muslim government. This choice was not too difficult for them to make, nor was it hypocritical. The two religions were similar, and some of the major concepts of their faith were almost identical. Both believed in one God, in Satan, in dualism, in eschatology, in high morality.

Those Zoroastrians who were determined to keep their ancient faith found life among the Muslims not impossible, but difficult. A few of them—some 14,000—have survived in Iran to this day.

They have large communities at Yezd and Kerman in south central
Iran, and small groups also in some other cities. The Muslims call
the Zoroastrians "Gabars," that is, infidels.

Most of the Zoroastrians who were determined not to be assimilated into the Muslim faith, however, from time to time since A.D.
651, have migrated to India, where they have found hospitality and
a new homeland. Settling first in the Gujarat region, they took up
farming, but later, under new Muslim pressure—for the Muslims
had come to power in India—they went on to Surat. There they
began to enter other vocations. In time some of them moved on to
Bombay, where opportunities for competent persons were more
plentiful. The practice of the high moral virtues of their faith soon
gained them respect from the Indian community. At the present
time many of the leaders in the commercial world of India are
Zoroastrians. They are noted for their generosity: they even send
financial aid to their poverty-stricken Gabar brethren of Iran. They
have also grown in numbers in India and now number approximately 150,000. While they have remained loyal to their ancestral
faith, they have also adjusted themselves to their Indian environment. Zoroastrians who reached India during previous centuries
are called Parsees, from the Indian word for Persia. More recent
arrivals are called Iranis, from the word *Iran.*

Zoroastrianism is primarily a priestly religion. Its best-known and
most significant rites are priestly functions—in particular, those
associated with their temples. *Magus,* the ancient priestly name, survives to this day in *mobed,* the general term for a Zoroastrian priest.
The priesthood is hereditary, and has descended through certain
families from ancient times. The priest has portable altars which
he may take into homes where he performs rites for individuals,
such as anointing the lips of a newly born infant, as well as those
of the dying, with Haoma, the sacred drink.

Training for the priesthood begins at the age of seven, after the
Nozud ceremony, in which the candidate puts on the sacred girdle,
the *kusti,* worn by all laymen between the ages of seven and fourteen. At fourteen, the candidate must pass an examination, the
Nabar, when he becomes a *Herbad* and is entitled to serve as
acolyte at the altar. On attaining a complete mastery of the Yasna
and Vendidad, he becomes a *mobed.* Upon being appointed to

FIGURE 8.2   A Zoroastrian altar in Iran. (*Inge Morath from Magnum*)

serve in a temple, he acquires the title of *dastur*, the highest priestly
rank. If his duties there are chanting prayers, he is a *zot*; if tending the fire, he is a *raspi*. In earlier days there were many priests.
When Mazdaism was the established religion in Sassanian times,
the High Priest, called the Zarathustratotema, stood next to the
great king himself in power. The High Priest in Yezd, Iran, today
is called Dastur-i-Dasturan.[25]

The Mazda temple today is called the Dahr-i-Mihr, the Gate of
Mithras; *fire temple* is its popular designation, deriving from the
fact that tending the holy fire is the main function performed there.
Fire is the symbol of God; this is a reflection of a spiritual view of
Ahura Mazda that goes all the way back to the Aryans (see Figure
8.2). No image, no statue of the gods, has ever been used in Zoroastrianism.[26] (By contrast, Hinduism, which also has an Aryan
background, has developed great temples and made elaborate use
of statues.) The fire temple is outwardly a plain structure, scarcely
distinguishable from business houses on the city streets.

Five times daily, at the traditional hours of prayer, priests go into the sanctuary, where the holy fire burns in an urn, standing on a square stone pedestal or on a metal tripod. The priest wears a mask over his mouth and gloves, and tends the fire with tongs and a spoon in order not to contaminate it with his breath or touch. The priests of Bombay renew the fire with sandalwood. The tradition has been to keep the fire burning always, never to let it die. Mazda worshipers brought the sacred fire with them when they fled from their Persian shrines to India twelve centuries ago. At least once in recent years, fire was sent back from India to relight the fire at Yezd. There is also a sacred fire burning in every Parsee home, lit from the fire in the temple.

The sanctuary in which the holy fire burns is designed so that no light from the sun or any other outside source may penetrate into its darkness. The temple also contains rooms for other purposes. In a room adjacent to the sanctuary, in a second chapel, the Haoma is prepared and the holy water as well as the flesh offering (today this is milk or cakes) is consecrated. In this chapel priests celebrate a liturgy, drinking the Haoma and eating the cakes, a practice that is somewhat parallel to Christian Holy Communion.

Laymen are also free to worship at the fire temples, and both men and women take part. At the entrance to the sanctuary where the fire burns, they recite a prayer, remove their shoes, approach the fire barefooted, and give an offering of holy water, barsom twigs, sandalwood, and money to the priests, who presumably derive their support from these offerings. With ashes ladled from the urn, the priest anoints the brows and eyelids of the worshipers, who then depart, moving backward from the fire; they never turn their backs toward it.

There are numerous occasions of a special character when Parsees attend their temples, but they also engage in their own individual devotions under the open sky, much as their ancestors did ages ago. At Bombay one may be seen standing on the beach in the evening, head uncovered and barefooted, adoring the setting sun, the most ancient symbol of Ahura Mazda. Kneeling on the sand until his chintz hat, *kaoka,* touches the wet sand, he then rises and advances to the edge of the sea, wets his fingertips in the salt water and touches his brow with the brine, worshiping in the sanctuary of nature, man's oldest temple.[27]

NOTES

1. Herodotus, *The Histories* (Baltimore: Penguin, 1954), I, 129–140.
2. *Ibid.*, p. 130.
3. A fuller account of the Aryans is given on pp. 359–360, 370–380.
4. Jacques Duchesne-Guillemin, *The Hymns of Zarathustra* (Boston: Beacon, 1963), p. 65.
5. Viraf's excursion through Heaven and Hell may be read in *The Dabistan,* translated by David Shea and Anthony Troyer (New York: Tudor, 1937), pp. 144–154.
6. James Darmsteter, trans., *Sacred Books of the East* (Oxford: Clarendon Press, 1880–1897), XXIII, 286–309.
7. The Gabar community of only fifty persons at Shiraz, Iran, has neither fire temple nor dakhma. They bury their dead in the ground and cover the grave with stones. Probably other very small communities of Zoroastrians have to resort to similar practices. Cf. A. V. W. Jackson, *Persia Past and Present* (New York: Macmillan, 1906), pp. 337–338.
8. Darmsteter, *op. cit.*, IV, lxxviii; Jackson, *op. cit.*, pp. 387–400, gives a vivid description of funeral rites of present-day Zoroastrians in Yezd, Persia.
9. Vendidad 3:14.
10. Vendidad 3:14–20.
11. Vendidad 6:44–48
12. Vendidad 8:16–18.
13. Vendidad 3:9.
14. Vendidad 3:13; 7:45–59.
15. L. H. Mills, trans., *Sacred Books of the East* (Oxford: Clarendon Press, 1880–1897), XXIII, 119–158.
16. Darmsteter, Yast 17, *op. cit.*, XXIII, 270–282.
17. Clement of Alexandria, *Protrepticus* 5; also Herodotus, *op. cit.*, I, 130.
18. Strabo, *Geography*, XI, 532; XII, 537.
19. Franz Cumont, "Anahita," in James Hastings, ed., *Encyclopaedia of Religion and Ethics* (New York: Scribner, 1908–1926), I, 414–415, gives a valuable collection of the classical references to the Anahita cult.
20. Darmsteter, *op. cit.*, XXIII, 159–167.
21. Franz Cumont, *The Oriental Religions in Roman Paganism* (Chicago: Open Court, 1911), p. 66; also, *The Mysteries of Mithra* (New York: Dover, 1956), p. 179.
22. Cumont, *The Mysteries of Mithra,* p. 152.
23. Cumont, *Oriental Religions,* p. 66.
24. Cumont, *The Mysteries of Mithra,* pp. 167, 191, 196.
25. Jackson, *op. cit.*, p. 357.
26. Anahita, who can hardly be considered a true Zoroastrian deity, is an exception.
27. John Clark Archer, *Faiths Men Live By* (New York: Ronald, 1934), p. 320.

9 Biblical Judaism

Judaism is the religion of the Jews—that is, the Jewish people, who are also called Hebrews, Israel, Israelites, and Semites. The oldest of these terms, in the biblical sense, is Hebrew. In the singular form, it occurs first in Genesis 14:13, where Abraham, the ancestral father of all Jews, Hebrews, or Israelites, is called Abram the Hebrew. The term probably means "one from across the river"—that is, an immigrant into Palestine, then called Canaan, from across the Euphrates River. All the descendants of Abraham were commonly called Hebrews in the Bible, and it is still correct to designate them in this way.

The word *Jew* is derived from Judah, one of the twelve sons of Jacob. He was the ancestral father of the tribe of Judah, which settled in the southern part of the land of Canaan. The name Judah was applied to the people who occupied the region, as well as to the region itself.

According to Genesis 32:28, Israel is a title of honor that God gave to Jacob because he had striven with both God and man and prevailed. Jacob's descendants were often called Israelites or, in a collective sense, Israel. But when the Hebrew kingdom was divided, on the death of Solomon in 922 B.C., the southern part took the name of Judah, the northern that of Israel.

After both nations had fallen, it was survivors of Judah who returned to their homeland, where they were probably joined by a few survivors of other tribes. Because this restored group lived in the land of Judah, they came to be called Jews; it is this group that preserved the Hebrew culture.

The Jews are also called Semites. A Semite is a person who speaks

FIGURE 9.1   A section of a Dead Sea Scroll of the Book of Isaiah. (*Keystone*)

one of the Semitic languages. But the Jews are descendants of just one of the groups who in ancient times spoke a Semitic language—others were the Canaanites, Phoenicians, Moabites, Ammonites, Arabs, Syrians, Babylonians, and Assyrians—so that the term *Semite* cannot be correctly limited to the Jews. The word Semite is derived from Shem. The ancient Hebrew ethnology held that all the peoples of the earth were descended from Shem, Ham, and Japheth, the three sons of Noah: the Shemites, or Semites, from Shem; the Hamites from Ham; the Japhethites from Japheth (Genesis 10:1–32).

THE HEBREW SCRIPTURES

One of the most characteristic elements of the Jewish faith is the belief that God has revealed himself to man and that he has done this most significantly through persons of unusual talents who are believed to be inspired by God. Such persons are called prophets, or spokesmen of God. Their utterances, either oral or written, are therefore believed to be divinely inspired, the real words of God. This belief in inspiration gave rise to the Bible, certainly one of the most famous collections of writings in the world.

For many centuries the stories, ballads, and laws of the Hebrews were transmitted orally from generation to generation. As early as 1000 B.C. a few individual pieces attained a fixed form and were probably put into writing. After the nation was founded and its culture began to develop, Hebrews began to take pride in their history; the increasing complexity of their culture required codification of their laws. They therefore began to write down what had previously existed only orally. This process continued until all the books of the Old Testament had been produced. The New Testament was written by Christians at a later period, and it has never been accepted as Scripture by the Jews.

The Old Testament, as it appears in the Christian Bible, contains thirty-nine books. It is an anthology of writings of many types and various lengths, none of them full-length books in our sense of the word, some of them only short pamphlets. In the Hebrew Bible the same writings are presented as only twenty-four books divided into three parts: the Law, the Prophets, and the Writings.

The Law, or Torah, as the Jews call it, contains five books: Genesis, Exodus, Leviticus, Numbers, and Deuteronomy, all associated by tradition with Moses, who lived a little before 1200 B.C. and may be regarded as founder of the Hebrew religion. Some of the basic ideas in these books are traced back to Moses, but the writings themselves, as we have them today, came into existence over a period of 600 or 700 years. In that respect, they are parallel to the law codes of other cultures, which also developed in response to the growing needs of the people.

Scholars have devoted an enormous amount of study to these Hebrew lawbooks and have discovered evidence of at least four editions and revisions of the material, much of which at first existed only orally. The earliest version was written in Judah, the southern kingdom, close to 900 B.C. It is called the J Version or Document because, throughout, the Hebrew God is called Yahweh (sometimes translated as Jehovah). Beginning with the story of Adam and Eve in the Garden of Eden in Genesis 2:4b, the J Document appears intermittently through the first four lawbooks and then continues at least through Joshua and Judges. It provides a vivid account of both the history and the social life of the Hebrews, as well as of their religion. God is often presented picturesquely in anthropomorphic form—that is, as having the physical form or attributes of a man.

The second version of this material was written in Israel, the northern kingdom, around 750 B.C. It has no creation stories and begins instead with Abraham. From the outset it uses the Hebrew word *Elohim* for God; for that reason it is called the E Version. It tells many of the same stories found in J, but shows an interest in events, places, and persons of Israel, by contrast with J. Furthermore, its view of God is more spiritual: God makes himself known to men in visions and dreams, not face-to-face, as in J.

The third edition of the old material was created in Judah about 621 B.C., in the days of King Josiah, long after Israel had fallen, as well as long after the time of Amos, Hosea, Isaiah, and Micah, some of the greatest prophets. It has to do mainly with the Mosaic laws, and omits most of the historical material in the other lawbooks. Because of its preoccupation with the Hebrew laws, it is called Deuteronomy, the Second Law. From the name Deuteronomy, this version of the Law is referred to as D. This work represents important advances in religion and morality, and reflects the influence of the prophets who lived about a century before it was produced. This code is permeated by a humane spirit, a sense of generosity and of justice. Another of its important features is that it outlaws religious sacrifices in the local shrines of Judah, thus consolidating all sacrificial worship in the Temple of Solomon at Jerusalem, and making it possible for the temple priests to eradicate many religious rites that the Hebrews had adopted from their Canaanite and other neighbors. Deuteronomy also presented a new philosophy of history: that the prosperity, even the survival, of the nation was dependent on loyalty to the covenant with Yahweh. Security and prosperity resulted from keeping faith with God. Famine, pestilence, military disaster, or any other catastrophe was interpreted as God's judgment on the nation because of its apostasy. Under the influence of this philosophy, the books of Judges and I and II Kings were edited and achieved their present form.

After the fall of Judah, probably during the Babylonian Exile, about 550 B.C., the priests undertook another complete revision of their books of law and history. The point of view reflects changes in theology and makes the history of the temple, the rituals, and the priesthood paramount. These changes appear in the Pentateuch —the five Books of Moses—as the Priestly Document, which now becomes the framework of the whole. The same priests or their followers then proceeded to rewrite later history, the new version appearing in I and II Chronicles, Ezra, and Nehemiah, all of which reflect the same priestly interests. I and II Chronicles are a revision of I and II Samuel and I and II Kings, but by no means always an improvement on those ancient records. Since this revision of the Law and other works was made by priests, it is abbreviated as P. I and II Samuel contain the best historical writing in the Old Testament.

The most characteristic legal part of the priestly work is the Book of Leviticus, which was primarily a manual used by priests in performing their duties, especially at the restored temple after the Babylonian Exile. But the priestly work also reflects a high theology, as presented, for example, in the first chapter of Genesis. This represents the maturity attained toward the end of the Old Testament period. In reediting the Pentateuch, the priests placed their creation story first, and they gave us the Books of Moses as we know them today. By 400 B.C. they had attained the status of Scriptures, the first Hebrew books to be so regarded.

In the meantime, many Hebrew prophets had lived, and either they or their disciples had edited some of their most important oracles. While these were not at first regarded as Scripture, they gradually won their place in the Hebrew culture. Joshua, Judges, and the Books of Samuel and Kings, which we now think of as history books, had come to be regarded as books of prophecy. Since the Hebrews believed that these four works were written by inspired men, they called them the Former Prophets. At the same time, the books Christians call the Prophets, but Jews call the Latter Prophets, were being assembled. They were Isaiah (see Figure 9.1), Jeremiah, Ezekiel, and the Twelve (a collection of the twelve shorter prophetic books), the entire group being considered as four books. By Hebrew reckoning, the two groups of prophetic writings constituted a collection of eight, all of which had attained Scripture status by about 200 B.C., although their authority was lower than that of the Law.

There remain a group of some thirteen books, as the Hebrews counted them, called the Writings, which gradually came into favor and authority, but certainly not as equals to the Law, and hardly as equals to the Prophets. Their recognition did not become final until about A.D. 100, when an assembly of Jewish scholars at Jamnia, Palestine, in response to the threat of emerging Christianity, drew up an official list of Jewish canonical books. The thirteen books in this last collection were the Psalms, Proverbs, Job, Song of Solomon, Ruth, Lamentations, Ecclesiastes, Esther, Daniel, Ezra, Nehemiah, I and II Chronicles, which the Hebrews reckoned as eleven by counting Ezra-Nehemiah and I and II Chronicles as one each. Thus the Jewish canon contained 24 books: Pentateuch, 5; Prophets, 8; Writings, 11. As edited in the Christian Bibles, however, they number 39.

The Jews believed that this canon, since it was produced step by step, gradually made further revelation unnecessary and that prophets ceased to appear with Ezra and Nehemiah about 400 B.C. This belief required them to reject from their Scripture any book known to have been written after that date, on the theory that such books could not be inspired. Many Hebrew writings of good quality therefore failed to find a place in the Jewish Scriptures. One group of such books, comprising some fourteen writings, is called the Apocrypha. The titles usually included in this collection are I and II Esdras, Tobit, Judith, Additions to Esther, Wisdom of Solomon, Ecclesiasticus or Wisdom of Sirach, Baruch, Susannah, Song of the Three Children, Bel and the Dragon, Prayer of Manasseh, I and II Maccabees.[1]

Another group of Hebrew writings from the end of the Old Testament period, of inferior literary quality but not without historical and religious importance, has been collected under the name of Pseudepigrapha. The title is derived from the fact that many of these writings were published under the names of well-known ancient persons in an effort to get them accepted. This was one consequence of the dogma that inspiration had ceased. Some of the best known of these books are: Jubilees, Aristeas, Books of Adam and Eve, Martyrdom of Isaiah, Testaments of the Twelve Patriarchs, Sibylline Oracles, Assumption of Moses, I and II Enoch, II and III Baruch, Psalms of Solomon, III and IV Maccabees.[2]

HEBREW THEOLOGY

In attempting to grasp the ancient Hebrew concept of God, we need to be on guard against the assumption that the leading Hebrew writers were philosophers or even theologians in the technical sense. Apparently the Hebrews never thought of religion as a philosophical or theological system, or even as a creed to be accepted. For them religion involved the whole life, including family, community, people, nation. At times they also caught a vision of the whole world under the rule of God.

We should also be on guard with reference to the sources we use. The Bible is, in effect, an anthology, gathered from all the periods of Hebrew history known to us, but with its roots in prehistoric periods. It is not difficult for a perceptive reader to detect in the Bible traces of primitive beliefs, remaining like fossils in rocks; such evidences of a past long dead can be paralleled in the ancient cultures of all peoples. The understanding of God that the Hebrews had attained by 500 B.C. is the faith that has inspired them from that day to this, and differs from the primitive faith that they left behind.

Primitive Survivals

Genesis 6:1–4 contains a notable primitive survival. It records that,

When men began to multiply on the face of the ground, and daughters were born to them, the sons of God saw that the daughters of men were fair; and they took to wife such of them as they chose. . . . The Nephilim were on the earth in those days, and also afterward, when the sons of God came in to the daughters of men, and they bore children to them. These were the mighty men that were of old, the men of renown.[3]

This is the only passage of its kind in the Bible, and we are taken by surprise when we come upon it. It reminds us of ancient Greek religion, in which it was a commonplace for deities, both male and female, to engage in affairs with human beings, with these affairs producing such men of renown as Heracles, Aeneas, and Achilles. This passage in Genesis was probably included in the Bible unintentionally, an example of oversight in the editing of old material taken over from some earlier culture.

Another example, exhibiting bold imagination and picturesque beauty, is the episode in Exodus 33:12–23, in which Moses, a timid man, in his desire for certainty about his own vocation, requests the Lord to grant him the privilege of an interview, face to face. The Lord declines, explaining that no one can see his face and live. Yet he says in 33:21–23:

Behold, there is a place by me where you shall stand upon the rock; and while my glory passes by I will put you in a cleft of the rock, and I will cover you with my hand until I have passed by; then I will take away my hand, and you shall see my back; but my face shall not be seen.

This is probably the most extreme example of anthropomorphism in the Bible. God is represented as having a real physical form. In a less startling way, anthropomorphism is assumed in such stories as the Garden of Eden (Genesis 3), where Adam hears God walking in the garden, and also in Genesis 18, when Yahweh and two angels, all in human form, call on Abraham as he sits at the door of his tent by the Oaks of Mamre, and again in Genesis 32:22–30, in which Jacob wrestles with God all night, striving for a blessing.

Judges 5:4, 5 presents Yahweh as a mountain god, residing on Sinai. The forces of nature shudder as the divine warrior marches by to aid the Hebrews.

> Lord, when thou didst go forth from Seir,
>   when thou didst march from the region of Edom,
> the earth trembled,
>   and the heavens dropped,
>   yea, the clouds dropped water.
> The mountains quaked before the Lord,
>   yon Sinai before the Lord, the God of Israel.

This extraordinary concept of a mountain spirit rushing into battle reminds us of the nature deities of the Rig-Veda of ancient India.

It is impressive in these poetic lines, but it has little in common with God as conceived by the great prophets, when Hebrew thought was reaching its maturity.

Equally remarkable is the description of the top of Mount Sinai, the holy mountain to which Moses brought the Hebrews to receive the Law, after they had fled from Egypt.

> On the morning of the third day there were thunders and lightnings, and a thick cloud upon the mountain, and a very loud trumpet blast, so that all the people who were in the camp trembled. Then Moses brought the people out of the camp to meet God; and they took their stand at the foot of the mountain. And Mount Sinai was wrapped in smoke, because the Lord descended upon it in fire; and the smoke of it went up like the smoke of a kiln, and the whole mountain quaked greatly. And as the sound of the trumpet grew louder and louder, Moses spoke, and God answered him in thunder. And the Lord came down upon Mount Sinai, to the top of the mountain; and the Lord called Moses to the top of the mountain, and Moses went up. And the Lord said to Moses, "Go down and warn the people, lest they break through to the Lord to gaze and many of them perish." [Exodus 19:16–21.]

This description is only the stage setting for what is to follow. For in the immediate sequel (Exodus 20:1–17), while all the people stand at attention at the foot of the mountain, they hear the thundering voice of God, out of the fire and smoke boiling from its summit, proclaim the immortal words of the Ten Commandments. They begin,

> I am the Lord your God, who brought you out
> of the land of Egypt, out of the house of bondage.
> You shall have no other gods before me.

This is certainly one of the most impressive passages of the Bible, as well as in the literature of all the world. Yet it presents God speaking as the fiery spirit of a volcanic mountain, like the voice of Vulcan roaring from the throat of Mount Etna. It may be that at one time there was volcanic activity in the peaks of the Sinai mountains.

The Creation

The later priestly editors of the Pentateuch thought it appropriate to begin their Scriptures with a passage presenting mature faith. So they therefore placed at the beginning of Genesis their magnificent story of creation. This presents God in action, and not as a philosophical concept or a metaphysical system. He is actually in process of creating the universe.

It may be that at some earlier time the Hebrews had been polytheists, believing in many gods. It is even probable that this creation story is a revision of an older Mesopotamian myth, although no polytheism remains here.[4] Every vestige of it has been purged away. *Elohim*, the Hebrew word for God, is a plural form, but in this chapter it is used with a singular verb. The idea is singular even in verse 1:26, where God says, "Let us make man." The *we* or *us* ought to be interpreted as a royal plural. God does not use helpers in his act of creation; he speaks as a king, who only needs to speak a word to get his will accomplished.

The second feature of this creation story is that God is all-powerful. He creates merely by issuing a command, rather than as an engineer, an artist, a laborer. His power is that of a person, of mind and will over matter.

Perception of God in the natural world was an early and pervasive feeling among the Hebrews; it was a reflection of their life close to nature and their fascination with the stars, and other phenomena of day and night, such as sunrise and sunset, wind and rain. Amos, a shepherd prophet (c. 760 B.C.), said,

> He who made the Pleiades and Orion,
>   and turns deep darkness into the morning,
>   and darkens the day into night,
> who calls for the waters of the sea,
>   and pours them out upon the surface of the earth,
> the Lord is his name. [Amos 5:8.]

The Hebrews saw God revealed in all the forces and sounds of nature, not merely in wonders of the sky. Psalm 29:3–10 illustrates this:

> The voice of the Lord is upon the waters;
>   the God of glory thunders,
>   the Lord, upon many waters.
> The voice of the Lord is powerful,
>   the voice of the Lord is full of majesty.
> The voice of the Lord breaks the cedars,
>   the Lord breaks the cedars of Lebanon.
> He makes Lebanon to skip like a calf,
>   and Sirion like a young wild ox.

The voice of the Lord flashes forth flames of fire.
The voice of the Lord shakes the wilderness,
    the Lord shakes the wilderness of Kadesh.
The voice of the Lord makes the oaks to whirl,
    and strips the forests bare;
    and in his temple all cry, "Glory!"
The Lord sits enthroned over the flood;
    The Lord sits enthroned as king for ever.

Omniscience, Omnipresence, Eternity

Psalm 139 is a meditative poem about the omniscience and omnipresence of God. The poet is overwhelmed by his apprehension of God's wonderful knowledge, and writes that the Lord knows every movement I make, all my thoughts, every word I speak. It is impossible to hide from God; the night is like day to him. God knew me, the poet goes on to say, even before I was born, the days I would live, one by one. God's omnipresence he expresses in the following words:

Whither shall I go from thy Spirit?
    Or whither shall I flee from thy presence?
If I ascend to heaven, thou art there!
    If I make my bed in Sheol, thou art there!
If I take the wings of the morning and dwell in the
    uttermost parts of the sea,
even there thy hand shall lead me,
    and thy right hand shall hold me. [Psalm 139:7–10]

The psalm has the form of a prayer throughout; these sensitive lines reveal the reality, the wonder of God.

Justice

The idea of justice was first grasped in full clarity by Amos, Hosea, Isaiah, and Micah during the last half of the eighth century B.C., the finest age of Hebrew prophecy. The concept that God is just became central to the mature thought of the Hebrews at that time, and it has remained so. Yahweh is intensely personal. He is just in mind, in understanding, but also in emotions and will. He does right because he loves right and wishes to do it, not because it would be impossible for him to do wrong. He has freedom and power to do wrong, but if he acted unjustly, he would no longer be a God that men could love; he would be a demon, a monster, and such a thought was intolerable to the best Hebrew thinkers.

This doctrine of God is equally important in its implications for man, who, in order to be acceptable to God, must himself be good, upright, just. What God desires most in man is not animal sacrifices or ceremonial forms; God loves the man who is good in mind and heart and will.

Amos, using the prophetic idiom in which "I" means God, proclaims to his people:

I hate, I despise your feasts,
    and I take no delight in your solemn assemblies.
Even though you offer me your burnt offerings and cereal offerings,
    I will not accept them,
and the peace offerings of your fatted beasts
    I will not look upon.
Take away from me the noise of your songs;
    to the melody of your harps I will not listen.
But let justice roll down like waters,
    and righteousness like an ever-flowing stream. [Amos 5:21–24.]

Hosea, a younger contemporary of Amos, took from Amos the idea that Yahweh is just, but added to it the insight that he is also a God of love. Amos writes as if God might be a judge who brings Hebrews into his court. Hosea presents God as a faithful and sorrowing husband, pleading with Israel, his faithless wife, to return. Or, to change the metaphor, Yahweh is the Father of Israel, the forgetful and rebellious son (Hosea 1:2, 3; 2:1–13; 11:1–4).

Isaiah supplements justice with holiness in his concept of God. He says:

Holy, holy, holy is the Lord of hosts;
    the whole earth is full of his glory. [Isaiah 6:3.]

Isaiah's favorite epithet for God is the Holy One of Israel; and he dreams of an age to come when the world will be at peace under the law of God (2:2–4; 9:2–7; 11:1–9; 65:17–25).

Micah, the last of these four prophets, although partly contemporary with Isaiah, has distilled the essence of their theology into the following lines:

"With what shall I come before the Lord,
    and bow myself before God on high?

Shall I come before him with burnt offerings,
  with calves a year old?
Will the Lord be pleased with thousands of rams,
  with ten thousands of rivers of oil?
Shall I give my first-born for my transgression,
  the fruit of my body for the sin of my soul?"
He has showed you, O man, what is good;
  and what does the Lord require of you
but to do justice, and to love kindness,
  and to walk humbly with your God? [Micah 6:6–8.]

The attributes of saintly character are justice, kindness, and humility.

Sovereignty and Universality

Judaism takes history seriously. In that respect, it is different from Hinduism and Buddhism with their idea of maya—the view that everything in the material, historical world is temporary, transient, unreal, of no ultimate value. By contrast, the ancient Hebrews believed that the present world is the real world and the present life is the real life; whatever happens in the hereafter is in a shadowy realm, of little consequence. Only toward the end of the Old Testament period did an interest develop in rewards hereafter. The usual view in the classical period of Hebrew faith was that religion is for the present life; its rewards and punishments are here and now. When man dies, the drama ends and the curtain falls. God is therefore the God of this world, this present life, the God of history. He makes himself known in affairs of the world. We learn about God by observing nature, but also by the study of history, for his will is always being realized in history. The idea that God controls the rise and fall of nations is fundamental in the Old Testament.

Oracles about foreign countries were a standard literary form in biblical times; some of them attained great beauty. One of the best is the lament over Tyre in Ezekiel 27. It presents a vivid picture of Phoenician ships and seamen and the rich merchandise they carried from port to port throughout the Mediterranean. All such poems show the Hebrew feeling that God is sovereign of all nations, just as he is of the Hebrews.

When the Hebrews forgot that Yahweh was the God of other nations also, the prophets did not hesitate to rebuke them. Amos says to the proud Hebrew nationalists of his time, in 9:7,

"Are you not like the Ethiopians to me,
 O people of Israel?" says the Lord.
"Did I not bring up Israel from the land of Egypt,
 and the Philistines from Caphtor and the Syrians from Kir?"

Here the poet is saying that God has no favorites among the nations. Ethiopians, Philistines, and Syrians mean as much to him as do the Hebrews.

Providence

God's primary concern, the Hebrews believed, was man—man as an individual person, not the natural world nor the rise and fall of nations. He is especially concerned about the happiness and welfare of the upright man, the good man. In the older and more primitive J account of creation (Genesis 2:4–3:24), with his own fingers Yahweh shapes the form of man from dust and then breathes life into his nostrils. In this case he makes man to be his servant, his duty being to care for the Garden of Eden, Yahweh's own favorite resort; he walks there in the cool of the day, like an Arab sheik in his desert oasis. In the later P story God creates man and woman at the same time, both in his own image. In J Yahweh creates man as male first, and places him alone in the garden. Only when Yahweh sees that man is lonely does he put him to sleep, take out one of his ribs, and build it up into a woman to be his companion.

All the stories of Genesis illustrate God's concern for individual persons. After Cain has killed his brother, God holds a personal conference with him (Genesis 4:8–16). When the Lord has determined to destroy the evil world with a flood, he warns Noah to build an ark for himself and his household (Genesis 7:1 ff.). He personally tells Abraham to leave the wicked country of Babylon and go to Canaan in search of a better life (Genesis 12:1 ff.). In the same intimate way, he gives personal direction to Isaac, Jacob, and Joseph, making certain that these good men attain happiness and prosperity.

Angelic beings are mentioned in Genesis, but they remain anonymous, shadowy figures. Two angels accompany God when he visits Abraham by the Oaks of Mamre; then they supervise the escape of Lot and his family from Sodom and the destruction of that wicked city (Genesis 19:1–28). The Lord sends an angel with Abraham's slave when he makes the long journey to Mesopotamia to find a wife for Isaac (Genesis 24:40 ff.). The Book of Tobit in the Apocrypha tells the story of Tobias, who, for business reasons, made a hazardous journey from Nineveh into Persia, with Raphael, an angel, as his guide. Raphael led the way over the mountains, made the business aspect of the trip a success, saved the life of Tobias when he was threatened by a demon, and then helped him obtain a wife.[5]

Psalm 91 takes the providence of God as its theme.

> For he will give his angels charge of you
> to guard you in all your ways.
> On their hands they will bear you up,
> lest you dash your foot against a stone. [Psalm 91:11, 12.]

Toward the end of the Old Testament period the Lord had delegated to angels the task of protecting the Hebrew nation. In the Book of Daniel, Michael and Gabriel have that function (Daniel 9:21; 10:13, 21; 12:1). Gabriel is the messenger; Michael, the fighter.

Just Recompense Repudiated

The theology of just recompense in this life had gained general acceptance among the Hebrews by the time their culture attained maturity. It may be summarized as follows: God is ruler of all the world, both nature and man; God is just; therefore everything that happens to man is just. Man always receives his just deserts: a good man prospers; a wicked man suffers, fails in business or loses his family, his health, or all these things. The ideal of the Hebrews was prosperity, a long life, and a good family. The philosophy of just recompense guarantees these blessings to an upright man.

In other words, honesty, industry, and fidelity are the best policy. In a broad sense, this philosophy was shared with other nations of antiquity, from whom it has come down to us. We still hold to this philosophy, believing that these virtues make a good, healthy society, and that a society degenerates and dies when they disappear.

Yet every perceptive person knows that, while this philosophy is valid for a society in general, it does not always correspond literally with the facts of individual life. Some of the Hebrews themselves came to question this doctrine, the best known of these being Job, hero of the book by that name. Job belongs to the wisdom literature, a semiphilosophical type of writing developed toward the end of the Old Testament period. The author of this book has written it in the form of a drama, but one that is intended to be read, not put on the stage. The characters are God, Satan, Job, Job's wife, and certain friends who come to comfort him, as well as to criticize him. This is Satan's first appearance of any length in the Bible. Here he enters as a son of God, although a rebellious son, an evil angel. Job is a good man, possessing all the Hebrew virtues. Because God loves Job, Satan is envious of him and doubts his integrity. Satan therefore challenges God to put Job to the test.

God believes in Job; yet because Job has a free will, even God does not know beyond question that Job will keep his faith when the worst forms of tragedy strike. For that reason, he gives Satan permission to afflict Job, and Satan gleefully undertakes his grisly task. First he causes marauders to destroy or steal Job's flocks and herds, leaving him in poverty. Then he causes all of Job's sons and daughters to meet sudden death. Finally he afflicts Job with a loathsome disease.

The author thus presents the case of a good man who encounters tragedy in its most cruel forms. It is in this extreme way that he challenges the accepted theology. If we believe that God is both just and all-powerful, how can we reconcile the way the world is with the way it is supposed to be? If God is good, is he all-powerful? If all-powerful, is he good? That is the theological problem of tragedy.

Throughout the story Job maintains his innocence, affirming that he has lived by the teachings of his faith, that he does not deserve the things that have happened to him. Moreover, he holds, the world is full of examples of the prosperity of the wicked and the affliction of the righteous. That, he says, is the kind of world we live in. Against the friends who come to accuse, he staunchly makes this defense. Even to God himself, he declares that he is not being justly treated, that he does not deserve the adversity visited upon him.

At the end of the story, God appears to Job and deals with him kindly. He does not rebuke him for repudiating the doctrine of just recompense, nor does he undertake to explain why tragedy comes upon good men. All he does is to remind Job of his limited knowledge: there are many things about the world and about God that he does not understand. He therefore cautions Job to use restraint when he challenges the goodness of the Almighty.

The action closes with Job bowed in humility in the presence of God, his question unanswered and the reason for the existence of tragedy in the world still shrouded in mystery. But the foundations of the traditional theology have been undermined.

Ecclesiastes, the Skeptic

Ecclesiastes, another example of wisdom literature from the late period, goes even farther than Job in his skeptical attitude toward conventional religion. Writing under the pseudonym of King Solomon, who lived several hundred years before his time, this author purports to have tested all things said to bring delight into the life of man and found them wanting: wine, great works, houses, vineyards, gardens, parks, pools, slaves, flocks, herds, silver, gold, male and female singers, concubines. In the end, they are only a dissipation of man's strength, a vexation of his spirit; they are vanity. Wealth is unable to make a man happy; neither can wisdom nor learning. The great Solomon had explored all these, but in vain. The wise man dies just as the fool does. Toil is folly; man collects wealth only to leave it to another when he dies.

Moreover, although God has given man the capacity for wisdom, he can never find out the ways of God. God made the world and established its order, but he takes no further personal interest in it, and shows no concern about what happens to man.

The sage sounds pessimistic, indeed. But he writes in a light vein, with a touch of humor. True, man can never know the infinite mysteries or understand the ways of the faraway God, and the world seems to run along, indifferent to the relative fortunes of the righteous and the wicked. Yet, some courses of action are better than others. Wisdom is better than folly. No man should be a fool. It is best to enjoy yourself while you are young, with the wife of your youth, with good food, and simple pleasures. This course is the greatest wisdom. For youth is soon past, strength of the body subsides, ears grow dull, eyes dim; man no longer enjoys beautiful sights and sounds; appetite fails, death comes, mourners go about the streets, and man goes to his eternal home. Death is a silver cord snapped, a golden bowl broken, a pitcher broken at the fountain, a wheel broken at the cistern (12:1–7).

Vicarious Suffering

The theory of just recompense was developed first as a philosophy of national history, then as an interpretation of the fortunes of individual persons. In the latter respect it was criticized by Job, as well as by Ecclesiastes. As applied to the nation, this view became a dogma with both prophets and historians; few thinkers dared to raise their voices against it. Yet the Second Isaiah, who about 550 B.C. wrote the chapters we know as Isaiah 40–55, had both the insight and the courage to reject this view. The Second Isaiah worked out a new philosophy to give hope to the exiles, whose faith grew dim while the prophets kept on saying that they were suffering for their own sins and the sins of their fathers.

The poet developed his new interpretation in four beautiful poems: Isaiah 42:1–4; 49:1–6; 50:4–9; 52:12–53:12, known as Poems of the Servant of Yahweh. The Servant is the Hebrew nation personified as one individual, as is clear in 41:8; 44:1, 2; 49:3. He is addressed as Israel or Jacob, ancestral titles commonly applied to the Hebrew people as a whole.

In 42:1–4, the first poem, the Lord addresses the Servant as one whom he has chosen, upheld, and anointed with his own spirit, to bring justice to the nations. The Servant is quiet and gentle, but not weak. His courage will not fail before he accomplishes his purpose.

The second poem, 49:1–6, allows the Servant himself to speak. Even before he was born, he says, he was set apart for his mission of bringing justice and light to the nations. In the third poem, 50:4–9, the Servant meditates on his role as a teacher and how God sustains him in his trials.

The culmination is reached in the fourth poem, 52:12–53:12, where the kings of the nations are startled by the Servant's appearance and by the meaning of his suffering, which at last dawns on them. Now they see that the Hebrews are suffering innocently, not for their own sins, nor for the sins of their fathers, but for the sins of other peoples. The goal of the national disasters of the Hebrews is ultimately to bring all nations to the true God.

MORALITY

Although the Hebrew faith gave a large place to priests, altars, shrines, sacrifices, it is primarily a religion of morality. Along with their preoccupation with God, the Hebrews were also concerned about the character of man. Biblical religion is like a drama in which only two actors appear on the stage; one is God, the other is man; from the beginning to the end of the play, there is a constant fellowship between these two actors. Each finds fulfillment in the other, which grows out of the fact that they are like each other. For, according to the biblical view, man was created in the image and likeness of God.

This view appears in the first creation story (Genesis 1:26, 27), where God creates man in his own image and likeness. The word "man" includes woman, since "man" is used here in the generic sense, man and woman standing equal: "Both male and female he created them." The creation story in Genesis should not be interpreted as meaning, however, that God has a physical body and that man's being made in God's likeness is to be taken in a physical sense. It means instead that man is created with intelligence and freedom of will, that he is a moral being, responsible for his actions. In that respect he is like God. This high conception of the nature of man is prominent in biblical religion. It is true, of course, that this first chapter of Genesis is from the late priestly story of creation. Nevertheless, the idea that man is responsible for his conduct is presupposed throughout the Bible.

The story of Adam and Eve in the second and third chapters of Genesis is older than the priestly story. It comes from the J writer. This time man is created first, then woman, to be his companion, which presents the Hebrew view of the origin of marriage as a divine institution. Neither man nor woman is complete without the other. The temptation story in the third chapter is based on the question of conscience and the nature of right and wrong— questions as old as human life and today still wrapped in mystery. Man's knowledge of what is right and wrong comes to him as a commandment from God, it is not his own invention or discovery; man falls into immorality when he rebels against his conscience.

The flood story is the third presentation of the moral theme on a grand scale (Genesis 6:1–8:22). This story, in a polytheistic form, had been known for centuries in the earlier Babylonian cultures before the Hebrew writers stripped it of its polytheism and adapted it for their own purposes.[6] We should read this story in its moral and theological sense, since basically it deals with man's morality. God destroys man because of his moral degeneration, which he can tolerate no longer. God is here the judge of man, another central concept of biblical faith. The idea seems to be that, by determined rebellion against God, man can bring about his own destruction.

The moral character of biblical religion is given its classical formulation in the Ten Commandments, which combine reverence for God with emphasis on the moral character of man (Exodus 20:1–17). Hebrew religion means to love God with all one's heart and one's neighbor as oneself.

Even the most distinguished kings of the Hebrews are used as examples to set forth this moral lesson. When King David committed adultery with Bathsheba, the wife of one of his army officers, the prophet Nathan boldly went into the king's presence and denounced him for it (II Samuel 12:1–12). And the prophet Elijah in a similar way condemned King Ahab for his villainous actions in murdering Naboth and taking his vineyard (I Kings 21:17–19). The biblical writers did not hesitate to record the immorality, the sins, the vices, as well as the virtues, of their heroes. This is one of the most unique aspects of the literature of the Bible.

SACRIFICIAL RITES

The Covenant with God

Judaism is based on a covenant with God—an idea that appears in the earliest literature of the Hebrews and has been a constant element in the Jewish faith. It is, in fact, the one irreducible component. Many other features of Judaism have been modified, but the covenant never; it is as unchangeable as God himself, who is its author.

A covenant is an agreement, a contract, a mutual understanding between two parties, usually on equal terms. But the covenant in Hebrew religion is not between equal parties; it is between God and man. God is a king who out of his own generosity gives man a covenant. He promises to bless man if he keeps the covenant, but only on that condition. Whenever man breaks the covenant, God punishes him, but he never repudiates his covenant. The covenant is therefore a landmark to which the Hebrews were able to return when lost, a foundation on which they could always rebuild their shattered institutions.

Covenants were also made between men, but always with God as witness. All covenants were therefore essentially religious. God was the executor of every covenant, visiting punishment on the party who broke it.

The way the Hebrews made covenants is shown by the ceremony

alluded to in Jeremiah 34:18, 19, in which both parties passed between the parts of a slaughtered animal. The meaning seems to be based on the Hebrew belief that blood belongs to God and that life resides in the blood, so that passing through the animal in this sacramental sense established a blood covenant between the two parties. The sacrament made them of the same blood, that is, blood brothers.

In primitive religions such a covenant is made when two parties drink blood from the same beaker or when both gash their arms and interchange drops of blood. According to Hebrew belief, however, since life resides in the blood and is therefore sacred to God, man must not eat it or drink it (Genesis 9:1–6). This was one of the most basic of Hebrew food regulations. Blood must be drained from the carcass of a slaughtered animal before it is suitable for food. Hence a blood covenant among Hebrews was made in a symbolical way, not by the physical act of drinking the blood. In walking between the parts of the sacrifice, they symbolically passed through the same blood.

God's Covenant with Abraham

The Hebrews traced their belief in a covenant with God back to Abraham, their ancestral father. Abraham's encounter with God, according to tradition, occurred in the picturesque covenant ceremony described in Genesis 15:1–20, which is from the somewhat revised J Document. The most relevant parts of the account are as follows:

But Abram said, "O Lord God, what wilt thou give me, for I continue childless, and the heir of my house is Eliezer of Damascus? . . . a slave born in my house. . . ." And behold, the word of the Lord came to him, "This man shall not be your heir; your own son shall be your heir." And he brought him outside and said, "Look toward heaven, and number the stars, if you are able to number them." Then he said to him, "So shall your descendants be." And he believed the Lord; and he reckoned it to him as righteousness.

And he said to him, "I am the Lord who brought you from Ur of the Chaldeans, to give you this land to possess." But he said, "O Lord God, how am I to know that I shall possess it?" He said to him, "Bring me a heifer three years old, a she-goat three years old, a ram three years old, a turtledove, and a young pigeon." And he brought him all these, cut them in two, and laid each half over against the other; but he did not cut the birds in two. . . .

As the sun was going down, a deep sleep fell on Abram; and lo, a dread and great darkness fell upon him. . . .

When the sun had gone down and it was dark, behold, a smoking fire pot and a flaming torch passed between these pieces. On that day the Lord made a covenant with Abram, saying, "To your descendants I will give this land, from the river of Egypt to the great River, the river Euphrates."

The essentials of this ceremony are the same as those described in Jeremiah. God and Abraham, represented respectively by the smoking fire pot and the flaming torch, pass between the two rows of freshly cut pieces of the sacrifice. Abraham's symbol, the fire pot, goes through first, thus showing his faith. The terms of the covenant are also clear. God promises to give Abraham a son, to make him a great nation, and to give him Canaan as his homeland. Abraham's commitment is shown in verse 6 as trust in the Lord, nothing more. The verse was later to be used by Paul in the New Testament as the foundation of his theology of salvation by faith. One might have expected Abraham to promise to keep the Law, except that, according to biblical tradition, the Law was not given until the time of Moses, centuries later. God therefore accepts Abraham's trust as sufficient to seal the covenant.

God's Covenant with the People

A second form of the blood covenant, with its own variations, occurs in Exodus 24:4–8. This time Moses has just received the Law from God on Mount Sinai, and the covenant ceremony shows the people formally accepting it. The essentials are as follows:

And Moses wrote all the words of the Lord. And he rose early in the morning, and built an altar at the foot of the mountain, and twelve pillars, according to the twelve tribes of Israel. And he sent young men of the people of Israel, who offered burnt offerings and sacrificed peace offerings of oxen to the Lord. And Moses took half of the blood and put it in basins, and half of the blood he threw against the altar. Then he took the book of the covenant, and read it in the hearing of the people; and they said, "All that the Lord has spoken we will do, and we will be obedient." And Moses took the blood and threw it upon the

people, and said, "Behold the blood of the covenant which the Lord
has made with you in accordance with all these words."

This time God is represented by the fire burning on the altar.
Moses throws half the blood on the altar, that is, on the symbol of
God. Then, after he has read the Law to the people, and they have
made their commitment to keep it, he throws the other half of the
blood on them. Thus he binds God and the people together in a
covenant made with real blood. This record is from E, although
it is inserted between sections of J, thus showing how the two documents are often interwoven.

God's Covenant with the Individual

The rite of circumcision is the sacrament by which individual
persons enter the Hebrew covenant with God. The origin of this
rite among the Hebrews is given in Genesis 17:1–14, in a section
incorporated from the late P Document. The essentials of it are
given in 17:9–14, as follows:

And God said to Abraham, "As for you, you shall keep my covenant,
you and your descendants after you throughout your generations. This
is my covenant, which you shall keep, between me and you and your
descendants after you: Every male among you shall be circumcised.
You shall be circumcised in the flesh of your foreskins, and it shall be a
sign of the covenant between me and you. He that is eight days old
among you shall be circumcised; every male throughout your generations,
whether born in your house, or bought with your money from any
foreigner who is not of your offspring, both he that is born in your
house and he that is bought with your money, shall be circumcised. So
shall my covenant be in your flesh an everlasting covenant. Any uncircumcised male who is not circumcised in the flesh of his foreskin
shall be cut off from his people; he has broken my covenant."

This is obviously a rite intended first of all for male Hebrew infants, but it also includes adult males who may be accepted as converts into Judaism, even slaves. An uncircumcised person was considered unclean and was therefore not permitted to reside in an
ancient Hebrew community. The origin of circumcision is unknown, although we do know that it was practiced by Egyptians,
as well as by western Semitic peoples, including Arabs (who practice

it to this day). The Philistines, who resided on the coastal plain between the Hebrews and the sea, did not practice circumcision, and for that reason were often referred to by the Hebrews with scorn as the "uncircumcised" Philistines.

Other Sacrifices

The covenant ceremonies based on walking between the parts of slaughtered animals are only one example of the elaborate sacrificial rites of Hebrew religion. Some of the sacrifices were rooted in their early nomadic life; sheep and goats were prominent in their rituals, but bulls and heifers also attained major importance, and some birds were used. These were blood sacrifices, based on the idea that blood is sacred, that it belongs to God. But these animal sacrifices were eventually supplemented by agricultural products— sheaves of newly ripened grain, flour, loaves of baked bread, olive oil, wine, incense, various herbs, all of which became standard items in the sacrificial rituals.

This transition from the blood sacrifices so common in the old nomadic life to the products of agriculture was not, however, accomplished without religious tension. The old tradition was strongly entrenched, and the peasant did not win an equal place alongside the shepherd without a bitter struggle. The story of the murder of Abel by his brother Cain probably reflects this conflict (Genesis 4:2–8).

The Paschal Lamb

The paschal (Passover) lamb is one of the most celebrated Hebrew animal sacrifices. The most complete account of this sacrifice, although it is one that combines early with late elements, is found in Exodus 12:1–49. The paschal lamb was an annual sacrifice in memory of the exodus from Egyptian bondage. The lamb could be taken from either sheep or goats (Exodus 12:5); it was usually taken from the sheep. The lamb was slaughtered on the afternoon of the thirteenth day of Abib (Nisan), a spring month. It was roasted and then eaten after sunset, that is, on the evening of the fourteenth day. This was a family festival; if a family was too small to consume the entire lamb, enough guests were invited in to eat all of it. The entire lamb had to be eaten, and if any was left over, it was destroyed. Some of the lamb's blood was smeared on the doorposts and the lintel of the house. On that night the death angel was scheduled to visit every home in Egypt, destroying the first-born of the family. When he came to the blood on the entrance of Hebrew homes, he passed them by, he passed over them—the traditional interpretation of the name Passover. The meal was eaten in haste, with loins girded, sandals on, staff in hand, in preparation for their flight from Egypt. The roasted meat was eaten with unleavened bread and bitter herbs.

As the account of the festival now stands in this text (Exodus 12:1–49), it includes the Feast of Unleavened Bread, which continues for seven days, the Passover itself being only one day. The Passover probably goes back to the nomadic period, an old festival that has been reinterpreted in order to celebrate the Exodus. The Feast of Unleavened Bread is an agricultural rite, which originated in the life of cultivators of the soil in Palestine.

The Atonement Goat Sacrifice

The two goats sacrificed annually on the Day of Atonement (Yom Kippur) are another example of a rite from the nomadic period. The he-goats selected for this sacrifice were as nearly alike as possible in appearance, size, and value and were bought at the same time. Lots were cast over them, one chosen for Yahweh, the other for Azazel. The rite was performed on the tenth day of the month Tishri in late summer, which was an annual fast day, the most solemn of the Hebrew year.

The High Priest first sacrificed a bull as a burnt offering and with its blood entered the sanctuary to make atonement for the priests. Next he slaughtered the goat chosen for Yahweh and first with its blood alone, then with its blood mingled with that of the bull, made atonement for the people, thus completing purification of the temple and of all ritual objects for both priests and people. The rite reached its climax when the High Priest uttered YAHWEH, the ineffable Name, and the worshipers fell prostrate.[7]

On coming out the High Priest placed his hands on the head of the goat for Azazel, thereby transferring to it the sins of the people. A previously selected man then led this goat away into a solitary region and let him wander away into the wilderness, bearing a load of sins, as the people's scapegoat (Leviticus 16:7–22). The tractate Yoma 6:6 of the Mishnah (about A.D. 200) explains that the man who led the goat away tied a rock to its horns with a cord of crimson wool and pushed it over a cliff, where it fell to its death.[8]

The Bible leaves the identity of Azazel a mystery, although in other passages reference is made to various spirits of the desert that had goatlike forms, usually translated as *satyrs*.[9] In the Book of Enoch[10] (6:1; 10:4, 8; 13:1 ff.), dating from the end of the Old Testament period, Azazel is a leader of the angels who before the flood seduced the daughters of men. He is credited with introducing all sin into the world. But at God's command (Enoch 10:4–5), Raphael, the angel who routs the demon Asmodeus in Tobit 8:3, binds Azazel hand and foot, digs a dungeon in the desert, throws the archdemon into it, and casts stones upon him. There he remains in darkness until the last judgment, when he is to be cast into fire. The roles of Azazel and Raphael in Enoch suggest their identity with Asmodeus and Raphael in the story of Tobit, as well as with Aeshma Daeva and Sraosha in the Avestan myth of the Zoroastrians. In late biblical stories, Raphael becomes the conqueror of demons, the Hebrew parallel to Sraosha.

The Five Types of Sacrifices

The rituals of Passover and the Day of Atonement illustrate only two of the impressive animal sacrifices performed by the ancient Hebrews; there were many others. Leviticus is the major source book for these sacrificial rituals, although other books of the Law add details and variations, and hardly a book of the Old Testament fails to throw additional light on them, the reason being that the sacrificial rituals are everywhere presupposed. Leviticus was prepared essentially as a handbook describing the sacrifices themselves, the parts that are taken by priests, and the things that are done by the laymen.

Five basic types of sacrifices are described. The first is the burnt offering (Leviticus 1:3–17). In this case the entire carcass of an animal is burned as an offering by fire, "a pleasing odor to the Lord." If taken from the herd or flock, the animal had to be a male, perfect in every respect. The layman who brought the animal as an atonement for himself first placed his hand on the victim's head, thereby transferring his own sin or guilt to the animal, and then himself killed it with a knife. The priest presented the blood, throwing it around the altar. The worshiper skinned the animal and cut it into the proper pieces. The priest put fire on the altar, added wood to the fire, and laid the flesh on the wood so that it was all consumed by the flame, as an offering by fire to the Lord. This offering was employed in times of great stress, when men were desperately seeking divine aid.

The second type of sacrifice was the cereal offering (Leviticus 2:1–16; 6:14–23), an offering of a product of the field and obviously not of such serious character as a burnt offering. Third was the peace offering (Leviticus 3:1–17; 7:11–18, 28–36), apparently the form of animal sacrifice for ordinary occasions. Fourth was the sin offering (Leviticus 4:1–5:13), made for sins committed unwittingly. Fifth was the sacrifice required when one committed a breach against God, or against his neighbor, through deception, perjury, or robbery (Leviticus 6:1–13).

What Did the Sacrifices Mean?

We need to keep in mind that both blood and agricultural offerings were common in all the religions of antiquity. They provided a tangible, practical, colorful means of articulation of religious emotions, of communication with the deities worshiped. The idea at the root of all such rituals is to interpret the gods in terms of human beings: men present to God the things they love best themselves.

In the case of the Hebrew rituals, the offerings consisted mainly of the good food the Hebrews enjoyed. A complete sacrifice often included all the elements of a full meal: meat, bread, sweetmeats, spices, vegetables, wine. The fat was consumed by the altar fire, which was God's symbol; the blood was cast against God's altar; the priests and people themselves ate the good food, rejoicing in a fellowship which included the divine presence. There was much joy in Hebrew religion, with lively singing and dancing. There was also awareness of the frailty of human life, of illness, death, national disaster, exile, loneliness in strange lands.

The sacrifices cannot be understood without a knowledge of the priestly chants, prayers, benedictions, and the supplications of the shepherds, peasants, merchants, and professional men who came up to worship. All was accompanied by both instrumental and vocal music, sometimes by great choirs (Psalm 150). And there was dancing in the religious folk festivals which at times reached ecstatic heights, as in the case of King David when he brought the Ark of the Lord into Jerusalem (II Samuel 6:12–23).

SHRINES

A sacrificial religion usually requires many shrines of different kinds, ranging from a simple object of nature up to a great cathedral. A rock, a tree, a stone, a river, a forest, a mountain, a volcano, the heavens, the earth, the universe itself—all these may be shrines. No one knew this better than the Hebrew poets. But men need accessible places, close to home, where they can find God. A shrine is a holy place, a house in which God dwells, where he receives his guests, where men come to call on him. The religion of the Hebrews cannot be understood unless we have some idea of the holy places where their rituals were performed.

The first reference to worship in the Bible is in the story of Cain and Abel (Genesis 4:3–7); the second comes at the end of the genealogy of Cain, where it is noted that at that time men began to call on the name of the Lord (Genesis 4:26). A third is Genesis 8:20, where Noah built an altar and offered sacrifices after the flood. But no permanent shrine is mentioned in any of these cases, except the altar in the instance of Noah. These allusions reflect the Hebrew view that God might be worshiped anywhere without benefit of the formalities and the apparatus of organized religion.

The first reference to permanent shrines in the Bible is in the story of Abraham (Genesis 12:4–9). When Abraham came into the land of Canaan, he arrived at Shechem and pitched his tent by the Oak of Moreh. There God appeared to him, so he set up an altar. Next he camped at Bethel, where God also appeared to him; therefore he set up another altar. We encounter this holy place again in the story of Jacob (Genesis 28:10–22). God appeared to him there one night as he slept with his head on a stone. When day dawned he realized he had slept in the house of God; so he set up the stone, anointed it with oil, and converted it into a pillar. It is probable that both Shechem and Bethel were already Canaanite shrines before Abraham arrived and that Abraham made his camp there because shrines were safe places for strangers; they were sanctuaries. In any case, these are the oldest shrines mentioned in the Bible. When the Hebrews displaced the Canaanites they took over these shrines for their own use, and thus they continued to be of some importance.

Other local shrines that existed during the ancient Hebrew period were Hebron, Beth-Shemesh, Kirjath-jearim, Gibeon, and Ramah in Judah; and Gilgal, Shiloh, and Dan, in Israel. Jerusalem was a Canaanite shrine long before the city was taken by the Hebrews. Abraham once had to pay tithes to Melchizedek, the priest-king of Salem, an early name for Jerusalem (Genesis 14:8–20). Jerusalem was, in fact, one of the youngest Hebrew shrines, It did not come into the possession of the Hebrews until David captured it about 1000 B.C. and made it his capital (II Samuel 5:6–10). Desiring to adorn his new capital by building a temple there, he bought the threshing floor of Araunah, a Canaanite of the city, as a site for it (II Samuel 24:18–25); he also collected a quantity of building materials and a considerable sum of money for the undertaking (I Chronicles 22:1–17; 29:1–8). But time was too short; he had to leave this dream to Solomon, his son.

Solomon's Temple

If David was the most colorful king the Hebrews produced, Solomon was the most splendid. The undertaking most closely associated with his splendor was the temple of Yahweh he built at Jerusalem (see Figure 9.2). David had brought the Ark of God into Jerusalem, so that Yahweh at least had a modest shrine there; when Solomon was crowned, however, the main religious aspects of the coronation celebration appear to have been held at Gibeon, a Canaanite shrine a few miles northwest of Jerusalem, which had been converted into a shrine of Yahweh (I Kings 3:3–14).

Solomon was famous for other achievements, too. He adorned Jerusalem with palaces and state buildings, built fortresses on the frontiers, developed the use of horses and chariots for military purposes, constructed a merchant marine on the Red Sea, operated commercial caravans with neighboring peoples, was successful in diplomacy, collected a harem said to contain a thousand women. With all this, he was the center of a brilliant court life at Jerusalem. Tradition honored him most for the temple he built, using the best stone, timbers, and metals, as well as the finest workmen available, including Phoenician artists.

But in one respect fault was found with Solomon. He made religious toleration one of the policies of his reign. Among the princesses he loved were women of other nations, who worshiped the gods of their own peoples. Solomon built shrines for their gods in the vicinity of Jerusalem. Among those mentioned in the Bible were Ashtoreth of Sidon, Milcom (also called Moloch) of Ammon, and Chemosh of Moab, for whom shrines were built on the Mount

FIGURE 9.2 A model of Solomon's Temple, Jerusalem (conceived by Hans Kroch). (*Consulate of Israel*)

of Olives. Solomon must have built shrines as well for his Egyptian wife and for his Edomite and Hittite wives. Solomon's wives are credited with turning his heart toward other gods. He had become a man of the world, and his religion was polytheism; but Solomon's religion was probably not merely a personal matter. Included in his kingdom were Edom, Moab, and Ammon, and he had close business relations with Phoenicians, Syrians, Hittites, and Egyptians. Solomon's religious philosophy must therefore have had some relation to his diplomacy.

As magnificent as it was, the temple of Solomon never won the loyalty of the northern tribes; it drew its support almost exclusively from Judah. When Solomon died in 922 B.C. the northern tribes rebelled and set up the kingdom of Israel, which had its own shrines,

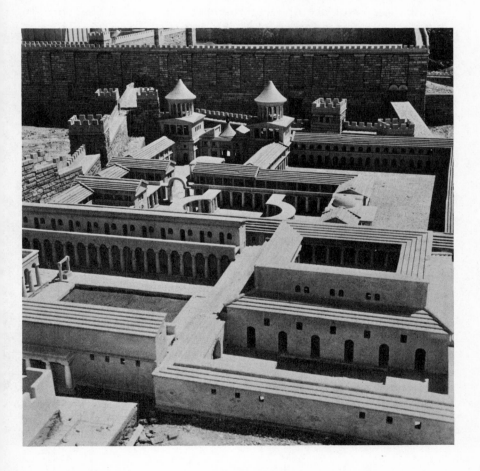

Bethel and Shechem being the best known; another was Dan in the far north. There was also a radical difference between the religions of Israel and Judah. The people of Israel used images, representing Yahweh in the form of a golden bull. One of the first acts of Jeroboam, the first king of Israel, was to set up golden bulls at Bethel and Dan (I Kings 12:25–33). Apparently the temple of Solomon never contained an image of Yahweh; yet the cherubim on the Ark of the Covenant were images (I Samuel 4:4), as well as the ephod (Judges 8:26, 27), the teraphim (Judges 18:20), and the brazen serpent (Numbers 21:9; II Kings 18:4). Opposition to images is based on the commandment in the Decalogue, "You shall not make yourself a graven image" (Exodus 20:4), although some scholars think that this was not added to the Decalogue until the time of Deuteronomy, in 621 B.C.

Under the influence of Deuteronomy, King Josiah immediately undertook a reformation in which he destroyed a remarkable number of foreign elements that had ben absorbed into Hebrew religion. The faith of Jerusalem had become a real syncretism; along with Yahweh, the Hebrews were worshiping Baal and Asherah, Canaanite deities. There was an image of Asherah in the temple. Assyrian deities were well represented, too, by cults of the heavenly bodies, including the sun. Canaanites held that agriculture depended on Baal and Asherah, so that the Hebrews were strongly tempted to adopt that worship. The presence of Assyrian deities resulted from the powerful influence of Assyria after 700 B.C., when Judah became an Assyrian satellite.

Josiah also destroyed the shrines of Ashtoreth of Sidon, Chemosh of Moab, and Milcom of Ammon, which Solomon had built east of Jerusalem three centuries earlier. In addition, Josiah demolished a second shrine of the Ammonite god Moloch, which was located in the Valley of Hinnom, just south of the city, where human sacrifices were offered (II Kings 23:10, 13). Even Manasseh, Josiah's grandfather, who preceded him on the throne by only two years, had "burned his son as an offering" there (II Kings 21:6). Earlier Hebrew examples of human sacrifice are Jephthah's daugher (Judges 11:29–40) and possibly the two sons of Hiel, who rebuilt Jericho (I Kings 16:34).

Moreover, for the first time in its history, the temple of Solomon now became the temple of all the inhabitants of Judah. Josiah destroyed all other shrines and limited the offering of sacrifices to Solomon's temple. This gave the temple priests control of religion everywhere in Judah. The priests of these destroyed shrines were called Levites; they were left with no opportunity to engage in their priestly profession until about 550 B.C., when Ezekiel's regulations permitted them to replace slaves in the restored temple (Ezekiel 44:9–14).

Josiah even found and destroyed houses of cult prostitutes in the temple, showing that this sexual worship, so common in the cults of Baal-Asherah of Palestine, Ishtar of Babylon, Anahita of Persia, and Aphrodite of Greece, had been accepted by the Hebrews. Deuteronomy 23:17, 18 prohibits both male and female cult prostitutes.

But the triumph that Solomon's temple had at last achieved was to be brief. Only thirty-five years later, in 587 B.C., after Judah rebelled against Babylon, Nebuchadnezzar captured Jerusalem, broke down its walls, and destroyed the temple.

The Temple of Zerubbabel

Jerusalem was left in ruins by this catastrophe, and Judah, broken and decimated by the war, was incorporated into a province of the Babylonian Empire. The discouraged community of Jerusalem had no leadership of its own, no place of worship, little hope of improvement. Matters remained that way for close to a half-century. But the overthrow of Babylon in 539 B.C. by Cyrus the Great of Persia brought new hope to the Jews, for this new king introduced a policy of allowing all exile groups to return and rebuild their homelands as parts of Persian provinces. Cyrus first authorized Sheshbazzar, a Jewish prince, to lead a return, but this effort appears to have come to nought (Ezra 1:1–11).

When Darius I (521–486 B.C.) came to the throne of Persia, a more serious effort was made in that direction. The leader was Zerubbabel, another Jewish prince, who led a caravan to Jerusalem in the second year of Darius, and, encouraged by Haggai and Zechariah, two Hebrew prophets, was able to rebuild the temple. The rededication took place in 516 B.C., approximately seventy years after the destruction of Solomon's temple.

While Zerubbabel's temple lacked the magnificence of the one it had replaced, it became a symbol of Jewish unity and provided a rallying point for those who desired to return to their homeland. In that respect, it served them well throughout the Persian period. But Jerusalem was poor: it had no walls as protection against raiders and little basis for economic security. It was in danger of losing its

Hebrew identity and of being absorbed into the surrounding cultures.

New life was injected into the community by the return of two more great Jewish leaders: Ezra, in 458 B.C. (or 398 B.C.), to revive religion and ban intermarriage with aliens; Nehemiah, in 444 B.C., to rebuild the walls. These two goals achieved, Jerusalem became prosperous again under Persian rule, and priests and teachers devoted themselves to adornment of the temple rituals and other ceremonials of Judaism, as well as to assembling and editing most of the Hebrew writings that are now found in the Jewish Scriptures.

When Alexander the Great overthrew the Persian Empire during his brief reign (336–323 B.C.), this marked the beginning of another era in Jewish religion, resulting from a struggle between Egypt and Syria for control of Judea. Antiochus IV Epiphanes, king of Syria (175–163 B.C.), who undertook to integrate his kingdom of different languages and cultures by imposing Greek culture upon them, forced the Jews to introduce Greek rites into the temple. In 167 B.C. the Jews rebelled, under the leadership of the Maccabean family. Judas Maccabaeus recaptured the temple and rededicated it in 165 B.C. He celebrated the event by a festive relighting of the temple lights; and it is still celebrated in the Feast of Dedication (Hanukkah, also called the Feast of Lights), which occurs during one week in early winter (I Maccabees 4:36–61). The Maccabean period came to an end in 63 B.C. when Pompey the Great conquered Jerusalem and annexed Judea to the Roman Empire.

Under Roman domination a new dynasty was installed in Jerusalem when Herod the Great, an Edomite, was crowned king, thus beginning another century of relative Jewish peace and prosperity, with Judea a Roman satellite. Herod did much to restore and adorn the culture of his kingdom. One of his main achievements was to take down the hastily constructed temple of Zerubbabel and rebuild it on a grand scale, using Roman architecture and methods of construction.[11] Herod's temple, which is the one that Jesus and the early Christians knew, probably outstripped even that of Solomon.

With their strength restored by the Herods, the Jews became more and more restive under the Romans. They therefore made a new bid for freedom in the rebellion of A.D. 66–70. When the Jews were finally crushed, the last act of the Roman soldiers was to burn down the temple. Some articles from the temple, including the golden candelabrum with its seven lamps, may be seen carved on the Arch of Titus in the Roman Forum, which shows the triumphal march of the victorious general.

Other Hebrew Temples

That some Hebrews did not accept the Deuteronomic view that sacrifices could be offered only in Jerusalem is shown by the construction of at least three temples elsewhere. The first was the Samaritan temple on Mount Gerizim, built at the time of Ezra and Nehemiah, about 440 B.C., when intermarriage with aliens was banned. Manasseh, a priest in the temple, had married Nicaso, daughter of Sanballat, governor of Samaria. Faced with making a choice between his wife and his position, he chose his wife. As a reward, Sanballat built for him a new temple on Mount Gerizim and installed him as High Priest. It may be that this temple points to a more ancient tradition than that of Jerusalem, since it stood near Shechem. The Samaritans accepted the Books of Moses as Scripture just as the Hebrews did, but not the remainder of the Hebrew canon. The Samaritan temple survived until the Maccabean period, when it seems to have been destroyed by John Hyrcanus.[12]

There were also at least two Hebrew temples in Egypt at different times. The first was on the island of Elephantine in Upper Egypt, which was destroyed by hostile Egyptians about 400 B.C., as shown by papyri letters from Hebrews there to Hebrews of Jerusalem asking for aid.[13] Another Hebrew temple was built at Leontopolis, in the delta, during the reign of Ptolemy VI Philometor (181–145 B.C.), which survived until the fall of Jerusalem in A.D. 70, when it was destroyed by order of Lupus, governor of Alexandria.[14]

The Synagogue

The synagogue, a major Jewish shrine for more than two thousand years, is the Jewish shrine with which the modern world is familiar. There are thousands in existence today. They can be called shrines, for a shrine is a place where men go to meet God, and certainly that is true of the synagogue.

A synagogue is first a community center, a place where officials of a Jewish community assemble to transact matters of interest to their people. It is also a place of assemblies of a social character, a place of play, of entertainment. Again, the synagogue is the center of education in a Jewish community, and the Jewish religion perhaps more than any other has emphasized the importance of education; the old as well as the young have gone to the synagogue to study. The synagogue is also a place of worship, a holy place. But its worship is different from that of the temple; no animal sacrifices have ever been performed in a synagogue.[15] Worship there is based on prayers, chanting the psalms, singing hymns, reading the Scriptures, sermons.

The synagogue, in a general sense, is similar to a Christian church or a Moslem mosque. Indeed, both the church and the mosque developed out of the Jewish synagogue, from which came the rudiments of their worship service.

The origin of the synagogue goes back at least to the Babylonian Exile, which began with the fall of Jerusalem in 587 B.C. It probably originated informally in the homes of individual Jews. Ezekiel, who was a prophet of the Exile, might well be called the father of the synagogue. At any rate, he was closely associated with it in those early days. There is a relevant statement in Ezekiel 8:1: "In the sixth year, in the sixth month, on the fifth day of the month, as I sat in my house, with the elders of Judah sitting before me, the hand of the Lord God fell there upon me." This shows that Ezekiel's house at the time was a meeting place for elders of the community. Similar meetings must have been held in other Jewish homes in many parts of the world. Out of such meetings the synagogue developed. It gradually took over many activities formerly carried on by the local shrines of Judah, as well as some from the temple itself. All the early shrines had assemblies for business reasons, a school, and an altar for sacrifices. The local shrines of Palestine were the forerunners of the synagogue, which was so important that long before the fall of Jerusalem in A.D. 70 it had found a place in Jerusalem itself. Numerous synagogues clustered about Jerusalem, and no sense of jealousy or competition appears to have been felt between them and the temple.

The strength of the synagogue lies in its inconspicuous character, its simplicity, its adaptability to all sorts of places and conditions of Jewish life. Great numbers of Jews left Palestine of their own free will in search of prosperous places, where they could find a better life. Wherever they went in the ancient Near and Middle East, because of common interest, they tended to form communities of their own. In the center of such a Jewish community, there was always a synagogue.

To the Jews of A.D. 70, when the temple was destroyed by the Romans, it may have seemed that all was lost. Yet we can see that in certain respects this was only the beginning of a greater life for the Jews than they had ever known. It had been a mistake to assume that the life and faith of the Jews were solely dependent on the temple. When the temple was destroyed, the synagogues continued, as for centuries they had been doing, to nourish and carry on Jewish life and culture. While their life was bound to the temple, Jews could never get far away from Jerusalem, but once the temple was gone, the world became their home and the synagogue became the center of their life.

PROFESSIONAL RELIGIOUS LEADERS

In the early days of their nomadic life the Hebrews had no professional religious leaders. The head of the family or sheik of the tribe, such as Abraham or Jacob, performed the sacrifices and other religious rites. As social life increased in complexity, it became necessary to divide the responsibility of leadership. This becomes clear in the story of Moses, in which priestly duties are assigned to Aaron, while Moses retains in his own hands control over political, legal, and military affairs. Before the end of his life, however, Moses had placed military command in the hands of Joshua.

The general theory was that God, as the ultimate authority, revealed his will to Moses, who then delivered it to the people. He was, in effect, God's official spokesman, which is the meaning of *prophet*, Moses' primary role. Thus, in the story of Moses, we already see emerging four different types of leaders: the prophet, the priest, the military commander, and the king, all of them divinely authorized. In Moses' own time they were all still in their incipient forms.

When the positions of priest and king came to be more clearly defined at a later time, jealousy arose between kings and priests. Such kings as Saul and David at times acted as priests, while the priests charged that the leprosy which afflicted King Uzziah was a punishment that God had sent on him because he had once acted as priest in the temple (II Chronicles 26:16–21).

The priest usually performed his functions at an altar; he was attached to a shrine or to the temple itself. It is true that he also interpreted and supervised laws relating to clean and unclean things, food regulations, and the like, but there is little place for a priest without an altar. The priests themselves were responsible for the elimination of local shrines in 621 B.C., when Deuteronomy was published. Thus, when the temple was destroyed in A.D. 70, the last refuge of the priests was gone; there was no longer a place where they could perform their sacrificial rites. The function of the priest was almost eliminated from Hebrew life.

There have been three types of prophets among Hebrews. The first was the ecstatic prophet, the *nabi*, who spoke by inspiration as the Spirit of God came upon him. These men induced ecstasy by forming themselves into groups and playing instruments of music. Such bands were known in the time of Samuel, before 1000 B.C. In their prophetic frenzy they would induce visions or lie in a coma. King Saul himself at one time was a member of a group of this type (I Samuel 19:18–24). The *nabis* also at times induced frenzy by dancing and gashing their bodies with knives (Zechariah 13:2–6). But this type of prophet at length lost status and was rejected by Hebrew religion.

The second type of prophet, of whom Amos was the first example, condemned every form of artificially induced ecstasy. He denied that he was a *nabi* (Amos 7:14, 15); God spoke to him, he declared, through his conscience, as he did in the cases of Hosea, Isaiah, Micah, Jeremiah, and others, who were the glory of Hebrew religion. The age of these prophets spanned the centuries from around 800 to 400 B.C. It came to an end when the prophetic canon was closed and the doctrine was formulated that all truth had already been revealed. This made it difficult for a prophet of the moral type to appear again. Thus there was a dearth of prophets toward the end of the Old Testament period.

While closing the canon of the prophets did not quench the prophetic spirit, prophecy did have to go underground. It became a secret vocation, that of the apocalyptists, who wrote under assumed names, usually an honored name from the Hebrew past, such as Daniel or Enoch or one of the twelve patriarchs, and whose writings came to be known as the Pseudepigrapha. Although the apocalyptists adopted the convention of using strange symbols, synthetic creatures, demons, and dragons, their weird figures represented real nations, persons, or spirits of the time. This school of writing flourished during the last two centuries B.C. and into the Christian period.

The apocalyptic writers reflect the dualism of Zoroastrianism, a religion encountered by Jewish exiles in Babylonia and Persia. God and his angels are on one side, Satan and the demons on the other; and they engage in war down to the end of time, when the dead are raised, judgment takes place, the righteous and the wicked are rewarded, and God is triumphant over Satan. These ideas attained some importance in Judaism, but the canon of Scripture served as a restraint against extravagance. Apocalyptic views never succeeded in displacing the faith of the classical period of the Old Testament.

Another type of religious leader to emerge as the prophetic period was coming to a close was the wise man or sage. He made no claim to divine inspiration, but spoke rather on the basis of wisdom that he had attained by his own intellectual labor and insight. The Hebrews of the biblical period produced no philosophers in the technical sense, yet the sages did have a semiphilosophical character. The best examples of their work are Proverbs, Job, Ecclesiastes, the Wisdom of Solomon, and the Wisdom of Sirach. These are great books, full of profound insight.

The collection of Hebrew writings into an authoritative canon of inspired Scripture resulted in the people depending on books for guidance rather than, as previously, on the inspired spoken word. One result of this development was the emergence of the rabbis, a new profession of scholars who specialized in knowing the sacred Scriptures. Some scribes, who made new copies of the sacred writings when the old copies wore out, became experts in the knowledge of the Torah and were able to teach it to others. These scholarly scribes became the rabbis. The rabbi was primarily a lawyer, not a writer, and he provided guidance for the Hebrews as they tried to live by the letter of the Law. Emerging slowly, as the prophets and the priests passed from the scene, the rabbi became the indispensable authority and guide of the Jewish people. The rabbi was not a priest, and he was not connected with the temple; instead, his sphere of operation was the synagogue and the community. He remains the one professional leader in the synagogue.

NOTES

1. Cf. E. J. Goodspeed, ed., *The Apocrypha: An American Translation* (Chicago: University of Chicago Press, 1938); R. H. Pfeiffer, *History of New Testament Times, with an Introduction to the Apocrypha* (New York:

Harper, 1949); B. M. Metzger, ed., *The Apocrypha, with an Introduction* (New York: Oxford University Press, 1965).

2. Cf. R. H. Charles, ed., *The Apocrypha and Pseudepigrapha,* 2 vols. (Oxford: Clarendon Press, 1913). This contains introductions to the individual books.

3. The Bible text in this publication is from the *Revised Standard Version of the Bible,* copyrighted 1946 and 1952 by the Division of Christian Education of the National Council of Churches, and used by permission.

4. Cf. "The Creation Epic" in James B. Pritchard, ed., *Ancient Near Eastern Texts,* 2d ed. (Princeton: Princeton University Press, 1955), pp. 60–72; also, *ibid.,* pp. 93–97, Tablet XI, the propotype of the Hebrew flood story.

5. The demon's name was Asmodeus. The story is a Hebrew version of the Persian combat between Aeshma Daeva and the angel Sraosha.

6. Cf. Pritchard, *op. cit.,* pp. 93–97.

7. Yoma 6:2. Herbert Danby, *The Mishnah* (Oxford: Oxford University Press, 1933), p. 169.

8. *Ibid.,* p. 170. This tractate is an authoritative collection of traditions about the Yom Kippur celebration as they had come down from the ancient period. The interpretation above is partly based on it.

9. Cf. Isaiah 13:21; 34:14; Tobit 8:3; Baruch 4:7; Matthew 12:43.

10. Charles, *op. cit.,* II, 163–277.

11. Cf. W. F. Stinespring, "Jerusalem Temple," in George A. Buttrick, ed., *The Interpreter's Dictionary of the Bible* (Nashville: Abingdon, 1962), IV, 534–560.

12. Josephus, *Antiquities of the Jews,* XIII, ix, 1; XIII, x, 1–3.

13. E. G. Kraeling, "Elephantine Papyri," in Buttrick, *op. cit.,* II, 83–84.

14. Josephus, *op. cit.,* XIII, iii, 1–3; *War of the Jews,* VII, x, 2–4.

15. The synagogues of the Falashas, an isolated and little-known Jewish sect of Ethiopia, afford an exception to this statement. See p. 219.

EARLY POST-BIBLICAL JUDAISM

Interbiblical Parties

By the end of the Old Testament period, certain organized groups of considerable importance had taken form in Palestine. First and most conservative were the priests associated with the temple, who were the core of a larger aristocratic group which included some wealthy business and political figures. This strongly entrenched group was called Sadducees, a term thought to be derived from *Zadok,* the title of the high priest under Solomon, under whom the high priesthood was made hereditary. They derived their income from temple sacrifices and concessions operated around the temple, and were therefore interested in preserving the temple rites, together with all the festivals that brought pilgrims to Jerusalem from many parts of the world. The Sadducees accepted as authoritative only the five Books of Moses and rejected all the others, especially the apocalyptic writings, with their teachings about angels, spirits, demons, resurrection of the dead, and so on.

The Pharisees, on the other hand, were a scholarly association of some 6,000 Jews, organized for the study and keeping of the Law. Their aim was to organize their own group so that all their dealings would be with Pharisees. Admission into the order was attained only after careful study and examination. They emphasized laws with reference to food, clean and unclean, tithing, Sabbath, and the like. At the same time they were strong supporters of the synagogue; most rabbis were Pharisees. Two of the best known of these were Hillel I and Shammai, who date from the time of Herod the

FIGURE 10.1 Displaying the Torah. Each of the men is wearing a tallith and tefillin. (*Yeshiva University*)

Great. They accepted not only the written Law, the Prophets and Writings, but also oral tradition, which consisted of decisions of judges and courts handed down orally. At the time it was considered unlawful to write down these traditions; only inspired Scriptures could be written. The Pharisees were the most progressive group of Jews.

The Essenes were similar to the Pharisees in their emphasis on foods and on the concept of clean and unclean, but in order to maintain ceremonial purity they organized communities in isolated places, where they could lead monastic lives, most of them being unmarried. The ruins of one of these communities was discovered in 1947 in the Wadi Qumran, which flows into the northwestern corner of the Dead Sea.[1]

The Zealots were an organization of extreme nationalists that agitated for rebellion against the Romans. They were the group that instigated the rebellions, so disastrous to the Jews, of A.D. 66–70 and 132–135.

These professional groups were relatively small. The majority of the Jews, the common people, were called the People of the Land. They were devout persons, industrious, struggling to gain a livelihood, not well enough educated to keep all the rules of the Pharisees, yet strongly influenced by their teachings.

In order to round out our characterization of the Jews at the end of the Old Testament period, we need to keep in mind the vast numbers of Jews who at that time made their homes in other lands. Just how many we are unable to say, but there were probably several hundred thousand. As early as 277 B.C., according to Josephus, when Ptolemy Philadelphus wished to secure from the high priest at Jerusalem a copy of the Hebrew Scriptures, and scholars to translate them into Greek, he set free 120,000 Jewish slaves in Egypt.[2] Some idea of the different lands where Jews lived may be gleaned from the Bible. The story of Esther is based in Susa, capital of Persia. It tells of the attempt of Haman, vizier of Persia, to destroy all Jews in the Persian kingdom. Tobit, in the Apocrypha, has as its hero Tobias, son of a distinguished Jew living in Nineveh, capital of Assyria, on the Tigris River. The New Testament adds much to this picture. The second chapter of Acts lists Jewish pilgrims at Jerusalem for the festival of Pentecost from the following places: Parthia, Media, Elam, Mesopotamia; Cappadocia, Pontus, Asia, Phrygia, and Pamphylia; Egypt, Cyrene; Rome; Crete; Arabia. Acts 4:36, 37 introduces Barnabas, a native of Cyprus. Paul, the famous missionary, was a native of Tarsus (Acts 22:3) in Asia Minor. In the course of Paul's travels, he found Jewish communities in Damascus, Antioch of Syria, Antioch of Pisidia, Iconium and Derbe in Asia Minor, as well as at Philippi, Thessalonica, Berea, and Corinth in Greece. There was also a large community of Jews in Rome.

This wide dispersion of the Jews had caused many of them to forget the Hebrew language, as well as the Aramaic of Palestine; their own speech was the vernacular of the lands in which they lived. This explains why no less than seven Greek translations of the Hebrew Scriptures were made by Jews,[3] Greek being the most widely used language of the time.

New Professional Leaders

The Nasi

The field of jurisprudence is another area in which Judaism developed eminent religious leaders. The Sanhedrin, the supreme court of Judaism in late biblical times, appears to have had its origin in the Maccabean period. Its membership was composed of seventy judges and the high priest who presided over them. The Sanhedrin had control over political as well as religious affairs. The office of high priest included both of these spheres. The same individual, therefore, might at the same time bear the title of high priest, as presiding officer of the temple priests, and the title of Nasi, as president of the Sanhedrin. When the Romans took over Palestine in 63 B.C. they stripped the Sanhedrin of some of its functions. The high priest held office by Roman appointment and could be deposed at will, although appointments to the high priesthood were always made from persons with hereditary qualifications for the office.

The right to bear the title of Nasi and preside over the Sanhedrin, however, appears not to have been the exclusive prerogative of the high priest. Hillel I (c. 60 B.C.–A.D. 10), who as a young man came from Babylonia to study in the famous schools at Jerusalem, was one of the most distinguished Nasis. Talmudic tradition holds that Hillel received the title of Nasi because he became president of the Sanhedrin. Some scholars hold that he received the title as head of a commission on temple ritual. Still others have concluded that the title went with his position as head of his own Torah school in Jerusalem. In any case, the title points to Hillel's distinction. As a teacher of the Torah, his philosophy of interpretation

was to begin with man himself and then to search for the humane
elements of the Torah which support the good qualities of man's
character.

Johanan ben Zakkai (c. A.D. 80), recognized as the most outstanding
Jewish scholar of his time, was a resident of Jerusalem when the
Jewish rebellion against Rome in A.D. 66–70 broke out. Realizing
the hopelessness of the rebellion, Johanan made his way out through
the Roman lines to the headquarters of Vespasian, the commander,
who was soon to become emperor of Rome. He asked Vespasian for
permission to go to Jamnia, a village on the coastal plain, to open a
Jewish school. Vespasian readily granted the request. Johanan had
little besides faith and courage with which to begin, but he opened
a modest school and finally succeeded in assembling the seventy
scholars necessary to reconstitute the Sanhedrin. The significance of
what Johanan had done in his inconspicuous way was soon recognized far and wide. As Palestine was devastated, the walls of Jerusalem broken down, and the temple destroyed, this great educator
and religious statesman had rescued from ruin the twin pillars of
Jewish culture: education and life under the Torah. The school
of Jamnia became a rallying point for the remaining Jews of Palestine and the Jews beyond its borders. By the end of the first
century A.D. the Jamnian Sanhedrin had been recognized by the
Romans and given authority to appoint judges and supervise schools
in Jewish communities.

Johanan ben Zakkai and his associates were concerned about the
qualifications of teachers in the schools which were conducted in
connection with the synagogues. The rabbis, or teachers, were
selected on the basis of their distinction as well as knowledge. Each
member of the Sanhedrin (*Beth Din*) was a rabbi, and the Nasi
himself was called Rabban.

Another significant action of Johanan and the Sanhedrin at
Jamnia (c. A.D. 90) was to select and canonize the third division of
the Hebrew Bible, which is called the Writings. In Christian Bibles,
this collection usually contains thirteen books: Psalms, Job, Proverbs, Ruth, Ecclesiastes, Song of Songs, Lamentations, Esther, Daniel, Ezra, Nehemiah, I and II Chronicles. But in Hebrew Bibles
Ezra-Nehemiah and I-II Chronicles are counted as one book each,
thus making only eleven books. The Sanhedrin took this action in
regard to the Hebrew Scriptures in an effort to provide support for
the Jewish people at a time when they had been shaken by the fall

of Jerusalem as well as to provide a more stable defense against the impact of emerging Christianity.

But Johanan ben Zakkai was already an old man when he attained the eminent position of Sanhedrin Nasi. When he and his court cast about for his successor, they deemed it wise to select a man who would win and hold the respect of the Romans as well as the Jews. Since Hillel was the most distinguished name in the line of Nasis, they decided to appoint a scholar from that family. The choice fell upon Gamaliel II of Jamnia, a man of sound scholarship, who was committed to Johanan's policy of working for the unity of the Jews.

What Johanan and Gamaliel II had accomplished in the restoration of Judaism, however, appeared to be lost in the second Jewish rebellion against Rome (A.D. 132–135). In addition to a second devastation of Judea and destruction of Jerusalem and the armies of Simon Bar Kochba, Emperor Hadrian required all surviving Jews to leave Jerusalem and outlawed the Beth Din and the practice of all Jewish rites in Judea. But when Antonius Pius (138–161), a man of deeper insight, became emperor of Rome, he relaxed the harsh laws against the Jews. The Beth Din was reestablished and Jewish schools were reopened.

The Patriarch

In the meantime, Nasi Gamaliel II had died. He was succeeded by his son Judah who, recognized as the most brilliant of all the Nasis, was called "Judah the Prince" by later generations. Rome awarded him the title of Patriarch (Latin and Greek rendering of Nasi) and made him the administrative head of the Jewish people in the empire. But Judah's greatest achievement was literary, not administrative. It was he who finally succeeded in codifying the great body of oral legal tradition in a form which won acceptance from Jews everywhere. Other rabbis had made efforts in this direction, but Judah's knowledge, literary ability, and reputation made his work successful where others had failed. Judah's book was the Mishnah, which won its place beside the Bible; these two were now the authoritative books of Judaism.

After the second rebellion against Rome, the Beth Din and most activities of Palestinian Jewish life were transferred to Galilee. But after the death of the Patriarch Judah in 219, the intellectual and spiritual life of Palestine began to decline. Judah's successors as patriarch continued to serve under the Romans as administrative heads of the Jews but they were less interested in Jewish culture than in their own prosperity and power. When Patriarch Gamaliel VI died in A.D. 425 without an heir to succeed him, political uncertainty about a patriarch ensued. Rome finally abolished the office in A.D. 429.

The Gaon

Babylonia became a center of Hebrew culture in very early times. Abraham, the ancestral father, came from Babylon to Palestine, and caravan trade kept the Hebrews in touch with their earlier homeland. When Samaria was conquered by the Assyrians and when Jerusalem was destroyed by the Babylonians, large groups of Hebrew exiles settled in Babylonia. The Mesopotamian Jewish communities were reinforced by immigrants from Palestine and Rome who sought refuge. It is estimated that by A.D. 70 the Jewish population of Mesopotamia had reached a million persons. They continued to prosper under the Parthians, Persians, and Muslims.

By A.D. 200 the Mesopotamian communities were equipped with good schools, synagogues, and strong academies devoted to advanced study of the Torah. The best known of the academies were those of Sura and Pumbeditha, each under the direction of a leader whose title was *Gaon* (plural, *geonim*). Saadia ben Joseph (A.D. 892–942) was one of the most outstanding geonim of Sura, and Hai ben Sherira (d. 1038) was notable among the geonim of Pumbeditha. The quality of scholarship of these academies may be judged by the Babylonian Talmud which they produced. Jews considered it superior to the Palestinian Talmud, which was being prepared at the same time.

The Exilarch

The exilarch was a Jewish official appointed by the successive governments of Mesopotamia and Persia to supervise the affairs of the Jewish communities. He was parallel to the patriarch who served the Romans in governing the Jews of Palestine. The position was hereditary, and the exilarchs claimed descent from King Jehoiachin, who was brought to Babylonia in 598 B.C. They collected taxes from the Jews for the state and had authority to appoint judges and teachers, including the geonim, to serve as judge himself, and to enforce all penalties. This arrangement made the Jewish communities essentially autonomous. They also liked to feel that they were ruled by a prince of the line of King David. At best, the exilarch was an important religious leader in the Jewish communities. At worst, he was avaricious and a source of discord.

Josephus the Historian

Flavius Josephus (c. A.D. 37–100) was a distinguished Jewish historian who was an eyewitness to the tragedies of the Jews during his time. He was a native of Jerusalem, from a priestly family, and had received a good education in warfare and government as well as in Greek and Roman methods of writing history. His mother tongue was Aramaic but he wrote most of his books in Greek. He is an example of the penetration of Hellenistic culture into Palestine and even into Jerusalem.

At the outbreak of the rebellion against Rome of 66–70, Josephus was made commander of Galilee, which he defended against the army of Vespasian. His eyewitness account of the defense of the city of Jotapata is one of the most vivid records in the annals of ancient warfare. When the city was captured, Josephus was taken prisoner, but he quickly won the confidence of Vespasian and entered into his service as counselor on Jewish affairs. He became such a favorite that he was permitted to adopt the name Flavius, Vespasian's family name, as his own. At the end of the war, Vespasian brought Josephus to Rome and established him in his own house, where Josephus wrote his *War of the Jews*. He then wrote the *Antiquities of the Jews,* his own *Life,* and *Against Apion*.

Philo the Theologian

Philo of Alexandria (c. 20 B.C.–A.D. 50) is the best known Jewish philosophical theologian of the ancient period. He read extensively in the Greek philosophers and was especially impressed with Plato and the Stoics. From Plato he took the concept of eternal ideas as existing in the metaphysical realm, of which everything on earth is only a reflection. From the Stoics he took the idea of the *Logos,* the reason that gives order to the world. In addition, he made use of the Greek philosophical virtues of wisdom, temperance, fortitude, and justice. As evidence of his Jewish training and his love of religion, Philo wrote his philosophy in commentaries on the Books of Moses. He had a fascinating ability to discover philosophical ideas in virtually every word of the Scriptures, by treating the Scriptures as allegories. For example, Philo made use of Plato's concept of eternal ideas by saying that before God created the world, he drew a blueprint as architects do, and then carried out creation according to his plan. In a similar fashion, he used the Stoic Logos as God's agent in creation, corresponding to the role of Wisdom in Proverbs 8:22–30 and to the role of Logos in the Gospel of John 1:1–14.[4]

Jews and Early Christians

At the time when Christianity was emerging under the leadership of Jesus and Paul, the Jews of Palestine, nationalistic and restive, were girding themselves for rebellion against Rome. The Christian movement began as a reform within Judaism, but the Jews rejected it. They found intolerable its Messiah, who declined to take up arms against Rome; its doctrine of salvation by faith, which challenged the sacrificial system of the temple and the legalism of the synagogue; and its gospel of a universal kingdom of God transcending all races and bloods. The Jewish rejection of Christianity was far advanced, but still tentative, before the wars with Rome, but the fall of the temple in A.D. 70 made that rejection final. The last symbol of a bond of unity and a common destiny of Jews and Christians was shattered.

At the same time, as so often in the past, when national catastrophes struck the Jewish people, their will to survive as a people, a religion, and a nation was not broken. They found hope in the foreign Jewish communities whose stability and prosperity had not been seriously affected by the wars in Palestine. Profiting from the wisdom their forefathers had gained from earlier exiles, the Jews rallied again, and this time rabbinic Judaism, which created the Jewish culture of the Middle Ages, emerged.

Judaism and Missionary Activity

Judaism contains a principle of universality in its faith, a principle that is implicit in the Hebrew belief in the one God who is the sovereign of the world. At the same time, Judaism has also included devotion to one people and one nation, ideas which have tended to inhibit outright missionary activity. The Maccabean High Priest John Hyrcanus (134–104 B.C.) conquered Edom and compelled the Edomites to be circumcised and keep the other rituals of Judaism, and Aristobulus I (104 B.C.) conquered Galilee and required its people to be circumcised.[5] But these actions should be regarded as ceremonials of naturalization by which these newly conquered peoples became citizens of Judea, not as examples of missionary activity in the usual sense. During the late pre-Christian period, however, some real missionary work was accomplished in connection with synagogue services and the Greek translations of the Hebrew Scriptures. Gentiles were welcome in the synagogues, where they admired the Hebrew theology and morality. While some did become outright converts to Judaism, most gentiles did not become proselytes, being deterred by Jewish ceremonialism and nationalism. Such devout gentiles were called "God-fearers." They were a ripe harvest, ready to be garnered by the early Christian missionaries, whose faith abandoned Jewish ceremonialism and nationalism, yet retained the essentials of Jewish theology and morality. The Jewish synagogue thus prepared the way for the Christian missions. (Since ancient times, conversion to Judaism has been limited almost entirely to gentiles who are contemplating marriage to Jews. Orthodox rabbis will not perform such a marriage until the gentile has become a convert to the Jewish faith.)

The Talmud

Although the Law as found in the Pentateuch, the five Books of Moses, is the ultimate authority for Orthodox Jews, what they accept as the final interpretation of the Law is found in the Talmud, an encyclopedic work which every Jewish scholar must know, and by which all Orthodox Jews attempt to live.

The oldest portion of the Talmud is the Mishnah, edited by Judah the Patriarch, who lived in Sepphoris, Galilee, about A.D. 200. The oral traditions giving interpretations of the Law had eventually become so extensive that it was impossible to carry them in memory, and so they were written down. The view that they could not be written because they were not inspired, as were the Scriptures, had to be abandoned. Judah wrote much of the material for the first time, but he also made use of some tentative collections made by earlier rabbis. This work marked the end of the period of oral tradition.

The Mishnah contains six divisions, with a total of sixty-three chapters or tractates. They are collections of sayings of Jewish scholars, especially of the preceding two centuries, beginning with Hillel and

Shammai of the time of Herod, and including such well-known rabbis as Gamaliel I, who was the teacher of Paul; Johanan ben Zakkai, who was the Sanhedrin Nasi c. A.D. 90; and Akiba, who in A.D. 135 lost his life in the second Jewish rebellion against Rome.[6] In the Mishnah one finds illuminating discussions of almost every vital subject in Judaism: such matters as the Sabbath, the Passover, the Day of Atonement, marriage, the Sanhedrin, hallowed things, clean and unclean.

The Mishnah, which is a commentary on the Law of Moses, had not been in writing long before interpretations of it also became necessary. Thus commentaries on the Mishnah began to be expounded, and these commentaries are called the Gemara. Two sets of these commentaries were made, one in Palestine and the other in Babylon, where a large community of Jews lived and scholarly rabbinic schools flourished. The Mishnah, together with its set of commentaries, is called the Talmud. Because of the two sets of commentaries two Talmuds came into existence: the Jerusalem Talmud (which was not well preserved[7]) and the Babylonian Talmud. The latter was the more authoritative, and it is accepted by Orthodox Jews to this day.

MEDIEVAL JUDAISM

The Middle Ages

The period called the Middle Ages, or the Dark Ages, spanned the time between the disappearance of classical civilization, approximately at the time of the fall of Rome in A.D. 476, and the rediscovery of that classical culture, about A.D. 1500, which was a time of renaissance of civilization in Europe. One of the characteristics of the ancient world as it moved into the Middle Ages was the fall of various nations. The Greek states were the first to fall, and although Rome stood longer than any other nation, it, too, fell. Europe had been conquered by younger peoples who had no interest in the classical cultures.

The experience of the Jewish people followed a somewhat similar pattern. Hebrew culture flourished in Palestine as long as the nation stood, but when the Romans first destroyed Jerusalem in A.D. 70, and finally expelled all Jews from the city in A.D. 135, the Dark

Ages for the Jews began. Their religion included a belief that God had guaranteed their existence as a nation. For a time, even for centuries, some Jews hoped that one of the Roman emperors would allow them to return to Jerusalem and rebuild the temple. But the hope of restoration under the Romans was an illusion. The Jews had to resign themselves to life without a national existence and without a temple.

Medieval Judaism is characterized by the realization of the Jews that for the time they could not become a nation again, and that all they could hope for in a national sense was that when the Messiah came he would restore their nation. It was this faith which kept a light burning in Jewish hearts during the Dark Ages. Most ancient peoples who found themselves in the situation of the Jews after their nation fell willingly allowed themselves to be assimilated into the cultures of their conquerors. Some Jews did this then and others have done it since that time. But a majority of Jews have rejected assimilation in order to preserve the uniqueness of their own faith and culture. One of the aims of the great Jewish teachers was to surround devout Jews with the protection of their own faith and ceremonials; to build a "wall of the Torah" around the Jewish people. In this, the rabbis were successful; they led their people through the Dark Ages and brought them into the modern world with their faith unimpaired.

For some 200 years after the fall of Jerusalem, Palestine itself was the center of Jewish intellectual life. The publication of the Mishnah around A.D. 200 by Judah the Patriarch, a resident of Galilee, demonstrates the superiority of Palestinian intellectual life at that time. This codification of the Torah was soon recognized as authoritative by the geonim of the Mesopotamian schools of Sura and Pumpeditha, as well as by most rabbis throughout the Jewish world. But following the publication of the Mishnah, the intellectual life of Palestine began to decline and Mesopotamia itself took the lead. The schools of Sura and Pumpeditha were the ones which created the authoritative Talmud in the fifth century, but the Palestinian scholars later produced their own, less renowned version of the Talmud. Both Mesopotamian and Palestinian scholars recognized the Mishnah which Judah the Patriarch had produced as authoritative and made it the foundation of their versions of the Talmud. The Talmud was the wall of the Torah within which the Jewish people lived during the Middle Ages.

The Karaites

The Karaite sect arose in Iraq and was reputedly founded by Anan ben David of Baghdad around A.D. 760, during the age when the Talmud was achieving its authoritative position in Jewish life. Karaism was a rebellion against the Talmud on the one hand and a return to the original text of the Scriptures on the other. The word is derived from the Hebrew *kara*, read. The Karaite ideology is to read the Scripture itself and interpret it in the light of reason, not to limit its meaning to the Talmudic interpretaton, which may be erroneous at worst and difficult for the uninitiated to comprehend at best. Karaism therefore reaffirms the freedom of the individual to study the Scriptures. At the same time, Karaism, idealistic as it was, overlooked the difficulty of arriving at a consensus of judgment as to the interpretation of a law so long as individuals are left free to make their own interpretations. A consensus is necessary if a society is to live by law. While individual freedom must be recognized, a court, indeed a supreme court, appears to be inevitable; every court decision adds another element to the legal tradition, which must be considered in interpreting either constitutional or statutory law. Inevitably, the Karaites built up a body of traditions of their own.[8]

In dogmatic theology itself, there is no important difference between Karaism and Orthodox Judaism, since theologically speaking, the Karaites are extremely conservative. The difference appears only in practical theology: the Karaite interpretation of the laws tends to be more severe than that of the Talmud. This applies, for example, to their ruling on marriage, which made it difficult for a Karaite to avoid incest, a ruling that they modified in the eleventh century. They also had to change their rule that prayer must consist solely of biblical quotations. In addition, they abandoned some of their extreme asceticism. These three changes, however, appear to be the only modifications they have made in their practices through the years.[9] Contrary to the Talmud, Karaites interpret "an eye for an eye" literally and are unwilling to accept financial compensation. On the other hand, there are respects in which they are more liberal than Orthodox Jews; they do not use either phylacteries (*tefillin*) or doorpost amulets (*mezuzoth*).[10]

The place allowed to reason in Karaite theology may show the influence of the Mutazilite movement in Islam, which was vigorous at the time Karaism appeared in Judaism. The Karaite rejection of the Talmud was somewhat like the Mutazilite criticism of the Sunna. The Karaite schism originated under the tolerant rule of the enlightened caliphs of Baghdad, and the Rabbinic Academy of Sura in Iraq attained its greatest eminence under that Muslim government. But the Karaites found themselves bitterly opposed by the Rabbinic Academy of Sura, especially by Saadia ben Joseph (892–942), one of its most distinguished geonim. They therefore gradually transferred their activities to Palestine and Egypt and established an academy in Jerusalem. They also founded colonies in both Moorish Spain and the Balkans, which at that time were under Christian rule.[11] Some Karaites survive to this day in Turkish and Russian lands. The wars of the Crusades brought a temporary halt to their life in Palestine, but with the establishment of Turkish rule in 1517 Karaite work in Jerusalem was resumed.

The Karaite literary activity enjoyed its golden age from 900 to 1200. Most of the writing was theological and philological, and its vigor aroused new life even in Rabbinic Judaism. But the Karaites also wrote good poetry, some of it of a simple, secular character.

The Cabala

The Cabala designates a mystical approach to an understanding of God which was adhered to by thoughtful Jews from early times, and has come down through the centuries, to our own day. It is not a well-articulated system and does not manifest the same doctrines in the various parts of the world in which it has appeared, including Palestine, Babylonia, Spain, Poland, and Galicia. It was at first associated with ecstatic visionaries among the apocalyptic writers of the late biblical period, perhaps under Zoroastrian influence. Aaron ben Samuel is said to have brought the Cabala from Babylon to Europe about A.D. 870. Solomon ibn Gabirol (1021–1058), a Spanish poet and philosopher, is credited with introducing Neoplatonic mysticism among the Jews. The most important literary work associated with the Cabala is the Zohar, a compilation of mystical writings published in Spain in the eleventh century. The Cabalistic movement reached its culmination among the *Hasidim,* a mystical sect of Poland and Galicia, founded by Israel ben Eliezer, known as Baal Shem-Tov (1700–1760), who was under the influence of Isaac Luria of Palestine (see Figure 10.2).

While the Cabala led some of its devotees into magic and divination, it was in the main a serious movement, emphasizing the immanence of God, rather than the traditional Hebrew concept of transcendence. Cabalists based their teaching on personal experience and regarded their immediate sense of God as the most certain proof of the truth of religion.[12]

The Jews in Spain

Traditionally, the Jews of Spain believed that their ancestors had come to that land in the days of King Solomon. It is well known from the Bible that Solomon allied himself with Hiram, king of Tyre, in commerce by sea, and that the Phoenicians were the best known merchants and seamen of that ancient period. Their ships sailed to every port on the Mediterranean and around to the British Isles. The Jewish settlers arrived in Spain while it was still a Roman province, and their descendants continued to live there until the Jews were expelled from Spain in 1492 by Ferdinand and Isabella.

The lives of the Jews of Spain continued without interruption during the wars in Palestine when Jerusalem was destroyed by the Romans. They continued to live in Spain under the Romans without difficulty until Spain was conquered by the Visigoths, a Teutonic tribe, in A.D. 412. The Visigothic kings were Aryan Christians who allowed their subjects freedom of religion. For a century and a half Jews prospered under Visigoth rule, exercising a considerable influence in the government. But when King Riccared came to power in 589, a struggle ensued in which the Christian clergy incited the king to issue a decree that Jews must either become Christians or leave Spain. Some Jews fled to France, some pretended to become Christians but practiced Jewish rituals in secret, and others sought the protection of powerful nobles. The struggle came to a climax in 700 when a decree was issued that anyone found guilty of practicing Jewish rituals in secret would be sold into slavery and his children would be brought up as Christians by the clergy.

After the Muslims conquered Spain in 711, another era of peace for the Jews began in Spain. The Muslims applied the Pact of Omar to the Jews throughout their dominions. This pact empha-

FIGURE 10.2   Hasidim dancing on a holiday. (*Paul Schutzer, Life Magazaine* © *Time Inc.*)

sized the superiority of Islam over both Judaism and Christianity, but it did not create an intolerable situation for either Jews or Christians. According to the pact, non-Muslims could not be disrespectful to Muhammad or his religion; they could not prevent one of their fellows from becoming a Muslim convert; they had to bear heavier taxes than Muslims; no new synagogues or churches could be built, but old ones could be repaired; no synagogue or church tower could be higher than the minaret of a mosque; non-Muslims could not ride horses, but they could ride mules; non-Muslims could not carry swords; and non-Muslims had to dress so as to be distinguishable from Muslims. In 850, 200 years later, Caliph Mutawakkil interpreted this last requirement to mean that non-Muslims must wear a patch of yellow on the sleeve and a yellow headdress.

These regulations were not strictly enforced in Spain. Jews were soon permitted to rise to positions of power under the caliphs. They were allowed to live in their own communities in accordance

with their own laws, and under a *nagid,* a Jewish official similar
to an exilarch. It was under this tolerant rule of the Muslims that
the Jews of Spain entered into a period of freedom, prosperity, and
cultural development which lasted for some 500 years. To this day
Jews look back on those centuries as a golden age.

During most of that period the Muslims ruled an empire which
reached from Spain on the west to Persia on the east. They were
the most enlightened people of that era. Spain became the wealthiest and most cultured land of Europe. The Moors of Spain took
over the science, art, and philosophy of the Muslims of Persia and
Mesopotamia as well as the classical learning of Greece, and the
Jews greatly benefited from the Muslim intellectual life. The Jews
were prepared for this intellectual life, since, from the time of the
emergence of the synagogue in late biblical times, they had placed
strong emphasis on education. They substituted the Bible for the
Koran, Hebrew for Arabic, and Jewish theology for Muslim theology. Muslim scholars translated the classics of Greece and India
into Arabic; Spanish Jews translated them into Hebrew; French
Jews translated them into Latin. The Jews, therefore, transmitted
the classical as well as Muslim cultures to Europe.

Hasdai ibn Shaprut (c. 925–975) was one of the founders of
Spanish Jewish culture. He was by profession a physician, but he
became an unofficial counselor and diplomat under the caliph. At
the same time, he gave support to Jewish scholars—especially to
Moses ben Hanoch, a messenger of the Babylonian academies, who
was laying a foundation for Talmudic study in Spain at that time.
Later, Isaac of Fez (also known as Alfasi) came from North Africa
to become an authority on the legalistic aspects of the Talmud in
the Talmudic academy which Moses ben Hanoch had since established. Samuel ibn Naghdela (993–1056), a grocer from Cordova
who became a scholar, moved to Malaga on the seacoast of Granada
during unsettled times, where he rose to the position of vizier of
the king of Granada. The king also made him nagid of the Jews.
In addition, Samuel established a Talmudic academy and wrote
an introduction to the Talmud and a dictionary of biblical Hebrew.
His son, Joseph, inherited his positions as vizier and nagid, but
he lacked Samuel's wisdom. As a result, some of his actions caused
riots in which he and thousands of Jews died.

Inspired by Muslim thinkers and writers of the time, Spanish
Judaism produced some eminent poets and philosophical writers
of its own. Among these were: the poet Moses ibn Ezra (c. 1080–

1139); Solomon ibn Gabirol (1021–1058), a poet who wrote *The Fountain of Life,* a religious book used by Christians as well as by Jews; Judah ha-Levi (1086–1145), another poet who wrote philosophy and was the author of *The Kuzari,* an account of the conversion of the Khazars to Judaism, which discusses the relative merits of Judaism, Christianity, and Islam; and Bahya ibn Pakuda (c. 1100–1150), a judge with a philosophical bent who produced *Duties of the Heart,* which shows that the heart has a duty to provide every act with the right feeling, the right emotion. However, the greatest philosopher to emerge out of Spanish Judaism was Moses ben Maimon, generally known as Maimonides.

Moses Maimonides

Moses Maimonides (1135–1204), one of the most renowned scholars of the Middle Ages, was a rabbi, first in Spain and then in Egypt. He was also a student of medicine and was at one time physician to Saladin, an Arab general during the time of the Crusades. Maimonides lived at the time when the Arabs had just rediscovered the Greek classical writers, and he was fascinated by the classics. His ideal was the philosopher Aristotle, who more than any other Greek philosopher emphasized reason in the search for truth, and who applied it to religion as he did to everything else. Unsatisfied with the bondage of rabbinic orthodoxy to the literal words of Scripture, Maimonides emphasized the methods of Aristotle instead. He believed that he was able by reason alone to prove the existence of God. In this, he was a pioneer in the field of philosophical theology, and all subsequent writers in this field, whether Jewish or Christian, are indebted to him. *The Guide of the Perplexed* is his best known work, and it is still regarded as one of the world's great books.[13]

Maimonides also wrote extensively about Jewish law, philosophy, and medicine. One of his most popular writings was a formulation of the Jewish faith into thirteen basic principles, which we abstract as follows:

1. We believe firmly in God, the Creator of all things;
2. We believe firmly in the unity of God;
3. We believe that God has no corporeal form of any kind;
4. We affirm the eternity of God, his priority to all things in existence;

5. We believe that the Holy One alone may be rightly worshiped and exalted, and that there is no intermediary between God and man;

6. We believe in the reality of prophecy and that the appearance of many divinely inspired prophets is attested in the Scriptures;

7. We firmly believe that Moses was the chief of all prophets, both of those who preceded him and those who followed him;

8. We believe that the Torah given to us by Moses was received from heaven, that Moses obtained it from God;

9. We believe in the immutability of the Torah and that no one should add to it or diminish from it;

10. We believe in the omniscience of God, in his unceasing awareness of men's actions;

11. We firmly believe in the principle of rewards and punishment; and the greatest reward, as well as the severest punishment, is in the world to come;

12. We believe in the coming of the Messiah, and also that he will be of the house of David, but we are not to set the time of his coming;

13. And we firmly believe in the resurrection of the dead.[14]

These principles of Maimonides are sometimes couched in liturgical form and recited today in Jewish worship services.[15]

Persecution of the Jews

The story of the persecution of the Jews begins with their first appearance in history, when Abraham departs from Ur of the Chaldees and sets out in search of a more congenial home. The first major episode of Jewish persecution occurred in ancient Egypt, where the Jews were enslaved, finally escaping under the leadership of Moses. The next chapters of persecution came with the destruction of Israel in 721 B.C. by the Assyrians and of Judah by the Babylonians in 587 B.C. In both cases important elements of the populations were carried away as prisoners into exile. Next we read in the Book of Esther of an effort of the Persians to destroy Jewish communities in their midst. This was followed by an attempt by Syria to uproot Jewish religion about 167 B.C., which provoked the Maccabean rebellion. Next the Romans destroyed Jerusalem and the temple in A.D. 70 and then further devastated Judea and dispersed the Jews in A.D. 132–135.

From this time on, Jews were scattered throughout most of the lands of the Near and Middle East and Europe. For almost 1,000 years they lived in relative peace and security. But overzealous Christian emperors intermittently sought to convert the Jews to Christianity, sometimes by force.

Dangerous persecutions of Jews began about the time of the Christian Crusades, which were undertaken with the hope of recovering the sacred places of the Holy Land from the Muslims, who had been dominant there since about A.D. 638. The Crusades continued throughout the eleventh and twelfth centuries, in nine or ten expeditions, motivated not only by intense religious devotion and the desire to make pilgrimages to holy places, but also by the love of military adventure and plunder. While there were some victories, most of the ventures ended in frustration, not to say disaster. It was in this connection that the Crusaders began to turn against the Jews of Europe as well as those of Palestine. The theory behind the massacres appears to have been that if they were out to destroy opponents of Christianity, why not begin with the Jews close to home?

Bitter hostility against the Jews, however, had arisen even before the Crusades began. The first Crusade occurred during the years 1096–1099, but the first legal ghetto appears to have been established in 1084 at Speyer, Germany. In this case, the ghetto was voluntary. Jews themselves asked the Bishop of Speyer to set aside a section of the city for them and to surround it with a wall for their protection. Rueddiger, Bishop of Speyer, granted this request and permitted the Jews to organize their own guard. Also he gave them control of life inside their walls and permitted them to carry on their business affairs outside in the city.[16] This arrangement was at first considered a great boon by the Jews.

But what was at first voluntary soon became compulsory. By the fifteenth century most of the Jews of Europe were compelled to live in ghettos and to wear a distinctive garb, so that they would be easily recognized by non-Jews. The ghettos often were overcrowded and unsanitary, and there were frequent fires. Jews could carry on their business outside the walls, but had to return within them by sunset and remain inside on Sundays and other Christian holidays. Yet the ghetto had its positive side. It was the center of Jewish intellectual and artistic life; the Jews were at home; and there they were further confirmed in their sense of being a unique people having a particular destiny.

The central institution of the ghetto was the synagogue. Long before the emergence of the ghetto, a Jewish community tended to become a circle with the synagogue at the center and the Sabbath-day's journey—2,000 cubits—as its radius, for every devout Jew went to the synagogue on the Sabbath. The ghetto also had its own council or court, a slaughterhouse, a bakery, a guesthouse, a dance house, a bathhouse, and a cemetery, the care of which was an important community responsibility.

The business life of Jews during the Middle Ages was limited almost exclusively to banking and moneylending, since they were excluded from most of the professions. Because Christian theology considered moneylending a sin, Christians were forbidden to engage in this business. However, since money was a necessary means of commerce and someone had to be the banker, Jews were allowed to engage in this practice, which explains why they have so often been associated in the popular mind with pawnshops and similar financial institutions. At the same time, this enabled some Jews to become wealthy, so that rulers turned to them for the financial resources they needed to operate their governments. For this reason Jews came under the protection of the medieval kings and bishops. Yet the wealth of Jews was also at times the cause of their undoing. They were regarded with suspicion and jealousy and accused of trickery, dishonesty, and ruthlessness. Whether or not such charges were true, they led the rulers from time to time to expel the Jews from their kingdoms and at the same time to expropriate their property. This tragic event has occurred many times; there is hardly a nation in the Western world, except the countries in North and South America, that has not at some time expelled the Jews from its borders.

MODERN JUDAISM

Baruch Spinoza

Baruch Spinoza (1632–1677) was born in Amsterdam, where he spent his life as a lens grinder. He was devoted to philosophy and became so well recognized that he was offered a professorship, which he declined in order to pursue his scholarly activity in a quiet way. Spinoza lived at a time when the age of science was just beginning and men were starting to see the world through its eyes. Spinoza was fascinated by the order he perceived. Although he remained a devout Jew, the orderly character he saw in the universe forced him to reject the stories of miracles that he found in the Bible. His views shocked the Jews of his community to such an extent that they excommunicated him, but he was not deterred.

The main point in Spinoza's philosophy was his sense of universal order. He saw no room for miracles in the sense of exceptions to this order; nor did he see any room for human freedom, except the freedom to submit one's will to the order he observed. The harmony of the universe was itself a continuing source of wonder to him, filling him with awe. The universe, he believed, was God. For the God of the Bible, who appeared to be continually breaking nature's order, he substituted the God whom he saw working through the observable order of the world. He was a pantheist, a naturalist. While he disturbed his contemporaries by denying the miracle stories, his view has helped restore the faith of many scientists since his time, and all theologians of the school of naturalism have profited from his work.[17] Spinoza was a signal that the Dark Ages were at an end and that the Enlightenment was at hand.

Liberation

The Age of the Enlightenment introduced a new era of freedom for the Jews. All the nations of Europe, although some reluctantly, tore down the ghetto walls and permitted the Jews to reenter the common life. This began about 1800, in connection with the wars of Napoleon. The Jews responded to the opportunity. They engaged in all forms of business and the professions, and enjoyed the rights and responsibilities of citizenship in the various nations of the world.

The reasons for the persecution that has followed the Jews like a curse throughout their history are difficult to grasp, for most often they have been innocent of the charges leveled against them. The causes of anti-Semitism are probably to be found along sociological lines. As we have seen, Judaism is at once a religion, a people, and a nation. The very essence of Jewish culture has made it necessary for Jews to resist all efforts to assimilate them into the surrounding cultures or to absorb them into the general bloodstream of mankind. The uniqueness which demonstrates the integrity of their faith and their moral character at the same time arouses suspicion on the part of their non-Jewish neighbors, from whom they tend to hold themselves apart.

Until the recent establishment of the Jewish state of Israel, Jews got along better with Muslims than with Christians. They even found refuge from Christian persecution among the Muslims. Jews rose to eminence and prosperity and participated in the finest cultural achievements under the caliphs of both Baghdad and Spain. It remained for Jews to undergo the most bitter persecution of their history in our own time, at the hands of the Nazis of Germany.

Calendar and Festivals

To this day Jews retain a religious calendar, the essentials of which have come down from ancient times, although its origin is shrouded in uncertainty and numerous modifications have since been introduced. It combines both solar and lunar features. The names of its lunar months are Nisan, Iyar, Sivan, Tammuz, Ab, Elul, Tishri, Heshvan, Kislev, Tebet, Shebat, Adar. In a leap year, Adar Sheni (Second Adar) is added to keep the seasons coming at the right time. In biblical days the year began with Nisan, near the spring equinox, but in our time New Year's Day, Rosh Hashanah, occurs on the first day of Tishri, the seventh month. According to Jewish reckoning, a day begins and ends at sunset.

The Sabbath is one of the distinctive observances of Judaism. It is the seventh day of the week, beginning at sunset Friday and ending at sunset Saturday, and is the most important holiday in the Jewish religion. The origin of the Sabbath is traced back to the creation, when God himself rested on the seventh day (Genesis 2:2, 3). This is the basis of the seven-day week, with one day of rest, in all Western cultures, although Christians observe the day of rest on Sunday, and Muslims on Friday. In order to preserve the sanctity of the Sabbath and to keep it as a day of rest, Jews have surrounded it by numerous prohibitions. Except in emergencies, Jews may perform no labor on the Sabbath; they are forbidden to build a fire, cook, use a telephone, or travel by any other means than by foot, and then for a distance of not more than 2,000 cubits (about 3,000 feet) one way. Orthodox Jews must live not more than 2,000 cubits from a synagogue.[18]

Pesach (the Passover; the Feast of Unleavened Bread) goes back to the preexilic period, when it was observed in the home as a celebration of the exodus from Egypt. The Book of Deuteronomy,

FIGURE 10.3   A Passover seder. (*Merrim from Monkmeyer*)

which was written in 621 B.C., transformed the festival into a national celebration which took place in Jerusalem as the culmination of a pilgrimage, with the sacrifice of the paschal lamb and the eating of the sacred meal. With the destruction of the temple in A.D. 70, the Passover became a home festival again. The sacrifice of a lamb was eliminated, but the symbolic meal, consisting of wine, the shank-bone of a lamb, bitter herbs, honey and nuts, and a roasted egg, continues to be eaten during the first night of the holiday. Each item of the meal recalls some aspect of the escape from Egyptian bondage or points to some other essential element of Jewish faith. Today the Passover is a time of family reunion. The meaning of these items is brought out during the seder, or ceremonial meal, in a dialogue between the senior member of the family and the youngest member present (see Figure 10.3).

Shebuoth (the Feast of Weeks; Pentecost) was a one-day wheat

harvest festival on the fiftieth day after the day following Passover
(Exodus 23:16; Leviticus 23:15–21). Today Pentecost is celebrated
as the time when God gave the Law (Torah) to the Hebrews. The
story of Ruth, the Moabitess who belonged to the ancestry of King
David, is read on that occasion. It symbolizes the universal element
in Judaism. The synagogue is decorated with flowers and plants as
a reminder of the ancient agricultural character of the festival.

Sukkoth (the Feast of Booths; Tabernacles) was a fall harvest
celebration which was observed for seven days, beginning on the
fifteenth day of Tishri. It was kept in memory of the wanderings
in the wilderness in the time of Moses (Exodus 23:16; Leviticus
23:33–36). This festival is celebrated today, when possible, with a
temporary booth set up in a home garden or in a synagogue courtyard in which some meals may be eaten. A portion of a synagogue covered by a removable panel in the roof to let in the sunlight or even a properly decorated window ledge may serve the
same purpose.

Yom Kippur (The Day of Atonement), observed on the tenth
day of Tishri, is a day of fasting and penitence and the most solemn
day of the Jewish year. It contains some elements that go back
to earliest times as well as elements of postexilic origin (Exodus
30:10; Leviticus 16:1–34; 23:26–32; 25:9; Numbers 29:7–11). See
pp. 174–175.

Hanukkah (the Feast of Dedication; the Feast of Lights) celebrates the rededication of the temple under Judas Maccabaeus in 165
B.C., when the lights of the temple, which had been put out by the
Syrians, were started burning again. A central feature of this celebration today is the relighting of the lights on an eight-branched
candelabrum, with one candle added each evening of the festival
until all the eight branches are ablaze. Hanukkah begins the twenty-
fifth day of Chislev, the ninth month, and lasts eight days (I Maccabees 4:52–59).

Purim, a joyous festival of one or two days beginning on the
fourteenth day of the twelfth month, celebrates the victory of the
Jews over their Persian enemies, as related in the story of Esther.

There are several other minor festivals and fasts relating to the
new moon, the seventh year, the pentecostal year, the giving of the
Law, and the destruction of the temple. The destruction of the
temple in A.D. 70 had radical effects on the ancient festivals because
some of them had been built around colorful pilgrimages to Jerusalem from all parts of Palestine, as well as from many foreign lands,

which culminated in sacrificial rites at the temple. The sacrifices and the pilgrimages were gone forever and the festivals had to be reinterpreted and adjusted to the synagogue and home. The feasts of Passover, Weeks, Booths, and Yom Kippur were most affected.

Bar Mitzvah (Son of the Commandment) is a ceremony that celebrates the coming to manhood of a Jewish youth and is observed on his thirteenth birthday. It means that now the youth has come of age, is able to make decisions, and assumes full responsibility for his religious life. According to traditional Judaism, the boy approaches the *bema,* the reading desk, in the synagogue that day and reads in Hebrew from the unpointed text of a scroll the portion of the Torah prescribed for that day as well as a similar portion from the Prophets. In order to make certain that the boy can accomplish this feat, it is the father's obligation to send him to a Hebrew teacher in preparation for the event. In some cases the youth delivers an address before the congregation. Following the synagogue service, the family, with relatives and friends, celebrate the noon meal at home. There was no similar ceremony for girls in traditional Judaism, since they were not expected to assume religious obligations outside the home. Today, however, they have a similar rite in Bath Mitzvah. Recently Reform synagogues have introduced a service of confirmation for both boys and girls in English. Bar Mitzvah first made its appearance in the synagogue no earlier than the fourteenth century A.D. and was probably introduced into Judaism under the influence of the Christian sacrament of confirmation.

Among the numerous Jewish ceremonial items are the *tallith,* a prayer shawl; the *tefellin,* cubical leather cases containing Exodus 13:1–10, 11–16, and Deuteronomy 6:4–9 and 11:13–20, which are used in connection with prayer, bound to the left forearm and about the forehead; and the *mezuzah,* a small metal case containing Deuteronomy 6:4–9 and 11:13–20, which is nailed to a doorpost of the home. Orthodox men wear hats or skullcaps during worship and sit separately from the women. During worship Scriptures are read from handwritten scrolls known as Torahs (see Figure 10.1). The scrolls often have beautifully ornamented covers.

Contemporary Jewish Groups and Movements

According to the Jewish Statistical Bureau report for 1967, there was a total of 13,782,500 Jews in the world, distributed by continents as follows: North America, 5,996,000; Central and South America, 731,450; Europe, 3,956,800; Asia, 2,785,650; Australia and New Zealand, 72,000; Africa, 240,000. New York, with 1,836,000 Jews, is the city with the largest concentration of Jews in the world.

Most Jews may be classified as either Sephardim or Ashkenazim. The Sephardim are Jews whose ancestors lived in Spain during the Middle Ages. The name is derived from *Sepharad*, the Hebrew word for Spain. When Ferdinand and Isabella expelled the Jews from Spain in 1492, some migrated to England, Holland, France, Greece, and Italy; others went to Turkey, Palestine, and North Africa; some even went to South America. And their descendants continue to live in most of these lands. The Sephardim have been characterized by the language they speak, which is Ladino—a

form of medieval Spanish with an admixture of Hebrew words written in Hebrew characters. The first Jews to arrive on the North American continent were a group of twenty-three Sephardic refugees from Brazil, who arrived in New Amsterdam, New York, in 1654. The Sephardim were the dominant element among American Jews until about 1830, when their population had grown to a total of about 10,000

The Ashkenazim are Jews whose ancestors lived in central Europe during the Middle Ages. The name is derived from *Ashkenaz,* the Hebrew word for Germany. Jews from Germany began to outnumber the Sephardim in America about 1830. During the period of 1881–1924 there was large-scale immigration of east European Jews into the United States. Another wave of Jewish immigration came to America as refugees from Nazi persecution before and during World War II. Ashkenazic Jews have usually spoken Yiddish, which is a form of German with an admixture of Hebrew and Slavic. Yiddish is the official language of Birobizhan, an autonomous Jewish district in central Siberia. Sephardim and Ashkenazim have merged in the United States, and there is no longer a sharp distinction between them.

Orthodox Judaism attempts to retain all the teachings and practices found in the Talmud. By contrast, Reform Judaism advocates abandoning restrictions in the Talmud that do not belong to the essence of Jewish faith. It thinks of Judaism as a faith one lives by; in this respect it gives less emphasis to nationalism as an essential item of Jewish religion and does not consider migration to Israel to be a necessary expression of Jewish faith. Reform congregations allow men and women to sit together during worship; the Orthodox require women to sit separately, if possible in a balcony or behind a screen. Both men and women must cover their heads in Orthodox synagogues (see Figure 10.4), but not in Reform temples. The Orthodox conduct their worship services in Hebrew, whereas Reform services are conducted in the vernacular speech. Reform congregations have introduced the use of instrumental music and choirs, both of which are unknown in Orthodox practice. Reform congregations often call their place of meeting a temple, that is, a holy place or house of God, not a temple in the ancient sense, where animal sacrifices were offered.

FIGURE 10.4   A gathering in an Orthodox synagogue in Tel Aviv. (*Consulate of Israel*)

Reform Judaism regards as its founder Abraham Geiger (1810–1874), a German rabbi, scholar, and author, who became the chief rabbi of Berlin congregations in 1870. Yet it is difficult to find the real beginning of reform in Judaism, which has been acquainted with change and reform of a radical nature from time to time all through its history. Certainly we should not overlook Philo, Maimonides, and Spinoza, men who found themselves uncomfortable in Orthodox Judaism and adopted novel and productive approaches to the study of Jewish religion.

Rabbi Isaac Mayer Wise (1819–1900), who was an outstanding leader of Reform Judaism in America, organized the Union of American Hebrew Congregations in 1873, the Hebrew Union College in 1875, and the Central Conference of American Rabbis in 1889. Since that time the Reform movement has grown rapidly in the United States. The membership, which has doubled in the last decade, has reached a total of about 1 million.

Conservative Judaism, developed in Germany by Nachman Krochmal and Zacharias Frankel, attempts to hold a mediating position between Orthodox and Reform Jews. It is progressive, yet at the same time retains as many of the traditional ceremonies as possible.

The Reconstructionist movement, which was developed in the United States by Mordecai M. Kaplan as a phase of Conservative Judaism, emphasizes the cohesive bond holding together Jewish congregations all over the world—a sense of world Jewry, especially in relation to Israel.

While there are real differences between Reform, Conservative, and Reconstruction, the three are nevertheless variations of a continuing reform movement in Judaism. All of them have recognized the necessity of adjusting Judaism to new developments in philosophical and scientific thought, as well as to the economic, political, and cultural changes that have been taking place in the world, in an effort to keep Judaism in a position to provide inspiration and to serve as a guide for its people.[19]

Exile Groups

THE FALASHAS. § The Falashas are Ethiopians residing in regions north of Lake Tana who practice a form of Judaism. In some respects their faith resembles the religion of ancient Hebrews more than it does that of modern Jews. The Falashas, who number 15,000 to 25,000, possess the Bible as it was known to Jews at the end of the biblical period, including the Apocrypha and much of the Pseudepigrapha, especially Jubilees, on which their laws are partly based, but they show no awareness of the Talmud or of other Jewish writings of the post-biblical era.

The Falashas center their life around a shrine that is somewhat similar to the synagogue, but also reminiscent of ancient Hebrew rural shrines at Bethel, Shiloh, Mizpah, Gilgal, and Shechem, which were presided over by such priests as Eli and Samuel (I Samuel 1:1–2:36); today the Falasha shrine is presided over by a priest, not a rabbi. Indeed, the Falashas appear to have no counterpart to the rabbi. Worship in the Falasha shrines consists chiefly of prayers and readings from the Scriptures, but offerings of beer, coffee, bread, and grain are also brought, and at times sheep, goats, and bulls are sacrificed on altars in their shrines and the flesh then eaten by the priests and the people. These are rites that would be unthinkable in the Jewish synagogue as it is generally known.[20]

The religion of the Falashas also includes monks and monasteries, which are no doubt the product of Christian influence. The language of the Bible used by the Falashas is Geez (old Ethiopic), which again shows indebtedness to their Christian neighbors. Their personification of the Sabbath as if it were a goddess, or at least an angel, throughout their Commandments of the Sabbath, is unique.[21] Another unusual element in their faith is the belief that the name of the angel who is to sound the trumpet for the resurrection of the dead and the Day of Judgment is Michael, not Gabriel, as it is in the Western tradition.[22]

The origin of the Falashas remains a mystery. It may be that the Falashas are descended from Jews who came into Ethiopia from Egypt or Arabia, but have since become assimilated into the racial stock of Ethiopia. Yet it is not impossible that the Falashas are descendants of persons of Ethiopian blood who were converted to Judaism by Jewish missionaries. (There was a considerable missionary interest among Jews about the time of the rise of Christianity.) The Falashas themselves say that they are descended from King Solomon and the Queen of Sheba, but scholars do not take this view seriously.[23]

INDIAN JEWS. § The various forces that led to the dispersion of Jews from ancient Palestine carried some of them into such remote parts of the earth that they lost contact with the mainstream of Jewish life. This is true of the early Jewish settlements in India, two of which have survived. One of these is in Cochin, on the Malabar Coast of south India, where about 1,000 Jews still reside; another is located in villages around Bombay, which include some 10,000 persons. There is no certainty about the dates or the manner of arrival of either of these colonies in India, but in both cases they have retained the essentials of Jewish faith, even though their members have taken on the brown color of the local Indian inhabitants.

The Jewish communities around Bombay are the better known of the two. They call themselves *Bene Israel,* "Sons of Israel," and until recently rejected the name Jew. They had lost their knowledge of Hebrew and had no copies of the sacred books. For centuries, without any synagogue, they lived solely by oral tradition. Their vernacular speech was the Marathi of their Indian neighbors.

The Bene Israel practice circumcision, keep the Sabbath, and observe important elements of the dietary regulations and several of the festivals, although they call them by Indian names. They do not show any familiarity with the Talmudic tradition, nor do they keep either Hanukkah or Purim. It may be that their separation from historic Judaism took place in pre-Maccabean times. Their color would seem to indicate much intermarriage with Indians; yet when they were discovered in modern times they were adhering strictly to marriage within their own group, and they frowned on mixed marriages to such an extent that they treated the offspring of such unions as if they were outcasts. The oldest synagogue of the Bene Israel was built in 1796. Renewal of contact with world Judaism has brought new life to the Bene Israel, and about 7,000 of them have migrated to the new state of Israel.[24]

CHINESE JEWS. § At some early time, another colony of Jews established itself at Kaifeng in the Honan province of China, where they apparently prospered for some centuries. Remains of their buildings, including a synagogue, have survived. But by the outbreak of World War II only a few of these Jews remained. Whether any survived the war and its aftermath is unknown. Since they lived in the midst of a Muslim population, it may be that they were finally absorbed by it.

THE YEMENITES. § The Jews of Yemen, on the southern tip of Arabia, are another important exile group which has survived to our time. They never completely lost contact with world Judaism, and they have retained a strict loyalty to the faith. Although they have kept a knowledge of Hebrew, they have adopted Arabic as their vernacular speech, and they live, dress, and look like Arabs. Many of these Yemenites have returned to Israel.

Martin Buber and Existentialism

Martin Bubar (1878–1965), of whose work we have taken note in Chapter 1, was born in Vienna and educated in Austria, Germany, and Switzerland. After a career in Germany as author, editor, and professor, he migrated to Israel in 1938 to become a professor at the Hebrew University at Jerusalem. Fifteen years later he retired to devote the remainder of his active life to literary work.

Known as a member of the existentialist school of religious thought, Buber achieved fame through his little book *I and Thou,* which has been acclaimed by both Christians and Jews, by psychiatrists and artists, as well as by philosophers and theologians. His thesis is that one becomes a person only in relation to other persons. Indeed, in his sense there is no such thing as the isolated existence of an I or a Thou, that is, of an I or a You. Confrontation with a Thou, in which the I fully recognizes the freedom and dignity of the Thou, Buber calls an event. Such an event has a revelatory character. The I reveals itself to the Thou, and the Thou reveals itself to the I. Neither could know the other except by a free and gracious act of revelation. The event is, moreover, a contact with the Eternal Thou, for the freedom that characterizes a person is the very essence of the Eternal.

What Buber calls an "event" in such an experience, Mircea Eliade would call a "hierophany," and Rudolf Otto a "vision of the Holy." For Paul Tillich it would be the new creation or contact with the Ground of Being. But Buber adds to the wonder of his insight by showing that a Thou can be transformed into an It, and an It into a Thou; furthermore, that an I which refuses to escape from its isolated loneliness by means of an I-Thou encounter deprives itself of the possibility of becoming a real person, gradually withdrawing into a void of hopeless mental illness, left with no one he can still address as Thou. In rejecting a free and equal encounter with every human Thou, such a person, at the same time, turns away from the only door that leads into the shrine where the Eternal dwells.

Buber has thus given a singular expression to the universal character inherent in his Jewish faith. Like the biblical prophets, he sees genuine hierophanies in the moral relations between persons, but God also speaks to him in luminous moments as he contemplates the wonders of nature. Buber's language has such clarity, such freedom, such universality that it offers authentic expression to high monotheism, wherever it is found and whatever name it bears.

Zionism

The ancient desire of the Jews to be a nation has caused a latent nationalism to survive among them, stronger among the Orthodox than elsewhere, and the structure of Zionism has this element of faith as its foundation. Also, some Jewish leaders, like Moses Mendelssohn (1729–1786), were alarmed by the effect of liberation; many Jews deserted Judaism, and became fully assimilated into the contemporary culture. Zionism was advocated as a means of reviving Judaism as a religion and culture which had a value worth preserving for its own sake.

The founder of modern Zionism was Theodor Herzl (1860–1904), a Hungarian Jew whose interest in a homeland for Jews in Palestine was aroused by anti-Semitism in Europe. Theodor Herzl called the first World Zionist Congress in 1897 at Basel, which marked the beginning of active work toward a restoration in Palestine.

During World War I, Great Britain, in order to gain assistance from Jews against Turkey, promised to support the establishment of a homeland for Jews in Palestine. When Britain received a mandate over Palestine at the end of the war, large numbers of Jews began to return to it. But it was the effort of Adolf Hitler to exterminate the Jews of Germany during World War II that finally aroused Jews, as well as many others, to the need for a Jewish homeland in Palestine. Much of the support for Zionism was therefore based on the humanitarian desire to find a place of refuge for persecuted and homeless Jews.

After Britain withdrew from the Palestine mandate, under pressure of hostility and violence from both Jews and Arabs, an independent Jewish state, under the name of Israel, was proclaimed May 14, 1948. A short war with Arab states followed, but an armistice was arranged by the United Nations.

While the Israelis have made substantial progress in rebuilding their homeland, the difficulties have been enormous. Much of their country is not suitable for agriculture, and other resources are limited. Arab hostility to Israel is strong; it has grown out of the feeling that the Jews are dispossessing the Arabs, who have been at home in Palestine, under one government or another, since Omar, one of Muhammad's generals, captured Jerusalem in A.D. 638. Besides, Arabs trace their lineage back to Ishmael, son of Abraham, so that Palestine is a holy land to Muslims as well as to Jews and Christians.

NOTES

1. W. R. Farmer, "Essenes," in George A. Buttrick, ed., *The Interpreter's Dictionary of the Bible* (Nashville: Abingdon, 1962), II, 143–149.
2. Josephus, *Antiquities of the Jews*, XII, ii, 1.
3. B. M. Metzger, "Ancient Versions," in Buttrick, *op. cit.*, IV, 749–760.
4. F. H. Colson and G. H. Whittaker, eds., *Philo, an English Translation*, 10 vols., Loeb Classical Library (Cambridge: Harvard University Press, 1929–1941).
5. Josephus, *op. cit.*, XIII, x, 1, and XIII, xi, 3. Cf. M. H. Pope, "Proselyte," in Buttrick, *op. cit.*, III, 921–931.
6. Herbert Danby, *The Mishnah* (London: Oxford University Press, 1933); George Foote Moore, *Judaism in the First Christian Centuries*, 3 vols. (Cambridge: Harvard University Press, 1927–1930).
7. H. L. Strack, *Introduction to the Talmud and Midrash* (Philadelphia: Jewish Publication Society, 1933).
8. Cf. Bernard Revel, *The Karaite Halakah* (Philadelphia: Press Cahan Printing Co., 1913).
9. Leon Nemoy, ed., *Karaite Anthology* (New Haven: Yale University Press, 1952), p. xxiii.
10. *Ibid.*, p. xxv.
11. Zvi Ankori, *Karaites in Byzantium* (New York: Columbia University Press, 1959).
12. Isidore Epstein, *Judaism* (Baltimore: Penguin, 1966), pp. 223–251.
13. Moses Maimonides, *The Guide of the Perplexed* (Chicago: University of Chicago Press, 1963).
14. This abstract of the thirteen principles is based on the text of Charles B. Chavel, *The Book of Divine Commandments of Moses Maimonides* (London: Soncino, 1940), pp. 400–408.
15. Cf. Joseph H. Hertz, *The Authorized Daily Prayerbook* (New York: Bloch, 1948), pp. 248 ff.
16. Louis Wirth, *The Ghetto* (Chicago: University of Chicago Press, 1928), pp. 21–32.
17. Harry A. Wolffson, *The Philosophy of Spinoza* (New York: Meridian Books, 1960).
18. On Jewish festivals and fasts, cf. Meyer Waxman, *A Handbook of Judaism*

(New York: Bloch, 1947), pp. 42–82. Waxman (pp. 33–37) explains that the rabbis devised interpretations of the Sabbath laws which make it possible to convert certain city streets into "private areas" by means of a legal fiction, so that burdens can be carried through them on the Sabbath; also he explains a similar fiction which makes it possible to travel more than 2,000 cubits on the Sabbath.

19. Epstein, *op. cit.*, pp. 287–318.
20. Wolf Leslau, ed., *Falasha Anthology* (New Haven: Yale University Press, 1951) presents a translation of all these writings together with an individual introduction to each document and a general introduction to the life and religion of the Falashas, also an up-to-date bibliography, pp. xxiii, xxvi, xxvii, xlii.
21. *Ibid.,* pp. 4–39.
22. *Ibid.,* p. 140, Prayer 38.
23. Solomon Grayzel, *A History of the Jews* (Philadelphia: Jewish Publication Society, 1947), pp. 735–737, 740–750.
24. E. Elias and E. Isaac, *Jews in India* (Ernakulam, India: Hindustan Printers), Vols. 1963 and 1964.

THE HEBREW LEGACY

Christianity began as a movement within Judaism. John the Baptist, Jesus, the Twelve Apostles, and Paul were Jews, as were apparently all the members of the first church in Jerusalem. Gentiles did not gain admission into the Christian churches for some time after that. What Jesus and Paul had in mind was to reform Judaism, not to replace it. Christianity emerged as a separate religion only when it had been rejected by the majority of Jews. The final bond holding early Christians and Jews together had been the temple at Jerusalem; many ancient Christians, including Paul, continued to worship at the temple, when possible, as long as they lived. When the temple was destroyed in A.D. 70, the last formal tie between Jews and Christians was severed, and the two faiths emerged as separate religions. Yet, even after the separation, Christianity retained the essentials of Jewish theology as fundamental to its own faith.

The Hebrew Bible was another one of Christianity's heritages. Christian faith has always been understood as a fulfillment and continuation of the prophetic hopes of Judaism itself, and its theology cannot be understood without the Hebrew Scriptures. The stories of the Old Testament, the Psalms, the wisdom literature, the prophets, and the moral codes are all indispensable for this purpose. There have been problems involved in taking over certain parts of the Old Testament, which have seemed primitive and barbarous to some Christians. Marcion, about A.D. 140, rejected the Old Testament entirely, holding that the God of the Old Testament was a monster, and certainly not the Father of the Lord Jesus Christ. Other Chris-

FIGURE 11.1 The figure of Christ on the fourth-century chalice of Antioch. (*The Metropolitan Museum of Art, The Cloisters Collection, 1950*)

tians, in a romantic frame of mind, have turned the primitive and barbarous features of the Old Testament into allegories of Christian truth by stripping them of their original meanings. But neither outright rejection nor pious allegory is satisfactory to sophisticated modern Christians, who recognize the primitive survivals for what they are: evidence of the early periods of Hebrew culture, corresponding to similar things in other cultures, but still having both historical and religious value. Most of the Old Testament is appreciated by rigorous scholarship for the excellence of its literary qualities and spiritual insights.

Another legacy of Jews to Christians was the synagogue. Jesus, Paul, and other Jewish Christians had learned how to worship in the synagogue, and they brought these forms of worship into the Christian churches. To this day a Christian church service follows the general pattern that is characteristic of the synagogue: one finds reading of the Scriptures, prayers, hymns, and a sermon. A few Christian churches follow the Orthodox synagogue in rejecting instrumental music; most churches, however, like the Reform synagogue, have enriched their worship by its use, as well as by choirs, in which they also follow the pattern of the Hebrew temple.

A CHRISTIAN SCRIPTURE

Christians have also followed Jewish precedent in creating a Scripture, the New Testament, which is somewhat parallel to the Hebrew canon. At the same time, they have retained a belief in the Hebrew Bible as inspired Scripture. Therefore they now have two groups of Scriptures, the Old Testament and the New Testament—both terms being Christian, not Jewish. Jews say only the Law, the Prophets, and the Writings. All of these, from the Jewish point of view, record the covenant (testament) between God and Abraham, which they regard as the *one* covenant God has made. They do not say *old* or *new*, but simply *the covenant*. By contrast, Christians believe that God made a *new* covenant with man through Christ. They therefore refer to the covenant with Abraham as the Old Covenant and to the covenant through Christ as the New Covenant. The writings that record the covenant through Abraham are the Old Testament. The Hebrew canon was formed in stages: Law about 400 B.C.; Prophets about 200 B.C.; Writings about A.D. 100.

The Hebrew Scriptures were the only Scriptures early Christians had up to about A.D. 150; and they usually read these Scriptures in Greek translations, the reason being that after about A.D. 50 most Christians spoke Greek, not Hebrew, and the Septuagint Greek translation had been available for a century or more. The Septuagint (LXX) is the best-known Greek translation of the Old Testament, but at least six more were made during the early Christian period.[1] The Septuagint was made in Egypt about 300–100 B.C. for Jews who had lost the knowledge of Hebrew; the name is derived from the tradition that seventy Jewish scholars collaborated in making the translation. During the second Christian century some translations of the Scriptures into Latin also began to appear.

The first indication in the Bible itself that Christians were beginning to consider some of their own writings as Scripture occurs in II Peter 3:15–16 as follows:

So also our beloved brother Paul wrote to you according to the wisdom given to him, speaking of this as he does in all his letters. There are some things in them hard to understand, which the ignorant and unsteadfast twist to their own destruction, as they do the other scriptures.

Here the author shows that when he is writing this letter, the letters of Paul have already attained the status of Scripture. When he says "the other scriptures," he means the Hebrew Scriptures.

Tradition has attributed a total of fourteen letters to Paul. They are I and II Thessalonians, I and II Corinthians, Galatians, Romans, Colossians, Ephesians, Philemon, Philippians, I and II Timothy, Titus, and Hebrews. But Hebrews, as shown by its literary style and thought, was not written by Paul, and we are not certain who wrote it. I and II Timothy and Titus, called the Pastoral Letters, we think, were written by Paul, but revised after they came from his hand. There is some doubt of the authenticity of Ephesians and Colossians. Otherwise the Pauline letters are accepted with reasonable certainty. They are genuine letters, all written between A.D. 50 and 64, in the course of his missionary journeys and imprisonment, to churches and individuals, concerning their religious problems.

The Gospel of Mark is the earliest of the four Gospels, written about A.D. 70. Matthew and Luke, which are probably independent revisions of Mark, appeared about A.D. 85–95. The Gospel of John, representing a sharply different tradition of the life of Jesus, was written around A.D. 100. The Acts of the Apostles was written by the author of Luke and is a continuation of his record of early Christianity. It should be dated about the same time as Luke.

The General Letters and the Revelation of John were written between A.D. 100 and 150. The General Letters include James, I and II Peter, I, II, and III John, and Jude.

There has been uncertainty about the inspiration of some of these writings. The Muratorian Canon, a list of the New Testament writings drawn up about A.D. 200, omits Hebrews, I and II Peter, and III John. On the other hand, it contains the Wisdom of Solomon and a late Christian book called the Revelation of Peter. The Clermont List, formulated in Egypt about A.D. 300, includes the Letter of Barnabas, the Shepherd of Hermas, the Acts of Paul, and the Revelation of Peter, all of which were later rejected by the church. The first time in Christian history that the New Testament writings are listed exactly as they now occur is in the Festal Letter of Athanasius of A.D. 367. It is nevertheless true that most items in the New Testament canon were fixed by A.D. 200.

The first effort to establish a New Testament canon was made by the heretic Marcion about A.D. 140. After discarding the Old Testament outright, he accepted the Gospel of Luke, Galatians, I and II Corinthians, Romans, I and II Thessalonians, Ephesians, Colossians, Philippians, and Philemon. Marcion's list was refused by the church, but its publication probably aroused the church to the need of setting forth a canon of its own as a guide in Christian doctrine.[2]

JOHN, THE FORERUNNER

The first person of importance introduced in the story of Christianity is John the Baptist. His name is John, the son of Zachariah (Luke 1:5) and he is called "the Baptist" because he baptizes people. Mark, the oldest of the four Gospels, introduces the prophet John as follows:

As it is written in Isaiah the prophet,

"Behold, I send my messenger before thy face,
who shall prepare thy way;
the voice of one crying in the wilderness:
Prepare the way of the Lord,
make his paths straight—"

John the baptizer appeared in the wilderness, preaching a baptism of repentance for the forgiveness of sins. And there went out to him all the country of Judea, and all the people of Jerusalem; and they were baptized by him in the Jordan, confessing their sins. Now John was clothed with camel's hair, and had a leather girdle about his waist, and ate locusts and wild honey. And he preached, saying, "After me comes he who is mightier than I, the thong of whose sandals I am not worthy to stoop down and untie. I have baptized you with water; but he will baptize you with the Holy Spirit." [Mark 1:2–8.]

The first two lines of this quotation from the Prophets are from Malachi 3:1, which, in its original context, is a prediction that before the coming of the day of the Lord, the prophet Elijah will return. Its location here shows the belief of the early church that John was in some sense Elijah.

The second part of the prophetic quotation is from Isaiah 40:3, a passage in which the Second Isaiah encourages the exiles in Babylonia to get ready for the coming day of the Lord, when they will be permitted to return home. Early Christians took this to refer to the coming of the Messiah; to them, the Lord in this passage meant the Messiah.

This same passage was used by a community of Essenes living in the Wadi Qumran on the Dead Sea.[3] They took it to refer to their own life there in the Wilderness, the name by which the barren region west of the Dead Sea was then known.[4] The use of this passage by John (John 1:23) suggests that he had formerly had some contact with that Essene community; he may even have been an Essene himself. Luke 1:80 says of the child John that he "grew and became strong in spirit, and he was in the wilderness till the day of his manifestation to Israel." Again, in Luke 3:2, "The word of God came to John the son of Zachariah in the wilderness; and he went into all the region about the Jordan, preaching a baptism of repentance for the forgiveness of sins."

This introduction of the prophet John at the beginning of the story of Christianity indicates that the dearth of prophecy felt in Judaism since about 400 B.C. had now come to an end. The new

Christian movement, especially during the first century of its existence, believed that all of its important leaders were endowed with
the gift of prophecy and spoke by inspiration of the Holy Spirit.

JESUS, THE FOUNDER

Jesus is recognized by his followers, as well as by historians of
religion, as the founder of Christianity. This places him in the company of Confucius, Gautama Buddha, Zoroaster, Moses, and Muhammad. But it is the judgment of other persons, not of Jesus himself. He nowhere refers to himself as the founder of Christianity or
any other religion. So far as we can tell, he understood his life and
destiny as the fulfillment of Judaism itself. It was only after his
death that conflicts of belief between the followers of Jesus and
the great body of Jews brought about the separation of these movements into two different religions.

For our knowledge of Jesus, we are dependent almost entirely
on the New Testament. Only a few scattered references to him are
found in other writings of his own time, and they add nothing of
consequence. Within the New Testament, we must base our historical knowledge of Jesus almost solely on what appears in the four
Gospels.

Mark, the earliest Gospel, introduces Jesus as a fully grown man,
about thirty years of age, coming from Galilee, along with other
pilgrims, to hear the prophetic preaching of John the Baptist. Mark
contains nothing about the birth or childhood of Jesus, except the
following statement in 6:3, "Is not this the carpenter, the son of
Mary and brother of James and Joses and Judas and Simon, and are
not his sisters here with us?" Nor does Mark give any information
about the genealogy of Jesus.

The Gospel of Mark was written at Rome about forty years after
the death of Jesus. During these forty years, the sayings of Jesus,
the deeds he performed, the stories about him, the things that
happened to him, were carried in the memory of his disciples. Oral
tradition, as a method of transmitting culture from one generation
to another, was well known to the ancient Hebrews.

All four of the Gospels were written anonymously, as were all
the other historical writings of the Bible. Such books were thought
of as community books, not as the property of individuals. Yet

Mark, a native Jew of Jerusalem, is believed to have written the Gospel that bears his name. He had not been one of the disciples of Jesus during his lifetime, nor was he one of the Twelve Apostles. He had never been present to hear Jesus teach, according to Papias about A.D. 140, who gives us our earliest tradition about the author of Mark. But he had acted as interpreter for Peter. After Peter's death in Rome, about A.D. 64, the church there requested that Mark write down what he could recall of Peter's teachings about Jesus.[5] Mark had evidently become a Christian during the early days of the church in Jerusalem. Later he became active as a missionary, along with Paul, Barnabas, and Peter.

But Mark's Gospel is brief and fragmentary as a biography of Jesus, as well as inadequate in presenting his teachings. When the Gospels of Matthew and Luke were written a few years later, based on Mark and other documents accessible to their authors, as well as on oral traditions, both of them supplemented Mark in these respects. John, however, a still later Gospel, also gives no information about the birth and childhood of Jesus. It may be that in some circles of the early church there was no interest in these matters.

Birth and Infancy

While both Matthew and Luke say that Jesus was born in Bethlehem, there is in other respects considerable difference between their accounts. According to Luke, Joseph and Mary, the parents of Jesus, lived in Nazareth of Galilee, about eighty miles north of Bethlehem, from which they went to Bethlehem to register themselves in compliance with a decree of Caesar Augustus. While they were there, Jesus was born. Matthew indicates that the parents lived in Bethlehem at the time Jesus was born, but later moved to Nazareth because they feared Herod Archelaus (Matthew 2:22, 23). Luke reports that the annunciation was made to Mary (1:26–28); Matthew, that it was made to Joseph (1:18–25). Luke gives an account of the birth of John the Baptist and Mary's visit with Elizabeth, John's mother (1:39–56), and several beautiful poems related to these incidents, but Matthew has none of these. Luke reports the appearance of angels to shepherds, announcing the birth of the Messiah, and the visit of the shepherds to see the child in a manger in Bethlehem; Luke tells of the circumcision of the child and his presentation in the temple.

Matthew, on the other hand, tells of the coming of Wise Men

from the East, the murder of the male children of Bethlehem, the flight of the holy family to Egypt, and their removal to Nazareth after returning from Egypt. Only Luke tells of the visit of the family of Jesus to Jerusalem when he was twelve years of age, where he engaged in discussions with distinguished teachers.

There is also some difference between Matthew and Luke, with reference to the genealogy of Jesus. Luke carries the genealogy from Joseph through seventy-seven generations all the way back to Adam, the son of God. This is the only place in the Bible where Adam is called God's son (Luke 3:38). Matthew goes back forty-two generations to Abraham, by three stages of fourteen each, from Abraham to David, from David to the Exile, from the Exile to Joseph. And the lineages themselves from David to Jesus are quite different. Luke traces the lineage through David's son Nathan, whereas Matthew traces it through King Solomon.

Both Luke and Matthew relate that Jesus was born of a virgin mother. Matthew 1:23 states that the virgin birth of Jesus was a fulfillment of a prophecy in Isaiah 7:14, as follows: "Behold, a young woman shall conceive and bear a son, and shall call his name Immanuel." Matthew quotes this passage from a Greek translation which renders "young woman" as "virgin" (*parthenos*).

The Baptism of Jesus

There are interesting variations in the four Gospels with reference to the baptism of Jesus. Matthew, Mark, and Luke, called the Synoptic Gospels because of the similarity of their accounts of Jesus, agree that Jesus was baptized by John the Baptist. The Gospel of John, however, does not report his baptism. The accounts in the Synoptic Gospels are found in Mark 1:9–11, Matthew 3:13–17, and Luke 3:21–22.

Mark presents the record as follows:

In those days Jesus came from Nazareth of Galilee and was baptized by John in the Jordan. And when he came up out of the water, immediately he saw the heavens opened and the Spirit descending upon him like a dove; and a voice came from heaven, "Thou art my beloved Son; with thee I am well pleased."

Jesus is presented as God's son in the New Testament in various ways. We have already seen how the infancy stories of Matthew and Luke explain this by the idea of a virgin birth. As Mark portrays the baptism of Jesus, the idea of adoption is implied. At that moment God adopts Jesus as his son. Adoption was well known in the ancient world and was considered an honor. Several of the Roman emperors adopted promising young men to succeed them on the throne.

The Gospel of John shows a preference for the figure of a spiritual birth (3:3–8). Paul and the author of Hebrews, neither of whom mentions the virgin birth, both think of Jesus as God's eternal Son (Colossians 1:15–17; Hebrews 1:2, 3). There were a number of persons in the early church, however, who assumed that Jesus was the son of Joseph, husband of Mary. This assumption is implied by the genealogies of Jesus in Matthew and Luke. Philip refers to Jesus in John 1:45 as the son of Joseph. In Luke 2:48 Mary implies that Jesus is Joseph's son. All these views existed side by side in the early Christian writings, expressing different ways of understanding Jesus; apparently no conflict was felt between them.[6]

The Temptation

The temptation of Jesus is recorded in all three of the Synoptic Gospels: Mark 1:12, 13, Matthew 4:1–11, Luke 4:1–13. Although Mark has reported the incident very briefly, Matthew and Luke have followed a fuller version available to them in another source. Their accounts agree closely, the only significant difference being that the second and third temptations are given in reverse order. Matthew's is as follows:

Then Jesus was led up by the Spirit into the wilderness to be tempted by the devil. And he fasted forty days and forty nights, and afterward he was hungry. And the tempter came and said to him, "If you are the Son of God, command these stones to become loaves of bread." But he answered, "It is written,

'Man shall not live by bread alone,
but by every word that proceeds from the mouth of God.' "

Then the devil took him to the holy city, and set him on the pinnacle of the temple, and said to him, "If you are the Son of God, throw yourself down; for it is written,

'He will give his angels charge of you,'

and

> 'On their hands they will bear you up,
> lest you strike your foot against a stone.' "

Jesus said to him, "Again it is written, 'You shall not tempt the Lord your God.' " Again, the devil took him to a very high mountain, and showed him all the kingdoms of the world and the glory of them; and he said to him, "All these I will give you, if you will fall down and worship me." Then Jesus said to him, "Begone, Satan! for it is written,

> 'You shall worship the Lord your God
> and him only shall you serve.' "

This story of the temptation of Jesus presents the moral struggle of the spiritual life with a clarity not attained in the Old Testament, although Hebrew writers did find ways of dealing with the moral struggle. The temptation of Adam and Eve in Genesis 3 is presented in the form of a fable, where the principle of evil is a talking serpent. Satan first appears in Job as one of the sons of God, although a villainous one, and able to do only what God permits him to do. But in the temptation of Jesus, for the first time in the Bible, Satan talks to a man face to face, entirely free, as the enemy of both God and man. Here he reminds us of the dualism of Zoroaster, where Ahriman sets himself against Ahura Mazda, or Aeshma Daeva against Sraosha, in a perpetual struggle.

Miracles

The Gospels record that Jesus did many wonderful things. He performed deeds of healing of different types. Among those recorded in the Gospel of Mark are fever (1:30, 31), leprosy (1:40–42), paralysis (2:1–12), a withered hand (3:1–5), demon possession (1:23–27; 5:1–20; 7:24–30), blindness (8:22–26; 10:46–52), epilepsy (9:14–29).

Other miracle stories Mark records are as follows: Jesus stills a storm (4:35–41), multiplies loaves and fishes (6:30–44; 8:1–9), walks on the sea (6:47–51), withers a fig tree (11:12–14).

This list of wonders performed by Jesus in relieving illness and in connection with inanimate nature is typical of miracles ascribed to him in the other Gospels; most of them are repeated in Matthew and Luke, although Matthew and Luke, as well as John, have unique miracle stories.

What Jesus called demon possession, the modern physicians would probably call mental illness. Some of the techniques Jesus used to cure demon possession have counterparts in modern therapy. Suggestion is close to the faith that Jesus used, the commands that he gave to the possessed. Jesus understood how to use his own strong personality in order to give strength and courage to the weak and the fearful (see Figure 11.1).[7]

We can understand some of the miracle stories associated with Jesus from the point of view of our medical knowledge. Physicians recognize the importance of trust, of faith, in a patient. Once he loses confidence in God as well as man, there is not much hope for a seriously ill man; on the other hand, a strong faith is conducive to good health. Many of the healings described in the Gospels may actually have occurred. Yet some of the cases, such as curing leprosy and raising the dead, are beyond our understanding.

Miracle stories similar to those associated with Jesus are encountered in the Old Testament in connection with such men as Moses and the prophets, especially Elijah and Elisha. Such stories were almost always associated with outstanding religious leaders of antiquity, and constituted a tribute to the man's greatness.

The Theology Jesus Taught

Since Jesus was a teacher, we should not expect to find his ideas presented in the form of a theological system. The common people usually made up his audiences, and even his apostles were simple laymen. At least four of them were fishermen from the Sea of Galilee, probably with little education. Apparently his plan was to reach the masses of the people; he did not concern himself very much with reaching the Scribes, Pharisees, Sadducees, and Essenes.

Jesus was born a Jew and was trained in all the institutions of Judaism, first in his family and the synagogue in Nazareth, and later in Jerusalem, where he made occasional trips and could see and participate in the great spectacle of the temple services. We would, therefore, be safe in assuming that the fundamental principles of Jewish thought and faith constituted the foundation of his own theology. As we have already stated, what he had in mind was to reform Judaism, not to replace it. His point of view comes out clearly in the following passage, from Matthew 5:17–19, where it stands in a prominent position in the Sermon on the Mount:

Think not that I have come to abolish the law and the prophets; I have come not to abolish them but to fulfil them. For truly, I say to you, till heaven and earth pass away, not an iota, not a dot, will pass from the law until all is accomplished. Whoever then relaxes one of the least of these commandments and teaches men so, shall be called least in the kingdom of heaven; but he who does them and teaches them shall be called great in the kingdom of heaven.

While Jesus mentions specifically his devotion to the Law and the Prophets, it is improbable that he meant to exclude the Writings. Indeed, in verse 18 he designates the whole by the word "law" alone. It is in this passage that Jesus introduces "the kingdom of heaven," a phrase that seems to have occurred frequently in his teaching, but is reported only in the Gospel of Matthew. It has the same meaning as "kingdom of God," "heaven" in this phrase being a metonym for "God."

The Great Commandment

It is not characteristic of the Bible, either the Old Testament or the New, to formulate systems of theology. The very idea of a system of theology derives from a culture familiar with philosophy; the word itself is a philosophical concept. But the Hebrews had never developed a philosophical tradition like that of the Greeks; they had no Socrates, no Plato, no Aristotle, all of whom proceeded on the assumption that truth is a discovery of the human mind, not a revelation from God. What the Hebrews believed was that all truth comes from God, that it is a divine revelation.

The difference between these two points of view is shown by the different ways in which they formulate truth. Philosophy speaks in terms of rational propositions and principles that are thought to be universal. Hebrew thought, by contrast, never mentions either propositions or principles of a secular character; instead, it formulates truth in the form of commandments, since it conceives of God as a king who issues decrees or commandments by which people are to live. The best instance of this is the Decalogue, the Ten Commandments, which in principle summarizes all Hebrew religion. The language of the prophets is also somewhat along these lines. The prophet delivered his oracles from God in the form of "Thou shalt" and "Thou shalt not."

This Hebrew method of formulating truth is illustrated in Matthew's version (22:35–40) of the question a lawyer asked Jesus:

And one of them, a lawyer, asked him a question, to test him. "Teacher, which is the greatest commandment in the law?" And he said to him,

"You shall love the Lord your God with all your heart, with all your soul, and with all your mind. This is the great and the first commandment. And the second is like it, You shall love your neighbor as yourself. On these two commandments depend all the law and the prophets."

In this passage Jesus indicates that love is the essential element of religion. First of all, man must love God; second, he must love his neighbor. In other words, all religion is grounded in man's love for God, an idea that is characteristic of the religion of the Bible. It is unlike philosophical ethics, which sets forth the virtues of temperance, prudence, fortitude, and justice on a purely rational basis. While these Greek virtues are good, what Jesus teaches is that we should practice them because we love God, because they are his commandments. We do our duty because we love God, not because it is pleasant or because it seems rational or wise to do so.

If we attempted to summarize the theology of Jesus, therefore, its first principle would have to be, to love God; and the second, to love man. This moral quality is at the heart of the theology of Jesus.

God's Love for Man

The principle of man's love, according to Jesus, is based on God's prior love for man; both of these principles he takes from Hebrew religion. At the beginning of their history, Hebrew writers hold, God himself took the initiative in forming a covenant with man, in this way surrounding the man he had created with a continuing expression of his concern. In regard to this latter point, however, Jesus goes beyond the teachings of Hebrew religion. According to Jesus, God's love is for man as an individual, as a person, not as a nation, not even as a people. This view also has its roots in the Old Testament: the prophets, in their maturity, saw God as universal, exercising dominion over all nations, loving them all just as he did the Hebrews. While this is especially clear in the Second Isaiah and in Jonah, such prophetic universalism was not fully accepted until it found expression in early Christianity.

In the teaching of Jesus, the survival of the Jewish nation and people, or of any other nation or people, has disappeared from the covenant of God with man. No nation or people, in any century or land, or any form of political government, has a right, according to Jesus, to hold that God has guaranteed its existence.

Jesus reflected the mood of the Hellenistic age, when a majority of men everywhere had developed a yearning for individual security, personal redemption, by contrast with the mood of the past when all the peoples of antiquity—Hebrews, Assyrians, Babylonians, Persians, Greeks—believed that the function of the gods was to protect their nations. Religion was in every case a state establishment, so that one of the main duties of government was to support the priesthoods and shrines. As the various nations collapsed and fell, however, this faith in the gods was shattered and lost its hold on the people. The religion of Jesus is oriented toward this new hunger of individual persons for redemption.

Jesus makes his appeal to individuals, not to nations. Some of his best-known parables were so formulated as to present God's love for individual human beings. The fundamental idea behind them was that God loves every person; that no one is ever so great or so small as to be beyond the need and the reach of God's love.

This principle is well set forth in the trilogy of parables in the fifteenth chapter of Luke. In 15:3–7 God is represented by a shepherd who cares for a hundred sheep, which he grazes in a wilderness. When one sheep gets lost, he leaves the other ninety-nine and goes in search of the one that has gone astray. In 15:8–10 God is represented by a woman with ten silver pieces. When she loses one, she immediately lights a lamp and sweeps the house until she recovers it. Then she calls together her neighbors to rejoice with her because she has found the lost coin. After each of these parables Jesus clearly states their point, "There is joy before the angels of God over one sinner who repents."

The third parable, 15:11–32, is the well-known story of the prodigal son. A man of some property had two sons. When the younger son had decided to go out into the world and try his fortune, he asked for his part of the estate, which his father gave him. Soon he squandered his money, and, finding himself in difficulties, he had to work at debasing employment to get bread. Then he realized what a foolish mistake he had made in leaving his father's home. Assuming that his conduct had put him beyond reinstatement as a son, he decided to return home and ask to be received as a slave. But his father welcomed him with joy and announced his return with a festive celebration.

The point of the parable is that God allows a man freedom; he never coerces man's will. Man is allowed to make his mistakes, yet God's love for him never dies. So in a highly theological passage, expressing early Christian faith, Jesus says,

Come to me, all who labor and are heavy-laden, and I will give you rest. Take my yoke upon you, and learn from me; for I am gentle and lowly in heart, and you will find rest for your souls. For my yoke is easy, and my burden is light. [Matthew 11:28-30.]

God as Judge of Man

God loves man, but he is also man's judge; his love is not a sentimental love. Since it is God's desire to develop moral character in man, his love is always accompanied by discipline. The father in the parable of the prodigal son does not forgive his son and receive him back until he returns in a penitent mood, disciplined by his own actions. God, therefore, combines in himself the loving father and the just judge. While he yearns to forgive man, forgiveness is possible only to the man who has given up his rebellion and defiance and submitted his will to the will of God. Submission is man's part; forgiveness is God's. Although God has created man free, he holds him responsible for what he does in his freedom.

Jesus formulates the principle of justice in terms of eschatology. He often refers to a last judgment at the end of time; in this respect he agrees with the thought of Zoroaster, which had already made its penetration into Jewish apocalyptic writings. In their classical period, the Hebrew prophets expressed the belief that every man gets his just recompense in this life. Some of the Hebrew thinkers, however, notably Job and the Second Isaiah, recognized that the idea of just recompense in this life is untenable; it simply does not correspond with what we actually see about us in the world. Yet they still believed in a just God—that in the end justice would prevail— and this view came to be formulated in eschatological terms, as represented in the teachings of Jesus.

Early in the Gospels we are introduced to the idea of a coming judgment by John the Baptist. In his prophetic language, he calls the multitude flocking to him a brood of vipers and warns them of a wrath to come:

Even now the ax is laid to the root of the trees; every tree therefore that does not bear good fruit is cut down and thrown into the fire. . . . He will baptize you with the Holy Spirit and with fire. His winnowing fork is in his hand, and he will clear his threshing floor and gather his wheat into the granary, but the chaff he will burn with unquenchable fire. [Matthew 3:10-12.]

The tradition of using fire as a symbol of judgment is carried on by Jesus when he speaks of those who are "thrown into hell where their worm does not die and the fire is not quenched" (Mark 9:48). The Greek word for Hell in this passage is *Gehenna*, a word derived from the "Hinnom" and referring to the Valley of Hinnom, south of Jerusalem, where people of the city dumped their trash and garbage. Flies bred there continuously, and the smoking flames never died out. In one of his parables Jesus pictures a rich man who lived luxuriously, while a beggar lay at his gate hungry and diseased. When the beggar died, he was carried by angels to the bosom of Abraham, but when the rich man died, he found himself engulfed in the flames of Hell (Luke 16:19–31).

This apocalyptic view of the kingdom of God, however, is not the one that is most common in the teachings of Jesus. The "kingdom of God" meant for Jesus the reign of God. As we have seen, Jesus had in mind the lives of individual persons, not the rise and fall of nations. Whenever a person brings his will into submission to the will of God, therefore, he enters into God's kingdom. It is this insight that lies at the heart of the gospel Jesus preached, and he expressed it in many ways.

Several of the beatitudes employ this theme. "Blessed are the poor in spirit, for theirs is the kingdom of heaven. . . . Blessed are the pure in heart, for they shall see God. . . . Blessed are those who are persecuted for righteousness' sake, for theirs is the kingdom of heaven" (Matthew 5:3, 8, 10). The poor in spirit, the meek, the pure in heart, the persecuted for righteousness' sake, have already entered into the kingdom. The kingdom of God, Jesus seems to say, is a new dimension added to the present life.

Similar ideas are evident in the parables of Jesus. The kingdom of God, Jesus says, is like a seed cast upon the earth. While men go about their own affairs, the seed, of its own strength, springs up, grows, and comes to maturity. This means that the kingdom of God is truth, which, planted in someone's mind, eventually transforms his life and so carries him into God's kingdom (Mark 4:26–29).

While Jesus at times marshaled the lurid apocalyptic imagery in order to drive home his message, he regarded its elaborate symbolism as a kind of poetry, which presents as a visible historical phenomenon something that in itself is invisible. The kingdom of God never takes material forms, except as it is incarnate in the lives of human beings.[8]

Mission and Destiny

All the Gospels present Jesus as the Messiah, as himself accepting the Messianic role, and the early church after his time believed that. Scholars who reject the notion of a Messianic consciousness on the part of Jesus believe that this was ascribed to him by the disciples after his death and then projected backward onto him. Yet the Gospels present evidence, some direct, some indirect, that Jesus accepted the Messianic role.

Jesus discovered his Messianic role, first of all, in the Hebrew Scriptures. In the Nazareth synagogue he read a notable Messianic Scripture, Isaiah 61:1, 2, and then said to the audience, "Today this scripture has been fulfilled in your hearing" (Luke 4:21). He finds in this Scripture that he is anointed to preach good news to the poor, proclaim relief to captives, restore sight to the blind, set at liberty the oppressed, and announce the year of the Lord.

The Messianic role was not one to be sought because of its prestige and power. Jesus understood that the Messiah was elected to die. The final decision that he was the Messiah was made at Caesarea Philippi, to which he had retired with his intimate disciples, according to Mark 8:27–30, when, with Peter as their spokesman, they confidently affirmed that he was the Messiah. This assurance brought forth his public decision. It meant, as Jesus must have understood the role of the Messiah, from reading Isaiah 53, that he would go up to Jerusalem, where he would be rejected and put to death. This is indicated in sayings of Jesus in Mark 8:31; 9:31; 10:32–34.

Jesus immediately confirmed his decision by leading his disciples back through Galilee, down the Jordan Valley, through Jericho, and up through the hills to Jerusalem. Arriving on the day later to be known as Palm Sunday, he was acclaimed Messiah by his disciples and also by the people (Mark 11:1–10).

Cleansing the Temple

Since it was late that afternoon when Jesus arrived at the temple, he merely strolled through the courts to see what was taking place, and then returned to Bethany for the night. Early the next morning, however, aroused by what he had seen the day before, Jesus returned to cast out the moneychangers, overturn their tables, and drive out those who bought and sold doves (Mark 11:15–19). To this last John adds sheep and oxen, saying further that Jesus took a whip of cords and drove them all out (John 2:13–16). Jesus resented the commercialism, the exploitation of pilgrims; he felt that it was a profanation of the temple.

The temple priests were angered and immediately laid their plans to get Jesus put to death. Since they were probably the most powerful group in Jerusalem, the priests had no difficulty in enlisting the support of the Pharisees, who had been developing resentment against Jesus for his condemnation of their teachings about tithing, Sabbath observance, food regulations, clean and unclean things, and association with the common people.

There is no evidence that the Essenes were involved; they are not even mentioned in the New Testament. Presumably their isolation in the Qumran settlement and other remote places allowed them little contact with events in Jerusalem.

The Zealots were interested in Jesus at first, but when they learned that he had no intention of leading a rebellion against Rome, they became indifferent. Yet one of the apostles was Simon the Zealot, and it may be that Judas, who betrayed Jesus, was a disillusioned Zealot (Luke 6:13–16).

The plot to put Jesus to death was far advanced by Thursday evening, when Jesus ate the Passover meal with his disciples in a private room in Jerusalem; Jesus was already at that time aware of the plot and of the fact that Judas was involved (Mark 14:12–31). At the close of the meal, Judas slipped away to the priests, but Jesus led his other disciples to a secluded garden named Gethsemane, outside the walls. There he earnestly prayed that he might be spared the coming ordeal, yet he was submissive to God's will. Soon Judas arrived with a police detail. After a skirmish, the disciples fled, and the police led Jesus away.

The Sanhedrin, hastily summoned by the priests to hold the trial that night, condemned Jesus on charges of blasphemy, because he had said he was God's son, which they interpreted to mean son in a physical sense, not in the Messianic sense, as Jesus used it (Mark 14:51–72). Early the next morning they delivered Jesus to Pilate, the Roman governor, this time charging that Jesus claimed to be king of the Jews. In the trial that followed, Jesus remained silent, and did not defend himself. Pilate could not get him to speak in his own behalf. Since the charge on the face of it involved sedition, that is, a threat against Rome, and since Jesus did not deny it, Pilate condemned him to death. He was therefore led to a hilltop outside the city and crucified, this being the form of execution that the Romans ordinarily used for rebels. Above the head of Jesus, they placed the charge on which he was executed: The King of the Jews.

There was a double irony in the trial and execution. Jesus had not blasphemed against God: to be God's son, as he understood it, had nothing to do with blasphemy; what is more, he had no intention of taking up arms against Rome.

The Resurrection of Jesus

The authorities of Jerusalem, both Jewish and Roman, assumed that they were through with Jesus when he died and was buried. But they were shocked and embarrassed, a few days later, to hear his disciples spreading the news that he had risen from the dead and that they had seen him alive. This report, and the faith based on it, spread like wildfire among the disciples of Jesus; it was to become a cornerstone in the faith of Christianity. The first one to report that he had seen Jesus alive appears to have been Peter, but it was not long before several individuals and even groups reported that Jesus had appeared to them.

Skeptics have treated these stories as legends, not to be taken seriously, but Christians have always accepted them as true. There are two ways in which the stories have been interpreted. One group has accepted them as true without question, as literal historical facts, recording Jesus' physical resurrection from the dead and his reappearance in physical form to his disciples. Some of the accounts in the Gospels appear to assert that this is what actually occurred. There are other accounts, however, which record only appearances to the disciples as visions of an ecstatic character. Thus, many Christians, although they doubt the physical resurrection, believe in a spiritual resurrection; they believe that, in some way they do not fully understand, the spirit of Jesus survived the grave and inspired his followers throughout their lives. This belief in the continuing presence of Jesus in the hearts of individual disciples, and in the churches, is held to this day.

The earliest written account of the resurrection of Jesus is found in the first letter of Paul to the church at Corinth (15:1–8). It records appearances of Jesus to his disciples as follows (verses 3–8):

For I delivered to you as of first importance what I also received, that Christ died for our sins in accordance with the scriptures, that he was buried, that he was raised on the third day in accordance with the scriptures, and that he appeared to Cephas, and then to the twelve. Then he appeared to more than five hundred brethren, most of whom are still alive, though some have fallen asleep. Then he appeared to James, then to all the apostles. Last of all, as to one untimely born, he appeared also to me.

Paul wrote this account about A.D. 54, some twenty-five years after the death of Jesus.

The next account, chronologically, is Mark 16:1–8, written around A.D. 70.[9] Like Paul, he says the first appearance was to be to Peter (Cephas), but he also adds that the appearance was to be in Galilee, about seventy miles from Jerusalem. Matthew 28:1–20, some fifteen years later, speaks of appearances in both Galilee and Jerusalem. Luke 24:1–53, at about the same date as Matthew, places all the appearances in Jerusalem. Around the turn of the century, John 20:1–21:25 reports appearances in both Jerusalem and Galilee. There is a considerable variation in regard to minor details in the different accounts.[10]

THE FIRST CHURCH

Whatever we know about the first church to be established has been gleaned from the Acts of the Apostles, especially Chapters 1–12, although this church reappears from time to time in the remainder of Acts, as well as Paul's letters, mainly in Galatians 1–2.

The first church was established soon after the death of Jesus, but it was not at first called Christian, nor indeed had the idea yet appeared that Christianity was a separate religion. The name *Christian* was first used in the church at Antioch in Syria, some fifteen years later (Acts 11:26). The name was rare in the early days; it appeared only twice more in the New Testament: in Acts 26–28, where King Agrippa scornfully asks Paul if he expects to make a Christian of him in such a short time, and again in I Peter 4:16, where the writer says that one should not be ashamed to suffer as a Christian.

The most commonly employed designation of the followers of Jesus at that time was *disciples,* according to Acts, where the term is used some thirty times. The disciples are also referred to as the "brothers." At least six times in Acts (9:2; 19:9; 19:23; 22:4; 24:14; 24:22), however, the early Christian movement is called the Way, a term that the Essenes of Qumran also occasionally used to designate themselves. In both cases, the term was drawn ultimately from "the way of the Lord" in Isaiah 40:3.[11] This word dropped out of use in the first century, however, and apparently its use is limited to the Acts of the Apostles.

From the beginning the word *church* seems to have been used for an early Christian congregation, although this word is taken from the Greek *ekklēsia,* which means an assembly for either secular or religious purposes. The church is therefore a Christian counterpart of the Jewish synagogue, which in Hebrew is called the *house of assembly.*

The Twelve Apostles selected by Jesus constituted the nucleus of the first church at Jerusalem, although Judas, the traitor, had either committed suicide or died by some other violent means (Acts 1:18; Matthew 27:3–10).[12] One of the first actions of the new church was to select by lot a successor to the traitor (Acts 1:15–26).

The entire group of brethren in the Jerusalem church numbered about 120 (Acts 1:15). Included in the group were Mary, the mother of Jesus, and his natural brothers (Acts 1:14), who apparently after the death of Jesus had become his followers. According to the earliest tradition in the Gospels, the family of Jesus did not become his disciples while he lived (Mark 3:31–35). Only in the late Gospel of John (19:25–27) is the mother of Jesus definitely identified as being present at the crucifixion. But from Paul's statements in I Corinthians 15:7 and Galatians 1:19, we know that James, one of Jesus' brothers, was one of those who saw visions of Jesus after his death. It was probably this experience that led the entire family of Jesus to become disciples.

The membership of the Jerusalem church rapidly increased in size. During the festival of Pentecost, about fifty days after the crucifixion, when Jerusalem was full of Jewish pilgrims, the new members of this church were so filled with enthusiasm that ecstatic phenomena began to occur. A crowd of the pilgrims gathered to see what was going on. Peter, who had been the leader of the Twelve, now arose to speak for the new church. He was the first important leader to emerge (Acts 1–2). He explained that the prophecy of Joel (2:28–32) was being fulfilled, that God was pouring out his Spirit on all flesh, both old and young, and that they were beginning to see visions, dream dreams, and prophesy.

At the close of his address, 3,000 persons (Acts 2:37–47) were added to the fellowship. While we may discount the statistics, we do have to recognize that rapid growth was taking place. The Jewish pilgrims soon left Jerusalem and returned to their homelands, about sixteen different regions in all.

The growth of the Christian movement aroused the Jewish leaders of Jerusalem, who saw the movement as a threat to Judaism. Jesus himself had been the first victim of the attempt to exterminate the sect; Stephen was the second. His martyrdom is described in Acts 7: he was stoned to death just outside the eastern gate of Jerusalem. The third martyr was James, son of Zebedee and brother of John, whom King Herod Agrippa executed about A.D. 44. Herod at the same time had imprisoned Peter, who escaped from prison and fled from Jerusalem (Acts 12:1–17). John the Baptist, the prophet who baptized Jesus, had been executed by Herod Antipas just before Jesus began his ministry (Mark 1:14; 6:14–29).

Peter

Peter's leadership in the Jerusalem church was terminated by his flight from persecution in A.D. 44. Where he went is not stated, but he was back in Jerusalem in Acts 15:7, when Paul and Barnabas appeared before the apostles and elders in Jerusalem to defend their missionary work among the Gentiles. On that occasion, it is evident that James (Acts 15:13), not Peter, was now the head of the church. This was James, the brother of Jesus, who apparently continued to be the head of the Jerusalem church as long as he lived.

Peter's career from that point on is not clear. Paul indicates in Galatians 2:11–21 that at one time Peter came to Antioch of Syria, where he had vacillated on the matter of associating freely with Gentiles and finally taken the conservative position, for which Paul rebuked him. It may be that Peter also visited Corinth at one time, for that church contained a faction who claimed to be followers of

FIGURE 11.2 A fourth-century etching of Peter and Paul. (*The Metropolitan Museum of Art, Rogers Fund, 1916*)

Cephas, just as other factions were followers of Paul, or Apollos, or Christ (I Corinthians 1:11, 12). Peter's presence in the Greek churches may be indicated in a remark that Paul makes in I Corinthians 9:5, "Do we not have the right to be accompanied by a wife, as the other apostles and brothers of the Lord and Cephas?"

Paul, at any rate, felt that Peter was the missionary to the Jews, just as he was missionary to the Gentiles (see Figure 11.2). In Galatians 2:7, 8, Paul remarks, concerning the officials of the church in Jerusalem, "When they saw that I had been entrusted with the gospel to the uncircumcised, just as Peter had been entrusted with the gospel to the circumcised (for he who worked through Peter for the mission to the circumcised worked through me also for the Gentiles). . . ."

Second-century tradition, nevertheless, reports that Peter was associated with the Church at Rome in his later years and executed there by Nero. But Paul's letter to the Church at Rome, written about A.D. 54 or 55, gives no indication that Peter is there at the time. And when Paul arrived in Rome as a prisoner, about A.D. 61, according to Acts 28:11–31, there is no evidence that Peter was

there. If Peter finally reached Rome, he must have arrived no earlier than A.D. 64. It is probable that Paul was executed there and fairly certain that Peter also was put to death there.

The Religious Life of the First Church

No complete account of the religious life of the first church has come down to us. The best we can do is to glean scattered bits of information from the Acts of the Apostles. We can supplement this from the Gospels, although what we find there relates primarily to the life of Jesus and can be applied to the church after his time only with caution. Letters of Paul throw some light on the first church in Jerusalem, although they were written to churches out in Greek lands, where the situations were different.

One practice in the first church at Jerusalem which strikes us immediately is the community of goods:

And all who believed were together and had all things in common; and they sold their possessions and goods and distributed them to all, as any had need. [Acts 2:44, 45]

.   .   .

Now the company of those who believed were of one heart and soul, and no one said that any of the things which he possessed was his own, but they had everything in common. [Acts 4:32]

This is followed by a story about Ananias and his wife Sapphira, who sold a piece of property and conspired together to hold back part of the price. But when they were denounced by Peter for their fraud, the Holy Spirit struck them dead (Acts 5:1–10).

It may be that this community of goods in the first church is related to the Essene practice of requiring all their communicants to donate their property to the order, after which they lived from the common fund. But there is no evidence that such generosity was compulsory in this early Christian community. It arose spontaneously out of the new faith, and in response to an emergency. In its early days, the Jerusalem church had large numbers of the poor, as well as many pilgrims from foreign lands. Even at the beginning, however, the story about Ananias and Sapphira, even if it is legendary, reflects unhappiness with the practice. At any rate, this community of goods did not become a general practice in the Christian churches, and we hear little about it after the first generation.

Baptism

The first religious rite to be given prominence is baptism, no doubt because it was the rite of admission into the church; this was, after all, an evangelistic church, and was therefore constantly receiving members. According to Acts 2:41, 3,000 persons were baptized at one time. Baptism is mentioned frequently throughout Acts, as being preceded by repentance and faith. It was a rite of purification, and may have originated in the Jewish baptism of converts to Judaism. The new element in Christian baptism was that it was required of Jews as well as Gentiles. At the beginning, Christians, like Jews, probably limited baptism to adults, among whom it took the form of immersion. As Christians ceased holding to the rite of circumcision, by which Jewish children were brought into God's covenant, however, they extended the rite of baptism to children in order to replace circumcision.

The Breaking of Bread

Another prominent rite in the Jerusalem church was the breaking of bread, also called the Eucharist, the Lord's Supper, the Holy Communion, or the Mass. Acts 2:42 states, "And they devoted themselves to the apostles' teaching and fellowship, to the breaking of bread and the prayers." The communion service is not described in this passage, but Acts 2:46 continues, "And day by day, attending the temple together and breaking bread in their homes, they partook of food with glad and generous hearts." This indicates that the breaking of bread may have been simply the giving of thanks in connection with regular meals in their homes and from house to house.

Certainly this church had at that time no church building. For a good many years in Judea and also in Gentile churches small congregations met for worship in private homes. This practice is apparently reflected in Acts 12:12. When Peter escaped from prison, he went at once to the house of Mary, the mother of John Mark, where many were gathered and praying. In Romans 16:3, 5, Paul sends greeting to his friends Prisca and Aquila and the church in their house. He sends a similar greeting to a church in the house of Philemon (Philemon 1:2).

In the early days, before the Christian movement became separate from Judaism, Christians continued day by day to attend the temple services (Acts 2:46). This practice was gradually discontinued as they began to adopt their own times, places, and methods of worship. The practice of giving thanks at meals in the home may have caused some families to feel that every meal was an adequate religious rite and that no additional building was necessary. Yet the congregations soon discovered a need for more formal assemblies, which required a church building.

Sunday

At first, like the Jews, Christians kept the Sabbath, but the Sabbath was soon replaced by Sunday, the first day of the week, which was observed by Christians as the day on which Christ arose from the dead. The use of Sunday as a day of worship is not mentioned anywhere in connection with the early days of the church at Jerusalem. This observance is encountered first at Troas, one of Paul's churches, on the coast of Asia Minor, site of ancient Troy. Acts 20:7, 8, states:

On the first day of the week, when we were gathered to break bread, Paul talked with them, intending to depart on the morrow; and he prolonged his speech until midnight. There were many lights in the upper chamber where we were gathered.

This passage indicates that Sunday was being adopted as a day of worship, the main rite being the breaking of bread; a sermon, as in this case, was also being introduced.

A similar observance of Sunday appears to be indicated also at Corinth, another of Paul's churches. In preparation for his last visit to that church, this time to raise money for the poor in Jerusalem, Paul writes in I Corinthians 16:2:

On the first day of every week, each of you is to put something aside and store it up, as he may prosper, so that contributions need not be made when I come.

This passage reflects a custom in this church of assembling on the first day of the week. By this time the break between Judaism and the Christian movement, while not yet complete, was far advanced.

The earliest written account of the communion ritual is given by Paul in I Corinthians 11:23–26:

For I received from the Lord what I also delivered to you, that the Lord Jesus on the night when he was betrayed, took bread, and when he had given thanks, he broke it, and said, "This is my body which is for you. Do this in remembrance of me." In the same way also the cup, after supper, saying, "This cup is the new covenant in my blood. Do this, as often as you drink it, in remembrance of me." For as often as you eat this bread and drink this cup you proclaim the Lord's death until he comes.

We feel certain that this form was already being observed in all the early churches, for it occurs in almost the same words in all three of the Synoptic Gospels. They are all based on a common tradition, which goes back to the Last Supper itself. Mark, the earliest Gospel, gives the tradition in 14:22–25, Matthew in 26:26–29, and Luke in 22:17–20. John does not record the origin of Holy Communion.

PAUL, THE THEOLOGIAN AND MISSIONARY

After Jesus himself, Paul was the best known and most influential early Christian. His importance is threefold: as a missionary, a writer, and a theologian. He was the first truly great Christian missionary, and set the pattern of Christian missions down to the present time. He was also the first Christian writer; all his letters were earlier than the Gospels, and constitute a major portion of the New Testament. His interpretation of Christ laid the foundation for most subsequent Christology, and he was the first to give clear expression to the universality of the Christian faith.

Although we know the essential facts of Paul's life, uncertainties remain. The Acts of the Apostles gives a reasonably full account of his life. The author of the Acts of the Apostles was probably the physician named Luke, who was Paul's companion at times during his travels (Colossians 4:14; Philemon 1:24; II Timothy 4:11), and also the author of the Gospel of Luke. But his record of Paul's life is selective and fragmentary, and in places disagrees with what Paul reports in his letters. Paul's own statements about his visits to Jerusalem after his conversion (Galatians 1:1–2:14) are useful in correcting statements in Acts 9:26–30. The fragmentary character of Acts is shown by Paul's own account of his travels and hardships in II Corinthians 11:21–33. He refers to imprisonments, beatings, shipwrecks, and numerous journeys and dangers not alluded to in Acts.

Such discrepancies between Paul's letters and Acts have caused some doubt that Luke wrote Acts. The author of Acts appears to have been unfamiliar with Paul's letters, which were written hurriedly and dispatched in haste because of urgent problems in the churches; for some decades, Paul's letters were probably unknown to the church at large. They were not published as a collection until around A.D. 100, and it was another half-century before they began to be regarded as Scripture.

Paul first makes his appearance in Acts at Jerusalem, where he was a leader of the persecution of the early Christians. He was standing by when Stephen was stoned to death; he approved the bloody deed and guarded the garments of the witnesses who had testified against the prisoner (Acts 7:58–8:1). The witnesses had to cast the first stones (Deut. 17:7).

Paul must, in fact, have been in charge of the execution of Stephen, for the record continues (Acts 8:3):

Saul laid waste the church, and entering house after house, he dragged off men and women and committed them to prison.

All of this occurred in and around Jerusalem, but the story continues (Acts 9:1, 2):

But Saul, still breathing threats and murder against the disciples of the Lord, went to the high priest and asked him for letters to the synagogues of Damascus, so that if he found any belonging to the Way, men or women, he might bring them bound to Jerusalem.

In all these passages Paul is called Saul, his Hebrew name (Paul is the Greek form of this name).

Not much is known about Paul's early life, but we get a few bits of information from his own words. He remarks in Acts 21:39, "I am a Jew, from Tarsus in Cilicia, a citizen of no mean city." He adds in 22:3 that he was born in Tarsus and that he studied under Gamaliel, a famous teacher at Jerusalem, before he became a persecutor of the Christians. Acts 23:6 reveals that Paul was a Pharisee, one of the proudest and most learned sects of the Jews. In Philippians 3:4–6 he speaks with pride of his circumcision on the eighth day, of his descent from the tribe of Benjamin, and says that he is a "Hebrew born of Hebrews." On one occasion, Paul remarks that he is a Roman citizen, which was uncommon for Jews of that time, and he adds that he has received his citizenship by birth, showing that he belongs to a distinguished family (Acts 22:25–28).

We may assume that Paul's education began in his home at Tarsus, with his father as teacher, which was the custom among the Jews.[13] But his education must have been continued in the Tarsus synagogue school. No doubt he demonstrated his superior ability there and was encouraged to go to Jerusalem for study, probably with the intention of becoming a rabbi.

One further bit of family information is provided by Acts 23:16, where a son of Paul's sister at Jerusalem comes into prison and warns him of a plot laid against his life. All that we know about the family, therefore, is that, beyond his parents, he had one sister and one nephew. There is no evidence that Paul was ever married. It is clear that when he wrote I Corinthians, about A.D. 54, he was not married. Some of his statements in I Corinthians 7:25–35 seem to imply that Paul has chosen celibacy for religious reasons. Yet Paul recognizes that few are able to live a celibate life and does not prohibit marriage.

We do not know Paul's age at the time he enters the biblical story. Acts 7:58 refers to him as a "young man named Saul." The responsible position as leader of the persecution of Christians, to which Paul was appointed by the high priests, suggests a considerable maturity. Paul himself states in a speech before King Agrippa, Acts 26:10, concerning Christians he had arrested, "When they were put to death I cast my vote against them." This might imply that he was a member of the Jewish Sanhedrin. We are not sure of this, but it seems reasonable to suppose that at the time he was at least thirty years of age. If so, his date of birth was not far from that of Jesus.

Paul's Conversion

The Paul who set out with a police detail from Jerusalem to Damascus, armed with warrants for the arrest of any Christians he might find there, was educated, arrogant, fanatical, but honest. As he went on his way, a journey of some four days, Paul reflected on the faith of Stephen, stoned to death before his eyes, and toward the end of his journey, suddenly discovered himself involved in an

experience like that of Jesus at his baptism and Moses before the
flaming bush: he heard Jesus himself speaking to him. This vision
of Christ was the turning point in Paul's life. Without hesitation,
he turned his back on his past and faced toward the future as a
Christian (Acts 9:1–19; 22:6–16; 26:12–18). In Galatians 1:12, Paul
refers to the experience as a revelation of Jesus Christ. He was
baptized in Damascus by a Christian named Ananias.

Paul's movements immediately after his conversion are confused
because of conflicts between the sources. Acts says that he immediately began to preach in the synagogues of Damascus (9:19–25),
but when a plot was made against him by Jews there, the brethren
let him down over the city wall and he escaped to Jerusalem. There
the disciples were at first afraid of Paul, until he was vouched for
by Barnabas. Then he began to preach his new Christian faith
boldly in Jerusalem (Acts 9:23–30). But when a plot against Paul was
made there, the brethren sent him away to Tarsus, his home.

In recounting the same events, Paul himself says, in Galatians
1:11–24, that immediately following his conversion he did not go
to Jerusalem, but into Arabia, and then returned to Damascus.
After three years he went to Jerusalem and spent fifteen days with
Peter and James, following which he went into Syria and Cilicia,
but he was still unknown by sight to the churches of Judea. At any
rate, both accounts start with Paul at Damascus, take him back to
Jerusalem, and finally to Tarsus.

Paul's Philosophy of Missions

Paul appears to have remained at Tarsus for about seven years, A.D.
37–44. Neither he nor anyone else has given us a hint as to what
he did during those years. Some have assumed that he was somewhere engaged in Christian missions. It may be that some of the
experiences recorded in II Corinthians 11:23–29 belong to this
period, since there is no other place in Paul's career into which they
fit with certainty; but there is no proof that they belong here. We
might have expected Paul to establish a church at Tarsus, his home
city, but there is no evidence of such a church. It is probable,
therefore, that this was Paul's time of temptation. He found himself
considered a renegade by his fellow Jews; he was driven out of
Damascus first and then out of Jerusalem by the powerful Jewish
community. And even the Christians of Jerusalem, whose cause he

had now espoused, had little confidence in him; they gave him a cold shoulder. He was forced to return for personal safety to his home city. Eventually Paul turned back to his Holy Scriptures, searching for meanings that would enable him to weave together the disordered strands of his life. Perhaps it was during these seven years that he arrived at some of his remarkable interpretations of the Old Testament.

In the meantime a powerful church had grown up at Antioch in Syria, and it was to set a new course for the entire Christian movement. Here, for the first time, Gentiles were freely admitted into the church on a basis of complete equality with Jews. This was the first truly integrated Christian church.

When news of the new development at Antioch reached Jerusalem, the elders of the conservative church there immediately decided to investigate. They therefore selected Barnabas, one of their most able members, a liberal-minded Jew from Cyprus, to go, and he was delighted with what he found. But realizing that this church would have unique problems and need leaders able to understand them, his mind turned back to his old friend Paul at Tarsus. So he went personally to Tarsus and got Paul to come with him. Then they spent a whole year at Antioch, with great success, and Acts 11:26 reports that the disciples were for the first time called Christians there.

The most important result of the year Paul spent in the new environment of this church at Antioch was that he caught a vision of the fulfillment of the dream of universality that he had long been finding in the Scriptures, but up to now he had not been able to understand. It was here that at last he grasped the idea of entirely freeing the Christian faith of all nationalistic and racial barriers and carrying it to everyone, Greeks as well as Jews. In this way, the kingdom of God, as the old prophets had dreamed, would fill the earth. This was Paul's new philosophy of Christian missions.

The Missionary Journeys

We can guess that Paul had assistance from Barnabas in arriving at this new point of view. At any rate, he had the sympathy of this generous man; and together they had no difficulty in gaining the support of the entire church at Antioch for their new program of carrying the Gospel to all the world. By a ritual of fasting, prayer, and laying on of hands, this church ordained Barnabas and Paul as missionaries (Acts 13:1–3). Throughout his missionary career, Paul regarded the Antioch church as his sponsor; after every journey he returned to it to give a report.

About the year A.D. 46 Barnabas and Paul, accompanied by Mark, a nephew of Barnabas, sailed from Seleucia, port of Antioch, for Cyprus. They traversed this island, apparently without establishing a church, and then set sail again. After landing at Perga on the southern coast of Asia Minor, they went northward into the Roman province of Galatia, where they quickly established churches at Antioch of Pisidia, Iconium, Derbe, and possibly Lystra, in each case (except that of Lystra) using a synagogue as their starting point. Then they retraced their steps, revisiting the young churches, and returned to Antioch. They had converted more Greeks than Jews. The Greeks were usually persons who had attended the synagogues and admired the Jewish faith and ethics, but refused to become proselytes because they disliked the ceremonial laws. Now that a version of this faith was presented that had discarded the ceremonialism, they accepted it with joy. So Paul and Barnabas returned rejoicing, feeling that they had demonstrated the soundness of the new missionary program. They had been away possibly a year.

Following this, about A.D. 48, Paul and Barnabas had to go to Jerusalem in person to defend their work among the Gentiles. The church in Jerusalem, because of its original association with Jesus and the presence of the apostles there, felt that it had authority over such matters. Some of these leaders were still close to Judaism and believed that Gentiles should be required to accept the ritual law before they could become Christians. But the glowing account Paul and Barnabas gave carried the day in Jerusalem, although Paul was to be troubled by the conservatives at Jerusalem as long as he lived.

By A.D. 49 Paul and Barnabas were ready for a second journey, but because of a disagreement over Mark, who had left them in the midst of the first venture, they separated. Barnabas took Mark and went to Cyprus, and we hear no more of their work. Paul took Silas and picked up Timothy, a devoted young Christian, half Jewish half Greek, at Derbe or Lystra, and together they presumably first revisited the Galatian churches and then went across the province of Asia to Troas on the coast of the Aegean Sea. There Paul in a dream heard a man calling upon them to go on to Macedonia. So they sailed again and soon had established good churches in Philippi, Thessalonica, and Berea, all of them in Macedonia, and each time beginning with a synagogue or Jewish prayer group. Recurrent hostility in the synagogues, however, kept them moving on.

Paul stopped next at Athens, where he preached with little success, since no church came of it. Then he went on to Corinth, the metropolis of Achaia, where he spent about two years and founded a large church. This was the end of the second missionary journey (Acts 15:36–18:21), and he had established four churches.

Returning by ship, Paul stopped briefly at Ephesus, then hastened on to Jerusalem for a visit, and soon was back in Antioch of Syria, his home base, ready to embark on a third journey. This time he went by land across Asia Minor, no doubt revisiting his Galatian churches, and arrived at Ephesus, the seacoast metropolis of Asia, where he founded another flourishing church, the only one he established on the third journey. After two years he felt that his work there, as well as in all the lands of Greece and Asia Minor, was done. So after raising a collection from his Aegean churches for the poor in the mother church at Jerusalem, he bade them farewell and returned (Acts 18:22–20:38). On this journey, we think, he wrote the letters to the Galatians, I and II Corinthians, and Romans. In this last letter, he had expressed a desire to see Rome and then to go on to Spain for new missionary ventures (Romans 15:18–24). This plan was never to be carried out, however, for he spent most of the remainder of his life in prison.

When Paul reached Jerusalem, he was attacked by hostile Jews and placed under protective arrest by the Romans (Acts 21:15–40). He was imprisoned at Caesarea, the Roman capital of Judea, for two or three years. Finally, in desperation, Paul appealed to Caesar (as a citizen he had a right to do so), and so was sent to Rome by ship in the care of a Roman centurion, about A.D. 58. The record of this memorable trip is preserved in Acts 27, the most vivid description in antiquity of a voyage and storm at sea.

After the ship was wrecked and the party had wintered on the island of Malta, Paul, in the care of the centurion, finished his voyage in the spring, stopping briefly at Syracuse, and then going on to Rome, where they were greeted by the church, about A.D. 59. Acts then closes its record by remarking that Paul spent two years in his own rented house, a prisoner under guard, but free to entertain guests and teach all who came to him (Acts 28:1–31). The tenses of the verbs used at its close show that Acts was written at a later time, but the author, for reasons known only to himself, closes his dramatic record with his hero still a prisoner in chains.

According to strong tradition Paul became a martyr (that is, a "witness" to his faith), in the Neronian persecution, soon after A.D. 63. But before he died, and while he was still a prisoner, he wrote the following letters, either in their present form or in an original draft which was revised by a later hand: Philippians, Philemon, Colossians, Ephesians, I and II Timothy, and Titus.

Pauline Chronology

The pivotal date of Paul's career is A.D. 50, the year he arrived at Corinth and wrote I and II Thessalonians. This date is established by an inscription found at Delphi, which contains a letter of Claudius Caesar in which he mentions Gallio, the proconsul at Corinth before whom Paul was brought for trial (Acts 18:12–17). The letter is dated A.D. 51–52 from the material that it contains about Claudius. Since a proconsul held office for only one year, and Paul had been at Corinth about a year and a half before the trial, the date is fixed, the only date in Paul's life that we know as certain. It also establishes the date of Paul's second missionary journey as approximately A.D. 49–53. By making use of several notes in Acts as to how long he was at Antioch of Syria, Corinth, Ephesus, Caesarea, and Rome, and combining these with Paul's own statements in Galatians 1:18 and 2:1, we can date the major events of his life with reasonable certainty, beginning with his conversion about A.D. 33 and concluding with the last reference to him in Rome about A.D. 63 (Acts 28:30).

Paul's Theology

Paul's theology has as its foundation the legacy he received from Judaism. He had inherited a belief in one God as well as the canon of Holy Scripture. Prophecy in the living sense had ceased to exist among the Jews, having been stifled by the canonization of the Scriptures. Their dogma held that all truth is contained in the Scriptures, and when new truth is needed, it can be found somewhere in the Scriptures, provided one searches long enough. All changes in belief or practice had to be vindicated by reference to the Scriptures themselves. The result of this doctrine was the rise of an allegorical method of interpretation, which found a second or third meaning in a Scripture, and showed little concern about its original meaning and historical context. We must keep this method in mind in our study of Paul. Some of his interpretations may appear to us to be remote from the real meaning, but we ought to judge the position he affirms on its own merits, not on his exegesis of a passage of Scripture.

Paul's first important theological effort was to prove that salvation is achieved through faith alone, not by observing the legal requirements of ceremonialism. This is the theme of his letter to the Galatians. He first defends himself against the conservative Jewish Christians at Jerusalem, who charge that he is not a true apostle, not being one of the Twelve. They are trying in this way to undermine all of Paul's missionary work. While he readily admits that he is not one of the Twelve, he cleverly turns that fact to his advantage, by asserting that he has not received his authority from the Twelve, or from any other man, but through a personal revelation of Christ, who appeared to him and gave him his commission as an apostle (Galatians 1:11–2:21).

As to the main thesis of his letter, first he bases his teaching about faith on the Scriptures, thereby showing that the current Jewish interpretation is false. He begins with the case of Abraham (Galatians 3:6–9), and quotes Genesis 15:6, "Abraham believed God, and it was reckoned to him as righteousness," to show that Abraham himself, long before the Law of Moses came, had been justified by faith alone. Next he quotes the prophet Habakkuk 2:4, "He who through faith is righteous shall live," to undercut the view of the Judaizing Christians. He uses Abraham again in Galatians 3:15–29, this time taking the promise made to Abraham and his offspring (Genesis 22:17–18) and arguing that since offspring is a singular, not a plural, noun, the singular offspring is Christ. Thus he has three Scripture arguments in support of his position: two which undercut the Jewish position, and one which introduces the role of Christ as the offspring of Abraham through whom all nations are to be blessed.

Paul then goes on positively to show that in the sacrament of baptism believers are baptized into Christ. This is true of Jew and Greek, free man and slave, male and female, but since they are in Christ, and Christ is Abraham's offspring (singular), therefore all Christians, regardless of race or national origin, are the offspring (plural) of Abraham. This is one of the best examples of Paul's use of allegorical interpretation. Although he knows, of course, that offspring of Abraham in the primary sense means his blood descendants, he develops a second meaning, which is limited to Christ, and a third, which includes all Christians. Thus he finds three different levels of meaning in the same passage.

Again, speaking in the mystical sense, in Galatians 4:1–7, he says that by faith God sends his Spirit into our hearts, crying Abba, Father! That is, all believers have an immediate sense of being sons of God. They are no longer slaves to law or any other sort of spiritual master; as Christians, they are sons and heirs of God. In 2:20, Paul bases his argument on his feeling of identification with the crucified Christ. He says, "I have been crucified with Christ; it is no longer I who live, but Christ who lives in me." Since Christ is God's Son, he continues, that also makes him God's son.

The strength of Paul's argument is found in these mystical insights—his feeling of identity with Christ, his sense of divine sonship—not in his allegorical interpretations of Scripture. This also shows the meaning of faith, as he uses the word. Faith is not the acceptance of a creed or belief in historical facts, but rather submission of one's will to the will of Christ. One identifies himself with Christ to such an extent that he becomes a new creation (II Corinthians 5:17), a new person. Faith is therefore a warm, profound, transforming, personal experience, whose validation one finds in one's own heart.

Romans

Paul wrote the letter to the Galatians in the heat of controversy. Evidently the Judaizers had sent emissaries to undermine him. Since he had to defend both his gospel and himself, the letter was written passionately.

Romans, by contrast, was written somewhat later, after his work in the east was finished, and he had made plans to go to Spain with a stop en route at Rome. The heat of conflict has subsided, and he writes in a thoughtful mood. The result is Paul's most mature exposition of his gospel.

The theme of Romans is succinctly stated in 1:16, 17:

For I am not ashamed of the gospel: it is the power of God for salvation to every one who has faith, to the Jew first and also to the Greek.

For in it the righteousness of God is revealed through faith for faith; as it is written, "He who through faith is righteous shall live."

The central idea here is similar to the theme of Galatians, yet not identical with it. The new element is the concept of universality: the Gospel is for Jews and Greeks, the latter representing all non-Jewish peoples. Also involved is the justice of God, and the fact that God's power is realized through faith. Habakkuk 2:4 is introduced here, as in Galatians, "He who through faith is righteous shall live." This must have been the prophetic basis of all of Paul's thought about the Gospel. He then continues in a logical way, in the letter to the Romans, to develop his thought along these lines.

Paul first shows how the Gentiles are also in need of the Gospel of Christ. Their situation is different from that of the Jews, since God has never sent them a Moses. They therefore have no Holy Scripture comparable to the Law, the Prophets, and the Writings. Recognizing this, Paul approaches the situation of the Gentiles in a new way, and sets them in a different religious perspective. God gives all men a revelation of himself through the world of nature, Paul says, and because of the creation of the universe, man is without excuse. His intelligence should infer the existence and nature of God; and this natural revelation should lead man to a life of reverence, humility, and goodness (Romans 1:18–32). Yet man has not responded to God's revelation in this way. Instead, he has practiced a debased religion and gone into moral depravity. Men in general are therefore under condemnation, desperately in need of redemption.

At the same time, Paul recognizes that some Gentiles do in fact live a life of enlightenment and high morality. This he explains by availing himself of the idea that God also reveals himself to man through his moral conscience (Romans 2:14–16), and he foresees that in the day of judgment God will deal leniently with such persons. The majority of the Gentiles, however, like the Jews, are in a hopeless plight.

Here also, as in Galatians, Paul argues that the Jews fall short of salvation because the Law makes demands upon them that they are unable to keep. He quotes from the Psalms to prove that all men, both Jews and Gentiles, are hopelessly corrupt (Romans 3:10–18).

This pessimistic assessment of human character leads Paul to probe deeply into man's nature, in search of the causes for his immoral actions. Why is it that, in spite of God's revelation to all men through nature and conscience and to the Hebrews through Moses and the prophets, men turn as if by compulsion to an evil life? Paul considers this question in Romans 7:1–25, framing his thoughts about man in general in the first person. He finds himself doing things he knows he should not do and not doing the things he knows he should do. He knows God's law, but he also knows that he does not keep it. What causes a man to act this way?

Paul's introspective analysis of human nature presents the self in four different roles. In knowing the law of God, the self is reason or intelligence. In struggling to obey the law of God, the self is will. In being led by the flesh to do things one should not do, the self is emotion, feeling, desire. The self thus has a shifting character: first it assumes one of these roles, then another, and another. At the same time, the self, that is, the "I," has the capacity to stand aside, as if outside itself, and to observe how it assumes and acts these three different roles. Indeed, it is aware that, in taking this position outside the self and looking on, it is taking a fourth role.

Paul finds that the cause of his predicament is bondage to his flesh; that is, he is a slave to sin, which resides in his flesh, in his desires of every kind and in the compulsive forces that are ever impelling him to rebel against law. His only possibility of freedom is for some generous person to purchase him from his hard master and set him free. This hope of freedom affords Paul his opportunity to present the gospel of Christ.

The key word in Paul's concept of salvation is *justification* (Romans 3:24, 28; 4:2, 25; 5:1, 9, 16; 8:30; 10:4, 10; Galatians 2:21), a legal term meaning acquittal. But it is not because man is innocent that he is justified, as Paul explains; it is because Christ has assumed man's guilt and paid the penalty at the cost of his own life. The forgiveness of sin is an act of the grace, the generosity, of God. Because of God's love for man, he permits his own Son to die in man's place, the innocent for the guilty. This makes it possible for God to forgive man's sin and to set him free—that is, to give him salvation (Romans 5:15–21). A just God cannot forgive an unexpiated sin; the debt must be paid. But it is Christ who pays the debt, and expiates the sin; this enables God, the judge, to declare the sinner justified. Paul always operates within a concept of justice. The Christian gospel therefore presents a God who loves man and suffers for him, by giving up his own Son to die as an expiation for sin. In effect God takes man's sin upon himself.

Yet God does not set man free unconditionally. He does not coerce man, nor does he ever invade his personality; he can set man free only when man submits his will to the will of God. Thus Paul shows the nature of faith, by which he means an act of total submission to God's will, which at the same time brings perfect freedom.

CHRISTIAN ESCHATOLOGY

The basic ideas of Christian eschatology are the kingdom of God, both present and to come; history as a continuing struggle between God and his angels, on the one hand, and Satan and his demons, on the other; the final triumph of God and the angels over Satan and the demons. This triumph involves a return, or second coming, of Christ; the resurrection of the dead; the final judgment; heaven and hell; eternal rewards and punishments.

Paul has included numerous apocalyptic passages in his letters. One of the best known is I Thessalonians 4:13–17:

But we would not have you ignorant, brethren, concerning those who are asleep, that you may not grieve as others do who have no hope. For since we believe that Jesus died and rose again, even so, through Jesus, God will bring with him those who have fallen asleep. For this we declare to you by the word of the Lord, that we who are alive, who are left until the coming of the Lord, shall not precede those who have fallen asleep. For the Lord himself will descend from heaven with a cry of command, with the archangel's call, and with the sound of the trumpet of God. And the dead in Christ will rise first; then we who are alive, who are left, shall be caught up together with them in the clouds to meet the Lord in the air; and so we shall always be with the Lord.

II Peter, the latest of the New Testament writers (c. A.D. 150), is so depressed by the depravity of the world that he feels the universe itself has been infected with evil and is now corrupt to its very core. It will therefore have to be burned up and replaced by another. He writes in 3:10, 13:

But the day of the Lord will come like a thief, and then the heavens will pass away with a loud noise, and the elements will be dissolved with fire, and the earth and the works that are upon it will be burned up. . . . But according to his promise we wait for new heavens and a new earth in which righteousness dwells.

But the fullest statement of early Christian eschatology is provided by the Revelation of John. In 12:7–12 this author gives a picturesque account of the beginning of the eschatological drama in Heaven itself:

Now war arose in heaven, Michael and his angels fighting against the dragon; and the dragon and his angels fought, but they were defeated and there was no longer any place for them in heaven. And the great dragon was thrown down, that ancient serpent, who is called the Devil and Satan, the deceiver of the whole world—he was thrown down to the earth, and his angels were thrown down with him.

This statement assumes that Satan and the demons were at first angels in Heaven but, being rebels, were cast out and then took up their evil designs against mankind—ideas taken from Jewish apocalypses.[14]

The end of Satan's reign of terror on the earth is forecast in Revelation 20:1–3 and 7–10:

Then I saw an angel coming down from heaven, holding in his hand the key of the bottomless pit and a great chain. And he seized the dragon, that ancient serpent, who is the Devil and Satan. . . .

. . . the devil who had deceived them was thrown into the lake of fire and brimstone where the beast and the false prophet were, and they will be tormented day and night for ever and ever.

This Christian eschatology may be taken in either of two ways. Traditionalists take it as literal and historical: they believe that the return of Christ, the resurrection of the dead, the final judgment and eternal rewards and punishment, will take place as facts of history; they also believe that Heaven and Hell are real places. But Christians of a more philosophical point of view interpret all these ideas in a moral and spiritual sense, not a literal, physical, historical one. They find support for this view especially in the Gospel of John, where most of the apocalyptic imagery has been replaced by the experience of eternal life as a present possession (see John 6:47–58). The concept of the warfare of God and his angels with Satan and the demons is understood as an allegory, a parable, a myth, which presents faith in the sovereignty of God. It shows God as King of the world, as the Sovereign of history, who is continuously working out his will.

NOTES

1. B. M. Metzger, "Ancient Versions": Section 2, "Greek Versions of the OT"; Section 3, "Latin Versions of the OT," in George A. Buttrick, ed., *The Interpreter's Dictionary of the Bible* (Nashville: Abingdon, 1962), IV, 750–754.
2. E. J. Goodspeed, *The Formation of the New Testament* (Chicago: University of Chicago Press, 1926). This gives a concise history of the New Testament canon, also important early lists of the canon.
3. W. R. Farmer, "Essenes," in Buttrick, *op. cit.*, II, 143–149.
4. S. V. McCasland, *The Religion of the Bible* (New York: Crowell, 1960), pp. 206–208; and "The Way," *Journal of Biblical Literature*, Vol. 77, Part iii (1958), pp. 222–230.
5. C. E. B. Cranfield, "The Gospel of Mark," in Buttrick, *op. cit.*, III, 267–277.
6. S. V. McCasland, *The Pioneer of Our Faith, a New Life of Jesus* (New York: McGraw-Hill, 1964), pp. 20–25.
7. S. V. McCasland, "Demon Possession and Exorcism in Early Christianity in the Light of Modern Views of Mental Illness," *By the Finger of God*, (New York: Macmillan, 1951).
8. S. V. McCasland, "Apocalyptic Symbols," *The Pioneer of Our Faith*, pp. 114–123.
9. What follows Mark 16:1–8 in most New Testaments is a late ending, compiled from the other Gospels. The original ending of Mark has been lost.
10. S. V. McCasland, "The Resurrection," *The Pioneer of Our Faith*, pp. 181–188.
11. S. V. McCasland, "The Essenes," *The Religion of the Bible*, pp. 206–208; "The Way," *Journal of Biblical Literature*, Vol. 77, Part iii (1958), pp. 222–230.
12. Cf. "Judas Iscariot," in S. V. McCasland, *The Pioneer of Our Faith*, pp. 166–172.
13. S. V. McCasland, "Education, NT," in Buttrick, *op. cit.*, II, pp. 34–38.
14. I Enoch, chaps. 6–11, 86–88; R. H. Charles, ed., *The Apocrypha and Pseudepigrapha*, (Oxford: Clarendon Press, 1913), II, 191–195, 250–252.

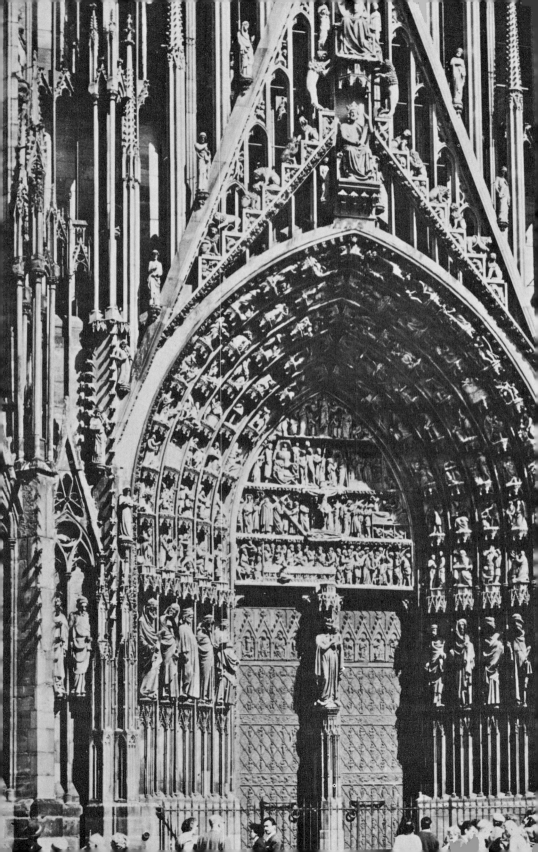

Christianity is a missionary religion, like Buddhism and Islam. It has never limited itself to one nation or one people as most other religions do; believing that it has a gospel for all nations, it has sought to become the faith of the entire world, and today there are large numbers of Christians on every continent (see Figure 12.2). Christianity remains a minority faith in Asia and Africa, but it is the most dominant religion of Europe and of North and South America. The 1968 yearbook of the *Encyclopaedia Britannica* estimates that in 1967 there were 969,591,000 Christians in the world, broken down as follows: Roman Catholics, 595,472,000; Eastern Orthodox, 144,829,000; Protestants, 229,290,000. Since Protestants usually list only adult members, while other denominations include entire families, these statistics would probably need to be somewhat adjusted.

CLASSICAL CHRISTIAN THEOLOGY

Creeds

A creed is a statement in a few brief sentences or propositions of the faith or belief of a church or religion. The brevity and clarity of a creed should make it possible for one to carry it in one's memory. It may serve as a basis for study for one who wishes to learn what a certain religious body believes; it may be chanted in the liturgy of a worship service; or it may be used as a test of ortho-

FIGURE 12.1   The main portal of the medieval Cathedral of Strasbourg. In the center is a figure of Mary holding the infant Christ. (*French Government Tourist Office*)

doxy. The use for which a creed is intended will usually determine its literary form.

Certain passages of the Old Testament were probably written for use in education or recitation in a liturgy. The Decalogue is an example. Each of the Ten Commandments is briefly and picturesquely stated and can be easily carried in the memory. Numerous statements in the Prophets may have been formulated with such use in mind. Micah 6:8 illustrates this: "What does the Lord require of you but to do justice, and to love kindness, and to walk humbly with your God?"

In the beatitudes of Matthew 5:3–11, Jesus carries on this Hebrew literary tradition. He follows this tradition again in Matthew 22:36–39, when he replies to the question of a lawyer about the

greatest commandment, and answers simply that to love God with all your heart is the first and greatest; and the second is to love your neighbor as yourself. Paul states the principle even more briefly in Romans 13:9 and Galatians 5:14, when he says that a summary of the entire Law is embodied in loving your neighbor as yourself. James (2:8) says that the love of your neighbor is the Royal Law. All these formulations from both the Old and the New Testament have a mnemonic purpose.

Yet formal creeds had only a minor place among the Hebrews, who were held together by strong ties of blood and nation, both of which were abandoned by Christianity. From early days, therefore, Christians have laid more emphasis on creeds as bonds to serve as a basis of union, although there is little evidence of a formal creed in the New Testament itself. While the Lord's Prayer, as formulated in Matthew 6:9–13, is not a technical creed, it was undoubtedly prepared for use in liturgies. The plural pronouns "our," "us," and "we" demonstrate that it was intended to be recited by a congregation, not an individual alone. Nevertheless this prayer does formulate certain affirmations of the early Christian faith. Note the creedal elements in it:

> Our Father who art in heaven,
> Hallowed be thy name.
> Thy kingdom come,
> Thy will be done,
>   On earth as it is in heaven.
> Give us this day our daily bread;
> And forgive us our debts,
>   As we also have forgiven our debtors;
> And lead us not into temptation,
>   But deliver us from evil.
> For thine is the kingdom and the power
>   and the glory, forever. Amen.

If not a creed, this prayer is certainly the nearest to one that Jesus ever formulated.

Other embryonic creedal and liturgical formulations occur in the letters of Paul. One of these is I Corinthians 11:23–26, in which he gives an ancient liturgy for the Lord's Supper. This had come

FIGURE 12.2   A missionary teaching the gospel in Africa. (*Maryknoll Fathers*)

to him in oral form from the time of Jesus. Paul's version of it follows (verses 23–25):

For I received from the Lord what I also delivered to you, that the Lord Jesus on the night when he was betrayed took bread, and when he had given thanks, he broke it, and said, "This is my body which is for you. Do this in remembrance of me." In the same way also the cup, after supper, saying, "This cup is the new covenant in my blood. Do this, as often as you drink it, in remembrance of me."

Variants forms of this ancient liturgy survive also in Mark 14:22–24; Matthew 26:26–28; and Luke 22:17–20.

I Corinthians 15:3–8, which gives the earliest summary of evidence for belief in the resurrection of Jesus, also comes from Paul; this, too, he has received from the oral tradition, as follows:

For I delivered to you as of first importance what I also received, that Christ died for our sins in accordance with the scriptures, that he was buried, that he was raised on the third day in accordance with the scriptures, and that he appeared to Cephas, then to the twelve. Then he appeared to more than five hundred brethren at one time, most of whom are still alive, though some have fallen asleep. Then he appeared to James, then to all the apostles. Last of all, as to one untimely born, he appeared also to me.

Paul received all of this from earlier times except the last verse, which is about his own encounter with the risen Christ. Since he believes that his own experience is like that of his predecessors in the faith, he adds it to the tradition. While all four Gospels give variant, but later, forms, Paul wrote his version considerably earlier than any of the Gospels. All studies of the resurrection of Jesus should therefore begin with Paul's summary of the evidence. Only in I Corinthians has Paul left a written account of this tradition, but he must have delivered it orally hundreds of times in the various churches he established. Most of his converts probably learned to recite it from memory; Paul's testimony about his own faith was a living link in the chain of evidence that reached back from his Greek converts to the first generation of disciples.

Paul has left us another embryonic creed in Ephesians 4:4–6:

There is one body and one Spirit, just as you were called to the one hope that belongs to your call, one Lord, one faith, one baptism, one God and Father of us all, who is above all and through all and in all.

I Timothy 3:16 also contains elements of a creed or hymn:

> He was manifested in the flesh,
> vindicated in the Spirit,
>   seen by angels,
> preached among the nations,
> believed on in the world,
>   taken up in glory.

The Apostles' Creed

It was not long after the close of the New Testament period that Christians found it necessary to state their faith in definite creedal forms. The most elementary and best known is the Apostles' Creed, also called the Old Roman Creed. It is still recited in many churches, as follows:

I believe in God the Father almighty, creator of heaven and earth;

And in Jesus Christ, His only Son, our Lord, Who was conceived by the Holy Spirit, born of the Virgin Mary, suffered under Pontius Pilate, was crucified, dead and buried. He descended to hell, on the third day rose again from the dead, ascended to heaven, sits at the right hand of God the Father almighty, thence He will come to judge the living and the dead;

I believe in the Holy Spirit, the holy catholic Church, the communion of saints, the forgiveness of sins, the resurrection of the body, and the life everlasting. Amen.[1]

The Apostles' Creed attained the form now used in churches about the year A.D. 700, but its essential elements can be traced back to Hippolytus about A.D. 215. According to legend this creed was written by the twelve apostles, each of whom contributed part of it. While the legend is now discredited, the creed does have an apostolic quality in the sense that it attempts to be strictly biblical, by limiting itself to items taken from the words of Scripure. On the whole, whoever first put it together achieved a remarkable success, attested by its acceptance by so many churches of different kinds through the centuries. The truth of several of its statements must be reinterpreted today, yet this applies to the Bible itself rather than to this creed, which only attempts to summarize items from the Bible. Elements to which some might now take exception are the virgin birth, the descent into Hell, the ascent into Heaven, and the resurrection of the body.

The statement that Jesus descended into Hell means only that he really died, that he went into the realm of the dead, not that he went into a place of torment. The English word *hell* has become an inaccurate translation of the Greek word *hades,* which was in the original text of the creed. Many Christians nevertheless take the language of the creed in a poetic sense and think of its general intent and mood, without being disturbed by its now somewhat archaic words and forms of thought.

Its strictly biblical character is both the strength and the weakness of the Apostles' Creed. It is simple, concrete, unspeculative, and it is this simplicity that has appealed through the years to a majority of Christians, who have felt no inclination to question what they have received from the Church as Holy Scripture.

Since early times, however, the Church has also gathered into its fold a considerable number of educated persons with scientific and philosophical interests, whose questing intelligence has impelled them to ask questions and search for rational answers. Such persons may read the Apostles' Creed with full appreciation of its liturgical qualities, yet feel themselves to be challenged by profound questions that the creed so easily by-passes and leaves unanswered. Quite without intending to, the simply worded creed, designed to bring peace to worshipers, for sophisticated persons may suddenly become a theological battleground.

Who are the different persons that are worshiped in the Apostles' Creed? Who are God the Father, Jesus Christ his Son, the Holy Spirit? How many Gods do Christians worship? One, two, three, or four? So far as the simple words of the creed go, one might infer three, possibly four Gods. This would seem to turn Christianity into a polytheism, although Christians have certainly never considered themselves to be polytheists. This shows why the Church has been driven time after time to formulate new creeds, in an attempt to answer these and similar questions. This philosophical interest is one of the characteristics of Chrisitanty, by contrast with Judaism and especially the Judaism of the ancient Hebrews, whose interests did not develop in philosophical directions. While the ancient Hebrews had great prophets, they had no philosophers like Plato and Aristotle.

The heritage of Christianity, however, is Greek as well as Hebrew, and this is reflected nowhere more clearly than in the creeds. By A.D. 100 Christianity had moved out of Palestine, and most Christians were Greeks or Romans.

The Nicene Creed

The Nicene Creed, whose purpose was to resolve the problem of the nature of Christ, was the first theological creed of Christianity. It was formulated in A.D. 325 at Nicaea, located in the Roman province of Bithynia in Asia Minor, by a council composed of 318 eminent prelates of the Church from many different parts of the Roman Empire. The council was assembled by the Emperor Constantine, who personally attended and presided over its sessions. He was eager to bring about peace in the Church, which was threatened with disruption by violent factions that had developed as the issue of the nature of Christ was being debated.

The basis of this issue is philosophical. The Christian Scriptures say that Jesus is God's son, or that God is incarnate in Jesus, as well as that Jesus, who is God's son, and an incarnation of God, died on the cross. All these statements raise questions: How can God become a man? How can God die? How can the Infinite become finite? Can the infinite God accept limitation in any way whatsoever?

The problem emerged in the early days of Christianity, when it was related to a larger movement called Gnosticism. One of the doctrines of this religious movement was the idea that the physical world, including the human body, is evil. The physical body appeared to be the source of man's moral and spiritual problems; it was a handicap to the soul. Even Plato had said that the physical universe was created by a demiurge, a sort of sub-God, not by God himself, and that the human spirit could never attain complete freedom until it was freed from imprisonment in the body. In apparent defiance of this doctrine, Christians were teaching that God had assumed a human form, had become incarnate as a man, and were offering a compromised and debased concept of God as a means of salvation.

As the debate over this issue developed, two definite positions with reference to Christ emerged. They revolved about the concept of the gulf between the infinite and the finite, the absolute and the relative, and the impossibility of integrating the two. On the one hand was a group of Christians called Ebionites, who affirmed that Jesus was a good and great teacher, a revealer of God, but not God himself. This position was finally championed by Arius, a brilliant presbyter of Alexandria, whose appeal was so powerful that it threatened the peace of the whole Church. This was the precipitating cause of the convening of the Council of Nicaea by Constantine.

On the other side were the Gnostic Christians, who affirmed the deity of Christ, but denied his humanity. He was not a man, but only appeared to be one; his flesh was an illusion. Some of them said that Jesus was the son of Joseph and Mary, but the Christ came upon him at his baptism and departed from him at the cross before he died. In this way, they avoided the necessity of saying that God died on the cross, which to them was unthinkable. Because of their assertion that the flesh-and-blood body of Jesus was illusory, that he only appeared to be a real man, those who held this view were called Docetae, derived from the Greek work *dokein,* meaning "to appear, to seem." The Council of Nicaea was summoned primarily for the purpose of trying to reconcile the conflicting positions of the Docetae and the Ebionites. The basic question was whether Christ is God or man. How could these contradictory views be brought together?

The answer of the Nicene Council was to refuse to be impaled on the horns of the dilemma. It did this by saying that it is not a question of asking whether Christ is God or man, but rather of affirming that he is both God and man, fully God and fully man. How this can be, they did not undertake to explain in a rational way. They held that the dogma of the nature of Christ, like all other dogmas of the Church, is a revelation of God, in the ultimate sense a mystery, beyond human power to comprehend. What they seemed to say was that the Church in its worship, in all its spiritual life, in its sense of redemption through Christ, knows that it confronts God in the full sense of the word. That is the essential affirmation of the Nicene Creed, the text of which is as follows:

We believe in one God, the Father All Governing, creator of all things visible and invisible;

And in one Lord Jesus Christ, the Son of God, begotten of the Father as only begotten, that is, from the essence (reality) of the Father, God from God, Light from Light, true God from true God, begotten not created, of the same essence (reality) as the Father, through whom all things came into being, both in heaven and in earth; Who for us men and for our salvation came down and was incarnate, becoming human. He suffered and the third day he rose, and ascended into the heavens. And he will come to judge both the living and the dead.

And (we believe) in the Holy Spirit.

But, those who say, Once he was not, or he was not before his generation, or he came to be out of nothing, or who assert that he, the

Son of God, is of a different *hypostasis* or *ousia,* or that he is a creature, or changeable, or mutable, the Catholic and Apostolic Church anathematizes them.[2]

The Holy Spirit

Both the Apostles' Creed and the Nicene Creed say simply, "I (or we) believe in the Holy Spirit"; they show that up to that time the nature of the Holy Spirit and its relation to God had not become a problem in Christian theology, presumably because the Old Testament had a doctrine of the Spirit of God. Christology, the question of the nature and significance of Christ, was the major concern in early Christian theology because Christ was the main new element Christianity introduced into the theology it had received as a legacy from Judaism. Nevertheless, once the deity of Christ had been clearly established in Christian thought, Christian theology began to show more concern about the Holy Spirit.

The creed associated with the Council of Constantinople in A.D. 381, fifty-six years after Nicaea, appears to have been the first to recognize that the doctrine of the Holy Spirit was in need of elaboration. A sentence in that creed says,

And in the Holy Spirit, the Lord and life-giver Who proceeds from the Father, Who is worshipped and glorified together with the Father and Son, Who spoke through the prophets. . . .[3]

Each item of this statement is significant. After calling the Holy Spirit the Lord and the life-giver it then goes on to explain that the Holy Spirit proceeds from the Father and is worshiped together with the Father and the Son. In that way it brings the three together. Yet it provides no clear statement as to the nature of the Holy Spirit in its relation to the Father and the Son.

Further progress on this point was made by the Second Council of Constantinople in the year 553, which says,

If anyone does not confess that the Father and the Son and the Holy Spirit are one nature or essence (reality), one power or authority, worshipped as a trinity of the same essence (reality), one deity in three hypostases or persons, let him be anathema. For there is one God and Father, of whom are all things, and one Lord Jesus Christ, to whom are all things, and one Holy Spirit, in whom are all things.[4]

In this statement the Father, the Son, and the Holy Spirit are said
to be one nature, one essence, one power; they are worshiped as
a trinity of the same essence, one deity in three persons. Further,
it says that all things are *of* God the Father, *to* the Lord Jesus Christ,
and *in* the Holy Spirit. This statement therefore elaborates on the
nature and the function of the Holy Spirit.

The Trinity

In this same paragraph, apparently for the first time, the word
trinity occurs in a Christian creed, and the concept is clearly stated.
This is an answer to the charge that Christians are polytheists:
here Christians reaffirm the monotheism that they have received
from Judaism.

The importance of the Trinity was to grow with the centuries.
The doctrine came to its culmination in what is known as the
Athanasian Creed (although it was not written by Athanasius, who
had been the chief opponent of Arius at the Council of Nicaea),
which came to its final form only in the ninth century. This creed
was not promulgated by a council and it was in that sense unofficial.
Yet it was widely accepted by the churches, and to this day is the
most explicit and exact definition of the Trinity. The part of the
creed that deals with the Trinity is as follows:

Now the catholic faith is this, that we worship one God in a Trinity and
a Trinity in a Unity, neither confusing the persons, nor separating the
substance. For there is one person of the Father, another of the Son,
another of the Holy Spirit, but of the Father and of the Son and of
the Holy Spirit the divinity is one, the glory equal, the majesty coeternal.

As the Father is, such is the Son, and such the Holy Spirit. The Father
is uncreated, the Son is uncreated, and the Holy Spirit is uncreated.
The Father is infinite, the Son is infinite, the Holy Spirit is infinite.
The Father is eternal, the Son is eternal, and the Holy Spirit is eternal,
and yet there are not three eternals, but one eternal, just as there are
not three uncreated nor three infinites, but one uncreated and one infinite. Likewise the Father is omnipotent, the Son is omnipotent, and
the Holy Spirit is omnipotent, and yet there are not three omnipotents,
but one omnipotent.

So the Father is God, the Son is God, and the Holy Spirit is God,
and yet there are not three Gods, but there is one God. So the Father

is Lord, the Son is Lord, and the Holy Spirit is Lord, and yet there are not three Lords, but there is one Lord. For just as we are compelled by Christian truth to confess each person singly both God and Lord, so by the catholic religion, we are forbidden to speak of three Gods or Lords.

The Father is made of none, neither created, nor begotten. The Son is of the Father alone, not made, nor created, but begotten. The Holy Spirit is of the Father and the Son, not made, nor created, nor begotten, but proceeding. There is therefore one Father, not three Fathers, one Son, not three Sons, one Holy Spirit, not three Holy Spirits. And in this Trinity there is no earlier or later, no greater or less, but the whole three persons are coeternal and coequal with each other; so that in all things, as is aforesaid, both a Trinity and a Unity and a Unity in a Trinity is to be worshipped.[5]

The Nature of Man

Christian views of the nature of man need to be seen in comparison with beliefs of the ancient Hebrews who wrote the Old Testament, where the most characteristic idea is that man is created in the image of God (Genesis 1:27). This view, which prevails throughout the Old Testament, means that he is created with intelligence and freedom of will and therefore with ability to be a moral person like God. God gives man commandments to obey, promising rewards to those who keep the commandments and punishments for those who do not. It is assumed that man has both the intelligence to know and the ability to keep the law that God gives him. God therefore respects man's autonomy; he never invades his personality, nor does he ever coerce his will.

This Hebrew view of the nature of man continues to appear in the teachings of Jesus. His sayings, such as those in the Sermon on the Mount (Matthew 5–7), and his parables always assume the full autonomy of man. Jesus appeals to man, inviting and persuading him to keep God's law, yet never compelling him to do so; neither does he ever feel that man lacks the ability to do so. Jesus holds in reserve a concept of ultimate justice, the certainty of that final judgment which man must face.

With Paul, however, we find ourselves in a new atmosphere. For Paul is overwhelmed by the evil, the wickedness that he sees in the world about him. So much is this so, that men's lives are full of immorality; they seem to be tainted by an innate depravity. More-

over, Paul believes, this depravity has afflicted man since the beginning of the race. Sin came into the world through Adam and passed
from him to his descendants, placing a burden on man he is unable
to bear, a bondage from which he is unable to free himself (Romans
5:12–17).

The Christian Doctrine of Sin

Primarily, sin means rebellion against God or a violation of the will
of God. More specifically, sin means violation of a commandment
of God. Sin is related to, but not identical with, immorality and
vice. Immorality becomes a sin when it is set in a religious perspective and seen as a violation of God's will. The Greek word for
sin, *hamartia,* means "to miss the mark." Therefore, if we consider
goodness, truth, and beauty as attributes of God, as well as of an upright person, any deviation from these attributes is a sin.

The main insight we derive from the teaching of Jesus on the
Christian concepts of sin is that sin is to be identified or recognized
by the intention one has in his heart, in connection with any act
he performs or intends to perform. Like other Jewish teachers of
his time, Jesus used the Ten Commandments as the basis for his
moral and ethical teachings.

The person who is angry with someone and wishes to kill him
has thereby already become morally guilty of murder. In the same
way, the man who has a lustful attitude toward a woman, in an
immoral sense, has become guilty of the act of adultery. This does
not mean that anger alone is murder, but when it reaches the point
of desiring to kill, it is, in a moral light, murder itself. Nor is sexual desire alone a sinful act, but when desire advances to the point
of readiness and determination to engage in sex relations at the
first opportunity, one is already guilty of the act (Matthew 5:27–
28).

Original Sin and Actual Sin

Christian theology distinguishes between *original sin* and *actual sin.*
Original sin does not become actual sin until man of his own free
will deliberately commits an evil act—an act that violates a commandment of God. Original sin has usually been interpreted in
one of two different ways, depending upon the way one interprets
the story of Adam and Eve, on which both Paul and Augustine
based the doctrine of original sin.

The first interpretation of the story of Adam and Eve takes it as literally true, as an actual historical record of the first two human beings. Their sin, according to this view, was the first, in a chronological sense, ever to be committed. Adam and Eve violated the commandment of God by eating the forbidden fruit, and this sin had a damaging effect on their will; their nature instantly became depraved, and they fell from the state of innocence in which they had been created. It was no longer possible for them to perform deeds of perfect goodness; they were no longer worthy to enjoy the immediate and intimate fellowship with God in his Garden. They were, therefore, driven out of Paradise, bearing their newly acquired depravity, as well as the guilt of their first sin. The children born to Adam and Eve and their descendants forever, the interpretation continues, were to inherit both the depravity and the guilt. They are born with the guilt of original sin and are therefore in need of redemption. If we state the doctrine in a legal way, this would seem to make every descendant of Adam and Eve the victim of a sin committed by his remote ancestors. Taken in this sense, the doctrine was rejected by Pelagius (see p. 283) and his followers, and it still continues to be repudiated by many persons.

Another way to understand the story of Adam and Eve is to regard it as a myth or allegory, in which Adam is mankind: every man that ever lived is Adam, every woman that ever lived is Eve, and the facts of all human existence are portrayed in the picturesque story.

The many desires that are deeply rooted in every human being have been given vivid expression in the theological concept of the *Capital* Sins, the *Cardinal* Sins, the *Deadly* Sins. They are called *capital* sins because all other sins are derived from them. They are called *cardinal* sins from the Latin word *cardo* (hinge) because so many specific sins are supported by these sins, as gates are supported by hinges. They are called *deadly* because of their destructive character. The seven cardinal sins are usually listed as pride, avarice, lust, anger, gluttony, envy, and sloth. These sins are all exaggerations of desires that, in their normal forms, are necessary components of human nature.

Augustine

The works of Augustine (354–430), which are the culmination of the first four centuries of Christian theology, represent a reconciliation of the ethical and theological thought of early Christians and

Hebrews with the philosophical and mystical thought of the Greek and Roman world. His writings are saturated with biblical quotations, but he is also familiar with Greek and Roman culture. In some ways he repudiates the Greek and Roman philosophers; yet he is also profoundly influenced by them, especially the Neoplatonists.

Augustine, bishop of Hippo in North Africa from 396 to 430 and the most influential theologian of the ancient church after Paul, was strongly influenced by Paul, in particular by his analysis of human nature. He made Paul's doctrine of original sin the foundation of his theology, but expressed Paul's thought more fully and systematically. Augustine says that Adam, the first man, was created with the ability not to sin (*posse non peccare*), as well as with the ability not to die (*posse non mori*), but through breaking the commandment Adam lost both. Therefore he became both mortal and sinful, and these consequences of Adam's sin passed on to all of his posterity. Man is therefore born in sin, original sin, just as he is born with mortality, destined eventually to die. But when, by the grace of God, man through faith receives the Holy Spirit, Augustine affirms, man attains the nature he had at his original creation: he once again possesses the ability not to sin and the ability not to die. This constitutes the eternal felicity of the City of God (*City of God* X:30; *Confessions* X:31). What we see here is that Augustine has rediscovered Paul and that through him Paul's analysis of human nature has become more pervasive and has penetrated more deeply into Christian theology.

Augustine's mother was a Christian, his father a pagan. In his youth, Augustine was energetic, brilliant, headstrong, and reckless. He lived a dissolute life for several years, but his conscience troubled him, and he began to give some thought to spiritual things. His mother sought to lead him to the Christian faith, but at first she met with no success. He was attracted instead by Manicheism, and for nine years he tried to be a Manichean and to find his inspiration in its dualistic interpretation of the spiritual lfe. He was impressed by the Manichean view that man is totally corrupt, and that view left its mark on Augustine. Eventually, finding the Manicheans superficial and unsatisfying, Augustine became a Christian. He took a vow of celibacy and soon after entered the priesthood. Several of Augustine's writings are against the Manicheans, while others are against the Pelagians, who emphasized the natural goodness of man.

It was this varied experience that prepared Augustine to accept the teaching of Paul about salvation by the grace of God. This idea so inspired Augustine that he gave it a philosophical setting and oriented all his theological thought with reference to it. Salvation is attained by faith, which is a gift of God, Augustine holds; man is unable to keep the moral commandments until God, through the supernatural gift of grace, enlightens his understanding, arouses in him a desire to live a virtuous life, and strengthens his will so that he is able to do so. It is the grace of God that implants in man delight in the life of virtue.

As a reflection of his Neoplatonism, Augustine permits mysticism to occupy a prominent place in his approach to God. His *Confessions,* an autobiographical account of his moral and spiritual struggles, are composed on the theme embodied in his famous words, "Thou hast made us for thyself, and our hearts are restless until they rest in Thee."[6] At the same time, the Bible is the basis of Augustine's faith, and, for his time, his understanding of the Scriptures is original and liberal. But above all, his authority is the Church, whose doctrines are guaranteed, he holds, by the episcopal succession from Christ, through the Apostles, especially Peter, down to his own time.[7]

Pelagius

Augustine's pessimistic view that man's nature is derived from the sin of Adam was not universally accepted in Christianity. The most notable critic of this idea of the natural depravity of man was Pelagius, a British monk who came to Rome in the year 400 and was distressed by the low level of morality that he found among churchmen there. He felt that it resulted in part from the theology of Augustine, which seemed to relieve man of any responsibility for his own evil deeds and to make him instead a victim of what Adam had done at the beginning of time. By contrast, Pelagius made a powerful reaffirmation of the biblical doctrine that man was created in God's image, with intelligence, freedom, moral autonomy, ability to understand God's commandments, and responsibility for every violation of them. He denied Augustine's concept of original sin, and held instead that every man is responsible for his own actions. No man has a right to blame another person for his immoral actions.[8]

Pelagius was popular in his time, but he was not able to compete with the powerful Augustine. His teachings were therefore rejected and condemned by the Church as heresy. To this day any Christian who holds that man is created with the intelligence to know God's will and the strength of will to keep it is called a Pelagian and in traditional circles is considered a heretic. Nevertheless, in spite of the influence of Paul and Augustine, there have always been staunch Pelagians, and they no doubt can be found in Christian churches today.

Scholastic Theology

For centuries theologians were inspired by the work of Augustine. However, despite their admiration for him, many of them had misgivings about this extreme view of the corruption of human nature and his repudiation of the ability of the human mind to discover truth. Pelagius, as we have seen, challenged Augustine in his own time, but was bested in the encounter. During the ensuing seven or eight centuries, few others had the desire or the courage to question the power that Augustine had acquired over the faith and thought of the Church.

The first important evidence of Augustine's decline appeared in Islam and Judaism. The Muslim Averroës (see Chapter 13) and the Jewish Moses Maimonides (see Chapter 10) were both born in Cordova, Spain, during the first half of the twelfth century and lived when Europe was just beginning to become aware of a new interest in science. Averroës wrote a widely influential commentary on Aristotle, and Maimonides wrote a series of learned works in which he too took his departure from the philosophy of Aristotle. Their books, which were eagerly read, made a substantial contribution to the recovery of confidence in the power of reason and in man's ability to discover truth. Many Christians were encouraged by the argument put forward by Averroës and Maimonides that reason is able to prove the existence of God.

Roger Bacon (c. 1215–1294) was the first widely recognized Christian theologian to come out boldly for a rational and scientific approach to truth. His work covered the entire field of science known in his day and advocated the empirical study of the phenomena of nature as a secure basis for the sciences. He even applied this method to the study of religion and became the first Christian scholar to attempt a comparative study of religion.[9] This led him to discover that primitive men, Muslims, Tartars, Buddhists, Jews, and Christians, have held in common, although with variations, a belief in God, a hereafter, and the human soul. He explained this by supposing that God, who desires the salvation of all men, has not left any race or nation without revelation. Thus the people of all religions share these elementary truths as natural revelations, or, as we might say, innate ideas.

The first Christian theologian who was able to make a successful challenge to the extreme position of Augustine in regard to human nature, as well as to his rejection of a rational approach to religion, was Thomas Aquinas (c. 1225–1274), who was born in Italy, but spent most of his mature life as a professor of theology at Paris. His best-known work is the *Summa theologica*,[10] in which he sets forth a systematic Christian theology, bringing together the results of Christian thinking from the early centuries down to his own time. Moreover, he does so in a creative way, by departing from some of Augustine's pessimism and showing a more balanced appreciation than Augustine does of philosophy.

As an admirer of Aristotle, Aquinas takes the position that reason is able to prove the existence of God. Nevertheless, he says, man does not know what God is like, for man's intelligence alone cannot discover this. Thus man is dependent on God's revelation of himself, which comes to him through the Church. In this respect Aquinas goes along with Augustine, who also held that the Church, rather than philosophy, is the guarantee of the truth of faith. Aquinas holds that there are certain truths of faith that are beyond the reach of reason—namely, the creation of the world out of nothingness, the doctrine of the Trinity, and the Incarnation, as well as inferences derived from these dogmas. These truths must be accepted on the authority of the Church. So Christian truth, therefore, as he formulates the system, rests on two pillars: one is reason; the other, revelation. Reason demonstrates the existence of God, but only revelation can tell us what God is like. Yet these truths, Aquinas holds, even though they are beyond the reach of rational demonstration, once they have been attained by faith are not unreasonable.

While this work of Thomas Aquinas was a systematic formulation of scholastic theology, it also marked the end of that period in the life of the Church. For in Aquinas, Christian theology achieved a new orientation toward human nature. It showed a new respect for man's rational ability in its recognition that reason has a place in theology itself. Moreover, it opened to Christian scholars the possibility of participating in the age of science just dawning. Man would now be able to look on his rational ability with more respect; he would be able to cast off some of the sense of depravity that had prevailed since Augustine's time.

Thomas Aquinas has had an enormous influence. The Council of Trent in 1563 decreed that he should be authoritative in all matters of philosophical theology, and he still retains this high position with most Catholic theologians. Moreover, his influence is by no means limited to Catholics.

THE ROMAN CATHOLIC CHURCH

The Roman Catholic Church is the common name of that worldwide organization of Christians who recognize the authority of the Bishop of Rome and give their allegiance to him. Other Christians often apply the word *Catholic* to themselves but say "Roman Catholic" when they are referring to those who recognize the Bishop of Rome. Roman Catholics, on the other hand, prefer to designate themselves simply as Catholics; yet they too find it increasingly necessary to call themselves Roman Catholics for the sake of clarity in their communications.

In its most complete form, the name of this body of Christians is the One Holy, Catholic, and Apostolic Roman Church, which its adherents also refer to as the One Church of Christ, and which, they believe, teaches the one completely true religion revealed by God for the salvation of man.[11] Each word of the title must be understood if one is to grasp its full meaning.

The most essential word is *Church,* a word that occurs frequently in English translations of the New Testament, where it is used to render the Greek *ekklēsia* (an assembly). In this case it refers to an assembly of Christians, although ancient Greeks applied the word to a public assembly of any sort. The English word *Church* is derived from *kyriakon,* which is itself derived from *Kyrios,* meaning Lord—that is, the Christian Lord Jesus. *Kyriakon* literally means the building, shrine, or temple, in which the Lord (*Kyrios*) is worshiped. There is no reference to a church building in the New Testament, but it may be that some large early churches, such as those in Jerusalem, Antioch, Corinth, Ephesus, or Rome, did own church buildings. The real meaning of *Church* in its primary sense in the New Testament is a group of Christians in one locality who constitute a congregation, a meaning that occurs very often in the New Testament. The word *Church* is also used there in a universal sense. When Paul says, "For the husband is the head of the wife as Christ is the head of the Church, his body, and is himself its Savior" (Ephesians 5:23), he uses the word in a universal sense, and that is how it frequently occurs elsewhere in the New Testament.

The word *Roman* in this title indicates that this particular religious body recognizes the supremacy of the Bishop of Rome.

Catholic is derived from the Greek adjective *katholikos* (universal), a word that does not occur in the New Testament. When Catholics use the word, they mean to say that their Church is universal not only in the sense that it is world-wide, but also in the sense that it embraces all truth.

The adjective *Holy* in the title is used by Catholics to indicate that their Church comes from God; that it is divinely authorized, founded, instituted; that it is sacred, consecrated, untainted by evil. *One,* as used here, means that there is only one Church that is at the same time holy, catholic, apostolic, and Roman.

Apostolic refers to the Catholic belief that the Roman Catholic Church was actually established by Christ himself with the Apostle Peter as its foundation. They base this on the words of Jesus in Matthew 16:18, 19, after Peter on behalf of all the disciples has affirmed that Jesus is the Messiah: "And I tell you, you are Peter, and on this rock I will build my church, and the powers of death shall not prevail against it. I will give you the keys of the kingdom of heaven, and whatever you bind on earth shall be bound in heaven, and whatever you loose on earth shall be loosed in heaven." In this passage, the name Peter, which is *Petros* in Greek, is a pun on *petra,* the Greek for "stone," that is, a foundation stone. Other Christians contest the Catholic interpretation of the words of Jesus to Peter. They point out that in Matthew 18:18 Jesus says to all the disciples, "Truly, I say to you, whatever you bind on earth shall be bound in heaven, and whatever you loose on earth shall be loosed in heaven."

Catholics also teach that Peter was the founder of the Church at Rome, a belief that is derived from tradition, not from any New Testament statement. They hold that the power Jesus gave to Peter was carried by him to Rome, where he became the first Bishop of the Roman Church, and that before he died, he transmitted this power to his successor. This power, Catholics hold, has passed down without a break, by direct succession of bishops, from Peter to the present Pope of the Roman Catholic Church, who is first of all Bishop of Rome. This belief is often called "episcopal succession."

The Catholic Faith

The Catholic faith is based first on the Bible, which includes the thirty-nine books of the Old Testament accepted by Jews and Protestants; they also accept the twenty-seven books of the New Testament, just as Protestants do. But Catholics add to their Old Testament seven books that are regarded by Jews and Protestants as being apocryphal and uncanonical: Tobit, Judith, Wisdom of Solomon, Ecclesiasticus (Wisdom of Sirach), Baruch, I and II Maccabees, and certain additions to Esther and Daniel. Catholics allow to them the same authority and inspiration as to other biblical books.

The faith of Catholics is therefore an outgrowth of the Bible itself, beginning with the legacy of Judaism and then going on to include the Gospels, which record the life and teachings of Jesus, the letters of Paul, and the other New Testament writings.

Catholics also hold to the theology that has been formulated all through the centuries by eminent Christian theologians, but especially in *ecumenical councils*. These are assemblies of bishops and other qualified spokesmen for the Church brought together from all over the world for the purpose of defining or redefining Christian faith in the light of new needs and new problems faced by the Church. The first of these ecumenical councils was held at Nicaea in A.D. 325; its deliberations were formulated in the Nicene Creed. There have been altogether some twenty-one' such ecumenical councils. Their decrees, when approved by the Pope, are considered infallible and binding on the Church. They constitute technical formulations of the Catholic faith.[12]

Catholics teach that the souls of men receive appropriate rewards or punishment in the hereafter. The righteous, who die in a state of grace, sins forgiven, immediately enter into eternal life in *Heaven*. Sinners, who die in a state of sin, of rebellion against God, and not in a state of grace, are condemned to eternal torment in *Hell*. Those persons who die without full remission of their sins must go for a time to *Purgatory*, where they suffer until their guilt is purged away before going to Heaven. All unbaptized children, and unbaptized adults who are not guilty of grievous sins, must go to *Limbo,* which is not a place of punishment, but one in which they will be deprived of a vision of God.[13]

Catholic Polity

The Catholic Church is governed through a world-wide hierarchical organization comprised of the Pope, cardinals, bishops, and priests, as well as orders of the clergy. The *Pope,* who is elected for life and is the Bishop of Rome, is its chief presiding officer. The word *Pope* is derived from the Latin *papa* and the Greek *papas,* meaning *father.* The Pope, also addressed as the Holy Father, is the head of the Roman Catholic Church and its official spokesman.

The *infallibility* of the Pope was affirmed by a decree issued by the Vatican Council in 1870. This means that he is considered infallible only when he speaks *ex cathedra,* that is, when he speaks in his official position as head of the Church on matters of faith and morals. This dogma is an expression of the general Roman Catholic view that the Church is the ultimate authority in religious matters. The Bible itself is to be interpreted by the Church. The layman must ask his priest for the correct meaning of Scripture, and the priest must state the interpretation that the Church authorizes him to give. This emphasis on the ultimate and definitive character of the Church is very important in Catholic doctrine.[14]

The *College of Cardinals* is the highest official body next to the Pope. It consists of more than 100 cardinals (who are also bishops, priests, or deacons) representing all Christian nations. Cardinals are appointed by the Pope himself, their function being to advise the Pope and to serve as administrators of the various activities and organizations of the Church. One of their main responsibilities is to elect a new Pope whenever a Pontiff dies.

The Seven Sacraments

The Roman Catholic Church employs seven sacraments in ministering to the religious needs of mankind. They are as follows: baptism, confirmation, Holy Communion (also called the Eucharist, the Lord's Supper or the Mass), penance, marriage, holy orders, and extreme unction. The sacraments are based on the belief that human nature is weak, characterized by desires which impel it to rebel against the laws of God as well as the laws of man. This rebellion of man is the result of the selfish character of his desires. Since man rebels against God and human society, he finds himself a sinner in need of reconciliation at both the divine and the human levels. As the creator of man, however, God is eager to assist man in his struggle for reconciliation; he is always ready to show his good will, his grace, to man, and to provide man with the power to achieve salvation from his human predicament. God has therefore established his Church, administered by its priests, whose responsibility is to offer the sacraments, through which his divine grace is made available. God offers salvation as an act of his own love; it is man's part to respond in faith by the submission of his will to the will of God. Baptism and confirmation are the rites which initiate man into the Church; a man receives them but once. Holy Communion (see Figure 12.3) and penance provide man with forgiveness for sins and awareness of the living presence of the Divine during his lifetime. The sacrament of marriage brings the blessing and grace of God to man and his wife as they enter the estate of matrimony. Holy orders is the sacrament which sets a man apart and equips him for a professional religious vocation. Extreme unction brings to man the support of God's grace as he dies and enters the life everlasting.

Catholics hold that when the bread and wine are consecrated in the sacrament of the Eucharist they are changed into the flesh and blood of Christ. This is the doctrine of *transubstantiation*. The miracle involves only the essence of the bread and wine. The change is not evident in appearance or taste, which remain as before.

Veneration of Saints

The veneration of saints is a prominent element in Catholic religion. One arrives at the status of sainthood through the stages of beatification and canonization after death, a process that may require several years. A saint is one who has demonstrated his qualifications, first by a holy life, second by his ability to perform miracles. Examinations of a rigorous character are made by the Congregation of Rites. Since 993, when the first solemn canonization occurred, a vast number of persons have received this honor.

FIGURE 12.3 A Catholic Mass. (*The New Catholic Encyclopedia*)

Such persons receive a feast day; their relics are publicly venerated; churches and altars are dedicated to them, and their statues and pictures are displayed.

The *Virgin Mother of Christ* is the most important of all the saints. According to Catholic doctrine, she became the mother of Christ by means of a virgin birth, as related in the Gospels of Matthew and Luke (see Figure 12.1). The dogma of the *Immaculate Conception,* proclaimed by Pope Pius IX in 1854, affirms that the Virgin Mother herself was conceived in the womb of her own mother Anna without sin. She and her son Jesus were therefore both born without the taint of original sin, the only human beings ever so born.[15]

The *Assumption of the Virgin* is the most recent dogma proclaimed with reference to the Virgin Mary. It was issued in 1950 and is in line with the earlier dogma of the Immaculate Conception, by which Mary was exempted from original sin. Her body was therefore not subjected to corruption in the grave. Her assumption into

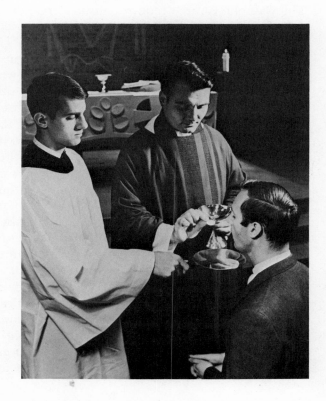

Heaven, both body and soul, was equivalent to the resurrection from the dead in the case of Jesus.[16] Since her assumption to Heaven, which occurred at her death, according to the dogma, the Virgin Mary has sat in splendor as Queen "at the right hand of her Son, the immortal King of the Ages."[17]

These last two dogmas—the Immaculate Conception and the Assumption of the Virgin—illustrate the Catholic view of the authority of the Church. Since neither of these dogmas is clearly articulated in the Scriptures, the Church promulgated them on its own authority. The first was by decree of Pope Pius IX, 1854, the latter, by Pope Pius XII, 1950, both without calling a Council. The power exercised by the Popes in proclaiming these new dogmas shows the increment of power which had come to the papal office, recognized by the dogma of Papal Infallibility adopted by the Vatican Council in 1870.

Celibacy and Monasticism

The Catholic Church requires all its clergy, except those of Eastern rites, from the rank of subdeacon up, to practice celibacy. They take a solemn vow to live a life of perfect chastity. This practice is based in part on the teaching of Paul in 1 Corinthians 7:32, 33, where he expresses the view that both men and women who are free of family anxieties are able to devote themselves more fully to the service of God; Jesus himself, in Matthew 19:12, notes with apparent approval the fact that some persons practice celibacy for the sake of the kingdom of Heaven. Celibacy was practiced by some members of the early church, but it did not begin to become a general institution until the fourth century, when it was first widely practiced in Spain and then became common throughout the Western Church. At the Lateran Council in 1139, marriage of the higher clergy was made unlawful and declared invalid.[18]

Monasticism is another well-known institution of the Catholic Church. A monastery is a place where a community of monks or nuns lives separated from the distractions of ordinary social and business life and therefore free to devote themselves to spiritual disciplines, as well as to various types of practical work. Monasteries have done much for general education and toward keeping scholarship alive, especially in Europe during the Middle Ages.

Some orders of monks, such as the *Franciscans* and *Dominicans,* have their own houses yet devote themselves to an active life outside the monastery; many of them are missionaries. Some monks, for instance the Franciscans, take a vow of poverty, following in the footsteps of Francis of Assisi (1182–1226), whose influence has been felt far beyond the ranks of Catholicism. The *Jesuits* are an order unique in the Church. Founded by Ignatius Loyola in 1534, this society places itself under the command of the Pope, and its members are noted for their scholarly achievements.

The Temporal Power of the Pope

The temporal power of the Pope is indicated by one of the titles ascribed to him. His full title is as follows: Bishop of Rome, Vicar of Jesus Christ, Successor of the Prince of the Apostles, Supreme Pontiff of the Universal Church, Patriarch of the West, Primate of Italy, Archbishop and Metropolitan of the Roman Province, and Sovereign of the State of the City of the Vatican. This last title derives from the fact that he is actually the monarch of the tiny State of the City of the Vatican, an area of just under one square mile, with a population of slightly more than 500 persons. It includes the Vatican Palace and its annexes, the Church of St. Peter, and adjacent buildings. As sovereign of this state, the Pope is responsible for all legislative, executive, and judicial powers of government.[19]

On the basis of his position as sovereign of the Vatican, small though it is, the Pope has a secretary of state and maintains diplomatic relations with at least twenty-five nations of the world, to which he sends ambassadors. The duty of a papal ambassador is to cultivate the good will of the foreign government and, at the same time, to watch over the welfare of Catholics in that nation. No other Christian denomination enjoys such a strategic relationship with foreign governments.

This temporal power of the Popes had no precedent in early Christianity. Neither Jesus, nor the Apostles, nor their successors for some 300 years either claimed or exercised such power. This unusual power of the Popes emerged at the time when the Roman Empire was beginning to collapse. From about the fifth to the ninth century, the Church was the only institution in Europe in a position to bring a measure of order and peace. Gregory I (590–604) and Gregory VII, also called Hildebrand (1073–1085), contributed most to this growth of temporal power. The Church gradually gained possession of large areas of Italy. By 1860 the papal lands had grown to 15,774 square miles, with 3 million inhabitants and large revenues. The Popes have at times provided military, financial, educational, moral, and spiritual stability to much of Europe, but in 1860 the papal states of Romagna, Marches, and Umbria were annexed by the emerging kingdom of Italy, leaving to the Pope only the City of Rome. In 1870 Italy seized Rome too, thus essentially bringing the Pope's temporal power to an end. However, in 1929 the Pope regained his temporal power in principle, when the government of Italy by the Treaty of the Lateran restored his sovereignty over the miniature State of the City of the Vatican.[20]

The Second Vatican Council (1962–1965)

The Second Vatican Council of the Roman Catholic Church made an important contribution to the ecumenical spirit among the various Christian Churches. Some of its decrees have particular relevance. The Decree on the Liturgy provides for the introduction of vernacular languages into the liturgy of the Mass, which has hitherto been conducted only in Latin. A democratic trend in the hierarchy of the Catholic Church is shown by the Constitution of the Church, which affirms that bishops in the various countries are to share the ruling power with the Pope. The Decree on the Laity gives more freedom and responsibility to laymen. Another decree recognizes the responsibility of the Church in regard to the moral issues of war and peace, poverty, industrialism, as well as social and economic justice. In the Decree on Ecumenism, for the first time in its history, the Catholic Church recognizes that Protestant Churches also share the grace and favor of God. Another decree of equal importance has to do with religious liberty, in which the Catholic Church recognizes the right of all men everywhere to freedom of conscience in religion and officially terminates the hostility toward other Christian Churches represented by the Inquisition and the Counter-Reformation. A step toward reconciliation between the Roman Catholic Church and the Eastern Orthodox Churches was taken when the Pope and the Patriarch withdrew the bans of excommunication which their predecessors issued against each other at the time of the separation centuries ago. The decrees also reflect a friendly spirit toward non-Christian religions, such as Judaism and Islam.

All this does not mean that the time has come for the union of all religions into one religion of the world, nor even that all

Christian Churches are going to unite. But it does recognize that all religions and all Christian Churches face the same ultimate problems, which means that each of them has an integrity of its own and is worthy of being treated with sympathy, respect, and dignity. Moreover, the Second Vatican Council provided a framework within which helpful collaboration of many kinds, such as will bring reciprocal benefits to all concerned, can take place.[21]

THE EASTERN ORTHODOX CHURCHES

The Eastern Orthodox Churches came into existence as a result of the division between the Churches of the east and those of the west, for which there were several causes. The division between the Churches was, to begin with, partially a result of the division of the Roman Empire between the east and the west, which began in the reign of Diocletian (A.D. 284–305). Owing to the vast size of the Empire, the difficulties of swift communication and administration of all matters of government from one capital became almost insurmountable. Diocletian concluded that one emperor could not successfully bear the responsibilities of the entire Roman world and therefore devised a new form of imperial administration. There were to be two capitals, with two emperors, one in the west, one in the east. Rome would continue to serve as the capital in the west; Constantinople would become the new capital in the east.

This division of the political powers of government set the pattern for rivalry, if not division, within the government of the Church.[22] The Bishop of Rome gradually strengthened his position as head of the universal Church, a claim that he had no intention of abandoning. When Constantinople was elevated to the position of a capital of the Empire, the Greek Patriarch of the Church of that city experienced an increase in prestige. The Churches of the east found it natural as well as convenient to turn to him for direction, rather than to the distant Bishop of Rome. The ensuing jealousy between the two powerful Church leaders did not immediately lead to a rupture, but the seeds of separation had been sown. The Patriarch resented and began to reject the claim of the Bishop of Rome to authority over the universal Church. Complete separation did not occur until A.D. 1054, and it became final only in 1453, when the Eastern Churches became independent and autonomous.

There were four main divisions of the Eastern Church: the Patriarchates of Constantinople, Alexandria, Antioch of Syria, and Jerusalem. In addition, however, each of these Churches extended its influence by missionary activities, which led to the founding of many new Churches. As a result, the following essentially Eastern Orthodox Churches have come into existence: Cypriote, Russian, Georgian, Sinai, Greek (see Figure 12.4), Bulgarian; Serbian, Croatian, and Slovakian; Roumanian, Ukrainian, Polish, Esthonian, Finnish, Czechoslovakian, Albanian, and North American.[23]

With slight and apparently insignificant exceptions, Orthodox theology is the same as that of the Roman Catholics. The Orthodox accept without question the first seven ecumenical councils, the last they accept being the one held at Nicaea in 787. Most of the

fundamental dogmas in this day held in common by Roman Catholics, Eastern Orthodox, and Protestants were formulated by these first seven councils. In that sense, all these groups have the same theological foundation and may properly be called Catholic, provided no sectarian adjective of differentiation is employed; in that sense, too, the Eastern Orthodox Churches are Catholic.

The claim of the Pope of Rome to universal sovereignty over all Catholic Churches has remained the main issue between the east and west; but there are also certain minor theological issues involved. The Eastern Churches repudiate the *filioque* clause which the Western Churches added to the Nicene Creed. This is the affirmation that the Holy Spirit proceeds from the Father *and the Son*. The Eastern Churches deny this, and affirm that the Holy Spirit proceeds from the Father alone, apparently more hesitant than the west in affirming the absolute deity of the Son. Yet this can hardly be said of the Eastern Churches in general. The Eastern Churches fully accept the dogma of the Trinity, and their liturgies and worship demonstrate that they go as far as the west in proclaiming that the Son and the Holy Spirit, as well as the Father, are God.

Another difference between east and west has to do with the use of statues in the Roman Catholic Churches. The Eastern Churches repudiate this practice, following the precedent of the Jews, who base their position on the commandment in the Decalogue, "You shall not make yourself a graven image" (Exodus 20:4). Yet the adoration of icons—paintings or mosaic portrayals of holy persons—by the east appears to be very similar to veneration of statues of the saints and the Holy Family in the west. At times, notably about 726, and again in 814, popular feeling against statues became so strong that mobs undertook to destroy all they could find in the Eastern Churches. The proximity of Jewish and Muslim communities to the Eastern Churches may have had something to do with these outbreaks of iconoclasm (attempted destruction of icons). Islam had conquered much of the territory occupied by the Eastern Churches, and the Muslims were bitterly opposed to the use of images of any sort.

The practice of celibacy by the Roman Catholic clergy is another issue that divides east and west: Eastern Churches permit

FIGURE 12.4   A Greek Orthodox wedding. (*Gordon Parks, Life Magazine* © *Time Inc.*)

their priests to marry. The form of baptism is a further issue: while
the Roman Church uses sprinkling or pouring, the Greek Churches
practice immersion. They even immerse infants, baptizing them
three times, in the name of the Father, the Son, and the Holy
Spirit. The Eastern and Western practices of observing the Holy
Communion also differentiate these two branches of Christianity:
Worshipers in the east receive both bread and wine; in the west,
laymen receive only the bread. Yet the east holds essentially the
same view as the west about transubstantiation. Eastern Churches
also reject the Roman Catholic doctrines of Limbo and Purgatory,
as well as the Roman Catholic dogma of the Immaculate Conception,
since they affirm that the Virgin Mary was freed from original sin
at the Annunciation. Finally, they reject the Catholic dogma of
the infallibility of the Pope, as well as the recently promulgated
dogma of the Assumption of the Virgin Mary.

The three most recently proclaimed Roman Catholic dogmas
have evidently widened the breach between west and east, and at
the same time the Eastern Churches appear to have drawn closer to
Protestants. The Eastern Churches have shown friendliness toward
Protestants by participating fully in the Protestant Ecumenical
Movement. They are members of the World Council of Churches,
which is the form the Protestant Ecumenical Movement has taken.
On the other hand, Roman Catholics recognize the validity of the
Orthodox Sacraments, and so consider them Catholics in a real
sense, except for their repudiation of the universal authority and
infallibility of the Pope, along with the minor deviations noted
above. The Eastern Churches, on their part, regard the claims of
the Roman Church to supremacy as unjustified by Holy Scripture
or in any other way.

PROTESTANTISM

Protestantism is the third major form of Christianity to emerge
since its inception. We are accustomed to associate Protestantism
with reform movements of the fifteenth and sixteenth centuries,
but there has never been a time in the history of Christianity when
it was completely unified, when there was no voice of protest
against the official formulations of faith. Reform movements began
to attain vigor in the twelfth century in southern France. The

Cathari were known in France, Italy, Spain, the Netherlands, and Germany. Their pessimism about the material world—their belief, for example, that matter was created by Satan, not by God—indicates a survival of an element of Manicheism in Christianity. The Albigenses and Waldenses were also important protest groups.

The Catholic Church organized the medieval Inquisition in 1229 in an effort to exterminate dissident movements. The Spanish Inquisition, organized in 1478, aimed to restore and preserve the unity of the Church. But the methods employed were at times extreme and the Inquisition with its cruelty constitutes a chapter of Church history that Catholics now look back upon with regret.[24] Many earnest Christians who refused to recant were put to death, had their property confiscated, or were punished in other ways. Although these severe methods may have succeeded in achieving a temporary repression of revolt, in the end they only increased resentment toward the Church by its own adherents.

Protestantism itself, for example, began as an effort to reform the Roman Catholic Church, yet it was the harshness that it encountered in this attempt that led to a complete break with the mother Church and the formation of independent Christian bodies. John Wycliffe (c. 1320–1384), of England, one of the pioneer reformers, made a translation of the Bible from Latin, which he placed in the hands of the common people; and he eloquently preached a return to the Bible itself as the chief authority in Christian faith. John Huss (1369?–1415), of Bohemia, who was burned at the stake, had been deeply influenced by the writings of Wycliffe and had thereafter become a leader of reform in his own country. Girolamo Savonarola (1452–1498), of Italy, another Catholic leader who was a bitter critic of abuses of the Church, was hanged in Florence. William Tyndale (1494–1536), an English reformer, was famous for his translation of the New Testament, which was eventually to become the basis of the King James Version of the Bible. He was burned at the stake in Antwerp.

Martin Luther (1483–1546) became the most famous of all the leaders of the Protestant Reformation, despite the fact that his activity was confined to his native Germany. In addition to his vigorous activity as a preacher and a leader of the new movement for reform, Luther found time to translate the Bible into German. He based his translation on the Greek New Testament just edited by Erasmus (1466–1536), the foremost classical scholar of the early Protestant movement.

Ulrich Zwingli (1484–1531) was a Swiss who was closely associated with Luther but did not entirely agree with him. He laid the foundation in Switzerland for John Calvin (1509–1564), the most eminent theologian of the Protestant Reformation.

The Church of England arose out of resentment of the fact that England was under the control of the Pope of Rome, although its actual separation from Rome was precipitated by the quarrel of Henry VIII (1509–1547) and the Pope over his desire for a divorce.

Some Protestant Denominations

LUTHERANS. § Lutherans are followers of the branch of the Protestant Reformation which had its origin in Germany under Martin Luther. The name Lutheran was applied to them by their enemies, although in time they wore it with pride. Luther's teachings were framed in terms of his rebellion against the Roman Catholic Church, of which he had been a priest. In place of the authority of the Church and the Pope, Luther substituted the Bible. For the Roman Catholic priesthood, he substituted the priesthood of all believers. For the sacraments and the purchase of indulgences, he substituted faith as the true and only means of salvation. Luther believed that the Bible is the inspired Word of God, and that every man has a right to read it for himself and to respond to it as he is prompted by the Holy Spirit.

BAPTISTS. § The first Baptist Church in America was founded in Rhode Island by Roger Williams in 1639. Like the Anabaptists, their predecessors in Europe, Baptists have continued to insist on adult baptism by immersion as well as on baptism of the Holy Spirit as the basis of church membership. Except for small dissident groups, Baptists of the United States are organized in the American and Southern Baptist Conventions, together constituting one of the largest Protestant fellowships in the world. They are evangelistic and missionary and have always stood for religious freedom and separation of church and state.

PRESBYTERIANS. § Presbyterians are the heirs of John Calvin (1509–1564) of Switzerland and of John Knox (c. 1505–1572) of Scotland. (The followers of Calvin in Switzerland, Holland, and Germany were called the Reformed Church; in France they were called the

Huguenots; in Scotland, the Presbyterians.) The name Presbyterian is derived from *presbyteros*, the Greek word for "Elder," the senior lay official in a Presbyterian Church. The basic concepts in the theology of John Calvin, and therefore of the Presbyterians, are the sovereignty of God in the universe, of Christ in salvation, of the Scriptures in faith and practice, and of the individual conscience in interpreting the Word and will of God. Closely related to these ideas are belief in the depravity of man and the election of certain persons to salvation and the predestination of others to be lost, doctrines which Presbyterians have modified. Man has a covenant with God which must be kept; he must trust in the goodness and grace of God; salvation is by faith, not by works. The Presbyterians have insisted on a well-educated ministry and have been a theologically informed people.

EPISCOPALIANS. § The Protestant Episcopal Church in the United States began as a branch of the Church of England. Its first congregation was situated in Jamestown in 1607, and by the beginning of the Revolutionary War congregations had been established in all the American colonies. Since the clergy had received their appointments in England, they remained loyal to England during the Revolution, despite the fact that their churches were destroyed and demoralized. But when the war was over, the churches were reorganized and became independent from the Church of England; they remain so today. The Episcopal Church regained its strength, adapted itself to American life and has become an influential denomination in the United States. Its continued use of the Book of Common Prayer has served as a bond with the Church of England in liturgy as well as in doctrine. While the Episcopal Church in the United States, like the Church of England, has maintained its organizational unity it nevertheless includes both an Anglo-Catholic party or High Church, which leans toward Roman Catholicism, and an evangelical party or Low Church, which leans toward Protestantism.

METHODISTS. § The Methodist Church began at Oxford, England, in 1729, when a group of students led by John and Charles Wesley and George Whitefield, impelled by the dryness of the Church of England and its lack of interest in the lower classes, organized regular times of Bible study, prayer, and discussion. Because of their regular habits, they were derided as "Methodists." John Wesley and George Whitefield became famous preachers, while Charles Wesley excelled as the hymn writer of the young Methodist movement.

Rejected by the Church of England, the Methodist preachers spoke at open air revivals and soon reached all of England. At the same time, John Wesley sent leaders to the American colonies. One of these leaders was Francis Asbury, who in 1771 became the first noted American Methodist bishop. Methodist evangelism was suited to the pioneer conditions in America and the Methodists manifested an interest in political, economic, and social life as well as in building churches and hospitals.

John and Charles Wesley lived in Georgia in 1736–1738, Charles as secretary to General Oglethorpe, and John as an unsuccessful missionary to the Indians. In the course of the trip, however, John Wesley came in contact with a group of Moravians, whose warm piety left its mark on him. He rejected Calvin's doctrine of predestination in favor of freedom of the will as set forth by Jacob Armenius (1560–1609).

QUAKERS. § The Society of Friends, better known as the Quakers, was founded by George Fox (1624–1691) of England, who denounced all religious ceremonies, sacraments, and creeds. He felt that he had had a personal encounter with Christ, who came to him as a quiet voice, an inner light. When Fox's followers met with persecution in England, several of them fled to the American colonies, where some were put to death in Boston, while others found refuge in Rhode Island and Pennsylvania. The Friends, preferring to live quietly, have never aggressively sought converts, but they have won high regard for their spirituality, devotion to peace, and works of charity. Although a small community, the Friends have made a large contribution to American life.

DISCIPLES OF CHRIST. § The Disciples of Christ are the largest denomination of purely American origin. Their first church was established in Pennsylvania in 1909 by Thomas Campbell and his son, Alexander, who came to America from a Presbyterian background in Scotland. The Campbells retained most beliefs shared by Protestants. Their specific aim was to unite all the denominations into one great church. The basis of the union of the denominations was to be primitive Christianity, which they planned to restore by teaching and practicing the New Testament. Like Baptists, the Disciples practiced adult immersion; like Presbyterians, they appointed elders and deacons as the lay officers of their congregations. They also adopted a weekly celebration of the Lord's Supper. Their polity is congregational.

UNITARIANS. § The Unitarians have no creed. They reject most Christian dogmas, such as the deity of Christ, the Trinity, and the inspiration of the Bible. Some do not believe in God. They believe in the natural goodness of man and in reason as an adequate guide for both religion and morality. In 1961 the Unitarians united with the Universalists, a group with similar beliefs, to form the Unitarian Universalist Association.

MORMONS. § The Church of Jesus Christ of Latter Day Saints (Mormons) was founded in New York State in 1830 by Joseph Smith, believed by his followers to have been an inspired prophet. He based his church on the Bible and the Book of Mormon, which he claimed to have translated from golden plates dug from the ground after their presence had been revealed by an angel. A Protestant denomination, the Mormons practice adult immersion and a weekly Holy Communion. They follow the New Testament, beginning with the Twelve Apostles, and teach that in Heaven God and angels as well as men and women have flesh and blood bodies and that a marriage contracted on earth continues in Heaven. Mormons practice baptism for the dead. At one time they also practiced polygyny, but this aroused hostility. They were forced to flee, first to Ohio, then to Missouri, and next to Illinois, where Joseph Smith, the prophet, and Hyrum Smith, the patriarch, were murdered. Led by Brigham Young, the Mormons migrated in 1844 to the territory of Utah and established a colony at what is now Salt Lake City. They abolished polygyny in 1890. The Mormons have a vigorous missionary program and teach that Christ himself was once a missionary to the American Indians.

CHRISTIAN SCIENTISTS. § In 1879 the Church of Christ, Scientist, was founded by Mary Baker Eddy (1821–1910) in Boston. It is based on the belief that God, the universal Spirit, is real; that matter is unreal; and that sin, evil, pain, and illness, which reside in matter, are therefore unreal. This faith is known for its cultivation of a spiritual life as well as for its practice of healing, which is accomplished through meditation on the unreality of illness and through prayer. Mrs. Eddy believed that she rediscovered the principles of divine healing which Jesus practiced in performing the cures attributed to him in the Gospels.

JEHOVAH'S WITNESSES. § Jehovah's Witnesses, founded by Charles Taze Russell (1852–1916), is based primarily on belief in the second coming of Christ.

Other Protestant leaders have continued to appear, especially on the continent of North America, representing new insights into the Christian faith or protesting abuses in older churches, whether Catholic or Protestant. The Protestant movement in principle seems to imply this process of continuous reform and renewal.

Protestant Faith

Protestantism as a religious phenomenon comprises many churches and has never been a single united movement. While the name it bears marks it as a protest movement, Protestantism has important positive elements which express its essential character. Up to the beginning of Protestantism, the Roman Catholic Church had been the main Christian church in Europe. The Pope of Rome claimed the power of giving or withholding crowns, with regard to the sovereigns of the nations of Europe. Protestantism was therefore at times an expression of rising nationalism and represented resentment of political control by the Roman Pontiff. At the same time, Protestantism served as protest against numerous abuses in the Catholic Church itself.

Of even greater importance is the fact that Protestantism emerged during a period when the learning of ancient Greece was being rediscovered and the importance of reason was being recognized. Men were turning to the natural sciences, and a new sense of man's own importance was making itself felt. A democratic spirit was moving through the scholarly atmosphere of Europe: man resented every form of authority that limited his freedom, whether political or ecclesiastical. All these factors had to do, in one or another way, with the Protestant repudiation of the authority of the Church of Rome.

Protestants differ among themselves on numerous questions of theology and church polity, yet there are some basic principles that most of them hold. They all agree in rejecting the authority of the

Roman Catholic Church and in turning to the Bible instead as their source of authority. Moreover, they affirm the right of every person to study the Bible himself, without intervention of church or priest, for they feel free to approach God directly. While Protestants believe in the inspiration of the Scriptures, they also emphasize the doctrine of the Holy Spirit, affirming that the Holy Spirit illuminates their minds when they read the Bible, as well as when they wrestle with problems of the moral life.

Most Protestant Churches observe only two sacraments—Baptism and the Lord's Supper (Holy Communion)—because they have concluded, on the basis of the New Testament, that Christ formally instituted only these two sacraments. Protestants hold that salvation is by faith alone, not by means of any sacrament; they regard a sacrament as no more than an "external and visible sign of an inward and invisible grace." In that light, Baptism does not bring about the forgiveness of sins, either original or actual. Both Catholics and Protestants believe that the efficacy of sacraments depends on the sincere intentions of the person receiving them. He must keep the rites for the purpose of fulfilling the will of God.

Protestants hold that the words of Jesus in instituting the Lord's Supper are metaphors, not to be taken literally. The bread and wine are symbols: while they represent the body and blood, they do not become flesh and blood. The symbols lay hold of the essence of the sacrament, Protestants teach, and enable worshipers to participate by faith in fellowship with their Lord, who is present as Host at the supper. The Protestant rite of Holy Communion therefore celebrates the presence of the living Lord, in addition to his death on the cross; but while it brings to mind his death, it does not repeat it. From the Protestant point of view, the mystery, the wonder, the miracle, of the sacrament occurs in the hearts of the worshipers, not in the elements of bread and wine.

Protestants do not deny the spiritual values represented by the sacraments that they do not observe, since they believe that all life may have a sacramental quality. Protestants regard marriage as a sacrament, but for them the sacrament is in the hearts of the persons entering into this union, not in the formal rites that unite them. They also believe that the grace of God comes through penance or, as they call it, repentance. Many Protestant Churches practice confirmation; those which do not usually emphasize conversion, which is a similar experience. Most Protestants also practice ordination for persons entering religious vocations. They have no formal rite called extreme unction, but it is their custom to bring the comforts of religion to the sick and the dying. Burial of the dead is an important religious rite in Protestantism.

This analysis shows that the differences between Catholics and Protestants in regard to the sacraments are more apparent than real. Both believe that their faith is a response to the grace of God, and both perform rites expressing the mysteries of faith. For Protestants the truly great sacrament is the sermon, in which they expect to hear the Word of God proclaimed. They believe that the Spirit of God enters their hearts as they hear the Word. They do not think of the sermon as a formal sacrament, and it is not usually called one. Yet a Protestant hardly feels that he has been to church unless he has heard a sermon (see Figure 12.5).

Emphasis on the Bible led Protestants to become diligent students of the Scriptures. Early in their development, the Protestants repudiated the Catholic attempt to limit the Bible to the Latin language and began to produce translations into the vernacular so that every person could read the Bible in his mother tongue. An interest in the Scriptures, similar to that of the Protestants, is being felt by the Catholics, who now have vernacular translations of their own and stress the importance of biblical studies.

Protestants have been heirs of the entire theological history of Christianity, beginning with the Bible itself and including all the creedal and theological developments up to their own time. They have shown a special debt to Augustine, insofar as faith is the main principle of Protestant theology, but they have rejected his emphasis on the authority of the Church. Although Protestants are also indebted to Thomas Aquinas, they have pursued their own theological studies in response to new developments in the sciences, philosophies, and cultural movements of their time. But it must not be assumed that the different Protestant Churches have always been in accord with one another in the formulation of their theologies. The fact is that they have sometimes been as hostile toward one another as they have been toward Roman Catholics. Controversy has been characteristic of Protestantism, and it is out of this that their new theologies have developed.

Luther was the first among the great reformers to make faith

FIGURE 12.5   A Protestant sermon. (*Southern Baptist Sunday School Board*)

the center of theology; he based his position primarily on Paul, but also reflected the thinking of Augustine. Calvin took Luther's position as a point of departure, but went on from there to emphasize the grace of God—again reflecting Augustine—and the sovereignty of God, election, foreordination, and predestination, all of which have continued to be important in such groups as the Presbyterians.

The coexistence of different schools of theology has been characteristic of Protestantism. Modernism and Fundamentalism arose out of the debate over the relative place of reason and revelation in the interpretation of the Scriptures. The Modernists made full use of reason, and did not hesitate to recognize elements of folklore, legend, and myth in certain parts of the Bible, as well as some in-

accurate historical statements and some erroneous scientific views. Fundamentalists, on the other hand, insisted on the inerrancy of Scripture in all respects.

The debate between Liberalism and Neoorthodoxy is a variant form of the same controversy. Employing a philosophical approach, Liberals have freely discarded some creedal statements and theological doctrines of the past; the Neoorthodox, by contrast, retain all the classical doctrines of Christianity, but nevertheless seek for new meanings and make frequent use of the concept of myth. The Neoorthodox treatment of original sin may be taken as one example of their use of myth. Original sin means those desires that are imbedded in human nature, desires with which all persons are born. Such desires are not actual sins, but are the basis of temptations and thus lead us to commit sin. Original sin is therefore a natural element in human nature, but actual sin is a violation of the moral law, which man commits of his own free will. Adam and Eve are type people; their story is an allegory, a myth. All men recapitulate the story of their primal sin. The Adam and Eve myth is a symbol of all moral experience.

The origins of Neoorthodoxy as well as of religious existentialism are traced back to the Danish Søren Kierkegaard (1813–1855). His work was a protest against humanism, which he denounced as a rebirth of Pelagianism. Karl Barth (1886–1968) has been the great exponent of Neoorthodoxy in Europe, and Reinhold Niebuhr (b. 1892) has been its chief spokesman in America.

Religious existentialism has been closely related to Neoorthodoxy. Most of the Neoorthodox theologians can also be classified as existentialists. The chief difference between the two movements is that while Neoorthodoxy is closely tied to biblical studies, religious existentialism is closer to philosophy. This movement which began in Denmark was cultivated by several German writers. Among them are the Jewish philosopher Martin Buber (1878–1965), whose *I and Thou* has had an influence far beyond Jewish circles; Rudolph Bultmann (b. 1884), who is a representative of both Neoorthodoxy and existentialism; and Paul Tillich (1886–1965), the most famous of the existentialist theologians, who also strongly reaffirmed the necessity of using reason in theology.

The existentialists describe the predicament of man in the machine age, where the danger exists that man himself will be interpreted in mechanistic terms. They are opposed to this mechanistic approach to man and affirm that the essence of man's nature is freedom of will and moral responsibility. These attributes of man must be defended, they say, against every form of mechanistic thought. Man today lives with the threat of nonbeing hanging over him, and anxiety is one of his characteristics. In this sense, he feels within himself an apprehension of death, a fear that his freedom is only apparent, that he cannot escape the compulsive forces of heredity and environment. This is contemporary man's predicament.

Paul Tillich held that man in his primary religious experience apprehends the Divine as personal—as is evident in all the religions of the world—but that this same man, who by faith apprehends the Divine as personal, is driven by his reason—which can operate only within the categories of causality—to grasp the Ultimate as impersonal. This is the basis of the doubt that every man knows: his reason always challenges the truth of faith. Yet faith is able, Tillich held, to absorb the doubt and to transcend it. Faith comes to man with a demand, a threat, and a promise: it demands complete submission of man's will to the will of God, and threatens nonbeing if man rebels. Yet faith also promises complete fulfillment through submission. It is in this way that a man becomes free in reality, inasmuch as God is perfect freedom.

The Social Gospel is a typical development of American Protestantism. This school of theology arose during the first half of the twentieth century, under the distinguished leadership of Walter Rauschenbusch (1861–1918) and Shailer Mathews (1863–1941). These theologians sought to enlist the churches in an effort to bring the ethical teachings of Christianity to bear on all the moral issues of contemporary society, such as the problems of capital and labor, war and peace, alcohol, poverty, and economic justice for minority groups. The Social Gospel movement reveals a kinship with the prophets of the Old Testament, who proclaimed to the people of their time: ". . . what does the Lord require of you but to do justice, and to love kindness, and to walk humbly with your God?" (Micah 6:8).

All the major branches of Christianity have shown interest in the Ecumenical Movement, which has gradually gained strength in the past half-century, and has led to organic union among some of the smaller Protestant denominations. This has been the result of the disappearance of the sectarian spirit of competition that previously existed. The contrasting spirit of friendliness has also brought about significant cooperation between some of the larger Protestant denominations, of which the World Council of Churches is the most evident example. This council is a loose collaboration which allows the individual churches to retain complete autonomy. As we have seen, the Eastern Orthodox Churches have also become members of the World Council. Up to the present, Roman Catholics have gone no farther than sending observers to the assemblies of the World Council, but they also invited other churches to send observers to their own Second Vatican Council at Rome.

Cooperation between Protestants, Catholics, and Orthodox has taken place for some years in the fields of Near Eastern archaeology. At the present time, such collaboration is being extended into the fields of biblical translation and even into the writing of biblical commentaries. This fellowship in archaeology and biblical studies also includes Jewish scholars.

NOTES

1. John H. Leith, *Creeds of the Churches* (Garden City, N.Y.: Doubleday Anchor, 1963).
2. *Ibid.*, pp. 30–31.
3. *Ibid.*, p. 33.
4. *Ibid.*, p. 46.
5. W. A. Curtis, *A History of Creeds and Confessions of Faith in Christianity and Beyond* (Aberdeen: The University Press, 1911), pp. 82 ff.
6. Augustine, *Confessions*, 1, 1.
7. Benjamin B. Warfield, "Augustine," in James Hastings, ed., *Encyclopaedia of Religion and Ethics* (New York: Scribner, 1928), I, 219–224.
8. Henry Bettenson, *Documents of the Christian Church* (New York: Oxford University Press, 1963), pp. 73–75.
9. Cf. Robert Belle Burke, *The Opus Majus of Roger Bacon*, a translation from the Latin (Philadelphia: University of Pennsylvania Press, 1928), II, 787–823.
10. S. Thomae De Aquino, *Summa Theologica* (Ottawa: Ottawa Institute of Medieval Studies, 1941–1945), 5 vols.; also, an English translation of important parts of St. Thomas, edited by Anton C. Pegis, *Basic Writings of Saint Thomas Aquinas* (New York: Random House, 1944), 2 vols.
11. Donald Attwater, *A Catholic Dictionary* (New York: Macmillan, 1931), p. 88.
12. *Ibid.*, "Oecumenical Councils," p. 131.
13. *Ibid.*, pp. 237, 238, 309, 437.
14. Leith, *op. cit.*, "The Vatican Council," pp. 454–457.
15. *Ibid.*, "Dogma of the Immaculate Conception," pp. 442–446.
16. *Ibid.*, pp. 458–466.
17. *Ibid.*, p. 463.
18. Attwater, *op. cit.*, pp. 90, 548.
19. *Ibid.*, p. 541.
20. *Ibid.*, pp. 502–503.

21. Cf. "How Vatican II Turned the Church toward the World," *Time*, December 17, 1965, pp. 24–25; and "On the People of God," *Vatican II Speaks to Lay People* (Washington: National Council of Catholic Men, 1965), pp. 20–25.
22. Robert H. Hastings, *The Growth of the Christian Church* (Philadelphia: Westminster, 1941), pp. 82 ff.
23. Attwater, *op. cit.*, p. 381.
24. *Ibid.*, p. 270.

13 Islam

RELIGION IN PRE-ISLAMIC ARABIA

The religion of the early tribes of Arabia was animism, like that of other early peoples. They believed in nature spirits called "jinn," which occupied springs, rocks, trees, and mountains. They also believed that some spirits were more important than others, indicating a development toward polytheism. In regions around Mecca there were gods called Allah and Hobal; a divine pair called Isaf and Nā'ilah; and the goddesses al-Lāt, Manāt, and al-'Uzza, as well as many other such gods.

Mecca, an oasis whose good spring Zemzem was regarded as sacred, was supported by trade carried on at this watering place, as well as by pilgrims who came to worship the spirit of a black stone that projected from the ground there. Arabs erected an unadorned cubical stone building, the Kaaba, over the stone and then draped the entire structure with a black cloth which is replaced each year. (Muslims say that the severe simplicity of the Kaaba, the holiest of their shrines, is intended to convey the indescribable, ineffable nature of the infinite God.) The Kaaba was supervised by the Quraysh tribe, who held a monopoly on the priestly rites performed there, and they developed the area surrounding the Kaaba into a sanctuary where peace reigned and where merchants from different tribes might safely come together for commercial dealings.

FIGURE 13.1 The Quba Mosque, Medina, the first mosque built by Muhammad. (*Arabian American Oil Company*)

MUHAMMAD

Islam, the youngest of the great religions, originated in Arabia, and was founded by Muhammad who was born in Mecca about A.D. 570 and died at Medina in 632. The English name for this religion is Muhammadanism, but the followers of Muhammad prefer to have their religion called Islam, and themselves Muslims. Islam is an Arabic word that means submission—submission, that is, to the will of God, whom the followers of this faith call Allah.

Muhammad (also spelled Mahomet and Mohammed), whose name means "the Praised One," is often addressed simply as "the Prophet" by the Muslims themselves, who say that the Prophet has as many as 30 to 300 or even 1,000 names. He was the son of Abdallah, a man of humble status who died before Muhammad was born; when Muhammad was only six years of age his mother died. The orphan was adopted first by Abd al-Muttalib, his grandfather, who died shortly thereafter, and then by abu-Talib, an uncle. Both of his adoptive fathers were sheiks of the Quraysh tribe, keepers of the holy places of Mecca, so that Muhammad's childhood and youth were spent in the vicinity of Mecca, in the most intensely religious atmosphere of Arabia.

When Muhammad reached maturity, he was a poor man. He had inherited from his father only five camels, a flock of goats, and one slave girl. Tradition relates that, as a young man, he became a camel driver, leading caravans in and out of Mecca to cities within reach of that area, but few actual details are known about this early period in Muhammad's life.

We do know that when Muhammad was twenty-five he entered the employ of Khadijah, a prosperous widow older than he, who had already been married twice. Khadijah soon fell in love with Muhammad and married him. Their marriage was happy; she was loyal to him, and her wealth gave him leisure and social position. She bore him one or more sons, all of whom died in infancy, as well as four daughters; but his daughter Fatima was the only child of that marriage that survived.

Until he was about forty years of age (in the year 611), Muhammad appears to have lived according to the traditional religious beliefs and practices of other Meccans and members of the Quraysh tribe. Yet he was a serious man who had already begun to withdraw from the social life of his community and retire to isolated and

secluded places, such as caves, where he devoted himself to meditation on religious questions. Moreover, his intensive preoccupation
with religion was marked by strange visionary experiences that left
him puzzled. The visions became more and more frequent, and he
found himself being addressed by Gabriel, an angel, which convinced him that he was receiving revelations from God. The angel
told Muhammad that he must carry these revelations to his people.

At first, Muhammad was almost completely unsuccessful as a
prophet. His old friends at Mecca scoffed at his stories about the
angel Gabriel and revelations from God. For some three years
Muhammad worked hard trying to propagate his new faith, but his
only converts were his wife Khadijah, a slave named Zaid, who had
been a Christian, and Ali, son of his uncle abu-Talib, whom he had
now adopted as his own son.

But Muhammad was not discouraged by the rejection of his revelations, and for ten years (611–621) he continued to preach in Mecca.
Gradually, however, his neighbors began to realize that Muhammad's
doctrine of one, and only one God, as well as his denunciation of
all other Gods and the use of images, was a threat to their own
religion and to the prosperity of Mecca, which was strongly supported by the local shrines. They therefore became increasingly
hostile toward the fiery new prophet and began to make his life in
Mecca intolerable.

In A.D. 621 Muhammad, who had probably already begun to
consider migration to some more friendly region in order to carry
out his religious mission, received an invitation from Yathrib, about
two hundred miles north, to come to that city. As a result, he for-
sook Mecca and went to Yathrib in 622. Soon he had established
himself so firmly as the leading citizen of Yathrib that its old name
was discarded, and Yathrib came to be referred to as Medina, which
means the City—that is, the City of the Prophet (see Figure 13.1).
Apparently the leaders of Yathrib were interested in new religious
ideas and therefore were ready to listen to the Prophet. Muhammad's departure from Mecca is called his Flight; the Arabic word
for it is *Hegira,* or *Hijra.* The Flight from Mecca was a turning
point in the career of Muhammad. Muslims consider the Hegira so
important that they have taken the date A.D. 622 as the beginning
of the Muslim Era.[1]

Muhammad had also expected to receive a welcome from the
Jewish community at Yathrib. He had even hoped that they would
accept him as the Messiah of whom their Scriptures spoke. But his

expectation turned out to be only a romantic dream, for the Jews were unimpressed by his Messianic claims and bluntly rejected him. Nevertheless, this rejection turned out to be another blessing for the Prophet. Up to that time he had been thinking of his new religion as a reform within the framework of the Jewish faith. The Jewish rebuff quickly disillusioned him, however, and for the first time he grasped the far more radical insight that the mission that Allah had given him was to found a religion essentially for Arabs, not for Jews.

The new religion would still have a biblical basis and it would trace its lineage back to Abraham and the Patriarchs, but the lines would be different: its center would now be Mecca, the holy place of the Arabs, not Jerusalem, the holy place of the Jews. Hitherto he had prayed facing toward Jerusalem; now he taught his followers to face toward Mecca, their very own holy city. This change had an enormous effect on the Arabs, for with one stroke Muhammad had given his new faith a solid Arab foundation. He now offered his people a new patriotism as well as a new faith, and the one was as important as the other. In Arabia the two were, in fact, so naturally welded together that they have never since been separated. Wherever Islam has gone, it has sought to be a total culture; where possible the faith and the state are yoked together, like two sides of the same shield.

Now that Muhammad had faced toward Mecca with his proclamation of the one God and his denunciation of idols, the Meccans grew more hostile than ever and laid plans to destroy him. Muhammad, in turn, upon realizing the new danger, issued a call to arms and began to convert his followers into soldiers. For the first time, the Arab tribesmen rallied to his cause with enthusiasm: those who had been lukewarm to the faith he preached were now thrilled by the possibility of plunder that it offered; Muhammad had tapped their love of raids, and his new militia hoped for rich booty in Mecca. Muhammad himself was without military training or experience, but men skilled in the arts of war took their places at his side. With little difficulty Muhammad's new recruits were able to withstand the force that the Meccans sent out to destroy them; and within a decade, by A.D. 632, the Prophet who had once fled from Mecca to save his life was able to return to the holy city in triumph. By this time all Arabia had given him its support. The Arabs recognized Muhammad as the Prophet, the head of their faith, as well as ruler of Arabia. Muhammad was so encouraged by this loyalty and felt himself so strong, as well as so certain of his divine destiny, that he dispatched letters to both the King of Rome and the King of Persia demanding submission to him.

But Muhammad's personal triumph was short-lived. Khadijah, his faithful wife, had died, leaving him without a son to succeed him, and he was greatly disappointed that he had no male heir. In his eagerness for an heir, Muhammad began to take other wives. Up to that time he had had only one wife but in his desperation he rapidly acquired eight or nine. He allowed his men to take no more than four wives; slaves were limited to two.[2] He had received a special revelation, he said, allowing him as many wives as he desired.[3] But Muhammad's spectacular career had reached its end. Returning to Medina from the brilliant triumph in Mecca mortally ill, he preached a final sermon in a mosque there. Then he died with his head in the lap of Aisha, his favorite wife.

Muhammad was truly outstanding, the most spectacular leader the Arabs have ever had, and one of the world's great men. He regarded himself simply as an inspired prophet, but as the greatest and last of the prophets of the biblical line, which began with Abraham and included all the Hebrew prophets as well as Jesus, founder of Christianity. Muhammad himself would have no successor until the coming of the Messiah, whom some Muslims call the Mahdi.

In later writings, however, Muslim piety soon began to elevate Muhammad to a higher position. Miracles somewhat similar to those in the Christian Gospels are attributed to him. His conception and birth were marked by signs and portents of both earth and sky. Wild animals rejoiced and told one another the good news. In the sixth month of his mother's pregnancy she heard a heavenly voice telling her of the greatness of the child she was to bear and instructing her to name him Muhammad. She required no human assistance when the child was born, for four angels came to receive him in a net of gold, and they covered him with fine Banaras cloth. He was born already circumcised and free from all impurity.

In some circles infallibility was ascribed to Muhammad, along with a high degree of moral excellence. Love and devotion were shown to him as if he were divine. This reverent attitude toward the Prophet was especially characteristic of the Muslim group known as Sufis, who regarded him as a manifestation of the divine essence, the core of reality, the perfect man, as well as a copy of God. It was through the light of Muhammad, they said, that the whole world was created. The angel Israfil, mightiest of all angels and nearest to God, was created from his heart. A kind of Logos doctrine developed about him, somewhat similar to the Incarnation of Christ.

In these devout groups, Muhammad became more and more an object of worship. One late story has Muhammad ascending to Heaven, riding Alborak, his favorite steed, from the rock in Jerusalem on which the temple of Solomon was built. In Heaven he is permitted to see the prophets of old and is taken on a tour of the celestial regions, after which he is escorted, like Dante, through Hell itself. The guide who takes Muhammad on this memorable journey is the angel Gabriel. Muhammad made no such claims for himself, however, as are ascribed to him in these popular stories.

THE QURAN

There is no good reason to doubt that the Qurān (also spelled "Koran") is composed essentially of the authentic words of Muhammad. Its 114 chapters are held together by a consistent unity of thought and style bearing the indelible stamp of the personality of the Prophet. Yet, although the Qurān is a genuine product of the mind and heart of Muhammad, who frequently refers to it as a book that God sent to him and to his people, just as he had given the Torah to the Hebrews and the Gospel to the Christians, Muhammad did not himself put it together in the form of a book.

It may be that Muhammad's sudden and unexpected death was the reason for this; after his death, however, abu-Bakr, his successor, in order to make sure that the scattered fragments were not lost, selected Zaid ibn Thabit, a native of Medina who had been closely associated with Muhammad, to collect and edit the oracles in the form of a book. Meanwhile rival copies of the sayings and traditions had arisen, and in order to prevent needless differences of opinion among the Prophet's followers, Uthman, who was Caliph from A.D. 644 to 656, prevailed on Zaid to reedit the entire work—after which all competing textual variants were destroyed.

When Zaid first undertook to put the Qurān together, it is said that he "gathered fragments from every quarter, from date leaves and tablets of white stone, and from the breasts of man."[4] Muhammad had apparently written different parts of his message at different times. All of it was then delivered orally as oracles or sermons, although some of the sayings had never been written down at all, having been preserved only in the memory of the faithful. In view of the extraordinary activity of Muhammad's prophetic life, it is not surprising that he had little time for literary activity. His career was not unlike those of Moses, Zoroaster, and Jesus, none of whom thought of themselves as men of letters; their sayings too were preserved mainly by their disciples.

Western readers often find the Qurān confusing, unintelligible, and dull. Muslims themselves, however, are eloquent in their praise of the profound truth of the Qurān and its literary beauty. Western scholars who have mastered the Arabic language and become expert in the life, customs, and thought of the Muslims generally add their own voices in praise of the literary ability of this fiery Arab prophet. They all agree that the Qurān is a classic of Arabic literature, and that it ushered in a golden age of Arabic poetry and music. They praise the rhythm of its lines, the elegance of its diction, the inspiration it imparts to the reader.

Like the prophets of the Old Testament, Muḥammad found it natural to speak, as he was moved by an ecstasy that overwhelmed him, and to give a poetic form to his oracles. Translators have only recently begun to print parts of Muhammad's discoveries as poetry, which gives the reader some hint of how one ought to approach the Prophet. Some of the beauty of the Qurān then becomes easily discernible.

The suras (chapters) vary in length: the first sura is very short, but leads us quickly into the beauty one may expect to encounter in the book. Nevertheless, some of the suras are repetitious, and lack real continuity. This disjointed nature of the work is probably due both to the original character of the book as independent oracles and to the way in which these oracles had been preserved. Zaid, who collected the fragments, seems to have put them together just as he found them, without seeking to give them a logical order. Had he been able to do this, however, and thereby restored them entirely to their original form, they would very likely still have seemed repetitious. The oracles were not composed as a systematic essay on religion or theology, and the Prophet did not seek to follow a carefully developed theme from the beginning to the end of the book.

The Qurān is neither a book of science nor a book of philosophy. We can understand it better as a collection of independent prophetic oracles or homilies, having the nature of sermons. It has often been remarked that a minister generally has only one sermon, which he preaches over and over. While he may use different illustrations and make new applications, this is always within the framework of the same central ideas. If the sermons were put down as a series and read through as a book, the reader would find himself weary with the repetitions. Muhammad is a preacher, an evangelist, always inspired by the same great themes. His object is to move his hearers to respond to the God who speaks to them through the Prophet, not to give them an organized course of lectures.

It is true that the Qurān is also a lawbook, just as the Bible is a code of law as well as a book of theology and worship. The Torah of Moses contains the laws by which the Hebrews lived, and in the same sense, the Qurān is the law by which the entire Muslim world lives. In short, it provides the structure of Muslim society. The strength of Muslim culture lies in the feeling that the Qurān is a book of divine truth. It speaks to their hearts as well as to their minds. Regardless of the practical laws he gives, Muhammad always brings his hearers back to the God who gives the laws, to the just God and the just man, to rewards of the upright and punishment of the wicked. He never tires of these theological themes.

MUHAMMAD AND THE BIBLE

One of the fundamental ideas of Muhammad was that Abraham, the ancestor of the Jews, was also ancestor of the Muslims, the difference between Jews and Muslims being that the Muslims were descended from Abraham through his son Ishmael, whereas the Jews were descended through Abraham's son Isaac. In his various prophetic oracles, Muhammad shows some familiarity with a considerable number of biblical characters, beginning with Adam. Yet his acquaintance with the people of the Bible is superficial, somewhat erratic, and clearly not based on firsthand knowledge. In Sura ii:250–254 he confuses the story of Saul and his troops facing the Philistines championed by the giant Goliath (I Samuel 17:1–54) with that of Gideon routing the Midianites (Judges 6:1–25). While Muhammad says that Saul selected his troops by having them drink from a brook, the Bible says that it was Gideon who did that.

Muhammad several times refers to the Virgin Mary, but his account of her is at variance with that of the Gospels. In her pregnancy,

Muhammad relates, Mary withdraws into a desert place and is resting under a palm tree when birth pangs come upon her. She almost perishes for water and food, but an angel calls her attention to a brook the Lord has placed by her feet, and when she shakes the palm trunk, as he tells her to, fresh ripe dates fall (Sura xix:20–25). Muhammad apparently even confuses Mary, the mother of Jesus, with Miriam, the sister of Moses and Aaron (Sura xix:29). This confusion may also explain why the Prophet traces the ancestry of Mary back to the ancient family of Imran, a variant of Amram, father of Moses, Aaron, and Miriam (Sura iii:36; I Chronicles 6:3).

Muhammad is not concerned about accuracy of details when he makes such use of the men and women of the Bible. He uses biblical characters for a homiletical purpose: he is presenting theological and moral ideas, not writing a history; he is concerned more with the effect of his ideas than with the facts of the stories. This is true of his treatment of the Bible as a whole. While he shows some degree of familiarity with many of the narratives of the Bible—in particular with the patriarchs from Adam to Moses—and makes occasional references to David or Solomon or Job, as well as to the prophets Elijah and Elisha, that is about the extent of his knowledge of the Old Testament. He shows no knowledge of it in depth, and there are no references to the writing prophets, such as Amos, Hosea, Isaiah, Micah, Jeremiah, and Ezekiel.

Similarly, Muhammad is familiar with the New Testament stories of the birth of John the Baptist and of Jesus, and he knows that Jesus was a teacher, that he was famous for his miracles, and that he was put to death by crucifixion. But he holds a Gnostic view of Jesus, and explains that the Jews did not slay the Messiah, nor did they crucify him, but instead crucified a likeness of Jesus that was shown to them (Sura iv:156). While Muhammad is aware that Jesus had apostles to assist him in his work (Sura lxi:14), he mentions none of them by name, not even Paul. There is no indication that he knows Paul's letters. His references to both the Old Testament and the New include only a few of the outstanding persons; he never indicates close familiarity with the Bible, and he never makes direct quotations from it.

On the other hand, Muhammad has great respect for the Bible, and expresses the view that God has given the Torah to the Jews and the Gospel to the Christians, although he seems to include all of the Old Testament under Torah (Law) and all of the New Testament under Gospel. He makes one or two references to the Psalms, but does not quote from them. Practically all the historical illustrations that Muhammad employs in his discourses are taken from the Bible. This preference for biblical stories reflects Muhammad's feeling that the Bible is a real Scripture, an inspired Book, and the fact that Jews and Christians are people of a Book causes him to deal with them in a laudatory fashion, whenever that is possible.

The Prophet derives Islam, his own religion, from Abraham and Ishmael, not from Moses and Jesus. In doing so, he shows awareness of the biblical view that Ishmael, the first son of Abraham, begotten of the Egyptian slave Hagar, is the father of the Ishmaelite tribes of Arabia. Numerous passages in his homilies show that the Prophet was involved in arguments with Jews and Christians, who tried to convert him to their faiths. But he cleverly argues that since he holds the religion of Abraham and Ishmael, his faith is older and truer than either Judaism or Christianity, having been founded long before either the Torah or the Gospel was given. Thus he says,

> People of the Book! Why do you dispute
> concerning Abraham? The Torah was not sent
> down, neither the Gospel, but after him. What,
>   have you no reason?
> Ha, you are the ones who dispute on what you
> know; why then dispute you touching a matter
> of which you know not anything? God knows,
>   and you know not.
> No; Abraham in truth was not a Jew,
> neither a Christian; but he was a Muslim
> and one pure of faith; certainly he was never of
> the idolaters. [Sura iii:58–60.][5]

In a similar way, the Prophet holds that Abraham (and Ishmael) had built the Kaaba, the holy shrine at Mecca to which all Muslims turn in prayer and go as pilgrims (Sura ii:118–124). He instructs people to make pilgrimages to this holy place as often as possible and while there to walk around Safa and Marwa, the two sacred hills at Mecca (Sura ii:145–153).

Muhammad's constant use of eschatology—in which he includes the ideas of Satan (whom he calls Eblis), angels with real names, Heaven and Hell—shows that his acquaintance with the biblical faith is mainly based on the Old and New Testaments, as they were known in his time. The Hebrew religion, in its classical period, had no Satan and no Heaven or Hell. Satan appears first in Job 1:6 ff.

and I Chronicles 21:1 ff., both of which are late books. Muhammad projects all these ideas back to the beginning of the Old Testament. Eglis is one of the angels of God, but when God commands all his angels to bow down to Adam, Eblis refuses and becomes an unbeliever (Sura ii:32), a role he takes ever after. God dooms all unbelievers to dwell in fire forever (Sura ii:37), an idea that is foreign to the early parts of the Old Testament. Similarly, Muhammad's ideas of Christian theology were drawn in part from apocryphal sources.

The Muslim practice of circumcision might perhaps be taken as evidence of biblical influence on Muhammad. However, the Arabs appear to have kept this rite long before the time of Muhammad, and Muhammad himself never mentions it in the Qurān, apparently because the rite was so familiar in his time that he assumed it as a matter of course. Moreover, the Arab custom varies from that of the Jews in that Arabs often postpone the rite until the boy is entering the age of puberty, or to whatever time appears to be least hazardous to his life for such an operation. It is also a fact that circumcision is practiced by many peoples whose ancestors had no contact with the Hebrews.

The ban on eating the flesh of swine is another instance that may or may not show Hebrew influence. Muhammad mentions swine as a forbidden thing (Sura ii:168), but swine were taboo in Egypt and used in the religious rituals of various cultures unrelated to the Bible, which would probably have made them taboo to the Hebrews as well as to the Muslims.

The use of alcohol is frowned on in Islam today. Muhammad calls wine a work of Satan and urges his people to avoid it (Sura v:93); yet he describes Paradise as a place flowing with rivers of delightful wine, along with rivers of water, milk, and honey (Sura xlvii:16–17). While the Bible teaches temperance it does not condemn the use of wine, nor does it put wine in Heaven.

THE CALIPHS

The word *caliph* means a successor of Muhammad. Since Islam is ideally a total culture, there is no such separation between church and state as is known in America. In a Muslim state, religion, government, economics, education, art, and literature are fused together, and an adequate history of Islam would have to keep all these elements of culture in balance. The head of a Muslim state is therefore a religious person, who exercises religious as well as secular authority. Muhammad was the founder of a religion; at the same time he established a government and became the ruler of a nation. It was this cultural concept that he bequeathed to his successors.

The problem of succession in Islam, however, has never been solved to the satisfaction of all Muslims, and this has been a cause of continuing weakness in Muslim states. The fact that Muhammad died without a son is the source of the problem. It is said that he adopted his cousin Ali, son of his uncle abu-Talib, with the intention of making him his successor, and with that in mind, gave his daughter Fatima to his adopted son as his wife. But Muhammad's sudden death, before careful preparation had been made, left a confused situation, and Ali lacked the ability to take immediate and decisive action. Aisha, Muhammad's favorite wife, who was a woman of strong will, easily pushed Ali aside and installed abu-Bakr, her father, as the first caliph. But abu-Bakr was an old man and he died within two years, in A.D. 634.

This aggressive act of Aisha in displacing Ali in favor of abu-Bakr created a division in Islam that has never been overcome. The partisans of Ali refused to accept abu-Bakr as caliph, regarding him as an impostor, and thus became a party or schism (*shia*, in Arabic) in Islam. These partisans of Ali are known to this day as Shiites. Those who accept abu-Bakr and his successors as legitimate caliphs are called *Sunnites,* from *Sunna,* which means custom, and especially any action or precedent of Muhammad; in other words, they are the traditionalists in Islam. The Sunnites constitute the vast majority of Muslims in the world and are found in Arabia, Syria, Jordan, Asia Minor, Egypt, North and East Africa, central Asia, Afghanistan, India, China, East Indies. The Shiites, who are concentrated in Iran and among the masses of India, number only about 15 million altogether, but they are noted for the tenacity of their devotion to the faith.[6]

Abu-Bakr, quite unlike Muhammad, did not set himself up as a prophet; he had no revelations, but was instead satisfied to follow the words of Muhammad. When abu-Bakr was dying, he selected Omar, a competent man and trusted friend, to succeed him as caliph. Omar was the ruler of Islam from 634 to 644, and although he apparently had not desired the office, he was a most successful ruler. Being a man of military ability, the first thing he did was to consolidate the conquests that Muhammad had made. But then his armies undertook new and ambitious campaigns of their own. He took Damascus, with all of Syria, in 635, and then captured Jerusalem in 637, thus beginning the Muslim period in Palestine. Since Muslims trace their origin back to Abraham, this conquest was something like a homecoming to them. They were especially gratified to recover Hebron, where Abraham is buried, for next to Mecca and Medina, Jerusalem and Hebron are the most holy sites of Islam. In 641 Omar went on to take Egypt and Persia, where Zoroastrianism was the established religion. Since Omar was growing old, he selected six electors to choose a caliph at his death—which took place when he was stabbed by an infuriated workman in a mosque.

Omar was succeeded by Uthman, son-in-law of Muhammad, who ruled from 644 to 656. A weak ruler, the one achievement for which he is honored is that of having stabilized the text of the Qurān by destroying all rival versions.

Uthman was succeeded in 656 by Ali, the cousin and adopted son whom Muhammad had desired to be his successor. But Ali also turned out to be an incompetent ruler, and he was killed by an assassin in 661. Throughout the period from the flight of Muhammad from Mecca to Medina in 622 to the death of Ali in 661, Medina was the capital of Islam. This period is referred to as the Medina Caliphate. (A caliphate is the period of time during which a series of caliphs used one particular city as their capital, the reign of a particular caliph, or the territory over which a particular caliph reigns.)

The next caliphate, a dynasty of great conquerors, was at Damascus from 661 to 750. The last of its line reigned over an empire reaching from Spain and North Africa in the west to India and China in the east and from Asia Minor in the north to Arabia in the south. During this period the Muslims came close to conquering all of Europe, but they were turned back by Charles Martel at the Battle of Tours in 732.

With the termination of the Damascus Caliphate in 751, the rivalry of political factions became so bitter that they were no longer able to live together in peace, and as a result Islam was divided into two Caliphates. One party established the Abbasid Caliphate at Baghdad, which lasted until 1258; another set up the Spanish Caliphate in 755, with Cordova as its capital, which continued until 1236, and was followed by the Moorish Caliphate at Granada from 1238 to 1492, when the Muslims were finally expelled from Spain by

Ferdinand and Isabella. These caliphates at Baghdad, Cordova, and Granada represent the most brilliant period in Muslim history, and some of the most beautiful architecture of Spain dates from that period. The Baghdad Caliphate became famous for its rediscovery and preservation of the learning of ancient Greece. It was through these Muslims that the Greek classics reached Europe, where their cultivation led to the Renaissance.

By 814 the Abbasid Caliphate had come to rule an enormous territory extending from India across Persia, Mesopotamia, Arabia, Egypt, and North Africa, while the Sunnite kingdom of Cordova remained limited to Spain. During the following centuries, however, the Muslim territories of Spain, North Africa, Egypt, Palestine, and Syria experienced numerous readjustments, including the Fatimid Kingdom of North Africa and Egypt, 909–1171, with Kairouan as its capital, and the period of the crusades when Christian armies from Europe, during the eleventh, twelfth, and thirteenth centuries, sought to recover the holy places of Palestine from the Muslims, although with little success.

The last important caliphate was established in 1517, when the Sultan of Turkey conquered Egypt. The rulers of Turkey continued to lay claim to the caliphate down to 1924, when this office was finally abolished by Kemal Atatürk, founder of modern Turkey. Since that date several important Muslim political leaders have emerged, but none has succeeded in being recognized as caliph. There is no head of all Islam at the present time.

MUSLIM LAW

The theory of Muslim law involves the Qurān, the Sunna, and the ijma. The Qurān is the word of Allah, the revelations given to Muhammad by the angel Gabriel and delivered at different times by the Prophet. This, Muslims believe, is Allah's infallible truth, the ultimate law that all Muslims must observe.

Sunna means "custom"—the customary way of acting—in particular, the actions and words of Muhammad. A tradition that embodies the Sunna of the Prophet is called a hadith. Muslims did not originally think of the Prophet as divine, or sinless, or free of error, yet the feeling developed that he had lived a perfect life and that what he did was a perfect example for others to follow. It is nigh impossible for people in any land to live permanently by the words of a book of law, since legal statutes lack the flexibility required by a dynamic culture and do go out of date. This is true of the Qurān, as of all other law codes. There must always be a way of adjusting and revising a written code.

Even before the time of Muhammad, Arabs were accustomed to follow the traditions of their fathers. Muslims adapted this ancient custom to their particular situation, by modifying their other traditions to the one that was related to Muhammad. Older persons, who had associated with the Prophet, retained a memory of actions he had taken and words he had spoken which had never been recorded. These recollected deeds and sayings provided a useful supplement to the written code.

Yet it was necessary for someone to decide in particular cases both the relevant statutes and how these were to be applied. According to the Sunnites, the community itself has this responsibility. Not the people as a whole, however, but rather scholars who have been trained in the law consider a case until they arrive at a decision. This decision is the ijma, the consensus; and a verdict is final. Muhammad himself, it is said, had expressed the view that his community could never be unanimous in holding to an error, and this consensus of the community provides the additional principle of flexibility that is needed by a society spread over so many lands and with such a variety of problems.

The Shiite Muslims, however, were more authoritarian than the Sunnites. They rejected the principle of consensus and instead placed the authority to make final interpretations and decisions in the hands of the imam, the divinely authorized and endowed spiritual leader of Muslims, usually descended by blood from Ali, who appeared age after age. When such a descendant of Ali was not available, the doctrine of a hidden imam was set forth, with the expectation that he might at any moment appear. This was the idea that gave rise to the Muslim belief in a Mahdi to come, somewhat similar to the Christian and Jewish Messianic hopes.

The Shiite imam was therefore parallel to the Sunnite caliph, except that he ruled by divine right, not by human choice, and was thus divinely preserved from error. The imam tended to be endowed with divine attributes, perhaps to be even an incarnation of God, a manifestation of the holy, to the devout Shiites. The hierophanies associated with the imams at times aroused in this phase of Islam a charismatic character, ecstatic emotions, and even violent

actions. This passionate faith has often assumed the form of political, revolutionary protest against what it took to be the worldly
character of the entrenched Muslim government.

There developed four well-known schools of law in Islam, each
of them deriving from one eminent scholar. One such school of
great influence was derived from abu-Hanifah, and is called the
Hanifitic system. This school was dominant especially in Turkey and
in lands under Turkish influence. Another important school of law
was that of al-Shafii, promulgated by the Abbasid caliphs of Baghdad and prevalent in Syria, Egypt, western Arabia, parts of India,
and the Malay States. The school of Malik ibn-Anas was based at
Medina and flourished in Spain, Tunis, Algiers, Morocco, Egypt,
and other Islamic areas of Africa. The school of ibn-Hanbal, whose
followers are known as Hanbalites, was of less importance. It flourished in central Arabia, Oman, on the Persian Gulf, and to some
extent also in central Asia. The Wahhabites of Arabia prefer this
school. Every Muslim community has a *mufti,* a legal authority, who
is expected to be expert in Muslim law and to be familiar with the
interpretations of these schools.

MUSLIM THEOLOGY

Muhammad's theology can be briefly stated; indeed, its strength lies
in large part in its brevity and clarity. The simplest man can understand it and respond to it. Most important of all, it is a powerful
affirmation of the one God, with total repudiation of polytheism and
all forms of idolatry, including the use of images. Further, Muhammad proclaims the justice of God and calls on man to practice justice. The essence of his theology is sovereignty of the one God and
submission of man's will to the will of God; Muhammad lays hold of
the doctrine of eschatology as his favorite way of expressing this divine sovereignty. He warns of an impending judgment, which includes a resurrection of the dead, heavenly rewards for the righteous,
and a hell of fire for the wicked. The chief attributes of a devout
man are humility and submission. Yet Allah is merciful: he knows
man's weakness and is always ready to forgive the penitent.

Muhammad was not a theologian in the technical sense and certainly not a philosopher. He never attempted to set forth his faith
as a theological system. Whatever systematic exposition we make of

his theology, it is a system that we extract from his words or impose upon them, not one that Muhammad himself developed. Nevertheless God was very real to the Prophet, as real as the air he breathed, the food he ate. Every word he uttered in his oracles is pervaded by this overwhelming awareness of God. In this respect Muhammad was like Zoroaster, Moses, and Jesus, all of whom had this sense of continuing hierophanies, apprehensions of the holy, of the divine presence.

The only way in which one can construct a system of Muhammad's theology is to glean it bit by bit from his individual poetic utterances. The theological wealth of his language may be illustrated from the first sura of the Qurān:

> In the Name of God, the Merciful, the Compassionate
> Praise belongs to God, the Lord of all Being,
> the All-merciful, the All-compassionate,
>   the Master of the Day of Doom.
> Thee only would we serve; to Thee alone we pray for succour,
>   Guide us in the straight path,
> the path of those whom Thou hast blessed,
> not of those against whom Thou art wrathful,
>   nor of those who are astray.[7]

These lines express the main elements of Muslim theology, and are reminiscent of the Twenty-third Psalm of the Bible. The poetic quality of the sura is obvious. It is addressed to God, and has the form of a prayer. God is the sovereign of history and judge of the world; but he rules with compassion and provides for those who trust in him, an idea that occurs in nearly every sura of the Qurān. Muhammad succeeds in conveying this high sense of the authenticity of his faith with remarkable frequency throughout his book.

The religious quality of the language of Muhammad is evident in the vividly personal character of his apprehensions of Allah. As both Martin Buber and Paul Tillich have pointed out, man in his primary religious experience always apprehends the ultimate, the holy, in personal terms. Muhammad's apprehension of Allah is a decisive confirmation of this insight. Not a word in the Qurān would seem to reduce Allah to a philosophical abstraction or to an impersonal ultimate reality. On the contrary, Muhammad without fail speaks of Allah as the Almighty, who is moved by concern for the faithful, since he understands man's weaknesses and stands ready to forgive the penitent. Allah hears; he sees; he feels. These are per-

sonal attributes, qualities that all men possess; and Allah deals with
man as an understanding judge might deal with men and women
who get into trouble with the law.

Muhammad's own personal theology is characterized throughout
by anthropomorphism; Allah is regarded as having qualities like
those of a man. The personality of Allah emerges therefore in vivid
and colorful ways, and this has been a source of strength wherever
Islam has gone. It has made Allah seem real; he is close and ap-
proachable. The ordinary man has not had to accept a complicated
creed or to struggle with ontological problems in order to approach
the God he worships and serves.

As Islam began to take on the character of a sophisticated culture,
this directness and simplicity of the thought and language of Muhammad was to create problems for his followers. The process of
sophistication was hastened by contact with the theologies of Jews
and Christians on the one hand, and with the philosophical culture
of the Greeks on the other. The Muslims were especially impressed
with the philosophy of Aristotle. Apparently before either Jews or
Christians had done so, Arab theologians began to make use of the
metaphysics of Aristotle in setting forth their own understanding
of God. Emphasis on reason was the leading element in Aristotle's
thought, and deeply influenced by the Aristotelian rationalism, Arabs
began to employ it in interpreting the poetic anthropomorphism of
Muhammad.

The Mutazilite Controversy

The enthusiasm of Muslim scholars for Greek learning, however,
was not to go unchallenged. In fact, it was only a minority of Muslims, a scholarly elite, who were inclined to approve of the Greek
learning. The mass of the Prophet's followers were suspicious of the
alien philosophy, for they saw it as a threat to their faith. Thus the
contact of Islam with Greek philosophy aroused a controversy that
raged for some decades and did not altogether subside for centuries.
The two parties to this controversy were the Traditionists and the
Mutazilites (from *mutazila,* which means "dissenters" or "seceders").

The Traditionists defended the literal text of the Qurān, as well
as the authenticity and accuracy of the Sunna and hadiths. They
even went so far as to affirm that the Qurān was uncreated, that it
had existed eternally, like all other attributes of Allah. It was therefore man's duty, they asserted, to accept and respond to these forms

of revelation without question. They clung to the idea of the absolute omnipotence of Allah and called for complete, unquestioning submission to him.

The Mutazilites, by contrast, affirmed the freedom of man's will and held that man is responsible for his conduct. The Qurān, the Sunna, and the Hadiths were created by man, they held, and they contended that man must make full use of his reason in interpreting them. This emphasis on reason was intended to introduce a flexibility into Islamic law that would be in keeping with the dynamic character of the young Muslim empire.

While al-Kindi (800–870), who was one of the first distinguished Arab philosophers, was devoted to Aristotle, he viewed him from the mystical vantage point of Neoplatonism, as did most of the other Muslim philosophers.

Al-Farabi (875–950) began with the absolute One from whom all other beings emanate, according to a hierarchy of power to command and obligation to obey, from the highest to the lowest forms. The aim of his philosophical thought was the creation of a metaphysical blueprint of the authoritarian state, by which he apparently meant the Shiite imamate. It vested final authority in the imam.

The Mutazilites enjoyed their greatest triumph during the reign of Caliph al-Mamum (813–833), who encouraged the translation of the Greek classics into Arabic and supported the use of reason in all the activities of his government. Indeed, in his effort to force Traditionists to adopt a philosophical interpretation of Muslim law, he even initiated an inquisition. The Mutazilite movement was important in the region of Baghdad, where Persian influence was strong. One of the greatest of the Mutazilite leaders was abu-Hanifah (d. 767), a Persian who lived far away from Mecca, the center of the Muslim tradition. Yet the Mutazilite triumph was relatively brief, even in Baghdad itself; the inquisition did not succeed in silencing the Traditionists. Ahmad ibn-Hanbal (d. 855), when put under pressure by the inquisition, would not recant; he refused to say that the Qurān was created. Thus the collapse of the Mutazila was inevitable, and when Caliph al-Mutawakkil (847–861) reversed the liberal government policy, the Mutazilite movement fell into disfavor. Yet the influence of this movement did not cease when the government withdrew its support. In a quiet way, Greek philosophy continued to engage the best Muslim minds, but in the role of handmaid of Muhammad's revelation rather than as its critic.

Al-Ashari (873–935) began his career as a student of the Mutazilite philosophy, but turned against it in disillusionment and concluded that revelation is superior to reason as a guide of life. Thus he became a defender of the traditions, yet this was a defense that made use of all the resources of reason. His example became a leaven, which spread throughout Islamic theology. He endeavored to assimilate the basic elements of Greek philosophy without compromising the central dogmas of Sunnite Islam.

Avicenna (980–1037), who was born on the southern coast of the Caspian Sea and lived in Bukhara, had memorized the Qurān and mastered all the sciences of his time, including medicine, by the time he was seventeen. His writings covered all these fields, as well as metaphysics and theology. His work was reminiscent of the Mutazilite point of view, and his writings were read with appreciation even by Jews and Christians.

Among the latter, the best known of the Arab philosophers was Averroës (ibn-Rushd, 1126–1198), a jurist of Seville and Cordova, who was a specialist on the philosophy of Aristotle. His commentaries on Aristotle were translated into Latin and Hebrew and thus made available to the scholars of Europe. Averroës took the position that both reason and revelation are valid and that these two different approaches to truth are the two pillars on which theology should be based—a view that was to have a strong influence on both Jewish and Christian theology.

MYSTICISM IN ISLAM

Mysticism appears to have been most congenial to the Shiite form of Islam and is known best in the Sufi movement, which flourished in Persia, Mesopotamia, and Turkey.[8] The word *Sufi*, whose origin has been much debated, was apparently derived from *suf*, the Arabic word for wool, and refers to the custom of holy men and prophets, among the ancient Hebrews and Arabs, of dressing themselves in rough woolen garments. The first stage of mysticism among the Muslims appears to have been represented by a class of ascetics similar to the rishis who wrote the hymns of the Rig-Veda. Such

FIGURE 13.2 Pilgrims praying at a mosque in Delhi during a celebration honoring the Sufi saint Hazrat Nizamuddin Aulia. (*Information Service of India*)

ascetics had been known among the Semites and Aryans for centuries. Through various forms of self-denial combined with meditation, these ascetics learned how to produce an ecstasy that led to illumination. They attained an experience of divine inspiration, communication, and even identification with the deity. In true mysticism in all religions, the meditating person gradually comes to recognize the unreality of the phenomenal world: all familiar forms finally vanish, leaving only the Infinite, the One, over against the meditating self, the I. Then, in a culminating flash of illumination, the self, the I, and the Infinite merge as One.

Men of the East have found this experience in the Dharmakaya, Nirvana, or Brahman, just as mystics in the monotheistic religions of the West have discovered it in God. Although students of the

Sufi mysticism of Islam have sought to show that it stands under the influence of prior mystical developments in other cultures, there is no reason why we should doubt the integrity of this mystical development in Islam. We would do better to seek out its origin in the primordial experience that is the common foundation of all religions.

The Sufi movement flourished especially in Persia. Qushairi published his *Risala,* a study of Sufism, in 1045. Some fifty years later, al-Ghazzali (1058–1111), one of the greatest Muslim scholars, who had been professor of theology in a college at Baghdad, retired from his position to become a Sufi. He did not go to the extreme of repudiating religious law, nor did he deny the personal nature of God, for he was not an outright pantheist. Yet he profoundly changed Islam by insisting that true religion is a matter of the heart, and not of rational knowledge or of the observance of external forms and ceremonies. Other famous figures among the Sufi theologians were Abd al-Karim al-Jili and ibn-al-Arabi; and a notable school of Persian poetry had its roots in the Sufi insight.

The Sufi movement became so important that a number of different orders were formed, with establishments for communal life and schools to train young men. Their moral ideals were renunciation, sincerity, patience, humility, charity, trust in God, and submission to his will.

The dervishes were related to the Sufi movement, but they had a special interest in the ecstatic disciplines. Along with meditation on the names of God, the disciplines might include control of breathing, and even flagellation, until a trance was induced. They also learned to induce ecstasy by means of music and dancing, and this is why they came to be called the whirling dervishes. They went from village to village, mixing with the people and bringing to them their gospel of the love of God. By both word and example they taught the average person how to cultivate an experience of God in the warm emotions of the heart. Their purpose was to reawaken a participation in the divine life that was wanting in the conventional prayers and rituals. Although Sufism developed in Shiite Islam, it became a movement in its own right and is not to be equated with the Shiite faith.

FIGURE 13.3 A muezzin calling people to worship from the minaret of a mosque in Jerusalem. (*S. Vernon McCasland*)

MUSLIM SAINTS

A cult of saints appeared in every Muslim land (see Figure 13.2), usually manifesting itself at tombs of famous persons. People of the adjacent region assembled at these tombs in veneration of the spirit of the deceased, and many of these tombs have become such famous shrines that they are objects of pilgrimage.

The list of venerated saints begins with the prophets themselves, the most important of whom is, naturally, Muhammad. But according to Muslim doctrine, there have been a total of some 124,000 prophets,[9] 313 of whom were outstanding. The prophets who are most highly venerated are Adam, Noah, Abraham, Moses, Jesus, and Muhammad. Each of these prophets superseded all those before him, and Muhammad was the last and the greatest of the line.[10]

The locations of the graves of Adam and Noah are unknown, but the burial places of the other major prophets are shrines. Abraham

is buried at Hebron. The grave of Moses, according to Islam, is located in the wilderness west of the Dead Sea, while according to the Bible it is on Mount Pisgah, east of the Dead Sea. The tomb of Jesus is at Jerusalem, and Muhammad's tomb is at Medina.

Next to these great prophets (*nabis*), each of whom was a messenger (*rasul*) from Allah to mankind, there was a large number of other persons so intimate with God that each of them was called a Friend (*Wali*). In almost any well-established Muslim cemetery, one or more of the tombs is likely to be that of a Wali. To these tombs people come for their devotions, bringing gifts and sacrifices, including the blood sacrifices of animals.

It is also true that some of these Walis are figures from old pagan cults which have been absorbed into Islam. In the case of people

whose conversion to Islam was superficial the Muslim faith is only a veil over an earlier paganism.

The Muslim cult of saints is approximately parallel to the veneration of saints in Christianity; it is also similar to the avatars of Hinduism and the Bodhisattvas of Buddhism. All these cults of saints relieve the austerity of theologies that are too abstract for the masses to comprehend. The saints are human beings, familiar with all the problems of mankind. They seem to be close to struggling, suffering people, and thus within the comprehension of ordinary persons. They can comprehend their petitions, and thus they make ideal intermediaries between men and God, or absolute reality, which is abstract, and far away. Although the cult of saints is not authorized by the Qurān and has often been condemned by such zealous groups as the Wahhabis of Arabia, it has been quietly accepted by the authorities of Islam. The flexible principle of the consensus has made this possible.

THE FIVE PILLARS OF ISLAM

Islam as a religion may be conveniently summarized under the Five Pillars used by Muslims themselves. The First Pillar is the creed which every Muslim holds and practices: he confesses that there is no God but Allah and that Muhammad is his Prophet. This confession of faith obligates one to keep all the commandments of Islam.

The Second Pillar is prayer, which must be both public and private. Islam has five well-recognized times of daily public prayer: daybreak, noon, mid-afternoon, just before sunset, and about dark. At each of these times of daily prayer the muezzin, or crier, climbs to the platform of the minaret, the tower attached to every mosque for this purpose, and chants the call to prayer in a melodious voice, which can usually be heard across the countryside (see Figure 13.3). Muslims take pride in the fact that, while Jews sound horns and Christians ring bells, they use only the unaided human voice to call men to prayer. The prayer call goes:

FIGURE 13.4   A man washing his feet before entering the Mosque el-Aksa, Jerusalem. (*Louise McCasland*)

Allah is great! Allah is great!
There is no God but Allah,
And Muhammad is his prophet!
Come to prayer! Come to salvation!
[Early mornings, the muezzin inserts:
Prayer is better than sleep!
Prayer is better than sleep!]
Allah is great! Allah is great!
There is no God but Allah!

Before entering a mosque for prayer, a Muslim must purify himself by washing his hands and feet in running water (see Figure
13.4). A mosque will usually have water flowing from a fountain

for that purpose in a convenient court. But when neither a fountain nor a faucet is available, a pitcher of water may be used or, in extreme cases, the clean desert sand. When it is not possible to come to the mosque, one may pause wherever he is when the time of prayer arrives—in home, field, on a rooftop, a highway, or on a train—and, facing toward Mecca, perform the genuflections and recite the petitions of the prayers. Muslims keep this impressive ceremony with great sincerity. Outsiders are not allowed to enter a mosque during the prayers, which Muslims say standing, kneeling, and reclining on their rugs, always facing toward Mecca.

There is a special service at the mosque on Friday, the Muslim Sabbath, which every healthy adult is expected to attend. Forty persons, Shafiites hold, must be present before a Friday service can be held, but Hanifites permit the service with only an imam and three others. The imam is the professional leader of worship in the mosques, although the word "imam" is also used as a title for various other spiritual and temporal authorities in Islam. The Friday service usually includes a sermon.

The Third Pillar is alms. A devout Muslim is expected to pay a regular alms tax. This is used for eight purposes: to cover the cost of collection, to aid the poor, to pay for missionary work, to ransom slaves, to aid persons unable to pay their debts, to support the Way of Allah, and to aid travelers.

The Fourth Pillar is fasting. This covers the entire month of Ramadan—the month in which the Qurān was sent down from heaven. From dawn till sundown during that month the believer is not allowed to eat, drink, or smoke. Exceptions are made for the sick, pregnant women, mothers, and travelers. Ramadan ends in the Lesser Bairam, a festival of much jollity. In Jerusalem it is customary to fire a cannon each morning at daybreak to indicate that the fast has begun and again at sundown to signify that the fasting time for that day is past. Some Muslims do a good deal of eating at night, often culminating in a feast before dawn, but devout Muslims eat only enough during the fasting period to sustain life. Because of the fasting, not much heavy labor can be carried on during the month of Ramadan.

The Fifth Pillar is pilgrimage to Mecca. Every faithful man and

FIGURE 13.5 The Kaaba, Mecca. The circles in the pavement indicate the seven circuits of the Kaaba each pilgrim must make. (*Arabian American Oil Company*)

woman hopes to make the pilgrimage to Mecca at least once in his life. The month Dhu-l-hijja is set apart for this pilgrimage. Muslims slaughter an animal as an offering on the tenth day of this month. This ritual is called the Greater Bairam. Before entering the sacred area of Mecca, a pilgrim consecrates himself and then refrains from all worldly affairs until he has completed the Meccan rituals. Seven times he makes a circuit about the Kaaba and then kisses the sacred black stone (see Figure 13.5). The next ceremony is to run seven times between Safa and Marwa, two sacred places near the great mosque of Mecca. When at last the pilgrim arrives at Marwa he goes to a barber, who shaves his head, thus ending the state of consecration. Numerous minor rituals connected with the pilgrimage precede and follow the major ceremonials at Mecca. After one has made the pilgrimage (hajj), he has the right to add Hajji to his name, as an honorary title.

The importance of the pilgrimage to Mecca can scarcely be over-emphasized. Devout Muslims come, at great cost and sacrifice, often extreme hardship, from many parts of the world to worship at this holy shrine. There they encounter pilgrims from every continent, every race. This meeting with so many strange peoples at the holy place may explain why in Islam there is no such thing as race prejudice. Men of every color meet there as brothers and bow down to worship God. In Islam men from all levels of culture and racial backgrounds stand on a basis of equality.

MISSIONARIES OF ISLAM

Since the time of Muhammad the adherents of Islam have increased to more than 400 million. This growth is in line with the belief of Muslims that their faith is a religion for all the world, and today they are still continuing to spread the frontiers of Islam by zealous missionary work.

The nature of the missionary work of Muslims has been misunderstood, however, owing to the fact that Islam views itself as a total culture. That is why, from the beginning, the expansion of Islam has involved wars of conquest. The Muslims' first desire was to escape confinement in the deserts of Arabia; and like many another people, they would not be satisfied until they had seized the lands of their richer neighbors; beyond that was the grandiose ambition of their conquering generals to overrun the most fertile parts of the continents of Europe, Asia, and Africa, and they almost accomplished this. The enormous Muslim conquest is without parallel in the annals of history. Not even that of Alexander the Great is equal to it. Alexander's kingdom fell apart when he died after a reign of only thirteen years, but the Arabs' conquest was permanent. The culture they spread has not been effaced, and some states they founded survive even in our own day.

It is obvious that the converts to Islam during these military campaigns were somewhat similar to the people of a conquered nation today who change their national allegiance when the treaty of peace is signed. This military and political action has led to the impression that converts to Islam have always been attained solely by the power of the sword, for such converts may not represent genuine religious conversion.

But that notion does not accord with the actual facts. Contrary to the general opinion, the attitude of Muslims toward other religions has on the whole been one of tolerance. In numerous places in the Qurān, Muhammad speaks of other religions with generosity and states clearly that religion must never be imposed by force. Moreover, no religion has a better record in this respect than Islam. There have been times of persecution in its history, but certainly Islam has as clean a slate in this respect as Christianity. It is a historical fact that large numbers of persons in the conquered lands accepted Islam of their own free will.[11]

The missionary work that Muslims carry on at the present time is done entirely by educational means; there is no military support whatever. The best example of this is Africa, where Islam has scored great gains. It is recognized that Muslims have been more successful than Christians in the field of African missions. From its very beginning, Islam has recognized the complete equality of the races. The Africans welcome missionaries who are ready to accept them as brothers in every sense of the word.

CONTEMPORARY ISLAM

Although Islam originated in Arabia, it now occupies parts of such widely separated lands as North and East Africa, Egypt, Jordan, Syria, Turkey, Iraq, Iran, Afghanistan, Turkestan, Pakistan, India,

Tibet, China, Malaysia, Indonesia, and the Philippines. A few Muslims are also found in the small European states of Albania and Bosnia.

The most zealous Muslim states today are Saudi Arabia, where the Wahhabi movement has sought to restore the faith of Islam to its original purity; Iran, where the Shiites are strong; and Pakistan, where the flame of Muslim nationalism has been fanned by competition with the emerging state of India, which is predominantly Hindu. Like other world religions, Islam is encountering difficulties as it seeks to adjust itself to the contemporary secular forces of philosophy, science, economics, and government.[12]

The total number of Muslims in the world is uncertain, but a recent survey by Muslims themselves arrived at the following results: North America, 40,000; South America, 405,000; Europe, 13,455,-000; Asia, 360,488,000; Africa, 100,382,000; Oceania, 115,000—a total Muslim world population of 478,885,000. These statistics make it clear that Islam is one of the major religions of the world.

The daily language of Muslims varies according to the countries where they live, but the Qurān, their sacred Scripture, is in Arabic, and that is their language of worship regardless of where they live. Arabic is also the vernacular speech of the Muslims of Arabia as well as those of adjacent lands, such as Egypt, North Africa, Jordan, Syria, and Iraq.

Although Islam has footholds in Europe and Africa, in addition to spanning all of southern Asia, Arabia deserves special consideration, for this peninsula has left its stamp on the Muslim faith: Arabia is its birthplace, and also its holy land. It has given Islam its language, its Scriptures, its greatest shrines—and, most of all, Muhammad, its Prophet. Wherever they have gone, the Muslims have remembered the homeland, and they try to return to it at least once in a lifetime. Arabia is therefore a possession that all Muslims share; it is their common heritage, a spiritual bond that holds them together; it is in a real sense part of the Muslim faith.

Mecca, which contains the Kaaba, the most sacred shrine in all Islam, is located in central western Arabia, only a few miles from the Red Sea. Thousands of pilgrims stream toward this holy shrine year after year, century after century. There at the ancient holy place they renew their faith. Like their inspired Prophet, Muhammad himself, in that desert oasis they feel the presence of God. Medina, the city to which Muhammad fled from Mecca, is located about two hundred miles to the north. It is next to Mecca in the hearts of Muslims, for this city had welcomed the Prophet; he had made it his home, and there he is buried. Pilgrims pause in Medina to honor Muhammad and to worship in the mosques he built.

NOTES

1. Muslims follow a lunar calendar which makes it difficult to convert their dates into ours and ours into theirs. But on the basis of the work of Wüstenfeld and Soret, the following formula has been attained. Given the Muslim date counted from the Hegira (A.D. 622), where the Muslim date is A and the Christian is X, the formula is

$$A - \frac{3A}{100} + 622 = X.$$

See "Muslim Calendar," in James Hastings, ed., *Encyclopedia of Religion and Ethics*, III (New York: Scribner, 1928), pp. 126–127.
2. Qurān, Sura iv:3.
3. *Ibid.*, Sura xxxiii:49.
4. *The Koran*, trans. by J. M. Rodwell (New York: Dutton, 1909), p. 1.
5. Arthur J. Arberry, *The Koran Interpreted* (London: Allen & Unwin, 1955), I, 82–83. Used by permission.
6. W. M. Patton, "Sunnites," in Hastings, *op. cit.*, XII, 114–119.
7. Arberry, *op. cit.*, p. 29.
8. Reynold A. Nicholson, "Sufis," in Hastings, *op. cit.*, XIII, pp. 10–17.
9. C. Snouck-Hurgronje, "Der Islam," in Chantepie de La Saussaye, ed., *Lehrbuch der Religionsgeschichte* (Tübingen: J. C. B. Mohr, 1926), I, 732.
10. *Ibid.*, p. 733.
11. Abd al-Rahman Azzam, *The Eternal Message of Muhammad* (New York: New American Library, 1964), pp. 171–183.
12. The Bahai faith, which began as a Muslim sect, was founded in Persia by Mirza Ali Muhammad in 1844. He taught the universal brotherhood of man and the unity of all religions and sought universal peace. But he was executed by Muslims in 1850, and his movement bitterly persecuted. The world headquarters is at Haifa, Israel; the American headquarters is at Wilmette, Illinois. Missionary centers have been established in many lands.

Bibilography

ZOROASTRIANISM

Bode, Dastur F. A., and Nanavutty, Piloo. *Songs of Zarathushtra*. London: Allen & Unwin, 1952.

Cumont, Franz. *Textes et Monuments relatifs aux Mystères de Mithra*. Brussels: 1896–1899.

———. *The Oriental Religions in Roman Paganism*. Chicago: Open Court, 1911.

———. *The Mysteries of Mithra*. New York: Dover, 1956.

Duchesne-Guillemin, J. *The Western Response to Zoroaster*. Oxford: Clarendon Press, 1958.

*———. *The Hymns of Zarathustra*. Boston: Beacon, 1963. Now the best translation of the Gathas.

Fani, Moshan. *The Dabistan*, trans. by David Shea and Anthony Troyer. New York: Tudor, 1937. This is a fascinating and informative study of Zoroastrians, Hindus, Jews, Christians, and Muslims, written about 1615. It includes Ardai Viraf's "Excursion through Heaven and Hell," pp. 144–154.

Grant, Frederick C. *Hellenistic Religions*. New York: Liberal Arts Press, 1953. A valuable collection of quotations from classical writers and inscriptions relative to religion in the Hellenistic Age. Pp. 112–149 are relevant to Zoroaster, the Magi, and Mithraism.

*Herodotus. *The Histories*, trans. by Aubrey De Selincourt. Baltimore: Penguin, 1954.

Herzfeld, Ernst. *Zoroaster and His World*, 2 vols. Princeton: Princeton University Press, 1947.

Jackson, A. V. W. *Persia Past and Present*. New York: Macmillan, 1906.

———. *Zoroaster: The Prophet of Ancient Iran*. New York: Columbia University Press, 1919.

* Indicates paperback.

Jackson, A. V. W. *Early Persian Poetry* New York: Macmillan, 1920.

Moon, A. Anthony. *The De Natura Boni,* Translation and Commentary. Washington: Catholic University of America Press, 1955. A useful study of one of St. Augustine's best minor works. Augustine was for a time a Manichean. This book is related to that experience.

Moulton, James Hope. *Early Zoroastrianism.* London: Williams and Norgate, 1908. Along with a good discussion of Zoroaster and many aspects of his religion, also of the times, this contains a translation of the Gathas and, in an appendix, passages from Greek authors relevant to Zoroaster.

Olmstead, A. T. *History of the Persian Empire.* Chicago: University of Chicago Press, 1948.

Pritchard, James B. *The Ancient Near East in Pictures.* Princeton: Princeton University Press, 1954.

————, ed. *Ancient Near Eastern Texts,* 2d ed. Princeton: Princeton University Press, 1955.

Rogers, R. W. *A History of Ancient Persia.* New York: Scribner, 1929.

Runciman, Steven. *The Medieval Manichee.* Cambridge: Cambridge University Press, 1955.

Sacred Books of the East, ed. by F. Max Müller, 50 vols. Varanasi, India: Motilal Banarsidass, 1963.

Vols. IV, XXIII. *The Zend-Avesta,* I, II, trans. by James Darmsteter.

Vol. XXXII. *The Zend-Avesta,* III, trans. by L. H. Mills.

Vol. XLVII. *Dinkard, etc.,* trans. by L. H. Mills.

Vols. III, V, XVIII, XXIV, XXXVII, XLVII. *The Pahlavi Texts,* trans. by E. W. West.

Vermaseren, M. J. *De Mithrasdienst in Rome.* Nijmegen: Centrale Drukkerij N.V., 1951. An up-to-date survey of archaeological studies of Mithraism in Rome. The main part is in Dutch, but it contains a summary in English, pp. 140–152. The author finds evidence that no less than 100 Mithreums of varying sizes existed in Rome between A.D. 100 and 400.

Willoughby, H. R. *Pagan Regeneration.* Chicago: University of Chicago Press, 1929.

ISM

Salo W. *A Social and Religious History of the Jews.* New York: bia University Press, 1952.

Bernstein, Philip. *What the Jews Believe.* New York: Farrar, Straus, and Cudahy, 1951.

Bevan, Edwyn R., and Singer, Charles, eds. *The Legacy of Israel.* Oxford: Clarendon Press, 1927.

Bewer, J. A. *The Literature of the Old Testament.* New York: Columbia University Press, 1944.

*Buber, Martin. *I and Thou.* New York: Scribner, 1958.

————. *Das Dialogisches Prinzip.* Heidelberg: Lambert Schneider, 1962.

Buttrick, George A., ed. *The Interpreter's Bible,* 12 vols. Nashville: Abingdon, 1951–1957.

Charles, R. H., ed. *The Apocrypha and Pseudepigrapha,* 2 vols. Oxford: Clarendon Press, 1913.

Danby, Herbert. *The Mishnah.* Oxford: Oxford University Press, 1933.

*Epstein, Isidore. *Judaism.* Baltimore: Penguin, 1966.

Finegan, Jack. *Light from the Ancient Past.* Princeton: Princeton University Press, 1946.

Finkelstein, Louis, ed. *The Jews: Their History, Culture and Religion.* New York: Harper, 1949.

Freehof, Solomon B. *Reform Jewish Practice.* Cincinnati: Hebrew Union College Press, 1944.

Goodspeed, E. J., ed. *The Apocrypha: An American Translation.* Chicago: University of Chicago Press, 1938.

Grollenberg, L. H. *Atlas of the Bible.* New York: Thomas Nelson and Sons, 1956.

Hartman, Louis F. *Encyclopedic Dictionary of the Bible.* New York: McGraw-Hill, 1963.

Abrahams, Israel. *Jewish Life in the Middle Ages.* London: E. Goldston, 1932.

Kaplan, Mordecai. *Judaism as a Civilization.* New York: Macmillan, 1934.

Kohler, Kaufman. *Jewish Theology.* New York: Macmillan, 1918.

Kraeling, E. G. *The Rand McNally Bible Atlas.* New York: Rand McNally, 1956.

Leslau, Wolf, ed. *Falasha Anthology.* New Haven: Yale University Press, 1951.

*McCasland, S. Vernon. *The Religion of the Bible.* Apollo. New York: Crowell, 1968.

Maimonides, Moses. *The Guide of the Perplexed,* trans. by Shlomo Pines. Chicago: University of Chicago Press, 1963.

————. *The Book of Divine Commandments,* trans. by Charles B. Chavel. London: Soncino, 1940.

Moore, George Foote. *Judaism in the First Christian Centuries,* 3 vols. Cambridge: Harvard University Press, 1927–1930.

Nemoy, Leon, ed. *Karaite Anthology*. New Haven: Yale University Press. 1952.

*Parkes, James. *A History of the Jewish People*. Baltimore: Penguin, 1964.

Pfeiffer, R. H. *Introduction to the Old Testament*. New York: Harper, 1941.

———. *History of New Testament Times, with an Introduction to the Apocrypha*. New York: Harper, 1949.

Philipson, David. *The Reform Movement in Judaism*. New York: Macmillan, 1931.

Pritchard, James B. *The Ancient Near East in Pictures*. Princeton: Princeton University Press, 1954.

———, ed. *Ancient Near Eastern Texts*, 2d ed. Princeton: Princeton University Press, 1955.

Revel, Bernard. *The Karaite Halakah*. Philadelphia: Press Cahan Printing Co., 1913.

Sachar, S. L. *A History of the Jews*. New York: Knopf, 1930.

Sandmel, Samuel. *The Hebrew Scriptures*. New York: Knopf, 1963.

Schauss, Hayyim. *The Jewish Festivals*. Cincinnati: Union of American Hebrew Congregations, 1938.

Waxman, Meyer. *A Handbook of Judaism*. New York: Bloch, 1947.

Wright, G. E., and Filson, F. V. *The Westminster Historical Atlas to the Bible*. Philadelphia: Westminster, 1956.

CHRISTIANITY

Adam, Karl. *The Spirit of Catholicism*. New York: Macmillan, 1962.

Aquinas, Thomas. *Basic Writings of Saint Thomas Aquinas*, 2 vols., ed. by Anton C. Pegis. New York: Random House, 1945.

——— (S. Thomae De Aquino). *Summa theologica*, Latin Text, 5 vols., ed. by the Instituti Studiorum Mediavalium Ottaviensis, Studii Generalis, O. Pr. Ottawa, 1941–1945.

Attwater, Donald. *A Catholic Dictionary*. New York: Macmillan, 1931.

Augustine, St. *Selected Works*, ed. by Philip Schaff, Vols. 1, 2, 3, 4 of the *Nicene and Post-Nicene Fathers*, first series. Buffalo: The Christian Literature Company, 1886.

———. *Basic Works of Saint Augustine*, 2 vols., ed. by Whitney J. Oates. New York: Random House, 1948.

Bacon, Roger. *Opus Majus*, 2 vols., trans. by Robert Belle Burke. Philadelphia: University of Pennsylvania Press, 1928.

Bainton, R. *Here I Stand: A Life of Martin Luther.* Nashville: Abingdon, 1950.

Barth, Karl. *The Word of God and the Word of Man,* trans. by Douglas Horton. New York: Harper and Row, 1957.

————. *Church Dogmatics.* Edinburgh: T. and T. Clark, 1949 to present.

————. *Dogmatics in Outline.* New York: Harper, 1960.

Bell, G. K. A. *Documents on Christian Unity.* Oxford: Oxford University Press, 1948.

Bettenson, Henry. *Documents of the Christian Church.* New York: Oxford University Press, 1963.

Brauer, J. C. *Protestantism in America.* Philadelphia: Westminster, 1954.

Brownlee, William H. *The Meaning of the Qumran Scrolls for the Bible.* New York: Oxford University Press, 1964.

*Bultmann, R. *Jesus and the Word.* New York: Scribner, 1934.

Burrows, Millar. *The Dead Sea Scrolls.* New York: Viking, 1955.

Case, S. J. *The Evolution of Early Christianity.* Chicago: University of Chicago Press, 1914.

Coulton, G. G. *Medieval Panorama.* New York: Macmillan, 1938.

Deissmann, A. *Paul.* New York: Hodder and Stoughton, 1926.

Enslin, M. S. *Christian Beginnings.* New York: Harper, 1938.

————. *The Prophet of Nazareth.* New York: McGraw-Hill, 1961.

Finegan, Jack. *Light from the Ancient Past.* Princeton: Princeton University Press, 1946.

French, R. M. *The Eastern Orthodox Church.* London: Hutchinson, 1951.

Gilson, Etienne. *History of Christian Philosophy in the Middle Ages.* New York: Random House, 1954.

Goodspeed, E. J. *The Making of the English New Testament.* Chicago: University of Chicago Press, 1925.

————. *The Formation of the New Testament.* Chicago: University of Chicago Press, 1926.

————. *Introduction to the New Testament.* Chicago: University of Chicago Press, 1937.

————. *A History of Early Christian Literature.* Chicago: University of Chicago Press, 1942.

————. *The Life of Paul.* Philadelphia: Winston, 1947.

————. *The Life of Jesus.* New York: Harper, 1950.

Grant, F. C. *Roman Hellenism and the New Testament.* New York: Scribner, 1963.

Grant, Robert M. *A Historical New Testament.* New York: Harper, 1963.

Hardon, John A. *Religions of the World*. Westminster, Maryland: Newman, 1963, pp. 382–474.

Hordern, William. *A Layman's Guide to Protestant Theology*. New York: Macmillan, 1957.

Jeremias, J. *The Parables of Jesus*. New York: Scribner, 1955.

Klausner, Joseph. *Jesus of Nazareth*. New York: Macmillan, 1934.

Kraeling, E. G. *The Rand McNally Bible Atlas*. New York: Rand McNally, 1952.

Latourette, Kenneth Scott. *A History of Christianity*. New York: Harper, 1953.

*Leith, John H. *Creeds of the Churches*. Garden City, N.Y.: Doubleday Anchor, 1963. Excellent for student use.

McCasland, S. Vernon. *By the Finger of God*. New York: Macmillan, 1951.

*———. *The Religion of the Bible*. Apollo. New York: Crowell, 1960.

———. *The Pioneer of Our Faith, a New Life of Jesus*. New York: McGraw-Hill, 1964.

May, H. G. *The Oxford Bible Atlas*. New York: Oxford University Press, 1962.

——— and B. M. Metzger. *The Oxford Annotated Bible with Apocrypha*. New York: Oxford University Press, 1965. Revised Standard Version, with good notes and maps. The best edition for students.

Mead, Frank S. *Handbook of Denominations in the United States*. Nashville: Abingdon, 1941.

Nichols, Robert Hastings. *The Growth of the Christian Church*. Philadelphia: Westminster, 1941.

Nock, A. D. *St. Paul*. New York: Harper, 1937.

Smith, George D. *The Teaching of the Catholic Church*. New York: Macmillan, 1960.

Tillich, Paul. *Systematic Theology*, 3 vols. Chicago: University of Chicago Press, 1951–1963.

———. *The Courage to Be*. New Haven: Yale University Press, 1952.

———. *The Protestant Era*. Chicago: University of Chicago Press, 1954.

*———. *Biblical Religion and the Search for Ultimate Reality*. Phoenix. Chicago: University of Chicago Press, 1955.

*———. *The Dynamics of Faith*. New York: Harper Torchbooks, 1957.

———. *Christianity and the Encounter of the World Religions*. New York: Columbia University Press, 1963.

*———. *The Eternal Now*. New York: Scribner, 1963.

*———. *Morality and Beyond*. New York: Harper and Row, 1963.

Throckmorton, B. H. *Gospel Parallels*. New York: Thomas Nelson and Sons, 1957.

Wright, G. E., and F. V. Filson. *The Westminster Historical Atlas to the Bible.* Philadelphia: Westminster, 1956.

ISLAM

Ahmad, Aziz. *Studies in Islamic Culture in the Indian Environment.* Oxford: Clarendon Press, 1964.

Andrae, Tor. *Mohammed, the Man and His Faith.* London: George Allen and Unwin, 1936.

*Arberry, Arthur J. *The Koran Interpreted.* New York: Macmillan, 1955. This is the best edition for students.

———. *Revelation and Reason in Islam.* New York: Macmillan, 1957.

Arnold, T. W., and Alfred Guillaume, eds. *Legacy of Islam.* Oxford: Clarendon Press, 1931.

Asad, Muhammad. *The Road to Mecca.* New York: Simon and Schuster, 1954.

Azzam, Abd al-Rahman. *The Eternal Message of Muhammad.* New York: New American Library, 1964.

Brockelmann, Carl. *History of the Islamic Peoples.* New York: Putnam, 1947.

Chand, Tara. *Influence of Islam on Indian Culture.* Allhabad: Indian Press, 1963.

Cragg, Kenneth. *The Call of the Minaret.* New York: Oxford University Press, 1956.

Fyzee, A. A. *Outlines of Mohammedan Law.* New York: Oxford University Press, 1949.

Gibb, H. A. R. *Mohammedanism.* New York: Oxford University Press, 1953.

——— and J. H. Kramers, eds. *Shorter Encyclopedia of Islam.* Leyden: Brill, 1953.

*Guillaume, Alfred. *Islam.* Baltimore: Penguin, 1954.

Hitti, P. K. *History of the Arabs.* New York: Macmillan, 1951.

Husain, S. Abid. *The Destiny of Indian Muslims.* London: Asia Publishing House, 1965.

Iqbal, Mohammed. *Reconstruction of Religious Thought in Islam.* London: Oxford University Press, 1934.

Jeffrey, Arthur, ed. *Mohammed and His Religion.* New York: Liberal Arts Press, 1958.

The Koran, trans. by J. M. Rodwell. New York: Dutton, 1909. Still a good translation, and with many good notes.

Levy, Reuben. *Social Structure of Islam*. Cambridge: Cambridge University Press, 1957.

Mahmoud, Zaki Naguib. *The Land and People of Egypt*. Philadelphia: Lippincott, 1959.

Morgan, Kenneth W. *Islam, the Straight Path*. New York: Ronald, 1958.

Nadwi, S. Abul Hasan Ali. *Muslims in India*. Lucknow: Academy of Islamic Research and Publications, 1960.

Rahman, Fazlur. *Islam*. London: Weidenfeld and Nicolson, 1966.

Smith, Wilfred Cantwell. *Islam in Modern History*. Princeton: Princeton University Press, 1957.

Watt, W. Montgomery. *Muhammad at Mecca*. Oxford: Clarendon Press, 1953.

————. *Mohammed at Medina*. Oxford: Clarendon Press, 1953.

————. *Islam and the Integration of Society*. Evanston: Northwestern University Press, 1961.

————. *Islamic Surveys*. Edinburgh: University Press, 1962.

————. *Muslim Intellectual*. Edinburgh: University Press, 1963.

————. *Muhammad: Prophet and Statesman*. London: Oxford University Press, 1964.

PART IV RELIGIONS OF INDIA

India is the largest part of a subcontinent that also includes Pakistan, Burma, and Ceylon, as well as the principalities of Nepal, Sikkim, Bhutan, and Assam. There is no barrier between India and West Pakistan except the Thar Desert; Burma is separated from the rest of the subcontinent by hills and a thick tropical jungle; Ceylon is cut off only by a narrow strait. In the northern part of the subcontinent are the high Himalayan ranges; the northwestern section of these ranges are known as the Karakoram and the Hindu Kush; Everest and other high peaks are in the northeastern part of the Himalayas. Both the high mountains and the mosquito-breeding jungles at their lower levels have served as barriers between the subcontinent and the regions beyond; even more significant as isolating factors are the vast plateaus—the Gobi Desert, beyond the desolate hills of Tibet, and the plateau of Afghanistan in the northwest. But the plateau of Afghanistan is not as impenetrable as the Gobi Desert, and it has always been through this easier barrier that new peoples have entered the country. On its other sides, the Indian peninsula is surrounded by the sea, a natural stimulus for trade and commerce.

India can be divided into four main regions. First, the mountains and hills of the extreme north. Second, the northern plains, which stretch for 2,000 miles in a crescent from the Arabian Sea to the Bay of Bengal and are watered by three river systems: the Indus, the Ganges, and the Brahmaputra. Today, only the Ganges plain is fertile. The entire plains region, known as Hindustan, has been the traditional center of Indian culture. The third main region is the Deccan, a plateau shaped like an inverted triangle with the Vindhya Hills as the base; its sides on the east and the west are chains of hills, called Ghats, which catch much of the monsoon rains before they are able to enter the plateau and prevent the

Deccan from being fertile. The fourth region is the coastal plains, long narrow strips of tropical country between the Ghats and the sea—the Bay of Bengal, the Arabian Sea, and the Gulf of Manar. The eastern coastal plain is known as the Carnatic Coast, the western as the Malabar Coast.

The climate of most of India is subtropical or tropical; only in the northernmost part (Kashmir) is it temperate. A continental climate, with hot summers and cool winters of about two months' duration (January and February), characterizes the northern plains from the Ganges Valley to the Indus. During the monsoon season (June through September) the weather is hot and humid. In the summers (April to June), which are dry and have temperatures as high as 120° Fahrenheit, dust storms add to the unpleasantness, and the land becomes parched. It is no wonder that Indra, the rain bringer, was the chief god of the early Aryans who composed the Rig-Veda; one could scarcely fail to do homage to the life-giving rain of the monsoons, as they followed upon the deadly drought.

The coastal plains extending into Gujarat on the western side and through Orissa to Bengal on the eastern are tropical regions. In these regions the products of nature grow lavishly, but the climate is humid and enervating. The tropical peoples are, on the whole, physically smaller and less energetic than those in the north; they have shown their genius in the quieter pursuits of commerce and the cultivation of religion, philosophy, art, and literature. The northern peoples, on the other hand, have been more active and aggressive and have produced more men of power, the political leaders of the country.

Peoples and Languages

The peoples of India can be divided roughly into the southern, Dravidian-speaking groups and the northern, Aryan-speaking groups. The peoples of the extreme north, the Kashmiris, are often Caucasian in complexion and build; the Punjabis and Rajasthanis, too, are frequently of lighter complexion and more powerfully built than the groups to the south of them. The Hindi-speaking peoples (one of the groups of Aryan-speaking peoples) of the northern plains are light brown to dark, and stocky in build. The Dravidian groups have dark skins, long heads, and broad noses and are small in stature; throughout the south, however, there are people of the higher castes who have the physical characteristics of the northern peoples.

At present, there is neither a Dravidian nor an Aryan race in India. Since a group of Dravidian languages with a family similarity does exist, however, there probably was a proto-Dravidian language spoken by people of a similar ethnic type whose prehistory is obscure. Apparently the Aryan invaders, who spoke an Indo-Iranian language, borrowed a group of sounds called "cerebrals" from this proto-Dravidian language and incorporated them into their language, thus forming Sanskrit. The "cerebrals," which do not exist in other Indo-European languages but are conspicuous in the Dravidian languages of India, must have come from the language of the indigenous peoples.

The Sanskrit language attained a fixed form about 500 B.C. Alongside Sanskrit there were spoken dialects called Prakrits; in the sixth and seventh centuries A.D., however, these old dialects began to disappear. By A.D. 1000 the modern Indian languages, formed by combining Sanskrit with words derived from foreign invaders or from local Dravidian dialects, had developed. Today fourteen regional languages have been given official status by the Indian government. These are Hindi, Urdu, Punjabi, Marathi, Gujarati, Assamese, Oriya, Bengali, Kashmiri, Tamil, Telugu, Kanarese, Malayalam, and Sanskrit. English is still the official national language for intercommunication between the various language-state groups, although efforts are being made to replace English with Hindi (an Aryan language). Such a move, it seems, will be postponed indefinitely because of the strong opposition of other language-state groups, especially in south India. In addition to the major languages listed above, there are many minor ones; one survey has counted 179 languages and 544 dialects; but many of these dialects are spoken by only a few tribes, and others among them are not culturally important. Nevertheless, the language diversity has been a source of disunity in the past, and today it is a divisive factor in the efforts of the central government to maintain Indian unity.

The Sanskrit cultural tradition has been the unifying factor of Indian culture, and the Vedic religion has been the foundation stone of this great tradition. From the Vedic religion have sprung India's dominant philosophies and religions and much of its significant literature and art.

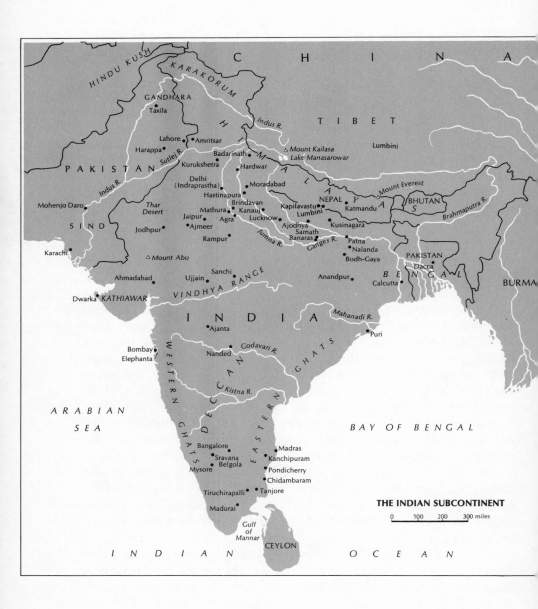

THE INDIAN SUBCONTINENT

0   100   200   300 miles

THE HISTORY OF INDIA

Prehistory and the Rig-Vedic Period

Research has barely begun on the prehistory of India. Enough has been completed, however, to show that the country has been occupied since approximately 400,000 B.C., the era of Paleolithic or Old Stone Age man. On the basis of the archaeological evidence, it appears that the plateau of Iran was occupied as early as the fifth millennium B.C. by small communities of farmers and shepherds. During the fourth millennium B.C. some of these people moved westward and settled in the Tigris-Euphrates valley; they were the forerunners of the Sumerian, Assyrian, and Babylonian cultures. Other groups of these same peoples of the Iranian Plateau moved eastward, first to Baluchistan, and then sometime in the third millennium B.C. into northwest India, where they occupied the valley of the Indus River and its tributaries. Rapidly an amazing civilization, called the Indus Valley or Harappan, developed; it flourished from about 2500 to 1500 B.C.

The civilization of the Indus Valley apparently centered around the cities of Mohenjo-Daro and Harappa. Harappa is in the Punjab, about 100 miles southwest of Lahore; Mohenjo-Daro is on the Indus in Sind, approximately 200 miles north of Karachi. Archaeological excavations at the sites of these two cities, which were not undertaken until the 1920s, revealed that a culture as great as the contemporary civilizations of Mesopotamia and Egypt had existed there. Heretofore it had been thought that the invading Aryans had encountered and overcome a primitive population. Now the opposite view had to be accepted: the Aryans were the barbarians, the Harappans the civilized people.

Unfortunately the script of this civilization has not yet been deciphered. But from studying the archaeological remains we know that the two capital cities were laid out in rectangular or square blocks that met at right angles. The houses were usually two stories high and were built around courtyards. The drainage systems in homes and buildings were connected with brick-lined sewers; this technique was lost with this civilization and nothing like it reappeared in India until recent times. The citadels of these cities contained palaces, halls, public baths, and granaries—all without sculptural decorations or paintings. However, other art forms were developed. The making of bronze sculptures, clay figurines, terracotta toys, and steatite seals, the last often of artistic excellence, were well known. Textile arts were also important, and cotton was carried to Mesopotamia.

The Indus Valley civilization flourished for about 1,000 years (2500–1500 B.C.). It was a prosperous and creative culture whose boundaries extended from Gujarat in western India to the banks of the Jumna at the borders of the Punjab. The cause of its decline and fall is uncertain, but one likely hypothesis is that it was destroyed by the incursions of Aryan invaders around 1500 B.C.

The early hymns of the Rig-Veda refer to battles against the enemy (the Harappans, no doubt); buildings were burned, inhabitants slaughtered, and treasures carried off. The Rig-Veda speaks disparagingly of the dark, flat-nosed elements of the population. These were probably the proto-Australoid racial types who, along with the Mediterranean ethnic type, were the dominant indigenous peoples; a blend of these peoples forms the dominant ethnic type in Dravidian-speaking south India today.[1] Perhaps some of the survivors of the Indus Valley culture escaped to the south. It is not only the ethnic types and the Dravidian languages that point toward this, but also such non-Aryan customs as bullfights and wild orgiastic fertility cults mentioned in early Tamil literature.[2] Sufficiently early documentary evidence of a conclusive kind is, however, lacking.[3]

There must have been intimate contacts, perhaps intermarriage, between the Aryans and the Harappans. This is evidenced by the incorporation of the "cerebral" sounds from the Harappans' Dravidian language into the Aryans' Sanskrit language.

The Aryans destroyed much of the high civilization they must have found in northwest India. These invaders were a barbarous people who knew agriculture, but held cattle, sheep, and goats to be of such importance that wealth was reckoned in them. They ate beef freely and drank intoxicating liquors other than soma (used only in religious ritual)—both of them forbidden in later Hinduism. Oxen were used to draw four-wheeled carts; the horse was used with two-wheeled chariots for sport or war. Gambling was indulged in, as we know from a poignant hymn, the "Gambler's Lament" (R.V. X, 34).

The Era Reflected by the Epics (c. 900–500 B.C.)

Although the two great Indian epics, the *Mahabharata* and *Ramayana*, were achieving their final forms sometime between 200 B.C.

and A.D. 200, some scholars think that parts of these narratives vaguely reflect the epoch between 900 and 500 B.C. By that period Indo-Aryan culture had moved from the Sind and Punjab south-eastward to the plains of the Ganges and Jumna rivers, where the two capitals of the war described in the *Mahabharata* are located— Hastinapura and Indraprastha. Kurukshetra, the battlefield itself, may have been situated about 100 miles south of the present Delhi. The social organization revealed in the *Mahabharata* indicates a change from the old tribal type of government, with chieftains, their councils of nobles, and a third estate of freemen, to a more developed society of numerous little kingdoms, with life at the courts much like that of kings and princes of later days.

A significant feature of Indian society that remains to the present time was becoming generally accepted in this era, the division into the four classes (*varnas*). First in rank was the Brahmin class whose duties were to study and teach the Vedas and preside over impor-tant rituals. Second in rank was the Kshatriya class of rulers and warriors whose duty it was to protect the people and administer a just government for their welfare. Third in rank was the Vaishya class who provided for the economic welfare of the community by engaging in such occupations as agriculture, cattle-raising, and trade and commerce. Fourth and lowest in rank were the Sudras who engaged in menial tasks. (See pp. 387–393 for a further discussion of varnas.)

Persians, Greeks, and the Mauryan Dynasty (500–183 B.C.)

Darius I of Persia (521–486 B.C.) completed the conquest of the Indus Valley and the Punjab begun by Cyrus and made these areas a satrapy of the Persian Empire. By the fourth century the Persians were no longer a power in these regions, yet aspects of Persian culture remained a permanent influence on Indian civilization. Persian influence is shown in the lion capitals of Asoka's pillars, and in the Persian pattern of political organization of the Mauryan Empire. Solar cults and the notion of the divinity of the ruler may also have been influenced by ideas from Persia.

One important result of the Persian Conquest was that India became known to the Greek world, although the impact of the Greeks was felt directly only in the northwest. Alexander the Great (336–323 B.C.) first conquered Bactria and then proceeded across the Indus River into northwest India. He was welcomed and entertained by the ruler of Taxila, but the chiefs of other Indian kingdoms united and halted his armies, forcing them to retreat. Alexander made no impression on the Ganges plain, where the important kingdoms were located, and is not mentioned in Indian literature. The only significant influence of Alexander on Indian culture was that he opened new routes of trade and travel, and it was along these routes that the Persian influences continued to be brought into India.

Recently, mainly through a study of Indo-Greek coins found in Afghanistan and northwest India, it has come to light that there were Greek invasions of India in the second century B.C. These Indo-Greeks came from Bactria, where there was a Greek colony that existed from early Achaemenian times.[4] This colony was strengthened by additional settlements established by Alexander. The Indo-Greeks declined in power toward the end of the second century B.C., and by the beginning of the Christian era they had disappeared. They left their mark, however, in the Gandharan style of Buddhist art and began the minting of coins in India.

More significant in Indian history and culture than the Persians and Greeks was Asoka (d. c. 226 B.C.), a ruler of the Mauryan dynasty, which was established by Chandragupta Maurya in 322 B.C. By the time of Asoka, grandson of Chandragupta, the Mauryan Empire included the territory from Herat to Bengal in the east, and the Deccan in the south. Asoka himself conquered Kalinga or eastern India (east of Andhra), and it was because of the slaughter of these conquered peoples that Asoka suffered remorse and became a convert to Buddhism. We have historical documentation of Asoka's reign in his Edicts on stone, which are the earliest surviving documents in Indian history except for the undeciphered materials of the Harappan culture. These documents of Asoka, filled with Buddhist ethical ideals, emphasize the Buddhist virtue of compassion for all living beings. Asoka almost eliminated the killing of animals for food in his kitchens and recommended vegetarianism to the people. In personal relations the Golden Rule was recommended, and the duties of a ruler were described as those acts that contribute to the welfare of his subjects. As much as possible, Asoka did perform these duties.

Asoka was such an enthusiastic Buddhist that he is said to have sent his son (some sources say his brother Mahendra) to Ceylon to preach Buddhism. The king of Ceylon was converted, and Ceylon subsequently became Buddhist.

Sungas, Sakas, and Kushanas (183 B.C.–A.D. 320)

The Mauryan successors of Asoka continued to reign for some fifty years. Then, about 183 B.C., Pushyamitra Sunga, the Brahmin general of the last Mauryan king overthrew the dynasty. Pushyamitra, who was a Hindu, persecuted Buddhism. Buddhism continued to flourish, nevertheless, as the remains at Bharhut testify.

The Sungas were displaced by invaders from the northwest, first the Bactrian Greeks, then the Scythians, known in India as the Sakas. By the middle of the first century B.C. the Sakas, who spoke an Iranian language, had stretched their power as far as Mathura. Then, toward the end of the first century B.C., a line of kings known as the Pahlavas (an Iranian name) came into control of northwest India. Among their rulers Gondophernes is best known because, according to legend, it was in his kingdom that the Apostle Thomas was supposed to have preached Christianity. The Pahlavas were conquered by the Kushanas, a tribe of the Yuechi, a people of Turkish type who spoke an Iranian language. Most important of the Kushana rulers was Kanishka, a patron of Buddhism.

The Golden Age of Ancient India (A.D. 320–450)

By the third century A.D. the power of the Kushanas had declined. Then began the rise of the Guptas and the Golden Age of Indian culture. Chandragupta II achieved an empire almost as great in its extent as the Mauryan Empire, although it was never as centralized; many of the subject kings were autonomous and merely paid tribute.

In this age, often compared with the Elizabethan age of England or the Periclean age of Greece, Indian culture reached its zenith. Sanskrit (a unifying factor throughout Indian civilization) became the official language, as well as the language of literature and philosophy. During this era intellectual and artistic activity reached its climax in the works of Kalidasa, the greatest literary figure of the period, who was famous especially for his lyrical poem the *Meghaduta* and his drama *Sakuntala;* Dhanvantari was a celebrated physician; and Bramagupta (born A.D. 588) made significant contributions to astronomy and mathematics. The teachers of the Golden Age were learned Brahmins who concerned themselves with the study of the four Vedas, the six Vedangas (phonetics, meter, grammar, etymology, astronomy, and the Kalpa Sutras), the Puranas, the Mimamsa philosophy, Nyaya (logic), Dharma or Law, and the *Maha-bharata*. The interest in education is evidenced by the founding of the University of Nalanda, which remained the most famous center of Buddhist learning until it was destroyed by invading Muslims around A.D. 1000.

The Golden Age was the period of the gradual ascendancy of Hinduism, under the patronage of the Gupta monarchs. Vedism (or Brahmanism), a religion that emphasized sacrifices and the Vedic gods, had by this time developed into Hinduism, a religion of devotion to deities, similar to the Hinduism of today.

During the Gupta era sculpture and painting flourished. Gupta art set the style for subsequent Indian works up to the ninth century. The Ajanta frescoes of about the sixth century represent the great beauty, grace, feeling, and skill achieved in this art.

The epoch of the Guptas was marked by material prosperity and well-being. Fa-hsien (fl. 399–414), a Chinese Buddhist pilgrim, in his record of his travels in India, tells us that India was peaceful, that serious crime was rare, and that one could travel from one end of the country to the other without fear of attack by robbers. He mentions also that vegetarianism prevailed; meat eating was restricted to the lower classes and the untouchables. Incidentally, he gives us our earliest reference to "pollution on approach," one feature of the social order in Hinduism. The laws were mild: offenders were usually fined rather than corporally punished, and the death penalty, known earlier in India, was abolished.

Incursions of the Hunas, a central Asian people (heretofore identified with the Huns of Attila, but according to certain modern scholars, a different people and of Iranian blood), brought an end to the Gupta Empire by A.D. 550.

Harsha and Indian Culture (606–647)

After a war between two of the more powerful northern kingdoms, Harsha (d. 646), another of India's great rulers, was able to bring some unity to most of northern India.

Another Chinese pilgrim, Hsüan Tsang, has left us an account of Harsha and his kingdom, which extended from Kathiawar to Bengal. Hsüan Tsang tells us that literature and the arts flourished again in Harsha's reign. Buddhism was declining, and certain aspects of later Hinduism were appearing, such as Tantric cults and the practice of suttee. Finally, law and order were not maintained as well as formerly.

The Medieval Period (c. 712–1565)

As soon as Harsha died, his empire fell apart. The subsequent history of northern India again shows political disunity and wars. Of importance in the history of Buddhism is the Pala dynasty, which flourished during the eighth and ninth centuries and was the patron of Buddhism in its Mahayana form. Apparently it was from the Pala kingdom that Buddhism was introduced into Tibet. Kanyakubja, controlled for a while by the Palas, was, during this time, the center of Sanskrit culture in the north. Kanyakubja remained the wealthiest city and center of Sanskrit culture in the north until the Muslim invasions brought about its destruction.

Wars and the political disunity of feudalistic states in northern India made the country an easy prey for the Turks of Ghazni in Afghanistan. Under Mahmud of Ghazni they made as many as seventeen raids into the western half of Indian territory between 1001 and 1027 with loot as their only object. These raids should have been a warning to the princes of the northern kingdoms to unite against the Muslim threat, but they were unable to. This disunity, in addition to the outmoded fighting machine of the Hindus, enabled Muslims to conquer India, which they ruled until the eighteenth century, when the British became dominant. Not until 1947 was India again to become an independent country.

After the Golden Age of the Guptas, when a decline in cultural creativity took place in northern India, the culture of the south continued to flourish. The contributions of the southern, Dravidian peoples to Indian culture have been great in literature, philosophy, religion, and art. Their literature dates back to at least the sixth century A.D. The greatest and most outstanding works written in Tamil (a Dravidian language) during the medieval era are the devotional hymns of the Shaivite and Vaishnavite singer-saints known, respectively, as the Nayanars and the Alvars.

Ramanuja (c. 1017–1137), one of India's outstanding philosophers, taught in the temple of Srirangam (near modern Tiruchirapalli) in Tamil Land (the far south). However, he was a Brahmin and his works are in classical Sanskrit. Shankara (788–820), the greatest of Indian philosophers, was probably a native of what is now called

Kerala, where Malayalam is the modern language. In Shankara's time Malayalam was just coming into being as an offshoot of the Tamil language. But Shankara also spoke and taught in Sanskrit. Both he and Ramanuja traveled widely throughout India, teaching, debating, and writing commentaries on the Brahma Sutras, Upanishads, and the Bhagavad-Gita. Their debating and writing in Sanskrit shows that this was the language of the learned all over India at that time, although it was most prevalent among the intellectuals of Banaras and the regions east of this city. Sanskrit culture—religion, philosophy, and literature—gave India unity, divided as it was politically.

The break in this cultural unity came with the Muslim conquest, which began around A.D. 1000.[5] Although during the centuries of Muslim occupation, Muslim culture and religion influenced the indigenous civilization somewhat, the Hindu traditions were still kept alive. Hindu and Muslim customs and traditions lived side by side, so that when independence came India was divided into two countries, India and Pakistan.

In the Muslim era some great art was created, notably the exquisite Taj Mahal, a combination of Hindu and Muslim styles. Akbar, one of the Muslim emperors and a contemporary of Elizabeth I, was a gifted man, a humanitarian ruler, and a brilliant statesman. He advocated religious toleration and intercommunal marriages, but his successor Aurangzeb reversed this policy and persecuted the Hindus, as well as the Sikhs.

The Modern Period (1600–1947)

In the seventeenth century Muslim rule was successfully resisted by the Maratha chief Sivaji (1627–1680). The Sikhs, too, formed a martial organization against the Muslims and by the end of the seventeenth century had built up an independent kingdom. Muslim power was broken.

The eighteenth century saw European influences brought into India by Portuguese, French, and British trading companies. The last gained the ascendancy, and by the middle of the nineteenth century Britain ruled India directly or through princely states with local autonomy. Missionary schools were founded, and began to educate some of the Indians along Western lines; the British began to employ clerks and subordinate officers who were trained in English, providing an incentive to Indians to acquire an education in this language; and many young Indians of the middle class were educated in England. It was from these contacts with Western culture that the Hindu Renaissance was born. This was an era when new social and cultural ideals were combined with Hindu religion, under the leadership of men like Rammohan Roy, founder of the Brahmo Samaj in 1830; Dayananda Sarasvati, founder of the Arya Samaj in 1875; the saintly Ramakrishna and the philosophical poet Rabindranath Tagore.[6]

These leaders and the societies or institutions they founded aroused a new devotion and pride in the traditions of their country among educated Indians and led the way for the nationalist movements soon to come. Gandhi and Nehru finally became the leaders of the movement for independence; but it was Gandhi who captured the devotion and imagination of the people that was essential for the success of the freedom movement.

In 1947 India again became a free country. The tragedy, when independence came, was the division of India into Hindu and Muslim states. If Hindu India and Muslim Pakistan could learn to cooperate as one nation, all India would benefit.

NOTES

1. A. L. Basham, *The Wonder That Was India* (New York: Grove, 1954), p. 24.
2. *Ibid.*, p. 185. Bullfights were prevalent among the Mediterranean peoples, notably the Cretans.
3. *Ibid.*, p. 25. Basham says that "the megaliths erected by the early Dravidians in south India have been shown to be not very ancient," and a recent theory dates the Dravidians as entering India during the second half of the first millennium B.C. It is certain only that descendants of the Harappans "must survive in the present-day population of India."
4. The Achaemenids reigned in Persia c. 550–330 B.C. See A. K. Narain, *The Indo-Greeks* (Oxford: Clarendon Press, 1957, 1962), and also Basham, *op. cit.*, pp. 58 ff.
5. Indian historians like R. C. Majumdar use "ancient" to refer to Indian history up to A.D. 1000, the beginning of what they term the "medieval" period. Western scholars, such as A. L. Basham, begin the medieval period after Harsha's reign in the seventh century. From the point of view of cultural unity, it seems that the Indian historians are justified.
6. See pp. 473–475 for more detailed information about these leaders and movements of the Hindu Renaissance.

15 Vedic Religion

RELIGION OF THE INDUS VALLEY CULTURE

The Aryans who entered India around 1500 B.C. came upon a highly developed civilization, the Harappan or Indus Valley culture. Its religion still remains somewhat obscure, mainly because of our inability to decipher its script; but from the archaeological remains and from what we know of other civilizations of the era in which this culture flourished (2500–1500 B.C.), it seems reasonably certain that the country was ruled by priest-kings and that a fertility cult was prevalent and popular. Most significant for us are the non-Aryan ingredients of later Indian religion that were probably derived from the fertility cult. Archaeological remains show worship of a mother goddess (see Figure 15.1) and of the phallus. Among the animals that were held sacred was the humped bull, which has retained his godlike position (along with the cow) in the contemporary Indian world. The bull and the phallus have been assimilated to the Shiva cult of Hinduism, the one as the mount of the god and the other as his mark (*linga*). Other aspects of Shiva were also contributed by this ancient culture. Steatite seals from both Mohenjo-Daro and Harappa show a male god, horned and perhaps three-faced, sitting in a yogi position (see Figure 15.2). On one seal the deity is surrounded by four animals: the elephant, the tiger, the rhinoceros, and the buffalo; at his feet are two deer. This is apparently the prototype of Shiva as lord of beasts (Pasupati) and prince of yogis.

No temple has been discovered on the sites of this civilization.

FIGURE 15.1 Mother-goddess figurine, Indus Valley culture. (*Museum of Fine Arts, Boston, Ross Collection*)

Unless further research reveals some such structure, it can only be surmised that religious rituals were conducted privately at small shrines in residences or perhaps under the open sky. Some of the baths that have been uncovered may have been used for ritual bathing, a custom that has been a characteristic feature of Hindu religion from early times.

ARYAN RELIGION: THE DEITIES OF
THE INDO-IRANIANS

Little is known about the Aryans who came into India around 1500 B.C. One authority comments that "we do not in fact know who the original Aryans were, or what they called themselves"; we know only that they spoke a group of related languages or dialects; it is best, therefore, "to refer to them as the 'Aryan-speaking' peoples."[1] The Aryan (also called the Indo-European) languages may have been evolved among tribes of the Russian and central Asian steppes.[2] During the second millennium B.C. many of these tribes migrated: some to Europe as founders of the Greek and other European civilizations; others went to Asia Minor; still another group, the Indo-Iranians, divided into two peoples, those who settled in Iran to found the Persian culture and those who entered India about 1500 B.C. These Aryans were seminomadic barbarians, predominantly fair, long-headed, and tall. They were mainly pastoral, but did a little farming; they had a definite tribal organization, and used horses and chariots.[3]

Male sky gods were the dominant deities of the Indo-European peoples. Linguistic evidence shows that the words for "god" in the different Indo-European languages have a common origin. In the earliest text of the Indian Aryans, the Rig-Veda (written in an archaic Sanskrit), this word is *deva;* in the Avesta (earliest text of the Iranians) it is *daeva.* Both of these are cognate with the Latin *deus.* The original great sky and father god of the Indo-Europeans turns up in the Rig-Veda as Dyaus-pitar (a god of very little im-

FIGURE 15.2   A Pasupati steatite seal from Mohenjo-Daro. (*Archaelogoical Survey of India*)

portance for both Indians and Iranians) and in the Greek and
Roman classics as Zeus and *Ju*-pitar (the great god of the Greeks
and the Romans).[4] Among the subjects of worship were the orb of
the sun (Greek—Helios, Vedic—Surya), storm gods (Teutonic—
Thor, Vedic—Indra), fire (Vedic—Agni, cognate with Latin *ignis,*
fire; in Greek religion note Hestia, goddess of the hearth fire), and
other important personifications of nature. The closest kinship is
between Avestan and Rig-Vedic deities—evidence of a common
Indo-Iranian religion and culture before this group divided.

The great sky god of the Aryan Indo-Iranians was Varuna,[5] who
was associated with both the cosmic and the moral order. Other
common Indo-Iranian deities were Mitra, Indra, the two Nasatyas
(also called the Ashvins), Vayu, Soma, and Yama, by their Rig-Vedic
names; their Avestan names are respectively Mithra, Indra, Nan-
haithya, Vayu, Haoma, and Yima. In the Rig-Veda Varuna and
Mitra are among the deities called *asuras,* while the other deities
mentioned belong to the class called *devas.* Far-off gods were mainly
asuras, the more intimate ones *devas.*[6] In later Indian religion

asuras became the name for demons and *devas* the word for gods; whereas in Iran *ahura* (same as the Vedic Sanskrit *asura*), which means "Lord," became the name for the one god Ahura Mazda (wise Lord), and the daevas were demoted by Zoroaster's reform. In both religions Varuna-Mitra and Rita (the Avestan Vouruna-Mithras and Asha), were grouped together as the powers of cosmic order and the Good (the moral Right, especially Truth).

Interestingly Indra, the boisterous war and storm god of the Indo-Iranians, becomes a demon in later Iranian religion; in the Rig-Veda he is foremost of the gods and in later Hinduism is god of the best of the sensuous heavens. However, under the epithet Verethraghna (same as the Sanskrit Vritrahan) he remained a god in the later Avesta.[7]

Vayu, the Indo-Iranian wind god, retained this role in the Rig-Veda; in the later Avesta and the Pahlavi books[8] there are two Vayus: a good Vayu, who protects Ahura Mazda's creatures, and an evil Vayu, who is mainly a demon of death.[9]

Haoma (Soma of the Vedas) was a plant revered by the Indo-Iranians. The Haoma of the Iranians seems to have been a juice, perhaps extracted from a plant like rhubarb, which is still found in the Iranian mountains.[10] This was consumed ritually as the elixir of immortality. It was even drunk by the gods for this purpose, as well as to increase their already supernatural power. In India, too, the same or a similar plant was ritually pressed, in order to extract the juice, which was also drunk as the elixir of immortality and in order to obtain godlike powers. A. L. Basham thinks, however, that the Indian plant must have belonged to the hemp family; today in India a juice called "bhang," with narcotic properties and made from hemp (the equivalent of the narcotic marihuana), is used in religious rites by some sects.[11] Yima of the Avesta parallels the Yama of the Vedas; in the former Yima, son of Vivahvant (Sanskrit Vivas-vant), was the first man and first king whose glory departs when the "lie" enters his mind; in the latter he is also son of Visvasvant—a sun god in both traditions—and again an Adam of some sort, the first man to die and become lord of the blessed dead in a place where feasting goes on forever.

For further discussion of the numerous deities of the Aryan-speakers see Chapters 5, 6, and 8 on the religions of the Greeks, Romans, and Zoroastrians; note especially the sky and other nature deities. The deities of the Aryans who came into India will be dealt with in the section immediately following.

VEDISM

Vedism (Vedic religion) is to be distinguished from Hinduism: the former is characterized by its emphasis on the ritual of sacrifices, the latter by devotion to particular deities. Although Hinduism may have been the dominant religion of the masses of the people from earliest times, our only sources of evidence of the religion of this era are the Vedas, which were in the charge of the priestly class who served the aristocracy. The religion of the common people may have included many elements that are not found in the Vedas.

The Vedas

There are four Vedas: the Rig-Veda, the Sama-Veda, the Yajur-Veda, and the Atharva-Veda. The Rig-Veda, composed between 1500 and 900 B.C.—that is, during an interval of 600 years—is the earliest of the Vedas and one of the oldest religious texts in the world still considered sacred. It consists of 1,028 hymns divided into ten books called *mandalas* and describes the religion of the Aryans who began their invasion of India around 1500 B.C. Books II-VII, which contain the oldest hymns, are called the Family Books because each is ascribed to a particular family of singers. The rishis—according to tradition the "fathers" of these singer families through which the hymns were handed down—are said in the Rig-Veda to have been seers of very ancient times. Elsewhere the rishis are heroes of myths and legends. Although the authorship of the Vedas is traditionally attributed to the rishis, the hymns of all ten books were probably composed by priest-bards who were attached to a princely family. The latest of the ten books is Book X, composed about 900 B.C.

The Sama-Veda consists of selected verses from the Rig-Veda, to be chanted during rituals by the chanting priest. The Yajur-Veda is a manual of sacrificial formulas in prose and verse, for the use of the priest who performed the physical operations in the sacrifices. The Atharva-Veda, the fourth of the Vedas, was late in gaining recognition, and its status has always been lower than that of the other Vedas. Much of its content is devoted to magical prayers and spells, which point to its derivation from the religion of the common people, both Aryan and non-Aryan. Only a few passages of the Atharva-Veda have philosophic meaning; for example, Book X, verses 2, 7, and 8, which describe the cow as a universal creative principle, and Book XIII, which glorifies the sun as the cosmic principle.

Each of the four Vedas has affixed to it the following sections of later writings: Brahmanas, prose writings dealing with the significance of sacrificial rites; Aranyakas (forest texts), religious and philosophical writings; and the Upanishads, philosophical works.

The word *Veda* may be used in two ways: it may refer to the four Vedas named above without their appendages (Brahmanas, Aranyakas, and Upanishads), or it may refer to the four Vedas plus all their appendages. All of the literature of the four Vedas, including Brahmanas, Aranyakas, and Upanishads, is considered sacred scripture in Hinduism and, according to tradition, was divinely revealed—heard or "envisioned" by the ancient seers called *rishis;* for this reason the Vedas are traditionally considered as *shruti* (a word meaning "that which is heard") or divinely revealed literature. The Sanskrit word *Veda* means "knowledge"—in this context, "sacred, religious knowledge." Each of the four core Vedas is called a *samhita.*

The Gods of the Rig-Veda

The hymns of the Rig-Veda honor the devas. *Deva,* the Sanskrit word for "god," is derived from the Sanskrit root *div* which has as one of its meanings "to shine with brightness and radiance"; the devas or gods are the "shining ones."[12] The important deities are the following:

INDRA. § Indra, foremost of the Vedic gods, was associated with creation and the rain. He was even more important to the early Aryans as their warrior-leader against the *dasas,* or native inhabitants of the lands of the Harappan civilization. As chief of the gods, Indra is given eloquent praise in hymn No. 12 of Book II of the Rig-Veda. He remains an important deity in the later religion, Hinduism, as king of the highest of the sensuous heavens, the heaven of the thirty-three gods.

Indra's myth is the central theme of the Rig-Veda.[13] The myth, largely concerned with creation, tells us that before the universe existed there were Asuras—some good, some evil. (In later Indian religion *asura* became a word for "demon.") Vritra and the Danavas were evil powers; the Adityas were good. According to the myth, there were seven or eight Adityas, all descended from the mother goddess, Aditi; among them were Indra, Varuna, and Mitra. Indra was miraculously born from Aditi's side. Through drinking Soma, he swelled to enormous proportions, which caused him to thrust apart heaven (sky) and earth and to fill the space between them. This region, henceforth known as the atmosphere, is the region occupied by gods and men. Thus the three worlds were created: sky, atmosphere, and earth.

The Adityas then asked Indra to become their champion against the archdemon Vritra and his cohorts, the Danavas. (This hero-fighting-the-dragon myth was a common one among the Indo-European peoples.) Indra consented, and Tvashtri, artificer of the gods, forged him a weapon called "vajra," the thunderbolt. Thus armed, he drank a huge quantity of Soma and went forth to battle with Vritra, an enormous serpent lying on the mountains. Indra succeeded in slaying Vritra, as well as his mother Danu. Then out of the mountains shattered by Indra—in other accounts out of Vritra's belly, and in still another version, out of a cave—there emerged the cosmic waters which flowed over the body of their demonic restrainer. These waters were pregnant with the sun.

All the essential elements were now present for an ordered universe: the three worlds—earth, atmosphere, and heaven—and the sun. A pathway was made in the stone sky for the sun to travel; the waters were in the sky to give moisture to the earth at regular seasons. Particular deities were given individual functions in this newly created order of the universe known as Rita, and the god Varuna presided over this cosmic order.

AGNI. § Agni is next to Indra in esteem in the Rig-Veda. He is the sacrificial fire and the fire on the hearth. In the latter capacity he is the intimate friend of the family and protector of the household and its prosperity. As the sacrificial fire, he is the messenger-mediator between gods and men; he is also the fire in the sun and the fire of lightning. Thus he is a god of all three worlds—earth, atmosphere, and sky. Oblations to him are still offered today.

SOMA. § As a personification, Soma is the god who animates the juice extracted from the soma plant. The whole of Book IX of the Rig-Veda is devoted to this god. All the hymns of this book have the same pattern of content: the pressing of the soma, its mixing and refining, the pouring of it into containers, and the calling upon Indra to drink it. As noted in the previous section, this narcotic drink, which gave rise to hallucinations and the feeling of consciousness-expansion, was also used ritually by the Iranians. In later Indian religion (Hinduism) Soma was also identified with the moon.

VARUNA. § In the Rig-Veda Varuna, who was the great sky god of the ancient Indo-Iranians, is the guardian of Rita, the cosmic order. The idea of Rita was extended into the moral sphere, as right order in the world of human relations. As guardian of this order Varuna had an army of spies, who flew about the world and brought to their lord reports of the conduct of men. He meted out punishments for evil deeds, and thus hymns to him are not only praises of his glory but also penitential psalms begging forgiveness for sins. The hymns to Varuna, although few in number, are the loftiest in the Rig-Veda, and he is the only Vedic deity who is approached with awe and humble reverence. Varuna was also a god of the waters. He punished sinners, afflicting them particularly with dropsy. As was mentioned above, Varuna is called an *asura,* which in later Indian religion had the connotation of demon.

MITRA. § Associated with Varuna is Mitra, guardian of vows and compacts. Varuna and Mitra are the chief figures among the Adityas, a group of seven or eight deities descended from Aditi, a mother goddess encountered above in the Indra creation myth. Mitra, one of the group of sun gods of the Rig-Veda, is, as mentioned above, identical with the Mithras of Zoroastrianism. His importance as a deity in the Roman world is discussed in Chapter 8.

SURYA. § Surya, the usual Sanskrit word for "sun," is god as the orb of the sun. He drives across the sky daily in his chariot. Other sun gods originated out of epithets of Surya. Very important among these is Savitar (inspirer, life-giver, or stimulator). In later times a prayer addressed to Savitar called the "gayatri mantra" was looked upon as the most sacred passage of the Vedas. This mantra is recited daily by all orthodox Brahmins even today.

ASHVINS. § The Ashvins are horsemen who drive across the sky in a three-wheeled chariot. As allies of Indra, their main function is the benevolent one of healing the sick and helping mankind in other ways. These twin gods, also known in Iranian religion, were probably related to the Greek Dioscuri.

MARUTS. § The Maruts are storm gods who ride in chariots behind Indra, their chief.

RUDRA. § Rudra is associated with the destructive aspects of the storm; he also has other fearsome aspects. His arrows bring disease and destruction, like the arrows of the Greek Apollo. He dwells in remote mountains and lacks the genial personality possessed by the other gods, with the exception of Varuna. Rudra does have a more attractive side to his character, as the possessor of valuable herbs that can bring health to those whom he favors. Sometimes Rudra is identified with Agni. In Hinduism, the god Shiva incorporates most of these qualities of Rudra, so that Rudra becomes another name for Shiva.

DYAUS and PRITHIVI. § Dyaus-pitar (sky father), an insignificant deity in the Rig-Veda, was probably the great sky father of the Aryans in prehistoric times. Prithivi (Earth) is Dyaus-pitar's wife.

PUSHAN. § Pushan is another sun god. His main function is to protect travelers and to reclaim lost cattle.

VISHNU. § Vishnu, destined to become one of the two greatest gods of Hinduism, is noted in the Rig-Veda for his three strides, which covered the universe.

USHAS. § Ushas is the lovely goddess of dawn. Gems of lyrical poetry are addressed to her.

VAYU. § Vayu is god of the wind.

TVASHTRI. § Tvashtri is the forger god, the Hephaestus of the Rig-Veda.

YAMA. § Yama was the first man to die. He rules as king in the highest heaven, the Heaven of the Fathers, the ancestral spirits. His equivalent in Iranian religion is Yima.

Minor Deity Groups

APSARASES. § The Apsarases are lovely nymphs who could become mistresses of gods and men.

GANDHARVAS. § The Gandharvas are heavenly musicians (male), partners of the Apsarases.

DASAS. § The dasas or dasyus—a name meaning "barbarian," "slave," or "servant" used by the Aryans to refer to the indigenous Indian peoples—are evil demons. Another name for evil spirits which became prevalent in later Hinduism is rakshasas.

Life after Death

The general Vedic view of life after death was that those who performed the proper rites during their lifetimes and had not offended Varuna beyond forgiveness went to the heaven of Yama, the delightful Heaven of the Fathers, and feasted joyously there forever. Evil men went to the House of Clay, an abode similar to the Greek Hades and the Hebrew Sheol.

Monotheism and Monism in the Late Hymns of the Rig-Veda

In Book X of the Rig-Veda we find the beginnings of philosophical thought, which was to reach a climax in Vedic literature in the Upanishads. Monotheism is shown in Hymn 121; here Prajapati, lord of creatures, is portrayed as creator of all things and the one God above all other deities. Monism (the doctrine that asserts that everything in the universe is part of, or in some way an emanation of, one substance) is brought out in the Purusha Hymn[14] (Hymn 90) and in the Hymn of Creation (Hymn 129). In the Purusha Hymn it is said:

> The Purusha is this all, that which was and which shall be.
> He is Lord of immortality. . . . One fourth of him is all beings.
> The three fourths of him is the immortal in Heaven.[15]

The hymn continues with a description of how all things, all regions in space, all time, and the four social classes were born of the sacrifice of this Purusha. This monistic idea of one Being (the cosmic Purusha) as the substance of the entire universe, both the concrete or manifested world and the immortal or unmanifested world, is repeated and elaborated in Upanishadic thought. The remarkable Hymn of Creation also posits a One as the source and substance of the created universe. But the unknown author of this poem had an unusual skepticism for a man of his time, and he questioned this monistic theory, as well as all others concerning ultimate origins and substances. He ends the hymn with the words, "None knoweth whence creation has arisen."[16]

The Sacrificial Cult

Vedic religion was primarily one of sacrifices to the deities, in order to obtain favors from them. There must have been domestic sacrifices performed by the head of the household, as there were in other early Indo-European communities, but there is no documentation of them until the *Grihyasutras*, written at a later period (about 500 B.C.). The Yajur-Veda is our source of knowledge of the larger-scale rituals performed by the Vedic aristocracy. In general the sacrifices were of two types: food offerings—usually milk, butter, cake, pulp, and grain; and Soma offerings. Animal sacrifices were included in both types, and the fire cult was an important preliminary to every sacrifice. The food or drink offered was divided into two parts; one part was thrown into the fire, and the remainder was eaten or drunk by the priests and the layman on whose behalf the ceremony was performed.

The fire (Agni) was prepared in accordance with a fixed ritual. Generally there were three fires arranged around an altar in the form of a rectangular pit in the ground. There were no temples and no images; the sacrifices took place on an open threshing floor. As many as sixteen or seventeen priests might participate, but the essential ones were four: the Brahmin, who was responsible for the entire performance; the Hotar, who recited passages from the Rig-Veda and made the offerings; the Udgatar, who chanted parts of the Sama-Veda; and the Adhvaryu, who performed the manual operations and recited the sacrificial formulas prescribed in the Yajur-Veda.

The most solemn of the sacrifices were the Soma rites. The Agnishtoma was the basic type. Prior to the ceremony the layman and his wife were consecrated and the soma bought in a prescribed manner. Then there were three pressings of the soma plant to extract the juice, each preceded by long preliminary rites.

The shortest rite, but a very important one, was the Agnihotra. This was a food offering of milk to Agni, an oblation performed by an Adhvaryu priest and the layman in whose behalf it was presented.

There were also new- and full-moon sacrifices in which vegetables

were offered along with oblations to the fathers (ancestors); sacrifices
of the seasons, which occurred every four months (in the spring, the
rainy season, and autumn); and lesser occasional sacrifices.

Special ceremonies for kings only were the Rajasuya, a king's inauguration ceremony, and the Ashvamedha, the great horse sacrifice
which only a conqueror-king could perform. The horse sacrifice was
a year-long rite. It had for its purpose the general welfare, fertility,
and prosperity of the kingdom. Its main feature was the letting
loose of a horse to wander whither it chose for a year, attended and
defended from capture and prevented from intercourse with mares
by a band of noble youths. When the stallion was brought back it
was strangled; then there was a fertility rite between the queen and
the dead horse, after which the horse was cut into pieces and parts
of it sacrificed.

Although the last king on record to perform the horse sacrifice
was a ruler of the Chola dynasty in the eleventh century A.D., the
public cult of sacrifice had actually begun to decline much earlier
and by the third century B.C. little of it survived. Only the domestic
cult of sacrifice, which must have existed in Vedic times alongside
the more public and large-scale ceremonies, continued; it is still
observed today in Hinduism.

The Brahmanas (c. 800–600 B.C.)

The Brahmanas are prose writings, composed between approximately 800 and 600 B.C., that deal with the sacrificial rites of Vedism. The
literature of the Rig-Veda and the Yajur-Veda is symbolic, but that
of the Brahmanas is much more so. The Brahmana whose symbolism
has greatest significance is the Shatapatha Brahmana of the Yajur-
Veda. The essential symbolic idea in this work is the identity between
the microcosmic individual and the macrocosmic Purusha called
Agni-Prajapati. This macrocosm-microcosm identity is the bridge
between Rig-Vedic and Upanishadic thought.

The Upanishads

The earliest books of the philosophical literature known as the
Upanishads were composed at the time of the writing of the latest
Brahmanas—in the seventh or sixth century B.C.[17]—but many of the
Upanishads are of much later date. Although according to tradition
there are only 108 Upanishads there are actually more than 200 of

them. Of these the following fourteen are usually considered the most significant: Aitareya, Kaushitaki, Chandogya, Brihadaranyaka, Isha, Katha, Prashna, Mundaka, Taittiriya, Mahanarayana, Mandukya, Kena, Svetashvatara, and Maitri.

The Upanishads came into being when sages arose who were dissatisfied with the ritualistic approach to man's nature and his immortality. These thinkers were for the most part members of the Kshatriya class (the class of warriors and the ruling aristocracy)[18] and included women philosophers.

Associated also with the Upanishads or included in them are the Aranyakas (forest texts). These works were concerned with the mystical meaning and symbolism of sacrifice and with priestly philosophy; their content was considered so secret and dangerous that they had to be studied in the forest.[19] The oldest Upanishads included Aranyakas either as a part of the main text or as appendices to it, so that it is often difficult to distinguish the Aranyaka from the Upanishad. The Aranyakas and Upanishads are attached to Brahmanas. For example, the first third of Book XIV of the Shatapatha Brahmana is an Aranyaka, and the end of this book is what is called by many the greatest and most important of all the Upanishads, the Brihadaranyaka Upanishad. The first section of the Chandogya Upanishad (which belongs to a Brahmana of the Sama-Veda) is an Aranyaka.

The word *Upanishad* may be analyzed into the following Sanskrit components: *upa,* "near"; *ni,* "down"; and *shad,* "sit"; "to sit down near or beside someone" is the complete meaning. This implies a secret session in which the pupil sat close to the teacher to receive a confidential communication. From the idea of a secret session developed the idea of a "secret doctrine," or that which is communicated at such a secret session. The Indians give as a synonym for the word *upanishad* the word *rahasya,* meaning "mystery" or "secret"; the words *rahasya* and *upanishad* are used together to mean "secret doctrine."[20]

The chief and most significant doctrine of the principal Upanishads can be expressed in a few words: the Atman is the Brahman; in Sanskrit this is the famous dictum: *tat tvam asi* (that art thou). Before this doctrine can be discussed further, the terms *Atman* and *Brahman* should be understood. The etymology of the word *Brahman* is uncertain; the word *Brahman* appears many times in the Vedas with the meaning of "prayer" or "magic formulas," and in this context its meaning centers on the magical potency of the prayers or magic formulas to operate in influencing or even coercing the gods to bestow the things requested.

Later, when the magic formulas and prayers were organized as the three Vedas (the fourth Veda, the Atharva, was not included), this literature was called "the Brahman" as well as the "threefold knowledge." The Vedas, now equivalent to "the Brahman," were believed to be of divine origin. The sacrifice—like the mana of the primitives —was considered superhuman in its power to bring about what was desired. The Vedas were the manual of these sacrifices filled with mysterious power. The next step was probably the combining of the idea of the divine origin of the Vedas with the idea of the deification of this magical power as Brahman. In this way perhaps there arose the concept of the Brahman as divine being.[21] Brahman was not a personal God like that of the Judeo-Christian, Muslim, and Zoroastrian religions, but a more impersonal divine principle.

In Sanskrit, *Brahman* is a neuter noun; *Brahma,* a masculine form of the word, denotes one of the personal gods, a creator-god of lesser power than and subject to Brahman.

The chief priests, as knowers and directors of the prayers, formulas and ritual of the magically potent sacrifice were called Brahmanas (written "Brahmins" in this text to avoid confusion with the Vedic literature of the same name—the *Brahmanas*). Because of their religious importance the Brahmins were the class with the highest social status of the four main classes of Aryan society.

Atman is the word used in the Upanishads to designate the individual soul or self. In Sanskrit, *Atman* clearly denotes "self," and there is a late passage in the Rig-Veda that mentions the Atman as "Self (Atman) of the world."[22] This is close to the theme of the Upanishads, viz., the individual self (Atman) is the Brahman (the universal Self).

In one of the earliest Upanishads, the Chandogya, the doctrine of "the Atman is the Brahman" is clearly expressed in several ways. All the examples illustrate the teaching that Brahman, the nondual ultimate reality, the One-without-a-second, is identical with the Atman, the individual self. The sage Uddalaka says to his son Shvetaketu: "That which is the finest essence—this whole world has that as its soul. That is Reality. That is Atman. That art thou, Shvetaketu."[23]

In another of the earliest Upanishads, the Brihadaranyaka, the sage Yajnavalkya in a philosophical discussion with his wife, Maitreya, describes the ultimate nature of Brahman, again equated with the Atman. Brahman is described by Yajnavalkya as "a mass of knowledge," as without self-consciousness and beyond all subject-object categories, the One-without-a-second, the only real Being. He explains to Maitreya that because the Absolute Reality is the All, he is beyond the duality of subject-object relationships and therefore beyond self-consciousness (feeling the self as an object). No qualities or attributes can be posited of It (the Brahman) because these would imply dualities and pluralities in the Absolute. The Brahman or Atman, therefore, can only be described negatively as *neti neti* (not this, not this); and this *neti neti* doctrine of nonduality (advaita) became the central principle of the later philosophical system, known as Advaita Vedanta, which was established by India's greatest philosopher, Shankara, in the ninth century A.D.[24]

The Brihadaranyaka Upanishad is also important for the first clear presentation of the doctrine of *karma* in relation to ethical action and the transmigration of souls *(samsara)*. In the four Vedas, including the Brahmanas attached to the nucleus of each, there is no doctrine of karma and samsara. The nearest approach to such a doctrine is found in the Shatapatha Brahmana's teaching of "re-death"—those who do not perform the rites correctly are born again and suffer death again.[25] The Brihadaranyaka Upanishad sets forth the doctrine of karma and samsara for the first time. Yajnavalkya explains karma as the law of the deed, a law of action, whereby good deeds result in a good rebirth "in a newer and more beautiful form . . . like that of the fathers, or of the Gandharvas, or of the gods, or of Prajapati, or of Brahma, or of other beings"; bad deeds result in rebirth as an evil being. The good or evil deeds are caused by a man's desires: "Where one's mind is attached—the inner self goes thereto with action, being attached to it alone."[26] Desires also cause rebirth, and determine whether the rebirth will be in a good or a bad form. The round of birth and death—with some rebirths better because of good deeds and some worse because of bad deeds—is called "samsara." To obtain release *(moksha)* from samsara one must eliminate desires, both good and bad. Desire is eliminated, according to the Upanishadic thinkers, by knowledge of the immortal Brahman and of the soul's essential identity with it. This knowledge is gained first with the help of a teacher, and then by one's own intuitive self-knowledge one achieves the direct experience of identity. When this self-realization is won, moksha, release from samsara, is gained. The philosopher who has experienced his identity with Brahman lives only until he completes his present life, caused by actions in previous lives and in this life before moksha was won. At death the unitive state already experienced by the sage becomes eternal.

Among other Upanishads important in later Hindu religion and philosophy are the Taittiriya and the Mandukya. The Taittiriya Upanishad contains the doctrine of the "sheaths" of matter, life, and mind surrounding the Atman (or Brahman). These sheaths are: the sheath of gross matter, the physical body in its gross form composed of the five elements (earth, water, fire, air, and ether) in their gross forms; within this is the vital sheath, the sheath of "breath" or life; within this is the sheath of the lower mind with its sense functions; and within this is the sheath of the higher mind (intellect). Within the sheath of intellect is the Self (Atman); this Self is Bliss, and is identical with Brahman.[27] In the philosophy of Advaita Vedanta (described below), however, the self of Bliss is interpreted to mean a fifth sheath, and the Atman-Brahman transcends even this. The general view in the Upanishads, as in later Hinduism, is that only the sheath of gross matter is shed at death; the other sheaths, composed of subtle matter (the five elements in their subtle forms), make up the body of transmigration until it is again reborn. The macrocosmic Brahman has a set of sheaths that correspond with those of the individual, the microcosm. The goal of the sage is to strip off these sheaths of the changing, phenomenal world and realize Brahman, the eternal core of his Being.

The Mandukya Upanishad is noted for its elucidation of the esoteric syllable OM, universally used as a symbol of the ultimate in religious meaning. OM probably originally meant simply Amen or assent, as in Hebrew prayer,[28] and was much used in this way by the priests in the Vedic rites. In the early Chandogya Upanishad,[29] as in later Hinduism, OM stands for the All, for total Reality. The Mandukya Upanishad explains how the OM is the total universe. The Mandukya Upanishad uses the A-U-M form of the word (in Sanskrit the letter O of OM is really the diphthong AU, so we have A-U-M from OM) to give the following explanation.

The letter A is the waking state, the "Common-to-all-men." This is the state of enjoyment of bodily pleasures—the "gross"—by means of the organs of the body, including mind. The waking state is the first fourth of the Atman (Brahman); on the macrocosmic scale, this is enjoyment of the concrete world of matter.

The letter U is the dreaming state. The bodily organs are again operative; but they enjoy a world of images and ideas, not material physical objects. This dreaming state, elsewhere often called the "subtle body," is common to both the macrocosm and microcosm and is the second fourth of Brahman.

The letter M is the deep-sleep state. There is no activity of the bodily organs; it is described as a unified "cognition-mass" consisting of bliss (*ananda*). This is the third fourth of Brahman, a higher state than the previous one because it is more unified; it has less reference to the multiple, separate objects of the first state, and gross material world.

The fourth, and highest state is silence. It is the goal of the philosopher and constitutes realization of the eternal, essential Self, the One-without-a-second. It can be described only in negative language because subject-object relations disappear in the All, the one eternal Real. The fourth state, called *chaturtha*[30] (the usual Sanskrit word for "fourth") in the Mandukya Upanishad, is called *turiya* in the Maitri Upanishad. Turiya is simply a variant of the same ordinal and is the word used for this fourth state in all later philosophical treatises.[31]

This explication of the meaning of OM as the All parallels in meaning the doctrine of the "sheaths" of matter, life, and mind of the Taittiriya Upanishad. These "sheaths" are called *maya* (here connoting illusory appearance) in some of the later Hindu philosophies; for example, in the Advaita Vedanta. The word *maya* is used first in the Upanishads in the Brihadaranyaka (2.5.19) in a quotation from the Rig-Veda: "Indra by his magic powers (maya) goes about in many forms."[32] This idea is developed into a theory of maya as cosmic illusion in the Svetashvatara Upanishad (4.9–10):

This whole world the illusion-maker projects out of this Brahma.
And in it by illusion the other is confined.
Now, one should know that Nature is illusion,
And that the Mighty Lord is the illusion-maker.[33]

This passage became a favorite proof-text for philosophers, who wished to appeal to the Upanishads as shruti, or divinely revealed literature, in support of their later maya concept.

Ethics is not emphasized per se in the Upanishads. There are important passages, however, that laud the virtues of truthfulness, reverence for parents, teachers, and guests, and generosity, modesty, pity, and self-restraint. The apparent reason for the scarcity of discussions of ethical values in this literature is that mention of specific moral precepts and values is superfluous in the light of the ethical implications of the general metaphysical teaching of the Upanishads —the teaching that the Self (Atman) is the Brahman. This implies that all men and all creatures are dear because the Self or Brahman underlies them all. All men, all creatures, have as their ultimate essence the same eternal Brahman; therefore all men and all living things are parts of oneself, the Atman, and the Atman is the Brahman. In ethical behavior, therefore, the man who has realized his identity with Brahman does not act egotistically because he has overcome the illusion that he is a separate self; he acts with the vision that all others are his own true self, the Atman-Brahman. This means that he acts with love and for the good of others. The Upanishads do not teach a life of service to humanity as a way of salvation (this concept did not appear until the Bhagavad-Gita); in human encounters between sages and others, the sage sees others as dear because of the Self (Atman). For example, in the Brihadaranyaka Upanishad (2.4.2– 5) the sage Yajnavalkya tells his wife that a husband, a wife, sons, the gods, and the creatures are all dear, not for themselves as separate beings but because they are the Self: "Verily, everything is not dear that you may love everything; but that you may love the Self, therefore everything is dear."[34]

The teachings we have mentioned—the *tat tvam asi* (that art thou) doctrine, the concept of the nondual Brahman, the meaning of OM, the idea of maya in the "sheaths" or coverings of the Atman-Brahman, the way of intuitive knowledge to attain moksha (release from karma and samsara)—these are the most important contributions of Upanishadic thought to later Hinduism.

The sages of Upanishadic thought—Kshatriyas as well as Brahmins —were thinkers who had abandoned the active life for one of meditation in the forest for the purpose of moksha, release from karma and samsara through union with the eternal Brahman. This new goal of life and the method of its realization were radical departures from the Vedic religion of sacrifice that had been accepted until then. Vedism[35] and Brahmanism are names given to the earlier sacrificial religion—Vedism because three of the Vedas (the Atharva-Veda had inferior status) were the handbooks for the sacrifices; Brahmanism because the Brahmin priests were the specialists who presided over the sacrificial rituals. The main purpose of the ritual sacrifice in Vedism was to bring about a happy, prosperous life in this world; moksha, the goal of the Upanishads, looks to release from the world. These new Upanishadic ideas began the break with Vedism and were among the first steps in the development of Hinduism.

NOTES

1. Percival Spear, *India: A Modern History* (Ann Arbor: University of Michigan Press, 1961), p. 32.
2. A. L. Basham, *The Wonder That Was India* (New York: Grove, 1954), p. 29, locates these Aryan-speaking tribes as occupying the land from Poland to the central steppes of Asia; Stuart Piggott in *Prehistoric India* (Baltimore: Penguin, 1952), p. 248, says that the Indo-European family of languages probably evolved among tribes of the south Russian steppes and the lands eastward to the Caspian Sea.
3. Basham, *op. cit.*, pp. 28 ff.
4. *Ibid.*, p. 233.
5. *Ibid.*, p. 236, comments that some scholars connect the name Varuna with Uranus, the Greek god, who was also a deity of the heavens.
6. R. C. Zaehner, *The Dawn and Twilight of Zoroastrianism* (London: Weidenfeld and Nicolson, 1961), p. 39.
7. *Ibid.*, p. 88.
8. These are Zoroastrian writings, later than the Avesta. See Chapter 8.
9. Zaehner, *op. cit.*, p. 88.
10. *Ibid.*
11. Basham, *op. cit.*, p. 236.
12. *Ibid.*, p. 233.
13. W. Norman Brown, "Mythology of India," in Samuel Noah Kramer, ed., *Mythologies of the Ancient World* (Garden City, N.Y.: Doubleday Anchor Books, 1961), pp. 281–330, describes this myth from which the account given is taken.
14. "Purusha" in this context means "Cosmic Man."
15. Quoted from Thomas' translation in Sarvepalli Radhakrishnan and Charles A. Moore, *A Source Book in Indian Philosophy* (Princeton: Princeton University Press, 1957), p. 19.
16. *Ibid.*, Macdonell's translation, p. 24.
17. The problem of dating the earliest Upanishads centers around the question of the relationship of the Upanishads to early Buddhism. All we can say with some certainty is that early Buddhism and the Upanishads "derive from a common source of ideas, which is not wholly Aryan . . . the date, often suggested, of 500 B.C. is reasonable" (Louis Renou, *Vedic India*, Vol. III, trans. by Philip Spratt [Calcutta: Susil Gupta Private Ltd., 1957], pp. 37–38). Basham, *op. cit.*, p. 249, suggests the "seventh or sixth centuries B.C."
18. See pp. 396 f. for an account of the four main classes in existence by 900 B.C. in Vedic times: Brahmins (priests); Kshatriyas (warriors and rulers); Vaishyas (farmers, shepherds, and merchants); Sudras (those who performed menial work).
19. Maurice Winternitz, *A History of Indian Literature*, trans. by Mrs. S. Ketkar, 3d ed. (Calcutta: University of Calcutta, 1962), I, 203.

20. *Ibid.,* pp. 211–212.
21. *Ibid.,* pp. 216.
22. *Ibid.,* p. 217.
23. "Chandogya Upanishad," *The Thirteen Principal Upanishads,* trans. by Robert Ernest Hume, 2d rev. ed. (London: Oxford University Press, 1931), p. 248.
24. For a brief description of Shankara's philosophy, see pp. 469–471.
25. Surendranath Dasgupta, *A History of Indian Philosophy* (Cambridge: Cambridge University Press, 1963), I, 25.
26. "Brihadaranyaka Upanishad," *The Thirteen Principal Upanishads,* 4.4.4, 4.4.6, pp. 140–141.
27. Dasgupta, *op. cit.,* I, p. 46, thinks *anandamaya* is the self. Others, notably the Advaita Vendanta school, interpret *anandamaya* as a fifth sheath.
28. Winternitz, *op. cit.,* I, 187, notes 1 and 2.
29. "Chandogya Upanishad," *The Thirteen Principal Upanishads,* 2.23.3, p. 201.
30. Spelled more properly "caturtha," but spelled phonetically on p. 387.
31. *The Thirteen Principal Upanishads,* p. 392, note 11.
32. *Ibid.,* p. 37.
33. *Ibid.,* p. 38.
34. "Brihadaranyaka Upanishad," trans. by F. Max Müller, in *Sacred Books of the East* (London: Oxford University Press, 1894), Vol. XV, pp. 108–110.
35. See Louis Renou, *The Religions of Ancient India* (London: Athlone, 1953), for a lengthy discussion of the distinction between Vedism and Hinduism, especially pp. 46–67.

16 Hinduism

HINDU RELIGION AND SOCIETY

One of the best, most concise abstract definitions of Hinduism[1] is the following: "Hinduism is that complex of culture, religious practice, myth, belief that are felt to be a continuation of the Vedic tradition."[2] Hinduism is a continuation of the Vedic tradition in that it holds sacred the four Vedas and the Vedic pantheon. It differs from that tradition, however, in its emphasis on meditation and release from this world and also in its devotional worship of deities, both in the home and in the temple. Vedic religion was, by contrast, primarily a religion of sacrifice; the sacrifice, performed in order to obtain desired goods, was almost magical in its compulsion. In Hinduism, loving devotion to Shaivite or Vaishnavite deities replaced Vedic sacrificial ritual. Worship of these deities at home or in temples is distinct from the domestic cult of sacrifice (the main aspect of Vedic ritual still observed today in Hinduism) that is described in the *Grihyasutras,* a part of the smriti literature noted below. Worship of Shiva and the mother goddess had probably continued at the popular level since the time of the Indus Valley civilization, but it was only after the era of the early Upanishads that these deities were accepted by orthodox Brahmins. The smriti literature of the Brahmins—the Epics and Puranas—absorbed these deities and the Vaishnavite gods into the religion known as Hinduism.

The doctrine of the ashramas, which adapted the new Upanishadic ideal—a life of renunciation for the purpose of moksha—to the

FIGURE 16.1 Boy receiving the Sacred Thread. (*Leonard McCombe, Life Magazine* © *Time Inc.*)

more traditional Vedic way of life, is a good example of the way
the Brahmins accepted new ideas and absorbed them into a continuing tradition. This doctrine, which was fully developed by
400 B.C., divides the ideal life of every man of the three "twice-born"
classes (varnas) —the Brahmin, Kshatriya, and Vaisya (members of
the Sudra class are not twice-born)—into four stages, or ashramas.
"Twice-born" means that a boy undergoes a second birth between
the ages of eight and twelve by participating in the *upanayana,*
a ceremony in which he becomes a full-fledged member of his class
and of society (see p. 441).

After the upanayana rite the youth is introduced to his teacher
(*guru*), with whom he lives for about twelve years. This is the first
ashrama, the stage of the Brahmacharin, or student. During this time
the pupil learns what he can of the Vedas. He must obey and serve
his guru absolutely; in return the guru must give him whatever
knowledge he possesses without withholding anything.

When the youth is somewhere between the ages of twenty and
twenty-four, he returns home, marries, and establishes a household.
This is the second ashrama, the Householder (Grihastha) stage. The
goals of the Householder are Dharma, the observance of religious
duties and generally accepted moral precepts such as those mentioned on pp. 385–386; Artha, the accumulation of wealth to provide
for his household, to provide gifts for Brahmins when they perform
domestic ceremonies, and to enable him to give alms to beggars and
holy ascetics; Kama, pleasure, sense pleasures including sexual pleasures of married life. There is a hierarchy in the three goals of the
Householder ashrama, with Dharma first, Artha second, and Kama
last in any conflict among these values. In the Householder stage of
life—longest of the ashramas—the Brahmins have reaffirmed the
ideal of a good life in this world, as it was glorified in the Vedic religion; for even Dharma, the highest value, like Artha and Kama, is
a goal that pertains to the temporal world. But the ultimate wisdom
is to seek release from the world, from karma and samsara. This final
aim of life, moksha, is reached in two stages: the ashramas of the
Forest Dweller (*Vanaprastha*) and of the Wandering Ascetic (*sannyasi*).

The ashrama of the Forest Dweller begins when the Householder's
first grandson is born or when his hair begins to turn gray. He
leaves home, joined by his wife if she wishes to accompany him,
and lives in the forest, in order to meditate on philosophical and
religious ideas and symbols. (Life in a forest hermitage in ancient

and medieval India was not incompatible with a certain amount of worldly activity. Sages and seekers of wisdom might visit the hermitage and hold lively discussions; family members, too, could be received for a short time.)

When the individual (or couple) feels that he is spiritually ready, or that life is coming to a close, he leaves the forest hermitage and begins the life of the wandering ascetic, the ashrama of the sannyasi. If the wife has been with her husband in the hermitage, she returns home; the husband, now a lonely mendicant, removes his Sacred Thread (see p. 441) as a sign of anonymity, of egolessness, of his shedding all social, all worldly ties. (This kind of "outcast" was and still is greatly respected in India.) The sannyasi's preoccupation is concentration and meditation on Brahman to attain self-realization. This is union with Brahman in Its eternal aspect. When this is effected, moksha, man's final goal, is won; never again will the spirit be entangled in the bonds of karma and samsara. In some Hindu philosophies the individual may attain moksha in one or more experiences of union with the divine. A person who has attained moksha is called a *jivanmukta* (a soul that is liberated while still alive). He lives until he works out the residue of karma accumulated before the experience of moksha; when this karma ceases, the man dies.

This ideal life of the Four Ashramas was seldom observed; most men were satisfied to remain in the Householder ashrama. Observance of the last two stages was largely confined to a few Brahmins; however, in early Hinduism a few Kshatriyas also observed it. In present-day India, when the ideal life is followed through, the third and fourth ashramas are often lived in a small place in the home compound or in a room in the home. There are sannyasis in India today, but most belong to religious orders and are not sannyasis as a result of following the sequential order of ashramas.

The hierarchy of values, in relation to the aims of human life, gives a humane, dignified, and ordered place to man's major desires, while it points to a final aim of high spirituality, to be achieved by those who desire this supreme good.

Ways to Moksha (Liberation)

All four of the varnas are eligible for moksha. Hinduism has, in fact, several paths (*margas*) by means of which individuals of differing social status, abilities, and personality types may seek and find moksha. The four principal margas are: the path of knowledge (*jnana-marga*); the path of works (*karma-marga*); the path of love (*bhakti-marga*); and the path of classical yoga (*raja-yoga*). These paths to moksha are also called *yogas. Yoga* is a cognate of the English word *yoke* and signifies a yoking or union of the soul with God[3] or with the Absolute Reality. All the margas enumerated are paths to this union or to a similar state of moksha. The word *marga* (literally "path") emphasizes the method used, the word *yoga,* the goal (union of the soul with the Ultimate Reality). Therefore the way of salvation by work (*karma*) can be called either *karma-yoga* or *karma-marga.* The same is true of the *jnana* and *bhakti* margas or yogas. Raja-yoga, however, is not called "raja-marga," although it, too, is a path (*marga*) to liberation.

A yogi is one who is seeking liberation by one of these four ways or by other less classical methods. Also the word *yogi* is used to denote a person who has extraordinary, supernormal powers (clairvoyance, clairaudience, omniscience, etc.) usually gained either by following the path of raja-yoga or by engaging in austere ascetic practices.

The Path of Knowledge (Jnana-Marga)

The marga of knowledge is chosen by the man whose interests are predominantly intellectual and contemplative. The great hindrance to moksha in the jnana-marga is ignorance—ignorance of the true nature of the soul. When ignorance is banished, the individual soul becomes identical with the eternal Brahman.

The way to attain knowledge of the Atman-Brahman is, first, discipline of the aspirant's moral and intellectual nature; this involves the renunciation of sense gratifications, an ardent desire for moksha, and the attainment of serenity. The second step is the study of texts from the Upanishads relevant to liberation (such as "that art thou") under the guidance of a guru who has himself attained moksha. The third step is reflection—cogitation on the significance of these texts. In step four, the stage of deepest contemplation, comes the immediate intuitive experience of identity with Brahman, the Absolute Reality. This is moksha. The aspirant then becomes a jivanmukta (a soul that is liberated while still alive). According to some views his body lives until his past karma is worked out; according to others, the individual may terminate his earthly life at will. Upon death there is only the Absolute Reality, Atman-Brahman, which he always was.

Sudras and women are not permitted to read the Vedas or to hear this literature read by anyone else, and the path of knowledge as a way to liberation is therefore closed to them, although it is appropriate for a Brahmin.

The Way of Work (Karma-Marga)

The karma-marga as a way of liberation was first expounded in the Bhagavad-Gita (c. 100 B.C.–A.D. 100). Before that time the renunciation of active life in the world was generally thought to be necessary for one seeking moksha. The Gita argues that such renunciation is not essential, and that moksha can be won through work in the world. The way of liberation through work is for the active man who chooses to perform his tasks in the spirit of an egoless renunciation of the rewards or fruits of his work.

A false ego sense leads one to the karma-causing actions that result in the continuous round of rebirths; as the Gita says, attachment to the sensual desires and ambitions of the ego, that is, selfish desire, causes the karma which leads to repeated rebirth. Salvation through the karma-marga comes about only by giving up the false notion that there is an ego. Egoless renunciation rids a person of the false view that there is a particular ego in whose interests work needs to be done. The fruits of work must be devoted to the Ultimate Reality; then work can be done unselfishly in a free and detached spirit and moksha attained through the labors of an active life. Gandhi is the great recent example of a karma-yogi.

The Way of Love (Bhakti-Marga)

The bhakti-marga is the way for emotional people to attain moksha, and it is the favorite marga of the Bhagavad-Gita. This method advocates warm, loving devotion to a personal god as the way of release. If the aspirant surrenders himself completely to the Lord, he will overcome selfish desire, all egoism, and devote all he has, all he is, to God, until in union with God egoism is abolished and swallowed up. The Gita declares that this way of salvation is open to Sudras and women.

The Path of Classical Yoga (Raja-Yoga)

The raja-yoga is the most scientific method of liberation and aspects of its discipline are used by the other margas also to aid in meditation on divine reality. It involves three main disciplines: moral purgation; control of the body, including the autonomic nervous system; and concentration of the mind. Moral purgation has two aspects: the restraints and the observances. Under restraints are rules against killing or injuring anyone, lying, stealing, sexual intercourse, and possession of anything beyond one's absolute needs; under observances are cleanliness, contentment, austerities (*tapas*),[4] study, and making the Lord the motive of all action.

Control of the body begins with postures (*asana*), physical exercises to gain control of the body. The next step is practice of the science of breath control. Then comes withdrawal of the senses from any and all external objects. Following that, the attention is turned inward and the fixation of the eyes on the tip of the nose or the navel is used as an aid to the next step, meditation (*dhyana*). Meditation is complete absorption, concentration of the mind on pure spirit in its true nature until the final stage of absorption, *samadhi* (trance), is reached. Samadhi, the goal of the three kinds of discipline, is realization of Brahman or union with Brahman.[5] This intuitive realization of the Ultimate Reality is moksha.

Varnas and Castes

The division of society into the four varnas (classes) was already fully developed by 400 B.C. The word *varna,* which means "color," perhaps first became associated with class when the invading Aryans used color as a distinguishing feature to separate themselves from the dark-complexioned dasyas, or indigenous peoples. The concept of four varnas was first expounded in a late hymn of the Rig-Veda (c. 900 B.C.) [6] and was generally accepted in the period during which the Brahmanas were composed (c. 800–600 B.C.). It was difficult for any individual to rise to a higher status, but it was easy enough for him to fall. A breach of any of the many regulations that had to be observed by particular groups (most of these involved impurity) could result in an outcasting, either temporary or permanent.

In the Shatapatha Brahmana the Brahmins, highest of the varnas, are called "human gods" to whom non-Brahmins must give presents. The duties of the Brahmin varna are primarily to study and teach Vedic learning and preside over important rituals. Today, as in earlier times, Brahmins make up the largest group of people who pursue intellectual callings. Since ancient times, however, Brahmins have been permitted to follow other callings by invoking the accepted principle of *apad* (economic need); there are Brahmin cooks, and members of this varna also engage in many other occupations.

The Kshatriya varna has for its traditional duty the protection of the people and the administration of a just and beneficent government. The Rajputs in India today are the chief representatives of this varna. The Vaishya varna provides for the economic needs of the community. Men of this class were to engage in agriculture, cattle raising, or trade and commerce in order to provide necessities and luxuries for the two higher varnas. They were heavily taxed and were not supposed to become rich themselves, although occasionally some did become wealthy. Today Vaishyas do not engage in agricultural occupations; most of the farm work is now done by Sudras, and the Vaishyas are mainly businessmen.

The Sudras were the menials among the social classes. They were usually domestic servants, whose duty was to work obediently for the other three classes. Sudras were forbidden to hear or to repeat the Vedas; for spiritual salvation they were to await rebirth in one of the three higher classes. Despite their social and religious handicaps, some Sudras apparently engaged in manufacture and commerce, and by Asoka's time many were free peasants. Shortly before the beginning of the Christian era, it became possible for them to attain religious salvation through hearing the Epics, and later, through hearing the Puranas. And when devotional religious sects for salvation became popular after the Mauryan dynasty, they were permitted to join these groups.

Untouchables

The origin of the groups known as Untouchables, Outcastes, Depressed Classes, or Scheduled Castes is difficult to ascertain. They probably originated from tribes that had been conquered by the Aryans. Several centuries before the Christian era there were people who were looked on as outside the Aryan order of the varnas. The *chandalas* were foremost among these, and their name was later given to many different kinds of Untouchables. The main duties of the chandalas, who had to live outside the boundaries of cities, were the carrying and cremation of corpses and the execution of criminals. They could not perform domestic work because this would involve proximity to the higher classes, which would pollute them. In Gupta times fear of pollution was so great that a chandala had to strike a wooden clapper when he entered a town to warn

the people of his approach. Included in the general class of Untouchables were hunters, fishermen, leatherworkers, sweepers,
basket makers, chariot makers, and *mlechchhas* (literally "barbarians") —the name given to foreigners of any race or color.

Castes in Hinduism

Early Indologists assumed that the modern complex system of castes,
numbering about 3,000, arose out of the confusion of classes, as a
result of class intermarriages. This theory is no longer accepted,
however.[7] First, class (varna) must be distinguished from caste. The
word *caste* is derived from the Portuguese *casta,* which means
"breed, race, kind." When the Portuguese entered India in the
sixteenth century they noticed the group divisions of Indian society
and called the separate groups *castas.* In Sanskrit the equivalent
word is *jati.* In ancient Sanskrit literature the word *jati* is rarely
found; but *varna* is found fairly often, and the two terms are always
sharply distinguished.

Only after A.D. 700 do we find caste (jati) beginning to take on
its modern meaning of a group that normally has the following
characteristics: endogamy (marriage permitted only within the
group); commensality (food may be received from, and eaten in
the presence of, members of the group or a higher group); and
occupational exclusiveness (each group must do its particular work
according to the occupation that is specific to it).[8] Varna, on the
other hand, the system of the four classes, does not have strict rules
of endogamy, commensality, or occupational exclusiveness. Moreover, the four varnas are stable and have not altered for over 2,000
years, whereas castes fluctuate: new ones come into being and old
ones die out.

If the definition of *caste* given above is correct, this institution
did not take form until late medieval times.[9] According to lawbooks
written a few centuries before and after the Christian era, a Brahmin
was allowed to take food from any Aryan, occupational exclusiveness
was frequently ignored (apad was invoked), and hypergamy[10] was
permitted. Hinduism in the later Middle Ages, when caste was an
institution, reconciled the conflict of caste rules with the lawbooks
by invoking the concept of *kalivarjya;* that is, the notion that some
customs, once permissible, could not be allowed in this present
wicked (Kali) age.[11]

By the beginning of the modern era many of the present-day

castes had appeared, and even the Brahmins were divided into many caste groups; the Vaishyas, Sudras, and Untouchables had each evolved hundreds of castes. Each caste group was governed by a local committee of elders, who could regulate caste rules and expel members who broke them. Expulsion was a calamity because it involved social ostracism. This effective kind of social sanction, in addition to endogamy, commensality, and occupational exclusiveness, made caste a powerful institution. On the positive side, caste has given each individual a place and definite status in the community and has prevented the conflicts and tensions caused by the competitiveness that has characterized other societies. On the negative side, the great blot on the caste system has been the degradation of a large human group, the Untouchables.

A recent eyewitness account describing the working of the caste system in a village in Malabar[12] which belongs to the more traditional and conservative Dravidian country is worth quoting:

A brief description of the working of the caste system in Malabar will be interesting. The Nayar is an untouchable to the Nambudiri [the highest Brahmin caste], but the latter can take to bed a Nayar woman in her own house, for which permissible defilement he purifies himself by a ceremonial wash in the morning, without which he is not allowed to enter his own house. Children born of such a union are Nayars and, as such, untouchable to their male parent. A Nayar, in conversation with a Nambudiri, is not allowed to refer to his own house in more flattering terms than as "my hovel" even if this be as good as a castle. A Nambudiri's residence, on the other hand, should always be mentioned as a palace. The Nambudiri should be addressed as a god, and the Nayar himself mentioned as a slave. The Nayar, while addressing a Nambudiri should cover his mouth lest spittle that might spurt out should defile the Brahmin. On seeing a Nambudiri, a Nayar should remove his upper garment and tuck it under his arm and stand at a respectful distance. There are numerous other courtesies of a similar nature a Nayar is expected to perform; these are duly performed even now by Nayars who are dependent on the Nambudiris; but others, under the influence of modernism, are inclined to treat the Nambudiris with contempt.

The Thiyas are untouchable to the Nayars. To a Pattar Brahmin a Thiya is unapproachable by twenty paces and to a Nambudiri by twenty-five. The Pulayas, Cherumars and Parayas are untouchable to one another, each one claiming superiority over the others and indulging in a ceremonial wash when touched and defiled. A member of any one of these communities is unapproachable to a Thiya by ten paces, to a Nayar by twenty, to a Pattar Brahmin by forty and to a Nambudiri by sixty. An Ulladah is "unlookable" to a Nambudiri and Pattar, and unapproachable to the others. Because of this, the Ulladahs seldom venture into a village, and when they do so utter mournful cries for others to take warning. The Nambudiris when moving about generally order a Nayar to go in front shouting at the top of his voice, "Ha-Ha," as a warning to the unapproachables to keep aloof. The unapproachables, when they are engaged in putting up fences or in other work which requires their continued presence in the village lanes, take care to put up, at the distance of about 60 paces on either side of them, a sign which usually consists of a couple of green branches kept down by a stone, as an indication of their presence to wayfarers. I have often seen in Malabar villages the Nayars accompanying their highborn Nambudiris chasing poor Pulayas all over the village so that their masters might go about without defilement, and detaining the work of putting up fences indefinitely. And I remember a case when a Pulaya, who was engaged by a Syrian Christian farmer, was thus stopped from his work for several hours by Brahmins who were on that day busy going to attend some feast; the enraged Syrian resented this and it led to a free fight among the villagers.[13]

The caste system has been defended on religious grounds as the result of the natural working of the law of karma. For example, an individual born into a caste of the Brahmin varna has earned this status because in former lives he has accumulated so much merit that he is ready for and entitled to the type of life conducive to moksha. The individual born into an Untouchable caste, on the other hand, has committed so many evil deeds in his former lives that he well deserves the misery of living the most degraded kind of human existence; moreover, if he lives this type of life as well as he knows how, then he can hope for rebirth in a higher caste and progress gradually in life after life until he, too, may be eligible for the Brahmin's existence with its opportunity for final salvation. It is on the basis of this religious idea and support for caste in relation to the order of society that many conservative orthodox Hindus—a few Brahmins and the many illiterates, especially in the villages—still support the caste system.

It is well known that Gandhi in his campaigns all over India did a great deal to break down untouchability, the worst feature of the system. Gandhi himself and his close followers did such things as clean out latrines, a job reserved only for Untouchables, to show

that no task made a man unclean; and to give this depressed, degraded group a respected human status, Gandhi christened them
Harijans, literally "children of Hari" (Hari is a word for God
used by Hindus). With this kind of leadership it is not surprising
that, when India gained her freedom, the Constitution of the new
Republic declared that the state cannot permit discrimination
against any citizen on grounds of caste, religion, sex, race, or place
of birth; that untouchability was completely abolished and any
practice of it punishable by law. In religious practices, this meant
that former Untouchables, who were to be so no longer, must be
allowed to enter the temples. Further, the central government has
designated the Scheduled castes (Untouchable castes) as the recipi-
ents of special concessions and privileges in educational, employment, and housing opportunities. In addition, a certain number of
seats are reserved for these castes in the Indian parliament, and
finally, these groups, which comprise almost 10 percent of the population, have the privilege of voting, which also makes them important in party platforms and politics.

What remains of caste today? In the villages, which are very
conservative, it will take a long time to eliminate a concept so
deeply grounded in religion. Nevertheless, some of the Untouchables, even in the conservative south, are absorbing the new ideas
of human equality and refuse to show the servile behavior before
Brahmins that was formerly demanded of them. In the large cities
and other industrialized communities, caste in general has broken
down occupationally; another factor in urban life that has greatly
weakened caste consciousness is the cinema—all individuals of
whatever social status must be admitted and seats assigned on the
basis of the price paid for the ticket. In public restaurants, too, a
similar situation prevails; but there are still a few orthodox Brahmins who might eat with a Christian in a public restaurant, yet
would not dine at home with a member of some other Brahmin
caste, let alone lower castes or Christians. Caste is still almost universally observed in marriage. The parents of every child desire
their son or daughter to marry within the caste group.

To conclude, it seems that caste has been eliminated in the
political sphere and has broken down occupationally in the industrialized urban centers. Like all customs that are grounded in a long
tradition and have a deep religious basis, it will take much education at the village level (the villages account for 80 percent of
India's population) to eliminate the more onerous features of the

caste system; but elimination of untouchability has in the past and can in the future move much faster. As for religion as a sanction for untouchability, one can refer to the authority of the Vedas themselves, the holiest of religious works. In the Vedas there is no mention of a class of Untouchables; only the four varnas are enumerated; it is only in the smriti literature that we find references to this aspect of the social system.

THE SMRITI LITERATURE OF HINDUISM

The word *smriti* in Sanskrit means "that which is remembered" in contradistinction to *shruti* or "that which is heard." The shruti is of the utmost holiness because it is thought to have been supernaturally revealed, "breathed" by the divine power at the creation of the world cycle and received or "visioned" by the rishis. All of the Veda, from the four core Vedas through their appendages— Brahmanas, Aranyakas, and Upanishads—is shruti. Smriti is next in holiness and includes the entire body of sacred tradition, what is remembered by human teachers. Included in the smriti are the Six Vedangas, the lawbooks (the *Laws of Manu* are most famous), the two great epics (the *Mahabharata* and the *Ramayana*), the Puranas, and the literature called *nitishastras* (literature dealing with worldly wisdom, such as the book of fables known as the *Panchatantra* and the great work on the science of polity, Kautilya's *Arthashastra*).

The Six Vedangas

The word *Vedangas* means "limbs of the Vedas." These six limbs are ritual, phonetics, grammar, etymology, metrics, and astronomy. All these studies were necessary for proper understanding of the Vedas (for instance, astronomy was involved in fixing the dates of rituals). The study of the Six Vedangas was attached to the Vedic schools; these schools developed manuals, in a short aphoristic style for easy memorization, called "sutras." The word *sutra* originally meant "thread"; it was later given the meaning "short rule" or "aphoristic precept," and a sutra work was a fabric woven of such precepts or "threads."

For the understanding of Hinduism, ritual is the most important of the Six Vedangas. The Vedanga of ritual is given the name *Kalpasutras*. This work contains three kinds of texts: *Shrautasutras,* texts of sacrificial instructions such as directions for the performance of the Agnihotra, the Soma sacrifice, and similar rites; *Grihyasutras,* directions for the performance of the rites that sanctify the individual in his life cycle from before his conception to his death[14] (this is the most important section of the Kalpasutras for Hinduism today); and *Dharmasutras,* the purpose of which is the preparation of the individual for a successful moral and ritualistic life as Householder, in order to obtain such goods as wealth, children, and a life in Heaven after death. The main classes of dharma taught in these sutras are three: the specific duties of each of the four varnas of society; the specific duties of each of the ashramas; and the common duties obligatory to all, such as self-control, kindness, and speaking truth.

The word *dharma* as it is used in these sutras denotes one of the most significant and all-pervasive doctrines of Hinduism. Literally the word means "what holds together," and as used in the literature of Hinduism, it has the connotation of "that which is the basis of all order," particularly social and moral order. Also, the term is applied to religious merit which operates causally to produce good results for the individual, both in this world and beyond. The concept *dharma* resembles the idea of Rita in the Rig-Veda. Both connote right order in moral and ritual life, which in turn is related to the general cosmic order of the universe by which all things maintain their right place and proportion.

Dharmashastras: Laws of Manu

The *Dharmashastras* are instructions in the sacred law and belong to the smriti literature, but not to the Vedangas, as do the Kalpasutras of which the Dharmasutras are a part. The Dharmashastras resemble the Dharmasutras in content, but are later in date and in a longer, versified form. Of the Dharmashastras the *Manu Smriti* or *Laws of Manu* is the most famous work. It was put into its final form about the second or third century A.D. It contains a philosophy of the varnas and ashramas similar to that of the Dharmasutras, but in addition there are other significant moral teachings. Most interesting of these, perhaps, are the verses that deal with the treatment of women. On the whole, women are to be honored; this is brought out in the following passage: "Where women are honoured there

the gods are pleased; but where they are not honoured no sacred
rite yields rewards."[15] In other places, however, we read that a wife
should rise before her husband, go to bed after him, and do the
fetching for him; she should never be independent, but in childhood subject to her father, in youth to her husband, and if her husband dies, then to her sons. But the *Mahabharata*, another smriti
work, says in praise of women:

The wife is half the man, the best of friends, the root of the three ends
of life, and of all that will help him in the other world. . . .
    Even in the grip of rage, a man will not be harsh to a woman, re-
membering that on her depend the joys of love, happiness, and virtue.
    For woman is the everlasting field, in which the Self is born.[16]

The Epics

The Mahabharata: The Bhagavad-Gita
Mahabharata means "the great narrative of the battle of the Bharatas." The Bharatas, a people whose territory was located in the
Upper Ganges plain and around the Jumna River, are mentioned
in the Rig-Veda; then, in the Brahmanas we meet Bharata, the
eponymous ancestor of the Bharatas. Around 900 B.C. or earlier[17]
a family feud arose among the Kauravas, the leading clan of the
Bharatas, which ended in almost complete annihilation of the tribe.
Bards composed and sang poems about this war. Then an unknown
poet combined these songs into a heroic poem of 90,000 stanzas.
    The most significant part of the voluminous poem known as the
Mahabharata is the Bhagavad-Gita, probably written between 100
B.C. and A.D. 100. This work (although it is smriti and not shruti)
is often called the New Testament of Hinduism. The greatest philosophers, notably Shankara and Ramanuja, have written commentaries on it. There is no greater work in the religion of Hinduism
today; the Upanishads are the only other Hindu works that compare
with it in importance for modern leaders of religion and philosophy.
    The charm and value of the Bhagavad-Gita, which for so many cen-
turies has appealed to all classes of Indians (as well as to Westerners), lies in its variety in theology and philosophy. The other source
of its wide appeal is its emphasis on yoga, especially the yoga of
action (karma-yoga or karma-marga). The Gita's idea of the karma-
yogi, the man who has attained complete control over his senses
and passions so that he can engage in egoless action in a detached,

serene spirit for the social good, has inspired many, notably Mahatma Gandhi, the greatest karma-yogi of recent times.

The setting for the Bhagavad-Gita, the great poem interpolated in the *Mahabharata,* is a scene at the beginning of the battle between the Pandavas (the five sons of Pandu) and their allies, and Duryodhana (son of King Dhritarashtra, brother of Pandu) and his allies. The cause of this war between cousins was the stubborn hatred and jealousy felt by Duryodhana toward his cousins the Pandavas, especially Arjuna and Yudhishthira.

ARJUNA'S LAMENT. § Arjuna in his chariot, with Krishna his cousin as charioteer, halts between the two armies to survey the troops on both sides. He sees "fathers and grandfathers, teachers, uncles and brothers, sons and grandsons, friends, fathers-in-law and companions." Horror overwhelms him at the thought of killing these people, who are all dear to him. He lets fall his bow and arrows; his heart is heavy with grief; he tells Krishna that he would rather die than slay his kinsmen. Then Krishna explains why he must fight and much more—an entire philosophy of man, nature, and God. Who is this Krishna?

KRISHNA THE TEACHER. § The Krishna of the Gita is not only a tribal chieftain and a cousin of the Pandavas, but an *avatar* of Vishnu. (*Avatar* means "descent, appearance, or manifestation of a deity on earth.") At the end of the second century B.C., and probably even earlier, the Vedic god Vishnu was identified with Vasudeva, the supreme god of a theistic sect called the Bhagavatas, which was prevalent especially in western India.[18] This sect taught belief in the personal god Vasudeva, and preached that salvation was to be attained by loving devotion (bhakti) to him.[19] The bhakti religion of the Bhagavatas is prominent in the Gita, although in some passages God is the impersonal Brahman of the predominantly monistic Upanishadic philosophy.[20]

Krishna explains to Arjuna three of the principal margas that lead to moksha: the karma-, the bhakti-, and the jnana-margas. He also mentions the fourth marga, raja-yoga, but does not explain it.

Krishna, himself, is a man of action and a great karma-yogi who descends as avatar to intervene actively in worldly affairs whenever human society deteriorates so badly that divine intervention is needed.

Krishna explains to Arjuna that egoless action—renunciation of the fruits of work—makes moksha (liberation) possible. (This is the earliest reference in Sanskrit literature to the karma-marga as a road to moksha.) Krishna goes on to enunciate the relationship between the karma-marga and dharma. Dharma, the ethical and general harmonious order of the universe, is preserved by the life of right action. Each man must perform the social duties of his varna and thereby uphold the order of society; he must not usurp the duties of another class. Krishna reminds Arjuna that he is a member of the Kshatriya varna. The duty of this class is to rule righteously and to defend just causes, by military force if necessary. It is, therefore, Arjuna's dharma, his duty, to fight in this righteous war. Retirement from the battlefield is not possible for a man of his dharma, despite the fact that he sees relatives and close friends on the opposing side. Besides, Krishna adds, to lay down arms is unenlightened; the enlightened man looks on all men as God sees them; that is, he sees them in God and God in them as the immortal core of their Being. The real, the immortal soul of man can never be slain; only bodies are slain; this is why Arjuna cannot kill his relatives and friends. For all these reasons Arjuna is admonished by Krishna to seek salvation through the karma-marga. In performing the work of the Kshatriya in a detached, egoless spirit, Arjuna may obtain moksha.

Another way of liberation recognized by Krishna is the jnana-marga (path of knowledge). Krishna praises the jnana-marga as a way of liberation, but he does not recommend it for Arjuna, the Kshatriya, whose dharma makes the karma-marga the appropriate path to release. The jnana-marga is the principal way of liberation expounded in the Upanishads, and it remains important in the Gita. The knowledge one needs to attain moksha by the jnana-marga is primarily knowledge of the difference between the soul[21] and the world of *prakriti*. Prakriti is composed of three *gunas* (literally "strands"): *sattva, rajas,* and *tamas.* Sattva is the lightest, most ethereal constituent of prakriti; rajas is characterized by energy and dynamism; tamas, by inertia and heaviness. At the beginning of each world cycle the equilibrium heretofore existing among the gunas is disturbed, and then prakriti evolves the essential principles for all the things that can come into being in the world cycle of 4,320,000,000 years. These principles are given in full and systematic form in the Sankhya philosophy;[22] in the Gita the following eight are named: intellect, the lower mind, the ego-principle and the five elements (earth, water, fire, air, and ether). All eight of these belong to the world of prakriti (or the gunas), and each thing in nature contains all three in varying proportions. Among the elements, ether and air consist primarily of sattva; in the individual personality, sattva is the primary constituent of intellect, and this guna is dominant in the type of man who is a thinker. Rajas is the guna of activity or energy and is dominant in the element fire. In the individual, rajas is the dynamic energy of action and shows itself in the passions; the passions need the guidance of sattva, for without such guidance the personality may show anger, lust, greed, and violence—qualities of impure rajas. The type of person dominated by the rajas guna is the doer, the man of action. The tamas guna is predominant in the element earth and is characterized by heaviness and inertia. The individual whose personality is dominated by tamas lacks self-harmony, and he is vulgar, arrogant, deceitful, malicious, lazy, and despondent.

Cosmic evolution takes place in every world cycle when the equilibrium of the three gunas (heretofore in a quiescent state) is disturbed, and the gunas then recombine in unequal proportions. Once intellect, mind, egoism, and the five elements evolve, the total universe appears again in the same pattern as always.

The aspirant for moksha who is following the jnana-marga realizes that the entire world of prakriti described above has nothing to do with purusha (the spirit or soul). Deep meditation on the pure purusha will ultimately yield the intuitive experience of being only the pure purusha, an eternal substance outside of prakriti (the matter side of the universe). The relationship between God and the soul is not clearly defined in the Gita and leaves the way open for interpretations in the light of varying systems of philosophy.

Another mode of salvation expounded in the Gita, and the favorite one, is the bhakti-marga. Karma-marga and jnana-marga are rather impersonal: karma-marga invokes such abstractions as dharma and the law of karma for its justification; jnana-marga invokes abstract knowledge of the absolute difference between soul and prakriti. Bhakti-marga ignores such abstractions and advocates loving devotion to a personal God as the way to liberation. Krishna says:

> Be Me-minded, devoted to Me;
>   Worshipping Me, pay homage to Me;
> Just to Me shalt thou go, having thus disciplined
>   Thyself, fully intent on Me.[23]

> Even if a very evil doer
> Reveres Me with single devotion, . . .
>
> •   •   •
>
> Quickly his soul becomes righteous
> And he goes to eternal peace.[24]

Vishnu, speaking through his avatar, is a god of grace when he says:

> Abandoning all (other) duties,
> Go to Me as thy sole refuge;
> From all evils I thee
> Shall rescue: be not grieved![25]

This verse and the second one quoted above mean that man's sins can be canceled out by complete love for and surrender to the Lord, for the Lord will then extend his grace and absolve such devoted souls from their rebirth-causing sins. Instead of a rebirth, such men will enter into the Being[26] or abide in the eternal presence of the Lord forever.

THE IDEAS OF ULTIMATE REALITY IN THE BHAGAVAD-GITA.   §   There is no one logically coherent idea of the Ultimate Reality in the Gita. The difference between God and the soul, between spirit and matter, and emphasis on loving devotion to God contribute to a theistic interpretation. These ideas would harmonize with the Sankhya-Yoga philosophy or with Madhva's dualistic Vedanta system.[27] The pure monism of Shankara's nondual (advaita) Vedanta, which views the Ultimate Reality as the impersonal Brahman, is also found in the Gita. But by far the dominant view is the easier and more popular one, viz., that the Ultimate Reality is a personal God of grace. Bhakti is the favorite and most adequate way to attain moksha, not Shankara's way of knowledge (the jnana-marga).

Ramanuja, the great systematizer of Vaishnavite thought, had little difficulty in finding his own philosophical system of qualified nondualism (*Vishishtadvaita Vedanta*) exemplified in the Gita. In his system the God concept is personal but more pantheistic than theistic. Ramanuja's God contains within himself all the matter of the physical universe and all souls; yet he is not just the universe. Only part of the deity is manifested; he transcends the world in his unmanifested aspect. His nature is sublimely expressed in the theophany of Book XI of the Gita. Krishna, as Vishnu the Supreme

Being (that is, Brahman), reveals himself to Arjuna as the whole universe with all its variety united in the body of the God of gods. Arjuna sees the "heroes of the world of men" enter into the "flaming mouths of Vishnu."[28] Vishnu says he is Time, which destroys all. The glory of Vishnu is likened to that of a thousand suns rising together; and all the multitude of creatures, including human beings and devas, are within his Being. He is million-armed in power; the sun and moon are his eyes; his form fills the total universe. The creator-god Brahma sits on his lotus within the body of the God of gods. Vishnu is all that is, all that is not, and all that is beyond. He is equated with the total universe both manifested and unmanifested; this concept of God is more pantheistic than theistic.[29]

The Ramayana

The *Ramayana* is an epic poem that is divided into seven books. It is only one-fourth the size of the *Mahabharata;* and unlike the latter, most of it appears to have been written by a single poet—the reputed author is Valmiki. Except for Books I and VII, the *Ramayana* was probably completed a little before the beginning of the Christian era.[30] There are also many interpolations in the *Ramayana*, although these are much shorter than those in the *Mahabharata.*

The epic story begins in the city of Ajodhya (about 125 miles north of the present Banaras). Rama (also called Ramachandra or "Ram"), eldest son of the king of Ajodhya and happily wed to the lovely Sita, is named heir to the throne. When this is announced, the king's second queen reminds the king of a boon he had promised her. She now requests its fulfillment in the banishment of Rama and the installation of her own son, Bharata, as the heir apparent. Against the wishes of both the king and Bharata, Rama, who was always a model of dharma (moral duty, righteousness), goes into exile voluntarily, in order that his father might keep his promise to his second queen. Soon the king dies and Bharata becomes king, but for Rama's sake assumes only the title of regent.

Rama and his wife have meanwhile retired into the forest. Lakshmana, Rama's brother, has chosen to join them, and the three dwell together as forest hermits. While they are living in the forest, Rama destroys many demons, until Ravana, the demon king of Lanka (Ceylon?) decides to avenge his demon kinsmen and he comes to the hermitage where Rama, Lakshmana, and Sita are staying. While the men are away on a hunting trip, Ravana forcibly abducts Sita and carries her all the way to his palace in Lanka.

Rama is much distressed to find his wife missing and seeks everywhere for her. He enlists the help of Sugriva, the monkey king, and the king's general, Hanuman. With Hanuman's help Rama conquers Ravana and his demon hosts in their stronghold in Lanka. (Because of the aid rendered by Hanuman to Rama in the war, Hanuman is a much-loved deity in Hinduism, and all monkeys are held in reverence. See Figure 16.2.)

After the victory of Rama and his allies over Ravana, Rama should have been happily reunited with Sita. But for a man of Rama's great virtue there are problems. Sita has been forced to live in the palace of Ravana. Although there have been no sexual relations between the two (Ravana treats Sita with respect after she refuses his advances), it is nevertheless Rama's duty under the Sacred Law to reject his wife because she has lived in another man's house. Sita then undergoes an ordeal by fire to prove her innocence: she throws herself upon a funeral pyre, but Agni refuses to burn her. Rama is now satisfied about her purity. The pair then go to Ajodhya to rule there, and Bharata voluntarily abdicates his regency.

According to what was probably the original ending of the epic, Rama and Sita live long and happily together. The last book of the *Ramayana*, however, which is apparently an addition to the original poem, shows a different and unhappy ending. The people of Ajodhya, unlike Rama, are not sure that Sita has retained her purity in Ravana's palace, and Rama, as the very essence of dharma, believes it to be his duty to please his people. Therefore, despite his love for his wife, he places dharma before his own and Sita's happiness and banishes her. In great sorrow, but with absolute obedience, as befits the ideal wife, Sita seeks refuge in the forest hermitage of Valmiki, the reputed author of the *Ramayana*, where she gives birth to two sons. Later Rama finds his wife and acknowledges the sons as his own, as further proof of her innocence. As final proof, Sita calls upon her mother, Earth, to swallow her up. Earth does so, and Sita disappears. Shortly after this, Rama "dies," but in this late story he is described as returning to Heaven to resume his universal form, Vishnu.

FIGURE 16.2   Rama, Sita, Lakshmana and Hanuman. (*Originally published by Sharma Picture Publication, India*)

In this last book and in Book I, which is also a later addition, Rama is described as an avatar of Vishnu. (Hinduism accepts Rama and Krishna as the two principal avatars of Vishnu.) The battle of Rama and his allies against Ravana and his forces is thought to be symbolic of the ever-recurring struggle between the powers of good and evil. Rama is dharma incarnate, and Sita, who is revered as an avatar of Vishnu's consort, Lakshmi, is the ideal of the Hindu wife, always obedient and faithful to her husband—always solicitous for his welfare, even to the point of giving up her life for him. In the *Ramayana*, Dharma (moral duty, righteousness), as a major goal in life, overrides Artha (pursuit of wealth, honor, and fame) and Kama

(pursuit of pleasure). Rama and Sita are the divine exemplars of Dharma.

The Puranas

Purana in Sanskrit means "ancient story." Traditionally there are eighteen Puranas, all later in date than the two epics, yet some of the legends incorporated in the Puranic literature are very old. Authorship of all eighteen Puranas is attributed to the sage Vyasa, to whom tradition also attributes the *Mahabharata.* Among the Vaishnavite Puranas, the Vishnu Purana and the Bhagavata Purana are the most popular. There are also important Shaivite Puranas.

The Vishnu Purana

The Vishnu Purana is one of the oldest of the Puranas and may be as early as the fifth century A.D. It is regarded as foremost among the Puranas by the Vaishnavites, and it conforms more closely than other works of this kind to the ancient definition of Purana as a work that should have for its content the following five subjects: creation; world cycles; genealogy of the gods and rishis; *manvantaras* (the Manu periods of time, each of which has a Manu or primal ancestor of the human race); and history of the dynasties. The Vishnu Purana contains six books. A brief review of each of these books will indicate the general content of the Puranic literature—a literature of importance because of its influence on popular Hinduism.

BOOK I: IDEAS OF TIME IN TRADITIONAL HINDUISM. § Book I opens with a hymn glorifying Vishnu, after which there is an account of the creation of the world, which includes a description of the cycles of time. In traditional Hindu thought, time is viewed as cyclical. The great and small cycles that are given in the Vishnu Purana have been commonly accepted in India and permeate Indian thought. The basic unit of time is the *yuga,* and there are four yugas in each Maha Yuga.

First is the Satya Yuga (also called the Krita Yuga), the Golden Age of the world. In this era there are no vices in the human race; all live harmoniously and happily and obtain all they desire by mere wish, without any labor. Disease and the decline of sense organs in old age are unknown. The length of this yuga is 4,800 divine years; a divine year is equivalent to 360 human years.

Next is the Treta Yuga. In this era human righteousness declines somewhat, so that Vedic sacrifices become necessary; men begin to act from selfish motivation and seek reward. This yuga endures for 3,600 divine years.

The third is the Dvapara Yuga. In this epoch righteousness is reduced by one-half. This causes diseases and many kinds of calamities; human suffering becomes great. It lasts 2,400 divine years.

The fourth and last yuga is the Kali Yuga. Righteousness has been decreased by three-fourths, and this results in extreme human misery, with anxiety, disease, hunger, and fear characteristic of this era. It is 1,200 divine years in length.

Then the Golden Age returns, and the entire cycle is repeated. Each cycle of yugas (maha yuga) is 12,000 divine years in length. One thousand of these maha yugas make up a *kalpa*—4,320,000,000 human years—which is also known as a day of the god Brahma (the creator god of Hinduism). Brahma has a night of equal length called the *pralaya*, the dissolution state of the universe. When Brahma's day again dawns, the universe is re-created and repeats the same cyclic pattern of yugas and maha yugas until another kalpa is completed. Time is infinite; no one can count the number of kalpas in the past or enumerate those to come in the future.

The total pattern of life, of all creatures on earth and of all the gods, is repeated in each cycle. Even the god Brahma has a life of only 100 Brahma years; after this time another individual in the samsara world, worthy because of his good karma to become a Brahma, takes his place in this position. The wise man is aghast at being caught on this relentless, repetitive wheel of time throughout countless rebirths; his ardent desire is liberation from this circular time process into the plane of eternity; he wishes to join Vishnu, the ultimate deity, and those wise and virtuous men who have already achieved moksha.

Complicating the simple pattern of the yugas is a system, probably of later origin, that divides the kalpa into fourteen manvantaras (Manu periods) each lasting 306,720,000 years; but this figure multiplied by 14 equals only 4,294,080,000 years. This is 25,920,000 years less than the kalpa of 4,320,000,000 years; the two schemes of the four yugas and the fourteen manvantaras do not fit together very well. The writers of the Puranas were aware of this discrepancy and added 1,851,428 years to each manvantara of 306,720,000 years, which multiplied by 14 yields the figure 4,319,999,992, close enough to the kalpa of 4,320,000,000 years; for absolute accuracy

further minute periods were added to make up for the small difference of only eight years.[31]

Each manvantara has its Manu, or progenitor of the human race.
We are now in the era of the seventh manvantara and the Kali Yuga.
This yuga began after the death of Krishna, as described in the
Mahabharata (traditional date about 3000 B.C.).

Among other intriguing materials in Book I are a flood story
involving the Manu of the present manvantara, a myth of the
churning of the ocean, the story of Prahlada's devotion to Vishnu,
and the myth of Dhruva, the Pole Star.

BOOK II: IDEAS OF SPACE IN TRADITIONAL HINDUISM.   §   Book II is
important for its general picture of the spatial universe of traditional Hinduism. According to this account, the earth has seven
continents, each surrounded by an ocean. Bharatavarsha (India)
is situated in Jambudvipa, the continent in the center of the earth.
Bharatavarsha is the most desirable of the regions of Jambudvipa

for rebirth, because it is the land of works. The other regions are for enjoyment; it is only after many thousands of rebirths that living beings may be born in Jambudvipa, where it is possible to attain final liberation. The gods themselves say that it is a great blessing even for gods to be reborn in this land.[32]

Mount Meru, the great mountain that is in the center of the earth and therefore in the center of Bharatavarsha, is a peak so high that it touches the sphere of the stars. The dwellings of the gods are on the slopes of Meru. There are also six heavens of the gods; the lowest is Bhuvarloka, which extends from the lower atmosphere to the sun; next is Svarga, in the upper air, home of Indra and many other gods; then there are four higher worlds where very superior intelligences dwell: Maharloka, where saints live for an entire kalpa; Janoloka, peopled with the patriarchs and progenitors of mankind— the pure-minded; Tapoloka, the place of ascetics; and Satyaloka (or Brahmaloka), the inhabitants of which are close to liberation; they live with the god Brahma until the end of his existence and then are united with the Ultimate Reality as Vishnu when Brahma is.

Beneath the earth are the seven regions of Patala, home of the Nagas (serpent deities). These are pleasant abodes. The sage Narada, who visited there, reported that Patala is more delightful than Indra's Heaven.

Below Patala are the twenty-eight hells or divisions of Naraka, where Yama rules. Here sins and crimes are punished with tortures that are adjusted to the seriousness of the crime; this is a purgatory, however, rather than a hell, because after the punishment has been suffered (in accordance with the law of karma), the person is again reborn.

Under the Patalas, and supporting them as well as supporting the Naraka world below them and all the regions above them, is the serpent Shesha. He is called Ananta (endless) by the gods, and is worshiped by them and by the sages. Shesha has 1,000 heads; from his mouths proceeds the venomous fire that takes the form of Rudra (or Shiva) to devour the worlds at the end of a kalpa.

BOOKS III-VI.   §   Book III gives an account of the Manus of each of the previous six manvantaras—we are at present in the seventh manvantara, over which the Manu named Vaivasvata presides—and

FIGURE 16.3 Krishna as cowherd. (*Vedanta Press*)

the names of the future Manus of each of the succeeding manvan-taras. About half of Book III is concerned with rituals, ceremonies, and ashramas, and the duties of each varna.

Book IV gives the genealogical lists of the ancient royal families—of the Solar Dynasty, which traces its origin back to the sun god, and of the Lunar Dynasty, which traces its origin to the moon god. Occasionally these lists are interrupted with a story about one or another of these kings, such as the famous tale of King Pururavas and his beloved Urvashi, a nymph.

Book V tells the complete story of Krishna. It covers his youth as the divine cowherd (see Figure 16.3), his heroic exploits in maturity, and finally his death (he was shot in the heel by a hunter), after which he again becomes one with Vishnu.

Book VI is important for its description of the dissolution of the world. Three kinds of dissolution are described: incidental dissolution, a destruction of the creatures, but not the substance of the world; elemental dissolution, the resolution of all the elements of the world into their primitive source, prakriti (primal matter), which occurs at the end of Brahma's life (the souls who have not attained moksha retain their karma and are reborn again in the next cycle of existence); and absolute dissolution, individual ego-annihilation and the end of a person's samsara as the result of the fact that his karma has been overcome. Absolute dissolution is moksha.

A method recommended for attainment of absolute dissolution is yoga, in the stages fixed in the yoga system of philosophy.[33] The samadhi is union with Vishnu, which destroys forever the false separation between the individual and the universal spirit (Vishnu); one lives eternally now as part of Vishnu, basking forever in his eternal presence.

At the end of this Purana, it is said that whoever has heard the reading of this work will have the contamination of the Kali Yuga removed and will be freed from all his sins; and whoever hears or reads this Purana with intense devotion acquires the state of perfection that is Vishnu's. Like the Bhagavad-Gita, this and all other Puranic literature, as smriti, could be heard or read by Sudras and women and could reveal the path to moksha to these groups excluded from study of the Vedas, which are shruti.

THE GODS OF MODERN HINDUISM

The personalities and iconography of many of the gods of Hinduism took shape in the Golden Age of the Gupta dynasty (c. A.D. 320–540). But some aspects of the god concepts date from very much earlier. For example, Shiva as yogi, lord of animals and phallic deity, and Devi, or Parvati, as mother goddess, are as old as the Indus Valley civilization (c. 2500–1500 B.C.). In the Rig-Veda (c. 1500–900 B.C.) other qualities of these deities appeared and many other gods took shape. The Brahmanas and early Upanishads (c. 900–600 B.C.) developed religious symbolism and a philosophy of religion. The smriti literature (the two epics and the Puranas) and the Tantric treatises (earliest c. A.D. 600) added still further to the god concepts. The following list of the major gods, with their chief attributes, will give some notion of the Hindu pantheon as it exists today.

BRAHMAN, THE ULTIMATE REALITY.   §   In nondual views of the Ultimate Reality, Brahman is impersonal and infinite, a *nirguna* (qualityless) Absolute referred to in the *neti neti* passage in the Brihadaranyaka Upanishad and later considered as the Ultimate Reality of Shankara's Advaita Vedanta philosophical system. In another prominent system, Ramanuja's qualified nondualism, the Ultimate Reality has attributes and can be called personal.[34] Although the Ultimate Reality may be called Brahman (an impersonal, neuter noun), Vaishnavites, whose greatest philosopher is Ramanuja, think of this Absolute as Vishnu, who is personal and both a transcendent and immanent deity. His immanent aspect is revealed most clearly in his powers of creation, preservation, and dissolution (or destruction) of the cosmos, in accordance with the time pattern described in the section on the Vishnu Purana (see pp. 412–414). These three powers may be personified as the Trimurti. The other dominant group of sectarian Hinduism, the Shaivite, gives Shiva the same place in its thought that Vishnu has in the Vaishnavite philosophies.[35]

THE TRIMURTI.   §   Trimurti means literally "three forms" and refers to the immanent or manifested aspects of the Absolute revealed in the powers of creation, preservation, and dissolution of the universe. The personifications of the three forms are Brahma, the creator; Vishnu, the preserver; and Shiva, the destroyer or dissolver of the universe at the end of each kalpa. The Trimurti as such has been of little religious importance. As we noted above, sectarian Hindus are mainly either Vaishnavites or Shaivites and their particular great deity, either Vishnu or Shiva, is believed to have all the powers of the Trimurti.

BRAHMA. § Brahma is the personification of the creative powers of the universe and the active immediate creator of the world in every new cycle of existence after a world dissolution. In iconography he is shown with four faces and four arms, and his color is red or pink (see Figure 16.4). In his hands he holds either the Four Vedas or four of the following articles: a scepter, symbolizing lordship or dominion; a sacrificial ladle, showing the importance of Vedic rites; a string of beads or a rosary, symbol of the necessity for repeating mantras or prayers—there are usually 108 beads because a mantra should be repeated 108 times (the beads tally off the number of mantras); a water jug, also used in religious rituals; and his bow, named Parivita (encompassing). Brahma represents the Brahmin and is the prototype of Brahmin priesthood; the ladle, rosary, and water jug are related to the priestly functions, as are the Four Vedas. It is said that the Four Vedas are breathed from Brahma's four mouths in every world cycle, and the rishis (seers) envision them and pass them on to mankind.

In the Vedas[36] and generally in the Brahmanas, Brahma is not the creator god; this function is assigned to Prajapati or Hiranyagarbha. Only in the Shatapatha Brahmana do we find a passage in which Brahma is referred to as the creator god. Brahma (the Prajapati of later Vedic literature) was important until the time of the Gupta dynasty, and although he then declined in popularity, there are nevertheless many representations of him in medieval sculpture. At present the only known place of Brahma worship is a temple by the sacred Lake Pushkar near Ajmer in Rajputana.

VISHNU. § In the personifications of the Trimurti, Vishnu is the preserver god. He is very popular; as mentioned above, for Vaishnavites he is the Ultimate Reality (Brahman), manifesting himself

FIGURE 16.4 Brahma, with three of his four heads showing. (*National Museum, New Delhi*)

in his immanent aspects in all three powers of the Trimurti: creation, preservation, and dissolution. In the Rig-Veda, where he is
not among the great gods, he is described as a manifestation of the
solar energy, and is depicted striding through the universe in three
steps; further he is called "the unconquerable preserver," and it is
this quality of preservation that became his major attribute. One
of his names is Narayana (moving in the waters); pictorially this
is shown in art as a reclining figure sleeping on the serpent Shesha
on the cosmic waters during the dissolution periods of the world
cycles. When the cycle is about to begin again, the icons show
Brahma the creator god at the tip of a lotus stem rising from Vishnu's navel. This means that Brahma's creative powers have their
source in Vishnu.

The iconographic portrayals of Vishnu show him as dark blue,
youthful, and in the garb of a king. He has four arms. The usual
symbolic articles he holds in his four hands are the conch shell, the
mace, the discus, the lotus, and sometimes a sword or a bow (see

Figure 16.5). The conch is a symbol of creation. The mace, scepter club of the deity, signifies his universal power and sovereignty. The discus, always shown with the god, is a sun symbol as wheel and a weapon as discus. The lotus is another symbol of creation; the unfolding of the many petals of the lotus parallels the unfolding of the many aspects of the world in the creative process. The sword is a symbol of wisdom and the sheath a symbol of ignorance. The Kaustabha jewel, which the deity wears on his chest, represents "the soul of the world, undefiled and void of qualities."[37] The Shrivatsa, a lock of golden hair on the left breast of the deity, represents *pradhana* (matter or prakriti), which is infinite and the boundless cause of all world eggs (universes), of which there are thousands of millions. The dark blue or black color of Vishnu is accounted for in several ways. Dark blue or black is the color of ether, the all-pervading element in the universe, and thus a

symbol of the all-pervading god; furthermore, deep blue sky represents infinite space, and this color thus symbolizes the infinity of the god. Also, *Krishna* means "black" in Sanskrit, and since Krishna is an incarnation of Vishnu, it would be natural to represent Vishnu as dark blue or black. Another probable significance of the dark blue or black is that this is the color of the welcome monsoon storm clouds, which make fertility possible. Still another interpretation related to fertility is the color assigned to fertile earth—black.

The mount of Vishnu is Garuda, a creature with human form but with wings and the beak of an eagle. Garuda is the enemy of serpents.

The Avatars of Vishnu. The Bhagavata Purana, popular with Vaishnavites and many others in India today, enumerates twenty-two avatars of Vishnu and then adds that the incarnations of Vishnu are really innumerable. Vishnu has altogether one thousand names, which are recited as a litany for the accumulation of religious merit. The number of avatars of Vishnu that is generally accepted is ten. These are:

1. Matsya (the Fish). In this incarnation Vishnu rescued Manu from a flood by telling him how he could save himself from a coming world deluge. Following the advice of this avatar, Manu built a ship and embarked with his family. Then Matsya appeared as a huge fish with a great horn; the ship was tied to the horn until the waters subsided. After the deluge was over, Matsya guided the boat to a mountain where Manu and those with him disembarked, to renew the human race and all other creatures.

2. Kurma (the Tortoise). Vishnu appeared as a tortoise to rescue some things lost in the deluge.

3. Varaha (the Boar). At the beginning of the present kalpa, Earth, a goddess, was submerged in the ocean. Hiranyaksha, a demon, had dragged her to the bottom of the sea. Vishnu took the form of a great boar to conquer the demon and effect a rescue.

4. Narasimha (the Man-Lion). Vishnu appeared as a man-lion to rescue the kingdom from Hiranyakasipu, a demon king.

5. Vamana (the Dwarf). Vishnu became incarnate in the deceptive form of a dwarf to rescue the world from Bali, a tyrant who had conquered the earth and was threatening the heavens of the gods.

FIGURE 16.5 Vishnu in meditation. (*Archaeological Museum, Mathura, India*)

6. Parashurama (Rama with the Ax). Vishnu appeared as Rama with the Ax to curb the insolence of the Kshatriya class and reinstate the Brahmins.

7. Rama (or Ramachandra). To overcome Ravana, the demon, Vishnu incarnated himself. This is the main theme of the *Ramayana*.

8. Krishna. The chief purpose of this incarnation was to rid the earth of Kamsa, the demon king. As a youth Krishna loved to play the flute and flirt with the Gopis, girl cowherds. The *rasalila* dance (a circle dance) in the moonlight described in the *Bhagavata Purana* was the special delight of the Gopis. The amorous adventures between Krishna and his favorite, Radha, are an important theme in the *Gita Govinda,* symbolizing the love between God and the soul. Krishna as avatar is best represented in the Bhagavad-Gita. Krishna and Rama are the two principal avatars of Vishnu.

9. Buddha. The common view is that Vishnu assumed the form of Buddha to delude the wicked, to lead them to deny the reality of one universal supreme Spirit and the authority of the Vedas. One authoritative work, the *Gita Govinda,* however, says that Vishnu assumed this form out of compassion for animals, to prevent their being slaughtered.

10. Kalki. This is the incarnation of the future. When the present Kali Yuga degenerates into the maximum of wickedness, Vishnu will take the form of Kalki on a white horse. With a flaming sword in his hand, he will come to judge the wicked, reward the good, and bring in a new Golden Age (Krita or Satya Yuga). This concept shows Zoroastrian and Buddhist influences.

LAKSHMI (OR SRI). § Lakshmi, the wife of Vishnu and mother of Kama, the god of sensuous pleasures, is often shown as a devoted wife massaging Vishnu's feet. By Vaishnavites she is considered God's Shakti. She is the goddess of fortune and beauty. Lakshmi has four arms, but because she is beauty itself, often only two arms are shown in her icons. She sits on the lotus or holds a lotus in her hand; this flower is a symbol of creation, the appropriate sign for the mother-creative aspect of Vishnu. Vaishnavites call her "mother of the world" and honor her especially at Divali, one of the four major religious festivals of the Hindu year. Lakshmi's avatars are the wives (or the chief wife when there was a plurality) of the avatars of Vishnu; the most important is Sita, wife of Rama.

SHIVA, THE GREAT GOD (MAHADEVA). § Shiva is the destroyer god of the Trimurti, but for Shaivites he is, as noted above, all three aspects of the manifestations of deity and also the nondual Absolute beyond them. Shiva is probably, along with the mother goddesses, the oldest deity of the Hindu pantheon.[38]

Other facets of the concept of Shiva come from the god Rudra of the Rig-Veda. In the Rig-Veda Rudra is lord of sacrifices; he is a healer who grants prosperity, gives nourishment, drives away disease, and removes sin. On the other hand, he wields the thunderbolt, shoots deadly arrows, and is terrible as a wild beast when he mounts his chariot in a fierce mood. In the Yajur-Veda he is called "auspicious" (*shiva*) "blue-necked," "red-colored," and "thousand-eyed," but also Tryambika (three-eyed). In the Atharva-Veda he is still called a protector of cattle, but in general his character is fierce, "dark, black, destroying, terrible." One of the later Upanishads, the Svetashvatara, identifies the Supreme Being with Rudra, calling him creator and protector of all things, as well as the one who dissolves them at the end of time. This gives Rudra all the aspects of the Trimurti. Another passage in this Upanishad calls Rudra "dweller among the mountains." In the epics, particularly in the *Ramayana,* Vishnu is exalted over Shiva; in the more heterogeneous *Mahabharata,* Shiva sometimes occupies the supreme place among all the gods. The Puranas, on the other hand, show a distinctly partisan preference between Shiva and Vishnu; Vaishnavite Puranas make Shiva subservient to Vishnu as the Supreme Being, and Shaivite Puranas take the opposite position. Over the course of many centuries the Rudra of the Vedas (including the Brahmanas and Upanishads) was probably synthesized with the ancient Shiva prototype of the Indus Valley civilizations into the concept of Mahadeva, the Great God, as Shiva is called by his devotees.

The Dancing Shiva bronze images of south India show Mahadeva dancing within a circle (or ellipse), bordered with flames which signify the illusory, transitory nature of the world. He has four arms (see Figure 16.6). In one left hand he holds a flame, symbol of the disintegrating processes of time, change, and death. But Shiva destroys to liberate souls from the illusory (maya) world of time, a beneficent function. The other left hand, extending downward, points to the raised left leg. This symbolizes release from the world of time and change, of karma and samsara. It is a symbol also of the grace of the deity who aids his devotees in obtaining moksha. In

one right hand he holds a drum, symbol of the rhythm of creation.
Shiva is creator of this world of maya (illusion) in all its aesthetic
harmony, which has its source in the rhythmic pattern of Shiva's
drum and dance. Another right hand is raised with the palm outward in the gesture "do not fear." Fearlessness comes from the
knowledge of the ephemeral nature of the world of change—the

world of the body, sense organs, and intellect—and the knowledge of one's identity with the eternal, unmanifest, formless, spiritual Shiva, the nondual Ultimate Reality. The man who realizes this, his true nature, has no fear of injuries to his body or his ego, for neither of these is his true self. No one can injure the true self; it is one with Ultimate Reality. The right leg stands on the back of the prone figure of the demon dwarf Muyalaka, another symbol of time, of maya (or illusion and delusion); Shiva crushes this ignorance for his followers; and the raised left leg, free from Muyalaka (or maya) shows liberation from its power. Muyalaka, as a demon, is also a symbol of evil, crushed by Shiva's power.

Shiva wears the crescent moon on his head and serpents coiled around his body. The moon may represent the measure of time (the lunar month) or Shiva's endless life-giving powers. The moon, like the serpent, is thought by many primitives to renew its life cycle endlessly: the moon through its limitless phases from crescent to full moon, the serpent by shedding its skin repeatedly. Another interpretation of the serpents coiled about the god construes them as symbols of life and death; the spiral coils of the serpent represent life, the poison fangs, death.[39]

The goddess Ganga (the personification of the Ganges river) is seen in Shiva's matted locks. This goddess has lived in Shiva's hair ever since the Ganges river descended to earth in the episode known as the "descent of the Ganges." The heavenly Ganges, Vaishnavites believe, flows from the nail of the great toe of Vishnu's left foot; Dhruva (the Pole Star) receives her on his head, whence she falls on the moon, and from there descends to Mount Meru. At Meru she divides into four rivers, which descend to the four quarters of the earth. Only the Ganges of India (one of the four rivers) was devoutly received by Mahadeva upon his head to prevent her flooding the earth. The Shaivites know nothing about the four rivers. They say that Shiva received the earthly Ganges upon his head to prevent a destructive flood, and ever since that event Ganga has lived in Shiva's hair, a cause of much jealousy on the part of Shiva's wife, Parvati.

The matted locks of Shiva signify that he is the Great Yogi and the archetypal ascetic; it is customary for yogis or ascetics to have

FIGURE 16.6   A Dancing Shiva. (*The Metropolitan Museum of Art, Harris Brisban Dick Fund, 1964*)

such tangled hair as one of the marks of ignoring attention to the body.

Another distinguishing attribute of Shiva as the Great Yogi is the third eye placed vertically in his forehead. From the philosophical point of view this is the eye of spiritual omniscience and insight which yields temporal omniscience also—complete knowledge of the present, the past, and the future. Another view interprets the third eye as fire and Shiva's other two eyes as the sun and the moon. A popular myth relates that when Kama, the god of love, attempted to distract Shiva from his meditations, Mahadeva burned him to ashes with the fire from his third eye.

The male and female earrings Shiva wears mean that he is the source of all reproductive forces, male and female. The great icon of the god that makes this meaning much more emphatic is the phallic symbol—the linga—in its receptacle base—the yoni, symbol of the female generative organ. Although Shiva Nataraja (Shiva, lord of the dance) is a favorite form of the deity, especially in south India, the object of ritual worship everywhere is invariably the linga (see Figure 16.7). The phallic symbol has been worshiped in India since the time of the Indus Valley culture, and even today the linga is the symbol of the god in the sanctum sanctorum of the great Shiva temples. It is the symbol par excellence of the creative powers of Mahadeva.

The creative power of Shiva is symbolized also by the type of image called Ardhanarisvara, "the Lord who is half female" (and half male). The icons of this type show one-half of the body in male form with male ornaments and the other half female with female ornaments.

Another name of Shiva related to his abundant creative energies is Pashupati (lord of animals). A steatite seal of the Indus Valley culture shows a horned deity seated in a yoga posture surrounded with animals (see Figure 15.2). There are many sculptures in south India that show a deer in one of the hands of the god.

One of the sublime epithets of Mahadeva is "Digambara," or the naked God. Literally, Digambara means "he whose garment or covering is Space." The Absolute Reality is purely spiritual, without the "clothes" of the "sheaths" of nature, which compose the vital mental, and physical coverings of spirit (the Atman-Brahman).

FIGURE 16.7 A linga with Nandi. (*Chevet's Photo Supply: Grace Cairns*)

A different aspect of Mahadeva is brought out in the name Bhairava. In this form the Great God is terrible and violent, and is the destroyer. He has a similar character in the form of Bhuteshvara, the lord of ghosts and goblins. In these two forms he wears garlands of skulls, smears himself with ashes, and haunts cemeteries and joins demons. This destroyer aspect symbolizes, on the spiritual plane, destruction of attachment to the illusory world of sense-gratifications, which brings suffering and causes incessant rebirth.

His title Yogeshvara distinguishes him as the archetype of all yogis. In this personification, he is seated in yoga posture on a tiger skin with cobras coiled about him; the crescent moon is on his head; his locks are matted and either coiled or flowing; the third eye is prominently shown. The tiger is the archetypal wild animal of the forest. As lord of animals, Shiva is the hunter who is victorious over the tiger, the wildest of beasts. This symbolizes the success of the yogi in restraining and harnessing the wild energies of the vital sheath (the biological energies) for use in progressive concentration until samadhi is experienced.

Another epithet, Nilakantha (blue-throated), is a reminder of the benevolence of the god in drinking the poison emitted during the churning of the ocean. He saved the universe from this deadly poison by drinking it himself.[40] As lord of death, he alone could drink such a potion and live.

Hara (the remover) is a name signifying death. Shiva as destroyer is death that removes all creatures and things. Hara is the bringer

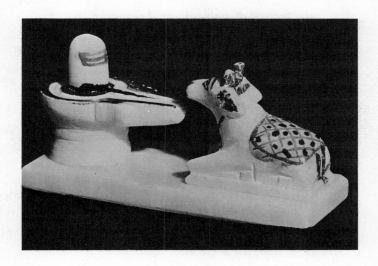

of disease that inflicts death on good and bad alike. At the end of every kalpa, he brings universal death to all beings.

Shiva is often seen with the trident. The three prongs symbolize the three powers of Shiva: creation, preservation, and destruction; they also represent the three gunas: Sattva, Rajas, and Tamas.

The Great God's mount is the bull named Nandi. The bull is another fertility symbol and stands for the male seed, the fire, the active creative power of Lord Shiva.

Mahadeva's heavenly residence is on top of Mount Kailasa, a high peak in the Himalayas; his royal earthly residence is in the Vishvanatha Temple in Banaras. This temple and the entire city are said to be supported by the trident of Shiva, which is immediately under them. Chidambaram in south India, however, claims to be the center of the universe as the earthly place of Shiva's cosmic dance; its heavenly counterpart is performed on Mount Kailasa. The more spiritual interpretation of the dance does not put the Lord in a physical center, but instead places him in the heart, man's spiritual center.

Mahadeva is the most versatile of the great gods: he can be all things to all men. At the popular level, under the form of the linga, he brings all the fruits of the reproductive powers of nature; as Bhairava and in other forms, he is destroyer of demons and lord of death, which brings the immortality of moksha; for yogis, sannyasis, and ascetics he is the archetypal model. On the whole, however, Shiva is the god of the intellectuals (the great philosopher Shankara, for example, was a devotee of Shiva); Vishnu is the more popular deity among the masses of the people.

HARI-HARA. § Hari-hara is a title that attempts to combine Vishnu and Shiva into one deity; Hari is a name of Vishnu the preserver, and Hara that of Shiva the destroyer. This deity has not received much worship.

DEVI, THE GREAT GODDESS (MAHADEVI). § Devi, like Shiva, is one of the most ancient deities of the living religions of the world. Many figurines of mother goddesses, her prototypes, have been found in the archaeological remains of the Indus Valley culture. Mother-goddess worship seems to have been universal among all ancient peoples. In Hinduism the mother goddess is called by many names, but all are ultimately designations of the one goddess, who is given the general name Devi (the Goddess) or Mahadevi (the Great Goddess).

Devi's ancient symbol, which is in the form of the female organ, is called the yoni; this corresponds in meaning with the phallus. The Shiva linga is, in fact, usually mounted on a receptacle base, either square or round and with a small groove, that signifies the yoni. The yoni represents the heavier material elements of the created universe, earth and water; the linga, the finer material elements—fire, air, and ether. The conjunction of the two symbols means that both the male and female aspects of creative power are essential in order to produce the manifested world, in all its various forms. Shakti, a term meaning the female creative power, is another name for Devi. Shakti is the female personification of the creative energy of the great gods. Mahadevi is also known by many names; one group is descriptive of her benevolent mother aspects: the other group, of her terrible forms.

The kindly aspects of Devi are represented in the following appellatives: Uma (light), a beautiful woman; Gauri (yellow or brilliant); Anna Purna (giver of food); Jaganmata (mother of the world), a very old attribute of the goddess, which signifies that she is "mother of all living creatures"; and Parvati (daughter of the mountain), her usual name as the woman who upholds wifely and motherly virtues in the home of her husband, Shiva. Of these names, Uma and Parvati are the most common. A more concrete idea of her character in its benevolent manifestations can be gained from two famous Puranic myths, one about Uma (or Parvati) as Sati and the other about Parvati. The myth about Sati is important to an understanding of Hindu views about the practice called *suttee*.

Uma (Parvati) was born as Sati (pronounced "suttee"), daughter of Daksha, who was a son of Brahma. When she came of age her father, Daksha, announced her *svayamvara* (a self-choice type of marriage). Sati was already in love with Shiva and had taken a vow to marry no one else. Daksha invited all the gods to the svayamvara so that Sati could select the one she preferred. However, Daksha omitted Shiva because he thought this deity an unsuitable husband for his daughter. Shiva was an irascible god, given to asceticism, and often ugly and untidy in his appearance. On the wedding day, Sati entered the hall to garland the god she desired as a husband. She looked everywhere for Shiva, but could not find him. Then she prayed loudly to Shiva to become manifest and receive the garland. At that she threw it upward, and lo! her beloved miraculously appeared and received it around his neck. Daksha had to yield and permitted his daughter to marry Shiva. Later there was an assembly of the gods. When Daksha appeared at this assembly, all the gods except Brahma and Shiva arose; Brahma was Daksha's father and did not need to rise; but Shiva, Daksha's son-in-law, should have risen. Daksha felt insulted and cried before all the gods that he was sorry that he had given his daughter to this haunter of cemeteries and wearer of garlands of skulls, this naked ascetic and mad dancer. Daksha angrily left the assembly. Soon he invited all the gods except Shiva to a sacrifice. Sati, sitting outside her palace on Mount Kailasa, saw throngs of gods passing by and inquired where they were going. When she learned that they were on the way to a sacrifice given by her father, she was hurt that her husband was not invited. She went alone to her father's house, but was not well received. She saw that the other gods were given their rightful portions of the offerings in the sacrifice, but none was given Shiva.[41] Sati was so offended at this heinous insult to her husband that she jumped into the sacrificial fire and burned herself to death.[42] She did this out of devotion to her husband, to protect his honor.

This story of Sati is used to vindicate the practice of *suttee*. The word *sati* in Sanskrit means "virtuous woman" and was applied in later Hinduism to a woman who immolated herself in the funeral pyre of her husband. The word is usually spelled by English writers phonetically as "suttee." The custom of suttee is foreign to the Vedas and was rare in the time of the composition of the two epics. The earliest occurrence of suttee of which we have a historical account was around the time of Alexander's invasion. The first memorial pillar commemorating such a sacrifice is dated A.D. 510. The nomads of central Asia practiced this rite and may have encouraged it when they came to India as invaders.[43] Since then the frequency of suttees increased and there are many suttee stones (memorial pillars commemorating suttees) all over India. Bana, a humanitarian poet, condemned suttee in the seventh century. The Tantric sects, which became important in the seventh century, prohibited it; they taught that a woman who immolated herself went to hell. On the other hand, some writers of the Middle Ages asserted that a suttee acquired religious merit sufficient to send both herself and her husband to a life in heaven lasting 35 million years.[44] The custom was prohibited by law in 1829.

Another episode was added to the story of Sati to explain the origin of the Shakta Pithas, fifty-one places of pilgrimage associated with Devi as the mother goddess under various appellatives. When Shiva learned of his wife's immolation, he flew in fury to Daksha's home, cut off his head, and quickly put the other gods to flight. Demons from Shiva's hair made havoc of the sacrifice. Then he took his wife's charred body out of the remains of the fire, addressed it lovingly, and in mad grief begged his beloved to return, but to no avail. Finally he flung the body over his shoulder and danced wildly over the earth. Fearing the fury of this god, the other deities plotted to put a stop to his madness. In one version, Vishnu followed Shiva and cut Sati's body in pieces with his discus or his arrows. The body now gone from his shoulder, Shiva came to himself. The pieces of Sati's body fell in various places throughout India. The usual number of pieces is given as fifty-one. Each place where one part of Sati's body fell became a Shakta Pitha, a sacred place devoted to her worship as mother goddess; and associated with Devi at these places is a Bhairava (the "terrible" form of Shiva).

The character and personality of Devi as Parvati (or Uma) are shown in another celebrated story. After the body of Sati was gone from his shoulders, Shiva went into seclusion and engaged in a life of meditation. Meanwhile Sati was reborn as Parvati (daughter of the mountain). Parvati again was in love with Shiva. She was encouraged by the gods, who feared that something might happen to the world if Shiva neglected his creative duties by devoting himself to yogi meditations and ascetic penances. Parvati enlisted the aid of Kama, god of love. Kama shot arrows of desire at Shiva, who became angry at these attempts to disturb his meditations. He caused fire emitted from his third eye to burn Kama to ashes.[45] Realizing that her beloved could not be won by appeals to desire, Parvati chose another method. She emulated her lord by engaging in yoga and asceticism herself, becoming emaciated and ugly. One day when she was engaged in ascetic practices, Shiva finally noticed her. He came in the form of a Brahmin and asked her why she was torturing her beautiful body. When she told him that it was because of her love for Shiva, the Brahmin said contemptuously that she should be aware that her beloved was notorious for his ugliness, unkempt appearance, irascibility, and macabre habits. Parvati, unable to hear any more of this blasphemy against her Lord, closed her ears. Then the Brahmin turned into Shiva himself. He sent Parvati back to her father and asked for her hand in marriage. As Parvati (or Uma) she became a devoted wife and mother. Her children by Shiva are the popular, benevolent deity Ganesha and the fierce god of war, Karttikeya.

Mahadevi takes her terrible forms to fight demons, symbol of evil in the world. The names of these major forms are Durga (the inaccessible), Kali (the black), Chandi (the fierce), and Bhairavi (the terrible). Kali is the most widely worshiped form of Mahadevi.

The myth that brings out Kali's major qualities describes her combat with the demon Raktavira, who was granted a boon from Brahma whereby every drop of his blood that fell on the ground became another Asura. To conquer him Kali held him in the air, pierced him with a spear, and drank all the blood that gushed from the wound. This is how she acquired her taste for blood. Animals are offered to her, especially goats; at one time human sacrifices were used as potent means to propitiate the goddess, but if such sacrifices still occur today, the secret is well kept. Bhavani, goddess of Thugs, was a form of Kali. The Thugs (the Hindi word for robber or deceiver) were a group of men engaged in ordinary occupations during most of the year, but in the fall they went about in bands dressed as religious mendicants or as merchants. In this disguise they approached wealthy travelers, strangled them, and took their goods. Women were exempt from such attacks. Around 1839 many of the Thugs were arrested and about 300 executed. This ended their terrorism.

A favorite portrayal of Kali in devotional pictures represents her nude, black in color, wearing a long garland of human heads around her neck and a short tunic of human arms with their hands (severed at the elbow) around her waist, with four arms, and with her long red tongue hanging out of her mouth. In her upper left hand she holds the head of a slain demon, dripping with blood; in her upper right hand is the sword of destruction; in her lower left hand she holds a plate of food; her lower right hand is extended in the gesture of giving or bestowing blessings. She stands on Shiva, with one foot on his chest and the other on one of his legs. The inert prone body of Shiva symbolizes that Shiva without Shakti is inert, "pure consciousness." Only with Kali, his shakti or energy

FIGURE 16.8   Kali with the head of a demon she has slain. Kali (a fearful manifestation of Devi) stands on the body of Shiva, her lord. (*Ajanta Art Calendar, Calcutta*)

aspect, can he act in the world either to create or to destroy (see Figure 16.8).

In the nineteenth century a great leader of the Hindu Renaissance, Sri Ramakrishna, a mystic and saint, worshiped Kali as the "Mother." His visions of the goddess were the initial steps in his extraordinary spiritual attainments.

Another form of Devi akin to Kali is known as Durga, and is very popular in West Bengal. The Devi-Mahatmyam, a sacred text devoted to her, is popular all over India today, but particularly in West Bengal. This text is chanted daily in her worship, as well as during the Durga Puja in West Bengal when Durga is worshiped for four days in the form of hundreds of earthen images.[46] Durga is represented in iconography as a beautiful woman with ten arms, in

each of which she holds a weapon. One foot stands on the buffalo demon, Mahisha (her foremost exploit is the slaying of this demon); the other foot stands on her mount, the lion. The lion is aiding the goddess by lacerating Mahisha. Bengali women today are proud of Durga. They think of her as an all-powerful destroyer of evil, and in this capacity they call her "symbol of Indian womanhood."

SARASVATI §   The lovely goddess Sarasvati is the wife of Brahma, the creator god. In the Rig-Veda she is a river goddess. The Sarasvati River has its source in the Himalayas and in ancient times flowed on to the sea, but now ends in the desert sands. In modern Hinduism, Sarasvati is the goddess of speech and learning and patroness of music and the fine arts. She invented the Sanskrit language and the Devanagari letters, the modern script of Sanskrit, Prakrit, Hindi, and Marathi. (This script was already in its present form in the late medieval period.)[47]

Sarasvati is worshiped by students, writers, and musicians. Every

year in February at Banaras Hindu University there is a grand
Founder's Day celebration. The queen of the pageant, enthroned
in a beautiful float, is a lovely college student representing Sarasvati.

In iconography the goddess is often represented with only two
arms; she is usually playing the vina, a stringed musical instrument.
Her mount is the swan or the peacock; her husband, Brahma, rides
the swan (or goose).

GANESHA. § Ganesha, one of the two sons of Shiva and Parvati, is
also called Ganapati (Lord of the Ganas). The Ganas are troops of
inferior deities, especially those led by Shiva. He is represented as
having an elephant head (see Figure 16.9). One well-known story
of how Ganesha acquired his elephant's head is a favorite tale. One
day Parvati asked her son to watch outside her door while she was
bathing and to admit no one. Shiva came home and insisted upon
entering. Ganesha refused to admit him, so Shiva angrily cut off
his head. Parvati rushed to the scene and wept over the death of
her son. Shiva repented and substituted the first head available, that
of an elephant, on the body of Ganesha to revive him.

A main function of Ganesha is the removal of obstacles that may
stand in the way at the beginning of any important undertaking.
He is therefore invoked by authors beginning a book, by students
about to take an examination, by devotees at the beginning of religious worship, and in general by those performing any significant
act in the business of life.

Ganesha has two wives, Siddhi (success) and Riddhi (prosperity).
His mount is the rat.

KARTTIKEYA. § Karttikeya, also known as Kumara (the Prince),
Skanda, and Subrahmanya, is the brother of Ganesha. Karttikeya is
god of war and general-in-chief of the celestial armies. He is often
shown with six heads and with his mount, the peacock. He is worshiped little in north India, but in south India, where he is usually
called Subrahmanya, he is popular.

INDRA. § In the Rig-Veda, Indra was the chief deity, leader of the
gods and of the Aryans against their enemies; he was wielder of the
thunderbolt and slayer of Vritra. In Hinduism, Indra is subordinated

FIGURE 16.9 Ganesha. (*Slade Studies: Grace Cairns*)

to the great gods Brahma, Vishnu, and Shiva. He is king in one of the lower heavens, Amaravati, but stays in office for only one lifetime (the life span of an Indra is 100 divine years, or 36,000 human years). Virtuous mortals who have not yet won liberation from samsara may go to Amaravati as a reward for their merit, but when this is expended, they are reborn again in the world.

Indra has 1,000 eyes; his deadly weapon is vajra the thunderbolt; he possesses the wonderful horse, Uchchairavas; and his mount is the elephant. He is guardian of the eastern quarter of the universe.

AGNI. § Agni, who was a great god in Vedic times, is still important in Hinduism because of the use of fire in many rites and also because he is identified with the sun (Surya) and with lightning. This makes him a deity in each of the three worlds: on earth as fire, in the atmospheric regions as lightning, and in the heavens as the sun (Surya). Hinduism still accepts him as priest, as messenger and mediator between men and gods. When a person dies his body is resigned to Agni's purifying flames; Agni has the power to purify both pure and impure things.

In art Agni is often shown as a red man with two heads and four arms and on or with his mount, the ram.

VARUNA. § In Hinduism Varuna, the Vedic sky god of impartial justice who was feared by sinners, has become a god of the waters without any concern for morality. His mount is Makara, a strange creature which has the head and forelegs of a deer and the body and tail of a fish. Varuna is the guardian of the western quarter of the universe. He receives no worship at present, except for prayers offered to him by Hindus before they take a sea trip or when they see the ocean.

YAMA. § Yama is the god of death. In the Rig-Veda he was the first man to die and ruled as king in the Heaven of the Fathers, but in Hinduism he supervises Naraka, the region of the purgatories (twenty-eight in number, according to the Vishnu Purana). In this destroyer aspect, he is considered a deputy of Shiva. When a person dies, he is taken before Yama. Some accounts assert that Yama then requests his clerk to read out the record of the person's deeds, and if the bad deeds outweigh the good, he is assigned to the appropriate tortures for his particular forms of wrongdoing.

Other accounts do not mention the weighing, but it is generally thought that Yama supervises punishment of the wicked in the purgatories. Although the Puranas mention horrible tortures for serious sins, the wicked are eventually released for some form of rebirth. The exception is in the dualistic philosophical system of Madhva, who taught that some very wicked souls are everlastingly doomed to tortures in Naraka.[48]

Yama's mount is the buffalo; he is also accompanied by two vicious dogs with four eyes. He is green in color, wears a red garb and holds a mace and a noose to capture his victims. He is guardian of the southern quarter; therefore, this is an inauspicious direction for Hindus; death is spoken of as "going south."

KUBERA. § Kubera is the god of wealth (gold, silver, jewels, metals, and the like). His heavenly city, Alaka, near Mount Kailasa is said to be the richest in the sensuous heavens; it is the dwelling place of the Yakshas, over whom he is king. Kubera is depicted as ugly; his name means "vile body" and refers to his ugliness. He is white in color and deformed in body, but covered with lavish ornaments. He guards the northern quarter of the universe.

KAMA. § Kama, whose name means "desire," is the charming god of love and sensuous pleasures. He is the most handsome of the male gods and carries an appropriate bow and arrow. His mount is the parrot.

HANUMAN. § Hanuman is the monkey god described in the *Ramayana*. He is worshiped in temples dedicated to him and is especially popular in the villages. He is noted for the virtue of faithfulness and has a reputation for kindness. He is learned in the Vedas and brilliant in elucidating their meaning, and Vaishnavite students pray to him rather than to Ganesha for success in examinations. His physical strength is prodigious; many of his feats are described in the *Ramayana*.

SURYA. § Surya is the sun god. The sun is worshiped in the *sandhya*, one of the most important thrice-daily ceremonies of the orthodox Brahmin. The gayatri mantra (prayer), recited 108 times during the sandhya rite, is addressed to the sun as Savitar (stimulator).

Surya, who has several wives, drives a golden chariot with seven horses across the sky. His twin sons, the Ashvins, are physicians of the gods and are invoked by men because of their healing power and benevolence. The most famous temple of Surya is at Konarak. Surya and the Ashvins were important Rig-Vedic gods.

VAYU. § Vayu is god of the wind and father of Hanuman.

Minor Deity Groups
There are many spirits, some good, some bad, and some ambivalent in character in the Hindu pantheon.

GANDHARVAS AND APSARASES. § The Gandharvas are the troops of heavenly musicians; they are male. Their female companions are the Apsarases, the heavenly nymphs, who are flirtatious and tempt ascetics.

YAKSHAS. § The Yakshas are the semidivine beings who are Kubera's attendants. They are generally looked on as inoffensive. The greatest poet in Indian classical literature, Kalidasa, in his delightful poem the *Meghaduta* (Cloud Messenger), has immortalized all Yakshas. The theme of this famous work is the separation between a Yaksha and his beloved wife; the Yaksha romantically sends a cloud to deliver his passionate message of love to his wife.

NAGAS. § The Nagas are half human and half serpent, have many magic powers, and can assume human form. They dwell in Patala, a beautiful realm. Some ancient Indian kings claimed descent from a human hero and a female Naga (Nagini).

VIDYADHARAS. § The Vidyadharas are heavenly magicians who can fly through the air. They are very wise, they dwell in magic cities in the Himalayas, and they are friendly to man.

ASURAS. § The Asuras are demons who are constantly at war with the gods. Sometimes they succeed in dethroning the gods (except Shiva and Vishnu), but the gods always vanquish them again.

FIGURE 16.10   Hindu snake worshipers. (*Keystone*)

RAKSHASAS.   §   The Rakshasas are divided into three classes. One corresponds to the Asuras, another to the Yakshas, and a third is described as a group of imps, fiends, or demons who haunt cemeteries, devour human bodies, disturb sacrifices, and generally afflict mankind. Ravana, who was finally slain by Rama, was chief of this third group.

PISHACHAS.   §   The Pishachas are among the malignant evil spirits.

SNAKES.   §   Snake worship has been common in India from very ancient times (see Figure 16.10). Manasa, the snake goddess of Bengal, is widely worshiped there.

COWS. § The cow has never been worshiped, but the cow and the bull as living beings are revered. To kill a cow is as heinous a crime as to kill a Brahmin. Cows wander unmolested through the cities of India today; it is the sacred duty of a Hindu to protect them. Philosophically minded Hindus often think of the cow as the great mother symbol, the epitome of gentleness, and the nourisher of mankind. Gandhi revered the cow as such a symbol.

GRAMADEVATAS. § The Gramadevatas are the local gods and goddesses of the villages and cities. Every village or city has its local god or goddess, often a fertility deity. The goddesses are frequently identified with some form of the Great Goddess (Devi), usually under her more fearful aspects. Mariamma, the smallpox goddess worshiped for prevention and cure of the disease, is an important local deity. Some villages have well-known deities as their chief gods. The village of Gopalpur, in south India near Madras, has Hanuman and Shah Hussein (a recently deified Muslim of the village) as its special deities. They stand ready to help the village in any emergency.[49]

Every Hindu, especially in the villages (80 percent are villagers), ordinarily has three gods: the village god, the particular family god, and a personally chosen deity, his *ishtadevata*.

RITES OF HINDUISM

The Life Cycle (Samskaras)

The rituals that mark the significant stages in the life cycle of the Hindu are hallowed with appropriate ceremonies called *samskaras* ("sacraments"). Today these rites are rarely practiced in their full form, and, as in the past, are normally for males. Girls are not legally excluded, however, even from the upanayana, the initiation ceremony (in Vedic times this was sometimes performed for girls[50]), but ordinarily the *samskaras* have been and still are performed only for the males of the family. The following are the more important of the sacraments that are practiced today.

The birth of the baby is celebrated with pomp; there are important ceremonies concerned with the subsequent health and intelligence of the child. Within ten days he is given both a secret and a public name. Then in the sixth month comes the ritual of the first feeding with solid food.

When the child reaches the age of three the tonsure ceremony is performed. His head is shaved, leaving only a topknot; the orthodox Brahmin does not cut this for the rest of his life.

Next is the *upanayana,* the initiation ceremony. This is an ancient rite, known before the division of the Aryans into the Iranian and Indian peoples[51] and still performed by the Parsees. Among Hindus the ceremony takes place between the ages of eight and twelve: at eight for a Brahmin, at ten or eleven for a Kshatriya, and at twelve for a Vaishya. An important part of the rite is the investiture with the Sacred Thread (see Figure 16.1), which the youth subsequently always wears under his right arm with the end lying over his left shoulder. The Sacred Thread has three strands,[52] symbolic of the three debts that the youth owes to society. These three debts are: to the rishis, who received and passed on sacred knowledge (the Vedas); to the gods, who bestow all good things; and to the ancestors. Another important feature of the upanayana rite is the whispering into the child's ear of the holiest mantra of Hinduism, the gayatri, which may be translated as: "Let us think on the lovely splendor of the god Savitar, that he may inspire our minds."[53] The upanayana is called the second birth of the boy; he is now eligible to learn the Vedas, which can lead to moksha. Only the three upper classes (varnas) are permitted to have this initiation; they are called the twice-born. (In Hinduism today the upanayana rite is practiced mainly by Brahmins.) After initiation the youth is led to a teacher chosen by his parents for education in Vedic learning. Prior to this, beginning at about the age of five years, he has learned the alphabet, as well as arithmetic and reading. He has, therefore, some background for his serious studies, which begin after his "second birth."

After about twelve years of study (the Brahmacharin ashrama), the young man is expected to marry and enter upon the life of the householder. Marriage is solemnized with sacramental rites. The bride must be offered in the proper way by her parents and accepted publicly by the bridegroom. The bride and groom take a vow of lifelong fidelity before the sacrificial fire (Agni). They then take seven sacred steps, which symbolize the seven responsibilities and pleasures of life. Next, the groom applies vermilion to the parting of the bride's hair; this is symbolic of fertility, conjugal love, and auspiciousness.[54] The couple then return to the groom's house, where sacrifice is made to the domestic fire. In the evening they are to look at Dhruva, the Pole Star, symbol of faithfulness.

Funeral rites are important for the welfare of the departed. Only a son can properly perform the rites for his father, and a son is therefore practically a necessity for Hindu families. The corpse is carried to the cremation ground, followed by the mourners, then sacred texts are read and the body is burned, and finally the mourners circumambulate the pyre, take a ritual bath, and return home.

Three days later there is a bone-gathering ceremony. A priest gathers the bones in a vase and presents them to the eldest son or nearest relative, who will, if at all possible, throw them into the Ganges River. Those too poor to journey to the Ganges throw the bones into some other body of water, for all water is symbolic of the Ganges. The Ganges purifies from sin and thus ensures the soul's passage to Heaven.

For ten days after death the family is impure. During this interval the spirit develops its subtle body out of the five elements. It is essential that the son or nearest relative perform the ceremonies on each of the ten days. If these are not done in the right way or are only partially performed, the soul acquires no body or else a deformed body; it becomes a wandering evil spirit, a threat to the family and others.

The *shraddha* is performed between the tenth and thirty-first day after the cremation. The shraddha consists of offerings of *pindas* (balls of rice) to sustain the deceased. The ceremony is performed by three Brahmins who represent the dead man's ancestors in a direct line. The Brahmins and relatives are feasted. Those who can afford it give the Brahmins gifts of money and metal vessels. The feasts and gifts are thought to nourish and aid the body of the departed on its journey to Heaven. Thereafter, there are periodical offerings of pindas to continue feeding the deceased. These later ceremonies are inexpensive; only a single Brahmin and a few guests need be present; the pindas (placed on grass outside of the house) are sufficient to feed the departed.

Daily Rites

The orthodox Brahmin performs a rite called the "sandhya," preferably three times daily—at sunrise, noon, and sunset; however, the noon ritual is usually omitted. Before beginning the sunrise sandhya the Brahmin takes a ritual bath. All three sandhyas, however, follow the same pattern.[55] (1) The Brahmin takes water in a spoon and sprinkles it on his head; meanwhile he says a prayer mentioning the name of God. This rite is called "purifying oneself with water." (2) Then water is sprinkled on either side of the seat while a mantra is recited; this makes the seat holy. (3) Next the Brahmin takes water in the palm of his hand and sips it three times. (4) He then sprinkles water on his head again to purify himself from sin. (5) He practices *pranayama* (breath control) by closing one nostril and exhaling, then closing the other and exhaling, then closing both nostrils and exhaling. While doing this, he recites mantras. (6) He takes water in the palm of his hand and puts it to his nostrils without breathing. This purifies the entire body. (7) He sips water again for purification from sin. (8) He places flour, rice, and sandal paste in a vessel and stands up to offer these things to Surya, the sun god; at the same time he recites the Gayatri mantra. (9) Still standing, with his hands in the posture of prayer (palms open upward), he recites four mantras asking for long life. (10) Then he sits down and recites the Gayatri mantra 108 times, keeping count with his prayer beads (rosary) under the cover of his tunic. (11) Finally he recites verses in praise of the Gayatri mantra.

The orthodox householder of the upper castes is also obligated to perform what are called the Five Great Sacrifices daily. These are: (1) the Brahma Sacrifice, the study and recitation of some part of the Vedas; (2) the Sacrifice to the Gods—in modern Hinduism, food offerings to deities that represent aspects of the divine, for example, Vishnu, Shiva, Surya, Parvati, and Ganesha; (3) the Sacrifice to the Ancestors—a libation of water mixed with sesame; (4) the Sacrifice to Guests—feeding of Brahmins, students, and ascetics; (5) the Sacrifice to All Living Creatures—the feeding of pet animals, sick people, insects, birds, and the spirits—symbolic of giving life to all.

Puja (the Ritual of Worship)

In *puja* rites the deity is represented by an image or an equivalent symbol. The image is made according to definite iconographic specifications for the particular deity. Then the image must be animated by a rite that brings into it the vitalizing presence of the god. However, even the lowliest worshiper does not take the image as the complete manifestation of the deity. He knows that his god is a divine being whose presence is also elsewhere; and if it is Shiva or Vishnu, he knows that the deity pervades the entire universe. The image is merely one center of the operation of the god's spiritual power, and an aid in devotion to, and concentration on, the deity.

Simple *puja* rites can be performed for symbols of a deity. For Shaivites this symbol is the *linga;* for Vaishnavites the *shalagrama* may be used. (The *shalagrama* is a black stone that contains a fossil ammonite with spiral marking symbolic of the creative powers of Vishnu.) Some families use both symbols. Puja for such symbols consists of such daily offerings as water, ghee, and food. Large pictures that even the poorest can afford are also used as aids in devotion. Flower and food offerings (later consumed by the family —the deity eats only the essence) are placed before the pictures. The full puja rite described below is performed at temples and in those households sufficiently affluent to support a household priest *(purohita)*.

The ritual of worship in the home resembles the receiving and entertaining of a guest. Temple rites are similar, but on a scale appropriate for a king. Both the private and temple *pujas* take the following general form:[56] (1) The presence of the deity is invoked; a seat is offered. Then the feet are washed. (2) Uncooked rice, flowers, and some sandal paste are mixed together with water in a spoon and offered. (3) Water is poured over the head of the image (to give the god a bath). (4) Clothing is offered. In daily pujas this need be only a piece of thread; on great occasions, it should be a lower garment and an upper garment. (5) Sandal paste is mixed with water, and some of it is put on the forehead of the god's image. (6) Rice (uncooked and washed in water) is put on the head of the idol. (7) Flowers: tulasi leaves, if possible, to Vishnu; bilva leaves to Shiva; all deities accept marigolds, which even the poorest can afford. (8) Incense: this rite is performed with a bell in the left hand held downward close to the side and incense in the right hand. The right hand circles incense around the deity while the bell is rung. (9) Lights: the procedure is the same as in (8), except that the right hand holds one light or a tray of several (instead of incense) which it circles around the god. Ghee (butter) is the fuel burned in the lamps. (10) Food, usually sweets and fruits, is offered to the god. On being offered it becomes *prasada,* that is, food that can be given freely to anyone. (11) Betel leaf and betel nut, which the deities (like the people) enjoy chewing, are proffered. (12) Money or gold is offered. (13) The lights are again circled around the deity. (14) In the temple, circumambulation of the holy image is performed; or if that is not possible, the worshiper may turn himself around several times. (15) Recitation of mantras. (16) Bidding farewell to the god.

In the richer temples the image of the deity may be taken out in the afternoon and entertained in the evening. At the birthday celebration in Rama's temple at Banaras in 1965, for example, there were about ten musicians to entertain the deities. The musicians stood in rows, five on each side in front of the niche that held the deities—life-size statues of Rama, Lakshmana, and Sita. These musicians struck gongs and clapped cymbals, making a loud noise. Two men with fly whisks (*chowries*) stood on either side of the gods, just outside the niche. The priest inside made the offerings, circled the incense, and then circled a large tray with twelve lights. At the end of the service this priest brought the tray of lights forward to a railing that would correspond to the Christian altar rail. The devotees pressed against the rail, eager to place their hands over the holy flames.

At the Vishvanatha Temple in Banaras the evening puja features circumambulation of the linga. There is loud ringing of bells and the clashing of other instruments for the entertainment of Mahadeva (Shiva). Emotional chanting, too, is part of the ritual. Worshipers circumambulating the linga offer flowers, money, and other things while the musicians who are close to the linga perform. Only Hindus are allowed inside, but there is a small window in the linga room through which non-Hindus may observe the rites. During the evening puja worshipers crowd so thickly that it is difficult to see the linga (usually covered with flowers) or the musicians and priests.

In some temples, the god is put to bed at night in an apartment with his wives, and waked in the morning with all the pomp of an earthly king. He follows the elaborate daily routine that a monarch would observe. He is entertained by musicians and, formerly, by women dancers (*devadasis,* literally "slaves or servants of the god"). In the Middle Ages it was the custom for a king to have among his salaried servants numerous female prostitutes who had various duties assigned them in addition to waiting on the king's person, and it seems that the king could bestow their favors temporarily on any courtier in the palace. Similarly in the Middle Ages the god in the temple had among his attendants a retinue of prostitutes. Some of these women were given to the temple as children by pious parents. The function of these girls and women was to dance and sing before the god and to bestow their favors on the god's courtiers, that is, the men who paid a fee to the temple.[57] This kind of temple prostitution was most prevalent in south India and continued to exist there until recent times; it is now no longer lawful anywhere in India for temples to use dancing girls in this way. It seems that there are dancing girls today at the temple of Lord Jagannath[58] in Puri, where the deity is daily given the elaborate ritual attention mentioned above and is attended to in the magnificent style of a potentate of bygone days; the entertainment portion of the ritual includes "dancing girls who sing and dance before the deity."[59]

Rites for the Principal Religious Holidays

The principal Hindu religious holidays celebrated throughout India are Divali, Holi, Dashera, and the Kumbha Mela.

Divali (a corruption of *dipavali,* "cluster of lights") comes on the fifteenth day of the month Kartika (October–November). This is also the New Year's festival for those Hindus who follow the widely used Vikram Era calender. The outstanding rite is lighting row upon row of lamps in as many places as possible: outside the house, on the roof, on the verandas, etc. The lamp is a symbol of prosperity, light, and brilliance. Lakshmi is the patroness of this festival because she is goddess of prosperity. On Divali, Vaishnavites hold a domestic rite (puja) in honor of this goddess: a variety of sweets are presented by the family to the goddess; afterward these are eaten by the family, guests, and neighbors. Children are permitted to light fireworks.

Holi is the most popular of all holidays. It is celebrated on the full-moon day of the month Phalgun (February–March), which is the first day of spring. Originally, it was a fertility festival, and it still has this character among the lower castes. Songs about the love between Radha and Krishna are sung by college students and many others. Colored water is thrown or squirted by mischievous boys everywhere on the streets, and in the gardens of homes men and women indulge in similar frivolity.

Dashera (also spelled Dussehra) comes on the tenth day of the bright half of the month Ashvin (September–October). This is the end of the rainy season and the beginning of autumn. The holiday celebrates the victory of good over evil and is based on the myth of

Durga's victory over the buffalo demon, Mahisha. Another myth that adds significance to the festival is the tale of the victory of Rama, avatar of Vishnu, over Ravana on that day. The Durga Puja is given its most spectacular annual celebration in West Bengal. For example, in the Belur Math temple compound in Calcutta (the place where the nineteenth century mystic Ramakrishna had his vision of Kali) a huge statue of the goddess is constructed and magnificently costumed.[60] There is prayer entreating the goddess to come to earth, while Indian style music is played. The chants ask Durga to drive away evil and bless the good. The intellectuals interpret this as man's need to arouse the Durga in himself to destroy evils within his own nature. At about 4:30 A.M., after the prayer session, Durga is carried in a gala procession before the temple of "the Mother" (deceased wife of Ramakrishna, now worshiped). In front of this temple two young men perform a dance with lights; then Durga, followed by musicians and crowds, is taken to the Ganges where she is submerged in the holy waters. This ends the Durga Puja. Durga has now destroyed evil and blessed the good, but she will need to come again next year and every year in this Kali Yuga, the epoch of darkness and evil.

The Kumbha Mela takes place once every twelve years in rotation in Allahabad, Hardwar, Nasik, and Ujjain. The occasion celebrates an episode in the myth of the Churning of the Ocean for the purpose of extracting the nectar of immortality. When the nectar was obtained, the gods and asuras who had performed the difficult churning operation fought for possession of the precious elixir. In one version of the story Vishnu in the clever disguise of a beautiful maiden entertained the asuras while one of the other deities ran off with the pot *(kumbha)* of nectar. When the asuras became aware of this they pursued the god. The chase lasted for twelve days of the gods (twelve human years). During the chase the deity rested at the four places where the Kumbha Mela is now held. Other accounts say that these towns are sacred because drops of the nectar fell into their rivers. The latter version adds to the significance of the main event in celebration of this holiday, ritual bathing. Such bathing is especially desired at Allahabad (Prayaga) at the Sangama, the confluence of the Ganges and the Yamuna rivers; and at the Triveni where a third river, the "invisible" Sarasvati meets the other two. The Triveni has another sacred significance; it is associated with the syllable AUM (described in Chapter 15 in the section on the Upanishads). Besides the other meanings of each letter of this syllable, the letter A is linked with the Sarasvati river and the god Brahma; the letter U with the Yamuna river and the god Vishnu; and the letter M with the Ganges river and the god Shiva. The Trimurti (Brahma, Vishnu, and Shiva), the manifested aspect of Brahman, the Ultimate Reality, abides in this way at the Triveni.

In 1954, 6 million Hindus are said to have bathed during the Kumbha Mela at Allahabad because of its superlative effectiveness for the purification essential for *moksha;* it is believed that even the gods desire to bathe in this place.

There are numerous other lesser holidays in Hinduism. Most important are: Vasanta Panchami, observed mainly by students, musicians, and intellectuals in general, the day being dedicated to Sarasvati, goddess of music and learning; Janmashti, Krishna's birthday, important for Vaishnavites and given a grand celebration at Mathura; Rama Navami, Rama's birthday, also a Vaishnavite holiday; Ganesha Chaturti, birthday of Ganesha, a great occasion in Bombay.

Shravani (now called Raksha-bandhana, Rakhi Purnima, and Narali Purnima) was a festival celebrated in ancient India on the full-moon day of the month Shravana (July–August) to mark the resumption of the educational year after the monsoon rains began. (Today in India the school-year also begins in July.) Associated with the rains, Narali Purnima (Coconut Full-moon Day or Coconut Day) is a contemporary name of the festival and is derived from the practice of throwing coconuts into a river or the sea as offering to Varuna, god of waters. The other names, Raksha-bandhana (protective-bond) and Rakhi Purnima (Amulet Full-moon Day) come from the popular rite of a girl tying a colored tassel or an amulet made of more precious materials such as gold, around the wrist of her brother (or a friend adopted as a brother) on this day; this symbolizes that the boy will henceforth be the sister's protector. Another rite is the changing of the Sacred Thread by the higher varnas on this occasion.[61]

Mahashivaratri (the Great Night of Shiva) is Mahadeva's festival. The day preceding it is one of fasting, and women especially keep a strict fast on this occasion. The Shiva temples have special pujas, in which snakes are sometimes used to add to the realistic manifestation of the god. Villagers sing about the god and go to the temple to present gifts and to circumambulate the linga. Musicians play percussion music, and everyone is expected to keep vigil on this night. As part of the holiday atmosphere, large fairs are often held near rivers or at the seashore, where people flock to bathe because it is meritorious to do so on the Shivaratri holiday.

There is no weekly holy day corresponding to the Jewish Sabbath or the Christian Sunday; religious Hindus may observe a fast day *(vrata)* or some other ascetic practice *(tapas)* at any time. The most important fast days are called Ekadashis because they fall on Ekadashi, the eleventh day of every fortnight of the lunar calendar. Many women of the three higher varnas fast on these days; religious men, too, keep this fast regularly if their work permits it. A vigil (wakefulness to God) is usually kept, and the individual devotes himself to pujas and prayer or, if he is more philosophical, purely to meditation.

Pilgrimage

Pilgrimages are a characteristic feature of Hinduism. While the entire land of India is sacred, particular cities and places possess a special holiness. Among the holy cities are seven perhaps most often regarded as guarantors of salvation; four holy Dhamas (places looked upon as houses of God) are regarded as having a similar function. The seven sacred cities are Banaras, Ajodhya (on the outskirts of Fyzabad in the province of Uttar Pradesh), Mathura, Hardwar, Kanchipuram, Ujjain, and Dwarka. The four holy Dhamas are Mount Kailasa, celestial abode of Shiva and Parvati in the Himalayas of Tibet (the highest point—altitude 22,028 feet—of a range north of Lake Manasarowar); Badarinatha, near the Ganges in the Himalayas, the dwelling place of Narayana (a name for Vishnu); Puri, where Vishnu is enthroned as Jagannath (Lord of the World); and Dwarka, city of Krishna, avatar of Vishnu.

The Sacred Cities

Of the seven holy cities, Banaras is the most sacred. One version of the myth of the cutting off of Brahma's head by Shiva symbolizes the spiritual values attached to this place.[62] The god Brahma, in order to show his superiority to Shiva, grew a fifth head. In anger, Shiva cut it off. But Mahadeva had committed one of the gravest sins of the moral code, killing a Brahmin (Brahma is chief of all Brahmins). Therefore Shiva was doomed to wander with the head of Brahma in his hand, in search of atonement. Finally he was released from carrying the head by bathing in the holy waters of the Ganges. Shiva was so delighted to lose the burden of his sin that he made the place, the present Banaras, his residence on earth and had the city built upon his trident. The power of the waters that flow by the city to remove sin, attested to by the Shiva story, is generally accepted, and this is the main reason why all Hindus desire to make a pilgrimage to Banaras (see Figure 16.11). Other sacred cities give a qualified *mukti* (liberation from rebirth again in this world), but Banaras gives nirvana mukti, absolute release, union with the Absolute Spirit.

The oldest name for Banaras is Kasi; the name means "to shine" and signifies that this region lights the way to ultimate realization of the Absolute Spirit. The city is called also Mahashmashana (*maha*, "great"; *shmashana,* "cremation ground"); this means that final destruction of the body is attained through the liberation won at Banaras. Final destruction of the body for liberation is related to the destroyer aspect of Mahadeva (he is both Creator and Destroyer). At Banaras he is called Vishvanatha (Lord of All) and enthroned in

symbolic form as the linga in the Vishvanatha Temple, his royal residence.

The individual is still more certain of absolute release if he can die and be cremated in Banaras and have his ashes thrown into the Ganges there. In addition to the many bathing ghats, cremation ghats, and temples that line the Ganges at Banaras, there are two houses for sick and aged people who come there to die. "See Banaras and die" is a maxim taken literally by these people.

Two of the other six sacred cities to which pilgrimages are made, Hardwar and Ujjain, are also, like Banaras, devoted to Shiva. Hardwar is a beautiful place in the hills of northern India. The Ganges comes down from the mountains to Hardwar and there enters the plains. Ujjain was known as Avantika in the Golden Age of Indian culture. At that time it was called the "great among the great," and it continued to be a flourishing center of Hindu culture until A.D. 1000. The attraction today for pilgrims is mainly the Mahakala Temple dedicated to Shiva.

Ajodhya, Mathura, and Dwarka are Vaishnavite cities. Ajodhya is sacred as the birthplace of Rama, who also ruled there as the most righteous of men and kings. Mathura is holy as the birthplace of Krishna, and it has the same significance for millions of Hindus that Bethlehem has for Christians. Dwarka is the city that was built by Krishna and in which he lived during the last part of his life.

Kanchipuram is the only one of the seven cities sacred to both Shaivites and Vaishnavites. Both deities, Shiva and Vishnu, have temples there.

The Hindu who is in search of salvation visits all seven sacred cities if possible, or at least Banaras, if he must limit himself to one.

The Holy Dhamas

Pilgrimages to the four holy Dhamas (abodes of God) are similar in religious function to pilgrimages to the seven sacred cities. Mount Kailasa, the high, snow-clad mountain in the Himalayas that is the celestial abode of Shiva and Parvati, is climbed by brave pilgrims. To die while climbing this peak means moksha, eternal union with Shiva. Badarinatha (also called Badarikashrama), another Himalayan peak, is the abode of Narayana, a name for Vishnu. A temple there

FIGURE 16.11   Ritual bathing in the Ganges river at Banaras. (*Information Service of India*)

contains an image of Narayana made of ammonite *(shalagrama)*, the black stone sacred to Vishnu. Eternal life in Vaikuntha (the name of Vishnu's heaven) is won by this pilgrimage.

Puri, located on a beach on the Bay of Bengal, is the abode of Krishna as Jagannath (Lord of the World); close by, at Konarak, is the temple of the sun (Surya). In the main temple at Puri, called the Sri Mandir, the principal objects of worship are three images in the sanctum sanctorum.[63] These represent Jagannath, his brother Balarama (also called Balabhadra), and Krishna's sister Subhadra.

The great celebration at Puri is the Car Festival. This commemorates the journey of Krishna from Gokul to Mathura to slay the wicked Kamsa. The three deities are drawn in separate chariots; Jagannath's chariot is forty-five feet high and thirty-five feet in length and width and it is supported on sixteen wheels, each seven feet in diameter. Formerly it was considered an act of supreme religious merit for devotees to throw themselves in front of Jagannath's car to be crushed to death; simply to die within sight of Jagannath guaranteed salvation. To have *darshana* (religious vision, illumination or insight) by looking at the deity or by participating in his festival is still considered to be potent for salvation.

Darshana is an important religious term in Hinduism. The Sanskrit root of this word means "to see," but it has the connotation of spiritual vision or realization; this is its meaning for the religious devotee who is searching for God-realization in a place that is rich with divine associations. Pilgrims go to all the sacred cities to visit not only the holy objects or images to have darshana, but also to contemplate the temple building itself in which such an object or image may be housed. Darshana in this context is insight into the temple structure itself as a symbol of divine reality and of the journey of the soul to union with it.

The two major styles of temple structure are the northern or Nagara style and the southern or Dravidian style. The northern style features the single temple with its tower called a *sikhara* (see Figure 16.12); the southern style, ornate high gateway towers called *gopuras* (see Figure 16.13) erected at the cardinal points of the temple compound with the temple of the deity in the center less imposing

FIGURE 16.12   Gopuram Ramesvaram Temple. *(Information Service of India)*

FIGURE 16.13   Jagannath Temple. *(Archaeological Survey of India)*

in height but often jewel-like in splendor, for example, the main temples of the Madurai temple-compound. The religious meaning of both styles is similar. The tower (sikhara) is the most important feature; as a whole it has two meanings: (1) it represents the Purusha or Cosmic Man as the entire universe, a notion as old as the Rig-Veda (see the account of the Purusha Hymn and Hymn of Creation in Chapter 15); (2) it represents Mt. Meru, the World-Mountain or axis-mountain of the universe on whose base is the earth-world and on whose slopes are the heavens of the gods at the appropriate various levels (for details of the sacred geography of Hinduism see the section on the Vishnu Purana). Then beyond the tip is the formless-spaceless world of the eternal spiritual reality. Both the Cosmic Man and Meru signify the macrocosm, the universe that parallels in its structure material and spiritual the individual man, the microcosm. The Cosmic Man or World-Mountain springs from the Divine Reality symbolized by the holy image or other symbol (such as the linga) in the cella (garbha-griha or womb-house) at the base of the sikhara. The divinity ensouls the entire temple just as the Divine Reality pervades or ensouls the universe and the Atman pervades the body of the microcosm, the individual. On the walls of the temple at the lower levels numerous gods and goddesses that people the lower, more sensuous heavens are sculptured. Even here many interpret the numerous couples engaged in erotic dalliance (mithuna couples) as symbols that remind the beholder of the love between the divine reality and the soul. All architectural lines of the sikhara carry the eye towards the crown (amalaka), a ribbed, ring-like decoration at the top of the tower called the "door to the sun." When one passes this door he enters the ethereal heavenly world whence his soul passes into unity with the Ultimate Reality. This passage to union is symbolized by the finial (kalasa), which ascends from the amalaka. The philosophical pilgrim may circumambulate a temple for concentrated meditation upon its religious symbolism, that is, for religious vision, darshana; and if he is acquainted with Indian philosophy he will know that the word darshana is used also to denote a system of philosophy because this, too, gives vision, or insight into reality.

The ultimate aim of the pilgrim visiting the sacred cities or the Dhamas with their great temples, holy rites, images or other sacred objects, whether he is mature or at a childish stage in his religious development, is darshana at his own level of comprehension; for with complete darshana comes moksha, release from karma and samsara.

The Place of Ritual in Hinduism

Many Hindu philosophers and others who are advanced in the spiritual life look on rituals as the mere outer trappings of religion, although they are useful to beginners and the immature. However, novices should strive to advance to the point in the spiritual life at which such props become unnecessary. The Ultimate Reality, which is purely spiritual and all-pervasive, cannot be represented in gross forms nor can it be approached by such external means as ritual performances. Such forms and performances are tolerated by the spiritually mature only because they are considered to be aids for those who are still children in the soul's search from birth to birth for enlightenment. The liberated souls, the jivanmuktas (those liberated while still alive), have attained the vision of Brahman or identity with Brahman. Such souls, as well as those that are close to this highest spiritual realization are ever conscious of the divine presence; they have no need for external observances. Step by step as the soul progresses, more and more of the external props can be dispensed with until none at all is needed by the sage or saint.[64] This is an orthodox view among the Shaivites and others. The Shiva Purana says: "The highest state is the natural realization of God's presence, the second in rank is meditation and contemplation, the third is worship of symbols which are reminders of the Supreme, and the fourth is the performance of ritual and pilgrimages to sacred places."[65]

SECTS OF HINDUISM

Sectarianism is not a characteristic of Hinduism. Many Hindus do not belong to a particular sect, and many of those who do are merely nominal members. The essential features of a sect are: a particular body of scriptures; a system of beliefs; and a method of salvation.

The sects of Hinduism, except for a few small, insignificant ones, fall into two main groups, the Vaishnavite and the Shaivite. A third important sect, the Shaktas, may be classified under Shaivism as a development out of it. Before we discuss these sects separately, however, we should be aware of the strong influence exerted on them and on all Hinduism today by the bhakti-poets of the Dravidian south.

Influence of Dravidian Devotional Literature on
Vaishnavism and Shaivism

Vaishnavism and Shaivism in their developed forms owe a great deal
to the poet-saints of Dravidian south India, who were the authors of
some of the world's greatest religious literature. The ecstatic songs
of these lovers of God arose out of movements that synthesized indigenous Dravidian cults with Aryan influences.[66] The poet-saints
(the Shaivite saints are known as the Nayanars, the Vaishnavite as
the Alvars) sang their inspired songs during the period from the
seventh to the tenth century. Their fresh, vital religion not only
aided in the ascendancy of Hinduism in south India in their own
time,[67] but exerted a strong and lasting effect on Hinduism as it
exists today.[68] These poet-bhaktis voiced a simple religion, one in
which the soul seeks the Lord and the Lord the soul. They were
God-intoxicated men and women of a variety of castes, from Brahmins to "untouchables,"[69] and this made it clear that there were no
artificial barriers between God and the soul; all were eligible for
salvation. Moreover, their songs, which were sung in the vernacular,
have influenced devotional Hinduism all over India and are still
sung today in the Tamil country in pious homes.[70] In northern
India poet-bhaktis flourished between the eleventh and eighteenth
centuries in Kashmir, Maharashtra, Rajputana (home of Mira Bai,
c. 1504, a woman who was one of the greatest mystic poets of the
world), Assam, Mathura, and West Bengal. Kabir and Nanak were
also bhaktis.[71] The Bauls today in West Bengal carry on the
tradition.[72]

The Vaishnavites

All Vaishnavites are worshipers of Vishnu as the Ultimate Reality,
and they all believe that bhakti is the ultimate way to God; hence
Vaishnavites are also called bhaktis of the Lord.

SCRIPTURES. § The god Vishnu is mentioned in the Rig-Veda and
in the Upanishads; and the Vaishnavites, therefore, like all Hindus,
regard the Vedas as revelation (shruti). But they also consider the
Mahabharata and *Ramayana* to be sacred: the Bhagavad-Gita in the
Mahabharata is a favorite Scripture, and the *Ramayana* is loved
because it is filled with examples of self-surrender to Rama, avatar
of Vishnu. The Bhagavata Purana is also enjoyed, because it is concerned with the boyhood and youth of Krishna, avatar of Vishnu,

and tells of his love affairs with the Gopis, which are interpreted as the love between God and the soul. The hymns of the Alvars, the Vaishnavite poet-saints, which are filled with the love of God, are also very popular. Another text loved by the bhaktis of the Lord is the *Gita Govinda* (Songs of the Cowherd) by Jayadeva, who lived in Bengal in the twelfth century. This lyrical poetry in rhymed verse celebrates the love between Krishna and his favorite, Radha. Interpreted as the love between God and the soul, these songs are still sung by Bengali Vaishnavite sects. In the bhakti path to moksha the highest stage of love is patterned after the ecstatic erotic relationship between Radha and Krishna so delightfully described in the *Gita Govinda*.[73]

The works of Ramanuja, the great philosopher of Vaishnavism, provide a systematic formulation for its doctrines. His *Commentary on the Vedanta Sutras* (verses that summarize the essence of the Upanishads) is especially famous.

Ramanuja, in his turn, founded his philosophy (one of the greatest systems of Indian philosophy—described later in this chapter) on the early Vaishnava Pancaratra Agamas (or Tantras).[74] These works originated in northern India, and additional material was later composed in south India, in the Tamil country, after the eighth century. Ramanuja's teacher, Yamuna, called the Pancaratra Agamas a fifth Veda. An Agama or Tantra, like the Vedas, contains both philosophy (beliefs) and ritual practices, with emphasis on the latter. The ritual practices are of primary importance to Vaishnavite sects. The system of beliefs on which they are based, as these are given in the Pancaratra Agamas, is as follows.

SYSTEM OF BELIEFS.   §   The Supreme God, Vishnu, as the transcendent source of all being has six attributes: omniscience, lordship, power (potency to become the material cause of the world), strength (power of preservation), power of dissolution, virility, and splendor. These qualities are the "body" of Vishnu (not a material body), as he is seen by the liberated souls in the highest heaven, Vaikuntha. Creation is conceived as a process of emanations from the divine source, Vishnu. The first emanation is a chaotic mass, the embryonic state of the universe; the second emanation is soul and matter, which emerge from the chaotic mass; the third is the emergence of gross matter and time out of the second emanation. These are all personified: the transcendent source or form of the Lord is called Vasudeva[75]; the first, second, and third emanations are named respectively Samkarshana, Pradyumna, and Aniruddha (these are the elder brother, son, and grandson of Krishna).

The next stage of emanation is the deity in the form of incarnations (avatars); the chief ones are ten in number: the Fish, Tortoise, Boar, Man-Lion, Dwarf, Parashurama, Rama, Balarama (elder brother of Krishna, in place of Buddha), Krishna, and Kalki. The Supreme God is also present in the heart as the *antaryamin,* which resembles the Holy Spirit in Christianity and is the form of the deity preferred by those who practice meditation. (The trinity of transcendent God, the incarnations, and the antaryamin resemble the Christian Trinity of Father, Son, and Holy Ghost.)

Finally there is the grossest, most concrete manifestation of the divine reality, the idol. This is called *archavatara* (descent into the idol). It is thought that God descends into the idol; the famous icons at the great Vaishnavite shrines are regarded as permanent incarnations.

METHOD OF SALVATION. § The goal of salvation is the liberation from karma and samsara and the everlasting enjoyment of Narayana (Vishnu) in his Heaven (Vaikuntha). God himself is love and yearns to save the soul. After Ramanuja's time theologians of the Tamil country debated the question of whether or not effort to attain liberation is required on the part of the aspirant. What became known as the Northern School teaches that some effort is necessary; this is called the "monkey's way"; the monkey performs some action in clinging to its mother when danger threatens and thus helps to save itself. The Southern School takes the position that no effort is necessary on the part of the recipient of grace. This is called the "cat's way." The mother cat picks up her kittens by the scruff of the neck to save them, without any effort on their part. Both schools agree that liberation is impossible without divine grace. God's Shakti (Lakshmi), as mother of all souls and wife of Vishnu, is important as an intercessor between the soul and God.

The method of the three margas (karma, jnana and bhakti) is potent for salvation and appeals to the more philosophical. Raja-yoga disciplines are used for concentration of the mind. Karma-marga gives self-control, and jnana-marga, self-knowledge; but these two margas are merely preparatory stages for bhakti-marga, because it is only through complete devotion to God that the soul can find the union with Him that is moksha. The highest stage of love is called *prapatti;* this is absolute self-surrender. All are eligible for prapatti, including the unlearned and the lowest in the social scale.

ETHICS.   §   The best summary of the highest ethical teachings of Vaishnavism is given by Prahlada in the Vishnu Purana:

Keshava [an epithet of Vishnu] is most pleased with him
    who does good to others;
Who never utters abuse, calumny, or untruth;
Who never covets another's wife or wealth,
And who bears ill-will to none.[76]

EXTERNAL MARKS OF THE VAISHNAVITES.   §   The most general mark of Vaishnavites is a U-shaped emblem on the forehead with a perpendicular mark in the center, but there are many others, totaling thirty-six altogether.

The Shaivites

Shaivite sects consider Shiva the Ultimate Reality and emphasize the jnana-marga as the supreme way of salvation. The two main sects of Shaivism in Hinduism today are the Shaiva Siddhanta and the school of Virashaivism, also called the Lingayats. A third school, that of Kashmiri Shaivism, does not flourish today, although there has been a revival of interest in it; its philosophy is felt in the Shakta schools.

EXTERNAL MARKS OF THE SHAIVITES.   §   The most general sign of Shaivites is an emblem of three horizontal white lines drawn across the forehead, but there are many others, totaling altogether about twenty-four.

The Shaiva Siddhanta
The Shaiva Siddhanta is the southern school of Shaivism.

SCRIPTURES.   §   The Scriptures of the Shaiva Siddhanta are the Vedas and twenty-eight Shaiva Agamas. Also much revered are the devotional hymns of the Nayanars, the Tamil Shaivite poet-bhaktis, and the philosophical works of later sages. The classical literature of the school was compiled in the eleventh century. The *Shiva-jnana-*

bodham by Meykandar, in the thirteenth century, is the earliest systematic statement of the doctrine of the Shaiva Siddhantas.

SYSTEM OF BELIEFS. § The Shaiva Siddhanta doctrinal system considers Shiva to be the Ultimate Reality. Shiva has attributes of omnipotence, omniscience, purity, and freedom. His divine power, called Shakti, is the material cause of the world. Shiva is creator, preserver, and destroyer of the universe, and in addition he has the functions of concealment (maya) and grace. All five functions are for the benefit of all souls.[77]

The material world of matter, sense-organ, and intellectual experience has its source in maya. The unmanifested form of maya is an eternal and invisible substratum; from it arise pure and impure principles. From the five pure principles Shiva produces worlds, bodies, and objects of enjoyment for the pure souls. From the impure comes prakriti-maya, which gives rise to the concrete material world of matter, life, and mind, the world for impure souls.

METHOD OF SALVATION. § The goal of man is realization of the true nature of his soul as Shiva. The hindrances to this realization are three bonds: ignorance, karma, and maya. The way of release from these bonds has four stages, beginning with external acts of worship and attendance upon the deity in temple worship, proceeding to more internal acts of worship and meditation, and ending (with the help of God's grace) with the fourth and final stage, knowledge. Knowledge is the direct way to God for which the earlier steps toward release are a preparation. Knowledge culminates in the ultimate goal, union with God. The union with God is called *advaita* (nondual), but the meaning of advaita in this system does not mean nondifference from God (as in Shankara's system described below); advaita here means nonseparateness from God. Whereas the soul formerly experienced through matter, in the released state it now experiences through God,[78] just as a blind man, when he regains his sight, sees only through the illumination of the sun. The notion of union with God must be interpreted in the light of the ecstatic experience of the Nayanar poet-bhaktis as a "mysterious communion" between God and the soul, "the former the source of bliss, the latter the recipient. . . . They are neither two substances nor one, but a two in one."[79] The supreme, ineffable bliss of this two-in-one unity can be known only through experiencing it. In this advaita union with Shiva the soul enjoys his omnipresence (all-

pervasiveness) and through him experiences something of his omniscience. As a jivanmukta he lives in Shiva and sees the Lord in
all things. He lives only until the karma he accumulated before
liberation is completed; when he dies he will be in union with
God forever.

ETHICS.   § One of the Shaiva Scriptures says, "Love alone is
God."[80] Thus unselfish love, as well as truth, is a great virtue.

The Lingayats (Virashaivism)

The Shaivite sect known as the Lingayats takes its name from the
fact that its members carry a linga (Shiva's phallic emblem) on their
persons. Basava, who lived in the twelfth century, is considered to
be the founder of this sect. However, the Lingayats claim an origin
in the ancient past; Basava may not have been the originator, but
a reformer of the sect, who made it a popular movement.[81] Basava's
teaching was very unorthodox; it rejected the Vedas and caste distinctions (social equality was to be practiced), and advocated re-
marriage for widows—in fact, social equality for women.[82] Since
the time of Basava the sect has compromised somewhat with orthodoxy. The Lingayats are found today in Hyderabad and Mysore.

SCRIPTURES.   § The Lingayats accept the Vedas, Agamas, and
Puranas as sacred and, in addition, accept the hymns of the Tamil
Shaivite saints and the sayings of mystics.

SYSTEM OF BELIEFS.   § The doctrine of the Lingayats, which resembles that of the Shaiva Siddhanta, is known as "Shakti qualified
nondualism." This term means that the Ultimate Reality, called
Para Shiva, is qualified by his power (shakti). Creation in all its
aspects is the manifestation of God's power (shakti); it is, therefore,
part of his being.

METHOD OF SALVATION.   § The goal of man is realization of his
essential nature as one with Para Shiva. The hindrance to this goal
is ignorance. In order to overcome this, the aspirant must seek the
aid of the guru, or spiritual teacher; of the *jangama,* the soul that
has realized union with God; and of the linga, Shiva himself. The
devotee must surrender himself to the three and worship them in
order to obtain divine grace, which will enable him to realize his
oneness with Shiva. Eight rites, including the rite of *japa*[83] (con-

tinuous repetition of a five-syllabled mantra—*namah shivaya* in the case of this sect), are designed for achievement of this goal. Observance of these rites is for the purpose of maturing the person spiritually so that he may obtain the illumination that brings the bliss of union with Para Shiva. This union is not one of identity; rather, the individual soul is a part of God, who is the Whole.[84]

The Shaktas

The Shaktas worship Devi, the Great Goddess, personified as the Shakti of Shiva. Often Devi as Shakti has taken precedence over Shiva. The beliefs and practices of the Shaktas have merged with Tantric beliefs and practices, so that Shaktism and Tantrism are almost synonymous. We shall treat them as identical.

SCRIPTURES.   §   The Shaktas consider the Vedas and Puranas to be sacred, but accept the Tantras as the most authoritative. The Shaktas believe that the Tantras have come directly from Para Shiva, the Divine Being. These Tantras are in the form of dialogues between Devi and Shiva; they are called *Agamas* when Devi asks the questions and Shiva answers, *Nigamas* when Shiva asks and Devi replies.

SYSTEM OF BELIEFS.   §   The view of the Ultimate Reality is advaita (nondual). The nondual One, neither male nor female, is the perfect oneness of inert consciousness (Shiva) and power (Shakti).[85] Because there is only the One, it has the power to manifest the universe; Shakti is, therefore, necessarily inherent in the One. She is conceived as mother of the universe; as the divine power, she is creator, preserver, and destroyer.

Since the universe is the divine Shakti, it is not a maya of illusion, but a maya that is a glorious aspect of divine being, Shakti, personified as the goddess Devi under her many names; and because the world is real and divine, the Shaktas take delight in it.

METHODS OF SALVATION.   §   The goal of the aspirant is liberation, becoming one with the nondual Ultimate Reality. There are three grades of aspirants for liberation: the creature, the hero, and the *divya* (godlike). The Creature (*pashu*, literally "animal") is bound by the bonds of existence. To release himself he makes use of three ways: the Vedic, the way of ritual (karma-marga); the Vaishnava, the way of devotion (bhakti-marga); and the Shaiva, the way of knowledge (jnana-marga). After the practice of these methods, a synthesis and harmony of all three is effected in the fourth way, called *dakshina*. *Dakshina* means "right-hand" and signifies that the three methods in their synthesis are the right-hand way of liberation. The higher, more adequate way is the "left-hand" way (*vama*).

The hero (*vira*) uses dakshina and then vama. Vama-marga (the left-hand way) is called the *"reverse* path" to salvation.[86] This means that the aspirant uses nature, the outward manifestation of Shakti, as a means for return to the One, the Ultimate Reality. Just as the macrocosm is a process of emanation from the One and returns in dissolution, so the aspirant who has been involved in the emanation process reverses it and returns to the nondual Source. In the return he uses Shakti (nature) herself as the divine means.

A badly misunderstood Tantric ritual practiced at the vama stage is the one called the Five M's because the Sanskrit words for the items used in the ritual all begin with the letter M—wine (*madya*), meat (*mamsa*), fish (*matsya*), parched or fried grain (*mudra*), woman (*maithuna*—the word in Sanskrit means literally "sexual union"). All five items have a spiritual meaning and symbolism, including maithuna, which in its highest interpretation means waiting upon the inner woman, the Shakti in the microcosm, the individual body. When this inner Shakti is aroused and unites with Shiva (consciousness), her Lord, the ananda (bliss) that is felt is the real maithuna. Any other maithuna is mere physical copulation. Shaktas of today do not, and many in earlier times did not, practice maithuna as a religious rite in the physical sense; but in the past some Tantric groups apparently misused the rites of the Five M's and indulged in nights of orgiastic intoxication and pleasure. It is this malpractice by some Tantrics plus the misunderstanding by outsiders of the higher, spiritual meanings[87] of the Five M's ritual that has given the left-hand Tantric method its bad name.

The divya (the godlike), third and highest of the three grades of aspirants, is able to follow the paths of Siddhanta and finally of Kaula. The Siddhanta is the stage of knowledge—the knowledge of all things in their true nature. The knowledge gained must be embodied in all of the devotee's being, all his acts and thoughts. Then he is prepared to follow the Kaula, the Royal Way, which is the highest path. This is a path of meditation and yoga, yet there is no denial of the world. The Kaula sees the universe in every aspect as the divine Shakti. He takes delight in the world at the same time as he beholds the nondual eternal One beyond its space-time manifestations. The world is real as the manifestation of the Shakti of the One; it is maya only in the sense that it *conceals* the nondual eternal One, its source. The divya following the Kaula path looks upon both the eternal One and its Shakti as divine. The Kularnava Tantra expresses this view when it says that Yoga and Bhoga meet in the Kaula doctrine. Yoga is union with the One, and Bhoga is enjoyment of its manifestation, Shakti.[88]

A graphic symbol of this doctrine much used by the Shaktas is the *Shri Yantra* (see Figure 16.14). A *yantra* is a diagram of spiritual reality. It may represent one or more particular deities or the entire macrocosm placed within a circle drawn on the ground or on some kind of writing material. Vaishnavite and Shaivite sects also use yantras. The Shri Yantra[89] diagrams the whole of reality. Its center is a dot called Bindu, which represents the Ultimate Reality, the complete nondual unity of consciousness and power (Shiva and Shakti). Emanating from the Bindu are a series of interlacing triangles, the upright ones symbolizing Shiva (consciousness) and the inverted ones Shakti (energy or power). Two circles of lotus petals symbolizing the created universe surround the ordered pat-

tern of interlacing triangles. Outside the lotus petals, as the external border of the entire diagram, is a square with "entrance gates"; this makes the square a swastika, for each gate has an arm or entrance in two directions—one to the left (the "reverse" path) and one to the right. These symbolize the two Tantric ways of salvation, the dakshina-marga (right-hand way) and the vama-marga (the left-hand or reverse path). Many Shaktas in the past, and the great majority at present, have practiced the dakshina-marga; but in the past the vama-marga was popular in either a literal or a symbolic form.

The divya is a yogi. He uses devices such as the Shri Yantra as aids in concentration and reintegration; but his primary technique for realizing union with the nondual One utilizes aspects of the method of classical yoga (described in the section "Ways to Moksha," pp. 395–396, and in the following section on Indian philosophies, pp. 468–469), but only as accessory to the Tantric practice called "kundalini yoga." In kundalini yoga, Kundalini (Shakti) is coaxed upward through six psychic centers of the body until she reaches the "thousand-petaled lotus" at the crown of the head. Here she is dissolved into the One, the nondual Ultimate Reality; the yogi (divya) becomes this One and is liberated.[90] Ramakrishna, greatest saint-philosopher of the Hindu Renaissance, used this form of yoga.

ETHICS. § The Shaktas admit all castes, foreigners, women, and outcasts as candidates for the highest knowledge. Women can become spiritual directors (gurus), and it is considered a special honor to be initiated into the mysteries of the cult by a woman. Woman is Shakti herself and therefore entitled to reverence. Shakta rites involve the worship of women and girls, and positively forbid any harm to them; even female animals cannot be sacrificed. Sacrifice of women in *suttee* has always been strongly opposed by the Shaktas; they worked actively to abolish this practice long before the British did.

CONTEMPORARY REVIVAL OF INTEREST IN TANTRA. § On March 8, 1965, the Governor of the state of Uttar Pradesh inaugurated a four-day all-India Tantric conference held at the Sanskrit Univer-

FIGURE 16.14 The Shri Yantra. (*Ganesh and Co., Madras*)

sity in Banaras. The conference was financed by the University Grants Commission, which shows the interest of the academic world of India in Tantric philosophy and practice.

THE GREAT SYSTEMS OF INDIAN PHILOSOPHY

The systems of Indian philosophy are divided into two groups, *astika* and *nastika*. The astika systems are those that accept the authority of Vedas; these are the Hindu systems of philosophy. The nastika systems do not accept the authority of the Vedas.

The Nastika Systems

The nastika include three philosophical systems: a school of materialism that is usually called *Charvaka,* after the founder of the school, but is also called *Lokayata,* which means "materialist, limited to this world"; Buddhism; and Jainism. The two latter systems are treated in the chapters on those religions.

The Charvaka (Lokayata) Philosophy

The metaphysical base of the Charvaka school is materialism, the belief that the material world perceived by the sense organs is the only reality. The basic elements of the world are earth, air, fire, and water, and there is no soul or other spiritual reality. What is called the soul is merely the body with an intelligence that is the result of the manner in which the elements are combined. The "soul" disappears, therefore, with the body. Moreover, there is no God, and no right and wrong in nature; virtue and vice are social conventions. The ethics of this school may be called hedonism, because it is founded on empirical pleasure and pain: the good is the pleasant and the bad the painful. The Charvaka system resembles logical positivism in recent Western philosophy, in its emphasis on empiricism and its polemics against rationalism and belief in spiritual entities.

The Astika Systems

The Hindu systems of philosophy are the Six Orthodox (*Astika*) Systems: Purva Mimamsa, Sankhya, Yoga (usually Sankhya and

Yoga are combined), Nyaya, Vaisheshika (usually Nyaya and Vaisheshika are combined), and Vedanta divided into three main schools
—Advaita, Vishishtadvaita, and Dvaita.

Purva Mimamsa

The *Mimamsa Sutras* of Jaimini (about 200 B.C.) are the foundation of the Purva Mimamsa system of philosophy. Kumarila and
Prabhakara, who flourished in about the early eighth century A.D.,[91]
are the outstanding Purva Mimamsa philosophers. In its metaphysics the school is atheistic, in the sense that there is no belief in a
Supreme Being, but the limited gods of the Vedas are accepted as
adjuncts to Vedic rites, and some later Mimamsakas do accept the
existence of God. The Vedas are regarded as fundamental in this
system of thought and are believed to be absolutely eternal and
uncreated.

For salvation, the Vedic rites must be observed. There are two
main kinds of Vedic rites: those that are obligatory and those that
are optional. Performance of such rites is the substance of Vedic
teaching according to Mimamsakas. To attain heaven, the goal of
the earlier school of Mimamsa philosophy, both obligatory and optional rites had to be performed. If obligatory rites were omitted
demeritorious karma would be accumulated; this would result in
an undesirable rebirth. If optional rites were performed in addition
to the obligatory ones, sufficient meritorious karma could be accumulated to gain heaven for the performer. The later school of
Mimamsa philosophy took moksha as the goal; in other words not
even rebirth in heaven was desired. To avoid *all* rebirth, both
demeritorious and meritorious karma had to be eliminated. This
meant that obligatory rites had to be performed to eliminate the
former and that the optional rites could not be performed to eliminate the latter. In release (moksha) the soul is all-pervasive.

Sankhya

The Sankhya philosophy is also atheistic. It accepts two ultimate
substances: a plurality of *purushas* (the word for souls or spirits
in this system) and *prakriti* (matter). As in the Bhagavad-Gita
(which reflects the Sankhya view of prakriti) prakriti's ultimate
constituents are the three gunas (strands) —sattva, rajas, and tamas
—explained above in the section on the Bhagavad-Gita. At the beginning of each world cycle, when the equilibrium of the gunas is
disturbed, prakriti evolves twenty-three *tattvas* (principles) in the

following order: (1) *mahat* (literally "the great"), referring to cosmic intellect; (2) *ahamkara* (literally "I-maker"), the ego-principle, which evolves the remaining tattvas which are its appendages; (3) *manas,* the lower mind: (4–8) the sensory organs (organs of sight, hearing, smell, taste, and touch); (9–13) the motor organs (hands for grasping, feet for locomotion, mouth for speech, genitals for reproduction, and anus for evacuation); (14–18) the *tanmatras,* subtle essences of the five elements (ether, air, fire, water, earth); (19–23) the *bhutas,* the five elements in their gross forms. Two other tattvas are prakriti itself and purusha, making a total of twenty-five.

Man's goal is to free his purusha from the false view that it is involved in prakriti (the whole matter-world of the twenty-three tattvas). When this is known and freedom from prakriti experienced, moksha is achieved. The soul has no qualities (it is regarded only as pure consciousness), and purushas are indefinite in number.

Yoga

Meditation techniques became important in the realization experience in Sankhya. Moreover, there were theoretical problems involved, such as: Why does the universe dissolve and reappear in cyclic rhythms? How can matter (which includes intellect) interact with an utterly different substance, purusha (spirit), and cause its ignorance, the source of its "fall"? Because of these problems and the adoption of yoga meditation methods, Sankhya was combined with theistic yoga. Yoga accepts the metaphysics of Sankhya, but adds God, who creates the world and dissolves it in order to aid souls in their efforts toward release. Since Sankhya and Yoga thus supplement each other, the two are usually considered as one philosophy, called Sankhya-Yoga.

The unique contribution of yoga to Indian philosophy and religion is its scientific meditation technique in eight stages: (1) *Yama* (restraints): one must not steal, lie, or injure anyone; sexual chastity and nonpossession of worldly goods are essential. (2) *Niyama* (observances): one must observe cleanliness and contentment, one must study and practice austerities (such as bearing heat and cold, keeping the body unmoved, maintaining silence for long periods), and deep meditation on God. (3) *Asana* (postures) : these are physical exercises for control of the body. (4) *Pranayama:* this is the science of breath control. (5) *Pratyahara:* withdrawal of the senses from external objects. (6) *Dharana:* fixation of the gaze usually on the tip of the nose or the navel. This is an aid in gaining one-pointedness of thought consciousness. (7) *Dhyana* (meditation) : complete absorption in a single object until (8) *Samadhi* is reached. There are two forms of samadhi. In the lower form there is complete absorption in a single object of consciousness contemplated by the intellect. But in the ultimate and higher form, the object disappears and with it activity of the intellect; only pure consciousness remains, and this is the naked purusha liberated from prakriti. The person who has attained this state may remain alive until whatever karma he may have left is worked out; he lives as a jivanmukta and when his body dies there will be no rebirth.

Nyaya-Vaisheshika

Nyaya is a celebrated school of logic, and Vaisheshika is a school of metaphysics. The two together form a systematic philosophy. Vaisheshika metaphysics is pluralistic: whereas Sankhya has only two ultimate substances, Vaisheshika posits nine—the five elements plus space, time, mind, and soul. Souls are indefinite in number and go through rebirths in accordance with their separate karmas. Release is attained through knowledge of Vaisheshika metaphysics, but merit must first be acquired through virtuous conduct before the saving knowledge can be attained. Moksha is the state of the eternal substance, soul, liberated from the other substances. After liberation the soul has no qualities; it is described as a state of cessation from pain.

Advaita Vedanta

Advaita Vedanta is the most famous school of Indian philosophy. The main ideas of this philosophy are found in early Upanishads, especially the Brihadaranyaka, Chandogya, and Mandukya. In the Brihadaranyaka it says that "this self is Brahman" and that this Brahman is without attributes (*neti neti,* "not this, not this"), which is an affirmation of the nondual Brahman. In the Chandogya Upanishad is the famous "that art thou" (*tat tvam asi*), a terse expression of the identity of the Atman (the soul or spirit in the individual) with the Brahman (the universal Spirit). However, there was no systematic formulation of Advaita Vedanta until Gaudapada (teacher of Shankara's guru) in the eighth century wrote his *Mandukya-karika.* This work develops its system around the four states described in the Mandukya Upanishad: the waking, dreaming, dreamless sleep, and the ultimate, nondual fourth state.

With this background as a foundation, the philosopher Shankara (A.D. 788–820), the greatest teacher of the system and responsible for its popularity among intellectuals, developed the greatest and clearest systematic formulation of the Advaita philosophy. Shankara argues that Brahman, the Ultimate Reality, is absolutely One (advaita or nondual). Attributes would destroy the absolute unity of the One and also impose limitations on it. The nondual One is infinite, beyond subject-object and all other relations, for these would make it finite being. Brahman is the absolute knower, pure consciousness itself, not consciousness dependent on objects, attributes, or relations. As the Brihadaranyaka Upanishad says, "Thou canst not see the Seer of seeing, thou canst not know the Knower of knowing." All that one can posit of the nondual One (and these are not attributes) are being (reality), consciousness (pure luminous intelligence), and bliss (serene joy). Shankara uses persuasive rational arguments to defend this view of the Ultimate Reality. He also appeals to the Great Sayings in the Upanishads. The method he advocates is mainly the jnana-marga, the way of knowledge, which he calls *atma-vidya* or *brahma-vidya*. But, as in most systems of Indian thought, theoretical knowledge is not sufficient; it must be verified in a direct, intuitive experience. Shankara, like the Upanishadic thinkers, teaches that the truth of the advaita nature of Brahman must be meditated on with such intense concentration that the philosopher finally *is* Brahman as the nondual One. The That and the Thou become absolutely identical. This immediate experience is ineffable and intuitive and is liberation. One may remain in the body as a jivanmukta for the benefit of the unreleased to teach them the way to moksha. But for the jivanmukta himself, there is no body as a real entity; only Brahman is real.[92]

If the One alone is real, what is the status of the world? Shankara says that the world is neither real nor unreal; it is an illusory appearance (maya). He uses the famous analogy of the snake and rope to clarify this concept. One sees what he believes to be a coiled snake in the road; but on closer inspection he sees that the "snake" is merely a rope. Similarly the world is illusory appearance, superimposed on Brahman just as the snake is superimposed on the rope. But the world is not unreal, because it appears and is a public world; and neither is it real, because it is negated in the knowledge and especially in the immediate intuitive experience of identity with the nondual Brahman. Maya is, therefore, said to be indeterminable. When the philosopher rises beyond maya (the world) to Brahman, the eternal nondual One, there is no problem of maya. The method of arriving at this goal is knowledge (jnana), because it is ignorance of the truth that makes one identify oneself, the Atman, with the body, the mind, and the vital functions. These "sheaths" of the Atman (or Brahman) belong to maya. Shankara does not advocate the karma-marga or bhakti-marga as paths to moksha because one is naturally in the state of moksha; that is, he is already Brahman; but one needs to know this in direct experience, and Shankara's method, therefore, emphasizes the jnana-marga.

Shankara traveled throughout India teaching his philosophy and established four "maths" (pronounced "mutts"), or monastic institutions, one in the north at Badari, one in the south at Sringeri, one in the east at Puri, and one in the west at Dwarka. Shankara himself, according to tradition, became a sannyasi at the age of nine. No one saw Shankara die; he disappeared at Kedarnath in the Himalayas. Pilgrims today visit the temple there that is dedicated to him. The Shaivites believe that Shiva, Lord of jnana-marga (or jnana-yoga), in his form of Dakshinamurti (teacher), came to earth in the avatar of Shankara.

Vishishtadvaita Vedanta

Ramanuja, who flourished around the twelfth century, is the greatest philosopher of the Vishishtadvaita Vedanta school. Vishishtadvaita means "qualified nondualism." Ramanuja disagreed with Shankara's view of the nature of the Ultimate Reality. He argued that Brahman without qualities (nirguna) is nothing; to be real, Brahman must have content (qualities); Brahman is Saguna Brahman (*saguna* means literally "with qualities"). Since Brahman has qualities, he is personal and is called Ishvara (the Lord or God) in this system; he is also One, and this makes the system a "qualified nondualism." The One Reality, God, includes in himself both the matter of the entire universe and the souls. These form God's (Ishvara's) body; he is immanent in the universe in these attributes. He is also transcendent in his eternal, unchanging aspect. He is perfect being with the attributes of omniscience, omnipresence, perfect beauty, infinity, and supreme bliss. The relation between Brahman and the world of matter and souls is analogous to the

relation between soul and body in the individual; matter and souls
are the "body" of the supreme self (Purushottama).

Man's goal is moksha, attained through the three margas of karma,
jnana, and bhakti in that order. Karma-marga is the path of selfless
service to God described in the Bhagavad-Gita; jnana-marga is the
way of knowledge, but not mere theoretical knowledge—yoga methods of meditation on God are essential to bring realization of God's
nature. The margas of karma and jnana are preparatory stages for
bhakti-yoga; service to God and knowledge of God lead to bhakti
(love for God). In bhakti-yoga the aspirant practices meditation
on the immediate presence of God as his inner self (and the self of
all); through self-surrender and complete devotion to the Lord,
God's grace comes to him. In this way moksha is won. The devotee
does not become a jivanmukta; but when he dies, he is liberated from
karma and samsara and dwells eternally in Vishnu's (God's or Brahman's) Heaven, Vaikuntha, basking forever in the divine presence.

Dvaita Vedanta
Dvaita Vedanta, founded by Madhva (1199–1278), is the form of
Vedanta that teaches theism and dualism. According to this philosophy, there are two kinds of substance in the universe: spirit and
matter. Spirit is divided into the Supreme Spirit (Vishnu or Brahman) and the indefinite number of souls, all dependent on Vishnu.
Matter, although a different substance from spirit, is also entirely
dependent on God. Vishnu (God) is creator, preserver, and destroyer, as well as absolute controller of the universe. He has the
qualities of omnipotence, omniscience, omnipresence, perfect bliss,
and all other perfections. Souls have the same qualities as God, but
only in a finite degree.

Bondage (karma and samsara) is caused by ignorance. To obtain
moksha the aspirant uses all the margas and ends with the bhakti-
marga. The bhakti-marga leads to prasada, the coming of God's
grace to the individual soul which is the major element in salvation.
Those who receive God's grace attain full liberation only at death;
then they live eternally in Vishnu's Heaven. Those who are not
liberated are divided into two classes: wicked souls doomed eternally to Hell, a place of blinding darkness (this is the only school
that posits Hell as everlasting); and souls who must migrate eternally.

Although there are followers of Madhva's system in south India
today, they are few in number; Advaita and Vishishtadvaita are by

far the most popular schools of philosophical thought throughout India.

LEADERS OF MODERN THOUGHT IN HINDUISM

Modern thought begins with the era known as the Hindu Renaissance of the nineteenth century. During this time Western cultural influences were felt, and in synthesis with the Hindu religion they gave rise to new emphases in the social and cultural ideals of Hinduism.

The first great name in this movement is that of Rammohan Roy (1772–1833), who had an excellent knowledge of Western ideas in addition to those of his own Hindu culture. He founded the Brahmo Samaj in 1830, which advocated social reform and monotheism; this society combined the best in Upanishadic thought with the best in Christian ideals. Rammohan Roy denounced abuses of caste, suttee, and idolatry and advocated civil liberty. Although the Brahmo Samaj still exists today, it has been too rationalistic to become a popular movement.

The Arya Samaj founded in 1875 by Dayananda Sarasvati, a Gujarati Brahmin, is somewhat more popular. Sarasvati advocated a return to the Vedas as the basis of religion. This involved the abolition of idol worship, which is a non-Vedic aspect of Hinduism. He also urged social reforms, such as abolition of child marriage and untouchability, pointing out that the Vedas do not sanction these things.

Ramakrishna and Vivekananda

Sri Ramakrishna (1836–1886) was the greatest religious leader of the Hindu Renaissance. He began his life of spiritual leadership at the age of twenty as a priest of Kali, the universal Mother (or Shakti), at the Dakshinesvar Temple in Calcutta. Ramakrishna could not be satisfied until he had obtained the vision of Kali. Eventually, the divine Mother revealed herself to him several times until he could, at will, envision her real presence. This success encouraged him to engage in many spiritual experiments to realize the divine in its many forms. He became an adept in the Tantric philosophy and rituals. Then he tried the paths to realization of the other major sects, the Vaishnava one of bhakti and the Shaivite one of jnana. He realized God as the Saguna Brahman of the Vaishnavites and then reached the grand heights of divine illumination, which is realization of the Nirguna Brahman (the nondual Brahman). It is this Nirguna Brahman which, for him and his followers, is the ultimate Divine Reality. He also continued to experience the Saguna Brahman (Brahman with Shakti or qualities) and continued to practice Tantric yoga (Kundalini yoga) for realization of both aspects of Brahman. This is significant because it puts emphasis on the world-and-life-affirming aspects of Reality.

Ramakrishna then went on to experience God through the disciplines of the Christian and of the Muslim faiths. He found that he could have the realization experience through following the theories and devotional practices of both these religions. He concluded that all the great religions are ways of experiencing God, and he taught that all Hindu sects and the other religions of the world should be tolerant of each other.

Ramakrishna and Vivekananda (1863–1902), a learned man who was completely devoted to Ramakrishna and who was his greatest disciple, were explicit in making clear the implications of God-consciousness. They reiterated the Upanishadic view that God is the real in every human being and in nature generally, but reveals himself most fully in man. Therefore the God-conscious individual reveres all human beings, even the most lowly or most wicked, as divine, and he shows his reverence by service to them. The Ramakrishna movement, in order to carry out service to man, has engaged in many philanthropic activities in India and has set up Ramakrishna Centers which are supervised by the Ramakrishna Order of monks. Attached to these centers, which number over 100, are dispensaries or hospitals, homes for the aged, the crippled, or hopelessly diseased, and rooms for distribution of food to the hungry. In developed foreign countries the Ramakrishna Centers (called Vedanta Centers) do not engage in these activities, but function as teaching and literature centers.

Vivekananda was a spokesman for the Ramakrishna movement and for Hinduism at the World Parliament of Religions held in Chicago in 1893. He remained in the United States for a while and was successful in popularizing the ideas of his master. He established a permanent center in New York, and later other centers were founded in California, Illinois, Massachusetts, Missouri, Oregon, Rhode Island, and Washington, D.C. Vivekananda also lectured in Europe, and there are centers in London and in Gretz, France. Although he did not lecture in South America, a center does exist in Buenos Aires. Ramakrishna proved that Hinduism has much to offer the modern industrialized, mechanized, commercialized world.

Gandhi

Mohandas Karamchand (Mahatma) Gandhi (1869–1948) is so famous for his practical accomplishments as the architect of Indian freedom that the religious doctrine on which his activity was founded is often overlooked. He was not a professional philosopher, but his views are, on the whole, closest to the Vaishnavite philosophy.[93] He called God or the Ultimate Reality *Truth*. He saw all beings, especially each human being, as a fragment of this Truth which is God, just as a wave is a part of the ocean. All men, therefore, are divine and should be served as one would serve God. Gandhi called the power of Truth *satyagraha* (Truth-force), and believed it to be far more potent than physical power.

Gandhi, who had learned from Christianity the New Testament ideals of nonviolence, universal love, and service that are expressed in the Sermon on the Mount, and who admired Tolstoy's efforts to put them into practice,[94] developed Ahimsa (nonviolence) as his second cardinal religious principle. Ahimsa follows directly from the view of Truth (God) as immanent in all men. Gandhi was eminently successful in living by the tenets of his religion; by nonviolent methods he won his first success in South Africa on questions of racial discrimination against Indian nationals, and later won the battle for Indian independence against the powerful British Empire.

Brahmacharya (self-purification or self-restraint) was the third cardinal principle of Gandhi's ethics. He thought that the principles of Satyagraha and Ahimsa could scarcely be put into practice without Brahmacharya. Gandhi's favorite religious text was the Bhagavad-Gita because it teaches self-restraint as the basic ethical principle. Gandhi's favorite passage in the Gita says, "The sense-objects turn away from an abstemious soul, leaving the relish behind. The relish also disappears with the realization of the Highest."[95] This doctrine of self-restraint, of self-purification in order to make possible selfless service devoted to God, included complete sexual chastity. Gandhi believed that only through complete detachment from all egoistic desires could he devote himself wholly to the service of man, to social service, and this for him was service to God.

Aurobindo

In the metaphysics of Sri Aurobindo (1872–1950), Brahman (God) is existence, consciousness, and bliss. Consciousness is interpreted as consciousness-force, and bliss as delight of existence. Universal history, both cosmic and social, is interpreted as an involutionary and evolutionary process. First there is an involution of the One into matter. Then comes the evolutionary process, which progresses through the stages of life and mind. The next stage, and the goal of the evolutionary process, is Supermind, a stage which will be attained eventually by all humanity. The method by which this stage is to be achieved is called an "integral" yoga. In this yoga, Spirit or Supermind has complete control over mind, life, and matter, because knowledge at the level of Supermind is knowledge by identity. There is no denial of the three lower levels; the integral yoga harmonizes the finite lower world of mind, life, and matter and uses it for the service of the infinite Spirit. In a society of superminds each person will be directly and intuitively aware of Brahman and of all other spirits, because all are parts of one Supermind, which in its turn is an aspect of Brahman. Brahman aids man to achieve this evolutionary level already attained by the great saints, but, ordinary man, too, must attempt through the integral yoga to reach the next and highest level of Supermind. As more and more God-conscious men or saints move in the supramental sphere of being, the new era for all humanity will be ushered in; and finally all life will have the illumination that once belonged to a few saints.

Rabindranath Tagore

Rabindranath Tagore (1861–1941), a poet of international fame, was the son of Debendranath Tagore, a leader of the Brahmo Samaj. Rabindranath's ideal was to combine Western science with Indian spirituality as the basis for a new world order. He believed that the fundamental contribution of Indian spirituality, stemming from Upanishadic thought, would be the teaching that wealth and similar worldly satisfactions are not ends in themselves, but subservient to the self; the goal of the self is union with the Infinite eternal Self that pervades nature and man.

Tagore's interpretation of Upanishadic metaphysics is Vaishnavite. He sees the Infinite Self as creator of all things in nature out of his joy and love; the world, therefore, is real and not maya. All evil and suffering are caused by egocentricity, by lack of union with the Infinite Spirit; when this union is attained, only serene joy remains.

This divine consciousness, which sees the universal Self in nature and in all men, can be expressed in social action, in love, in art, and in religion. All life becomes a harmony. This, Tagore says, is the basic teaching of the saints and seers of India for all the world. Tagore himself established a cultural and educational center, the Vishvabharati at Shantiniketan in West Bengal, to encourage and develop talent in art, music, dancing, and literature, as well as in more academic subjects. This center is now one of India's best universities.

Nehru

In religion Jawaharlal Nehru (1889–1964) was an agnostic. At the same time he had deep respect for the founders of the religions of the world and for sincere men of religious faith like Gandhi. In his book *Glimpses of World History* he points out the vices of much of institutional religion in India and the rest of the world: he writes, "In the name of religion many great and fine deeds have been performed. In the name of religion also thousands and millions have been killed, and every possible crime has been committed."[96] In 1944 he wrote, "Whatever gods there be there is something godlike in man, as there is also something of the devil in him."[97] As a humanist and liberal interested in the freedom of the individual he praises "the old Hindu idea that if there is any divine essence in the world every individual possesses a bit of it."[98] Therefore every individual is important and has the right to develop his potentialities. Nehru sees history as the struggle for a classless society in which every individual will have access to spiritual (intellectual and artistic) development and economic goods, and there will be no exploitation of anyone. Politically, Nehru was a democratic socialist, not a doctrinaire Marxist. He abhorred tyranny and violence as methods of attaining freedom, and he had faith that India and other developing countries would be able to achieve the good society by democratic processes.

Nehru's non-religiousness is representative of the attitudes of many young Indian intellectuals. But a good many of them, including science students, are deeply religious, and so are the vast majority of Indians, both educated and uneducated. Only in a country as religious as India could a man like Gandhi have gained mass support for the spiritual teachings of Satyagraha and Ahimsa.

NOTES

1. The name "Hindu" is derived from the name the early Indians gave to the Indus River, "Sindhu." The Persians pronounced it "Hindu." The Greeks received "Hindu" from the Persians and called the entire subcontinent by this name. The Indians themselves called their land Jambudvipa or Bharatavarsha. After the Muslim invasion there was a revival of the Persian name in the form Hindustan, and the inhabitants of the country were called Hindus, that is, those who observed the indigenous religion. It is interesting to note that the government of independent India has been trying to revive the ancient name of the land, Bharatavarsha. See A. L. Basham, *The Wonder That Was India* (New York: Grove, 1954), p. 1, note.
2. A definition given by the Indologist Professor J. A. B. van Buitenen, Department of South Asian Studies, University of Chicago, in a lecture in the series "Sanskrit and Indo-Aryan" during the summer of 1963.
3. In the Sankhya-Yoga system of philosophy the aspirant devotes himself to God and in a sense "yokes" himself to him; but moksha is not union with God: it is isolation of the individual soul from the matter world. Yoga in this system really means "restraint"—restraint of the body and sense organs that must be "yoked," as one yokes a wild steed, if moksha is to be gained.
4. Austerities *(tapas)* means mortification of the flesh. It is an ancient idea in Indian religion that a great yogi accumulates extraordinary physical and mental powers by observing austerities such as exposure to the "five fires" (one in each of the four directions of space and the sun above), fasting, holding a limb in one position for an indefinite time, or disregarding the body in other ways. Yogis at the highest spiritual level, however, have no interest in displaying extraordinary powers and do not observe bizarre austerities; they aim only at complete control over the sense organs and body.
5. Raja-yoga is a discipline used in part or in its entirety by aspirants of varying religious or philosophical viewpoints. It belongs essentially and originally to the Sankhya-Yoga, and in this system moksha is not union with the Absolute, but isolation of spirit from matter. A fuller account of Sankhya-Yoga is given on pp. 467–469.
6. This is the Purusha Hymn described in Chapter 15, in the section on "Monotheism and Monism in the Late Hymns of the Rig-Veda."

7. Basham, *op. cit.*, pp. 147–148.
8. *Ibid.*, p. 147.
9. *Ibid.*, p. 148.
10. This is a marriage of a man to a woman below his class. Only marriage between a Brahmin and a Sudra woman was considered impure.
11. Basham, *op cit.*, p. 148.
12. Malabar is located in the southwestern coastal region in the Dravidian country.
13. P. Thomas, *Hindu Religion, Customs and Manners* (Bombay: D. B. Taraporevala Sons and Co., Private Ltd., 1960), pp. 18–19. Used by permission.
14. The section on "Rites of Modern Hinduism," pp. 440–442, describes these rites as they are observed today.
15. Quoted in Sarvepalli Radhakrishnan and Charles A. Moore, *A Source Book in Indian Philosophy* (Princeton: Princeton University Press, 1957), p. 172.
16. Quoted from *Mahabharata* 1, 74.40 ff., in Basham, *op. cit.*, pp. 181–182.
17. William T. de Bary, ed., in *Sources of the Indian Tradition* (New York: Columbia University Press, 1958), p. 1, gives the date as 900 B.C. Percival Spear, *India: A Modern History* (Ann Arbor: University of Michigan Press, 1961), p. 35, gives the date as about 1000 B.C.
18. Basham, *op. cit.*, p. 298, also p. 328. Basham says that we know "little about the early history" of this sect. The Besnagar column was erected to this god of the Bhagavatas, Vasudeva, at the end of the second century B.C. by the ambassador, Heliodorus, of the Greek Bactrian kingdom. This shows, says Basham, that this god was by then important even among the ruling classes. (It also shows the absorption of Indian religion by the Greeks.)
19. The original edition of the Gita may have been written as an Upanishad of the Bhagavatas in the second century B.C. See Maurice Winternitz, *A History of Indian Literature*, trans. by Mrs. S. Ketkar (Calcutta: University of Calcutta, 1962), II, 384–385.
20. Some scholars account for such inconsistencies by positing interpolations made in the original poem. *Ibid.*, p. 383.
21. As in the Sankhya Yoga philosophy the Sanskrit word used most often for the eternal spirit in man is *purusha;* sometimes *atman* also is used. *Purusha* can be translated "soul," "man," "person," "spirit."
22. See below, pp. 467–469, for an account of this philosophy.
23. *The Bhagavad Gita*, trans. and interpreted by Franklin Egerton (Cambridge: Harvard University Press, 1952), I, Bhagavad Gita IX, 34.
24. *Ibid.*, IX, 30–31.
25. *Ibid.*, XVIII, 66.
26. The Gita says, "Through devotion he comes to know Me. . . . Then, knowing me in very truth, he enters into (Me) straightway." *Ibid.*, XVIII, 55.
27. A brief description of these systems will be found on pp. 467–469, 472.
28. *Op. cit.*, Bhagavad Gita, XI, 28.
29. In theism the world is separate from God, though dependent on him. Pantheism, narrowly defined, equates the universe with God. Ramanuja's view is like that of the Purusha Hymn of the Rig-Veda, described on p. 378, wherein only one-fourth of God is manifested in the universe; three-fourths "is the immortal in heaven."
30. Winternitz, *op. cit.*, II, 453, says that it is likely that Valmiki composed an original *Ramayana* in the third century B.C., using ancient ballads as his materials.

31. See *The Vishnu Purana,* trans. from the Sanskrit by H. H. Wilson (Calcutta: Punthi Pustak, 1961), Book I, pp. 19–24, for a discussion of the yugas, kalpas, and manvantaras.
32. *Ibid.,* Book II, p. 145.
33. See the section "The Great Systems of Indian Philosophy," pp. 468–469, for a brief account of Patanjali's yoga; also see the section "Ways to Moksha (Liberation)," pp. 395 f.
34. See pp. 469–472 for a fuller account of the Ultimate Reality in the classical philosophical systems of Shankara and Ramanuja.
35. See the section "Sects of Hinduism," pp. 455–462, for a further discussion of Shaivite and Vaishnavite thought.
36. "Vedas" here is being used in the narrower sense, the core collections of materials in each Veda, called *samhitas.*
37. *The Vishnu Purana, op. cit.,* p. 129.
38. See the section "Religion of the Indus Valley Culture" in Chapter 15.
39. For a full account of the symbolism of the Dance of Shiva see Ananda Coomaraswamy, *The Dance of Shiva* (Bombay and Calcutta: Asia Publishing House, 1948). For the interpretation of the serpent symbolism as life and death see also E. B. Havell, *The Ideals of Indian Art* (London: John Murray, 1920), p. 50. See also Stella Kramrisch, *Indian Sculpture* (Philadelphia: University of Pennsylvania Press, 1960), p. 80. Dr. Kramrisch, in her description of a Karttikeya representation in which a serpent appears, comments that "cosmologically the serpent is a symbol of the cycle of the year and of recurrent time."
40. The gods and demons were churning the ocean to recover the nectar of immortality. The serpent, used as the rope around the churning stick, emitted poison. Shiva drank it to save the others and the universe.
41. D. C. Sircar points out that the conflict between Shiva and Daksha reflects the conflict between Aryan religion and the non-Aryan cult of Shiva. The Shiva cult was not "respectable." However, the ending of the story shows the victory of the Shiva cult and its absorption into Hinduism. See D. C. Sircar, *The Sakta Pithas* (Varanasi, India: Motilal Banarsidass, 1948), p. 6.
42. This story about the sacrifice of Daksha evolved from a legend in the *Mahabharata.* Many Puranas, written later, tell the story in modified form; in these versions Sati dies by yoga or of a broken heart, or as the great poet Kalidasa writes, Sati immolated herself. See Sircar, *op. cit.,* pp. 5–6.
43. Basham, *op. cit.,* p. 188.
44. *Ibid.*
45. Ashes are smeared on the body by yogis and by Shiva worshipers. The symbolism, especially in the light of this story, is plain. Ashes signify the death or conquest of lust, of all sensuous desires, and also the ephemeral nature of all bodies, which end in decay and dissolution.
46. *The Devi-Mahatmyam* or *Sri Durga-Saptasati,* trans. by Swami Jagadisvarananda (Madras: Sri Ramakrishna Math, 1955).
47. Basham, *op. cit.,* p. 398.
48. See p. 472 for a brief account of Madhva's philosophy.
49. Alan R. Beals, *Gopalpur: A South Indian Village* (New York: Holt, Rinehart, and Winston, 1962), p. 47.
50. Basham, *op. cit.,* p. 162. L. Renou tells us that in Vedic times the rituals of the *samskaras* were simplified "or even abolished" for girls. Louis Renou,

Classical India, Vol. III, *Vedic India,* trans. Philip Spratt (Calcutta: Susil Gupta Private Ltd., 1957), p. 114.

51. Basham, *op. cit.,* p. 161.

52. Each thread consists of nine twisted strands made of cotton for a Brahmin, of hemp for a Kshatriya, and of wool for a Vaishya. See Basham, *op. cit.,* p. 162.

53. *Ibid.,* p. 162, gives this translation of the Sanskrit verse.

54. Raj Bali Pandey, *Popular Hinduism at a Glance* (Varanasi, India: Kashi Cultural Publications, 1963), has a good account of the main samskaras as they are observed today in Hinduism.

55. This description of the sandhya ritual was supplied by Pandit Upadhyaya, an orthodox Brahmin who is a professor in the Sanskrit College of Banaras Hindu University.

56. Based on an account of the rite received from Professor Upadhyaya of the Sanskrit College of Banaras Hindu University.

57. Basham, *op. cit.,* pp. 184–186, points out that the *devadasis,* like the hetaerae of ancient Greece, were trained in literature and the arts, as well as in the sphere immediately related to their profession. A Buddhist legend tells us that the Buddha, on his last journey to the hills, stopped at Vaishali. Here he preferred to accept the invitation of the talented prostitute Ambapali rather than attend a civic reception to which he was invited by the city fathers. Ambapali is said to have later become a Buddhist nun.

58. Jagannath is a title of Vishnu and means Lord of the World. Only Hindus, Buddhists, and Jains are permitted to enter this temple.

59. *Visit Orissa, A Hand Book for Tourists* (Bhubaneswar: [Home Public Relations Department], Government of Orissa, 1958), p. 116.

60. For a full account of the Durga Puja at the Belur Math see "The Durga Puja" by Dorothy Mercer in *Vedanta and the West,* No. 148 (Hollywood: Vedanta Society of Southern California, 1961), pp. 34–42.

61. For a description of this festival see R. B. Pandey, *Popular Hinduism at a Glance,* 2nd rev. ed. (Varanasi, India: Kashi Cultural Publications, 1964), pp. 17 f.; also Thomas, *op. cit.,* p. 126.

62. Heinrich Zimmer, *The Art of Indian Asia,* ed. by Joseph Campbell (New York: Pantheon Books, 1955), I, 209 ff.

63. See *Visit Orissa, op. cit.,* for a good account of the temple and the images.

64. T. M. P. Mahadevan, ed., *Outlines of Hinduism,* 2d ed. (Bombay: Chetana, 1960), p. 53.

65. Quoted from the Shiva Purana in *ibid.,* p. 48.

66. Basham, *op. cit.,* p. 298.

67. R. C. Majumdar, ed., *The History and Culture of the Indian People* (Bombay: Bharatiya Vidya Bhavan, 1954), Vol. III, *The Classical Age,* pp. 432 ff. Jainism and Buddhism were dominant in south India when these saints began their work.

68. Basham, *op. cit.,* p. 298.

69. Majumdar, *op. cit.,* p. 332.

70. *Hymns of the Tamil Saivite Saints,* trans. by F. Kingsbury and G. E. Phillips (London and New York: Oxford University Press, 1921), p. 1. Kingsbury writes about the Shaivite songs, but the same would apply to the Vaishnavite.

71. See Chapter 18, on the Sikhs, for further information about these men.

72. See K. M. Sen, *Hinduism* (Baltimore: Penguin, 1961), pp. 103–107, for a good short account of the Baul singers, who, though not nominally Vaishnavite, participate in Vaishnavite festivals.

73. See M. S. Randhawa, *Kangra Paintings of the Gita Govinda* (Honolulu: East-West Center Press, 1963), for an account of this poem and lovely plates of the miniatures inspired by the poem.

74. See F. Otto Schrader, *Introduction to the Pancaratra and the Ahirbudhnya Samhita* (Madras: Adyar Library, 1916), for an account of this literature. See also M. Yamunacharya, "The Vaishnava Scriptures," in T. M. P. Mahadevan, ed., *The Great Scriptures* (Madras: G. S. Press, 1956).

75. Vasudeva was the supreme god of the Bhagavata theistic sect at least as early as the second century B.C.

76. M. Yamunacharya, "The Vaishnava Scriptures," in T. M. P. Mahadevan, ed., *The Great Scriptures* (Madras: G. S. Press, 1956), p. 46.

77. See Mahadevan, *Outlines of Hindu Philosophy*, pp. 167–172, for a good account of this system. See also S. Satchidanandam Pillai, "Shaiva Scriptures," in *ibid., passim*.

78. Mahadevan, *Outlines of Hindu Philosophy*, pp. 171–172.

79. V. Paranjoti, *Saiva Siddhanta*, 2d rev. ed. (London: Luzac, 1954), p. 109.

80. Pillai, *op. cit.*, p. 67.

81. Louis Renou, *The Nature of Hinduism*, trans. by Patrick Evans (New York: Walker, 1962), p. 113.

82. Basham, *op. cit.*, p. 335.

83. The rite of *japa* is the continuous repetition of a mantra or of the name or names of God. It is a common practice in Hinduism to attain nearness to God.

84. Mahadevan, *Outlines of Hinduism*, p. 173.

85. Mahadevan, *Outlines of Hinduism*, pp. 205–206.

86. *The Kularnava Tantra*, trans. by M. P. Pandit (Madras: Ganesh, 1965), pp. 30 f.

87. For a full account of all the significant, symbolic, spiritual meanings assigned the Five M's and the ritual centered on them, see *ibid.*, Chapter IV, "The Five M's and Their Full Significance," pp. 47–54.

88. *Ibid.*, p. 32.

89. For a full description and discussion of this yantra see Sir John Woodroffe, *Tantraraja Tantra* (Madras: Ganesh, 1954).

90. For an account in some length of this form of yoga, see Arthur Avalon (Sir John Woodroffe), *The Serpent Power*, 6th ed. (Madras: Ganesh, 1958).

91. It is difficult to date these philosophers and also Jaimini's Sutras. S. Dasgupta, *A History of Indian Philosophy*, 5 vols. (Cambridge: Cambridge University Press, 1963; 1st ed., 1922), tells us that traditionally Kumarila has been considered an older contemporary of Shankara who perhaps flourished around 788 A.D. Prabhakara was a pupil of Kumarila. See Vol. I, p. 370. Radhakrishnan and Moore, *op. cit.*, p. 486, gives the date of the Sutras as 400 B.C., and the philosophers' dates as the seventh century.

92. Mahadevan, *Outlines of Hinduism*, p. 149.

93. Dhirendra Mohan Datta, *The Philosophy of Mahatma Gandhi* (Madison: University of Wisconsin Press, 1961), pp. 64 f.

94. Ruskin's work *Unto This Last* was another crucial influence on Gandhi. Upon reading this, he says in his *Autobiography*, he realized that a life of labor (farmer, handicraftsman, and the like) is the life worth living. He

realized that this was implied in the principle he had known, viz., that the good of the individual is contained in the good of all (sarvodya). This implication was made clear to him by Ruskin's book.

95. Mohandas K. Gandhi, *An Autobiography*, trans. by Mahadev Desai (Boston: Beacon, 1957), p. 211. Gandhi is quoting a favorite passage from the Bhagavad-Gita.

96. J. Nehru, *Glimpses of World History* (New York: John Day Company, 1942), p. 37.

97. Quoted in Michael Brecher, *Nehru: A Political Biography*, abridged ed. (Boston: Beacon, 1962), p. 232.

98. *Ibid.*, p. 235.

17 The Jains

According to traditional Jain history the first teacher of the Jain religion, Rishabha, lived countless years ago, in the third period of Avasarpini, the half of the world cycle that begins with a best period and ends with a worst period. Unlike the first paradisiacal epoch of the cycle, the third period of Avasarpini saw sorrow and evil beginning to mar happiness. A teacher, called by the Jains a Tirthankara (ford-maker), was therefore needed to cope with these blights on life in the world. In the fourth period evils increased so much more that twenty-three other Tirthankaras were born in order to teach men how to overcome these evils and to attain moksha. The fifth period is the present time and is wholly evil. In this epoch, men live no longer than 125 years. Yet the next, the sixth epoch, will be still worse. Man's life span will be only sixteen to twenty years and his height will be reduced to the size of a dwarf. (Rishabha's height, like that of all men of his era, was two miles.) Disease, natural disasters, and vice will plague him. But then the slow upward movement of the second half of the world cycle, Utsarpini, will begin. There will be steady improvement until, in the sixth era, man's needs will be fulfilled by wishing trees, man's height will be six miles, and evil will be unknown. Then again degeneration will gradually set in during the next five periods, a repetition of Avasarpini; Utsarpini will follow, and the pattern of cycles will be repeated everlastingly. This is not a belief in the creation and destruction of the world at regular intervals, such as one finds in Hinduism. The Jains believe that the world has never had a beginning and will never come to an end. There is no supreme spir-

FIGURE 17.1 The Temple of Vimalasaha at Dilwara. At right is a statue of a Tirthankara. (*Keystone*)

itual being or God; the world process operates in accordance with its own innate laws. While the gods of Hinduism are accepted, they are given a subordinate position. The twenty-four Tirthankaras are the major objects of worship.

The name of the first Tirthankara, Rishabha, means "bull." This animal was revered in the Indus Valley civilization, and it is possible that some aspects of the religion of the Jains may be very old. However, the impossible date of Rishabha's activity—oceans of billions of years ago—and his incredible life span—8,400,000 years—make scholars skeptical of his historicity. The dates of activity and life spans of the other Tirthankaras from the second through the twenty-second, although gradually coming somewhat closer to the realm of possibility, are still too impractical to make their existence plausible. Arishtanemi, the twenty-second Tirthankara, for example, is said to have lived 84,000 years before Mahavira, who lived c. 540–468 B.C. and was the last Tirthankara of this half-cycle of the world. He is supposed to have attained the age of 1,000. The twenty-third Tirthankara, Parshva, is accepted as probably a historical person. He is said to have lived about 200 or 250 years earlier than Mahavira,[1] that is, during the eighth century B.C., and to have died at the age of 100. It is not clear what his teachings were. He founded an order called the Nirgranthas (Free from Bonds), and is usually shown in iconography in meditation posture, with hooded serpents about his head. A legend, similar to one told about the Buddha, narrates that these serpents, befriended by Parshva in a former existence, protected him from a great storm caused by an enemy.[2]

The life, in its main outline as well as the teachings of Mahavira —the twenty-fourth and last Tirthankara of this half-cycle of the world—are fairly well established. He was the son of a Kshatriya who was a chief of the Jnatrikas in a suburb of Vaishali (about twenty-five miles from the present city of Patna). His given name was Vardhamana, but he was later called Mahavira (great hero) because of his spiritual victory in attaining kevala[3] and moksha. He married and had a daughter, but when his parents died he renounced the world. He was then thirty years old. He joined Parshva's Order of Nirgranthas, which wore clothes; but after thirteen months Mahavira adopted nudity and retained this custom for the rest of his life. During the following six years, he traveled about with a fellow ascetic named Gosala, but the two parted over a philosophical dispute. Gosala maintained an absolute determinism in relation to karma and samsara; the individual could not influence his destiny in any way in order to obtain a better rebirth or moksha, but was under the complete control of an impersonal cosmic principle, destiny (Niyati). Mahavira took the opposite position—namely that man was free to overcome karma by his own persistent efforts. This is the general view in Hinduism, too. Gosala, then, separated himself from Mahavira and the Nirgranthas to found the Ajivikas, whose religion survived until the fourteenth century A.D.[4] Mahavira remained with the Nirgranthas and gave new life to this group; he contributed so much that he was regarded almost as the new founder of the religion, soon called the Jainas (or Jains). Mahavira became a *jina* ("conqueror" or "victor") in the thirteenth year of his life of asceticism. His victory was the winning of full enlightenment, called *kevala*. He gathered many followers about him and became a well-known teacher in the kingdoms around the Ganges River. Some of the same kings in the area gave aid to both him and his contemporary, the Buddha. Mahavira died of self-starvation at the age of seventy-two in the small town of Pava near Rajagriha, capital of Magadha.

The Jains began to gain strength during the Mauryan dynasty (c. 322–183 B.C.). It was during this era that the Jain community was divided into the two major sects that prevail today. The occasion of the division was the exodus (because of a famine around 300 B.C.) of many Jain monks from the Ganges to the Deccan, where the faith now spread. The emigrants retained the rule of nudity established by Mahavira; those who remained in the more northerly region disregarded this rule and allowed the wearing of clothes. Thus arose the division into Digambaras (literally "space-clad" or nude) and the Svetambaras ("white-clad"). This is the only fundamental difference between the two sects, and even this difference is now vague because eventually most of the Digambara monks began to wear clothes in public, as they do today, observing nudity only when feasible. Another difference between the two groups is the belief among the Digambaras that women must be reborn as men in order to be candidates for liberation. This is related to observance of nudity; women cannot go about unclothed. The belief that women must be born as men to be eligible for moksha matters little from the practical point of view, because in this era of vice and degeneration in world history, no one can attain enlightenment; the last man who did so was a saint who lived sixty-four years after Mahavira.[5] More minor are such differences as the rule of the

Digambaras that images of Mahavira and the other Tirthankaras must be represented nude, and the denial of Mahavira's ever having married.

Today the Jains number about 2 million souls, most of them prosperous merchants. They are found all over India, but are mainly concentrated in Kathiawar, Gujarat, and Rajasthan, where the Svetambaras are dominant, and in south Hyderabad and Mysore state, where the Digambaras prevail.

SACRED TEXTS OF THE JAINS

The tradition reports that an oral sacred literature, the fourteen Purvas (former texts), was passed down from Mahavira's time, but Bhadrabahu (c. 300 B.C.) was the last to have memorized it. After the death of this venerable elder, a council was called and the texts were reconstructed as well as possible in twelve Angas. These Angas were not accepted by the Digambaras, who declared that the Purvas were hopelessly lost and began to compose new texts. The Svetambaras, some time in the fifth century A.D., called a council at Valabhi to reduce the current oral texts to writing. By this time the texts had become rather corrupt and one of the twelve Angas had been lost completely; new materials were added also—viz., the twelve *Upangas* and other minor texts. Despite the textual difficulties and the late date of the Scriptures as they were finally formulated, they seem to contain the basic teachings of Mahavira and possibly even go back to Mahavira himself.[6] Otherwise it would be difficult to account for the fact that the fundamental teachings found in these Scriptures are accepted by Digambaras and Svetambaras in common.

The eleven Angas are concerned with such matters as rules of ascetic life, heretical views of Hindus and Buddhists, Jain doctrines, didactic tales, ethics for laymen, glorification of asceticism, and death by voluntary starvation.

The twelve Upangas deal with such subjects as Heaven and Hell, proofs of the existence of the soul, and other religiophilosophical beliefs of the Jains; cosmogony, geography, astronomy, and divisions of time are also covered in the Upangas.

During the Middle Ages much commentarial material on the Scriptures was written by the monks. Another form of Jain literature

corresponds to the Hindu Epics and Puranas in function and importance. These works are called Puranas by the Digambaras and
Charitas by the Svetambaras. The best-known work of this type is
Hemachandra's *Trishashti-shalaka-purusha-charita,* a compendium
of the biographies of the Sixty-Three Excellent Men. These Sixty-
Three Excellent Men appear in every half-cycle of the endless
revolutions of the time wheel. They are: twenty-four Tirthankaras,
twelve Chakravartins (universal emperors), and other great leaders,
totaling sixty-three all together. Hemachandra's work has an appendix, which contains numerous tales.[7]

RELIGION AND PHILOSOPHY OF THE JAINS

The entire doctrinal system of the Jains is contained in seven
tattvas (principles). These are *jiva, ajiva, asrava, bandha, samvara,
nirjara,* and *moksha.*[8]

Jiva

Jiva is soul.[9] The permanent, essential nature of soul is pure omniscient consciousness. Lesser kinds of extraordinary knowledge[10]
in the progress toward the pure state are "limited immediate knowledge," that is, knowledge of objects too distant or too small to be
observed by ordinary sense organs; and knowledge of other minds.
The pure state of omniscience, reached when all karma is lost, is
called *kevala.* No one, however, achieves kevala in the current
dark epoch of world history; as mentioned above, the last man to
attain this highest knowledge, which occurs immediately before
moksha, was a man who lived sixty-four years after Mahavira.

Although in the pure state souls are absolutely equal, in their
embodied condition they are graded in accordance with the number
of sense organs that they possess. Lowest in the scale are the non-
moving jivas who have only one sense: that of touch. Jivas in the material elements (earth-bodied, fire-bodied, water-bodied, air-bodied)
and plants occupy this category. The plant-embodied fall into two
classes, the gross and the subtle. Gross plants are those that contain
only one soul; subtle plants are invisible and are called *nigodas.*
A nigoda is composed of an infinite number of souls, which form
a tiny cluster. Vast numbers of these clusters form a globule. The

entire space of the universe is tightly filled with these globules. When a soul is liberated, another takes its place from this infinite supply of nigodas.[11]

The moving jivas of two senses, touch and taste, are creatures such as snails and other mollusks; those of three senses, like ants and leeches, add the sense of smell; those of four senses, such as gnats, bees, mosquitoes, add the sense of sight; those of five senses possess hearing and include birds, men, and other mammals. An "internal organ," mind, is added to the higher animals, men, gods, and those in Hell. These beings alone are called rational.[12]

Ajiva

In the category of ajiva (nonliving nature), matter (*pudgala*) is basic and is like the prakriti of the Sankhya-Yoga, except that it is fundamentally atomic and composed of atoms of fire, water, air, and earth. Atoms of these four elements combine in various ways to form the bodies of jivas and all the objects of nature.

Other nonliving substance categories are *dharma, adharma*, and *akasha*. Just as water is a condition for the swimming about of fish, so dharma is the necessary condition for movement. Adharma is the essential condition of the static, or immobility; it enables an object to come to rest. Outside the enormous universe of the continents, heavens, and hells, dharma and adharma are absent; therefore no being, not even a liberated jiva, can get outside the universe, because the substrata of motion and rest are absent; outside the universe there is only absolute nothingness.

Akasha is space; its function is merely to make room for all objects. Time (*kala*) is mentioned by some authorities as a nonextended substance whose nature is continuous and cyclical.

Moksha (Liberation)

Moksha involves the tattvas (principles) of asrava, bandha, samvara, and nirjara. Bandha (bondage) is caused by an influx of karma into the soul, called *asrava*. Karma is conceived, rather materialistically, as forming a kind of subtle body within the soul. The subtle matter that becomes the karma body (*karmanasharira*) is enabled to enter the soul because of its vices (anger, pride, greed, hypocrisy). These vices are called the *kashayas;* they act like sticky substances that cause the influx of subtle matter to adhere to the soul and form the karma body. Souls take on a definite complexion and related qualities in direct relation to the vices that caused the karma body; this complexion, with its concomitant qualities, is called a *lesya*. Worst of all is the black lesya; a soul of this kind performs deeds of extreme wickedness. The blue and gray lesyas are also bad. Then, in ascending order there are the good lesyas— the fire-coiored, the lotus-colored, and the white, the best. Although invisible, the soul has the color that manifests its moral condition. The karma body fills the soul, migrates with it, and causes its rebirth in a form appropriate to its moral condition, from the lowest to the highest form in the graded embodiments of jivas.

To be a candidate for moksha, one must be born a human being and live the life of a monk or a nun. Initiation into this life of striving for moksha involves pulling out the hair of the monk by the roots (the Buddhists merely shave their hair). The severity of this initiation is a foretaste of further ascetic practices designed to stop further accretion of karma to the soul. This stoppage, called *samvara,* is accomplished by ridding oneself of the kashayas that cause the karma body to form. The soul has the qualities of action and of freedom; both are needed to free itself from the kashayas.

The three main steps in the samvara process are called the Three Jewels (Triratna) of Jainism. The first jewel or step in liberation is faith. The second jewel, right knowledge, can be obtained only by studying the teachings of the omniscient Tirthankaras, masters of liberation, and faith in these teachers is therefore prior to study of their teachings. When the essential knowledge is gained, it must be realized concretely in practice, in action directed outward and inward, in order for the aspirant to rid himself of the kashayas. This is done by observing the third jewel, right conduct, which is control of the thoughts, words, deeds, emotions, and senses in the light of knowledge and which centers upon what are called the Five *Mahavrata* or Great Vows. These are: (1) Ahimsa, noninjury to all forms of life. The theory that there are souls in such substances as air causes the Jain monk to breathe through a piece of cloth in order to prevent injury to the jivas in the air (see Figure 17.2), and to strain drinking water. Jains of lesser virtue (the laity) try not to injure jivas of two or more senses (the moving ones). Ahimsa also involves (2) Truthfulness, the second Great Vow. Idle gossip, malicious, vulgar or frivolous talk, are forbidden. Complete silence for long intervals is a practice recommended for monks. (3) Nonstealing. This means not taking what is not given and affirms, on the positive side, the sanctity of property. The Jains relate this to ahimsa; taking a man's property is an injury to him. (4) Chastity. This is generally interpreted as celibacy (for monks), but the meaning is extended to cover all forms of sensual indulgence. (5) Abstinence from all attachment to sense objects. This includes nonownership of property for monks and limitation of property and possessions for the laity.

Other requirements essential to samvara (stoppage of karma formation) are: (1) Meditation on the Jain truths about the nature of the jiva and the world; the posture for meditation is ordinarily the seated yoga position, but the son of the first Tirthankara, Gomateshvara, is shown in a colossal sculpture in a rigidly upright standing posture, which he is said to have maintained uninterruptedly for a year, oblivious to the vines and insects over his body. (2) Ascetic practices; for example, endurance of long fasts (all Jains are supposed to fast frequently), of extreme temperatures— exposure to the sun in the hot Indian summer, and to the cold of the Indian winter in the north. (3) Internal austerities, such as penance and confession. (4) Attainment of serenity, purity, greedlessness, and perfect conduct.

Such knowledge, practices, and right attitudes prevent the formation of further karma, but it is essential also to rid oneself of the karma already accumulated. This process, called *nirjara,* is effected by the same means as samvara, but heavily emphasizes such ascetic practices as prolonged endurance of hunger, thirst, heat, and cold. It is said that a monk, by four and one-half days of fasting, can annihilate more karma than a jiva in Hell (purgatory) in millions of years.[13] Fasting to death is, in fact, a requirement for moksha. Confession, penance, study of Jain texts, and meditation are very important, too, in ridding oneself of the karma body. When nirjara (wearing away of the karma body) is complete, moksha is attained. Since this path to moksha is very difficult, it is believed that many jivas will never succeed in liberating themselves, but must migrate throughout everlasting time.[14]

Moksha is always preceded by kevala knowledge (omniscience). This is realized in a yoga meditation state, when all but a small residue of karma has been expelled from the soul. The kevala annihilates in a few seconds the residue of karma.[15] Now, freed from the karma body, the soul sheds at the same time its physical body. Then, because it is naturally buoyant, it ascends in a straight

FIGURE 17.2   Jain monks wearing masks. (*Keystone*)

line up to the top of the universe where all the released jivas (called Siddhas) dwell. This umbrella-shaped region shines like white gold in its brilliance. Although the soul in this, its pristine state, is invisible and intangible, it is said to be two-thirds the size of the body it occupied immediately before moksha. Individuality, dependent on the physical and the karma bodies, is lost in this absolute equality of souls. All Siddhas have the identical, purely spiritual quality of omniscient consciousness, a blissful state. All objects of the universe are known in both their abstract-universal and concrete-particular attributes and characteristics. This life of omniscience is the eternal bliss of the Siddhas. The Siddhas are called "jinas" (conquerors or victors) because of their spiritual feat in the conquest of karma.

The victory in Jainism (the religion of conquerors or victors)

is won through self-help and is therefore a heroic feat. No God or Supreme Being of any kind plays a part in the doctrinal system. From this point of view, Jainism is atheistic. The gods of Hinduism are accepted by the Jains, but they are given a subordinate position in rites of worship, for they, too, need liberation, which is attainable only by one who is in the human state. All objects and processes in nature, including the liberation process of jivas, are controlled by laws that are inherent in the cosmos.

Although the road to moksha is for monks and nuns alone, lay members of the community have always been considered members of the order. Jain laymen have always been encouraged to observe periodical retreats, in order to live the monk's life.[16] In addition, they were and still are expected to observe what are called the Five *anuvrata* or Small Vows, as distinguished from the Great Vows (*mahavrata*) of monks and nuns. The anuvrata are the same as the five mahavrata listed above for monks, except that they are adjusted to the laymen's life in the world as a householder. The

close relationship between laymen and monks in fulfilling the ideals of Jain teachings has helped the religion to survive and maintain its identity since the time of Mahavira. Buddhism, on the other hand, which separated monks and laymen more fully, eventually died out in the land of its birth and, in its Mahayana forms, diverged considerably from its original doctrines.

Jain religion places major emphasis on ethics. The strong interest in the major ethical principle of ahimsa (nonviolence or nonkilling) among contemporary Jain leaders is brought out in a recent pamphlet, *Pacifism and Jainism,* published by the Jain Cultural Research Society of Barnaras Hindu University.[17] This pamphlet discusses ahimsa in relation to its use by Gandhi in his program of social reform. The author comments that although the Jains always stood for ahimsa, they nevertheless performed all their social duties, even participating in armed defense; but now that Gandhi has shown the way for implementing the ideal of ahimsa, the Jains are participating in large numbers with great enthusiasm in all the Gandhian nonviolent movements. In this pamphlet there is also a discussion of "nonpossession of property" (emphasized in the fifth of the Great Vows listed above), especially in relation to ahimsa. The author writes that the necessity for observing nonpossession of property, or at least limited possession of property, is urgent at the present time. Greed, he thinks, is at the root of the world crisis. Without control of this vice, world conflicts are bound to increase. The nonviolent way to solve the world's social and economic problems is observance by the Jains and by others of the voluntary vow of nonpossession or limited possession of property.

RITES AND CUSTOMS OF THE JAINS

The Jains observe the Hindu domestic rites of birth, marriage, and death. They follow the caste system of Hinduism, too, in their prohibition of marriage between certain of their groups, despite the fact that the Jains belong almost entirely to the upper classes.

Hindu rites of worship (puja) have also been adopted by the Jains, together with the Hindu gods and goddesses, although these

FIGURE 17.3   Gomateshvara at Shravana Belgola. (*Archaeological Survey of India*)

have been placed in a position much subordinate to the Tirthankaras. Despite the fact that the Tirthankaras in their aloof abode
and released state have no concern for human beings and their
affairs, prayers are offered to them daily by devout Jains.[18] Temple
worship, too, is important. The central idol in the temple is a
Tirthankara. The favorites are the first Tirthankara—Rishabha—
and the last three—Arishtanemi, Parshva, and Mahavira.

There are also a few temples to the other Tirthankaras. As idols,
the Tirthankaras are represented seated in a yoga meditation posture. All are alike except that Parshva has snake hoods over him;
in the Digambara sect the seventh Tirthankara, Suparshva, too, has
a snake-hood cluster, although a smaller one, over his head. The
Digambara idols are nude, but the Svetambara images are clothed
and wear ornaments and crowns. The Tirthankaras, other than
Parshva and Suparshva, can be distinguished only by the emblems
carved on the cushions of their thrones or by their attendant yakshas
and yakshinis. Rishabha's emblem is the bull. Arishtanemi's is the
conch shell, Parshva's is the snake, and Mahavira's is the lion.

Beautiful temples have been built by the Jains for the worship
of the Tirthankaras; most renowned are the lovely marble Dilwara
temples (Mount Abu) of Vimalasaha (see Figure 17.1) and Vastu-
pala. The most famous Jain sculpture, erected in the tenth century,
is the colossal (fifty-seven feet high) nude image of Gomateshvara,[19]
son of the first Tirthankara, Rishabha. This, the largest sculpture
in India and one of the largest in the world, is located at Shravana
Belgola in Mysore state, south India (see Figure 17.3). Every twelve
years there is a great celebration for the bathing of the image with
ghee (clarified butter).

The Jains are proud of their contributions to the public welfare
and culture of their country, India. They have founded such welfare institutions as public dispensaries, public lodgings and board-
ings for the poor and helpless, and schools. Because of strict observance of ahimsa, they could not engage in agriculture (which would
necessitate the killing of creatures in the soil); householders therefore resorted to trade and commerce for a living. In this way the
Jains became, for the most part, a well-to-do merchant class able
to support the welfare institutions mentioned above. Their cultural
contributions have also been numerous not only in religion and
philosophy but in other fields as well. They have established libraries; the big jnanabhandaras (depositories of ancient literature, not
only of Jain but of Buddhist and other valuable non-Jain works)

are storehouses for scholarly research. They have contributed to secular literature, to the poetry and drama of their country, and to art. Altogether they are among the leading contributors to Indian religion, philosophy, literature, and art.

NOTES

1. Walther Schubring, *The Doctrine of the Jainas,* trans. by Wolfgang Beurlen (Delhi, Varanasi, and Patna: Motilal Banarsidass, 1962), pp. 28 ff., gives Parshva's date according to Jain sources as 250 years earlier than Mahavira. A. L. Basham, *The Wonder That Was India* (New York: Grove, 1954), says that Parshva, "some two hundred years" earlier than Mahavira, founded the order of Nirgranthas.
2. Johann Georg Buhler, *The Indian Sect of the Jainas,* 2d ed., trans. and edited with an Outline of Jaina Mythology by James Burgess (Calcutta: Susil Gupta Private Ltd., 1963), pp. 49 ff.
3. *Kevala* is explained below.
4. Basham, *op. cit.,* pp. 294–296. Basham has made the definitive study of the Ajivikas in his *History and Doctrines of the Ajivikas* (London: Luzac, 1951).
5. Hermann Jacobi, *Studies in Jainism,* ed. by Jina Vijaya Muni, No. 1, Part one (Ahmedabad, India: Jaina Sahitya Samsodhaka Karyalay, 1946), p. 36.
6. Basham, *The Wonder That Was India,* p. 290. For a lengthy discussion of the entire canon and process of its formation, see Schubring, *op. cit.,* Chapter III, "The Canon," pp. 73–125.
7. Maurice Winternitz, *The Jainas in the History of Indian Literature,* ed. by Jina Vijaya Muni (Ahmedabad: Jaina Sahitya Samsodhaka Pratisthan, 1946), pp. 12 ff.
8. Amulyachandra C. Sen, *Elements of Jainism* (Calcutta: Indian Publicity Society, 1953), p. 52.
9. Jacobi, *op. cit.,* pp. 53 ff., points out the likeness between the Jain and Sankhya metaphysics in the dualism between soul and matter.
10. Satischandra Chatterjee and Dhirendra Mohan Datta, *An Introduction to Indian Philosophy,* 6th ed. (Calcutta: University of Calcutta, 1960), pp. 76–78.
11. Jacobi, *op. cit.,* p. 23.
12. *Ibid.,* p. 22.
13. Schubring, *op. cit.,* p. 325.
14. Basham, *The Wonder That Was India,* p. 291.
15. Schubring, *op. cit.,* p. 328.
16. In Buddhist countries, too, lay members have lived the monk's life for short intervals. However, such retreats are not ordinarily observed throughout the layman's life in Buddhism as they are, theoretically at least, in Jainism.
17. Pandit Sukhlal Sanghavi, *Pacifism and Jainism.* Bulletin No. 25 (Varanasi, India: Jain Cultural Research Society, 1950).
18. Chatterjee and Datta, *op. cit.,* p. 110.
19. The meaning and significance of the standing yoga posture of Gomateshvara have been explained above, p. 492.

18 The Sikhs

The forerunners of the Sikh religion were two teachers, Ramananda and Kabir. Ramananda, a poet-bhakti, lived in the first half of the fifteenth century and taught in Banaras. His teaching combined Vaishnavism with Muslim theism. In a hymn that was later incorporated into the Granth Sahib (the Sikh bible), he says that God is in the heart and everywhere—all-pervasive. Ramananda abolished caste distinctions by having his followers eat together, a custom still observed by the Sikhs.

Kabir (d. 1518), a disciple of Ramananda, has about 1,000 of his verses included in the Granth Sahib. Kabir, like Ramananda, combined Hindu and Muslim ideas. He taught that all men should worship the one God, who should be called Sat Nam (True Name), True Guru, or Rama. He denied the efficacy for salvation of ritualistic practices such as idol worship and pilgrimages. In his view the way to salvation is bhakti, complete devotion to God. Only by this method is immediate apprehension of God to be won. Kabir took over from Hinduism the belief in karma and rebirth. The sect he founded, the Kabirpanthis, still survives; it now has about 650,000 members.

NANAK

Nanak (1469–1538), founder of the Sikh religion, was born in the village of Talwandi, about thirty miles from Lahore, now in Pakistan. The town, later named Nankana in honor of Nanak, is a

FIGURE 18.1   Reading from the Adi Granth. (*Keystone*)

hallowed Sikh shrine. Nanak's father was the village accountant, an educated man of the Kshatriya varna. Many stories are told of the precocity in religious matters of Nanak as a child. At the age of nine he rejected the ritual of the Sacred Thread; he called it a meaningless practice. When he was fourteen, his parents arranged his marriage, but Nanak took little interest in it, or in any other secular affairs. His pursuits lay in meditation and the search for religious truth. After his marriage he did not change; he still declined to follow any secular occupation, an embarrassing situation for his family. After the birth of his second child, he left his family and his village to take a position as keeper of the storehouse of a Muslim governor (he had already become proficient in Persian, a requirement for his duties), but he soon gave up this work for the life of a religious devotee and teacher. The occasion for his abandonment of all secular life, according to the Sikh accounts, was a crucial experience, a vision of God. One day after his early daily bath, he retired into the forest for meditation. While there he was taken into God's presence and given a cup of nectar. Then God told him to practice repetition of his name, charity, ablutions, worship, and meditation.[1] Nanak replied by singing verses about the nature and glories of God. At the end of the vision God said to Nanak, "Thou art the divine Guru."[2]

Nanak remained in the forest for three days. When he returned, he gave up his position and distributed all that he had among the poor. He associated only with religious men and donned a religious costume. After an entire day of silence he made the famous declaration, "There is no Hindu and no Muslim."[3] By this apparently heretical saying, Nanak only meant to draw the logical conclusion from his faith in the one God that there can properly be only one religion, that in essence all religions are one. He had in mind, of course, the bitter animosity between Hindus and Muslims, which he believed resulted from the irrelevant externals of these religions, not from the eternal truth which he thought they both held in common. He hoped, therefore, that his new religious insight would provide a common ground on which all religions could reconcile their differences and live together in peace.

Nanak then began an extended preaching mission. He is said to have traveled throughout India, and also to have visited Mecca, Medina, and Baghdad. It is reported that there is an inscription commemorating Nanak's visit to the latter in 1521.[4] On a trip to Brindavan, India, Nanak is said to have worn a costume symbolic of his view that his new religion was one acceptable both to Hindus and Muslims; he wore the Hindu dhoti and a saffron jacket with a long, white sheet thrown over both, a Muslim hat, and a necklace of bones. On his forehead he painted an emblem in Hindu fashion. Accompanying Nanak on his travels was his loyal disciple and friend Mardana, who had originally been sent to him as a servant when he held the position of storehouse-keeper for the Muslim governor. Mardana played an Arabian stringed instrument, the rebec, and accompanied Nanak when he sang the hymns he composed. These hymns form the nucleus of the Granth Sahib.

When Nanak returned from Mecca[5] and Baghdad, he changed his pilgrim's garb for worldly dress. This was to illustrate his teaching that he did not want his disciples to abandon the world.[6]

Nanak spent the last years of his life at Kartarpur in the Punjab. By this time he had made many converts, called Sikhs (learners); he was also revered by many Hindus and Muslims.[7] When he felt that he would soon die, he appointed Angad, a disciple, as his successor in the guruship; neither of his own sons, Nanak thought, was capable of filling that office.

As Nanak was dying, there was a dispute between his Muslim and Hindu followers over the disposal of his body; the Hindus wished to cremate him, the Muslims to bury him. Nanak ruled that the Muslims should place flowers on his left, the Hindus on his right. Those whose flowers were found fresh in the morning could dispose of his body. Then the Guru drew a sheet over himself, uttered a prayer to God, and "blended his light with Guru Angad's."[8] All were surprised the next morning to find the flowers on both sides fresh; and when the sheet was lifted, nothing was under it! Both the Sikhs and the Muslims erected monuments in his honor, but these have since been washed away by the Ravi River. (The Sikhs have adopted cremation as the mode of disposal of the dead.)

NANAK'S SUCCESSORS

Guru Angad was leader of the religion from 1539 to 1552. His most noteworthy accomplishment was the beginning of the compilation of the Granth Sahib. Angad wrote down what he had learned from Nanak and added some devotional passages of his own. He also de-

signed a unique script worthy of the sacred character of Guru
Nanak's hymns. The entire Granth Sahib is written in this script,
which is named Gurmukhi (the Guru's tongue); Angad created it by
modifying a Punjabi alphabet.

Angad appointed Amar Das to the guruship. Amar Das was a
good organizer and established a Sikh Church by creating a system of
parishes under lay preachers. He set up an important Sikh center
at Goindwal, on the Beas River in the Punjab, and there installed
a *langar* (free kitchen), an institution that had already been begun
by Nanak, in order to show the equality of men. It is said that
Akbar, the liberal Muslim emperor, had to dine in this community
kitchen where men of all classes ate together as brothers.[9] Amar
Das made another contribution to his religion by instituting new
rituals for marriage and death in place of the Hindu rites; he also
established new Sikh religious festivals in spring and fall, to replace
Hindu celebrations at these times.

Amar Das appointed Ram Das, his son-in-law, to the guruship.
Under Ram Das a piece of land was acquired from Emperor Akbar,
who was noted for his religious tolerance, for the founding of the
temple at Amritsar. Amritsar became the holy city of the Sikhs and
their religious capital.

The guruship now became hereditary. Ram Das designated his
youngest son, Arjan, as his successor because he was the most able.
Arjan completed the Golden Temple at Amritsar and built another
Sikh center at Tarn Taran, fifteen miles from Amritsar. A further
aid to Sikh strength was the inauguration, by this Guru, of a regular
system of tax collection. But Ram Das's most important contribution was the compilation of the Adi Granth (Granth Sahib), the Sikh
Scripture, in 1604. Included in the collection were the materials
gathered by Angad—the hymns of Nanak and some of Angad's
own; the hymns of Gurus after Angad; verses by Hindu bhaktis
(1,000 of Kabir's verses were selected) and of Muslim Sufis (lovers of
God). Emperor Akbar's successors persecuted non-Muslims, including the Sikhs, and when Arjan aided Khusru in his rebellion against
his father, Emperor Jahangir, the latter found the occasion to arrest
the Guru. Arjan was given the choice of accepting Islam or torture
and death. Courageously he chose the latter and was tortured to
death in 1606.[10] Thus Arjan became the first Guru martyr of the
faith. An account given in Max Macauliffe's *The Sikh Religion*
says that Jahangir imposed a heavy fine on Arjan for his participation in the rebellion. When he was unable to pay this, he was put in

prison where he died from the heat and the tortures to which he was subjected.[11]

Before his martyrdom, Arjan foresaw the peril to the Sikhs of persecution by Jahangir and later Muslim rulers. Arjan therefore had his successor son, Hargobind, educated as a soldier. Hargobind engaged in several skirmishes with government troops and found refuge in a retreat in the foothills of the mountains near Rupar. He and the next four Gurus—Har Rai, Har Krishan, Teg Bahadur, and Gobind Singh—were of necessity military leaders. Har Rai and Har Krishan were not particularly noteworthy Gurus.

Teg Bahadur, the ninth Guru, led the Sikhs between 1664 and 1675. He was the youngest son of Hargobind. Teg Bahadur was very active in religious matters and founded many new Sikh centers. The reigning Muslim fanatical emperor, Aurangzeb, began a program to exterminate Hinduism. Teg Bahadur went to the aid of the persecuted Kashmiri Hindus, for which he was publicly beheaded in 1675.

Gobind Singh, only son of Teg Bahadur, became the next Guru and held the office from 1675 to 1708. By this time the Sikhs were trained soldiers, and were feared by the Muslim rulers who sought to exterminate them. Guru Gobind Singh, in preparation for a crisis, organized the Khalsa (Guru's Own). The Khalsa had a dramatic beginning. During a fair at Anandpur in 1699, Gobind stood before an assembly of the Sikhs. Brandishing his sword, he fiercely demanded a head. All were startled, but one man volunteered. He and the Guru went into a tent, a blow was heard, and blood gushed out from under the tent. Appearing again, but this time with a bloody sword, the Guru demanded another head. Most of the Sikhs left, but one volunteered, and the process was repeated until a total of five had gone into the tent, presumably to give their heads to the Guru. Then the Guru opened the tent. Five headless goats were seen; the five men were whole. They were given the title of the Five Beloved Ones and were adorned with splendid robes. Next, all five were baptized by the Guru, and they in turn baptized him. The baptism ceremony was a sprinkling of sweetened water stirred with a dagger over the initiates. After baptism all added the name Singh (lion) to their personal names. All swore always to wear the Five K's: *kes* (long, uncut hair), *kangha* (a comb), *kirpan* (a sword or dagger), *kara* (a steel bracelet), and *kachh* (shorts). In social class one was a Brahmin, one a Kshatriya, and three were Sudras; but now all were equal and able to intermarry freely. While tobacco was forbidden (this prohibition was observed by all Sikhs), hemp (marihuana) was allowed; meat was permissible, so long as the animal was not killed in the Muslim manner. The Gurus' hymns were to be read or sung at regular times daily; public congregational worship, too, was recommended, with men and women worshiping together on an equal basis. Such was the origin of the Khalsa brotherhood. Despite persecution by the Muslims, the brotherhood has survived and is still the major unifying force among Sikhs today.

Guru Gobind Singh's Khalsa was vastly outnumbered by the Muslims who fought against them. The Guru's small sons were put to death, and the Guru himself fled to south India. He was assassinated there, probably by a fanatic who thought his teachings heretical.[12] Before his death he proclaimed that the line of Gurus would stop with himself. Henceforth, he declared, the Adi Granth (Granth Sahib) would be the Guru.

SCRIPTURES OF THE SIKHS

In the Sikh temples, the only object of worship is the Granth Sahib (or Adi Granth: *granth* means "book," and *sahib*, "holy"; *adi* means "first" or "primordial"). Sikhs bow before this sacred book and circumambulate it with the book always on their right side. There are readers whose regular occupation is that of reading it at the main temples. Although Gurmukhi is the script of the entire work, the languages used are Persian, Arabic, Marathi, Multani, and others; there are also numerous dialects among the main language forms. Much of the content is in the Punjabi tongue, but even this is not the Punjabi spoken today.[13] Macauliffe comments that because of the variety of languages involved there is scarcely a single Sikh who can make a correct translation of his sacred writings; neither can most scholars.

The first section of the Granth Sahib is called the Japji. The Sikhs consider it to be the epitome of their teachings. The author, Nanak, probably composed it in his late years.[14] All orthodox Sikhs must memorize the Japji even though it is long (it occupies about twenty-two pages in English translation).[15] This "creed" is repeated daily early in the morning.

After the Japji come the four main books. These are called *ragas* or tunes: the *Srirag, Majh, Gauri,* and *Asa.* Next are twenty-six minor books, which are elaborations on the preceding four books. Each of the four major books (ragas) is arranged in accordance with the thirty-one ragas or tunes to which they are sung, not according to authors. Each Guru has the *nom de plume* of Nanak; therefore, in the Granth each Guru is given a designation called a Mahalla; for instance, Nanak's hymns are assigned to Mahalla I, Angad's to Mahalla II, and so on.[16] Meter, however, is all-important in the arrangement of the materials, and a page may contain three or four hymns on different subjects by different writers; this mars the coherence of the work. However, the Granth does not profess to be a philosophical treatise, but a devotional book similar to the Song of Songs or Psalms of the Old Testament.

There is another Granth that is honored by the Sikhs. This is the Granth of the Tenth Guru, which is almost as long as the Adi Granth. The Granth of the Tenth Guru, although not accepted as genuine Scripture like the Granth Sahib, has had an important influence on the Sikhs and is a respected work.[17] Its purpose is militant. Less than one-tenth of it consists of poems by the tenth Guru; the balance was compiled under his direction from Sanskrit and Persian literature. There are heroic tales about Rama and Krishna and about wars between gods and demons, praises of the exploits of the Hindu goddess Durga, a group of tales about the deceitfulness of women, and a letter in Persian to Aurangzeb. All of this is written in the Gurmukhi script. Macauliffe thinks that the Guru's purpose in collecting these tales was to have them recited on the eve of a battle in order to inspire bravery in the soldiers. The praises of Durga were translated by the Guru himself. He reasoned that if a woman could show such daring and courage, men would be ashamed not to be able to match her bravery.[18]

DOCTRINES OF THE SIKHS

The main religious doctrines of the Sikhs are found in the Japji, the opening portion of the Granth Sahib. The religious philosophy expressed is monotheistic for the most part, yet there are passages that are definitely pantheistic. Nanak declares that there is but one God, called the True Name (Sat Nam) or True One. The True One is immortal, unborn, self-existent, and creator of the universe.

He is omniscient, omnipotent, omnipresent, and infinite. Although he is personal, he is not made in man's image, but is formless. Karma and samsara are taken over from Hinduism; however, God has ultimate control over both. The supreme will of God rules all— which is reminiscent of the supreme will of Allah in the Muslim faith. Nanak says that by God's order some are rewarded, while others "must ever wander in transmigration."[19] God is also full of love and compassion; man is asked to put God's love into his heart. His grace may be freely granted to those who are without virtue in order to change them into virtuous souls. The practice of repeating and hearing the True Name (Sat Nam) brings closeness to, and knowledge of, God. (This practice of uttering the name of God is a favorite device of the bhakti-marga of Hinduism.) Devotion to God must manifest itself in right attitudes and conduct. The virtues of the righteous are contentment, patience, compassion, honesty, and sincerity; they do not commit the vices of stealing, murder, lying, greed, slander, idolatry; their only ritual practice is repetition of the name of the One God. Nanak denounced Hindu ritualistic practices, as well as the view of Hindus and of Muslims that their Scriptures, the Vedas and the Qurān, respectively, were divine revelations. The only truth that is contained in these Scriptures is the reiterated view that the ultimate principle is One. Nanak says in the Japji that the Hindu gods and goddesses, including Shiva, Brahma, and Devi, adore the True One.[20]

As Macauliffe points out, no religious teacher has been successful in logically separating theism from pantheism. The Sikh Gurus, beginning with Nanak, express both monotheistic and pantheistic views of God. Nanak says that God is "contained in everything." Guru Gobind Singh affirms that God and his devotee, although two, are really one, just as bubbles arise in water and merge with it again. (This resembles the Upanishadic and Shankara's Atman-Brahman doctrine.) Men err, Gobind Singh declares, in believing they are separate from God. He teaches that this error is caused by human passion and spiritual ignorance, which are the causes of evil in the world and of the soul's transmigration.[21]

Final salvation, Nanak and the other Gurus teach, is *nirvan* (the same as the Sanskrit *nirvana*). This is absorption in God, a state compared by the Sikhs to water blending with water. Individuality is completely lost in God's being. Nirvan is attained by meditation on God (repetition of God's name is an aid to this) and by following the pattern of conduct advocated by the Gurus as described above.

The life of the householder is preferable to asceticism for salvation. To make this clear, Nanak chose the married Angad as his successor instead of his own celibate son. However, a righteous life without meditation on God results only in another human rebirth after a period in purgatory. The soul will either attain nirvan in this next human rebirth or again have to endure countless numbers of re-births. Evil men must be reborn as lower animals and endure in-numerable kinds of existences until they again have the opportunity of rebirth in the human state for another chance to attain nirvan.[22]

There is also belief in a paradise called Sach Khand, where souls recognize each other and enjoy eternal bliss. Some of the learned Sikhs, who are aware of the discrepancy between nirvan and Sach Khand, teach that nirvan and Sach Khand are "practically the same."[23]

A Sikh belief, similar to the Hindu concept of avatars, is the notion that the Ten Gurus are "revelations of one Light and one Form."[24] In pictures of the Gurus each is represented with a halo of light about his head.

THE SIKHS IN THE CONTEMPORARY WORLD

The Sikhs have contributed much to Indian culture in their re-ligion and ethical ideals, and many of the hymns of the Granth Sahib are poems of high literary merit. The cultural level of the Sikhs is, in general, high. In India literacy among the Sikhs is higher than in any other Indian community except the Parsees and Anglo-Indians.

Sects of the Sikhs

A Sikh encyclopaedia enumerates three main divisions of Sikhs: the Udasis, the Sahajdharis, and the Singhs.[25] All three groups have the same fundamental beliefs: they accept the Granth Sahib as Scripture and acknowledge the same Ten Gurus.

UDASIS. § The Udasis are an order of sadhus (holy men) founded by the older son of Guru Nanak. They are celibate, wear yellow clothes or go about almost nude, carry a gourd begging bowl, and avoid accepting gold or silver. The Udasis have been active missionaries in the spread of the Sikh faith. Although formerly they were unshaven, many today are shaven or have adopted the matted hair of Hindu ascetics. Some follow the Hindu customs of wearing the Sacred Thread, carrying a rosary, and painting an emblem on the forehead.

SAHAJDHARIS. § The Sahajdharis ("slow adopters" or "easy-goers") include several sects. They are shaven like Hindus, and like them often smoke tobacco. They do not observe the new rites and militant teachings of Gobind Singh.

SINGHS. § The Singhs or Keshadharis (hair-wearers) are divided into several subsects including the Nihangs, Nirmalas, and Kukas or Namdhari.[26] All observe the rite of baptism *(pahul)*, as well as the Five K's instituted by Gobind Singh.

The Nihangs are the most militant sect of the Singhs. Their dress, which is blue, is worn with a high blue and yellow turban; they carry martial implements—spears, swords, daggers, and shields. They do not smoke or drink intoxicating beverages, but use bhang (hemp).

The Nirmalas, by contrast, are a contemplative and learned order of celibate ascetics. They are especially learned in the Hindu monistic Vedanta philosophies.[27] The members live in monasteries and emphasize personal purity in their lives. Gobind Singh sent the five founding members of this group to Banaras to study Sanskrit and Hindu philosophical theology.

The Kukas or Namdhari Singhs derive their name of Kukas (crowers) from the piercing shriek they utter when excited. They dress in white and marry, and they oppose asceticism, Hindu idol worship, and other Hindu rites. They differ from most Singhs in that they have a series of their own living gurus. The Nirankaris, another sect, also have a succession of living gurus, and, like the Kukas, oppose Hindu idolatry and rites.

Doctrines and Conduct Contained in the Official Book
of Worship and Discipline of 1950

The official book of worship and discipline disseminated by the Parbandhak Committee of Amritsar in 1950 gives a short summary of Sikh beliefs.[28] These are: (1) Only one Immortal Person is to be worshiped. (2) The Ten Gurus are saviors and "worthy of worship."

They are "revelations of one Light and one Form," a concept that corresponds to that of the avatar of Hinduism. (An inscription on the Golden Temple at Amritsar asserts that Nanak is an incarnation of Rama.)[29] (3) The Granth Sahib and the word of all Ten Gurus must be accepted. (4) There must be no belief in Hindu literature, in the Qurān of Islam, or in the New Testament of Christianity. (5) Caste distinctions must not be observed. (6) Hindu ceremonies and pilgrimages must not be performed.

In matters of conduct, the book of worship and discipline teaches that the Khalsa should not offend those of other faiths. Sikh men and women should permit their hair to grow long; they must not pierce their ears or noses; men should wear the kachh (short drawers) and a turban, in addition to any other clothes they may choose. Opium, liquor, and tobacco are forbidden. Stealing, adultery, gambling, slaying girls, and selling off girls or boys in marriage are also prohibited. There is also a rule against dyeing the beard.

Rituals

BAPTISM.   § Sweetened water, stirred with a dagger, is prepared in an iron bowl; passages from the Granth Sahib are read during the stirring. Then each of the Five Beloved—those chosen to administer this ritual—in turn sprinkles the *amrit* (sweetened water) in the eyes and on the long hair of the candidates. After the sprinkling each candidate drinks of the amrit.[30] Then each candidate is admonished to observe the doctrines and ethical teachings of the Sikh religion. Special mention is made of the sins that the average man is apt to commit: the cutting of long hair, eating meat from an animal killed in the Muslim fashion, adultery, and smoking tobacco.

THE FIVE K'S.   § This rite, instituted by Gobind Singh and already described above, is observed by both men and women. The rite for women is similar to that for men except that women take the name *kaur* (princess) instead of *singh* (lion).

DAILY DEVOTIONS.   § Every Sikh should bathe early in the morning, then repeat God's name devotionally and say the Sikh Prayer. Next, he must read and recite the morning prayers (this includes the memorized Japji mentioned above). At night he worships again, reading the Sohila hymn[31] and again reciting the Sikh Prayer.[32]

The Sohila hymn consists of three hymns of Guru Nanak, one of Ram Das, and one of Arjan. It is filled with ecstatic praise of the One God and of the beatitude of the repose of the soul in Him. The Sikh Prayer praises God and all the Gurus, those who were martyrs for the faith, the Four Takhts, or Thrones, the *gurdwaras* (see below), and glorifies the Khalsa. It is also recited in congregational worship.

RITES OF THE LIFE CYCLE. § Rites of the life cycle in the Sikh religion are much simpler than in Hinduism. This is conspicuously true of the marriage ceremony, where the prohibitive expense of the dowry and elaborate feasting employed in Hinduism has been abolished by the Sikhs. The funeral rites, too, are simple. No loud lamentations are permitted because the soul has gone to bliss. The Psalm of Peace is read to the dying person by a relative or friend. Cremation is the mode of disposal of bodies.

Congregational Worship

Congregational worship is held in temples called *gurdwaras*. The sacred object in the gurdwara is the Granth Sahib, which is always kept in "clean clothes"[33] and under a canopy. Sikhs feel toward the Granth Sahib much as Jews feel toward their holy scroll, the Torah. The Granth Sahib must be covered with a scarf when no one is reading it, and someone must sit before it. The Sikh, upon entering the gurdwara, bows before the book, then salutes the other members with the words, "Wah Guru ji ka Khalsa, Wah Guru ji ki Fateh!" ("The Khalsa are the chosen of God; Victory be to God.")[34] The service begins[35] with the opening of the book; then there is music and a sermon. Next come the Anand ("Song of Joy," a hymn of thanksgiving to God), another prayer, and the reading of a passage from the Granth. The service concludes with *Karah Prasad,* a communion rite. Karah Prasad is a kind of pudding made of flour, sugar, and ghee mixed in equal proportions and prepared in an iron vessel. Some Karah Prasad is given to each member of the congregation, and all eat it together—no caste distinctions are made. Another element of equality in the service is the equal participation

FIGURE 18.2   The Golden Temple of Amritsar. (*Information Service of India*)

of men and women. Also, there are no priests, and even a boy or young girl may lead the worship service.

The Four Thrones of the Sikhs

The Sikhs have four main Takhts (Thrones). The most important one is at Amritsar (the "Mecca" of the Sikhs), where the chief authorities of the religion furnish guidance on matters of ritual and doctrine. There is also one at Keshgarh in Anandpur for the guidance of the Sikhs in the eastern Punjab, one at Patna for the Sikhs of eastern India, and another at Nanded in Hyderabad for the Sikhs of the Deccan.

All Sikhs like to go to the Golden Temple of Amritsar despite the rule against ritualistic pilgrimages. The temple itself, a gem in the center of a lake-like pool of crystal-clear water, is a beautiful domed building whose lower part is made of marble and whose upper part is covered with gold leaf (see Figure 18.2). The interior of the central dome is tooled in fine filigree and enamel work in gold. Sacred texts in golden characters decorate the walls. On the ground floor the central object is the Granth Sahib under a canopy, and musicians alongside it sing the hymns from the holy book. There is no form of worship on the main floor of the Golden Temple other than obeisance to the Granth Sahib and circumambulation around it; also Karah Prasad may be received by those who request it.[36] A hall close by, called the Akal Takht, is used for preaching, committee meetings, and the business of this Throne. In the upper story of the dome there are relays of readers who read the Granth Sahib continuously day and night. In the cupola on the roof there is another reader who is engaged in reading another copy of the Granth Sahib (see Figure 18.1).

In the temple compound is a langar,[37] or free kitchen. This institution, described above, was established to promote equality among the Sikhs and discourage the caste consciousness of their Hindu background. At the big langar close to the Golden Temple, large buckets of lentil soup, chapatis (a form of bread shaped like a pancake and cooked on an enormous griddle), and other simple dishes are prepared by volunteers, both male and female, for the crowds of men and women of all classes who eat there together and thus participate in an essential rite in the interest of social equality. Around the temple building one sees well-dressed Sikh ladies sweeping (a job usually reserved in India for outcastes) and Sikh men of all classes carrying bricks and doing other work ordinarily assigned to the lower social ranks. Such volunteer work is done in the interest of human equality. Outside of temple worship, however, it is said that many Sikhs, like the Hindus and the rest of mankind, observe social distinctions. A contemporary Sikh writer tells us that the " 'caste system' current today divides the Sikhs into three: agriculturists (Jats), non-agriculturists and Harijans."[38] He adds that among the upper castes (jatis) distinctions are observed only in arranging marriages. The Harijans (outcaste groups), he says, have equality in the gurdwaras, but "still suffer from discrimination" in the villages.

There are Sikh temple compounds (gurdwaras) all over India and throughout the world; they are found in Malaya, Thailand, Singapore, Indonesia, Afghanistan, Iran, Great Britain, Canada, and the United States (in Stockton, California).

NOTES

1. Max Arthur Macauliffe, *The Sikh Religion,* 6 vols. (Oxford: Clarendon Press, 1909; republished, New Delhi: S. Chand and Co., 1963), I, 34.
2. *Ibid.,* p. 35.
3. *Ibid.,* p. 37.
4. C. H. Loehlin, *The Sikhs and Their Scriptures,* 2d ed. (Lucknow: Lucknow Publishing House, 1964), p. 4, note.
5. Macauliffe, *op. cit.,* pp. 175–179, has a description of the visit to Mecca. Macauliffe's life of Nanak is based on an account by a Sikh author who wrote in 1588.
6. *Ibid.,* p. 180.
7. *Ibid.,* p. 188.
8. *Ibid.,* p. 190.
9. Loehlin, *op. cit.,* p. 5. However, Macauliffe's account, *op. cit.,* II, 97, says merely that Akbar had to partake of this Guru's food before seeing him. Akbar asked for the food, and some coarse, unseasoned rice was brought to him, which he ate. It is not said that he dined with a heterogeneous social group.
10. Loehlin, *op. cit.,* p. 6.
11. Macauliffe, *op. cit.,* III, 100, note 1. This account is the statement, Macauliffe says, of the author of the *Dabistan-i-Mazahib.*
12. *Ibid.,* V, 241.
13. *Ibid.,* I, Preface, vi.
14. *Ibid.,* p. 195, note 1.
15. For a translation in English see Khushwant Singh, *The Sikhs Today,* rev. ed. (Bombay, Calcutta, Madras, and New Delhi: Orient Longmans, 1964), Appendix III, pp. 112–133. Also see Macauliffe, *op. cit.,* I, 195–217, for a very good English translation.
16. Macauliffe, *op. cit.,* I, Introduction, li.
17. Loehlin, *op. cit.,* p. 37.
18. Macauliffe, *op. cit.,* V, 83.
19. *Ibid.,* I, 196 (in Macauliffe's translation of the Japji).
20. *Ibid.,* pp. 207 ff.
21. *Ibid.,* Introduction, p. lxiii.
22. *Ibid.*
23. *Ibid.,* p. lxv.
24. Loehlin, *op. cit.,* p. 42, includes this in a summary of the statements in the official book of worship and discipline issued by the authorities at Amritsar in 1950. It is interesting to note that the Shiite Muslim's belief about the Imams succeeding Ali is similar to the Sikh's concept of the Gurus succeeding Nanak.
25. *Ibid.,* p. 67. Loehlin mentions Kahn Singh's *Encyclopaedia* as his authority.

26. *Ibid.*, p. 67.
27. *Ibid.*, p. 69.
28. *Ibid.*, pp. 42 ff.
29. John Clark Archer, *Faiths Men Live By*, rev. by Carl E. Purinton (New York: Ronald, 1958), p. 341. Khushwant Singh, *op. cit.*, p. 20, denies avatar status for the gurus.
30. *Amrit* means "immortality" and is borrowed from the Sanskrit word *amrita* (immortality).
31. Macauliffe, *op. cit.*, I, 258–260, has a good translation of the Sohila.
32. Loehlin, *op. cit.*, p. 39.
33. Teja Singh, *Sikhism,* rev. ed. (Bombay: Orient Longmans, 1951), p. 101.
34. *Ibid.*, p. 102.
35. *Ibid.*, pp. 102 ff., gives a brief account of the congregational worship service.
36. Loehlin, *op. cit.*, p. 73.
37. See Parkash Singh, *The Sikh Gurus and the Temple of Bread* (Amritsar: Dharam Prachar Committee, 1964), for a full account of this important institution of the langar and how it is implemented at the Golden Temple of Amritsar.
38. Khushwant Singh, *op. cit.*, p. 24.

Bibliography

HINDUISM

Agrawala, V. S. *Siva Mahadeva*. Varanasi, India: Prithivi Prakashan, 1966.

*Archer, William George. *The Loves of Krishna*. New York: Grove, 1958.

Atharva Veda Samhita, 2 vols., trans. with commentary by William Dwight Whitney. Varanasi, India: Motilal Banarsidass, 1962.

Aurobindo. *Essays on the Gita*. Sri Aurobindo Library. Calcutta: Arya Publishing House, 1950.

————. *The Life Divine*, 3d ed., 2 vols. Calcutta: Arya Publishing House, 1947.

————. *The Synthesis of Yoga*. Madras: Sri Aurobindo Library, 1948.

*Bary, William Theodore de, *et al.* *Sources of the Indian Tradition*, 2 vols. New York: Columbia University Press, 1958.

*Basham, A. L. *The Wonder That Was India*. New York: Grove, 1954.

*Beals, Alan R. *Gopalpur: A South Indian Village*. New York: Holt, Rinehart, and Winston, 1962.

The Bhagavad Gita, trans. and interpreted by Franklin Edgerton. Vols. 38 and 39 of Harvard Oriental Series. Cambridge: Harvard University Press, 1952.

The Bhagavad Gita, trans. by Franklin Edgerton. New York: Harper and Row, 1965. One volume, translation only, of the edition mentioned above.

*Bhandarkar, Ramkrishna Gopal. *Vaisnavism, Saivism and Minor Religious Systems*. Varanasi, India: Indological Book House, 1965.

*Brecher, Michael. *Nehru: A Political Biography*, abridged ed. Boston: Beacon, 1962.

*Brown, W. Norman. "Mythology of India," in Samuel Noah Kramer, ed. *Mythologies of the Ancient World*. Garden City, N.Y.: Doubleday Anchor, 1961.

* Indicates paperback

Coomaraswamy, Ananda. *The Dance of Shiva*. Bombay: Asia Publishing House, 1948.

Danielou, Alain. *Hindu Polytheism*. London: Routledge and Kegan Paul, 1964.

*Dasgupta, Surendranath. *Hindu Mysticism*. New York: Frederick Ungar, 1927; reprint 1959.

*———. *Indian Idealism*. Cambridge: Cambridge University Press, 1962.

———. *A History of Indian Philosophy*, 5 vols. Cambridge: Cambridge University Press, 1963.

*Datta, Dhirendra Mohan. *The Philosophy of Mahatma Gandhi*. Madison: University of Wisconsin Press, 1961.

The Devi-Mahatmyam, trans. by Swami Jagadisvarananda. Madras: Sri Ramakrishna Math, 1955.

Dowson, John. *A Classical Dictionary of Hindu Mythology and Religion, Geography, History and Literature*, 10th ed. London: Routledge and Kegan Paul, 1961.

Eliade, Mircea. *Yoga, Immortality, and Freedom*. New York: Pantheon, 1948.

Eliot, Sir Charles. *Hinduism and Buddhism*, 3 vols. London: 1921; New York: Barnes and Noble, 1954.

Embree, Ainslie T., ed. *The Hindu Tradition*. New York: Modern Library. 1966.

Filliozat, Jean. *India: The Country and Its Traditions*, trans. by Margaret Ledesert. Toronto: George G. Harrap, 1962.

*Gandhi, Mohandas K. *An Autobiography*, trans. by Mahadev Desai. Boston: Beacon, 1957.

Goswami, Mahamahopadhyaya Bhagabat Kumar. *The Bhakti Cult in Ancient India*. Varanasi, India: Chowkhamba Sanskrit Series Office, 1924; reprint 1965.

Hiriyanna, M. *The Essentials of Indian Philosophy*. London: Allen and Unwin, 1949; fourth impression 1959.

Hooper, J. S. M. *Hymns of the Alvars*. Calcutta: Association Press, 1929.

Hopkins, E. Washburn. *The Great Epic of India*. New Haven: Yale University Press, 1913.

Hymns of the Rig Veda, 4th ed., 2 vols., trans. with commentary by Ralph T. H. Griffith. Varanasi, India: Chowkhamba Sanskrit Series Office, 1963.

Hymns of the Sama Veda, 4th ed., trans. with commentary by Ralph T. H. Griffith. Varanasi, India: Chowkhamba Sanskrit Series Office, 1963.

Hymns of the Tamil Saivite Saints, trans. by F. Kingsbury and G. E. Phillips. London: Oxford University Press, 1921.

Isherwood, Christopher. *Ramakrishna and His Disciples*. New York: Simon and Schuster,, 1965.

Jayadeva. *Gita Govinda,* trans. by George Keyt. Bombay: Kutub, 1947.

Keith, Arthur Berriedale. *The Religion and Philosophy of the Veda and Upanishads*. Harvard Oriental Series, Vols. 31, 32. Cambridge: Harvard University Press, 1925.

Lin Yutang, ed. *The Wisdom of China and India*. New York: Modern Library, 1955.

*Macnicol, Nicol. *The Living Religions of the Indian People,* 2d ed., rev. by M. H. Harrison. New Delhi: YMCA Publishing House, 1964.

Mahabharata, 2d ed., 12 vols., trans. into English from the Sanskrit by Pratap Chandra Roy. Calcutta: Oriental Publishing Co., 1962.

Mahadevan, T. M. P., ed. *The Great Scriptures*. Madras: G. S. Press, 1956.

————. *Outlines of Hinduism,* 2d ed. Bombay: Chetana, 1960.

Majumdar, R. C., ed. *The History and Culture of the Indian People,* 6 vols. Vol. II, *The Classical Age;* Vol. IV, *The Age of Imperial Kanauj*. Bombay: Bharatiya Vidya Bhavan, 1954, 1955.

Morgan, Kenneth W., ed. *Religion of the Hindus*. New York: Ronald, 1953.

Narain, A. K. *The Indo-Greeks*. Oxford: Clarendon Press, 1957; reprint 1962.

Naravane, V. S. *Modern Indian Thought*. New York: Asia Publishing House, 1964.

Paranjoti, V. *Saiva Siddhanta,* 2d rev. ed. London: Luzac, 1954.

*Piggott, Stuart. *Prehistoric India to 1000 B.C.* Baltimore: Penguin, 1952.

Radhakrishnan, Sarvepalli. *Indian Philosophy,* 2 vols. New York: Macmillan, 1923–1927.

*————. *Eastern Religions and Western Thought,* 2d ed. New York: Galaxy, 1959.

———— and Moore, Charles A. *A Source Book in Indian Philosophy*. Princeton: Princeton University Press, 1957.

———— and Muirhead, J. H., eds. *Contemporary Indian Philosophy,* rev. ed. London: Allen and Unwin, 1952.

———— et al., eds. *History of Philosophy, Eastern and Western,* 2 vols. London: Allen and Unwin, 1952.

Ramakrishna Monastic Order. *Life of Sri Ramakrishna Compiled from Various Authentic Sources* (a collective work by members of the Ramakrishna Monastic Order). Almora: Advaita Ashrama, Mayavati, 1925; 2d rev. ed., 1928.

Ramanujacarya (Ramanuja). *Vedarthasamgraha,* trans. by S. S. Raghavachar. Mysore: Sri Ramakrishna Ashrama, 1956.

————. *Ramanuja's Vedarthasamgraha*. Introduction, critical ed., and annotated trans. by J. A. B. Van Buitenen. Poona, India: Deccan College Postgraduate and Research Institute, 1956.

Randhawa, M. S. *Kangra Paintings of the Bhagavata Purana.* New Delhi: National Museum, 1960.

———. *Kangra Paintings of the Gita Govinda.* Honolulu: East-West Center Press, 1963.

Renou, Louis. *The Religions of Ancient India.* London: Athlone, 1953.

———. *The Nature of Hinduism,* trans. by Patrick Evans. New York: Walker, 1962.

——— and Filliozat, Jean. *Classical India,* Vol. III: *Vedic India,* trans. by Philip Spratt. Calcutta: Susil Gupta Private Ltd., 1957.

Rolland, Romain. *Prophets of the New India.* New York: Albert and Charles Boni, 1930.

Sacred Books of the East, ed. by F. Max Müller, 50 vols. Varanasi, India: Motilal Banarsidass, 1963. The titles indicated as paperbound are available from Dover Publications, Inc., 180 Varick Street, New York, N.Y. More of these titles will soon be published.

*Vols. I, XV. *The Upanishads,* trans. by F. Max Müller.

Vols. XXXII, XLVI. *Vedic Hymns,* trans. by F. Max Müller and H. Oldenberg.

Vol. XLII. *Hymns of the Atharva Veda,* trans. by Maurice Bloomfield.

Vols. XII, XXVII, XLI, XLIII, XLIV, *The Satapatha Brahmana,* trans. by Julius Eggeling.

*Vol. XXV. *The Laws of Manu,* trans. by Georg Buhler.

Vols. XXIX, XXX. *The Grhya Sutras,* trans. by H. Oldenberg.

Vol. VIII. *The Bhagavad Gita,* trans. by K. T. Telang.

*Vols. XXXIV, XXXVIII. *The Vedanta Sutras with Commentary of Sankaracarya,* trans. by George Thibaut.

Vol. XLVIII. *The Vedanta Sutras with the Commentary of Ramanujacarya,* trans. by George Thibaut.

Schrader, F. Otto. *Introduction to the Pancaratra and the Ahirbudhnya Samhita.* Madras: Adyar Library, 1916.

*Sen, K. M. *Hinduism.* Baltimore: Penguin, 1961.

Sircar, D. C. *The Sakta Pithas.* Varanasi, India: Motilal Banarsidass, 1948.

Siva-Nana-Bodham: A Manual of Saiva Religious Doctrine, trans. from the Tamil with synopsis, exposition, etc. by Gordon Matthews. Oxford: Oxford University Press, 1948.

Spear, Percival. *India: A Modern History.* Ann Arbor: University of Michigan Press, 1961.

Tagore, Rabindranath. *Sadhana; the Realisation of Life.* New York: Macmillan, 1913.

*———. *The Religion of Man.* Boston: Beacon, 1961.

The Thirteen Principal Upanishads, introduction and trans. by Robert Ernest Hume, 2d rev. ed. London: Oxford University Press, 1931.

Thomas, P. *Hindu Religion, Customs and Manners,* 4th rev. ed. Bombay: D. B. Taraporevala Sons and Co. Private Ltd., 1960.

————. *Epics, Myths and Legends of India.* Bombay: D. B. Taraporevala Sons and Co. Private Ltd., 1961.

Tripathi, Rama Shankar. *History of Ancient India.* Varanasi, India: Motilal Banarsidass, 1942.

The Upanishads, 4 vols., trans. and ed. by Swami Nikhilananda. New York: Harper and Row, 1949–1959.

The Vishnu Purana, 3d ed., trans. and commentary by H. H. Wilson. Calcutta: Punthi Pustak, 1961.

Vivekananda. *The Complete Works of Swami Vivekananda,* 7 vols., 6th ed. Almora: Advaita Ashrama, Mayavati, 1940–1946.

————. *Raja Yoga.* Almora: Advaita Ashrama, 1947.

*Wallbank, T. Walter. *A Short History of India and Pakistan.* New York: Mentor, 1958.

Wheeler, Sir Mortimer. *The Indus Civilization,* 2d ed. Cambridge: Cambridge University Press, 1960.

Whitehead, Bishop Henry. *The Village Gods of South India.* New York: Oxford University Press, 1916.

*Winternitz, Maurice. *A History of Indian Literature,* 2 vols., 3d ed., trans. by Mrs. S. Ketkar. Calcutta: University of Calcutta, 1962.

Woodroffe, Sir John. *Tantraraja Tantra.* Madras: Ganesh, 1954.

————. *Introduction to Tantra Shastra,* 3d ed. Madras: Ganesh, 1956.

———— (Arthur Avalon). *The Serpent Power,* 6th ed. Madras: Ganesh, 1958.

————. *Shakti and Shakta,* 5th ed. Madras: Ganesh, 1959.

*Zaehner, R. C. *Hinduism.* New York: Galaxy, 1966.

*Zimmer, Heinrich. *Myths and Symbols in Indian Art and Civilization,* ed. by Joseph Campbell. New York: Harper Torchbooks, 1962.

————. *The Art of Indian Asia,* 2 vols., completed and ed. by Joseph Campbell. New York: Pantheon, 1955.

*————. *Philosophies of India,* ed. by Joseph Campbell. New York: Meridian, 1956.

JAINISM

Buhler, Johann Georg. *The Indian Sect of the Jainas,* 2d. ed., trans. by James Burgess. Calcutta: Susil Gupta Private Ltd., 1963.

*Chand, Bool. *Lord Mahavira.* Varanasi, India: Jain Cultural Research Society, 1948.

*Jacobi, Hermann. *Studies in Jainism,* ed. by Jina Vijaya Muni, No. 1,

Part One. Ahmedabad, India: Jaina Sahitya Samsodhaka Karyalay, 1946.

The Jaina Sutras, trans. by Hermann Jacobi with critical introduction and notes. *Sacred Books of the East,* Vols. XXII and XLV. Varanasi, India: Motilal Banarsidass, 1963.

Jaini, J. *Outlines of Jainism.* Cambridge: Cambridge University Press, 1916.

Mehta, Mohan Lal. *Outlines of Jaina Philosophy.* Bangalore: Jain Mission Society, 1954.

Sanghavi, Pandit Sukhlal. *Pacifism and Jainism.* Bulletin No. 25. Varanasi, India: Jain Cultural Research Society, 1950.

Schubring, Walther. *The Doctrine of the Jainas,* trans. by Wolfgang Beurlen. Varanasi, India: Motilal Banarsidass, 1962.

*Sen, A. C. *Elements of Jainism.* Calcutta: Indian Publicity Society, 1953.

Stevenson, Mrs. Sinclair. *The Heart of Jainism.* London: Oxford University Press, 1915.

Williams, R. *Jaina Yoga.* London, New York: Oxford University Press, 1963.

*Winternitz, Maurice. *The Jainas in the History of Indian Literature,* ed. by Jina Vijuya Muni. Ahmedabad: Jaina Sahitya Samsodhaka Pratisthan, 1946.

THE SIKHS

Archer, John Clark. *The Sikhs.* Princeton: Princeton University Press, 1946.

Loehlin, C. H. *The Sikhs and Their Scriptures,* 2d ed. Lucknow: Lucknow Publishing House, 1964.

Macauliffe, M. A. *The Sikh Religion,* 6 vols. New Delhi: S. Chand and Co., 1963.

Singh, Khushwant. *A History of the Sikhs,* 2 vols. Princeton: Princeton University Press, 1963–1966.

*———. *The Sikhs Today,* rev. ed. Bombay, Calcutta, Madras, and New Delhi: Orient Longmans, 1964.

Singh, Parkash. *The Sikh Gurus and the Temple of Bread.* Amritsar: Dharam Prachar Committee, 1964.

Singh, Teja. *Sikhism: Its Ideals and Institutions,* rev. ed. Bombay: Orient Longmans, 1951.

PART V RELIGIONS OF EAST ASIA

East Asia can be designated in three ways: geographically, referring to the region east of the Himalayas; ethnologically, referring to the area populated mainly by the Mongoloids; and culturally, referring to the area under the influence of Chinese civilization. China, Mongolia, Korea, and Japan are the countries that make up East Asia. This region has traditionally been called the Far East, which implies an attitude of Europe-centeredness. In order to avoid this implication, the term East Asia is preferred. The East Asian countries with which we are primarily concerned are China and Japan.

CHINA

China is bordered by Korea and the Pacific Ocean on the east, the Himalayas on the west, Mongolia and Siberia on the north, and Burma, Laos, Vietnam, and Thailand on the south. Two mountain ranges—one stretching from southwest to northwest and the other extending from south to northeast—are intersected by three parallel mountain chains reaching from the west to the east coast. Between these mountain ranges lie the plains where the population centers are located. The rivers of China have their sources in central Asia and flow eastward to the coast. The Yellow River, which is 2,700 miles long, is not navigable; at times it changes its bed in certain sections as it enters the north China plain, and this has been a perennial cause of flooding in Chinese history. The Yangtze River, which is 3,200 miles long, is navigable and flows across western, central, and eastern China, where much of the Chinese rice grows. The West River flows in south China, and most of its fertile soil produces two crops a year.

The economy of China is primarily agricultural. Four-fifths of the Chinese are farmers and live from the soil. Since farmers traditionally depend upon the forces of nature, the Chinese, from the beginning of their history, have given much attention to these forces. (It is not surprising that the revisions of the lunar calendar were a major concern of Chinese rulers, who wanted a calendar that could provide a better guide for agricultural activities.) Out of this dependence upon the forces of nature came some of the germinal ideas of the Chinese religions and cosmology, such as the viewing of earth as a fertility deity to whom sacrifices must be offered. A chief attribute of the Ruler-Above (Shang Ti), the ancestor deity, is the power to assure good crops. A persisting cosmological notion is that agriculture and human affairs depend upon the harmony of natural forces (heaven, earth, and man) or the interplay between the passive (Yin) and active (Yang) forces of the cosmos.

Since Chinese civilization arose in the Yellow River Valley, water control for the benefit of farming has been a major task of the government from early times. In order to prevent flooding, the state had to conscript the masses by means of coercion, to work on drainage and irrigation. Various bureaus were established to organize the people to perform prescribed labors. The origin of bureaucratic government in China may be traced to the practice of irrigation in ancient China. Moreover, the cosmic order is a reflection of the imperial order in that the hierarchical nature of the Chinese government also influenced the religion of the masses, which views gods as officials who perform specific duties and who are related to each other in terms of a hierarchy.

The Formation of Chinese Civilization (c. 1994–221 B.C.)

The traditional history of China began at the turn of the second millennium B.C. During the first several centuries the center of China was in the present province of Shansi, and the country was composed of a group of city-states. Although tradition has called this period the Hsia dynasty (c. 1994–1751 B.C.), archaeological evidence has yet to be discovered to support the historicity of this dynasty. During this period bronze weapons and written symbols were in use, agriculture and the cultivation of silk worms were adopted, and the initial phases of civilization began.

The actual history of China, based on archaeological findings, began with the Shang dynasty (c. 1751–1112 B.C.). At that time, the house of Shang was dominant over the other city-states. The cult of the royal ancestor was practiced, and the succession of Shang kings followed either from father to son or from elder brother to younger brother. During this period, a priestly-made lunar calendar was adopted for use in agriculture and religion, the basic structure of the ideographic script was introduced, the best Chinese bronze vessels were made, and the two-wheeled chariot was introduced. By the end of the Shang dynasty, Chinese civilization was dominant in most of the area that is present-day China.

The long Chou dynasty (c. 1111–221 B.C.) saw the rise, growth, and decline of feudalism. It also witnessed the laying of the philosophical foundation of Chinese civilization. The founders of the house of Chou introduced the concept of the virtuous king, who makes the welfare of his subjects his chief duty. In the Early Chou (c. 1111–722 B.C.) the kings parceled out fiefs to their relatives and subordinates, and as a result, feudal lords arose whose lands were passed on to their descendants.

In the Middle Chou (722–481 B.C.) the lords became semi-independent rulers who gave only nominal allegiance to the house of Chou. The first Chinese literary works, *Shih Ching (Book of Songs)* and *Shu Ching (Book of History)* were products of the Middle Chou; these books are the earliest records of Chinese religious beliefs and ethical ideas.

Toward the end of the Middle Chou period, when the Chou dynasty was declining, Confucius lived and taught, and feudalism was breaking down. By that time, the practice of giving out fiefs had been discontinued. States were becoming semi-independent, and were vying with one another for power. Kings of the Chou house continued to exist, although without actual power; they were able to survive chiefly because no state was strong enough to unite the country. The main interest of the rulers of states was to build military power and acquire wealth. In order to achieve these goals, they were eager to employ able men for office. Scholars traveled from one state to another seeking opportunities for political appointment. Confucius was one of them, although his philosophy was unacceptable to the existing rulers.

One evidence of the decline of feudalism was the rise of ministers who were not of noble descent. These men rose to power by ability and shrewdness, and then became the actual leaders of several states.

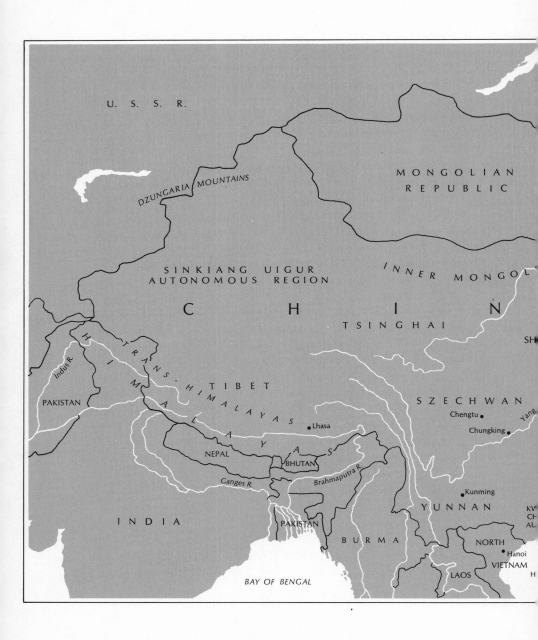

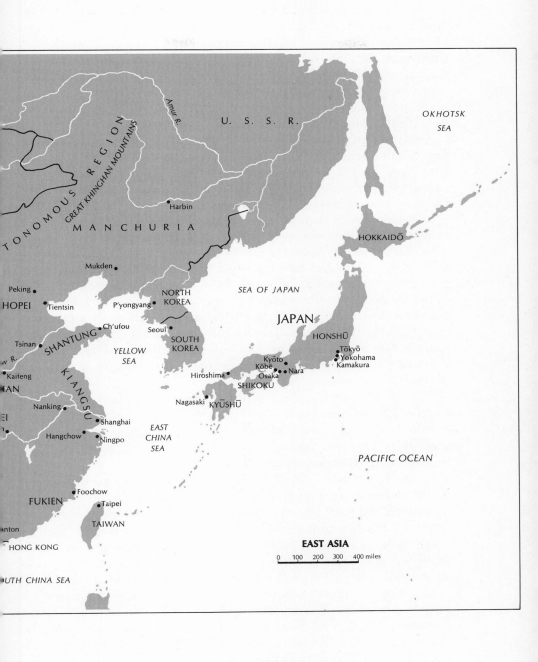

EAST ASIA

0   100   200   300   400 miles

Their children continued to hold important offices, and powerful families arose from this group. Their households rivaled the courts of nobles; they even employed officials and retainers. State policies were often decided in those households, rather than at the courts of the princes. Within each of these families there was a struggle between relatives for important offices. During the time of Confucius his home state was actually under the control of one of these families: its arrogance and greed were a constant target of his criticisms.

Another sign of the collapse of feudalism was the increasing numbers of poor aristocrats who were descendants of nobles. These men, who were skilled in reading and writing, did not own fiefs, but neither were they peasants. In order to earn a living, they trained themselves as experts in ceremony and ritual, and because of their proficiency in such matters, many of them became retainers of nobles or ministers of state and they assisted in sacrifices. They soon became a mediating group between the aristocrats and the commoners: as descendants of nobles, they respected the feudal tradition, but being poor, they understood the needs of commoners. These men were called by their contemporaries *ju* (weaklings). This derogatory term may have had to do with their involvement in ceremony and ritual. After Confucius' death, his followers were called ju, probably because he was a member of ju. As Confucians filled important posts in states and became increasingly influential, the derogatory meaning of the word *ju* was dropped.

The age of Confucius thus witnessed the disintegration of a feudal society. The humanitarian tradition of the Early Chou was no longer followed, and old moral concepts came to be badly in need of clarification. It fell upon Confucius to revive the early tradition of Chou by redefining its ideas and beliefs.

In the Late Chou (481–221 B.C.)—the greater part of this period is also known as the period of the Warring States (403–221 B.C.)—the domains of the lords became independent states competing with each other for the hegemony of China. Kings began to employ men of talent rather than their relatives for high posts and qualified commoners thus became eligible for governmental service, thereby causing the distinction between aristocrats and commoners to diminish. Many original thinkers arose who founded major philosophical schools, as well as Taoism, and who produced the most important Chinese classics. This final stage of the Chou, together with the Ch'in period (221–206 B.C.), was the most productive time in traditional China and is comparable to the Golden Age in Greece.

The Consolidation of Chinese Civilization (221 B.C–A.D. 220)

After long years of division China was reunited by Shih Huang Ti, the first emperor, who founded the Ch'in dynasty (221–206 B.C.) by organizing the country into thirty-six military districts under a central government. For the first time in Chinese history, the government had direct control over the local districts through military forces and could apply the same laws to all people. Among the legacies of the Ch'in dynasty were certain legalist features of bureaucratic administration, the standardization of the Chinese script, the standardization of weights and measures, and the Great Wall, which is some 1,400 miles long and was built for protection against the northern nomads. They were called the Hsiung-nu, which is the Chinese equivalent of Hun.

But the Ch'in dynasty came to an abrupt end in 206 B.C. Its harsh and regimental method of governing from the start did not gain the support of the Confucian leaders, who preferred a government of benevolent rulers to that of law. The Ch'in rulers' large-scale building programs—irrigation systems, palaces, roads, and the Great Wall —depleted the strength of the masses, and the hearts of the masses then deserted the state. Hence, both the Confucian elites and the peasants desired a change of government. It is no surprise that the Ch'in dynasty collapsed so suddenly and that it was followed by the Han dynasty (206 B.C.–A.D. 220) which was founded by a peasant.

During the Han period the national boundary was extended to include Korea in the northeast, Sinkiang in the northwest, and Tonkin-Annam (North and South Vietnam) in the southwest. Emperor Wu Ti (140–87 B.C.) also maintained the "silk routes" between central Asia and China, by means of which some goods were exchanged between the Roman and the Chinese empires. Confucianism and bureaucracy were wedded under Wu Ti, who sponsored Confucianism as a state teaching and at the same time introduced civil service examinations as a means for recruiting able scholars for high posts. In the first century A.D., Confucianism became a state cult; Confucian temples were built in cities and towns, where officials periodically offered sacrifices to the sage. Both the civil service examinations and the Confucian cult continued in China until the turn of the present century; the cult of Confucius was still being practiced even after the fall of the monarchy in 1912. The lasting influence of the Han period can be seen in the fact that the Chinese today still call themselves the people of Han.

Many new books, which ascribed their authorship to Confucius, appeared in the Han dynasty. These writings defended the absolute right of kingship and exalted the virtue of obedience to the emperor. During this period the character of Confucianism underwent a change: early Confucian thought had considered man himself as the source of morality; now morality was viewed as being cosmically centered and thus arose Confucian metaphysics, which emphasizes the complementary relation between nature and man.

The Han dynasty was interrupted by a brief reign (A.D. 9–23) of a usurper, who made an attempt to establish a socialistic state; land was nationalized and distributed equally among the people. But his reign collapsed abruptly, as a result of strong opposition of the laissez-faire Confucians.

The Era of Buddhist Influence (A.D. 220–1279)

Following the collapse of the Han dynasty, China was again divided, at first between three kingdoms and later among several states. Both the north and south underwent a series of dynastic changes. In the north several groups of nomadic barbarians, all of whom eventually became Chinese, succeeded one another in establishing regimes. Among these groups were the Hsiung-nu, or the Huns, whose rulers, converted by Buddhist missionaries from India, sponsored the spread of Buddhism. In the south, the Chinese dynasties reigned under the constant threat of northern enemies. This period of great upheaval is called the Political Disunion (A.D. 220–589).

It was during the Political Disunion that Indian Buddhism caught the imagination of the Chinese and began to grow in China, although according to tradition it had reached China in the first century A.D. Confucianism had exhausted its energy after the efforts at systematization during the Han period; its rational metaphysics offered no spiritual consolation to the people, who were now suffering from social disruptions. While philosophical Taoism attracted the intellectuals, it did not appeal to the masses. Buddhism spoke to the intellectuals through its imaginative ideas and to the masses through its cult of Bodhisattvas, savior-gods.

The Sui dynasty (A.D. 590–618) at last united China after more than three centuries of political chaos. The Sui rulers invaded Taiwan in A.D. 610 and sent envoys to India, Turkestan, and Japan. They also sponsored huge building programs which included palaces, roads, parks, canals, and the canal system which were undertaken in order to transport grains from the Yangtze River Valley to north-west China, where the political center was located. The Sui dynasty, which attempted to renew the imperialism of early China, was brought to an end because of extravagance, military adventures, and oppression.

In the Tang dynasty (A.D. 618–907), probably the most brilliant era in Chinese history, Buddhism reached its peak of growth. Several Chinese monks went to India, by way of central Asia, to collect sutras. The best known of these monks is Hsüan Tsang, who left China in 629 and returned home sixteen years later. In this period a number of Buddhist Scriptures were translated from Sanskrit into Chinese, which not only gave China a new body of literature but also greatly influenced her indigenous thought. Toward the end of the Tang period, the printing industry flourished and books became easily accessible.

By the eighth century A.D., Buddhist temples and shrines were beginning to appear throughout China, and many people were joining the priesthood. Monasteries owned huge tax-free lands, and monks were exempted from conscription. Meanwhile, after centuries of oblivion, Confucianism began to reassert its influence. The Confucian leaders were alarmed by the domination of Buddhism and, with the cooperation of Taoist advisers at the court, they instigated the emperor in A.D. 845 to issue an edict for the confiscation of Buddhist properties, the destruction of temples and shrines, and the secularization of monks and nuns. Although the growth of Buddhism was halted by this persecution, it was far from being stamped out, for by then Buddhism was already well rooted in the Chinese soil. Temples and shrines continued to be built after A.D. 845, but the intellectual leadership that Buddhism had enjoyed for centuries was soon taken over by Confucianism.

Zoroastrianism, Nestorian Christianity, and Manicheism also came to China in the Tang period. These religions, which were brought in chiefly by Persian and Syrian traders and for the most part confined to them, became victims of the same persecution. Since then, they have virtually disappeared.

The Sung dynasty (A.D. 960–1279), which succeeded the Tang rulers, was militarily weak, and during the second half of its reign was able to control the south only. During the same period, northern China was ruled by the Khitan, a tribe of nomadic Mongols who established the kingdom of Liao. Liao was eventually conquered by the Jurchen, a Tungusic people who founded the kingdom of Chin, which rivaled the Sung dynasty in the south. At the same time, northwestern China was ruled by a Tibetan people who founded the kingdom of Hsi Hsia.

The military weakness of the Sung dynasty was compensated for by a renaissance in poetry, art, history, and philosophy. This renaissance was climaxed by the growth of neo-Confucianism which, as a system of ethics, government, and metaphysics, reflects the influences of Buddhism and Taoism. Private academies, designed for mature students who desired philosophical and literary studies rather than preparation for the civil service examination, also grew during this period.

In the Sung period, the bureaucracy deteriorated and the economic conditions of the people were bad. In the face of these crises, Wang An-Shih (1021–1086) launched several reforms in 1069. In economics, he established government loans with low interest to the poor, graduated land taxes on the basis of the productivity of the soil, enforced price control, and instituted government buying and selling in order to regulate prices. In education, he advocated practical learning in such fields as medicine, political economy, and military science instead of the memorization of classics. He also proposed the reform of the civil service examination. But Wang An-Shih's reforms failed because of oppositions from Confucian leaders who represented the interests of large landowners and wealthy merchants.

Contact with Foreign Powers (1260–1912)

The Mongols were nomadic Asians who lived in what is present-day Mongolia. At one time their empire, launched by Genghis Khan (c. 1167–1227), covered a territory from Korea to the Danube, an area larger than that of Alexander's empire. Kublai Khan, a grandson of Genghis Khan, conquered China and established the Yüan dynasty (1260–1368). It was during Kublai Khan's reign that Marco Polo visited China.

The Mongols built a system of highways that connected China, Persia, and Russia. Gunpowder and printing techniques were transported from China to the West, while traders, engineers, and mathematicians came to China from central Asia and the West. The hospitality of the Mongols and their tolerance toward different religions facilitated a cultural interchange between Europe, central Asia, and China. Some Mongol generals became Muslims, through contact with Arabs who worked under them. As a result, mosques appeared in the Yüan period, and Islam became a permanent religion, especially in the northwestern region of China. Roman Catholicism came to China through the Franciscan monks in the fourteenth century.

The Mongol dynasty was overthrown by the Chinese, who were led by a Buddhist monk. This monk founded the Ming dynasty (1368–1644). The busy traffic over the Eurasian continent declined in the Ming period, while sea communication with the world began. At one time, the Chinese fleet of junks made seven expeditions to the ports of southeast Asia, India, and Africa. These marine expeditions sowed the seed for the migrations of Chinese to the trading centers of southeast Asia and also caused peoples south of her border to hear about China.

Western powers, through seaborne commerce, began to exert their economic influences on China in the Ming period: the Portuguese came to the Chinese coast in the early sixteenth century; Spanish influence was felt by China in the same century when Chinese traders sold silk to the Spaniards in Manila and returned with Spanish silver dollars; Russian envoys came to Peking in the seventeenth century requesting trade; Dutch and English arrived in China in the same century. On the whole, the Ming rulers' attitudes toward the Western powers were negative. The foreigners who came to the Chinese shores were merchant sailors who desired trade, but traditional China, being agriculturally oriented, did not place a premium upon commerce. She considered profit making an unworthy pursuit, fit only for inferior men—an attitude that was reflected in early contacts with the Western powers. Neither the Western nations nor China understood the other.

The Jesuit missionaries were another group of Westerners who arrived in China in the seventeenth century. They were men of high character and dedication, and officials at Peking were greatly impressed by their Chinese and their scientific learning. They were revered as scholars, the elite of China. Matteo Ricci, a noted Jesuit, spent his last years (1601–1610) at Peking, where his house was frequently visited by the scholar-officials. The Jesuits were also the first translators of the Confucian classics into Western languages. Through their writings Chinese government and philosophy became topics of interest among the European intellectuals.

Another nomadic people, the Manchus, descendants of the Jurchen inhabitants of Manchuria, overthrew the Ming rulers and founded the Ch'ing dynasty (1644–1912). After an initial prosperous reign of 150 years, this regime was weakened by two continuing disturbances:

rebellions inside and pressures from outside. The rebellions, spreading intermittently in different regions and often lasting for years, caused the death of millions and paralyzed the economic life of the nation. It was at such a time that the Western powers intensified their demand for trade and Christian missions.

In the second half of the nineteenth century, China suffered military defeats which resulted in concessions to foreign powers. Following the Opium War of 1839–1842, treaties with Britain made Hong Kong a British colony, and extraterritoriality was granted to England. The same privilege was soon extended to other European nations, as well as to America and Japan. In 1884–1885, France conquered Tongkin-Annam, which was nominally under Chinese control. In 1886 Britain annexed Burma, a Chinese protectorate. Following China's defeat in the First Sino-Japanese War, 1894–1895, Japan took Korea, another Chinese protectorate. A treaty with Japan in 1895 resulted in the cession of the island of Taiwan by China to Japan. Meanwhile, Russia gained military and economic access to Manchuria, in addition to leasing the Liaotung Peninsula of south Manchuria. In order to protect their gains, these nations imposed their "spheres of interest" upon China. Practically all major nations had their particular spheres of interest in China in the late nineteenth century. China's sovereignty was badly infringed and her territories reduced.

Chinese resentment against foreign powers led to the Boxer Rebellion in 1900, which was aimed at driving out the foreigners, but was quickly subdued by an international army. Decay from within and infringements from without quickened the fall of the Manchu dynasty. The revolutionary forces finally rallied under the leadership of Sun Yat-sen, a physician of Western medicine, who became President of the Provisional Government in 1911. The following year the last Manchu emperor abdicated and the Republic was founded.

The Republic (1912 ——)

The history of China in the twentieth century is the story of the making of a modern nation out of an old one. Since the founding of the Republic in 1912, China has come through a number of national crises. Viewed from a historical perspective, they are but different stages of a continuing national revolution.

The new Republic from the outset was divided among the semi-independent military governors of the provinces. These provinces did not become subordinate to the central government until 1928, when Chiang Kai-shek, of the Nationalist Party, restored unity. Henceforth the central government became steadily stronger, although it was unable to subdue the Communist Party, founded in 1921, which had its own army first in central China and later in northwest China. Despite insurmountable obstacles, the central government under the Nationalist Party labored for the modernization of China. This was a time of widespread Western influence, and important Western books were translated into Chinese.

Japan was the chief enemy of China in the thirties and forties. The Japanese army gained control of Manchuria and gradually advanced to north China. The Sino-Japanese War began in 1937 and eventually developed into a part of World War II. During all these years the Nationalist Party and the Communist Party were united in name, but were in fact hostile to each other. The economic stability that China had briefly enjoyed was now badly shattered. Although Japan surrendered in 1945, China was paralyzed as a nation.

Immediately after the defeat of Japan, open conflict between the Nationalist Party and the Communist Party increased. It should be noted that, while the Nationalist Party was engaged in war with Japan, the Communist force was steadily growing in power, and by the time of the Japanese surrender, it possessed a disciplined army and a corps of dedicated cadres. In contrast, the Nationalist Party's soldiers were worn out after years of war. Corruption in high places further deteriorated the morale of the government. When civil war broke out in 1947, the government army was no match for the Communists, who won control of China in late 1949. The new government, called the People's Republic of China, is attempting to apply an indigenous version of Communism in order to build a modern nation. Meanwhile, the Nationalist government of China has reestablished itself on Taiwan, an island about a hundred miles off the coast of mainland China.

TIBET

Tibet, the roof of the world, extends for 1,500 miles between other Chinese provinces on the east and Kashmir on the west. It varies in

length from 600 to 800 miles between Sinkiang on the north and
Assam and the Himalaya kingdoms of Nepal, Sikkim, and Bhutan on
the south. The Tibetans, who number about 5 million, are nomads,
most of them living in tents that are made of materials woven out of
yak hair. They dwell on high plateaus which average 16,000 feet
above the sea. Many Tibetans have never been to places below 12,000
feet. Villages are few and are separated by mountains and unbridged
rivers. Monasteries serve as centers for the cultural and communal
life of nearby camps and villages.

Meat, milk, butter, barley, and tea form the staple diet in Tibet.
Although much of Tibetan land is pastoral and unproductive, agriculture does exist in eastern and southeastern Tibet, where barley,
wheat, peas, maize, and even rice grow. The institution of polyandry,
as well as a large number of celibate monks, has helped to limit the
birth rate. By and large, Tibetans have an adequate supply of food
in spite of their meager produce.

In winter Tibetans combat screaming winds which, raging from
noon to sunset, frequently blow horses and their riders off the
ground. In summer, they face dreaded floods and hailstorms which
destroy cattle and crops and damage tents and horses. Between midnight and noon, temperature varies as much as fifty or sixty degrees
Fahrenheit.

While physical environment cannot fully explain religion, the
unusual conditions of life in Tibet are definitely a determining factor. Nature is a perpetual adversary. Its inhabitants are constantly
threatened by extreme weather, and in their everyday life are surrounded by hanging cliffs, deep gorges, vast bogs, and narrow passes.
The reason why Tibetans developed an elaborate demonology is
therefore obvious: nature possesses demonic forces. It is also under-
standable why Tibet abounds in magic, which is a means of placating
or counteracting the adversities of nature, as well as of enabling men
to cast off fear and live courageously. The Tibetan emphasis on self-
mastery is also related to the surroundings; only men of strength can
survive here. But it is mental or spiritual exertion that is the special
gift of Tibetans. Since overcoming the physical environment involves
insurmountable difficulties, they turn instead to the cultivation of
spiritual disciplines. Much of Tibetan Buddhism emphasizes meditation as a means to self-realization. This process of involution is a way
to fulfillment, under circumstances in which the hostile conditions of
the external world have denied people security and comfort.

The Kingdom of Tibet

Beginning in the seventh century, Tibet flourished as an independent kingdom. Relations between China and Tibet were first established during the Tang dynasty (618–907).

In the thirteenth century, when Kublai Khan conquered China and established the Yüan dynasty (1260–1368), Tibet came under the influence of Mongolia.

At the turn of the eighteenth century, when China was ruled by the Ch'ing dynasty, Tibet was still under the political influence of the Mongols. But the Ch'ing emperor in 1720 dispatched an army to Tibet and installed the seventh Dalai Lama to be the ruler of the land. A Tibetan civil war broke out in 1727–1728, whereupon a new troop was brought in from China. This time the Ch'ing government appointed two imperial residents to oversee the administration under a lay Tibetan ruler. Two decades later, in 1750, civil disorder again plagued Tibet. The Ch'ing ruler then restored the temporal power of the Dalai Lama. A council of four ministers was established to assist the Dalai Lama under the supervision of two imperial residents.[1] From then on, until modern times, Tibet was run by a theocratic government with the Dalai Lama as its spiritual and temporal head. For all practical purposes, the Tibetans considered Lamaistic rule a continuation of the tradition of earlier Tibetan kings. The ancient kings were descendants of the gods of Heaven, and the Dalai Lamas were the incarnation of Bodhisattva Avalokitesvara; both were ascribed to a divine origin.

JAPAN

Japan lies off the east coast of Asia, surrounded by seas and 115 miles from the continent; its four main islands—Hokkaidō, Honshū, Shikoku, and Kyūshū—form a rectangular shape spreading from north to southwest. In terms of latitude and climate, Japan resembles the east coast of the United States from New England to the Carolinas and Georgia. In terms of size, Japan is larger than the British Isles and smaller than France. Its present population is more than 90 million. Four-fifths of the country is mountainous, which leaves only one-fifth of the land for agriculture. On the basis of

cultivated acres, however, Japan has been the most productive agricultural country in the world because of intensive rice farming,
favorable weather, and plentiful rainfall. Although Japan is deficient
in natural resources, the seas have provided her with an unlimited
food supply.

Villages in Japan are separated by mountains, and most of the
country's rivers are unnavigable; hence, communities in traditional
Japan were not easily accessible. This accounts for regionalism and
conservatism in Japan's history. Japan's geographical isolation from
the continent also enabled it to preserve traditional customs and
practices without the intrusion of continental culture.

Pre-historic Japan was a land of numerous autonomous clans, each
rivaling the other for control of larger territories. Eventually, the
Yamato clan subjugated many other clans and established the Yamato
dynasty at the turn of the fourth century A.D. By the seventh century,
Japan was united under a central government, largely due to the
efforts of Prince Shōtoku (A.D. 573–621) who was the regent from 592
to 621. He adopted Confucianism as the national ethic and Buddhism as the state's metaphysics. After the time of Shōtoku, the history of Japan may be divided as follows.

The Nara Period (710–794)

The government, which was then in the city of Nara, was acutely
aware of the inferiority of Japan's culture as it came into contact
with the continental culture of China. In this period, the central
concern of the state was the adoption of the civilization of Tang
China. Envoys were sent to China to gather knowledge about institutions and learning. Since this was the time of Buddhist ascension in
China, Japan was particularly attracted by this religion. It was during
this period that Japan began to build Buddhist temples, which was
also motivated by a desire to exalt the imperial house. Several ancient
Buddhist schools were then established: (1) the Sanron (three-treatise)
School, which emphasizes the philosophy of the Indian Buddhist
Nagarjuna, according to whom truth lies between affirming and denying, (2) the Hossō (Consciousness Only) School, which teaches that
ideas are the basis of external reality; (3) the Ritsu (*vinaya* or discipline) School, which emphasizes the proper administration of the
ordination ceremony as a means of admitting monks into the order;
and (4) the Kegon (Flower Splendor) School, which holds Lochana

as the Supreme Buddha and Sakyamuni (the founder of Buddhism) as the manifestation of Lochana. The Kegon School compares the Lochana Buddha to the emperor of Japan. Although Buddhism was the spirit of the Nara culture, it was essentially confined to the members of the court and aristocrats.

Writing in this period among the aristocrats was done mainly in the Chinese language, which is monosyllabic, but efforts were also made to use the Chinese script to express the Japanese language, which is polysyllabic. The *Man'yōshū* (Collection of Myriad Leaves), an anthology of poems, was written in the latter fashion during this period.

The Heian Period (794–1192)

The imperial government was in the city of Heian (Kyōto) during the era when Chinese civilization in Japan underwent the process of Japanization. Although the Heian government formally adopted the political system of the Tang dynasty in China, in practice it created offices to meet the actual conditions of the Japanese society. The hereditary office of regent also arose during this period; the regent acted for a child emperor who had succeeded a retired emperor. By this time there existed a dual system of the state: the emperor was its nominal head and the regent its actual head. A prominent regent's house in this period was the Fujiwara family, many of whose members intermarried with members of the imperial house.

Two important Buddhist schools arose in this period: (1) the Tendai School, which accepts the Lotus Stura as the supreme truth of salvation; and (2) the Shingon School, which adheres to esoteric rites as the vehicle of salvation. These schools had huge monasteries that possessed great estates. Like the Church in medieval Europe, they became wealthy and their prelates frequently interfered with the affairs of the state. In the Heian period, the leaders of these two schools behaved much like their contemporary feudal lords.

It was in this period that genuine native literature developed. By the ninth century, a system of much simplified phonetic symbols derived from Chinese characters, the *kana* syllabary, came into use, which was a far more suitable medium for writing Japanese poems and popular literature. Many court ladies used this medium for writing. The *Tale of Genji* and the *Pillow Book* were written by two court ladies in this period.

The Kamakura Period (1192–1336)

The decadence of the imperial house and the political interference of the clergy caused the rise of shōguns, generalissimos, who became the heads of the government in this period causing a rise of military men who held the real power of the state. Kamakura, a town in eastern Japan, away from the corrupting influences of Heian, was the seat of the shōgunate. Although the Kamakura government was founded by Yoritomo of the Minamoto clan, during most of this period the administration was in the hands of the Hōjō family whose heirs served as regents of shōguns.

A significant historical event of this period was the invasion of Mongols, who were then the rulers of China (the Yüan dynasty), in 1281. For once, different regional lords were united under the government against the invaders. The Mongol ships, together with a force of 140,000 men, attacked the Hakata Bay in north Kyūshū for two months without being able to land. Then a typhoon destroyed most of the Mongol force. Although the Japanese government won the victory, the nation suffered great financial loss on account of the war, which was a vital cause of the eventual collapse of the Kamakura shōgunate.

In this period, Buddhism penetrated the Japanese interior and became a religion of the masses, rivaling Shinto, the native religion of the land. Three schools arose: (1) Pure Land (Jōdo), (2) Zen, (3) Nichiren Buddhism. All three groups (see Chapter 21, Buddhism in East Asia) offered practical assistance to people who suffered from the threat of war and economic upheaval.

The Ashikaga Period (1338–1593)

Ashikaga Takauji founded a new shōgunate in 1338 and established his headquarters in Heian (Kyōto). This period is also called the Era of Civil War, as Japan was in fact divided between several powerful families of territorial lords which fought against each other for suzerainty, while the Ashikaga shōguns existed as the nominal heads of the government. The characteristic political phenomenon of the day was the loyalty of the vassals to their respective lords, not to the shōguns, while the characteristic social phenomenon was the rise of small household families as social units instead of clans—the basis of earlier Japanese society. This change was largely due to the need for economic security which necessitated the keeping of land within the immediate family instead of bequeathing it to relatives. One son was chosen to own the family land while the other sons would either work for their brother or leave the family. Daughters were denied the right to land inheritance; consequently, beginning with the Ashikaga period, the status of women deteriorated. This was also the era of the introduction of the Nō plays, which became a popular form of entertainment among the aristocrats.

Japan once again looked to China for national stimulation after the long years of seclusion during the Kamakura period. Trade with China was sponsored by the Ashikaga shōguns and managed by Zen Buddhist monks who were sent to China because of their knowledge of Chinese. Both the Kamakura and the Ashikaga periods were times of feudalism during which Japanese society was characterized by lord-vassal relationships, in which the lord protected the vassals' lands in exchange for their allegiance to him.

The Tokugawa Period (1603–1867)

After the fall of the Ashikaga shōgunate and immediately prior to the Tokugawa period, Nobunaga (1534–1583) and Hideyoshi (1536–1598) controlled Japan. Nobunaga was noted for his suppression of Buddhism, wiping out the military power of the monasteries once and for all. Hideyoshi is noted for his suspicions of the motives of Christian missionaries, and he made efforts in 1587 to deport them. In addition, his Korean invasions in 1592 and 1597 were unsuccessful. In 1603 Tokugawa Iyeyasu united Japan and founded the Tokugawa shōgunate, whose seat was in Edo (Tōkyō), his former headquarters. Japan enjoyed more than two centuries of peace and prosperity during the Tokugawa regime; meanwhile the imperial court continued in Kyōto. Although the Tokugawa government voluntarily isolated the nation from the world for two centuries (see Chapter 25, Shinto), commerce and cultural contact with the Netherlands and China continued during this period. It was actually an era of economic expansion; cities grew, a merchant class developed, a money economy arose, and large family-owned firms spread. An urban culture also developed, publishing houses, public bathhouses, theaters, and brothels became commonplace in the cities, and a new type of drama, *Kabuki,* and puppet plays arose for commoners. Neo-Confucianism became the philosophy of the state and Shinto became the politico-religious ethos of the nation (see Chapter 25, Shinto).

The nineteenth century saw the rapid decline of the Tokugawa regime. The government, with its conservative ideology, was at odds with the changing, commercial society of Japan. The growth of the merchant class, the increasing power of the lower warrior-officials, the autonomy of prominent regional lords, and the deteriorating economic condition of the peasants were among the factors that threatened the government. The prestige of the regime also suffered under an incompetent shōgun who reigned for half a century during this crucial epoch. A change at the top was imperative, and it was at this time that the restoration of the imperial administration became a foremost consideration. Factors such as the revival of Shinto, national learning, and the Royalist movement all contributed to the restoration of imperial rule. Thus in 1867 the last shōgun bowed out and returned the administration to the emperor, who was then fifteen years of age. The following year, 1868, Mutsuhito, later known as Emperor Meiji, began to rule.

The period was also one in which the previously self-imposed seclusion ended. In 1853 Commodore Matthew Perry and his squadron had reached the Edo Bay and requested trade on behalf of the United States. Upon his return the following year, a treaty between Japan and the United States was signed. A more specific treaty of commerce between these two nations was made in 1858. Similar agreements between Japan and the European powers were signed during the same decade.

The Meiji Period (1868–1912)

During the Meiji period (literally, Enlightened Rule), which was the era of modernization, Japan returned to imperial rule under the Emperor Meiji. The primary task of the government was to build a new nation out of a feudal society. The imperial house was moved to Edo which was now named Tōkyō (Eastern Capital). Leaders of diverse ideologies and inclinations were united under the young emperor. This time the imperial house again led Japan toward national rejuvenation, but now its model was the West, not China, and its aim was the transformation of the country into a world power. For this purpose the government adopted the slogan, "Enrich the nation and strengthen its arms." In less than half a century, Japan succeeded in becoming a world power: in 1895 it won the Sino-Japanese War and took possession of Taiwan; Japan's victory in the Russo-Japanese War of 1904–1905 enabled it to gain special rights over Manchuria;

and in 1910 it annexed Korea. Domestically, a constitution was enacted in 1868; this was replaced by a new one in 1889. A parliament, composed of the House of Peers and the House of Representatives, was convened in 1890.

The Modern Period (1912 ———)

After the Meiji era, Japan entered a period of imperialism during which it followed other world powers and concentrated on commercial and military expansion. Japan occupied Manchuria in 1931 and created the "Manchukuo" in 1932. In 1937 a war with China commenced, and in 1941 Japan entered the Pacific War, which precipitated the attack on Pearl Harbor on December 7, 1941. The Japanese defeat in World War II, in August 1945, resulted in Allied occupation of the land under the Supreme Commander, General Douglas MacArthur. A new constitution in 1947 made the sovereign power of the nation reside with the people and renounced Japanese participation in future wars.

NOTE

1. Edwin O. Reischauer and John K. Fairbank, *A History of East Asian Civilization*, Vol. I, *East Asia the Great Tradition* (Boston: Houghton Mifflin, 1958 and 1960), p. 363.

Buddhism is today a principal religion in Ceylon, Burma, Thailand, Cambodia, Laos, Vietnam, China, Korea, Japan, and Mongolia. It is here placed within the context of East Asia (China, Korea, Japan, Mongolia) because Mahayana, the most popular form of Buddhism, prevails in this region. But Buddhism is, in fact, the most widespread religion throughout Asia and, with Christianity and Islam, one of the three most influential religions of the world. It arose about twenty-five centuries ago in the Ganges Valley of northeast India. Vedism (the Hinduism of the Vedas, Brahmanas, Upanishads) and Jainism were already in India when Buddha began his teaching, and in the following section we shall point out their influence on him and how his teaching differed from theirs.

THE INDIAN LEGACY

In the time of Buddha, the Vedic gods were already widely accepted in India and the Upanishads had become the philosophical study of the higher castes in some places. Although Buddha's teaching and Vedism differed, they nevertheless shared some beliefs. Buddha assumed the basic Hindu doctrine of rebirth, samsara, although he interpreted rebirth as the entrance of the karmic matter (the residual effects of the previous life) into the new body, not the continuity of the same permanent self (*atman* in Sanskrit or *atta* in Pali). But the view that something is transmitted indefinitely from one body to an-

FIGURE 20.1 Buddhist monks in front of the Dhamek Stupa at Sarnath. (*Government of India Tourist Office*)

other until one attains Nirvana was basic for Buddha, who also accepted the Hindu belief in the law of karma (the moral law of cause and effect). However, Buddha's attitude toward the inexorable law of karma was more optimistic than that of Vedism; he worked out a definite philosophy and a practical method (the Four Noble Truths) of overcoming the law of karma, whereby, instead of submitting oneself to a series of rebirths before reaching emancipation, one could attain emancipation in the present life. Buddha's own life is a clear example of this philosophy.

Buddha's view of the cosmos also shows Hindu influence; it conceives time in terms of cycles of eons, kalpas, each consisting of millions of years, in which rebirths take place and the law of karma affects all sentient beings.[1] Gods of the Vedic pantheon are also subject to rebirth and the law of karma. These gods are superior to ordinary men, but not equal to men of enlightenment, and in Buddhist Scriptures, there are many references to gods who pay homage to enlightened men.

Buddha wanted to eliminate the metaphysics and sacerdotalism of Vedism. First, Buddha denied the reality of Atman and rejected the monism that views changeable phenomena as appearances of the unchanging Absolute. A unique emphasis of Buddha was his insistence on the impermanence of all things. He refused to admit a metaphysical Being beyond the changeable process. His religion was neither monistic nor theistic; instead, he confined himself to a program of personal enlightenment. His interest was practical and therapeutic rather than metaphysical, and in that regard he differed clearly from the speculative approach to religion as it was seen in Upanishadic thought, with which he was probably unfamiliar (he lived in a region where Upanishad doctrines reached later). Second, he offered a practical program (the Four Noble Truths) for salvation, in which there is no need for divine and priestly assistance, and one relies exclusively on personal efforts. Although the religion of the Upanishads also minimized sacrifices, it recognized the privilege of the Brahmin priests and was not opposed to divine assistance. Buddha's religion was by contrast iconoclastic. Third, his program was for men of all castes; his monastic order was inclusive and welcomed many non-Brahmins. This was in contrast to the Vedic religion, which favored the Brahmin caste. Although Buddha himself did not explicitly repudiate the caste system, his movement, in practice, broke down the division among castes by admitting members from various groups and by offering a universal standard of ethics for monks, instead of varied standards for different caste members, as in Vedism.

Mahavira, the twenty-fourth Tirthankara of the Jains, and Buddha were contemporaries,[2] and there are also many resemblances between this religion and Buddha's teaching. Indeed, although Buddha's new religion included both Hindu and Jain elements, it was closer to Jainism. Since some recent scholars view Jainism as reflecting aspects of Dravidian culture, the rise of Buddhism can be interpreted as a resurgence of indigenous religion through the stimulations of Aryan culture.[3]

Both Jainism and Buddhism repudiated the idea of a Supreme Ultimate, supported a dynamic materialism and monastery life, and believed in salvation through personal efforts and in liberation. The Jain savior, or Tirthankara (literally, the ford-maker), is one who has reached the other shore of the river, that is, he has reached Nirvana by liberation from rebirths and by overcoming the law of karma, and in many respects he seems to be a predecessor of Buddha. In fact, the life of Buddha is almost parallel to the life of the legendary twenty-third Tirthankara, who lived about two centuries before him. Furthermore, the first four of the five Buddhist precepts for householders (no injury, no lying, no stealing, no adultery, no intoxication) are the same as the vows for Jain believers, and are in the same order of importance.

But early Buddhism also differed from Jainism. First, Jainism believed in the indestructibility of the two primordial cosmic elements: nature (*ajiva*), and soul (*jiva*). But what Buddhism believed in was the impermanence of all things. Second, *ahimsa* (noninjury) for the Jain meant refraining from both intentional and unintentional injury; he could not eat meat, and neither was he supposed to destroy any form of life. It was extreme asceticism. The Buddhist held to ahimsa less rigidly than did the Jains. A Buddhist monk avoided intentional injury only; he was permitted to eat meat as long as he himself had not killed the animal. He was not held responsible for insects that were unintentionally destroyed by him. Third, the Jain monk took a mechanistic view of the law of karma in relation to ahimsa; he automatically took a step downward on the ladder of salvation when he destroyed a life. On the other hand, the Buddhist monk let intention govern ahimsa and the law of karma; when a life was destroyed by a man unintentionally, his future was not affected by that deed.

The Life of Gautama

Buddhist Scriptures, the Sutras (*Suttas* in Pali), were not written until sometime between the first century B.C. and the first century A.D., when Buddha had already been elevated to divine status. For four centuries the tradition of the life and teaching of the founder had been transmitted orally. What we read about the life of Buddha in the Scriptures is an interpretation, involving a mixture of the historical with the nonhistorical, and it is impossible to distinguish the one from the other.

At the outset, two things should be considered in connection with the life of Buddha. First, all ancient religions of India shared a common view of history, a view that sees history as including both empirical and nonempirical events; the former deal with what actually happened in human history, the latter with imaginary and mythological events before and within human history. The Indian view of history is larger in scope and longer in duration than that of the West, and it includes stories of gods and other mythological beings, both on this and on other planets, and their relations with men. Buddhism is rooted in this tradition. Second, although Buddha was regarded as human, his followers believed that he possessed supernatural qualities; he assisted both men and gods to salvation; he was omniscient and possessed power even to subdue gods. The mythological and legendary aspects of his life not only put Buddha in a cosmic setting, but also provided clues to Buddhist theology and philosophy.

The term *Buddha* (the Enlightened One) was used in early Buddhism to designate beings of a certain type—the number of such beings varies, according to different schools—who attained enlightenment after numberless rebirths on this and other planets, through which they progressed toward Buddhahood. There may be one Buddha, several Buddhas, or none at all in a span of millions of years. Because of the infinite number of years required for making a Buddha and because of the aspirant's austere preparations for the final triumph, his arrival is an event of cosmic significance. A Buddha was called Bodhisattva (Buddha-to-be) during his previous lives, beginning with the time when he took a vow to be a Buddha. Accordingly Gautama was a Bodhisattva in his past lives as a monkey, a peacock, an ascetic, a king, and so on. Dipankara was the Buddha who preceded Gautama. In that infinite past, Gautama was a Brahmin who, having met Dipankara, made a vow to become a

Buddha in the future.[4] The next Buddha after Gautama is to be Maitreya, who will appear at the end of the present eon.

Although there are many Buddhas, they all reveal the same Truth taught by Gautama Buddha. Buddhists believe that the Truth deteriorates in cycles of time. When it is at a very low ebb, a Buddha arrives in the world to revive it. All Buddhas emanate the spiritual principle called *Tathagata* (literally, "thus come, *or* thus gone") which is incarnated in a Buddha from time to time. Insofar as this principle is manifested in a Buddha, he is called the Tathagata.

Gautama Buddha (c. 560–480 B.C.) was the only child of Mahamaya and Suddhodana, ruler of the small Principality of Shakyas at the foot of the Himalayas in northeast India. He was born near Kapila-vastu, the capital of the principality (modern Padaria in southern Nepal). Before his birth, his mother dreamed of a white elephant entering into her side, and wise men predicted that the child would be either a Universal King or a Universal Teacher. Immediately after birth, the boy walked seven steps, declaring that this was his last time of birth. He was named Siddhartha Gautama. Siddhartha (wish-fulfilling) was his given name and Gautama was the name of the clan to which he belonged—although later he was called Shakyamuni (the Sage from the Tribe of Shakyas). His mother died soon after he was born, and he was cared for by his aunt until he was married at the age of sixteen.

When he was a child soothsayers foretold that, if Siddhartha ever saw signs of miseries or a monk, he would become a religious teacher. From that point on his father confined him to the palace compound, and kept all unpleasant and repulsive sights away from him.

One day, as Siddhartha was riding around the palace park, he saw four sights: an aged man in the last stage of infirmities, a sick man with high fever, a human corpse, and a mendicant monk in search of salvation. The last scene awakened his desire to leave home. One morning he was told that a baby boy was born to his wife. This news increased his fear of family bonds which must be relinquished in order to obtain liberation. That night, after bidding good-by to his child and wife, who were asleep, Gautama left home. Out in the country, he cut off his hair, removed his princely dress, and put on the monk's robe, thus beginning his new life as a wandering ascetic.

Siddhartha tried different means to find Truth. He studied the Vedic philosophy and attempted to reach understanding by way of meditation and knowledge—the way of the Brahmins. But he was not satisfied and soon gave it up. Then in the company of five monks he practiced fasting and self-mortification, seeking to discover the secret of salvation through extreme self-abstinence—the way of the ascetics. He tortured himself for six years until he looked like a skeleton and eventually fainted because of hunger and exhaustion. When he recovered, he gave up self-mortification and resumed his life as a wandering beggar, gradually regaining his strength. His five friends left him when they saw that Siddhartha had not been able to attain enlightenment through the method of severe austerities.

One day, at the age of thirty-five, Siddhartha was sitting under a fig tree in the town of Gaya nearing the climax of spiritual struggle. He decided then that he would never leave his seat, though his flesh and bones were to dry up, until he found the secret of salvation. Sitting in the same place for forty-nine days, he was first surrounded by gods and later tempted by Mara, the Buddhist Satan. One time Mara informed him that Devadatta, a cousin and archenemy of Siddhartha, had revolted at home, imprisoned his father, and taken his wife. Siddhartha was undisturbed. Another time Mara had his three beautiful daughters, Desire, Pleasure, and Passion, dance before the sage and try different means of seduction, but they were not successful. At dawn on the forty-ninth day, Siddhartha solved the riddle of suffering and discovered the method for its elimination. He reached Nirvana, that is, cessation from craving and release from rebirth. He became Buddha, the Enlightened One. His enlightenment was accompanied by celestial and terrestrial events: the sky shone bright, the earth swelled, blossoms and fruits fell, evil thoughts and deeds instantly departed from men everywhere. Siddhartha spent another forty-nine days sitting under the Bodhi Tree (Tree of Wisdom), where he meditated on the Truth he had found.

For a while he hesitated about teaching the wisdom to others. But Brahmā urged him to do so.[5] He then left Gaya and came to the deer park (in modern Sarnath, see Figure 20.1) near Banaras, where he met his former friends, the five ascetics, who became his first disciples, after he preached to them his first sermon, thus setting "the Wheel of Wisdom" in motion. Next, he went home and converted his father, wife, son, and cousin Devadatta, who, however, remained jealous of him.

Buddha and his disciples traveled for eight months of the year, and spent the remaining four months, the rainy season, in monasteries. They traveled extensively in northeast India (the present provinces of Bihar and Uttar Pradesh, and southern Nepal), making new converts and building monasteries. A community of nuns was also established. The length of Buddha's ministry was forty-five years. Finally, at the age of eighty, suffering from dysentery, he arrived at Kusinara (east of modern Gorakhpur). That night he lay down under a tree and died. His death was called *Parinirvana,* "Final Blowing-out."

The Four Noble Truths

The sermon Buddha preached at the deer park was undoubtedly closely related to the Four Noble Truths. However, the concise form of the Four Noble Truths indicates that they are a product of a later period than the sermon. But since they succinctly depicted the basic core of truth, as accepted by all present-day Buddhists, they must have been evolved from the sayings of the founder. It should be noted, to begin with, that the Four Noble Truths are not a metaphysical statement; they are a therapeutic prescription to be put in action for attaining enlightenment. Their concern is not theoretical, but practical.

The first truth is that life is suffering (*dukkha*). There are seven universal elements of suffering: (1) birth—the baby's first cry is indicative of the beginning of a painful life, (2) sickness, (3) old age, (4) death, (5) separation from what one loves, (6) desire for what one is unable to get, and (7) bondage to what one dislikes (for example, a permanent impairment one has to live with). As can be seen from this list, suffering in Buddhism is basically mental; it is sorrow, despair, or anxiety. Buddha did not say that life is equivalent to suffering; he said that as one lives in the world, he necessarily experiences suffering. Reflection is necessary to be able to see its universality.

The second truth is that desire (*tanha*) is the cause of suffering. The word *tanha,* which implies intensity, encompasses the concept of persistence and insatiability. A normal desire, such as hunger, does not fall into the category of tanha, because although a person desires food when he is hungry, once he has eaten, his desire is satisfied. Tanha should also be viewed in the context of two other ideas: impermanence, *anicca,* and no-self, *anatta.* Impermanence is the belief that all things change and decay, that nothing is stable—neither physical things nor thoughts (ideas). No-self means that every entity is of a composite nature, that its every part is dissoluble. There is no self in it, if by self is meant an unchanging or indestructible soul. Tanha is the result of refusal to accept impermanence and no-self as necessary conditions of life. When one thinks that the desired object —which may be either a concept or belief or a physical object—is permanent or the self is real, he becomes attached to it. But such attachment entails suffering, since all things change and decay. Because all Buddhist doctrines are "vehicles" only, that is, they are means to ends, they too are not considered absolute or permanent.

The third truth is that there is a method for the elimination of suffering. The fourth truth is that the Eightfold Path is the way to eliminate suffering.

The Eightfold Path is as follows: (1) *Right knowledge* is an adequate understanding of the Buddhist philosophy, which includes the Four Noble Truths and the principles of impermanence, no-self, and suffering. (2) *Right thought* refers to thought that is free from craving, lust, ill will, or cruelty. (3) *Right speech* involves avoidance of falsehood and vain talk. (4) *Right conduct* means refraining from taking life, from appropriating things not one's own, and from sexual misconduct. (5) *Right livelihood* refers to occupations that do not bring harm to others. Trades such as butchering or selling alcoholic beverages should be avoided. (6) *Right efforts* involve the avoidance of evil thoughts not yet arisen, the elimination of evil thoughts that have already arisen, the cultivation of good thoughts not yet arisen, and the conservation of good thoughts that have arisen. (7) *Right mindfulness* refers to meditation on the body, on mental activities, and on thought or ideas. One continuously reminds himself that his body is composed of discrete parts, which are reducible to segments of earth, water, heat, and wind. One constantly examines his mental activities, discovering whether or not they are lustful, hateful, or deluding. One subjects his thoughts or ideas to introspection, realizing that they are mere mental constructs, impermanent and motivated by craving. (8) *Right concentration* refers to the culminating state of meditation that follows upon the practice of right efforts and right mindfulness. It leads toward an intuitive and mystic experience, called "samadhi," which results in the extinction of craving and the elimination of the cause of suffering.

The Five Aggregates

The doctrine of no-self (anatta) was fundamental for Gautama. As long as one holds the view of the self—thus making it an object of craving—no enlightenment is possible, and hence one will continue to be reborn. Gautama was aware of the difficulty of explaining no-self, partly because he still accepted the doctrine of rebirth, samsara, and partly because the belief in self, atman, is a Hindu heritage. But since Buddhist salvation required the negation of self, it was imperative for him to explain why self is nonexistent. This resulted in his doctrine of the five aggregates (skandhas) in order to explain the unreality of the self.

Man, for Gautama, is composed of the five aggregates—body, feelings, perceptions, dispositions, consciousness. Body refers to material or corporeal parts of man. Feelings refer to sensations: pleasant, unpleasant, and neutral. Perceptions are mainly sense perceptions: sight, hearing, touch, taste, smell, although in Buddhism sight and hearing are preeminent and touch is subordinate. Dispositions refer to broader mental activities, which are composed of simple feelings and perceptions, and include such impulses and emotions as fear, hatred, empathy, love, or drives and tendencies. Consciousness refers to thoughts or reason—to mental activities of a higher order than dispositions. Gautama believed that what man ordinarily calls "self," "ego," or "personality" is nothing more than the combination of these five skandhas, which change from moment to moment; there is no permanent entity lying behind them. It should be noted that Gautama had no quarrel with self, if it means nothing more than the five aggregates, or the continuity of consciousness. What he was opposed to is the belief in self as the indestructible soul, whether it be the atman of Vedism, the jiva of Jainism, or the purusha of Sankhya philosophy. There were early Buddhist personalists, however, who believed in an enduring entity in man which bears the burden of the five skandhas.[6] But they were considered heretics in early Buddhism and never exerted much influence on subsequent history.

One problem that puzzles students of Buddhism is how Buddha can repudiate the reality of soul while still accepting the doctrine of rebirth. Is not that which is reborn the antecedent self? Buddha's reply is that what passes on from the old to the new body is not the soul, but the karmic matter. As was said earlier, Buddha accepts the law of karma as conditioning man's life and determining his next birth; it serves as both the self-judging and self-determining factor in man. When death does take place, the cumulative effects of man's previous conduct do not perish with him; they are stored as karmic matter, an invisible force or energy, which immediately passes on to a new body. The reason why karmic matter is not a soul is that it is changeable and destructible: it changes from moment to moment under the influence of man's conduct and does not remain identical within the succession of births. When one is completely freed from desire, then his karmic matter is dissolved. The necessity for rebirth is now terminated; one has reached Nirvana. For Gautama, rebirth is neither the reappearance of the same identical soul nor the emergence of an existence that is completely different from the previous one. Since the karmic matter of each existence differs, there is no identity between antecedent and subsequent lives. But, since the karmic matter of the previous life is inherited by a new body, there is that degree of identity between the preceding and the succeeding lives. The line of births is analogous to the different stages of one's present life: the infant becomes a youth; the youth becomes a man; the man reaches old age. No stage is the same as any other; yet there is some identity between the different stages. Likewise, each karmic matter is different from the others; yet there is some likeness between them in the succession of births. The relation between karmic matter and rebirths is analogous to the lighting of individual candles: each is kindled by the flame of the preceding one, and hence there is continuity of light; yet the flame of each is separate and distinct.

In essence, the doctrines of no-self and rebirth, as expounded by Buddha, point up two assumptions of Buddhism. First is the assumption that nothing is permanent in empirical existence; objects that appear to be "permanent" are but combinations of skandhas which are in continuing flux. Although Buddha discussed skandhas as the constituents of man, in Buddhism they are the constituents of virtually all living things: gods (devas), celestial spirits (asuras), men, ghosts, and high-level animals are all products of skandhas and share perpetual rebirths. Second is the assumption that there is a continuity between successive births, which is explainable in terms of the law of karma; an antecedent life is always the cause of the subsequent one. These relations are ideally traceable to the infinite past, as well as the infinite future. However, the locus of life is the *present,* in which man can change his karmic matter by practicing the Four Noble Truths. In Buddhism it is ideally possible for a man to remember his previous lives; he is unable to do so only because of his fallen condition, and through meditation and concentration one can gradually restore memories of one's previous births. The Buddhist

Scriptures are filled with accounts of enlightened men, including Buddha himself, who recalled what they did in previous lives.

THERAVADA BUDDHISM

Buddhism in India

Buddhism spread widely in India after the death of its founder. Although early Buddhism was essentially a religion of monks, even during the life of Buddha, laymen appeared among its followers. Its open, casteless policy was a positive asset for recruitment. Rulers (kshatriyas) and merchants (vaishyas), who resented the superior status of Brahmins, were attracted by the fraternal spirit of the new religion. Its Middle Way, neither extreme indulgence nor extreme asceticism, suited the interests of merchants, who contributed funds for building and supporting monasteries. Many were impressed by the selfless and compassionate lives of the monks. The growth of Buddhism reached its peak during the reign of Asoka (c. 274–226 B.C.), king of the Mauryan dynasty, whose empire reached from northwest to south India. Having been converted to the new faith, Asoka became a sincere follower. Through his efforts, monasteries and shrines were erected at places associated with the life of Buddha, as well as numerous stupas[7] and cylindrical mounds commemorating the death of Buddha, which were built in all parts of India. Asoka's famous Edicts, which were the earliest written records of India and are inscribed on rocks and pillars, tell of his conversion eight years after his inauguration, of his many conciliatory and beneficent policies designed to promote peace and good will, and of his personal example as a humanitarian and a righteous ruler. His promotion of ahimsa (noninjury of animals and men) resulted in the reduction of animal sacrifices in Hinduism, restrictions on animal slaughtering, and the growth of vegetarianism in India. He introduced Buddhism into Ceylon, where the Theravada Scriptures, written in Pali, were originally recorded in the first century B.C. He also sent Buddhist missionaries to Syria, Egypt, Cyrene, Macedonia, and Greece. Although the effects of Buddhist missions to the West are difficult to assess, he definitely laid the foundation for spreading Buddhism to southeast Asia. During his reign, Buddhism ceased to be a sect and began its career as a world religion. About A.D. 100 Kanishka, a king of the Kushanas, a Turkish people, whose kingdom embraced the western half of northwest India and central Asia, became a patron of Buddhism and supported Buddhist missions in central Asia. Kanishka's contact with China enabled Indian and central Asian monks to reach China through the silk routes, thereby laying the ground for the spread of northern Buddhism (Mahayana) to China, Japan, and Korea.

In the second century after the death of Buddha, division arose among his followers. According to tradition, there were at one time eighteen groups. The school of Theravada (the Way of the Elders, called *sthavira* in Sanskrit) persisted in India for several centuries and developed a base in Ceylon, Burma, Siam (Thailand), and other parts of southeast Asia, while other schools either disappeared or were merged into the Theravada or the Mahayana school.[8] Since the Theravada school through its canon[9] represents early Buddhist thought, as well as the teaching of Buddha, it can be regarded as embodying the essential beliefs of early Buddhism.

The Mahasanghikas (the Great Assemblists), who arose as a dissenting group in the third century B.C., were the forerunners of the Mahayanists (followers of the Great Vehicle, Mahayana). They spoke against the Theravada and other schools. The Mahasanghikas adopted a more flexible attitude toward the interpretation of Buddha's teaching, especially its monastic rules, than did the Theravadins; they accepted later Buddhist Scriptures as part of the canon; and they gave greater recognition to lay believers. By the second century B.C., Mahayana became a distinct group. On the other hand, the Theravadins, who wanted to maintain a strict interpretation of Buddha's teaching, refused to accept later Buddhist writings as part of the canon and did not consider lay believers capable of pursuing the life of enlightenment.

The Mahayanists prevailed in north India in the early centuries of the Christian era. The Sarvastivadins, a group theologically akin to the Theravadins, were also active in the same region, and because of the use of Sanskrit as the common language of Buddhists in north India, and as the result of mutual influences, the Sarvastivadins were eventually assimilated by the Mahayanists. In the north, Mahayana philosophers and Brahmin scholars debated continually on intellectual issues; as a result, each group was stimulated by the other, and the philosophical writings of both groups flourished. The Mahayanists were willing to adopt Hindu elements as a way of broadening their theological basis—which probably explains why their writings were synthetic and speculative. Meanwhile, Theravada Buddhism, which continued to prevail in south India, regarded itself as the legitimate guardian of the pure Dharmas (Doctrines) of Buddha and resisted the infiltration of alien elements; for example, they considered Mahayana Buddhism to be impure and heterodox. Because of their intense interest in maintaining the purity of Buddhism, rigidity and insulation came to be reflected in their way of life.

By A.D. 400, Buddhism in India was showing signs of decay, although great monasteries and universities still continued to exist. The Chinese monk Hsüan Tsang, who visited India in the seventh century, reported the steady decline of Buddhism, particularly the Theravada branch. Between A.D. 1000 and 1200, Buddhism virtually disappeared in India, although by that time it had become firmly established beyond India's borders. Theravada eventually became the permanent religion of Ceylon, Burma, and other regions in southeast Asia, while Mahayana was carried to China, Japan, Korea, and Tibet.

The disappearance of Buddhism in its homeland remains a baffling problem. It can perhaps be attributed to three factors: the decline of vigor in monastic life, the resurgence of Hinduism, and Muslim persecution. Much of the vigor of early Buddhism was due to the renunciation of the monks, who lived as mendicants. Later, Buddhism won the favor of kings who sponsored the building of temples, and as these temples acquired wealth, the monks learned to live in comfort rather than to pursue the life of wandering beggars. Among the consequences were that the monks lost close contact with the people and that the chief activity of the monastery shifted from moral discipline and spiritual cultivation to academic studies. At the same time, there was a renaissance of Hinduism, which had undergone the assimilation of Buddhist thought and practice. The philosophy of Shankara had much in common with Mahayana thought, and the Hindu conception of an incarnated god, avatar, enabled Hinduism to appropriate Gautama Buddha as the ninth avatar of Vishnu. As far as laymen were concerned, what took place was a fusion of Hinduism and Buddhism: it was common for lay Buddhists to attend ceremonies at Hindu temples and to invite Brahmins to conduct Hindu rituals. Buddhist devotion was absorbed into Hindu Bhaktism, and Buddhism came to be regarded by Hindus as one of their sects. When Muslim invaders conquered India, beginning about A.D. 1000, they ransacked Buddhist temples, and massacred the monks. Although both Hinduism and Buddhism were persecuted during the early Muslim conquest, Buddhism suffered irreparable loss because its activities were centered around the monastery, whereas Hinduism survived because its nucleus was the family. Without the leadership of monks the lay Buddhists eventually became absorbed into Hinduism.

THE THERAVADIN TRADITION

Since Theravada represents the early phase of Buddhism as well as a present branch, what has been said about Gautama's teaching may also be said about Theravada. In contrast to Mahayana, Theravadin thought is analytic rather than synthetic: its chief interest is the development of a method for attaining enlightenment. As has already been said, for four centuries there was no written teaching of Buddhism. Before the death of Buddha, Sariputra, his brilliant disciple —the St. Paul of Buddhism—arranged the knowledge of the Master in such a manner that it could be easily remembered and taught from generation to generation. Sariputra organized Buddhist thought in simple and precise terms, often numerically, for purposes of memorization.[10] One of the consequences was that he sacrificed imagination for clarity and brevity. Although his version of Buddhism was regarded as authoritative by Theravadins, it was considered inferior by the Mahayanists.

Theravada was basically a religion of the monks, who were able to attain enlightenment primarily because of their full-time devotion to morality, concentration, and wisdom. Lay believers could hardly attain this goal because they were involved in mundane affairs; their duty was therefore the support of monasteries, by giving alms to the monks, in return for which they acquired merit for better rebirths. The ideal man in Theravada Buddhism was called Arhat (*arahat* in Pali), literally, "a slayer of the foe," that is, one who through vigorous discipline and study has conquered passions and desires and has reached enlightenment. For the Theravadins, Gautama Buddha was the model Arhat, an object of emulation. The balance of this chapter provides a summary of the basic Theravadin beliefs and practices.

Twelve Links of Causation

Causation in Buddhism requires some explanation. To begin with, Buddhism emphasizes multiple causes for every effect. For instance, when a boy is hit by a ball, there are more causes than the throwing of the ball by his playmate. Other factors such as his playmate's eyesight and the reflection of the sunlight in his eyes, the topography of the ground, the physical and mental condition of the playmate prior to the act, and the karmic forces of his present and previous lives must also be taken into consideration. Similar factors could also be applied to the injured boy himself in order to determine why he was hit at that particular moment. The effect is always the convergence of many causes. Buddhists do not accept the linear view of causation—that an effect is the result of a single cause in time sequence. Second, since Buddhism views time in terms of cycles, it understands causation in the same way; causal relations follow cycles of repetition. So long as one is not enlightened, he is caught in the cycles of craving, attachment, suffering. Third, because of the Buddhist emphasis on the law of karma, causation is closely associated with the moral and spiritual conditions of man's past, present, and future. Just as his present life is the result of multiple causes of his past, so his future life will be the effect of multiple causes of his present. Causation in Buddhism is not a term of physical science; it is related primarily to man's existence, that is, his condition of misery.

The twelve links of causation are usually presented as follows: (1) ignorance, (2) karma formations, (3) consciousness, (4) body-mind, (5) six senses, (6) contact, (7) feeling, (8) craving, (9) grasping, (10) becoming, (11) birth, (12) aging and death.[11] These are called links because they serve as causal connections in the individual's life. The present arrangement reflects later Theravadin scholasticism. It should be noted that this chain of causation is essentially a restatement of the second and third Noble Truths: the cause of suffering and the cessation of suffering; it is not an analysis of causation of the cosmos. This chain of causation is also called the Wheel of Becoming; as long as the individual is unenlightened, he is subject to the cycles of these twelve conditions, which are like the spokes of a wheel that is in perpetual motion.

The first link in the chain of causation is ignorance (avidya), Since causation is understood in cyclical terms, there is no fixed point at which causation begins, although the chain itself begins with ignorance because that is the root of man's misery. Avidya means blindness: one does not see the true nature of the self or the world; he mistakes the five skandhas for the indestructible self, and ascribes permanence to things of flux. Since blindness permeates all his thoughts and actions, he accumulates karmic forces which in turn stain his skandhas. This brings us to karma formations, the second link, denoting the karmic forces that enter into new birth. Karma formations include all voluntary actions and thoughts produced under conditions of ignorance. The two links of avidya and karma formations refer to one's past life, which causes rebirth in the present.

Consciousness, the third link, refers to subliminal consciousness or subconsciousness, at the point of conception in the womb, as a result of karma formations in a previous life; it is rebirth consciousness. This stage corresponds to the living embryo, which forms the basis, but not the actuality, of individuality. Body-mind, the fourth link, refers to the five skandhas. Body *(rupa)* denotes matter, and mind *(nama)* refers to the four immaterial elements: feelings, perceptions, dispositions, and acts of consciousness. The five aggregates form the new individual in the stage of prenatal growth. The six senses, the fifth link, are the five physical senses (sight, hearing, touch, smell, and taste) and mind. The fourth and fifth links are actually conjoined, though the latter suggests a more completely developed personality parallel to the stage in which the baby is already separated from the mother. Contact, the sixth link, corresponds to the bridge between the outside world and the child, and it refers to impressions of objects on senses. Feeling, the seventh link, is the result of contact; it refers to pleasant, unpleasant, and neutral sensations derived from impressions of objects. This stage corresponds to the completion of childhood. The preceding five links, from the third to seventh, are called the effects of the past life on the present. Their formations in the present are due to the past life. The present individual is not entirely responsible for them. He is, however, henceforth a self-acting being, responsible for his own actions and thoughts.

Craving, the eighth link, is the result of feelings derived from impressions. It is a reference to the second Noble Truth: the cause of suffering is desire. Craving nourishes man's ignorance: it increases his belief in the permanence of things. The consequence of craving is grasping, the ninth link; one becomes attached to objects of desire. Craving and grasping result in becoming, the tenth link, which is desire for future existence. Thirst for existence necessarily entails future birth, the eleventh link. Aging and death, the twelfth link, are the result of birth.

The first two links refer to past life, the next eight to present life, and the last two to future life. Although this chain of causation explains the cycles of rebirth, its basic intent is the analysis of the cause of suffering. These cycles can be stopped, however, if and when one follows the method of salvation in the present life.

Morality, Concentration, Wisdom

Theravadins aspired to enlightenment by adhering to the threefold method of salvation—moral discipline, concentration, and wisdom. Although these three monastic disciplines were different from each other, they were interdependent and reciprocally enhancing; they were meant to be practiced alternately. A basic Theravadin assumption was faith in man's potentialities to overcome evil within and to actualize good without. In order to carry out this faith, a single-minded, around the clock attention to the threefold method was necessary, which meant that monks were the only ones who had the time and perseverance to do it. Salvation in Theravadin thought required the exclusive efforts of the monk himself; neither god nor friends could help him.

Moral discipline, the lowest of the three, involves the elimination of evil actions. The principal cause of evil actions is the delusion that self is real. Acts of hostility, injury, greed, or passion are the result of attachments to self either as a subject or an object. If one truly believes in the insubstantiality of things, he has no desire to possess them, and has thus eliminated the cause of immoral actions. A practical way to begin the process of subjugating the self is to take a low estimate of one's body. A monk constantly reminds himself of the thirty-two repulsive parts of his body, such as sinew, bones, marrow, intestines, pus, blood, tears, urine, and its "nine apertures" (two eyes, two ears, two nostrils, mouth, urethra, anus) from which filthy substances flow. The Buddhist deliberately stresses the disgusting parts of his body in order to overcome self-attachment. His body is a mere example of all other bodies, which are composed of like elements, All so-called "selves" are mere appearances of aggregates. When one is continuously reminded of the unreality of objects, he will react to stimuli differently. For instance, when a Buddhist's passion is aroused by an alluring object, he immediately begins to break down its image, and once the image of the object has been broken down, his passion subsides.

Moral discipline can eliminate evil actions only; it cannot remove evil thoughts or feelings. That is the task of concentration, which has to do with mind control. One practices concentration in order to

overcome the impact of sense stimuli and to rise above ordinary reactions to the environment. Concentration is divided into three parts:
(1) the eight *dhyanas,* (2) the four unlimited states, (3) the occult
powers. Dhyana *(jhana* in Pali) means meditation. One begins by sitting before an object (such as a bowl of water or an image of Buddha)
and gazing at it. By concentrating on one single sense object, one
eliminates ill will, sense desire, restlessness, sloth, or other undesirable feelings. The second step is the elimination of any specific feelings or thoughts in connection with the sense object. One experiences
elation and delight in going beyond discursive thoughts toward something that one cannot describe yet which one knows would be more
satisfying than things one knows discursively. The third and fourth
dhyanas involve mental efforts for the removal of dual feelings, such
as elation and dejection, pleasantness and unpleasantness, comfort
and discomfort. Contradictory feelings need to be eliminated in order
for one to be able to arrive at even-mindedness. Whereas the first
four dhyanas are for the overcoming of ordinary responses to outside
stimuli, the last four are for the removal of any trace of attachment
to things, either physical or mental. The fifth stage involves meditation upon endless space. The sixth stage passes beyond endless space
to unlimited consciousness. In passing beyond the unlimited consciousness one dwells on the attainment of nothingness, the seventh
stage. Finally, in the eighth stage, one dwells on neither consciousness
nor unconsciousness, a state of emptiness wherein one is not even
attached to his own feeling of emptiness.[12] At this point, the adept is
said to have touched the abyss, the mystic union of nothing with
nothing. This state does not guarantee the attainment of Nirvana,
which cannot be reached without a thorough study of wisdom. The
practice of dhyanas requires years of training, and even then one may
never succeed in reaching the last stage. On the other hand, meditation is a universal discipline among Buddhists; much of Buddhist
thought presupposes personal experience of it.

The four unlimited states—friendliness, compassion, sympathetic
joy, even-mindedness—are methods for the cultivation of emotions;
they reduce the distinctions between self and others. Friendliness
means good will toward people, whether enemies, friends, or
strangers. Compassion means identification with the suffering of
others as one's own and a willingness to help remove suffering. Sympathetic joy taking account of the successes of others and joining
them in happiness. Even-mindedness comes only after one has practiced the early stages of dhyanas, in which the contradictory feelings

have been eliminated. It means cultivating a neutral attitude: one is neither dejected because he is humiliated nor elated because he is honored. He is indifferent to the reactions of others toward him. Even-mindedness presupposes the absence of "I" or "not-I" in one's relations with others, even though one acts as if there were both "I" and "not-I."

Occult powers are the third aspect of concentration and come as a result of the fruitful practice of meditation. After years of training in concentration, a monk may gradually attain psychic powers, such as clairvoyance, recollection of previous births, and mind reading. There are accounts of monks who even attained such feats as levitation, passing through a wall, entering into and coming out of the earth. Here Buddhism was wedded with magic. Occultism later became a central feature of Tantric Buddhism, the religion of the Tibetans.

Although concentration removes evil thoughts and feelings, it does so only temporarily. As long as there is latent evil in man, evil thoughts and feelings will return. Removal of this latent evil requires the mastery of wisdom. In Theravada Buddhism, wisdom generally refers to the books of Abhidhamma (Further or Supreme Doctrines), the third Basket of the Pali canon. But wisdom in the technical sense means the methodical contemplation of the ultimate substances of things; it attempts to reduce things to their basic elements, such as matter, feeling, sense, emotion, reason, in order to discover the fictitious character of "self" or "person." The Abhidhamma books deal chiefly with this latter kind of analysis. Latent evil disappears when one realizes fully the illusory character of self or others. When the reality of persons or things is dissolved, then the causes of craving are also removed.

The threefold method of salvation is often made to correspond with the Eightfold Path in Theravadin scholasticism: moral discipline is equivalent to right speech, right conduct, and right livelihood; concentration means right efforts, right mindfulness, and right concentration; and wisdom involves right knowledge and right thought.

Nirvana

The Sanskrit word *Nirvana* (*Nibbana* in Pali) is composed of the root *va,* which means "to blow," and the prefix *nir,* which means "out" or "off." Etymologically, then, *Nirvana* means to "blow out."

This word was already known before the time of Buddha by both Jains and Brahmins. Jainism used it to designate the state of release (moksha), when the adept broke the chain of rebirth. Buddha also adopted it as a designation for release. But within the framework of his new teaching, and because of his polemic with Jainism and Vedism, his understanding of Nirvana differed from that of his rivals. Basically, Nirvana for him meant the cessation of cravings as a result of pursuing the Four Noble Truths, particularly the Eightfold Path; the flame of desire was now "blown out." Yet cessation of craving is not synonymous with extinction after death. On several occasions, in the Pali canon, disciples showed concern about the destiny of an enlightened man. They came to Buddha with this question: Does the enlightened person have an existence after death or is he annihilated? Buddha persistently refused to comment on these alternatives.[13] The Hindus believed that the atman (soul) of a released man united with Brahman at death; the Jains believed that the jiva (soul) of an enlightened man dwelt forever at the top of the universe. There were also pure materialists, called Charvakas and Lokayatas, who believed that the soul was identical with the body and that it died with the body.[14] Buddha wanted to distinguish his own beliefs from those of such groups. He refused to comment on existence or annihilation of the saint after death because, for him, religion did not depend on the truth of these alternatives. Religion deals with suffering, the causes of suffering, the cessation of craving, and the attaining of Nirvana. Some modern interpreters of Buddhism nevertheless identify Nirvana with annihilation, a view that was explicitly avoided by Buddha himself.

Although Buddha refused to discuss the destiny of the enlightened person, he and his disciples did give positive affirmation to Nirvana as the final goal of life. Epithets used to describe this state were:

The harbour of refuge, the cool cave, the island amidst the floods, the place of bliss, emancipation, liberation, safety, the supreme, the transcendental, the uncreated, the tranquil, the home of ease, the calm, the end of suffering, the medicine for all evil, the unshaken, the ambrosia, the immaterial, the imperishable, the abiding, the further shore, the unending, the bliss of effort, the supreme joy, the ineffable, the detachment, the holy city.[15]

Nirvana was also described as the "unborn," the "uncompounded," "not made," "not become."[16] These names and descriptions suggest that whatever Nirvana is, it is the opposite of the empirical world of pain, sense pleasure, and impermanence. As to its conceptual nature, however, Gautama said nothing. All we can say is that early Buddhism, whose tenets were authoritative to the Theravadins, understood Nirvana in essence as cessation of craving. They also conceived it as the state of the unconditioned and permanent. Early Buddhists, however, persistently refused to consider Nirvana metaphysically. That task was undertaken later by the Mahayanists.

Theravadin scholasticism distinguishes four groups of monks according to their advancement toward Nirvana and in connection with their overcoming of the Ten Fetters. (1) The aspirants are those who have broken the first three of the five lower fetters: self-illusion (belief in a permanent self), doubt, and clinging to vain rites. They have entered the stream that leads to Nirvana (like the ocean) and have been assured of the final goal, but they will be reborn several times before reaching enlightenment. (2) Once-returners are those who have overcome the first three fetters, but have not completely destroyed the next two: sensuous craving and ill will. They will return once to the world of desires before reaching Nirvana. (3) Non-returners are those who have completely destroyed the five fetters. They will be reborn once in a higher world and attain Nirvana from there. (4) Arhats are those who, in addition to the five lower fetters, have destroyed the five higher ones: craving for rebirth in worlds of forms, craving for rebirth in formless worlds, pride, restlessness, and ignorance. They have won enlightenment and are higher than celestial beings and gods.

Buddha

Gautama was believed to be human by his disciples during his own ministry. No divine origin was attributed to him.[17] Although the Pali canon ascribed to him such powers as knowledge of his own previous existences as well as those of others, knowledge of causal phenomena in the world, and the gift of miracles, these powers were also shared by other enlightened persons. The only difference between Gautama and others who also reached Nirvana was that he was the founder of the Path: he discovered the way of salvation, whereas the others were followers of the Path. However, the fact that within the Theravada tradition no enlightened person was called a Buddha after Gautama is an indication of the unique place it gave to Gautama.

The disciples viewed the death of Buddha as an empirical fact; he departed from the world and existed no more. He could neither hear prayers nor assist men, and he was not made a god. On the other hand, there is ample evidence in the Pali canon to show that Buddha was a very special person. The places in which he was born, attained enlightenment, set in motion the Wheel of Wisdom, and died soon became holy places. Pilgrimages to these places were considered meritorious, and believers paid homage to the relics of Buddha, which were enshrined in stupas.

Nowhere was the high esteem of Buddha better seen than in the devotion of the Buddhists to the "Three Refuges," also called the Three Jewels: "I go to the Buddha for refuge. I go to the Dharma for refuge. I go to the Sangha for refuge." This formula was recited by all Buddhists, a practice that probably began soon after Buddha's death. It says: one has faith in the founder of the Path, in the Truth taught by him, and in the community of monks who perpetuate it. Here Buddha became the Revealer of Truth and the object of faith. In these three sentences we catch a glimpse of Buddha as the Dharmakaya (Body of Truth) developed by the Mahayanists. In Theravada Buddhism, however, there was no doctrine concerning the divinity of Buddha; technically speaking, he was not divine. Yet, in terms of devotion, divine attributes were implicitly ascribed to Buddha by the Theravadins.

MAHAYANA BUDDHISM

Although Mahayana (Great Vehicle) Buddhism was eventually brought to East Asia, its basic doctrines and practices were developed in India between the third century B.C. and the fourth century A.D. Our purpose in this section is to trace its formation in India. Theravada and Mahayana recognized each other as branches of Buddhism, even though each claimed its own Scriptures as the direct teaching of Buddha. Historically speaking, however, the Theravadin claim bears more truth, since its Pali canon was an earlier product. Although the Mahayana Scriptures, written in Sanskrit, reflect a departure from the Theravadin tradition, most of their important beliefs reveal Theravadin origins. However Mahayana Buddhism was more adaptable than Theravadin Buddhism, and it also reflected the metaphysical influence of contemporary Hinduism.

Bodhisattva

A basic change from Theravadin tradition was the emphasis of Mahayana on the doctrine of Bodhisattva (the Enlightenment Being). The emergence of this concept was due to a number of religious considerations faced by early Mahayanists. Several ideas which had to do with the concept of the *arhat* (one who has attained Nirvana through individual efforts alone) now came under attack. The Mahayanists felt that an exclusive concern for one's own Nirvana indicates one's selfishness; he has not completely got rid of the self. Members of the new movement wanted to emphasize compassion, which implies personal sacrifice, that is, helping others reach Nirvana by postponing one's own. The shift from seeking one's own Nirvana to helping others reach it, as a condition of salvation, necessarily modified one's attitude toward the question of rebirth. Although the Mahayanist still considered rebirth as pain, he welcomed it in order to continue his work of salvation. The Theravadins, on the contrary, regarded the desire for rebirth in any form as detrimental to enlightenment. In accepting rebirth as a legitimate way of life, the Mahayanists, especially the laymen, were less interested in attaining Nirvana in present life than they were in rebirth in heavens, although Nirvana remained the ideal goal. Popular Mahayanism believed that, by having faith in a Buddha or Bodhisattva, one could be reborn in a heaven—an idea that was unacceptable to the Theravadins.

The ideal life of Mahayana was embodied in the concept of Bodhisattva or future Buddha. The Bodhisattva could have reached Nirvana if he so desired, but because of his compassion for others he postponed it. The Bodhisattva made a vow saying:

I take upon myself the burden of all suffering. . . . The whole world of living beings I must rescue, from the terrors of rebirth, of old age, of sickness. . . . And why? Because it is surely better that I alone should be in pain than that all these beings should fall into the states of woe. I must give myself away as a pawn through which the whole world is redeemed from the terrors of the hells . . . and with this my own body I must experience, for the sake of all beings, the whole mass of all painful feelings.[18]

It may be recalled that the term *Bodhisattva* also appeared in later Pali Scriptures; there, however, it referred to the past existence of Gautama, at a time when he was still a future Buddha. Theravadins also believed in the coming of Buddha Maitreya at the end of the present world; hence he is at present a Bodhisattva. Other than with these meanings, however, Bodhisattva played no important part in Theravada thought. In Mahayana Buddhism, by contrast, it attained preeminence. Mahayana Scriptures contained a profusion of Bodhisattvas in different worlds, each aiming at fulfilling his vow. They stored up infinite merits which could be shared with believers at the latter's request. These merits assisted believers toward rebirth in the heavens, so that, for all practical purpose, the Bodhisattvas were saviors.

The prominent Bodhisattvas were actually personifications of certain Buddhist qualities or beliefs. Manjusri, the Bodhisattva of wisdom, symbolizes the teaching of Buddhism. The sword he carries cuts off the cycles of birth and the bond of attachment. Mahasthamaprapta (one who has attained great power), the Bodhisattva of strength, symbolizes the power of wisdom, which prevails in all worlds and is accessible to all sentient beings. Avalokitesvara (*ishvara* means "lord," and *avalokita*, "one who looks down with compassion"), the Bodhisattva of compassion, is the personification of mercy. Maitreya, the Bodhisattva of the future Buddha, personifies the view that all sentient beings will be enlightened at the end of the present world. These and other Bodhisattvas are objects of worship.

Although Bodhisattvas are in principle divine beings, in essence they are not different from men. It is the Mahayana belief that every man can begin his career as a Bodhisattva, in the same way as Buddha did in the infinite past. Buddha was a Bodhisattva until he became enlightened, and during these numberless years he helped others attain salvation. The Mahayanists emphasized Buddha's Bodhisattva career as an example for all men; their goal was the pursuit of Bodhisattva careers in order to become Buddhas. According to Mahayana theology, Buddha as a Bodhisattva had in fact attained Nirvana. Nevertheless, he continued to be born in order to teach and save others. Siddhartha Gautama was but Buddha's apparitional body; his entrance into Nirvana was a demonstration to the world that Nirvana is attainable. His enlightenment did not prevent him from continuing rebirth for the purpose of assisting others. A Mahayana sutra says: "Although the Tathagata (Buddha) has not entered *Nirvana,* he makes a show of entering *Nirvana,* for the sake of those who have to be educated . . . for by this method I (Buddha) bring beings to maturity."[19] Although Mahayana thought made a technical distinction between Buddha and Bodhisattva, for all practical purposes Buddha was like a Bodhisattva who was merciful and continuously assisted others to reach salvation. Thus Nirvana in Mahayana thought implies the negation of Nirvana. When one is truly enlightened, one sees no difference between samsara and Nirvana. The central aim of Mahayana is the practice of the career of Bodhisattva in order to be a Buddha.

Philosophical Schools

Mahayana philosophy consisted of two major schools: the Madhyamika (Middle Way) and the Yogacara (Consciousness Only).

Middle Way

The term *Madhyamika* means "one who takes the middle way." Madhyamika philosophy probably began in the first century B.C. Its literature was called Prajna-Paramita (Transcendental Wisdom), the most important portion of the Mahayana Scriptures. According to Mahayana tradition, these sutras are a record of Buddha's teaching in Heaven after his earthly career; they are superior to Theravada Scriptures, which embody only the teaching of Buddha's earthly career. As a distinct school, Madhyamika was founded around A.D. 150, largely due to the efforts of Nagarjuna, who wrote a number of commentaries of first importance on Prajna-Paramita Scriptures.

The basic philosophical principle of Madhyamika is *sunyata* (emptiness). It is derived from *sunya*, which literally means "relating to the swollen."[20] Etymologically, *sunyata* means that a thing is swollen but is hollow inside. Emptiness in Madhyamika thought does not connote "nothing"; it refers to a thing's lack of substantiality, even though it appears to be real. Sunyata in the broad sense is thus another way of stating the universal phenomena of no-self and impermanence; it is not an entirely new concept.

Emptiness in Madhyamika philosophy has four levels of meaning. (1) Dharmas, the ultimate elements of the world, such as the skandhas (aggregates), are empty because they are impermanent.[21] A dharma is conditioned, that is, it is caused by others: the rise of a dharma is due to the convergence of many conditions. The dissolution of the supporting conditions necessarily results in the disappearance of the dharma. (2) An object or self is empty because it is composed of dharmas; it has no substantiality. *Object* or *self* is merely a delusion of man, which is due to ignorance. All so-called objects or selves are reducible to dharmas, which in turn are perishable. (3) Emptiness refers specially to the philosophy of Nagarjuna, who considered this word in terms of three levels of truth. At the lowest level, all phenominal things are real. At the second level, phenomenal things are empty—devoid of substantiality (hollow inside). Here what is affirmed at the first level is denied. At the highest level, truth lies between affirming and denying the first level; that is to say, it neither affirms nor denies the phenomenal things. This implies the negation of the second level of truth; that is, phenomenal things are empty. The highest truth, or the Middle Way, avoids one-sidedness, neither affirming nor denying; for in either case it involves attachment. To say a thing is real implies attachment; but to say that it is empty is attachment in the inverse sense. The purpose of avoiding one-sidedness is to overcome discrimination of things ("it is real" or "it is empty"). The Middle Way is the truth of nondiscrimination, which enables one to live in the world with the attitude of nondifferentiation. To hold the truth that all dualities (life and death, impermanence and permanence, rebirth and Nirvana) are not only nonessential but identical is to grasp the meaning of sunyata, emptiness. According to the Middle Way school, the understanding of this truth requires meditation; it is not the result of intellectual analysis. (4) Emptiness refers to Nirvana as inexpressible; it cannot be described, for any description implies its opposite. The Middle Way school calls Nirvana "Suchness" (*Tathagata*), which has no specific meaning. At this point emptiness or sunyata resembles the Infinite.

Although the Middle Way philosophy appears to be an analysis of the nature of reality, it is not intended to be theoretical. Emptiness is basically a practical concept, used for the purpose of meditation. The Madhyamika methodically contemplates the emptiness of things and persons in order to realize Nirvana. Since Nirvana implies its negation (what is affirmed must be denied), one reconciles oneself with the world and lives at peace with it. One who truly sees the identity of affirming and denying lives in nonassertion; he is sympathetic and friendly to all individuals precisely because he is not attached to things and persons. Hence, for the enlightened person, emptiness and compassion are identical, as can be seen in the career of a Bodhisattva. It is because the Bodhisattva is conscious of the emptiness of things that he is able to be compassionate, forgetting self and becoming involved in the welfare of others.

Consciousness Only

The very name of the second school of Mahayana philosophy, Yo-gacara, suggests that the practice of yoga, techniques of meditation, is a basic requirement for this school. Much of its philosophy presup-poses the experience of meditation. Like the Madhyamika, this school arose in the first century A.D., although its philosophy was not fully developed until A.D. 400, when two brothers, Asanga and Vasubandhu, made it prominent.[22] Both schools emphasized sunyata, emptiness, but they approached it differently. The Madhyamikas used emptiness as a logical concept to negate what is affirmed; the Yogacarins treated emptiness in terms of pure consciousness or thought. Hence Yogacara (same as *Vijnana Matra*) was called the Consciousness Only or the Thought Only (*Citta-Matra*) school.

The Yogacarins held that mind was prior to matter. All phenom-enal objects are mental constructs and are the result of craving. It is the self-centered mind, *manas,* that produces objects of discrimina-tion and projects them externally. External objects are comparable to ocean waves; it is the wind which causes the waves. When the wind (the discriminate thoughts) ceases, the waves (external objects) also disappear. Just as the waves disappear when the wind ceases, so ex-ternal objects cease to exist when there are no discriminate thoughts in the mind. Names or ideas are given by the mind to phenomenal matters that by themselves are nothing but transient, impersonal ele-ments. Mind forms representations of things because of its self-centeredness, which posits duality between self and the world. Con-sciousness of self is the result of craving. The unenlightened person's mind is by nature self-centered, and this conditions everything he perceives and thinks. The primary task of the Yogacara school is therefore the removal of ego consciousness from the mind. This school is sometimes called subjective idealism in the West, and that appellation is somewhat correct. But subjective idealism, as in the philosophy of Berkeley, assumes the absoluteness of ideas, whereas the Yogacara school regards ideas as the delusions of man prior to his awakening.

Man's essential nature is the original or absolute mind, *alaya-vijnana* (store consciousness), which by itself is empty and pure, that is, without ego consciousness or discriminate thoughts. But an un-enlightened individual's store consciousness contains the residual effects of actions, called seeds, or *bija,* which is another designation for the karmic matter. These seeds give rise to the self-centered mind

(manas) which makes the store consciousness discriminative, resulting in the duality between self and world. In Yogacara thought mind
as self-consciousness is derivative, while the store consciousness is
original; the former is empirical, whereas the latter is metaphysical.
Through meditation the adept gradually causes the seeds to dis-
integrate; once this has been accomplished, the self-centered mind is
also dissolved. What remains is the pristine nature of man, the pure
and empty store consciousness. When one attains this original state,
he realizes the voidness of phenomenal things, and thereby the duality between self and the world is also removed. This pure state of
store consciousness is called sunyata, or emptiness, the Nirvana of the
Yogacara school.

So long as one lives in ignorance, one's mind undergoes the "three
transformations." The first transformation refers to the store consciousness as the mind evolves from it. The second transformation
refers to the mind as ego consciousness. The third transformation
refers to discriminate thoughts as the mind produces individual
images and perceives in terms of sense objects. These three transformations take place simultaneously and continuously, making up
the phenomenal world which is but the manifestation of the store
consciousness. Salvation in Yogacara thought involves a revulsion
from the phenomenal world. This can be achieved through meditation whereby one gradually removes ego consciousness until the pure
nature of store consciousness is restored.

Like the Middle Way philosophy, the Consciousness Only school
also accepts the relative value of the phenomenal world; hence ideas
and concepts do express relative truth. But for one who has awakened, things, including the empirical mind, have no self-existence.
Of course, the saint still lives in the phenomenal world; but he sees
the emptiness behind the phenomenal objects and ideas. For him
there is no basic distinction between the "inside" and the "outside,"
between self and others. Pure consciousness is the Infinite.

Trikaya

Theravada discussion on Buddha was centered around the historical
Gautama Buddha, although references were made to other Buddhas.
The term *Dharmakaya* (Dharma body) appeared in late Pali Scriptures, but there it meant the body of doctrines. There was no interest
in the metaphysical meaning of Buddha. In Mahayana Scriptures
there was a profusion of Buddhas and Bodhisattvas, who reside in

imaginary worlds. A need was then felt to relate these supernatural beings to the founder and to consider them under an overall concept. The outcome of this endeavor was the doctrine of Trikaya, the three-body of Buddha, comparable to the Trinity in Christianity.[23] In the doctrine of Trikaya. Dharmakaya is the Absolute or the Ultimate Reality, which refers to Suchness (Tathagata) or sunyata. It is form-less, incorporeal, inexpressible, eternal, and omnipresent and lies behind particularities and individualities. Since Mahayana thought considered all sentient beings to be potential Bodhisattvas or Bud-dhas-to-be, the Dharma body is present in them as the Buddha nature.

Since the Dharma body is formless, it cannot be perceived or con-ceived as a distinct or finite entity. Buddha as a distinct object is the function of *Sambhogakaya* (body of bliss), which is an emanation of Dharmakaya. Body of bliss is corporeal and divisible and can be infinitely multiplied. It refers to the numerous imaginary Buddhas depicted in the Mahayana Scriptures, for instance the Buddha in the Pure Land. Body of bliss appears in various worlds as different Buddhas, and in a state of bliss each addresses an assembly of Bodhi-sattvas; Buddha is in such a state because he enjoys his own message of truth, and the Bodhisattvas are so because they share the same truth with him. Body of bliss is specially related to the Bodhisattvas, for only they can see this magical or transfigured body, which has thirty-two marks (long ear lobes and so on). Body of bliss also speaks different kinds and levels of truth, relative to the spiritual conditions of the audience of Bodhisattvas. This body, however, is not visible to ordinary sentient beings, whose spiritual conditions are too low to perceive it. This mythological account about body of bliss can be translated into empirical terms: the Sambhogakaya is actually the creation of high-minded persons, Bodhisattvas, who are enlightened and follow the truth of Buddha. But since the Buddha nature, Dharma body, is formless and inexpressible, it cannot be a finite object of faith. Sambhogakaya as the emanation of Dharma body means that Buddhas are mental products of spiritually minded per-sons, who use them as objects of faith; they are the representations of Dharma body, the eternal Buddha. The inability of ordinary sentient beings to see Sambhogakaya means that their conditions of existence prevent them from forming a proper image of Buddha; they do not know truth.

Nirmanakaya (body of transformation) refers to the empirical or historical person, Siddhartha Gautama. It also emanated from the Dharma body; the truth was now actually transformed into a person, whose deeds and life were seen even by ordinary sentient beings in India at one time. This body as a religious phenomenon is comparable to Jesus Christ in the Christian Trinity. But, according to Yogacara theology, Buddha as Dharma body is eternal, not subject to the processes of life and death. On the other hand, Buddha as Gautama was subject to life and death; this was a mere demonstration that Nirvana is attainable for men everywhere. Hence Dharmakaya as body of transformation is only an apparition, finite and transient. It can be seen that Gautama Buddha as a part of the Trikaya has a less exalted place in Mahayana Buddhism than has Jesus Christ as the third person in the Christian Trinity.

The doctrine of Trikaya is traditionally associated with the Yogacara school of Buddhism. Dharma body is pure consciousness or sunyata. Body of bliss as an emanation of Dharma body exists in the mind of Bodhisattvas. Body of transformation is Dharma body as an apparition. In the final analysis, both body of bliss and body of transformation are finite and impermanent; they are manifestations of the absolute Dharma body.

Pure Land

The growth of Mahayana Buddhism coincided with the spread of the bhakti (devotion) movement in Hinduism, which emphasized faith in the personal god Krishna, who promises salvation to all who have faith in him. Mahayana Buddhism also taught salvation for all, as well as faith in a Buddha or Bodhisattva as savior. This was especially true in the Pure Land sect. The first phase of Pure Land theology was represented by the Lotus Sutra (Saddharma-Pundarika), in which the historical Buddha was depicted as the Eternal One who was addressing a huge assembly of 80,000 Bodhisattvas, together with some unenlightened persons, about universal salvation. Some followers who favored salvation for the few left the assembly in disgust—much to Buddha's delight. Two Bodhisattvas, Avalokitesvara (compassion) and Manjusri (wisdom), who later became popular in China and Japan, were also present. On the same occasion Buddha through his supernatural power made the assembly see the 18,000 Buddha fields, future abodes of bliss for those who have faith in him. This new motif in Buddhism, universal salvation by faith, was probably stimulated by the Krishna cult of Hinduism.

The second phase of the Pure Land sect was represented by the longer and the shorter versions of the Sukhavati-vyuha, or the Pure

Land Sutra, in which Buddha mentioned a list of eighty-one Buddhas. The last Buddha on the list then appeared on the scene and described to his disciple Dharmakara the perfections of the many Buddha fields. After listening to this instruction, Dharmakara told his master that he could imagine a land eighty-one times more excellent than all the fields hitherto described. He then made a wish to be an ideal Buddha in the ideal Buddha field envisaged by him. After the passing of many eons, Dharmakara finally attained his wish and became Amitabha Buddha in the Sukhavati, the Pure Land, also called the Happy Land of the West. Amitabha was the Buddha of Infinite Light *(Amitabha)*. He was also called Amitayus, Infinite Life Span.[24] Both the longer and the shorter versions of the sutra describe Amitabha as the God of unlimited compassion, who promises devotees rebirth in his land, where evil and pain are completely absent and happiness reigns. The only difference between the two versions is that whereas the longer one demanded both meritorious deeds and faith from a devotee, the shorter one required only faith in Amitabha; rebirth in the Pure Land was not a reward for good deeds, but rather a divine gift for one who trusted Amitabha as his personal savior. The shorter version of the Pure Land Sutra, which expressed Buddhism as faith, enjoyed greater popularity. In the longer version, there was scant mention of Avalokitesvara and Mahasthamaprapta, the two Bodhisattvas who together with Amitabha later formed the Trinity in Pure Land theology, while the shorter version did not mention the two Bodhisattvas at all. It is most probable that at one time the Pure Land sect regarded Amitabha Buddha as the only savior-god. The Pure Land sect gradually expanded, however, the status of Bodhisattvas increased, and the Bodhisattvas became the active earthly agents of Amitabha.

The third or full-grown stage of the Pure Land sect corresponded with the increasing popularity of Avalokitesvara, the Bodhisattva of compassion whose task was to rescue beings from many worlds to the Pure Land. Avalokitesvara was reborn in many forms (as Brahmā, Shiva, man, horse, and so on), to save not only men but also beasts and insects[25] in order to accomplish his duty. So long as there was a single individual unrescued, he would return to the world. As for the condition of salvation, all it required was faith in Avalokitesvara or Amitabha as the savior. Although three deities (Amitabha, Avalokitesvara, Mahasthamaprapta) constituted the Pure Land Trinity, they all conveyed the ideal of compassion. Amitabha was the resident Buddha of compassion. Avalokitesvara was the incarnation of compassion, and Mahasthamaprapta was its power. According to Pure Land theology, rebirth in Sukhavati was not the final end. The ultimate end was to become a Buddha. The Pure Land was the realm where individuals continue to hear the words of Amitabha and prepare themselves for Buddhahood, or enlightenment.

Our first reaction to Pure Land theology, with its graphic descriptions of the land of bliss and other Buddha fields, may be the impression that the Buddhism of faith is incongruent with the Buddhism of wisdom. Actually, this is not so. From the viewpoint of Mahayana philosophy, the Pure Land is but a creation of the mind. Since a Buddhist in Mahayanism is by definition a Bodhisattva—a future Buddha—the Pure Land exists in the mind of a Bodhisattva. For the follower of the Consciousness Only philosophy, all external objects are creations of the mind, including the Buddha fields. The Absolute Reality transcends any particular form of consciousness. For the student of the Middle Way philosophy, ultimate truth stands between affirming and denying; hence what is affirmed must be denied. Once a man has been enlightened, samsara is no different from Nirvana; the world in which he lives is really no different from the Pure Land beyond. Mahayana wisdom does not reject the Pure Land theology; it simply regards it as one aspect of relative truth. There is no contradiction between wisdom and belief in the Pure Land when one acknowledges that one's devotion to Buddha and Bodhisattvas, along with one's vision of the Pure Land, is but a means for salvation.

MANTRAYANA BUDDHISM

Mantrayana (esoteric words as a vehicle of salvation), which began in India during the seventh and eighth centuries, represented the third and the last stage of Buddhism in India. In contrast to Theravada and Mahayana, both of which emphasized knowledge as an ingredient of salvation, Mantrayana stressed spells, magic, and rituals as means of salvation; it represented a fusion between Buddhism and certain magical aspects of Hinduism. Although Mantrayana is the third branch of Buddhism, it must be viewed within the context of

FIGURE 20.2 A Buddhist mandala of the Wheel of Becoming (Bhavacakra) held by the Demon of Impermanency. (*Information Service of India*)

Mahayana; for it presupposes the emptiness of the Middle Way school and the concentration of the Consciousness Only school.

Mantra literally means a group of esoteric words or syllables; mantras can be used as prayers. For the uninitiated, these syllables are completely meaningless, but for one who has carried out proper ritual observances with right concentration, these syllables can produce intended effects of good and evil in the external world. There were mantras for different purposes.

A *mandala* is a picturesque symbol which usually contains the images of a group of Buddhas and Bodhisattvas who symbolize the cosmos. The presupposition is that the universe is a manifestation of these divine beings. Since man is a microcosm of the universe, he is in essence identical with them. Furthermore, since Buddhas and Bodhisattvas are really identical with the Supreme Buddha, man is in

essence also identical with it. When one draws a mandala in ritual ceremony, he experiences the mystic union between himself and the Supreme Buddha. A mandala can be drawn on cloth, on paper, or on the ground. The drawing of a mandala, a cosmic diagram (see Figure 20.2), was an integral part of the Mantrayana school.

We have discussed the three Buddhist vehicles (Hinayana, Mahayana, Mantrayana) of salvation; each of them is actually a particular expression of the same truth. This notion is conveyed by the term *Ekayana* (one vehicle), which means that diverse Buddhist expressions and practices all lead to the same salvation.

NOTES

1. This cosmology, also shared by Jainism, was probably indigenous to India.
2. For information on the pre-Aryan or Dravidian origins of Jainism and its affinity with Buddhism, see Heinrich Zimmer, *Philosophies of India,* Joseph Campbell, ed. (New York: World, 1956), pp. 181–262.
3. *Ibid.,* pp. 218–219.
4. Such information is contained in the *Jataka* (Stories of Former Lives of Gautama Buddha). See *Buddhist Scriptures,* trans. by Edward Conze (Baltimore: Penguin, 1959), pp. 19–66.
5. In Buddhist Scriptures Brahmā (masculine gender) is referred to as a personal god who rules in a separate region of the cosmos; he is not to be identified with Brahmā (the creator-god) of Hinduism.
6. The Personalists (Pudgalavadins) were divided into two groups: the Vatsiputriyas and the Sammitiyas. See: Edward Conze, *Buddhist Thought in India* (London: Allen & Unwin, 1962), pp. 122–130.
7. *Stupas* later became popular sacred objects in Buddhist countries. They were erected by believers in order to secure merit for themselves. Many stupas contained relics of Buddhism.
8. The Mahayanists referred to Theravada as Hinayana (the Lesser Vehicle), an uncomplimentary term disliked by the Theravadins. Although "Hinayana," as contrasted with "Mahayana," is better known in the West, we prefer the use of "Theravada" in compliance with the wish of its present followers.
9. The Theravada canon is called the Tipitaka (Three Baskets), and is composed of three parts: (1) Vinaya Pitaka (Basket of Monastic Rules), (2) Sutta Pitaka (Basket of Discourses), (3) Abhidhamma Pitaka (Basket of Wisdom) and is written in Pali.
10. For example, he categorized Ten Fetters (self-illusion, doubt, clinging to vain rites, sensuous craving, ill will, craving for rebirth in worlds of forms, craving for rebirth in formless worlds, pride, restlessness, ignorance), Ten Perfections (liberality, morality, renunciation, wisdom, energy, forbearance, truthfulness, resolution, good will, equanimity), and Ten Precepts (no injury, stealing, adultery, lying, intoxication, overeating, enjoyment of

dancing, singing, or dramatic spectacles, refraining from using garlands, scents, or ornaments, sleeping in soft beds, accepting gold or silver).

11. The twelve links of causation appear in the *Majjihima-nikaya*. See Edward Conze, ed., *Buddhist Texts* (New York: Harper, 1964), pp. 67–68.

12. For eight dhyanas, see Edward Conze, *Buddhist Meditation* (London: Allen and Unwin, 1956), pp. 113–118.

13. Edward J. Thomas, *The History of Buddhist Thought* (London: Routledge & Kegan Paul, 1933), pp. 124–126.

14. A. B. Keith, *Buddhist Philosophy* (Oxford: Clarendon Press, 1923), pp. 135–136.

15. T. W. Rhys Davids, *Early Buddhism* (London, 1908), quoted in Thomas, *op. cit.*, p. 128. Used by permission.

16. Conze, *Buddhist Texts*, p. 95.

17. According to the *Jataka*, Buddha's previous existence was as a god in the Tushita heaven. But such an existence cannot be considered divine in the proper sense, since it is subject to impermanence and pain.

18. Conze, *Buddhist Texts*, pp. 131–132. Used by permission.

19. *Ibid.*, p. 142. It is from Saddharma-Pundarika Sutra (Lotus Sutra).

20. Edward Conze, *Buddhism: Its Essence and Development* (New York: Harper Torchbooks, 1959), p. 130.

21. Sarvastivada, a school eventually merged with the Mahayana, enumerated seventy-two compounded things (dharmas); forty-six of them are mental qualities, such as feeling, volition, intellect; dharmas as matter are the five sense objects, five sense organs, and latent matter, that is, the impressions left on the bodily organs as a result of physical actions.

22. Some basic Yogacara Scriptures are *Lankavatara, Trimsika* (Thirty Verses), and *Shraddhotpada* (Awakening of Faith).

23. For a lucid discussion of trikaya, see D. T. Suzuki, *Outlines of Mahayana Buddhism* (New York: Schocken, 1963), pp. 242–276.

24. The Pure Land sect arose between the first century B.C. and the first century A.D. in northwest India bordering Persia. At that time Zervanism, a Persian religion, held that Zervan (Infinite Time) was the divine principle that created both the good and evil gods. Some scholars believe that since Amitabha was also called Amitayus (infinite life span), the worship of Amitabha was influenced by Persian religion. But the evidence is inconclusive.

25. The career of Avalokitesvara was depicted in the Karandavyuha, a sutra that shows the full development of Bodhisattva worship.

21 Buddhism in East Asia

Before dealing with the religions of China, a brief definition of religion in the Chinese tradition is necessary in view of the fact that much of the discussion to follow pertains to ethics, philosophy, and metaphysics. In a broad sense, religion is man's apprehension of and participation in the cosmos, which is conceived of either as the source and the totality of moral order, as in Confucianism, or as the source and totality of nature, as in Taoism. In either case, religion is a consideration of the relationship between man and the cosmos; the harmony between them is deemed supremely important for man's destiny. This somewhat inclusive definition of religion will enable us to include not only the traditional religious entities such as divinities and cultic practices but also philosophy and metaphysics, insofar as these bear a reference to the Ultimate.

The apprehension of the cosmos in Chinese religion is accomplished by means of a large number of modalities. It can be apprehended through the polytheistic modes such as ancestor-deities, gods, or demons, or through a single Being such as Shang Ti (Ruler Above). It can also be apprehended in terms of metaphysical concepts such as T'ien (Heaven), Tao, or Buddha.

So far as the expressions of man's relations with the cosmos are concerned, these take at least three forms: cultic expression (rituals and ceremonies), sociological expression (family, clan, state, the Confucian shrine, the Taoist or Buddhist temple), and intellectual expression (ethics, philosophy, metaphysics). In the discussions of Buddhism, Confucianism, and Taoism that follow, religion is understood mainly in two senses: as cultic and sociological expression and as ethics, philosophy, and metaphysics.

FIGURE 21.1   The image of Buddha at Kamakura. (*Japan National Tourist Organization*)

BUDDHISM IN CHINA AND JAPAN

Although Buddhists from India and central Asia began to reach China in the first century A.D., during the Han dynasty, the new religion did not gain momentum in China until the third century. It spread widely during the period of the Political Disunion (A.D. 220–589), when China was divided between north and south and there were dynastic changes and wars in both regions. Morale in government and society was low, and the earthbound Confucian ethics

could not meet the deepest needs of the people, but Buddhism could. Buddhas and Bodhisattvas could be prayed to for protection and strength, and the Buddhist heavens, as eternal abodes for men, gave the Chinese a transcendental hope that Confucianism did not provide. The Buddhist doctrines of rebirth and karma offered the Chinese a cosmic outlook and moral incentive.

When Mahayana philosophy first reached China, the Taoists were surprised to find that there was a similarity between Buddhism and the philosophy of Lao-tzu and Chuang-tzu. Many Taoists were converted to the new religion, and some collaborated with foreign Buddhists in translating Buddhist works from Sanskrit into Chinese. The outstanding translator was Kumarajiva (344–413), an Indian-Kuchean Buddhist, who under imperial patronage spent his last years at the Chinese capital where, assisted by 1,000 monks, he translated seventy-two philosophical texts into Chinese. These translations of literary works, together with Chinese commentaries on them, constituted a major intellectual production in China from the third to the tenth century, during which period Confucian philosophy remained dormant and stagnant. The influence of Buddhism in China can be seen in a Chinese work entitled *Lives of Eminent Monks,* completed in A.D. 519, in which biographies of nearly 500 monks were recorded. By the Tang dynasty (618–906) Indian Buddhism was influencing every aspect of Chinese culture—architecture, painting, sculpture, music, literature, philosophy, and religion. In architecture, for example, the pagoda, which is a common Buddhist symbol in China, was derived from the stupa of India. But a pagoda, unlike a stupa, does not contain relics; it usually stands on top of a hill near an important temple, and it symbolizes man's aspiration for Buddhahood.

Buddhism was introduced to Japan in the sixth century by a Korean king. The early history of Japanese Buddhism is characterized by imperial enthusiasm and patronage. The court believed that this new religion was culturally superior to Shinto, the native religion of Japan. The magical and esoteric aspects of Buddhism had a strong appeal for the rulers from the very beginning, but it was not until the regency of Prince Shōtoku (ruled 592–621) that the spiritual and ethical import of this new faith was appreciated. Shōtoku was not only a sincere believer; he was also a Buddhist scholar who wrote and

FIGURE 21.2   A Buddhist temple at Nara. *(Japan National Tourist Organization)*

lectured on the sutras. He wanted to make this new religion the faith of the people and Confucianism the philosophy of government, and so he sponsored the building of Buddhist temples. The famous Horyuji, a temple at Nara, was completed in 607 and is the oldest wooden building in the world. Buddhist history in Japan after Shōtoku's time can be summarized in three periods—the Nara, Heian, and Kamakura periods—each is designated by the place where the national government was located.

During the Nara Period (710–794) the imperial court continued the expansion of temple building (see Figure 21.2); it appointed state masters to supervise temple affairs in provinces and sent monks to China to study and acquire Buddhist documents. The huge statue of the sitting Lochana Buddha, a manifestation of Buddha Sakyamuni, who was considered to be the Supreme Buddha by the Kegon school of Buddhism, is fifty-five and one-half feet high and was erected in this period. Because of the close relations between government and Buddhism, some priests became influential ministers, and their power began to threaten the royal house. Clerical interference with state affairs was one reason for changing the capital from Nara to Heian (Kyōto).

A major characteristic in the Heian Period (794–1192) was the reciprocal influence of Shinto and Buddhism. Shinto adopted Buddhist deities, and Buddhism assimilated Shinto gods. From the time that Buddhism was first introduced into Japan, it enjoyed a greater prestige than Shinto; there developed the view that Shinto gods were incarnations of Buddhas and Bodhisattvas, a view that was even held by Shinto priests. This phenomenon shows the high status of Buddhism, as well as the interpenetration of these two religions. Toward the end of the Heian Period Buddhism became decadent and there was a general disintegration of morals: the court became weak and powerful families arose; monks became materialistic and different sects rivaled each other; and people felt that the "end of the Law" was at hand. The later Heian Period also saw the rise of clerical militarism, with various monasteries arming themselves in rivalry, and occasionally, monastery troops even marching to the capital against the government.

The Kamakura Period (1192–1336) was the era in which Japan was governed by shōguns, who had their headquarters in the town of Kamakura while the court existed in Kyōto. The shōgunate was plagued by war among factions led by feudal lords, and impermanence and vicissitude characterized the general mood of the time. New Buddhist sects emerged to answer the needs of warriors who were facing hardship and death and were therefore looking for a faith that could give them immediate comfort and personal security. Three new sects appealed to the common people: Pure Land, which emphasized faith; Zen (Ch'an), which stressed simple and ordinary living; and Nichiren, which taught personal efforts and the unification of Japan. For the first time in Japan, Buddhism became truly a religion of the people, whereas it had formerly been mainly the religion of the court and the aristocrats. The famous Kamakura Buddha (Daibutsu or Amida) was constructed in 1252 (see Figure 21.1).

Sects

Although Theravada did exist in both China and Japan in early times, our discussion of sects is confined to the Mahayana tradition because Buddhism in these countries has developed primarily from Mahayana. Two basic phenomena characterize Buddhist schools in China and Japan: one is the overlapping of beliefs among different sects, and the other is the adjustment of Buddhism to the cultural milieu of East Asia. Each sect maintained its distinct features while sharing some beliefs with others. The dominant sects were Chinese and Japanese in character, although the classical Mahayana thought of India was presupposed.

The Middle Way (Madhyamika) school, called the Three Treatise[1] (Sanlun) in China, was founded by Chi-tsang (549–623), who used Taoist terms to expound the philosophy of emptiness. This school, which owed a great deal to the translations of Kumarajiva, was introduced to Japan in 625 and was there called the Sanron sect. The Middle Way school as a distinct religious body eventually died in both countries because its philosophy of negation was too Indian for the East Asians. Many works of the Middle Way philosophy, however, continued to be studied by leaders of the larger sects, particularly Ch'an Buddhism, to which most of the eminent monk-philosophers belonged.

The Consciousness Only school, founded in China in the seventh century, was called the Fa-hsiang sect. It was particularly associated with an eminent monk, Hsüan Tsang (596–664), who set off on his famous journey to India by way of central Asia in 629 in order to pursue further Buddhist study. He did not return until 645, after spending sixteen years abroad; when he did return, he brought home 657 Buddhist works. Under imperial sponsorship and with the assistance of a large group of monks, he devoted some twenty years to translating seventy-five documents, principally of the Consciousness Only philosophy. He also wrote an important commentary on a work of Vasubandhu, in addition to a memoir on his travel abroad; the latter stirred up the imagination of the Chinese. The Consciousness Only school was called Hossō in Japan, where it was founded in the seventh century by Dōshō (628–700), who went to China in 653 and studied under Hsüan Tsang for ten years. The Consciousness Only school, which disappeared in China after the Tang dynasty, survived in Japan, although it remained small in size. The view of this school that some people are too evil to be saved is contrary to the idea of universal salvation which was held by other sects in China and Japan. It taught the separation between the phenomenal and the noumenal worlds, whereas other sects in East Asia maintained the unity of these two realms. As philosophy, however, the Consciousness Only school continued to influence other sects, particularly the Pure Land. It should be remembered that both the Middle Way and the Consciousness Only philosophies remained the backbone of Mahayana thought in the two countries, although as religious sects they have only historical interest.

T'ien-t'ai (Tendai)

The T'ien-t'ai sect was founded by Chih-i (515–597), a monk, and named for Mount T'ien-t'ai in east China, where he taught. By the sixth century China already possessed a proliferation of translated sutras, both Theravada and Mahayana. These embodied contradictory beliefs, although they were all supposed to have originated from Gautama Buddha. With much labor and ingenuity Chih-i worked out a scheme whereby Scriptures were arranged according to the chronological life of Buddha after his enlightenment. Buddha's ministry was divided into five stages, in all of which, with the exception of the first stage, he preached doctrines that ranged from the elementary to the profound, in accordance with the spiritual and intellectual qualifications of his listeners.

In the first stage, immediately after his enlightenment, Buddha spent three weeks in a state of bliss preaching the Avatamsaka (Flower Splendor) Sutra. But his audience left in despair because they could not comprehend what he had said. Buddha realized that mankind was not ready for such profound truth. Hence he decided to teach the Theravada doctrines instead.

In the second stage, which lasted for twelve years, he taught about the Four Noble Truths, including the Eightfold Path and the Twelve Links of causation. Although many were converted, Buddha considered these beliefs to be for the less gifted only.

In the third stage, Buddha compared Theravada doctrines with Mahayana beliefs, pointing out that the arhats had not yet cleansed themselves of selfishness because they were preoccupied with self-salvation, whereas the Bodhisattvas who postponed their own salvation for the sake of others were truly selfless. Hence the Theravada truths are not final. Although Buddha spent eight years comparing these two branches of truth, he did not teach higher Mahayana doctrines in this period.

In the fourth stage, he taught the Madhyamika philosophy as embodied in the Prajna-Paramita (Transcendental Wisdom) Sutras. For twenty-two years he preached about sunyata, pointing out that all dualities such as life and death, samsara and Nirvana, are non-existent.

In the fifth stage, the last eight years of his life, Buddha preached the Saddharma-Pundarika (Lotus) Sutra, which embodied the essence of Buddhism. This sutra taught the doctrine of *Ekayana* (one vehicle)—that is, Theravada and Mahayana are united, and salvation is for all sentient beings.

Chih-i's theology of Scripture, which is based on the ministry of Buddha, is a gigantic attempt to show the universalism and inclusiveness of Buddhism: different doctrines are made to suit peoples of diverse gifts and backgrounds, and they are simply different levels of the same truth. This theology also demonstrates the Chinese interest in books, which is a heritage of Confucianism.

The T'ien-t'ai school closely follows the Middle Way philosophy of Nagarjuna; it is indeed its Chinese version. According to Chih-i, reality can be interpreted in terms of a threefold truth: (1) Reality is empty because things are nonsubstantial and lack independence. (2) Reality is not nonexistent because things have temporary existence. (3) Reality is between emptiness and temporariness, which means that reality is the identity between these two.

The T'ien-t'ai school was introduced into Japan by Saichō (767–822), who founded the Tendai sect in 806, after his journey to China; its center was at Mount Hiei near Heian. Since it arose during the Heian period when Buddhism was politically powerful, the Tendai sect produced a military clergy and gained wealth. It was the mother of three important new schools, namely, Amidism (Pure Land), Zen, and Nichiren Buddhism.

Hua-yen (Kegon)

The Hua-yen sect was based on the Avatamsaka Sutra which, according to Chinese tradition, Buddha preached immediately after the enlightenment and which was too difficult to be understood by his audience. Although this Scripture was a text of the Consciousness Only school in India, the Hua-yen sect, like the T'ien-t'ai, had no counterpart in India. It was established by Fa-tsang (643–712) during the Tang dynasty.

This school advocated the fusion between the Buddha mind and the phenomenal world; since the former contains the latter, the myriad things are but manifestations of the Buddha mind. Once Fa-tsang was called to preach to Empress Wu. In order to illustrate the fusion between the Buddha mind and the world, he pointed to a statue of a golden lion, saying that the different parts of the lion are but manifestations of the same gold. The Hua-yen sect also emphasized the doctrine of inclusion of the whole in the part: all things are interrelated; the analysis of the part discloses the whole. For example, let a bright jewel be attached to each intersection of a net; each jewel will reflect the images of the others, and each reflected image will in turn contain the images of the rest. This example shows the inclusion of the whole in the part, as well as the reciprocal immanence of things. As a philosophy, the Hua-yen school represented organismic thought, which later influenced neo-Confucian philosophy. As a religion, this school held, through the doctrine of interfusion, that the Buddha mind is present in each thing; hence every man can attain Buddhahood.

Although the Hua-yen sect was close to the Consciousness Only school in emphasizing mind as the basis of things, it gave greater value to the phenomenal world as the concrete expression of the Buddha nature; whereas in the Consciousness Only school, the phenomenal world is a mere reflection of the Buddha. The interfusion between the Buddha mind and concrete things in the Hua-yen sect reflects the Chinese attitude of world affirmation, that is, the world embodies the Buddha mind and hence is not illusory. This probably explains why the Hua-yen sect survived the Consciousness Only school in China.

According to Japanese tradition, the Hua-yen sect, called Kegon

(Flower Splendor) in Japan, was founded by Bodhisena, an Indian monk who arrived in Japan around 736 and taught the Avatamsaka Sutra at Nara. A more reliable tradition attributed the establishment of this sect to Dōsen (596–667). Emperor Shōmu (ruled 724–748) was attracted by the Kegon theology and built the Todaiji Temple at Nara in order to propagate its teaching. Todaiji was historically the center of Kegon, and it was at this temple that the huge statue of Lochana Buddha was erected. The Kegon sect declined after the capital was moved from Nara, but the Avatamsaka Sutra continued to be studied by other sects in Japan.

Chen-yen (Shingon)

The practice of magic was known in early Chinese Buddhism, but Mantrayana was not founded in China until the eighth century. This school was called Chên-yen (true or esoteric words), a translation of the term *mantra*. Its establishment was largely due to the activities of three outstanding Indian monks who came to China during this period. Subhakarasimha, who arrived in 716, together with a Chinese monk, translated the Mahavairocana (the Great Brilliant One) Sutra, which became the principal text of esoteric Buddhism in China and Japan. It inspired the creation of a famous mandala in the Tang dynasty called *garbhadhatu* (womb element). This mandala depicted Mahavairocana as the Supreme Buddha surrounded by four other Buddhas of the four directions. These five Buddhas are the cosmic counterpart of the five earthly skandhas.[2] Vajrabodhi arrived in 720 and was active in instituting initiation rites and painting mandalas. His disciple Amoghavajra came with him and expanded the work after his death. The numerous miracles of these three Indian teachers, all of whom died in China, were recorded. The Chinese emperors were particularly impressed by their success in invoking rainfall through magical syllables. Amoghavajra was a favorite monk of three successive Chinese emperors. The Chên-yen sect suffered great losses during the great Buddhist persecution of 845–870. Forty-six hundred monasteries were destroyed, and 260,000 monks and nuns were forced to return to laity. Chên-yen virtually disappeared as a sect when the Tang dynasty fell in 906. The rise of neo-Confucianism, which was rationalistic and anti-Buddhist, was another factor in its downfall. But the magical practices of this school did not die; they were incorporated by other Buddhist sects.

Traces of esoteric Buddhism existed in the early history of Japanese Buddhism, although Mantrayana as a sect was not estab-

lished until the ninth century. It was called Shingon (true words),
a reference to mantra. This sect owed its development to Kūkai
(774–835), a versatile scholar and artist and an important figure in
Japanese history. He became a student of Buddhism after having
studied Confucian and Taoist classics. By the time Kūkai started
his journey to China in 804 in search of the right school, he was
already a learned monk. The following year he met Hui-kuo (746–
805), a Mantrayana master, who initiated him into esoteric rites.
Kūkai returned home in 806 and began conducting Shingon rituals
under imperial sponsorship. In 816 he received a land grant to
build a temple, and this date is commonly associated with the
founding of the school. He built the monastery on Mount Koya,
near Osaka, which has been a major Shingon center to this day.

Although the Shingon sect included Indian esotericism, it was a distinctly Japanese school, for it followed the syncretistic theology of Kūkai. A good example of this theology is Kūkai's work in Chinese entitled *Treatise on the Ten Stages of the Heart,* in which he develops a view of religious consciousness in terms of ten progressive levels; one moves upward by degrees from sensuous desire to Confucian morality, Taoist spirituality, Theravada self-denial, Mahayana metaphysics, until finally one reaches Shingon mystic truth, which is the height of man's attainment. The ultimate end of Shingon theology is identity with the Supreme Buddha Mahavairocana, which can be achieved through esoteric rites. Today the Shingon sect has more than 3 million followers.

Ching-t'u (Jodo)

Pure Land Buddhism was active in northwest India in the beginning of the Christian era, and its missionaries reached China around A.r 150. However, there was no formal organization of this school in China until 402, when Hui-yüan (334–417), a Taoist scholar, founded the Ching-t'u sect, and it did not spread widely until the Tang dynasty (618–906). The theology of the Pure Land school of classical Mahayana had a special appeal for the Chinese, who until the Tang dynasty did not have a doctrine of a heavenly realm as a future abode for men. In the Tang dynasty, bliss of the Happy Land and miseries of Hell became popular themes of painting. In addition to Amitabha Buddha, the most popular deity of the Pure Land sect was Avalokitesvara (Kuan-yin in Chinese and Kuannon in Japanese, Figure 21.3), who in early times was depicted as a male. In the eighth century images of a female Kuan-yin began to appear, most probably as a result of the influence of Tibetan Buddhism. Both Chinese and Japanese Pure Land devotees emphasized invocation of the name of Amitabha Buddha. The recitation form in Chinese is "O-mi-t'o-fo"; it is "Namu Amida Butsu" in Japanese.

Amitabha (Amida) Buddha was known in Japan in the Nara period. But the Jōdo sect did not exist there until 1175, when Hōnen (1133–1212), formerly a monk of the Tendai sect, formed this school as a reaction against the corrupt monastery life of his time. A disciple of his, Shinran (1173–1262), founded the Shin

FIGURE 21.3 A statue of Avalokitesvara (Kuan-yin). (*The Metropolitan Museum of Art, Purchase 1934, Joseph Pulitzer Bequest*)

(True) sect, which held a radical view of faith: man was basically evil and incapable of doing good. It is therefore utterly impossible for man to reach the Pure Land by work; salvation depends entirely on the grace of Amitabha. The Jōdo sect believed that practices other than that of invoking the divine name can also be a way to rebirth in the Pure Land, whereas the Shin sect abandoned all requirements except invoking the divine name. Lectures and ceremonies, such as weddings, were held at Shin temples, although worship of Buddhas or Bodhisattvas was not practiced. Because they believed that special practices were futile, followers of this sect simply lived normal lives. Their priests were married, but worked full-time as leaders of the sect. Today, more than half of the Buddhists in Japan are members of Pure Land sects, about 18,500,000 strong.

Ch'an (Zen)

The Japanese term *zen* was derived from the Chinese *ch'an,* which was a translation of the Sanskrit *dhyana* (meditation). In our discussion of Ch'an Buddhism, Ch'an is used in the Chinese context, whereas Zen is used for the same school in Japan. Although Ch'an was the name of this sect, we should avoid regarding meditation as its essential feature; meditation is practiced by most Buddhist sects. What is unique in this sect is the realization of one's true nature through intuition rather than through scriptural knowledge. The Ch'an school traces its origin to Gautama Buddha. One day Buddha was approached by the god Brahmā, who offered him a flower and asked him about Truth. Buddha accepted the flower and gazed at it in silence. Only one of his disciples understood why he did so, and this was Kashyaka, who smiled. Recognizing that Kashyaka understood what Truth is, Buddha appointed him as his successor in the order. Through intuitive understanding between a master and his disciple, the wordless wisdom of Ch'an was transmitted from one generation to another. The same tradition mentions twenty-eight Indian Ch'an patriarchs, including Nagarjuna and Vasubandhu.

The founder of the Ch'an sect in China was Bodhidharma (460–534),[3] the twenty-eighth patriarch, who came to China around 520. He taught that truth could not be obtained by studying Scriptures, nor be told directly by words; it must be discovered by the seeker himself. Tradition says that Bodhidharma retreated to a monastery in north China, where he practiced meditation in front of a wall for nine years. Hui-k'e, a Confucian scholar, hearing of his reputation, came to him and asked to be a disciple. The recluse made him wait outside in the snow for seven days and nights before accepting him. Bodhidharma then gave him a copy of the Lankavatara Sutra (a Scripture about Buddha's entry into Lanka), which contains the secret teachings of Ch'an and which has remained a favorite book of this school. Hui-k'e was the first Chinese Ch'an patriarch to die as a martyr.

By the seventh century the Ch'an school was divided into two groups. The northern school, headed by Shen-shiu (605?–706), was prominent and had the support of the court; the southern school, headed by Hui-neng (638–713), was beginning to teach a new type of Ch'an. The latter gained popularity in the eighth century under Shen-hui (670–762), a charismatic monk, who vehemently attacked the northern school for its belief in gradual enlightenment by meditation. Shen-hui insisted that meditation alone would not lead to enlightenment; enlightenment might come instantaneously and take place at the least expected moment. It was mainly through his efforts that the southern school eventually prevailed over its rival. Earlier, Hui-neng, the founder of the southern school, had revolted against meditation as the condition for enlightenment, and had said: "Sitting motionless is no *dhyana;* introspection of your own mind is no *dhyana;* and looking inward at your own calmness is no *dhyana.*"[4] He was the one who laid the foundation for Ch'an Buddhism as it is practiced today. Since the eighth century, the Ch'an school has been identified with the southern group, and it is out of this group that all Japanese Zen sects grew.

Suspicion of words was characteristic of Ch'an. Ma-chu, an eighth-century master, developed this idea into a teaching method; he stressed nonverbal communication—gesture, motion, beating, and so on—in order to help students gain the insight that leads to enlightenment. Once a disciple asked him about the essence of Buddhism. Ma-chu responded by giving him a box on the ear. The nonverbal method is a reminder that logical or philosophical scrutiny, which emphasizes the use of words, is an obstacle to reality; instead one must go behind the conventional language of duality (subject-object, internal-external, life-death, and the like) in order to perceive reality as it is. The master's gestures or motions are intended as clues to the perception of reality once the student has given up reliance on intellectualism. Ch'an's distrust of words is similar to the spirit of Taoism which says, "He who knows does not talk, and he who talks does not know." Both Ch'an and Taoism emphasized spontaneity and activities in accordance with the rhythm of nature. The two leading Buddhist schools, T'ien-t'ai and Hua-yen, emphasized scriptural learning and metaphysical speculation respectively; they associated Buddhism with intellect or thought. Ch'an, which reflected the convergence of Indian Buddhism with Chinese culture, represented a reaction against the rationalistic trend in Chinese thought as well as an indigenous development in Chinese Buddhism. Hwei-hai, a disciple of Ma-chu, was credited with founding the first Ch'an monastery in which the lecture hall replaced the sanctuary and discourse took precedence over rituals and ceremonies.

By the ninth century, the Ch'an school took a new turn. Two great masters, Hsüan-chien and I-hsüan, prepared the way for a blending of Indian negation with Chinese affirmation. Hüsan-chien and I-hsüan taught immediately after the great persecution of Buddhism in 845. Ch'an Buddhism, relying on no externalities, endured hardship in good spirit, and was, in fact, the only Buddhist school that continued to flourish after the great persecution.

Hsüan-chien taught inaction *(wu-wei);* spiritual cultivation means "no cultivation." Conscious efforts for Nirvana would never lead to it. Nirvana means there is no Nirvana to attain. He said: "Put on your clothes, eat your food, and move your bowels. That's all. No death to fear. No transmigration to dread. No *Nirvana* to achieve and no *bodhi* (wisdom) to attain. Try to be just an ordinary man having nothing to do."[5] This statement indicates that Ch'an Buddhism was no longer aimed at winning Nirvana in the metaphysical sense; it was interested in attaining a way of life that involves participating in one's daily activities while at the same time not becoming attached to them. Participation and detachment take place simultaneously. A person who lives in such a spirit is like one who has eaten rice and worn clothes all day without feeling that he has taken a grain of rice or touched a thread of silk.[6] But for the Ch'an follower, this way of life cannot be demonstrated; it cannot be taught through ordinary language. Óne must discover this truth by oneself; it comes like a flash of light, sudden and instantaneous, although years may pass before one receives such an experience. This sudden enlightenment is called *wu* in Chinese and *satori* in Japanese. Wu and satori are symbols that refer to the new viewpoint discovered by the student. Literally, both mean "awakening." In the light of the student's new perception, conventional truth (including Buddhist doctrines) has no worth. Although each student receives his satori differently, relative to his background and training, all experiences of satori imply the identity of the opposites (participation and detachment, self and world, enlightenment and non-enlightenment, sacred and profane, and so on). It is the discovery of this radical truth that often makes a Ch'an Buddhist iconoclastic. Once one attains the new viewpoint, even Buddhas or Bodhisattvas amount to nothing. As Hsüan-chien said, "Old Barbarian rascal [the Buddha] claims that he has survived the destruction of three worlds. Where is he now: Did he not also die after eighty years of age?"[7]

I-hsüan, the Ch'an master who was contemporary with Hsüan-chien, taught in the same vein, pointing out that there are no crutches in Ch'an Buddhism. If one's own learning or belief in Buddha is a crutch, then it is a hindrance to one's enlightenment. One must experience the sense of utter defenselessness, as if there were nothing to lean on, prior to the occurrence of new perception. This idea is implied in I-hsüan's following statement:

Here in my place there is no truth to tell you. My duty is to lighten the heavy burden of dead weight on your back. My mission is to free men from their bondage, to cure the sick, and to beat the ghosts out of men. . . . My duty is to kill everything. When the Buddha is in my way, I'll kill the Buddha. When the Patriarchs are in my way, I'll kill the Patriarchs.[8]

I-hsüan was also noted for making howling and shouting, both non-verbal methods of communication, aids to instruction. He was the founder of the Lin-chi school, named after a mountain in Hopei where he resided. This school was called Rinzai in Japan.

By the tenth century, all the features of Ch'an as we know them today were completed. The final development of Ch'an was its unique literary works called *kung-an* (public documents) in Chinese, and *kōan* in Japanese. It is worth noting that although Ch'an Buddhism was anti-intellectual and skeptical about learning, it eventually produced its own literature, however strange and abstruse the kōan appears to be. A kōan usually is a brief account of a dialogue between the master and his student; the master's question or answer is purposely bizarre in order to direct the student toward the truth of Ch'an. A simple kōan usually given to a beginner is: "You can hear the sound of two hands when they clap together. Now show me the sound of one hand."[9] Of course, from the conventional viewpoint, it is impossible to produce a sound with one

hand. But Ch'an experience demands that one must move beyond
the logic of two hands clapping; he must give up the ordinary
reasoning process and move into the reason of Ch'an. "The sound
of one hand" suggests that the student must enter into his own
inner life and discover his true mind.

Once a student asked his master, "Who is Buddha?" The master
answered, "The flax weighs three pounds." (The master was then
weighing some flax.)[10] "Who is Buddha?" is tantamount to saying,
"What is the ultimate nature of Buddhism?" which is an intellectual
problem. Ch'an Buddhism avoids the intellectual approach to truth,
because it leads one away from the actualities of the world. "The
flax weights three pounds" does not mean that the Buddha nature
is in the flax, which would imply pantheism—a speculative concept.
"The flax weighs three pounds" indicates the master's attempt to
lead the student back to the world of concrete things. Ch'an neither
affirms nor denies the world; it simply accepts the world as it is.
The performance of one's daily work in a straightforward manner
is the secret of Ch'an.

The following is a more advanced kōan in the form of a question
put forward by a master:

Zen is like a man hanging in a tree by his teeth over a precipice. His
hands grasp no branch, his feet rest on no limb, and under the tree
another person asks him, "Why did Bodhidharma come to China from
India?" If the man in the tree does not answer, he fails; and if he does
answer, he falls and loses his life. Now what shall he do?[11]

This kōan indicates that concern with either silence ("hanging in a
tree by his teeth") or eloquence ("if he answers, he falls") implies that
one is still caught in the world of duality (negation and affirmation,
life and death, and so forth), which Ch'an attempts to transcend. A
student of Ch'an must learn to remove the dichotomy of the opposites by seeing their identity. One should realize that silence and
eloquence, denying and affirming, life and death, are essentially
identical. Once one overcomes the world of duality, one is able to
live in the world without being trapped by it.

Kōan literature served a practical purpose; a kōan was to be meditated on in order to open one's mind for sudden enlightenment. The
use of kōan was practiced by the Lin-chi (Rinzai in Japan) sect.

The systematization of the kōan literature began at the end of
the tenth century, but was not completed until the Sung dynasty
(960–1279). While this literature gave Ch'an Buddhism a basic char-

acterization, it also represented the last phase of Ch'an development in China. The systematization of kōan corresponded with the decline of Ch'an Buddhism in China.

Although Ch'an Buddhism declined in the Sung dynasty, it did not die out in China subsequently, as some writers on Chinese Buddhism have indicated. A few large monasteries continued to practice meditation as a way of life and kept the Ch'an tradition alive until 1949.[12]

Zen Buddhism was introduced to Japan in the seventh century by Dōshō, the founder of the Hossō (Consciousness Only) school. But there were no independent Zen sects until the Kamakura period (1192–1336). The Rinzai sect, which stresses satori and the use of kōan, was founded in 1191 by Eisai (1141–1215), a monk of the Tendai school. Prior to this date, he visited China twice and found Zen still influential, although by then the intellectual leadership in China had been taken over from Buddhism by neo-Confucianism. Eisai was also credited with the introduction into Japan of both tea ceremonies and Chu Hsi's neo-Confucianism.[13] Dōgen (1200–1253), another Tendai monk, founded the Sōtō sect in 1244, after spending several years in Ch'an monasteries in China, where the same sect, founded in the ninth century, was called Ts'au-tung. His school emphasizes meditation (zazen), but does not use kōan. The Sōtō school believes in the gradual approach to enlightenment and rules out sudden enlightenment. It also gives a greater place to the study of Scriptures and the performance of rituals than does the Rinzai sect.

It was no surprise that the founders of both Rinzai and Sōtō were members of the Tendai monasteries. The prominent Tendai school had become worldly and power-hungry, and as has been mentioned earlier, several new Buddhist sects arose in Japan during the Kamakura period as a reaction. The founders of Rinzai and Sōtō were attracted by certain Zen features, for instance, simplicity, courage, discipline, sudden enlightenment, freedom from scriptural study or elaborate rituals. Bushidō, the ethical code of warriors, was influenced by the Zen spirit.

Zen Buddhism continued to grow and expand in subsequent Japanese history. Many customs and arts that were originated by Zen sects in Japan have now become a national heritage, for instance, the tea ceremony, Nō drama, haiku (short poems), black ink painting, swordsmanship, interior decoration, flower arrangement, temple architecture, gardening.

What is known as Zen Buddhism in the West is represented pri-

marily by the Rinzai school. In Japan, however, Sōtō is larger than
Rinzai; the former has more than 6,750,000 members, whereas the
latter has some 2,350,000 members. Throughout the history of Zen
in Japan, Rinzai has always attracted the intellectuals and the upper
class, whereas Sōtō has drawn its adherents from the commoners.
This and the fact that until recently Zen was known in the West
primarily through the writings of D. T. Suzuki, the eminent Rinzai
philosopher, and his students, explains why Rinzai is better known
in the West than Sōtō.

Nichiren

Nichiren Buddhism is a purely Japanese movement. It was the last
of three new Buddhist sects, the others being the Pure Land (Jōdo)
and Zen, that were founded in the Kamakura period (1192–1336)
when older schools, especially Tendai and Shingon, became decadent
and new spiritual vitality was badly needed. All three were reform
groups designed to give Buddhism new emphases and directions.
The Nichiren sect was named after its founder, whose career was
inseparable from the inception of this religious group.

Nichiren (1222–1282) was ordained at the age of fifteen and subsequently spent ten years in a Tendai monastery, where he discovered that the truth of Buddhism is found solely in the Saddharma-Pundarika (Lotus) Sutra, which was translated into Chinese
by Kumarajiva around 406. It was his contention that the Tendai
school had failed to follow the teaching of this sutra as it was originally intended; Tendai had instead become involved in abstract
ideas and esotericism. He wanted to lead Tendai back to this
Scripture, which teaches of the historical Buddha as Dharmakaya,
the Buddha essence, and of the austere and sacrificial life of the
Bodhisattvas. In 1253 he began teaching and making converts, and
it was at this time that he acquired the name Nichiren (*nichi* means
"sun" and *ren* "lotus flower"). This name was based on two passages
in the Lotus Sutra: one must remain as pure as a lotus flower in
muddy water; and one must live like the sun and moon, which bring
light to darkness.

After 1253 Nichiren lived a life filled with polemics, persecution,
and humiliation, all because of his uncompromising spirit and dogmatism. He believed that since about 1050 Japan had been in the
age of the decline of law; his calling was to revive and purify the
teaching of Buddha. He accused other leading sects in his day of
teaching false doctrines. The Pure Land followers were in Hell

because they taught salvation by faith; the Zen devotees were devils because they advocated sudden enlightenment; the Shingon practitioners were the cause of national ruin because of their love for elaborate rituals. Nichiren became the center of controversy and abuse. He was twice banished and once narrowly escaped death. But nothing could stop him. A passage in the Lotus Sutra predicts persecution against those who teach its doctrines; hence what happened to him was viewed as fulfillment of the Scripture.

The Nichiren sect taught three Great Mysteries: (1) The Great Mandala, a cosmic diagram designed by the founder, symbolizes the universal presence of Sakyamuni Buddha. It is an object of worship. (2) Repetition of the Lotus Sutra leads to enlightenment. (3) The sacred place is where Nichiren ceremonies are performed. Wherever Nichiren truth is embraced, there is a sacred place, and Nichiren ceremonies are therefore not confined to temples. This school also believes that Japan is the land where Buddhism will prosper and from there will spread to the world.

The Nichiren sect's polemical and uncompromising spirit has continued throughout its history, and the leaders have constantly been persecuted. Today Nichiren has more than 2,250,000 followers. There are also subsects of Nichiren, which have over 2 million members; one of them, the Soka Gakkai (value-creating study group), has been active in politics in modern Japan.

TIBETAN BUDDHISM

Pre-Buddhist Religion

The pre-Buddhist religion of Tibet was called Bön. Although the meaning of the word *Bön* is lost today, there are two related terms that shed light on it: one is *Bon-pa,* which means "to murmur spells;" the other is *Bon-po,* which means "the Bön one," referring to the one who performed the Bön rituals.[14] Whatever the original meaning of Bön was, this religion primarily involved priests who performed spells. Some scholars believe that the founder of Bönism was a shaman (medicine man-magician).[15] Shamanism originated in Siberia and northeast Asia, and it is very possible that it also spread westward to Tibet. Bön iconography shows its founder wearing a blue robe and carrying a dagger; the latter symbolizes the killing of victims, animal or human, as sacrifices to gods. Whether the Bön founder was a historical figure or a collective symbol of their priests, he is associated with shamanism. Tibetan records describe Bön priests as long-haired wizards who were skillful in black magic; their curses inflicted disasters on enemies. They were also necromancers who delivered messages from spirits of the dead. Bönism viewed divinities in two categories: gods who bless and demons who destroy. It had a belief in an afterlife in Heaven. Both Bönism and Tibetan Buddhism practiced magic. But while the magic of Bön was oriented toward success and happiness in this world, the magic of Buddhism was essentially an aid to personal salvation; one was mundane, the other transmundane.

The more primitive and crude features of Bönism were definitely softened by Buddhism, which helped to lay the foundation of Tibetan civilization. Even the pre-Buddhist myths of Tibetan origins were subject to Buddhist interpretation by the time they were put into writing. (The Tibetan script, formulated in the seventh century A.D., shows an indebtedness to the Sanskrit of Kashmir, India, which was then a Buddhist center.)[16] The Bön religion regarded the ancestors of Tibet as kings who descended from Heaven by a magic rope; the monkey hermit was one of these kings.[17] But Buddhism interpreted the monkey king as an emanation of the Bodhisattva of compassion. According to one account of the origin of Tibetans, a monkey hermit was emanated from Avalokitesvara, the Bodhisattva of compassion. Out of compassion the monkey hermit allowed himself to cohabit with an ogress of the rock, and the children of their union became the ancestors of Tibetans. Here we have an example of the fusion between the Bön and Buddhist elements in Tibetan cosmogony. These cosmogonic accounts generally disclose two sources of Tibetan origins: the pre-Buddhist source describes the ancestor kings as divine beings who descend from Heaven; the Buddhist source depicts the ancestor kings as emanations of Buddha or Bodhisattva.

Tantrism

Historically, Tantrism was a branch of Hinduism that was related to Shaivism and that influenced the development of Tantric Buddhism. Tantrism takes both Hindu and Buddhist forms. Although most of the rituals in Buddhist Tantrism were derived from Hindu Tantrism, the discussion that follows concerns Buddhist Tantrism in Tibet.

Tantra means esoteric knowledge and Tantric Buddhism is the Buddhist school that practices the mastery of esoteric knowledge as a means to salvation. Generally speaking, tantras refer to the Scriptures of this school. The same school is also called Mantrayana (see pp. 576–578) and Vajrayana. Vajra, in the specific sense, refers to Indra's thunderbolt; while it causes destruction when it strikes things, it is itself indestructible. In the broad sense, vajra is identical with the Ultimate Reality, or the Buddha body. This school believes that through ritual practice and proper training one can attain the vajra nature or the diamond body. Hence Vajrayana means salvation through attaining the diamond body. In China and Japan, this school had to combat other Buddhist sects and native religions for survival. In Tibet it absorbed the native Bön religion and became the leading faith of the land.

In terms of philosophy Tantric Buddhism in Tibet accepts the general Mahayana principle that the Absolute (sunyata, or emptiness) and the relative (samsara, or the phenomenal world) are essentially identical. Despite the incorporation of numerous gods into its pantheon and notwithstanding its concern with female divinities, Tibetan Buddhism affirms this basic Mahayana truth. What distinguishes Tantric Buddhism from Mahayana is its emphasis on practice, or the pursuit of methodical actions or contemplative exercises (sadhana) in order to become a Buddha. In Mahayana Buddhism identity between the relative and the Absolute is primarily a theoretical conviction, but in Tantric Buddhism this view is put into practice through the unification of all possible polarities (active-passive, male-female, terrifying-benign, profane-sacred, Buddha-self, Nirvana-samsara, and so on).

The Tantric rituals or contemplative exercises are basically a combination of (1) ritual gestures (the body acts through gestures), (2) recitation (speech acts through spells) and (3) concentrated thought (the mind acts through mystic union with a divinity). Through the coordination of the body, speech, and mind the adept experiences identity with the divinity of his choice.

Ritual gestures (mudras) of hands and figures are imitations of the posture of a Buddha or Bodhisattva as depicted in a statue or mandala.

Recitation refers to the chanting of mantras (spells). A mantra consists of a series of syllables which are based on transliterations of Sanskrit words. The potency of a mantra lies in the sound of the syllables rather than in the sense; it is secondary whether or not the meaning of the words is understood. In fact, since most Tibetan monks today do not know Sanskrit, many mantras are but strings of meaningless syllables. Although different mantras are addressed to different deities—mantras addressed to male deities end with HUM or PHAT, those addressed to female divinities end with SVAHA, and those addressed to neuter gods end with NAMAH—their ultimate effect is the same: identification with a divinity. But mantras can also be recited for worldly purposes such as protection, success, health. The most popular mantra is "OM MANI PADME HUM" (O the Jewel in the Lotus), which is believed to be a special gift of Avalokitesvara to man, and in Tibet it is seen as a sign everywhere.

Concentrated thought or meditation (dhyana) is the most important aspect of the contemplative exercises; it is presupposed in ritual gestures and recitation. In chanting a mantra, the adept should contemplate the shapes of the letters, distinguish the sounds of the syllables, and regulate breathing while meditating on the ultimate union. In order to facilitate this union, a mandala (cosmic diagram) is used. There are different mandalas for ritual practices. In Tibet a mandala in the form of a painting is called a *thangka*. Despite the fact that mandalas vary greatly in the number of divinities that they depict and in the arrangement of those divinities, they all convey the same meaning: the cosmos and Buddha are basically one.

A familiar mandala is called the Five Buddhas. The following table is a summary of the elements included in this mandala and their symbolic meanings:

THE FIVE BUDDHAS AND THEIR CORRESPONDENCES

Buddhas	Directions	Colors	Types of Evil	Aggregates of Personality
Brilliant (Vairocana)	Center	White	Stupidity	Body
Imperturbable (Akshobhya)	East	Blue	Wrath	Consciousness
Jewel-Born (Ratna Sambhava)	South	Yellow	Desire	Feelings
Infinite Light (Amitabha)	West	Red	Malignity	Perception
Unfailing Success (Amoghasiddhi)	North	Green	Envy	Impulses

Source: This table is a condensation of a larger table in D. L. Snellgrove, *Buddhist Himalaya* (Oxford: Bruno Cassirer, 1957), pp. 66–67.

As the table on p. 602 indicates, the Five Buddhas symbolizes the cosmos. The Brilliant (Vairocana) is in the center, representing the notion of sovereignty; the other four Buddhas are Vairocana's manifestations. Each human aggregate (skandha) corresponds to one of the Buddhas; hence personality and Buddha(s) are basically identical. Each type of evil corresponds with a respective Buddha, which means that evil and goodness are also identical; evil can be transmuted into goodness. On the basis of his own evil propensity the adept chooses one of the five Buddhas to identify with; if he has the propensity to hurt others, then he chooses Amitabha, the Buddha of the Infinite Light, as his favored divinity. No matter which Buddha one selects, the ultimate purpose is the same: homology with the divine.

Each of the five Buddhas has a feminine partner. And emanating from each of the same Buddhas is a Bodhisattva, who also has a feminine partner. The pairing of male and female Buddhas and Bodhisattvas is characteristic of mandalas. This art form is simply a confirmation of the principle of the identity of opposites; the male and female divinities are one in essence. Tantric Buddhism's view of divinity in terms of bisexual relation was definitely influenced by Indian Shaivism, which considered the Ultimate in terms of the union between Shiva and his partner Shakti. But there is a basic difference between Shaivism and Tantric Buddhism with regard to the attributes of each gender. In Shaivism, Shiva is passive and static, and Shakti is active and dynamic. But in Tantric Buddhism the male divinities are active and dynamic, and their female partners are passive and static. The Absolute or the Buddha nature is viewed as the union between the female Prajna (wisdom) and the male Upaya (method or skill). Upaya refers to the Tantric rituals, which symbolize the dynamic aspects (compassion) of the cosmos. Prajna refers to the passive nature (emptiness) of the cosmos. Buddhahood is the identity between these two natures, which is symbolized by the Yab-Yum (male-female) icon. This iconography depicts the mystic union between the male and female Buddhas. As the adept meditates on this union, he realizes the identity of these two forces within himself.

The initiation rite represents the height of contemplative exercises, which involves the partaking of the five sacraments (wine, meat, fish, parched grain, sexual union).[18] Tantrism made these into ritual acts precisely because they were taboo for a good Hindu sadhu or a Mahayana monk. These rituals demonstrate the view that the hor-

rifying and the benign are identical; one should enter the profane
in order to realize the sacred. These five sacraments are symbolic
of the identity between the sinful and the holy. However, substitutes can also be used for these five sacraments.[19] Those who use
substitutes are called Right-hand Tantrists. Those who do not are
called Left-hand Tantrists. Whether or not the initiate uses substitutes, the import of these acts lies in their symbolic meaning. In
Left-hand Tantric Buddhism the adept in going through the fifth
sacrament retains his semen, which symbolizes Nirvana. Since the
participants of the initiation rite are sworn to secrecy, it is difficult
for outsiders to gain information concerning its procedures.

Lamaism

According to Tibetan records, Tantric Buddhism began with King
Song-tsan-Gampo (ruled A.D. 620–650), who married a Nepalese
woman and a Chinese woman, both Buddhists, and himself adopted
the new faith. The same records attribute the beginning of Tantric
Buddhism to an Indian monk, Padmasambhava, who arrived in

Tibet in 747 and is described as a miracle worker who inaugurated Tantric beliefs and rituals with phenomenal success. This history was written in the twelfth and thirteenth centuries, when Tantrism had already become the national religion of Tibet. What was supposed to have taken place in the lifetime of Padmasambhava was actually a history of several centuries of Buddhist development, which involved the gradual assimilation of the indigenous divinities and rituals of Bön. The arrival in 1038 of Atish, another Tantric master from India, began a new phase of Buddhism; this resulted in the institution of Lamaism. *Lama* means "the superior one"; strictly speaking, only leading monks could be called lamas, although subsequently, for the purpose of courtesy, this term was applied to all ordained monks.

Atish's ministry gave impetus to the rise of several new schools in the eleventh century. Marpa founded the Kagyupa (Successive Order) school (see Figure 21.4), which emphasized meditation. One of its subsects, Dikhung, practiced extreme asceticism. Many of its members pursued voluntary incarceration; they lived in separate cells for years, or even for life, as solitary monks, and their only outside contact was the daily reception of a meager meal which was brought in through an opening in the wall.

The Sakya (Gray-Colored Earth) was also founded in the eleventh century. The group, whose monastery had married abbots whose succession was hereditary, emphasized scriptural learning. In the fourteenth century its members collected Tantric works and compiled them into more than 300 volumes. Most of these volumes, which constitute the Scriptures of Tibetan Buddhism, are not yet well known to the world.

In both the eleventh and twelfth centuries, the Tibetan kings were the chief patrons of Tantric Buddhism. They sent monks to India to collect Tantric Scriptures and sponsored their translation into Tibetan. They also contributed generously toward the construction of huge monasteries. A monastery was usually a large compound, consisting of temples and houses, in which lived lay members who served as attendants, as well as monks. When requested, monks conducted special services on behalf of families, for which they charged fees. Tibetan families usually sent their young-

FIGURE 21.4   Tibetan Buddhists of the Kagyupa sect and their leader. (*Wide World Photo*)

est sons to be trained as monks. As a rule, monks took the vow of celibacy. However, it was considered proper for Tantric yogis who were not required to take the vow of celibacy to have families, while devoting themselves to the life of self-realization. The monastery was the only educational institution in Tibet; there young men learned the basic skills of reading and writing. It was also the place where people came for counsel. The monastery served as a communal center, at which people gathered for festivals on religious holidays.

In the thirteenth and fourteenth centuries, when the Mongols conquered China, a close relation was established between Tibetan lamas and Mongol rulers. The Mongols and Tibetans were culturally and ethnically close, both being pastoral peoples. The Mongol rulers favored Tibetan Buddhism and sponsored the building of lama temples in Tibet, Mongolia, and China. This was also the time when Tibetan Buddhism spread to Mongolia and eventually replaced its shamanism. In 1247 the Mongol authority granted Sa-pan, an abbot of the Sakya monastery, the right to rule over Tibet. This was the first time a spiritual leader was made the temporal head of all Tibet. When Kublai Khan became emperor of China and the founder of the Yüan dynasty in 1260, he appointed Sa-pan's nephew the imperial preceptor. At the same time, Lamaism was declared the national religion of the Mongols. Lamaism, which was then at its zenith, enjoyed special privilege in Mongolia and China. A Mongol edict in 1309 specified that anyone who insulted a lama would have his tongue cut off.[20]

The prestige and power of Lamaism resulted in the corruption of monastery life in the fourteenth century; monks became worldly and violated the vow of celibacy. Near the end of the century a reform movement was led by Tsong-kha-pa (1357–1419), who advocated a return to a spiritual and ethical religion. He restored celibacy and prohibited sexual union as a ritual. The new school he founded was called the Yellow Hats because its members wore yellow robes and hats; its Tibetan name was Gelukpa (Virtuous Custom).

The increasing popularity of the reform movement alarmed one of the old schools, commonly called the Red Hats,[21] whose leaders allied themselves with a king of central Tibet in opposition to the

FIGURE 21.5 The Dalai Lama receives devotees. (*Information Service of India*)

Yellow Hats. Meanwhile in 1578, the third successor of Tsong-kha-pa of the Yellow Hats made an alliance with the Mongol authority for protection, and a few years later the Mongol ruler conferred on him the title of Dalai Lama, or the Great Ocean Lama (his two predecessors were also given the same title retroactively). The struggle between these two sects continued for many years. When the Red Hats rallied other schools and the king of central Tibet to its support, the Yellow Hats called on the Mongols for help. The showdown came in 1641 when the Mongol army subdued the king-dom of central Tibet and crushed the force of the Red Hats. With the backing of his ally, the fifth Dalai Lama in the following year established his group in Lhasa, which became the capital of Tibet.

The next most important person after the Dalai Lama, who

traditionally resides in the Potala, the palace in Lhasa, is the Tashi Lama (or Panchen Lama), who heads the Tashi Lumpo monastery near Shigatse, where at one time more than 3,000 monks resided. The Tashi Lama is an incarnation of Amitabha Buddha and a member of the Yellow Hats. The present Tashi Lama is the tenth.

The succession of a Dalai Lama, as well as of a Tashi Lama, is a unique phenomenon in Tibet. A mission of priest-officials, aided by astrologers, is responsible for the task of selection. This process involves being aware of portents that indicate the candidate's location as well as other factors. The selection of a new Dalai Lama is an event of cosmic significance involving cooperation between gods and men. The boy candidate must show signs of unusual gifts to be worthy of being considered the successor of the preceding lama. The present Dalai Lama, the fourteenth (see Figure 21.5), as a boy was able to identify the officials of the party that was sent to find the new lama and was able to recognize articles that belonged to his predecessor. He was able to speak in Tibetan when the party visited him, even though his family did not. (He was born and lived in the Chinese province of Chinghai, bordering northeastern Tibet.) After the installation, the new Dalai Lama undergoes years of rigorous spiritual and intellectual training under an appointed lama. A number of eminent lamas are believed to be incarnations of Bodhisattvas, and nearly every Tibetan monastery has one or more such incarnate lamas. It is estimated that prior to 1951, when the Chinese army entered Tibet, one-sixth of the male population were found within monasteries; many of them, however, were lay members.

NOTES

1. The three treatises refer to: *Madhyamika Shastra* (Treatise on the Middle Way) and *Dradasanikaya Shastra* (Twelve Gates Treatise), by Nagarjuna, and *Sata Shastra* (One Hundred Verses Treatise), by Aryadeva, his disciple. These three works are the foundation of the Middle Way school because they represent the philosophy of Nonbeing of Nagarjuna, the founder of this school in India.
2. This mandala is popular in Tibetan Buddhism. See the table on the Five Buddhas, p. 602.
3. Some Western writers doubt the historicity of Bodhidharma, but both Chinese and Japanese authors accept him as a historical figure.
4. Hu Shih, "The Development of Zen Buddhism in China" in William Briggs, ed., *Anthology of Zen* (New York: Grove, 1961), p. 21.

5. *Ibid.,* pp. 26–27.

6. Fung Yu-lan, *The Spirit of Chinese Philosophy,* trans. by E. R. Hughes (Boston: Beacon, 1964), p. 173.

7. Hu Shih, *op. cit.,* p. 27. The three worlds refer to the world of sense desire, the world of form (fine materiality), the formless world.

8. *Ibid.,* pp. 27–28.

9. Compiled by Paul Reps in collaboration with Nyogen Senzaki, *Zen Flesh, Zen Bones: A Collection of Zen and Pre-Zen Writings* (New York: Doubleday, 1961), p. 25. Used by permission of the original publisher, Charles E. Tuttle.

10. *Ibid.,* pp. 104–105.

11. *Ibid.,* p. 94.

12. Holmes Welch, *The Practice of Chinese Buddhism* (Cambridge: Harvard University Press, 1967), p. 47.

13. Joseph M. Kitagawa, *Religion in Japanese History* (New York: Columbia University Press, 1966), p. 125.

14. Robert B. Ekvall, *Religious Observances in Tibet* (Chicago: University of Chicago Press, 1964), p. 16.

15. *Ibid.*

16. D. L. Snellgrove, *Buddhist Himalaya* (Oxford: Bruno Cassirer, 1957), p. 141.

17. *Ibid.,* pp. 129–130.

18. These five sacraments are also called the Five M's, for each of the five terms in Sanskrit begins with M: (1) wine *(madya),* (2) meat *(mamsa),* (3) fish *(matsya),* (4) parched grain *(mudra),* (5) sexual union *(maithuna).* For a full discussion of the Five M's, see A. Bharati, *The Tantric Tradition* (London: Rider, 1965), pp. 228–268.

19. Milk, ghee, or rice liquor can be substituted for wine; salt, ginger, or garlic for meat; eggplant or red radish for fish; rice or wheat for parched grain; conjoining between two kinds of flowers for sexual union.

20. Kenneth Ch'en, *Buddhism in China* (Princeton: Princeton University Press, 1964), p. 420.

21. The Red Hats historically were the Karma Kagyu school, a subsect of the Kagyupa school founded by Marpa, although today this group is indistinguishable from the old Tantric Buddhism founded by Padmasambhava in the eighth century.

RELIGION BEFORE CONFUCIUS

The greatest difficulty in studying the pre-Confucian religion of China is that books written in the Shang period disappeared while those written prior to the time of Confucius were revised and altered by Confucians to suit their purpose. As a result, the early conditions of religion, most of which were unacceptable to Confucianism, were either deleted or rationalized. Fortunately, modern archaeological researches in Anyang and elsewhere in northern Honan have found several collections of objects, including oracle bones and tortoise shells inscribed with words, skeletal remains of men and animals, and bronze utensils, that were buried some 3,000 years ago, during the Shang and Chou periods. These objects, together with the *Book of History* and the *Book of Songs,* in which a veiled record of early religious life is still discernible, furnish us with clues about the rituals and beliefs of pre-Confucian religion.

The Shang Period

Ancestor worship was a dominant cult during the Shang period (c. 1751–1112 B.C.). It was first practiced by members of the royal family, and other officials soon adopted it. Kings and princes were regarded as heroes, and hence demigods; when they died, they became spirits who controlled the destiny of the royal house. Nobles as a rule offered sacrifices to their more recent ancestors, although

FIGURE 22.1 The teacher Confucius lecturing to his pupils. (*Howard Sochurek for Life Magazine*)

remote ones were worshiped too. Sacrifices were also offered to female ancestors, particularly for childbirth and harvest.

The royal ancestors were assumed to possess superhuman power and knowledge. The Shang rulers consulted their ancestral spirits when faced with every type of problem—diplomatic relations, war, hunting, fishing, crops, illness, and so on—and offered sacrifices to these spirits on such occasions. By examining the formations of the cracks on the oracle bones and tortoise shells which were used for divination, a diviner was able to learn the will of the gods. The chief method of consultation was divination; often both the question and the actual occurrence were recorded on the bone or shell, such as "Will it rain tonight?" "It really didn't rain."[1]

There is strong evidence, based on the skeletal remains in graves, that human sacrifice to royal ancestors was practiced in this period.[2] Victims were either captured enemies, retainers, or relatives close to the deceased. In either case, this was regarded as the highest form of religious ritual, since nothing could be more valuable than human life. From the viewpoint of early man, human sacrifice was an act of the greatest devotion to a divinity.

The most prominent ancestor was called Shang Ti, the Ruler Above; he was sometimes referred to as Ti, the Ruler. Since *ti* was also used to designate a king in this period, Shang Ti was associated with deceased royalty. Scholars have given different explanations of this term. One view has it that Shang Ti referred to the founder of the dynasty; as the progenitor of the royal family, he was the principal deity and headed the council of ancestors. Another view is that Shang Ti was a collective term, designating all the royal ancestors. A third view is that the term *ti* was originally the name of a sacrifice used for the ancestral cult,[3] and as time went by, the name of this sacrifice became associated with a deity. None of these views is conclusive, although the first one enjoys wide acceptance. It is certain, however, that Shang Ti was an ancestral god during this period. He gave rain, crops, and other favors to man, but his chief function was to grant victories in war. Shang Ti cannot be considered a monotheistic god since other ancestors also possessed these powers, and furthermore, he did not create the world. (Christian missionaries in China have used the term Shang Ti for the God of their own faith and hence Christians in modern China associate the name Shang Ti with a monotheistic god.)

Numerous bronze household and sacrificial utensils found in Shang graves, including the small ones, suggest that the ancestral cult was practiced extensively, and even commoners took part in it. The worship of the dead appears to have been a probable source of Chinese religion.

Earth was worshiped as a fertility deity. In every village there was a mound called *shê*, where sacrifices were offered to Earth. This cult was not developed in full, however, until the Chou period.

Two words were used to designate spirits: *kuei* and *shih* (better known as *shên* in later times). Kuei referred to demons or unfriendly ghosts; shên denoted benign gods. It is most probable that in the beginning both terms were applied to ancestral spirits. As time went by, each became a generic term for spirits: good divinities were called shên; evil ones were called kuei.

The Chou Period

The Chou dynasty (c. 1111–221 B.C.) institutionalized the ancestral religion of the Shang period. Ancestral temples were erected by aristocrats of all levels and important state and family events took place in such temples. There was no priestly class. Rather, the master of the household officiated at ceremonies in his temple; he was helped by someone versed in rituals who held an inferior position in the household. An official's temple served as a sacrificial place for both the official and his retainers. On the occasion of a sacrifice, the official sought ancestral guidance either about his own affairs or the affairs of a retainer, and the retainers assisted him in the ceremony. Officials in turn assisted the ruler of the state in his temple when he made new appointments, held state banquets, installed his heir, sent off armies to battle, and celebrated victories. In the center of the whole country was the king's temple, where the king was assisted by the rulers of the various states.

The belief in nature spirits (such as hill and river gods) was also common in the Chou period. Sacrifice was regularly offered to the Yellow River. It was generally believed that spirits who dwell in important localities could be pacified by sacrifice. The usual attitude toward nature spirits was one of fear and dread, and, by and large, there was less affection for them than for ancestral deities. Intimacy with spirits was undesirable, and one was to keep a proper distance from them, except in order to make sacrifices. And since shamans and wizards were considered as being very close to the spirits, they too were not respected in the Chou period.

Akin to nature spirits were the hungry ghosts; they were ancestors who did not have offspring to make sacrifices to them. As a result, they became wanderers in search of food. They haunted villages and stole sacrifices that had been made to other spirits. For that reason, special sacrifices were made to them.

In the Chou period the worship of Earth was further developed beyond the practices of the Shang era. The *shê,* mound, which was the altar of the Earth, now became the center of religious activities in every village; on it sacrifices were made for rain and good crops. But the Earth cult in this period was more than just a fertility cult; it was also a state cult. The shê was a symbol of the territory possessed by a ruler: the mound in the capital of a state was the symbol of the land over which the ruler held power, and likewise, the mound in the capital of China symbolized the terrestrial right of the king. From the Chou period on, each dynasty in China erected a new mound in its capital.

The chief ancestral deity of the Chou dynasty was called T'ien (Heaven). In the Chou period, the character for this word was written in the form of a man, and probably referred to a great man such as the king.[4] T'ien was either the name of the first ruler of the Chou dynasty or a name used to designate all the deceased Chou kings. Since the Chinese script does not make a distinction between singular and plural nouns, T'ien could mean both. In either case, it was an ancestral deity. The Chou masters used the names Shang Ti and T'ien interchangeably for the same deity. As time went by, T'ien was used more frequently than Shang Ti.

By the time of Confucius, the anthropomorphism of Heaven was replaced by a moral or rational apprehension; this was so, at least, among the sophisticated class. Later, Shang Ti was identified with the T'ien (Heaven) of the Chou house, being still conceived anthropomorphically. But at some time during the Chou dynasty, T'ien received a moral connotation and became associated with the Mandate of Heaven.

The term *Mandate of Heaven* was first used in the *Book of History,* a pre-Confucian work of the Chou period. This document regards the Duke of Chou, a brother of the founder of the dynasty and the regent of the boy king, as an early exponent of the concept of the Mandate of Heaven.[5] It states that according to the Duke of Chou, Heaven took the Mandate away from the last king of Shang because he was wicked and oblivious to the welfare of his subjects, and gave it instead to the founder of the Chou dynasty, who was virtuous and kind to the people. After the time of the Duke, kings in China considered themselves Sons of Heaven, whose duty it was to actualize the Mandate by being benevolent in state affairs and virtuous in personal conduct. The Confucians in later times projected this belief back to the beginning of Chinese history when legendary kings reigned.

The introduction of the Mandate of Heaven was a step forward in the religious consciousness of ancient China, insofar as it made the ancestral cult an ethical religion. Heaven was no longer the guarantor of human fortune, but rather the overseer of man's thought and actions, particularly those of the kings. In making virtue the chief qualification of rulers, the Mandate of Heaven suggests that all ancestors, whether royal or plebeian, were concerned with the moral life of their posterity.

In addition to its high ethical standards, the Chou dynasty was also known for its humanitarianism. The Duke of Chou, the greatest of the Chou humanitarians, felt that military might could never win the hearts of subjects, and therefore, after he defeated the Shang masters, he advocated a policy of conciliation toward the conquered and benevolence to the populace. He also called attention to such ideas as filial piety and family loyalty, which were later to be emphasized by the Confucians. As the Chou house began to decline, this humanitarian tradition was eclipsed. One major concern of Confucius was to revive it—that is why the Chinese say that Confucianism began with the Duke of Chou, 500 years before Confucius.

CONFUCIUS

It is difficult to give an accurate account of the life of Confucius because his biographies were written three or four centuries after his death, when he had already been elevated to a semidivine status. Naturally these works contain legendary elements, and he was idealized in them. The best source of information about his life is the *Analects,* a collection of his own sayings and those of his disciples and their contemporaries. These sayings were recorded, edited, and made into a book some time after Confucius' death. Other sources of information about his life must be checked against this work, as well as against other historical documents of the time.

Confucius was born in 551 B.C. in the state of Lu, the present province of Shantung in northern China. Lu had originally been a fief of the Duke of Chou and was currently being ruled by his descendants. This may explain why the early humanitarian tradition was better known there than in other states.

Both of Confucius' parents died while he was a child. All that we know about other members of his family is that he had one elder brother, a daughter, and a son whom he survived; we know nothing about his wife. As a young man Confucius was a keeper of stores for the state or for some official. At one time he was in charge of pastures, a responsibility that included the supervision of cattle. Apparently he was of humble origin, even though a descendant of an aristocratic family. Probably he was a member of *ju* (a scribe or expert in rituals), although there is no evidence that he ever served in the household of a ruler. His early positions were no higher than that of government clerk. He was most likely self-taught, perhaps with some tutorial assistance from his supervisors.

Confucius felt that the basic problem in his day was the moral deterioration of the ruling class, and that this in turn contributed to the degeneration of the common people. His conviction was that the moral conduct of the rulers has a contagious effect on their subjects: when rulers and officials cultivate virtue and are concerned with the welfare of the people, subjects will respect their leaders and be inspired to follow their examples. This view of government was embodied in the culture of the Early Chou, and Confucius, therefore, wanted to revive that culture. In order to be able to reform the government and to revive Early Chou culture, he wished to be appointed as a minister.

According to tradition, Confucius was at one time a prime minister or a minister of justice in Lu, but this cannot be supported by the known facts. If he had ever held such an important position, it would surely have been mentioned in the *Analects*. Indeed, he was concerned as to whether he had those qualities that would entitle him to hold office.[6] He most probably held a minor position in the court of Lu in later life, when several of his disciples had become officials in the state; for he said that he trailed behind other officials at the ducal court of Lu.[7] This means he was at one time a low-ranking official who had access to the court. But the post he held did not carry actual power and out of frustration he resigned his post.

Confucius was most successful as a teacher, and it was in that capacity that his talents were best displayed (see Figure 22.1). Before his time, a teacher was usually hired by an aristocratic family to tutor its children. But the school that Confucius established was open to men of all classes, and most of his students did not come from the aristocratic class. Tuition was charged according to a student's financial ability; he would not refuse a student who could pay no more than a package of dried meat. On the other hand, he was demanding as a teacher. He would teach "only those who burst with eagerness" for enlightenment.[8] "If I hold up one corner and a man cannot come back to me with the other three, I do not continue the lesson."[9] Confucius was probably the first teacher in history to start a school for commoners.

A few classics already existed in his day. For instance, the *Book of Songs* (*Shih Ching*), the *Book of History* (*Shu Ching*), the *Spring and Autumn Annals* (*Ch'un Ch'iu*, a history of Lu from 771 to 579 B.C.). However, these books did not at that time possess the same contents that they do today, for they were later expanded and revised. While these books were Confucius' literary sources for teaching and were used as a basis for discussion, he did not stress book learning. His interest was in eliciting the desire of students to think and reason for themselves on matters pertaining to government and other relationships among men. The personality of the Master must have had a strong influence on his students.

During his late fifties, Confucius, accompanied by a few disciples, spent some ten years visiting rulers and advocating his philosophy. His hope for an appointment was, however, not realized. Rulers received him politely, but were unresponsive to his counsel. In one state, he almost lost his life because a degenerate noble did not like his presence.

Finally he returned to Lu, where he resumed teaching. He died in 479 B.C. at the age of seventy-two. By then some of his disciples had become officials in different states. Others had established schools to teach Confucian ideas. In these and other ways his thought began to spread.

Tradition regards Confucius as the author or editor of such classics as the *Spring and Autumn Annals* and the *Book of Rites* (*Li Chi*), but evidence in support of this view is inconclusive.[10] It is doubtful whether Confucius wrote or edited any known book.

The Philosophy of Confucius

Man

The central problem that confronted Confucius was man. He did not regard man as an insignificant being in the vast universe. Neither did he conceive of man as an individual for and by himself.

Confucius viewed man always in relation to other men, that is, from the viewpoint of man-in-society. Although he stressed the importance of man's place in society, he never said that society is preeminent and that man should submit himself to it. He took it for granted that man is inescapably bound to his fellow-man, especially to members of his family. That much he inherited from early tradition.

His ethical structure rests on empathy for the other person. In assessing the adequacy of one's conduct, he believed that one should place himself in the position of the other person, and ask himself: "If I were he, would I like being treated this way?" If the answer were Yes, then the action was good. If the answer were No, then the action was bad. The criterion of ethics is therefore that of enlightened self-interest, that is, putting the self in the position of the other and then treating the other accordingly. Two sayings of Confucius can best illustrate the ethics of enlightened self-interest. One is: "Do not do to others what you would not like yourself."[11] This calls for refraining from action; it is a passive principle called *shu* (reciprocity). The other saying is:

As for Goodness [jen]—you yourself desire rank and standing; then help others to get rank and standing. You want to turn your own merits to account; then help others to turn theirs to account—in fact, the ability to take one's own feelings as a guide—that is the sort of thing that lies in the direction of Goodness.[12]

This requires action; it is an active principle called *chung* (conscientiousness).

Many passages in the *Analects* discuss the word *jen,* which has several possible translations: goodness, benevolence, humanheartedness, man-to-manness. This word is composed of two characters: "man" and "two." Thus jen in the generic sense refers to moral qualities that one exercises in his relations with another. Although Confucius never defined the term, since he thought that its perfection was rarely attained by men, yet he always understood jen as being rooted in man's social nature, that is, man-in-society. Once he asked his disciples what they thought was the inclusive principle of his teaching, and one disciple answered that chung and shu embraced this principle.[13] This means that when one practices both the active and passive sides of ethics, he approximates jen.

There is a statement in the *Doctrine of the Mean (Chung Yung),* a third century B.C. Confucian classic, which is attributed to Tzu Ssu, the grandson of the Master, that neatly combines the passive with the active aspects of the ethics of Confucius:

What you do not like done to yourself, do not do to others. . . . Serve your father as you would require your son to serve you. . . . Serve your ruler as you would require your subordinate to serve you. . . . Serve your elder brother as you would require your younger brother to serve you. . . . Set the example in behaving to your friends as you would require them to behave to you.[14]

This is a summary of the Confucian meaning of jen.

Propriety
The term *li* in its broad sense means propriety, the outward norm of human conduct. Although Confucius assumed its meaning to be primarily ritual, he considered li to mean much more than a display of jade and silk to be offered to ancestors or other divinities. While Confucius accepted the importance of ritual, he felt that it is the inner attitude of the worshiper which makes a ritual meaningful; its outward display is unimportant. Hence he condemned pompous ceremony. He was critical of those who took part in sacrifices without reverence and who attended mourning rites without the feeling of grief. For him the motive of the worshiper determines the value of ritual. When the worshiper is sincere, then the outward sign becomes an expression of his inward feeling; otherwise, it is meaningless. Sincerity and reverence in ritual are the essence of li, which should permeate man's other activities. For example, the Master said that an official should treat the common people as though he "were officiating at an important sacrifice."[15]

Li was also used by Confucius to mean proper conduct in one's relation with others, especially members of one's own family. Hence the son is obedient to his father, and the father is kind to his son; the husband is considerate of the wife, and the wife is subservient to her husband; the elder brother is helpful to his younger brother, and a younger brother is respectful to his elder brother. The li practiced within the family was also extended to society. Hence the ruler acts beneficently to the subject, and a subject is obedient to his ruler. The senior helps his junior friend, and a junior friend respects his senior.

Confucius believed strongly that rulers and officials should govern in terms of li instead of law. Li involves a personal relationship, whereas law is impersonal. Right emotion expressed through li by the ruler would touch the hearts of subjects, thus enabling them to have confidence in the government. Law, on the other hand, merely forces people to do things, without appealing to their will.

In the most general sense, li signifies the entire body of manners, customs, and institutions prescribed by Confucianism. It conveys the idea of a convention—a convention that has molded the Chinese and distinguished them from other peoples.

Education

The aim of education for Confucius was to make gentlemen (*chün-tzu*). Although the term originally signified sons of rulers, and hence men of noble descent, Confucius used it to mean men of noble character, who cultivated goodness and practiced propriety. Although he was for universal education, he believed that it was only those who have will power, intelligence, and talent who could be educated. The duty of a gentleman is to exemplify morality. He should strive for a position in government, for the service of people, and if for any reason he is unable to do so, he should maintain integrity and should influence people as a private citizen.

Confucius was a believer in natural aristocracy: he felt that men of superior endowment and character should be educated and become leaders of government. This also meant that it is a duty of the ruler to educate the gifted poor, who otherwise would have no means for an education.

Confucius' curriculum consisted primarily of history and literature. While he used ancient ideas, he gave them a fresh interpretation. He conceived of knowledge (*chih*) as an instrument for the development of the good life rather than as something to be acquired for its own sake. Thus knowledge in the impersonal, scientific sense was not his concern.

Since the aim of education was to develop the moral nature of man, Confucius did not believe that practical skill or specialization had any place in an educational program. One student wanted to learn the art of agriculture from Confucius. The Master refused to teach it to him, not because he despised farming, but because the arts of agriculture did not fall within the purview of his concept of education.

One aspect of education consisted of what Confucius called the rectification of names. Every name embodies certain attributes;

their sum total corresponds to its meaning. For instance, the word *ruler* contains attributes such as "man of highest virtue," "benevolent to his subjects." The noun *father* implies "kindness to his son," "parental responsibility for educating his child"; and so on. Every man has several roles to perform in family and society, and each of these roles bears a name. One should constantly examine himself to see to it that in performing each of these roles he realizes the attributes of the name of that role. Since most men do in fact fall short of the implications of these words, they must "rectify" them, that is, they must live according to their attributes. Confucius believed that, if every man thus "justified" the names he carried, society and institutions would be in harmony, since right men produce right society. Once a disciple asked the Master what he should do first if he became a minister of a state. His reply was, "It would certainly be the rectification of names."[16] On another occasion a ruler asked Confucius about the art of government. His answer was, "Let the ruler be a ruler, the minister a minister, the father a father and the son a son."[17] Although rectification of names resembles what we would describe as the definition of concepts in Western thought, the interest of Confucius in this doctrine is moral and social, not intellectual.

Government
Confucius understood government in terms of rulers and officials, not of institutions. He was not concerned with theoretical problems of state, such as policy, law, and forms of government. His main interest in this area was who should be the rulers and how they should behave. Government under the leadership of good men was the key to the solution of problems of the state.

The Master believed strongly that rulers should exercise moral force (*tê*). If men in authority were virtuous, the commoners would feel their benevolence and would follow suit. When those above conduct themselves in accordance with moral precepts and treat their subjects in terms of li, then those below will respect the rulers and support the government. Confucius said, "Moral force never dwells in solitude; it will always bring neighbors."[18] Once a prominent official asked Confucius what to do about the burglars in his state, and the Master replied, "If only you were free from desire, they would not steal even if you paid them to."[19] The same official was told by Confucius that the moral force of rulers is like wind and the subjects are like grass: "And when a wind passes over the grass, it cannot choose but bend."[20] The moral force of the ruler is a manifestation of the cosmic morality, or Heaven, which is numinous, or sacred. Under the contagious influence of this force, the subject cannot but follow the ruler.

Although Confucius believed in an aristocratic ruling class, it was an aristocracy based on education and character. Anyone may belong to the aristocracy, so long as he has the moral and intellectual qualifications—so long as he belongs to the natural aristocracy. The difference between aristocrats and commoners lies in their abilities, not in their wealth and inheritance. Confucius did not envisage any form of government other than monarchy, and he was not opposed to the hereditary right of kingship. But he applied the concept of natural aristocracy to the king, as well as to other government officials; in his eyes moral and intellectual qualifications are among the prerequisites for that office. Such a view of kingship was articulated further by Mencius about two centuries later, and it profoundly affected the political thought of China.

The Way

Before the time of Confucius, the word *tao* meant a road on which one walks; it conveyed the meaning of "way." But it was largely used in the specific and descriptive sense; for example, the way of the knight or the way to banish discontent.

Confucius at times also used tao in the specific sense. What was new in this word as used by Confucius was that it meant the Way in the ideal and normative sense. A typical example is as follows:

Wealth and rank are what every man desires; but if they can only be retained to the detriment of the Way he professes, he must relinquish them. Poverty and obscurity are what every man detests; but if they can only be avoided to the detriment of the Way he professes, he must accept them.[21]

Hence the Way conveys the meaning of that truth to which one is committed. Confucius said that there are times when a man should be ready to die for the good Way. He regarded the understanding of truth as a very precious attainment. One is ready to die in contentment at the end of the day if he has understood the Way in the morning.[22]

Confucius never defined the Way, but yet it is clear that he felt that his teaching approached it. In fact, his whole career was spent helping people to realize it. His ultimate hope was to bring this concept to the world. One might say that for Confucius the Way will be realized when the following conditions are met: (1) duties and responsibilities between family members are carried out reciprocally; (2) these duties and responsibilities are extended to include all human relationships and activities, wherein enlightened self-interest is used as the guide of life for everyone; (3) human conduct is performed along the lines of propriety and moderation; (4) the most talented and virtuous men become leaders of states—men who exercise their duties by relying on personal morality rather than law or regulations; and (5) qualities such as sincerity, integrity, consideration, and modesty are pursued by men everywhere. In summary, Confucius understood truth as a vision of a perfect society.

Religion

Confucius accepted the ancestral cult and sacrifices to nature spirits, but his approach to them was different from that of his contemporaries.

Heaven (T'ien) was the ancestral deity (deities) in the Chou period. Confucius conceived of it as the moral principles instituted by ancient kings. When these ancient kings were deified, their principles also attained a cosmic status. Other than this moral connotation, Confucius did not venture into the nature of T'ien. Once he was asked whether or not the ancestral deity was present at sacrifice. He replied, "I do not know. Anyone who knew the explanation could deal with all things under Heaven as easily as I lay this here"[23] (while speaking, he laid his fingers on the palm of his hand). At another time, he was asked whether or not the dead have consciousness. His answer was that, since man does not fully understand the living, how can he know about the dead? In either case, Confucius did not repudiate Heaven or spirits. What he refused to speak about was the manner of their existence. He avoided metaphysical discussion because it was outside of his province: he did not conceive of religion as a theological issue but as an ethical one. What was important in religion was not the nature of divinity, but the nature of man's moral response to it.

Heaven stood as the cosmic counterpart of man's ethical sensibilities, the guarantor of man's moral strivings. Man desires to act right not only because it is self-satisfying, but because Heaven demands it. Right actions are in accord with the cosmic will. Confucius did not believe that religious rituals have any influence on

Heaven; they are symbolic acts expressive of man's emotional and moral sentiments. Toward the end of the Master's life, a disciple asked permission to perform the rite of expiation for him at his sick bed. Confucius replied, "My expiation began long ago!"[24] What he meant was: if the rite in question is for the expiation of sin, then it is useless, for sacrifice has no effect on Heaven. What justifies a man in the eyes of Heaven is the life he has lived; an expiation rite at the end of his life would not change his destiny. Religion without ethics is meaningless. Hence Confucius remarked, "He who has put himself in the wrong with Heaven has no means of expiation left."[25] Man's day-to-day conduct is expiation itself. Sacrifice to ancestors does not minimize or purify one's sin.

Confucius was not opposed to religious rites. What he was against was their performance for utilitarian or selfish purposes—the expectation of reward or of exemption from misfortune. The real purpose of religious ritual was the expression of li, the attitude of sincerity and reverence. Whether or not a spirit was present was unimportant; the main thing was whether or not the heart of the worshiper was there. He said that one should sacrifice to a spirit as though it were present.[26]

Confucius accepted sacrifices to nature spirits. The popular view was that sacrifices should be regularly offered to the spirits who resided in hills and rivers so that harmony between them and men might be maintained. Confucius said a wise ruler "by respect for the Spirits keeps them at a distance."[27] He meant that by offering regular sacrifices to spirits, an official gives them what they want, and they will not disturb man. Man should not be intimate with spirits, and sacrifices to spirits enable man to keep his distance from their realm by pacifying them.

Although Confucius did not conceive of Heaven as a spirit, he felt that his own life was especially related to it. Once he was besieged by the army of a general who could not stand his teaching. In the face of imminent danger, he wondered whether or not it was the will of Heaven to let the ancient culture of Chou die. He came up with this conclusion: if Heaven had really so intended, then it would not have been possible for him to be engaged in the revival of the ancient culture for so long.[28] Convinced that his effort in renewing the Chou culture was a mission entrusted to him by Heaven, he felt that no one was going to stop him and he should not be afraid. At another time, he was despondent because his knowledge and talent were not being used by the rulers. But he was consoled by the conviction that those of lower status who do pursue the ancient culture of Chou are known on high and that Heaven appreciates their work.[29] These two instances show that Confucius accepted a sort of ethical providence; the thought of his work as being coextensive with the will of Heaven.

By and large, Confucius viewed religion as a factor that contributed to man's ethical and aesthetic life. When religion is properly pursued, it offers man both emotional satisfaction and moral aspiration. His view of religion is in accord with his philosophy.

THE UTILITARIAN SCHOOL OF MO-TZE

The time between the death of Confucius (479 B.C.) and the end of the Ch'in dynasty (206 B.C.), a matter of less than three centuries, is referred to as the Classical Period, for it was the most creative era of Chinese thought. Various philosophical schools emerged and offered ideas for the solution of China's problems. Whether they were for or against Confucian thought, they all assumed an acquaintance with it. These schools, which together with Taoism constituted the intellectual foundations of China, were primarily interested in ethics and government, although they also discussed theoretical and logical problems.

The Utilitarian school of Mo-tze and the Legalist school of Han Fei were rivals of Confucianism. The Idealist school of Mencius and the Realist school of Hsün Tzu represented two wings of Confucian thought. Although the first two were outside of Confucianism, they are here treated together with the Confucian schools because they were closely related to Confucianism in both their origin and their history.

Mo-tze and the Mohists

Mo-tze (478–381 B.C.) lived immediately after Confucius. A native of Lu, the home state of Confucius, he later moved to Sung (present-day Honan) where he became an official and developed his own philosophy. Mo-tze came from the lower stratum of Chinese society, and his followers, the Mohists, were also drawn from that class. The Confucians by and large were members of the upper and middle classes. This accounts for some fundamental differences

between the Confucians, who valued such things as music and ceremony, and the Mohists, who regarded these things as extraneous
and of no practical value.

Mo-tze believed that his philosophy of love and antimilitarism
could end war and unify China. He organized his disciples, at one
time 300 strong, into a religious association dedicated to austere
living, combating aggressors, and spreading Mohism. The head of
the organization, who was called the Leader, enjoyed absolute
authority over his members, including the power of life and death.
Mo-tze was the first of these.

The Mohists were skillful warriors and were frequently sent out
by rulers to defend their states. After the death of Mo-tze, there
were at least three successive Leaders who continued his teachings.
At one time the Mohists exerted great influence in China, but their
extremism did not outlive the Confucian spirit of moderation and
compromise. By the first century B.C., Mohism had ceased to be
influential, although its writings continued to attract attention.

The Philosophy of Mo-tze

Utilitarianism

The underlying principle of Mohism is utilitarianism: whatever
is useful is worth pursuing. The term "useful" refers to those
activities which would increase the wealth and population of the
state. Mo-tze believed in the primacy of the state; its welfare is
what determines what is useful for the individuals. But he was also
a moralist; he did not say that *any* means for the furtherance of
national goals is desirable. Although he parted from Confucianism,
he nevertheless accepted some Confucian principles. For instance,
he recognized the importance of benevolence (jen) and righteousness (*yi*). However, the welfare of the state gets more emphasis
in his thought than in that of Confucius. For Confucius, the practice of benevolence and righteousness are intrinsically worth pursuing; Mo-tze would say instead that conduct of that sort enables
the nation to prosper. Morality, in short, serves a useful purpose
for the state.

Universal Love

Both Confucius and Mo-tze agreed that love is a fundamental principle of life. They differed, however, in its starting point: the
former said that it should begin in the family, whereas Mo-tze said
that it should start universally. Confucius said that one should

love members of his family first, and then extend his love to include persons beyond the family. It was against the principle of propriety for one to love others before he loves those in his family or to love others in the same way one does his parents. In other words, love should be exercised in the order of parents, relatives, and persons beyond the family; it is graded and preferential; filial love is its basis.

Mo-tze advocated universal love; the distinction between one's own family and persons outside it should be removed. His conception of love still recognized the basic human relationships of Confucianism, although he interpreted them differently. His argument was that parents, children, brothers, and friends of others should be treated as one's own. Universal love means

to regard the state of others as one's own, the homes of others as one's own, the persons of others as one's self. When feudal lords love one another there will be no more war; when heads of houses love one another there will be no more mutual usurpation; when individuals love one another there will be no more mutual injury.[30]

Graded love entailed partiality and resulted in war between states. Universal love was the solution to the problem of China in his day.

But Mo-tze's universal love is motivated by utilitarianism; it is urged not because of the demands of conscience, but because of the benefits to be derived from it. Mo-tze asked: suppose a man is drafted to war, leaving his parents and family at home, would he entrust them to a friend who practices graded love or to one who practices universal love? He was certain that the departing warrior would leave them in the hands of the latter. Universal love involves reciprocity: when one takes care of one's friend's family as one's own, the friend will reciprocate. He was certain that "whoever loves others is loved by others; whoever benefits others is benefited by others; whoever hates others is hated by others; whoever injures others is injured by others."[31] Furthermore, the universal love of Mo-tze was pursued not for personal satisfaction, but for the welfare of society. If there is universal love, families in need will be supported by those who are able to give such support, and war will be eliminated.

In order to pursue universal love, according to Mo-tze, one must eliminate emotion, which entails preferential love. Emotion makes one love one's family or state more than others. Hence the Mohist conception of love is dictated by reason alone, without the support of feelings; it is a calculated effort to attain an ambitious social goal. There is no room for spontaneous and personal response in Mohism.

Religion
Because Mo-tze was a plebeian in origin and preference, he was critical of the aristocratic tradition of Chou. He sought a society in which there was uniformity of treatment, and he found that tradition in the culture of the Hsia period. While Confucius identified the ideal age with the time of the Duke of Chou, Mo-tze called for a return to the culture of the Hsia dynasty, which is supposed to have existed before Shang, although its historicity is now questioned.

Shang Ti, the ancestor deity of the Shang dynasty, was, for Mo-tze, identical with Heaven. To him this divine being was anthropomorphic, and his will was universal love. Heaven exercises rewards and punishments: "He who obeys the will of Heaven, loving universally and benefiting others, will obtain rewards. He who opposes the will of Heaven, by being partial and unfriendly and harming others, will incur punishment."[32]

Mo-tze also accepted the belief that spirits and ghosts existed literally as local divinities who watched the behavior of men closely and assigned rewards and punishments. As a result of the rational influence of Confucian thought, many Chinese during Mo-tze's time no longer believed in spirits and ghosts. He regarded the rejection of this belief as a cause of moral decadence, and he wished to revive it, so that men might be motivated to pursue universal love.

Although Mo-tze paid a good deal of attention to religious belief, his intentions were not theological, but utilitarian; he invoked the gods in order to promulgate his doctrine of love. For Confucius, religion was an attitude of reverence and respect; for Mo-tze, it was an absolute command for man to obey.

Government
Mo-tze advocated a government of pyramidal hierarchy in which monolithic command is strictly observed. In order to achieve uniformity of opinion, subordinates must obey their immediate superiors. Thus a son submits to his father, who follows the instruction of a district officer. The policy of the latter conforms to the direction of the state ruler, who obeys the king. And the king brings his policy close to the will of Heaven, which is universal love. This

upward movement of administration was called "the principle of agreement with the superior." Its ultimate aim was obedience to universal love. In theory, people exercised love through reason; in practice, however, it was imposed on them by the state.

Since the king represents Heaven in his establishing of universal love, it becomes his duty to reward those who practice it and punish those who do not. The king, being akin to Heaven, can always justify his actions and his policy in the name of God. Thus, according to Mo-tze, it takes a totalitarian state to enforce love in order to achieve a peaceful and prosperous society.

Frugality
Utilitarianism made Mo-tze advocate economy of expenditure at all levels of life. He condemned excessive indulgence in comforts, pleasures, rituals, and music, feeling that they wasted both money and time.

His criticism of the rites of mourning was aimed at the Confucians, who observed a three-year period of mourning after the death of parents. During that period, a filial son was required to withdraw from active employment and to live in semiseclusion. Although Mo-tze was not against filial love, he felt that that practice was detrimental to society, which needed men to work. He disapproved of it also on the ground of its effects on population, inasmuch as mourners refrained from sexual relations during the period of mourning. "To seek to improve the population in this way is like seeking longevity by thrusting one's self upon a sword."[33]

Mo-tze regarded music as useless, since it did not contribute to the wealth and population of the country. He saw no connection between music and the welfare of the state. Here he was again at odds with the Confucians, who believed in the value of music for the emotional life of man. Confucians associated music with rituals and ceremonies, a necessary aspect of li. Since Mo-tze wanted to eliminate emotion, he denied the value of music.

THE IDEALIST SCHOOL OF MENCIUS

Mencius (371–c. 289 B.C.) was born a century and a half later than Confucius in what is now the province of Shantung. He studied under a disciple of Tzu Ssu, a grandson of Confucius. His life resembles that of the Master—as a teacher, as a wandering scholar seeking office, and as a disappointed man, because no state would offer him a position to try out his philosophy. This similarity is not accidental; Mencius regarded himself as an exponent of the teachings of Confucius. In his day different philosophies such as Mohism, Taoism, and Legalism were competing with one another. He represented the orthodox view of Confucian thought. His position of moderation made him critical both of Yang Chu, an early Taoist, who expounded the doctrine of "each for himself," and of Mo-tze, who preached the subordination of individuals to the state.

Our knowledge of Mencius comes from the book known by his name. It is a record of conversations between him and his contemporaries—rulers, disciples, friends, and opponents. This work represents Confucian idealism, and it is therefore more discursive and extensive than the *Analects*. But it did not attain canonical status until the Sung dynasty (A.D. 960–1279), when Confucians selected it as one of the Four Books for students.

Mencius' thought reflects the social and political situation of the Warring States, when rulers were resorting to military power in order to attain control of all of China. They were willing to adopt any policy for that end. By contrast with the general mood of conspiracy, Mencius said that only a benevolent and righteous ruler could unify China. While the chiefs of state listened to him politely, none of them took his advice. Ironically, the first emperor, Shih Huang Ti, who did unite China in 221 B.C., was anything but a ruler of the Confucian persuasion.

Human Nature

Mencius is the first important Chinese thinker who held that human nature is originally good. Although such a view is implied in the thought of Confucius, he never stated it explicitly. Mencius explained it by way of a metaphor, saying that any man who sees a child about to fall into a well will without exception have a feeling of alarm and distress, along with the desire to rescue him. This feeling, as well as the desire to help, is instantaneous; it is not prompted by a wish for reward, a desire for praise, or a fear that he will be criticized if he fails to rescue the child.[34] It is not mediated by ulterior motives, nor is it learned from society; it therefore demonstrates the innate good nature of man.

There are four inherent feelings of men: commiseration, shame and dislike, modesty and yielding, and the feeling of approving and disapproving. Mencius called these feelings the Four Beginnings, because they are the source of human virtue. Hence benevolence (jen) is derived from commiseration, righteousness (yi) from shame and dislike, propriety (li) from modesty and yielding, and wisdom (chih) from approving and disapproving. Although these four virtues are to be cultivated, they are latent in the four feelings that constitute the good nature of man.

These four virtues were discussed separately by Confucius. Although he regarded them as necessary qualities for a gentleman, he did not discourse on their origin. It remained for Mencius to connect them with human nature and to give them a schematic interpretation. These virtues are potentially present in man, but they need to be developed. While Confucius refrained from a metaphysical analysis of man, Mencius did just that. With him the rationalistic trend in Confucian thought began.

If man's nature is innately good, how did Mencius account for the presence of evil in man? Mencius regarded man's evil aspects as attributes that he shares with the beasts. They are befitting the nature of animals, and hence do not properly belong to the essential nature of man. Mencius ascribed the absence of human virtues to bad environment, which prevents man from developing them. A bad environment is one that encourages the rise of animal nature in man; a good environment is one that encourages man to develop his virtues. Mencius also believed that individual differences with regard to the realization of virtue are due to differences in the extent to which men exert themselves; the more one acts to develop his good nature, the more virtuous he becomes. Mencius believed that the attainment of perfection is a real possibility for man.

Education
Although Mencius emphasized the good nature of man, he was fully cognizant that in his time the moral condition of men was bad; their animal nature had the upper hand. The remedy was education, which means drawing out men's good nature by the study and the practice of Confucian moral philosophy. The Chinese regarded the human heart as the dwelling place of man's nature; now one speaks of the mind in that regard. Education involved the cultivation of mind (heart), which is a moral rather than a mental enterprise. This remains the principal purpose of education in the Confucian tradition.

Mencius was the first important thinker in China to recognize

the place of environment in education; he believed that the best
way for one to develop virtue is to be among virtuous men. He
illustrated this by reference to learning a new dialect: if a native
of the state of Ch'u (in central China) wants to learn the dialect
of Ch'i (in north China), it would be far better if he went to Ch'i
and learned it there than to study it at home, for no matter how
hard this person studies the Ch'i dialect, so long as he remains in
his home state, hearing only the speech of his fellow citizens, he
cannot master the dialect.[35]

A legend has it that while Mencius was a boy, his mother had
to move the family twice in succession before she found a good
location near a school for her son. Needless to say, this story arose
out of Mencius' teachings on the importance of environment.

Government and Economics
In Mencius' day, the tradition of the three legendary kings Yao,
Shun, and Yü as the founders of the Chinese nation and the origi-
nators of Confucian moral principles was already established. But
it was left for Mencius to use this legend for an explanation of the
legitimacy of kingship according to the Mandate of Heaven. This
he stated as follows: When Yao was on the throne, he chose as his
assistant Shun, who exemplified virtue and was benevolent to the
people. After the death of Yao, Shun was chosen by the people as
his successor for his moral and administrative qualities. Shun had
an assistant, Yü, who was later made king by popular consensus
for the same reason. But after the death of Yü, his son was chosen
by the people as the successor, not because he was the heir, but
because he was qualified. In this account, Mencius showed that
Yao, Shun, Yü, and also his son, were all virtuous and wise; that
they became kings by popular consensus because of their qualifications; that their approval by the people is indicative of being appointed by Heaven; and that it is the Mandate of Heaven, not
hereditary right, that determines the legitimacy of kingship. Mencius cited as an example the case of Chow, the last king of the
Shang dynasty, who was dethroned and killed because he was devoid
of virtues and rejected by Heaven. Hence Chow should be treated
as a "mere fellow." Actually, no killing of a sovereign was involved
in the Chow case.[36]

Although it is difficult to determine the right holder of the
Mandate of Heaven, Mencius believed that confidence of people

in their ruler is an essential criterion. In the account above, of legendary kings, each became sovereign because he had won the hearts of people. Mencius elsewhere quoted a saying from the *Book of History,* "Heaven sees according as my people see; Heaven hears according as my people hear."[37] Popular opinion with regard to the ruler is an indication of whether or not he has received the blessing of Heaven.

The welfare of the people should be the primary concern of the ruler. Mencius said: "The people are the most important in a nation; the spirits of the land and grain are the next; the sovereignty is the lightest. Therefore to gain the peasantry is the way to become an emperor."[38] Here Mencius laid down three principles that a ruler should follow. First, he must win the hearts of the people, principally the farmers, by attending to their welfare; next, he should offer regular sacrifices to agricultural spirits; only lastly may he take care of his own needs.

China was at that time ruled by a handful of feudal lords, who through military might had subdued the lesser states. These rulers were called *pa.* Their policy, in the eyes of Mencius, was certainly contrary to what a virtuous ruler should do. Disgusted with their behavior, Mencius advocated the kingly way, *wang tao,* according to which a ruler conducts his state affairs through personal virtue, in contrast to the existing way of force, *pa tao.* Even though the kingly way was not practiced in Mencius' time, it did become an ideal in Confucian political philosophy and as such has molded the political institutions of China.

Mencius was much concerned with the condition of the peasants, whose welfare, as he saw it, determines the destiny of their ruler. He introduced a land reform whereby a unit of land was divided into nine squares in the shape of 井 , which is the Chinese word for a well. Hence this was called the "well-field" system. These nine squares are to be given by the state to eight families who live close together. Each family cultivates its allotted land and receives the produce from it. But all eight families jointly cultivate the central "public field," the produce of which serves as a tax to the state.

In the time of Mencius, land was privately owned: it belonged to the rulers and nobles. Mencius believed that the land should be state-owned, but should be distributed to the people. Although his agricultural policy has remained no more than an ideal, it has been frequently cited by land reformers in Chinese history.

Religion

Like Confucius, Mencius believed in ancestral spirits and nature spirits. He dispelled the older belief in Heaven as the royal ancestor deity and interpreted it instead as the divine appointer of human kings and as the source of human virtue.

Mencius rationalized the legitimacy of kingship, as the Duke of Chou had before him, through the doctrine of the Mandate of Heaven. A king, in his view, was in theory appointed by Heaven and was therefore called Son of Heaven. It is largely through the school of Mencius that the religious context of the government was firmly established in Confucian thought. The emperor was responsible to Heaven for his administration and personal virtue, and he ruled his country on the basis of divine authority. In this regard, there is a resemblance in the attitude toward kingship between the Hebrew religion and Confucianism.

Mencius held that man is endowed by Heaven with his good nature. This nature consists of the four innate virtues—benevolence, righteousness, propriety, wisdom. By connecting human nature with Heaven, Mencius started the tradition in Confucian thought of metaphysical inquiry into the nature of man. Here Mencius departed from Confucius, who had no interest in the discussion of metaphysical problems.

Mencius conceived of the nature of man as being identical in principle with that of Heaven; both are essentially moral. He arrived at this conviction through intuition: "He who has exercised his mind (*hsin*) to the utmost, knows his nature (*hsing*). Knowing nature, he knows Heaven. To keep one's mind preserved and nourish one's nature is the way to serve Heaven."[39] Man possesses the four virtues in potentiality, but Heaven has them in actuality. If we postulate Heaven as the ground of man's nature, then man has a duty to develop his nature.

Since Heaven is known to man through his own nature, Mencius understood man as a microcosm of the universe. Conversely, the universe is a macrocosm of man: the world is reflected in man. This kind of thinking led Mencius to say, "All things are already complete in us."[40] When one understands one's own nature, one understands the cosmos. By stressing the immediate relationship between man and Heaven, Mencius embraced one strand of mysticism. This is discernible in his remark on the "vital force" of man, which denotes man's cosmic feeling as he becomes one with Heaven. But since Heaven is moral in essence, what the mysticism of Mencius affirms is the ultimacy of morality; it is different from the Taoist mysticism, which transcends morality.

THE REALIST SCHOOL OF HSÜN TZU

Hsün Tzu (298–238 B.C.) survived Mencius by half a century; he was a native of present-day Shansi. At one time he was an official in the state of Ch'i, whose government was well known for its hospitality to scholars. Of the many disciples whom he taught, Han Fei and Li Ssu, two of the best known, were Legalists; both of these thinkers made helpful contributions to the policy of the state of Ch'in.

Hsün Tzu's life preceded by just a few years the unification of China in 221 B.C. The period of Mencius and Hsün Tzu was a fertile era of Chinese thought. Mohism, Taoism, the School of Logic, Legalism, and others flourished alongside the idealism of Mencius, each influencing the others. Hsün Tzu was exposed to these rival views. Although he stood within the mainstream of Confucianism, his ideas reflect the influences of other contemporary thinkers; they are eclectic. Basically he represents the rational, realistic wing of Confucianism.

Our knowledge of him is derived from his own writings, which have been collected in *The Works of Hsün Tzu*. This is a closely reasoned book, containing features comparable to the ethical and political writings of Aristotle. It represented the most comprehensive Confucian philosophy up to its time.

The early rulers of the Han dynasty adopted the political and social philosophy of Hsün Tzu. But his thought gradually lost its influence when the Han Confucians turned to metaphysics and Buddhism took hold of Chinese thought. The neo-Confucians, beginning with the twelfth century, preferred Mencius to Hsün Tzu, whose thought was pushed into the background until the late Ch'ing dynasty, when empiricism prevailed.

Human Nature
The word *hsing* (nature) was used by Hsün Tzu to mean what is original, that is, prior to change. When he said human nature is evil, he meant that such is man's inherent condition; man is by nature selfish, profit-seeking, and aggressive. Although human na-

ture is evil, man is nevertheless capable of good. Evil is inborn, but goodness can be acquired through efforts. This view of human nature does not negate man's freedom.

Hsün Tzu contrasted the inborn nature of man with his acquired goodness. He believed that these two aspects are in constant tension, but it is the latter that makes a person truly human, by contrast with the brutes. He said:

Now the nature of man is that when he is hungry, he desires repletion; when he is cold, he desires warmth; when he labours, he seeks rest. This is man's natural feeling. But now when a man is hungry and sees food, he dares not rush in ahead of others; instead the eater yields to others. When working, he dares not seek rest, instead he works for others. The son yielding precedence to his father; the younger brother yielding to his older brother; the son working for his father, the younger brother working for his older brother—these two kinds of actions are contrary to original nature and antagonistic to natural feeling.[41]

As a biological species, man is egoistic; as a moral being, he is capable of good. For Mencius, man begins as a moral being, and evil is learned. For Hsün Tzu, man begins as a creature of nature, and it is goodness that is learned.

What happens to man's evil nature when he becomes good? It cannot be eradicated, because it is inborn; yet this nature can be brought under control by the acquired character of man. One learns the Confucian virtues and practices them daily until they become "second nature." He thus gets into the habit of being good. Man's original nature is now subdued by his moral reason. Hsün Tzu's moral reason resembles the "oughtness" of Immanuel Kant.

Education

Since the nature of man is evil, the task of education becomes the making of a good man. This is the most important aspect of Hsün Tzu's teaching. Man differs from brutes in that he is able to develop a moral conscience through education. Hsün Tzu believed that the Confucian documents must be earnestly studied, for they are the intellectual and spiritual sources for making a good man. Since they are difficult to master, a teacher is imperative:

Therefore if a man is without a teacher or precepts, then if he is intelligent, he will certainly become a robber; if he is brave, he will certainly become a murderer; if he has ability, he will certainly go far from the truth. If he has a teacher and precepts, then if he is an investigator, he will quickly arrive at all truth; if he is a dialectician, he will quickly be able to determine the truth or falsity of all things. . . . If a man is without a teacher or precepts, he will exalt his original nature; if he has a teacher and precepts, he will exalt self-cultivation.[42]

The Confucian documents that Hsün Tzu specifically referred to are the *Book of Songs*, the *Book of History*, the *Book of Rites*, the *Book of Music*, the *Spring and Autumn Annals*. Hsün Tzu said that the study of these works is a lifelong process. "To do that is to be a man; to stop is to be a bird or beast."[43] Book learning, as the essential part of education in the Confucian tradition, began with Hsün Tzu. Prior to his time, it was the personal thought of a teacher himself that constituted the basic element of instruction. The career of Hsün Tzu marked a shift in Confucianism from emphasis on the teacher himself to stress on a body of written records. The exalted status of a teacher in the thought of Hsün Tzu indicates this shift. The teacher has now become the transmitter of a revered written tradition; his role is comparable to that of the Brahmin in India.

Since man is by nature evil and his goodness depends on the aid of a teacher, how did the first teacher acquire his goodness? Hsün Tzu touched on this question indirectly when he said that the Confucian precepts and standards of justice were formulated by ancient sages—the legendary culture heroes of China. Being sages, they did not need the assistance of teachers; they developed their goodness by themselves and laid down the foundations of Confucian culture. Hsün Tzu felt, however, that in his day people needed teachers.[44]

Hsün Tzu's view of human nature, together with his esteem of teachers, shows that he stressed outside authority for the accomplishment of man's goodness. In this regard, he differs from Confucius and Mencius, who emphasized the ability of man to develop goodness himself, and is closer to Mo-tze and the Legalists. His preference for external authority resulted in his authoritarian political philosophy.

Although Hsün Tzu and Mencius seemed to hold opposite views of human nature, in the end their views of man were not far apart. For Hsün Tzu, education conquers the evil nature of man; by unceasing self-cultivation, one forms a trinity with Heaven and

Earth. For Mencius, education develops the good nature of man;
by continuing self-development, one reaches unity with Heaven.

Government and Society
Hsün Tzu's view of government and society was predicated on his
theory of human nature. Since man's original nature is selfish, he
has unlimited wants and desires. If these are not restricted, chaos
follows: the satisfaction of desires becomes impossible, and the
supply of goods will soon cease. Government arose to establish the
rules of conduct (li) and standards of justice (yi) so as to set limits
to men's desires. In that way, the supply of things is able to continue, and men's proper needs can be met. Peace and harmony in
society are thus guaranteed. Hsün Tzu identified the origin of the
state with the formulation of rules of conduct and standards of
justice by the legendary sage-kings. His theory of state resembles
that of Thomas Hobbes. Both believed that the state is necessary
to protect people from annihilating one another, since man is selfish
by nature. Their differences lie in their understanding of the nature of the state. For Hsün Tzu, the state enforces precepts and
justice through the personal virtue of rulers. For Hobbes, the state
receives its right to rule from people who by agreement surrender
their natural rights for protection over their individual needs.

According to Hsün Tzu, once the state was established, its chief
function was to maintain social distinctions among individuals regarding rank, vocation, morality, intelligence, education, and other
factors. Men's achievements vary because they differ in background,
and apply their talents differently. Furthermore, the five human relationships (father and son, husband and wife, elder brother and
younger brother, ruler and subjects, junior and senior friends)
necessitate distinctions concerning the role one plays in relation to
another. On the other hand, men tend to have the same likes and
dislikes. If these are not curbed, confusion arises. The state enforces
social distinctions and sees to it that the rules of conduct and standards of justice are practiced according to one's position in family
and society. The standards are learned from Confucian classics and
nurtured by society. He says:

Work is what people dislike; gain and profit are what they like. If
there is no distinction of occupation, then people will have difficulty
in getting work done and the calamity of striving in order to obtain

any desired result. If the union of male and female, the separation from other males and females inherent in the relation of husband and wife, the making of engagement by the relatives of the groom and bride to be, the sending of betrothal presents and the going to get the bride, are not according to the rules of proper conduct; then men will have the trouble of losing their mates and the calamity of having to struggle to gain any sex relation. Hence for this reason wise men have introduced social distinctions.[45]

Hsün Tzu's theory of society assumed that men are unequal in their moral, intellectual, and social attainments. On the other hand, such a society implies differences in treatment in the eyes of law; the same crime committed by a well-to-do member of the gentry would receive a more severe punishment than if it were committed by a poor plebeian.

The society he prescribed is authoritarian; the state makes laws about right and wrong to be obeyed by people, and the Confucian classics offer precepts to be learned as infallible truth. For Confucius and Mencius virtue means the actualization of man's inner qualities. For Hsün Tzu it is the practice of a body of truth under the control of the state. Morality is now institutionalized.

In the philosophy of Hsün Tzu, we catch a glimpse of two later traditions concerning government: one is the emphasis on the personal virtues of rulers as the criterion of a good state, and the other is the interest in bureaucracy, in terms of rules and organizations, as the means of achieving a good government. The first tradition is represented by the right wing of Confucianism; the second is represented by Legalism. It is no surprise that some of Hsün Tzu's students turned out to be Legalists.

Religion

Both Confucius and Mencius accepted Heaven as a cosmic morality to which man looks for guidance. This was not so for Hsün Tzu, who equated Heaven with nature which for him means the recurrent phenomena such as the cycle of seasons or the alternation between the passive force (Yin) and the active force (Yang). (Although the concepts of Yin and Yang were developed earlier by the School of Yin-Yang, by the time of Hsün Tzu these ideas were incorporated into the writings of Confucianism and Taoism.) Heaven, as the primary cause in nature, is beyond man's reach and unobservable.

But Heaven as the effects of the primary cause—that is, the secondary cause in nature—is observable. His view of Heaven is summarized as follows:

The fixed stars make their round, and sun and moon alternately shine; the four seasons succeed one another; the *yin* and *yang* go through their great mutations; wind and rain are widely distributed; all things acquire their lives; each gets its nourishment and develops to its appointed state. We do not see the cause of these occurrences, but we do see their effects. This is what is meant by being spirit-like. The results of all these changes are known, but we do not know the invisible source; this is what is called Heaven.[46]

Hsün Tzu's interpretation of Heaven resembled that of nature in Taoism. But the Taoists posited Tao as the source of nature. Although Tao is unknowable, they constantly spoke of it, referring to it by metaphors (the uncarved block, the infant, the valley, water, and so forth), and taught man to be in tune with it (see Chapter 24, Taoism). Hsün Tzu parted company with the Taoists by not attempting to allude to the primary cause of nature, and thereby avoiding their mysticism. That is why he said that a sage "does not seek to know Heaven"; he wanted man to turn away from seeking to know the cause of nature. He further differed from the Taoists by emphasizing man's need for moral attainment.

Heaven, being the automatic process of nature, is devoid of moral and spiritual attributes; it neither gives rewards nor inflicts punishments. Man should not seek nature's cause (like the Taoists) nor should he look for its moral attributes (like the Mencians). The function of Heaven is to regulate the natural processes, while that of Earth is to produce; man's task is to utilize Heaven and Earth for his advantage. When each functions properly, a harmonious triad is established.

Although Hsün Tzu's understanding of Heaven is materialistic, this does not mean that he is not religious. Religion for him belongs to the realm of li, which includes sacrifices to Heaven and ancestors as well as birth, funeral, and other rites. He understands religion in terms of rituals and ceremonies. These activities are good for man's emotions. The need for religion is not theological, but aesthetic. Religious and secular rituals, "if for the service of the living, are to beautify joy; or if to send off the dead, they are to beautify sorrow, or if for sacrifice, they are to beautify reverence, or if they are military, they are to beautify majesty."[47] Religion adds an aesthetic dimension to human existence, which would otherwise be drab and arid.

Hsün Tzu was critical of Mo-tze, who opposed costly rituals. He felt that Mo-tze had failed to see the value of emotion in religion. On the other hand, to some extent he shared the utilitarianism of Mo-tze by stressing the usefulness of religion.

THE LEGALIST SCHOOL OF HAN FEI

The Legalists were a new breed of specialists in government affairs during the third century B.C. who advocated the power of state and its expansion. Their thought was in every way contrary to the Confucianism of their time, particularly with reference to political philosophy. Legalism centered around the belief that law (fa) prescribed by the state should regulate individual lives; whereas Confucianism believed that moral principles (li) should guide individuals and the state should never do anything contrary to these principles. Legalism became influential at this time because it was a means to an end for rulers who were desirous of uniting divided China.

The tradition of Legalism goes back to Kuan Chung, a seventh-century minister of the state of Ch'i. Shang Yang (d. 338 B.C.), who was at one time a prime minister of the state of Ch'in, and whose teaching was preserved in the *Book of Lord Shang,* a notable Legalist document, also was part of this tradition. His connection with Ch'in indicates that that state had been under the influence of the Legalist philosophy for some time.

Han Fei (c. 280–233 B.C.) was a prince of the state of Han, adjacent to Ch'in in present-day western Honan. He was a student of Hsün Tzu. Handicapped by a speech impediment, he resorted to writing. He digested the Legalist ideas and put them into the book known today as *Han Fei Tzu,* which became a classic handbook of this school. Although this work was unacceptable to Confucians, it was read continually, for it served as an antidote to Confucian verbosity. At length it came into the hands of the Ch'in ruler, who admired it greatly. In 234 B.C. the home state of Han Fei was invaded by Ch'in. Han was sent by his king as an envoy to negotiate peace. Li Ssu, his fellow student, a Legalist, who was then a minister in Ch'in, out of jealousy succeeded in persuading the king to have

Han arrested, and he was forced to die by taking poison. Nevertheless, his theories were put into practice by the ruler of Ch'in.

China was united by Ch'in in 221 B.C. But the dynasty, and with it the dominance of Legalism, came to an abrupt end in 206 B.C. However, the Ch'in rulers left the standardization of script, measures, weights, and techniques of government as a permanent legacy to China, and Legalism persisted as a substratum in Chinese political institutions.

Government

The purpose of the state in Legalism is to control power; the welfare of the individuals is subordinate to that of the state. The purpose of the state in Confucianism is to benefit individuals; the welfare of the ruler is considered only after that of the individual members of the state.

In a Legalist society the power (shih) of the king is undivided; ministers carry out his orders, but do not share his power. If this power is divided, it prepares the way for dissension and coups d'état. The authority of the ruler has nothing to do with virtue or talent. The high office he holds entitles him to this power. Han Fei said: "When a weight of thirty thousand catties has a boat, it floats. When a trifling weight is without a boat, it sinks. . . . Thus what is short can see over what is tall, because of its position, and one who is unworthy can rule the talented because of his *shih*."[48]

The Legalists substituted law (fa) for the personal virtue of the ruler, as taught by the Confucians. The king, with the assistance of his ministers, enacts statutes that regulate the public and private lives of his subjects. He needs no moral qualifications. All he needs is to see to it that the law is uniformly present and obeyed by all, including his relatives and ministers. Han Fei said that the ruler governs through inaction (wu-wei); that is, he lets law function by itself; he does not interfere with it personally. Han Fei conceived of human law as the counterpart of the law of nature.

The ruler enforces law through administrative techniques (shu). A cardinal technique is that of reward and punishment, which serves as the "two handles" of the ruler. Since human nature desires gain and shuns punishment, if the government rewards those who adhere to duties and obligations and punishes those who violate them, people will be motivated to work for their gain and to avoid punishment. In that way, both the state and the individual will profit. Legalism believed in equality of law; that is, the same reward and punishment is applied to all persons, regardless of rank or education. It differs in this respect from Confucianism, which holds that reward and punishment should vary according to the status and education of a person.

In Confucianism it was the responsibility of the state to teach virtue, encourage learning, and safeguard li, the conventions of a civilized society. All these were discouraged by the state in Legalism. If people followed the practices advocated by Confucianism, they would neglect farming and other works that are beneficial to the state. Furthermore, learning results in diverse opinions, which endanger the state.

Human Nature

Han Fei's view of human nature follows that of Hsün Tzu. The belief that human nature is evil or selfish determines his political theories. A recognition of man's desire for profit is a prerequisite for effective government policies. Han Fei used the employer-employee relationship as an example of his argument:

When a man sells his service as a farm hand, the master will give him good food at the expense of his own family, and pay him money and cloth. This is not because he loves the farm hand, but he says: "In this way, his ploughing the ground will go deeper and his sowing seeds will be more active." The farm hand, on the other hand, exerts all his skill cultivating the fields. This is not because he loves his master, but he says: "In this way, I shall have good soup, and money and cloth will come easily." Thus he expends his strength as if between them there were a bond of love such as that of father and son.[49]

Like the farm owner, the ruler should recognize the profit motive of man and act accordingly. If the ruler sees that the principle of reward and punishment is followed strictly but justly, people will then work hard for him. Han Fei said:

All ruling of the empire must be done by utilizing human nature. In human nature there are the feelings of like and dislike, and hence rewards and punishments may be employed. When rewards and punishments are employed, interdicts and commands may be issued, and the way of government attained. The ruler holds on to these handles so as to rest in his power (shih), and hence his orders operate and his interdicts serve to prevent. These handles consist in the control of death and life; power *(shih)* is the means of maintaining supremacy over the masses.[50]

Arguing in the same vein, Han Fei said that the ruler should avoid intimate contact with his ministers. Officials covet such situations for gain, and when they are permitted favoritism and factionalism follow. Officials prefer the cultivation of personal relationships to adherence to law, and the allowance of such relationships would thus upset the automatic function of law. Besides, human nature being evil, the most favored minister would eventually usurp the throne and make himself the king.

Economics

Mencius proposed the system whereby land is evenly distributed among families. Equal distribution of land remained a Confucian ideal for agricultural economy.[51] The Legalists, on the other hand, were opposed to it. Since man is motivated by self-interest, Han Fei felt, free competition is the best agricultural policy. It encourages people to work harder. Barring uncontrollable circumstances, the diligent person tends to increase his land, while the idle man's land decreases. Han Fei felt that the poverty of the wasteful and lazy person is the result of his own making, whereas the wealth of the industrious and thrifty person is the reward of his hard work. To take away the land from the rich so as to distribute it to the poor is unjust.[52] Moreover, equal distribution in the long run is harmful to the national economy.

The economic factor was one reason for Han Fei's opposition to learning. The pursuit of Confucian studies resulted in idle talk and abandonment of farming. If scholars were to quit farming, there would be a shortage of workers. At the same time, there were not enough government posts to absorb them, and, as a result, many of these men became parasites, to the detriment of the national economy. Han Fei was in favor of keeping the people ignorant so that they would remain in the field.

History

Han Fei's understanding of history is different from that of Confucianism. The latter posited an age of perfection under the reigns of the legendary kings as the embodiment of Confucian virtues. Subsequent governments were often urged by Confucians to return to the practices of these ancient kings. Confucians believed that an absolute standard of morality and government existed from the beginning and was valid at all times. Han Fei, while not denying the virtues of the sage-kings, refused to accept the idea of the standard of antiquity being suitable to his time.

The difference between the age of the sage-kings and the present age, according to Han Fei, was not one of morality, but one of change in social and economic conditions. In the earlier period, there was no need for competition, because the supply of materials was plentiful and the population was small. Under these circumstances it was easier to practice virtue. But in his time the supply of materials was scarce because of the increase in population. It was imperative to encourage free competition, and to enforce reward and punishment, in order to build national wealth. He remarked that the contemporary society was in fact better than the earlier one, because its standard of living was higher: a common laborer in his day lived as well as a sage-king of yesterday. If the latter were living at the present, he would not practice the virtues of antiquity.

Han Fei told a story to show the obsolescence of the practices of antiquity. There was a farmer who tilled his field daily. The stump of a tree stood in the field. One day a rabbit ran at full speed against the stump, broke his neck, and died. The farmer thereafter quit work and stood beside the tree, expecting another rabbit to do the same. Han Fei commented: "If, however, you wish to rule the people of to-day with the methods of government of the early kings, you do exactly the same thing as that man who waited by the tree."[53]

The Legalists believed that change is the essence of time: each age must form new policies of government and face novel situations. Taoism, a contemporary philosophy, also advocated change, but it was the Legalists who put this idea into practice in government. Their school arose in a time of social change, and what they offered was a rational explanation for the necessity of these changes.

Influences of Mohism and Taoism

The Legalist's emphasis on the useful and the nonaesthetic, as well as his prohibition of waste, is close to the utilitarianism of Mo-tze. Curiously enough, both schools are predicated on man's self-interest. Mo-tze said one should love the parents of his friend because in that way he ensured that his own parents would be looked after when he was away; it pays to practice universal love. Han Fei said that the ruler should enforce rewards and punishments because people are motivated by the desire for gain. In fact, the principle of reward and punishment even antedated Mo-tze; it was the chief function of Shang Ti, the God of Mohism.

The differences between Legalism and Confucianism are basic: one holds a materialistic view of nature and man, the other gives a moral interpretation of nature and man; one denies, whereas the other accepts, a divine being. Incompatibility is also seen between Legalism and Taoism: one advocates a totalitarian state, the other teaches laissez-faire individualism; one makes nature subordinate to man, the other makes man subordinate to nature. But a closer look discloses that Han Fei used Tao to elucidate the law of the state. Tao and law are both impersonal and both function automatically. Tao is the eternal principle manifested through cycles of natural forces; it rules over nature and man. Law for Han Fei, once established, operates by itself. Both Tao and law are indifferent to men's feelings and preference, yet their powers are present everywhere.

In Taoism the natural order finds its source in Tao; in Legalism the state finds its power in law. In either case, the source of law, natural or human, is to be found in a ruling power that partakes of wu-wei, inaction or effortless action. The difference is that in Taoism the ruling power is a metaphysical being, whereas in Legalism it is the king himself. Han Fei conceived the ruler as the embodiment of Tao. The *Tao Te Ching* says:

> The Way is like an empty vessel
> That yet may be drawn from
> Without ever needing to be filled.
> It is bottomless; the very progenitor
> of all things in the world.[54]

Again:

> Tao never does;
> Yet through it all things are done.[55]

Han Fei applied the same meaning to the king:

The enlightened ruler reposes in inaction above, and below his ministers tremble with fear.[56]

The Way lies in what cannot be seen, its function in what cannot be known. Be empty, still and idle, and from your place of darkness observe the defects of others.[57]

Although Han Fei denied a metaphysical reality, by incorporating the function of Tao in the king he made the latter virtually a divine ruler. He unwittingly identified the metaphysical being with the human ruler, and thus he was not entirely free from religion, as he had intended to be.

NOTES

1. Herrlee G. Creel, *The Birth of China* (New York: John Day, 1937), p. 190.
2. *Ibid.*, pp. 204–210.
3. *Ibid.*, p. 182.
4. *Ibid.*, p. 342.
5. *The Chinese Classics,* trans. by James Legge, Vol. III, *Shou King* (Hong Kong: University of Hong Kong, 1960), pp. 495–502.
6. *The Analects of Confucius,* trans. by Arthur Waley (London: Allen & Unwin, 1938), Book IV, 14, pp. 104–105.
7. Herrlee G. Creel, *Confucius and the Chinese Way* (New York: Harper, 1960), p. 39.
8. *The Analects of Confucius,* trans. by Arthur Waley (London: Allen & Unwin, 1938), Book VII, 8, p. 124. Used by permission.
9. *Ibid.*
10. Creel, *Confucius and the Chinese Way,* pp. 100–108.
11. *The Analects of Confucius,* Book XII, 2, p. 162.
12. *Ibid.*, Book VI, 28, p. 122.
13. *Ibid.*, Book IV, 15, p. 105.
14. Fung Yu-lan, *A Short History of Chinese Philosophy* (New York: Macmillan, 1948), p. 44. Used by permission.
15. *The Analects of Confucius,* Book XII, 2, p. 162.
16. *Ibid.*, Book XIII, 3, p. 171. Waley's translation is, "It would certainly be to correct language."
17. *Ibid.*, Book XII, 11, p. 166. Waley used "prince" instead of "ruler."
18. *Ibid.*, Book IV, 25, p. 106.
19. *Ibid.*, Book XII, 18, p. 167.
20. *Ibid.*, Book XII, 19, p. 168.
21. *Ibid.*, Book IV, 5, pp. 102–103.
22. *Ibid.*, Book IV, 8, p. 103.
23. *Ibid.*, Book III, 11, p. 96.
24. *Ibid.*, Book VII, 34, pp. 130–131.
25. *Ibid.*, Book III, 13, p. 97.
26. *Ibid.*, Book III, 12, p. 97.
27. *Ibid.*, Book VI, 20, p. 120.
28. *Ibid.*, Book IX, 5, p. 139.
29. *Ibid.*, Book XIV, 37, p. 189.
30. *The Ethical and Political Works of Motse,* trans. by Mei Yi-pao (London: Probsthain, 1929), p. 82. Used by permission.
31. *Ibid.*, p. 83.
32. *Ibid.*, p. 137.

33. *Ibid.*, p. 129.
34. *The Works of Mencius,* in the *Four Books,* trans. by James Legge (Shanghai: Chinese Book Co., n.d.), II A, 6:3.
35. *Ibid.*, III B, 6:1, pp. 666–667.
36. *Ibid.*, I B, 8:1–3, pp. 493–494.
37. *Ibid.*, V A, 5:8, p. 795.
38. *Ibid.*, VII B, 14:1–2, p. 985.
39. Fung Yu-lan, *A History of Chinese Philosophy,* trans. by Derk Bodde (Princeton: Princeton University Press, 1959–1960), I, 129.
40. *The Works of Mencius,* VII A, 4:1, p. 935.
41. *The Works of Hsüntze,* trans. by Homer H. Dubs (London: Probsthain, 1928), p. 304. Used by permission.
42. *Ibid.*, p. 114.
43. *Ibid.*, p. 32.
44. H. G. Creel, *Chinese Thought from Confucius to Mao Tse-tung* (Chicago: University of Chicago Press, 1953), p. 115. Used by permission.
45. *The Works of Hsüntze, op. cit.,* pp. 152–153.
46. Fung Yu-lan, *A History of Chinese Philosophy,* I, 285.
47. *Ibid.*, p. 237.
48. *Ibid.*, p. 326.
49. *Ibid.*, p. 327.
50. *Ibid.*, p. 326.
51. *Ibid.*, p. 328.
52. *Ibid.*
53. *Ibid.*, p. 317.
54. Lao Tzu, *Tao Te Ching, The Way and Its Power,* trans. by Arthur Waley (London: Allen & Unwin, 1934), p. 146. Used by permission.
55. *Ibid.*, p. 188.
56. Han Fei Tzu, *Basic Writings of Han Fei Tzu,* trans. by Burton Watson (New York: Columbia University Press, 1964), p. 17. Used by permission.
57. *Ibid.*, p. 92.

CONFUCIANISM IN THE HAN PERIOD

Eclecticism

When the Han dynasty (206 B.C.–A.D. 220) succeeded Ch'in, Confucianism was restored to prominence. Kao Tsu, the first emperor, who had been a commoner, won the throne through military might and wise statesmanship. In order to be thought a legitimate holder of the Mandate of Heaven, he sought the support of the Confucian gentry, although he himself was not a follower of that tradition. Also, because of the popularity of Confucian ideas among both the commoners and the literati, rulers were compelled to appoint Confucian leaders to government posts. But since the Han rulers possessed a large empire, they had to resort to law and its corollary of reward and punishment for administrative purposes. As a result, both Legalism and Confucianism came to be adopted: the former represented the interests of the state; the latter, those of the people. The state needed the Confucians in order to ensure popular support; the Confucians needed the state in order to be able to hold office. On the whole, the Confucians at the court acted as a restraining influence. The sudden collapse of the Ch'in dynasty was a reminder to the Han rulers of the dangers of the outright use of Legalist methods. Hence they applied those methods with caution, and Legalist devices were often even dressed in Confucian language when they were employed in government edicts. As a result of this mutual confrontation, Legalist ideas were absorbed into Confucianism.

FIGURE 23.1   An old woman lighting candles in a Confucian Temple. (*Henle from Monkmeyer*)

The school of Yin-Yang was also assimilated by Confucian thought during this period. That school grew out of astrology and divination, but by the third century B.C. it had become a theory of cosmology. Since then both Confucianism and Taoism have made use of it.

Because of the high prestige Confucianism enjoyed during the Han period, the sage was exalted by Confucian writers to the status of a divine being. A body of apocrypha, attributed to Confucius, appeared at this time. In one document it was said that Confucius had received the Mandate of Heaven to be a king, and that his kingship was stated in the *Spring and Autumn Annals,* a historical record of Lu, his home state.[1] In another work Confucius was described as the son of a god, the Black Emperor, and miracles were said to have filled his life.[2] But these views did not remain prominent in later times.

Confucianism as a State Teaching

The rise to power of Confucianism was associated with the reign of Wu Ti (140–87 B.C.), who became king at the age of fifteen. A group of Confucian advisers served at his court during the early part of his reign. On their recommendation, the king issued an edict in 136 B.C. making Confucian classics a requirement of education and the basis for recruitment. The Six Disciplines were made the core of the curriculum.[3] Wu Ti began the practice of sponsoring imperial examinations at the capital, attended by scholars who were recommended by officials in the provinces. Those who were selected were then appointed to office. He initiated a civil service system that was refined in later times and became an institution in the Sung dynasty (A.D. 960–1279). He was also credited with opening a national academy where scholars were employed to investigate Confucian texts, many of which had been lost during the burning of books in the Ch'in dynasty.

Although Wu Ti later in his reign introduced Legalist measures and indulged in religious Taoism, his contribution to Confucianism was permanent. It was he who started the cooperation between the government bureaucracy and the Confucian literati. Canonization of early Confucian classics also took place during his reign and while priority was given to books of Confucianism, the works of rival schools were not prohibited.

A Confucian temple existed during the reign of Wu Ti in the home town of the sage, where ancestral sacrifice was made by his descendants. Despite the high regard paid to him at this time, no official sacrifice was offered regularly. A state-sponsored Confucian cult did begin in A.D. 59, when Emperor Ming Ti ordered animal sacrifice to the sage by officials of different schools in the empire. From that time on, Confucian temples were erected in the provinces, and sacrifice at temples and schools continued. Even on such occasions, the sage was honored as the patron saint of learning rather than as a god.

Tung Chung-shu

Tung Chung-shu (c. 179–104 B.C.), the most influential Confucian of this period, represented the eclectic trend of Han Confucianism. He was an adviser and a teacher of Emperor Wu Ti and twice served as a minister; he espoused Confucianism as a state teaching. His own thought reflects a transition from Confucius, Mencius, and Hsün Tzu to Confucian metaphysics; political, moral, and religious teachings were now wed with the cosmology of the Yin-Yang school. He derived his knowledge of the Yin-Yang school from the *Book of Changes (I Ching),* the basic text of Yin-Yang thought.

What Tung did was to provide a theoretical basis for the existing political and social order; his metaphysics was designed to justify the Han institutions, and particularly the role of the king. This he did in the *Luxuriant Dew of the Spring and Autumn,* an elucidation of the *Spring and Autumn Annals,* which was attributed to Confucius and from which he felt that his own thought was derived.

Metaphysics

The concept T'ien (Heaven) occupies a central place in Tung's metaphysics; it serves both as nature and as deity. As nature, Heaven is the alternative movements of the forces of Yin-Yang. The Yang waxes and expands; the Yin wanes and condenses. Through the expansion and condensation of these forces in cyclical movements, individual entities come into being and pass into nonbeing. Heaven is here the creative and destructive processes in nature.

The Yin-Yang forces were further explained by Tung in terms of the theory of the Five Agents (wood, fire, earth, metal, water), which were protoscientific categories describing the basic forces in man and nature. These agents were used to explain the phenomena of both production and destruction in the cosmos, which occur as endless cycles of movement. Hence wood produces fire, fire produces earth (soil), earth produces metal, metal produces water, and water produces wood. While the productive process goes on, the destructive process also continues at the same time: wood overcomes earth, earth overcomes water, water overcomes fire, fire overcomes metal, and metal overcomes wood.

The Five Agents were also correlated with seasons and directions: wood corresponds to spring, which prevails in the east; fire corresponds to summer, which prevails in the south; metal corresponds to autumn, which prevails in the west; water corresponds to winter, which prevails in the north; and earth corresponds to the center, which assists the four seasons.

Although Tung did not emphasize the correlation between the Five Agents and the five virtues (faith was added as the fifth virtue by the Han Confucians), most Han Confucians accepted this concept, according to which wood corresponds to benevolence, fire to propriety, earth to faith, metal to righteousness, and water to wisdom. We thus have in Han Confucianism a complex theory of correspondence which shows the correlations among the Five Agents, the five virtues, the five directions, and the four seasons:

THE CORRESPONDENCES

Agents	Virtues	Seasons	Directions
Wood	Benevolence	Spring	East
Fire	Propriety	Summer	South
Earth	Faith		Center
Metal	Righteousness	Autumn	West
Water	Wisdom	Winter	North

This theory depicts Heaven, or the cosmos, in terms of harmony achieved by way of complement or influences; it also emphasizes the correspondence between the natural and the moral, since the five virtues are related to the basic physical forces as well as to time and space.[4]

Fearing that Heaven as the cosmic reality might not convey the sense of divinity, Tung Chung-shu also regarded Heaven as the divine personality, capable of pleasure and displeasure. In this context, he interpreted the two cosmic forces as two modes of divine power: Yang refers to Heaven's beneficent power; and Yin refers to its chastising power. The growth and fruition of things reflect the beneficence of Heaven; the decadence and dissipation of things mean chastisement by it. Harmony and orderliness in nature and society indicate Heaven's pleasure; disruption and chaos, its displeasure. Natural phenomena may be signs of Heaven for man; wonders, such as snow in summer, and disasters, such as famine and flood, are indicative of Heaven's anger, particularly against the ruler.

Tung understood man as a miniature of Heaven, cosmos, or deity:

Man's head is large and round, like Heaven's countenance. His hair is like the stars and constellations. His ears and eyes, with their brilliance, are like the sun and moon. His nostrils and mouth, with their breathing, are like the wind. The penetrating understanding that lies within his breast is like the spiritual intelligence [of Heaven]. . . . Within [the body] there are five viscera, which correspond in number to the Five Agents. Externally, there are the four limbs, which correspond in number to the four seasons. . . . The alternation of sadness and pleasure corresponds to the *yin* and *yang*. The mind possesses the power of thinking, which corresponds to [Heaven's] power of deliberation and calculation.[5]

This shows Tung Chung-shu's interest in homology, man's desire to be close to the Divine. Earlier, Mencius had also regarded man as a microcosm of Heaven and had emphasized that the virtues in man were a heavenly endowment. But Tung's man as a miniature of Heaven goes beyond this; man is ideally, in his view, a copy of the heavenly or cosmic model.

Human Nature

In Tung's system, the polarity of Yin and Yang underlies all things, including human nature. Human nature in the broad sense includes both potential good and covetousness; in the narrow sense, it refers only to the former. Tung, who preferred the broad meaning of human nature, used two words, nature (hsing) and feeling (ch'ing), to designate man. Hsing refers to a man's potential good, and ch'ing to his covetousness; they constitute the Yang and Yin aspects of human nature. Although the Yin in this particular instance is equated with evil, it does not have that meaning in Tung's metaphysics.

Human nature is not evil since it has potential good, nor is it good since it contains covetousness. Whether man is good or evil depends on the actual use to which he puts his nature. The relation of goodness to man's nature is analogous to that between the silk fiber and the cocoon, or the chicken and the egg. The cocoon has silk fiber as potentiality, and the egg has the chicken as potentiality; but one is not the other. However, the cocoon may produce silk and the egg the chicken. Man actualizes his goodness through education. It is the duty of the state and the family to educate man, so that his goodness can be materialized and his evil subdued.

Tung Chung-shu's understanding of human nature stands between that of Mencius and that of Hsün Tzu: with Mencius, he stressed man's possibility for good; with Hsün Tzu, he recognized man's tendency toward evil. But he differed from both in recognizing both elements in man.

Social Ethics

Tung's ethical views again show his dependence on the metaphysics of Yin-Yang. Tung considered three of the five Confucian human relationships to be essential: ruler and subject, father and son, husband and wife. The ruler, father, and husband partake of the Yang force; the other three reflect the Yin. Since the Yin is passive and the Yang active, the subject should submit to the ruler, the son to the father, and the wife to the husband. Tung called these three relationships the "three cords." As strings are attached to the cord in a net, so are subject, son, and wife attached respectively, to ruler, father, and husband. The "three cords" idea which has been an ethical standard since the Han period, represents the loyalty of a subject, the filial love of a son, and the chastity of a wife. These three concepts—loyalty, filial love, and chastity—have constituted a great ethical force in Chinese society.

The three cords and five virtues formed the basis of orthodox Confucian ethics. These human virtues and relationships, which related to the principle of Yin-Yang and the Five Agents, came to be viewed as cosmic; they are the law of Heaven and are comparable to natural law in the West.

History

Tung conceived of history in terms of cycles. Three consecutive reigns constituted a cycle, and each reign was symbolized by a color. The first three reigns, Hsia, Shang, Chou, were represented by black, white, and red respectively. The dynasty superseding Chou would again start with black, and another cycle would thus begin.

This view of history is another illustration of the Yin-Yang theory. The three-reign span, according to Tung, corresponds to the completion of a cycle: the waxing of Yang and the waning of Yin. The adoption of a color by a new dynasty signifies the receiving of the Mandate from Heaven. Change of color is also accompanied by change of dynasty name, change of the capital, and change of the color of the official costume, as well as by other innovations, such as reducing the penalties of prisoners.

The cyclic view of history has had a profound political effect on the Chinese. It means that a dynasty, however good and strong it is, will eventually decay and be replaced by another; no dynasty can hold the Mandate permanently. It also means that when the existing reign undergoes deterioration, a new dynasty may be anticipated. This view of history implies historical determinism, but that determinism is always accompanied by hope for the future. The cyclic view of history also has religious significance: the beginning of each cycle is the reenacting of the cosmogonic act, that is, the creation of the cosmos. A new cycle is a renewal of history comparable to creation out of chaos; it is a national participation in the cosmos.[6]

NEO-CONFUCIANISM

The period between 220 and 589 is known as the Political Disunion, a chaotic time in Chinese history. After the fall of the Han dynasty in A.D. 220, constant warfare and frequent change of dynasties made people feel uncertain about their future; they were looking for something beyond this world for support. Confucianism, which was committed to family and social responsibility, did not meet their spiritual needs. Philosophical Taoism with its emphasis on quietude and resignation, did offer some consolation to the intellectuals, but it did not speak to the masses. On the other hand, Buddhism, the new religion, through its saviors, Buddhas and Bodhisattvas, spoke to the hearts of common men. Meanwhile, Confucianism suffered stagnation and remained powerless for centuries.

Buddhism came to China from India during the reign of Ming Ti (A.D. 58–75), but it did not have a large following until the third century. The translation of Buddhist texts from Sanskrit into Chinese was done mainly with the use of Taoist philosophical terms, since the early leaders of Buddhism were for the most part Taoists. A Chinese legend of the second century made Gautama Buddha a disciple of Lao-tzu. It says that Lao-tzu disappeared from China and found himself in India, where he taught the Buddha Taoism, and hence, Buddhism is simply a foreign version of Taoism. This legend shows the Taoist influence in this period as well as its affinity to Buddhism.

By the Tang dynasty (618–907), Buddhism had grown to be a nationwide religion. Its most popular branch, called Ch'an (Zen), or the Meditation sect, was able to adjust Indian thought to both the mysticism of Taoism and the this-worldliness of Confucianism. It became truly, as Fung Yu-lan says, a "Chinese Buddhism," rather than Buddhism in China.[7] The Ch'an philosophy represents the culminating phase of Buddhist development in China. Meanwhile, toward the end of the Tang dynasty, Confucianism began to awaken, and its leaders expressed views that were critical of Buddhism.

But the real renaissance of Confucianism had to wait for the arrival of the Sung dynasty (960–1279). Sung Confucianism came on the scene after almost a millennium of Buddhist intellectual leadership, and it is no surprise that it contains hidden features of Buddhist and Taoist thought. This intellectual movement, from the Sung to the Ming period (1368–1644), is called neo-Confucianism. Its spirit is different from that of both pre-Han and Han Confucianism, for although thinkers of Sung and Ming continued the perennial Confucian interest in society, government, and ethics, they also emphasized man's spiritual cultivation and a sense of cosmic mysticism. They attempted to stand within the Confucian tradition, while giving it a new spiritual orientation. Their aim was to overcome Buddhism.

The Ch'eng Hao and Ch'eng Yi Schools of Neo-Confucianism

The Sung neo-Confucianists preferred certain Confucian works as the basis of their philosophy: the *Book of Changes,* the *Analects,* the *Mencius,* the *Great Learning,* and the *Doctrine of the Mean*—the last two are chapters of the *Book of Rites.* A central hermeneutic principle of the neo-Confucianists is the desire to relate rationality with spirituality, the internal with the external, or the self with the cosmos.

The two main schools of neo-Confucianism were initiated by two brothers, Ch'eng Hao (1032–1085) and Ch'eng Yi (1033–1108).

Ch'eng Hao believed in the oneness of all things: there is no essential distinction, he held, between the self and the world. When one's mind does not function properly—is dominated by selfish desire—then the sense of distinction between self and world arises. The first act in philosophy is to discover one's original mind (heart), which is identical with jen, the inner connection of all things. Ch'eng Hao took this word from Mencius, who understood it as the innate goodness of man. Ch'eng Hao, however, interpreted jen as the unselfish mind. Mencius had said that one cannot bear to see a child fall into a well, and that this feeling reflects man's basic goodness. Ch'eng Hao used the same metaphor to show that the original mind is unselfish. Once this mind has been restored, one can respond to objects instantaneously. The original mind, through intuition, connects all things; there is no real separation between self and the world. Rectification of mind is the beginning of philosophy. Ch'eng Hao's teaching was followed by Lo Chiu-yüan (1139–1193) and culminated with the thought of Wang Yang-ming (1472–1529). Their philosophy was called the Lo-Wang School or the School of Mind.

The other school, initiated by Ch'eng Yi, stressed the reality of principles or ideas. A passage from the *Book of Changes* says, "What is above shapes is called the *Tao;* what is within shapes is called the implements."[8] Ch'eng Yi took these words as the basis for his thought. Tao for him refers to the abstract principles that exist in eternity; implements are concrete and exist in time. A physical thing has two aspects: the concrete matter and the abstract principle. The concrete becomes a thing by embodying its principle, and the beginning of philosophy is therefore to investigate the principles of things. It is through this process that one eventually understands the world. First one must investigate the world; then he can understand himself. Ch'eng Yi's philosophy was systematized by Chu Hsi (1130–1200). Their thought was called the Ch'eng-Chu School or the School of Ideas.

The Rationalist School of Chu Hsi

Chu Hsi, the outstanding neo-Confucianist, lived in the twelfth century during the Sung dynasty (960–1279). In addition to administrative posts, he held several government research positions which enabled him to study, write, and teach uninterruptedly. As a result, he wrote voluminous books and produced a philosophy that synthesized Confucianism with Buddhist and Taoist thought. The key Confucian concepts were all embraced in his system; for instance, the jen (goodness) of Confucius, the four virtues of Mencius, the investigation of things of the *Great Learning*, the sincerity of the *Doctrine of the Mean*, the Yin-Yang and the five elements of Han Confucianism.

Principle and Matter

Chu Hsi posited two dipolar concepts, Li[9] and ch'i. Li refers to the eternal, incorporeal principle(s) or idea(s); ch'i refers to the temporal, material force. A physical thing contains both; Li is its principle, and ch'i is its material embodiment. Ontologically, Li exists a priori, even before the world was formed. It is comparable to Plato's eternal ideas.

Ch'i, matter, is understood dynamically; it is explained in terms of Yin, the passive force, and Yang, the active force. Through the flowing and ebbing movements of ch'i, the five elements—water, fire, wood, metal, and earth—are produced, and through their interaction an individual thing comes into being. These forces and elements constitute the physical nature of a thing, and Li is its principle.

Li, being abstract and devoid of physical elements, is by itself without evil. Evil is due to the possession of a physical body. The principle is present in all men, but men differ with respect to its actualization because of differences in their physical endowments; some possess coarser elements and are less responsive to Li, whereas others possess finer elements and are more responsive to it. The physical nature of man is like water in a container: it involves degrees of clarity from very muddy to very clear. The principle of man is like a pearl in the water: its visibility depends on the clarity of the water. Although every man is endowed with the same Li, it is not actualized to the same extent in every individual. The realization of Li depends on the purification of man's physical nature, which can be improved by study and spiritual cultivation. Although the evil in man is caused by ch'i, goodness is also inherent in him. How to realize the latter is a major concern for the neo-Confucians.

The Supreme Ultimate

Chu Hsi called the totality of principles *T'ai Chi*, the Supreme Ultimate, which denotes the realm of ideas existing a priori. It is supreme because it embraces standards in the ultimate sense. The Supreme Ultimate was also called the *Wu Chi*, the Nonultimate, which refers to its emptiness and its lack of physical form. Li, as the ontological structure, is identical with the Supreme Ultimate; it too is without form.

Li, understood in terms of the Supreme Ultimate and the Nonultimate, is comparable to the concept of Buddha in terms of the dual nature of Being and Nonbeing. The Being nature refers to the manifestations of Buddha in the phenomenal world and corresponds to the realization of Li in individual things. Mahayana Buddhism believes that each phenomenal thing contains the entire Buddha nature. Chu Hsi expressed a similar view:

There is but one Supreme Ultimate, which is received by the individuals of all things. This one Supreme Ultimate is received by each individual in its entirety and undivided. It is like the moon shining in the heavens; though it is reflected in rivers and lakes and thus is everywhere visible, we would not therefore say that it is divided.[10]

The Nonbeing nature of the Buddha for the Buddhists refers to its emptiness; it is uncontaminated by the world and evades man's comprehension. Chu Hsi also said that the Supreme Ultimate, as the Nonultimate, is devoid of physical character and beyond the phenomenal world.

According to Chu Hsi, the emptiness of the Supreme Ultimate is different from that of the Buddha nature in one respect: the emptiness of the Buddha nature is without principles and standards, and for that reason is completely incomprehensible, whereas the emptiness of the Supreme Ultimate contains principles. For instance, the Li of the father-son relationship as an abstract idea is conceivable. Chu Hsi said:

When the Buddhist speaks of "emptiness," this does not mean that they are (entirely) incorrect. And yet for there to be this "emptiness," there must be with it some kind of normative Principle. For what use can there be in merely saying that we are "empty," without understanding that there is a genuine Principle (lying behind this "emptiness")?[11]

Chu Hsi's criticism of Buddhism shows that he wanted to distinguish his concept of the Supreme Ultimate from that of the Buddha nature (see Chapter 21).

Spiritual Cultivation

Although Chu Hsi's philosophy is rationalistic, its ultimate aim is personal enlightenment. The first step in philosophy for him is the quest for knowledge; it begins with the "investigation of things" and the "extension of knowledge," a concept that is derived from the *Great Learning*. One studies things outside of oneself in order to discover their principles. In this way one gradually enlarges one's knowledge. On the other hand, all principles are potentially within the self, since one's nature contains the Supreme Ultimate, which is no other than the totality of principles. Hence the study of things is tantamount to self-discovery. Chu Hsi believed that "investigation of things" leads to the discovery of the original nature of the mind. This nature, like a pearl, is obstructed by the physical endowment of man, which is like muddy water. By means of investigating the principles of things, man's physical endowment can be purified; and if the muddy water is distilled, the pearl can shine forth.

One should not begin one's philosophical inquiry by investigating Li as such, for it is abstract and difficult to take hold of. One must therefore start with a concrete thing. Through what is "within shapes" one arrives at what is "above shapes." One moves from the known to the unknown. Chu Hsi went on to say:

When one has exerted oneself for a long time, finally one morning a complete understanding will open before one. Thereupon there will be a thorough comprehension of all the multitude of things, external or internal, fine or coarse, and every exercise of the mind will be marked by complete enlightenment.[12]

Chu Hsi's rational philosophy begins with the world, but ends in man's sudden enlightenment. Although he was aware of knowledge in the scientific sense—for instance, he mentioned the concept of a ship or a cart—he conceived of knowledge primarily in the ethical sense. Basically, the same moral nature underlies the cosmos and man.

Elimination of Selfish Desires

Chu Hsi and other neo-Confucians regarded selfish desires as a basic obstacle to enlightenment. Once enlightenment has been attained, there is no barrier between the external world and the internal mind. This is the state of freedom in which one can respond to an event or object with immediate identity. Selfish desire leads to the alienation of the self from the world; it has to do with the attachment of the ego to a physical or mental object. As a result, the mind loses its capacity to receive phenomena instantaneously. It is egoism that creates the duality between the self and the world. By contrast, an enlightened person has no attachment to objects, and his mind is ever free to receive new experience.

Chu Hsi compares the original mind to the mirror which, when inactive, is completely clear and devoid of traces of image. Centuries before him. Chuang-tzu, the famous Taoist, said:

The Mind of the perfect man is like a mirror. It does not move with things, nor does it anticipate them. It responds to things, but does not retain them. Therefore the perfect man is able to deal successfully with things but is not affected by them.[13]

Chu Hsi said likewise:

But when your encounter with the thing is over, you must not let this experience remain on your mind. . . . While receiving a phenomenon, the mind should stay on it. But when the thing has been dealt with, the mind must not continue to busy itself with it.[14]

Both statements show that the function of the mind is to respond immediately to an object, like the mirror which receives the image of the object instantaneously. It should be noted that Chu Hsi at this point was not advocating the discard of knowledge or the elimination of ideas from the mind as the early Taoists (see Chapter 24) did. He was speaking about the immediate function of the mind, which is the reception of experience; on such occasions the mind should not be preoccupied with thought or past experience. Egoism or selfish desire has no place in the reception of experience, for it reduces the degree of attentiveness to the object. This is why Chu Hsi advocated "self-mastery"—that is, the removal of selfish desires—for the reception of experience. The influence of Buddhism is noticeable at this point.

The Mind School of Wang Yang-ming

As has been said, the School of Mind was originated by Ch'eng Hao and developed by Lo Chiu-yüan, a contemporary of Chu Hsi. But its best spokesman was Wang Yang-ming (1472–1529), of the Ming

dynasty (1368–1644). Unlike Chu Hsi, Wang was not only a philosopher but also a practical statesman who held several important
civil and military posts. He was banished for three years among the
aborigines in southwest China for his attack against a certain
powerful eunuch. While in lonely exile he one day received sudden
enlightenment and discovered that the mind was all one needed to
know. His philosophy, developed from his busy career, was a
testimony to his personal struggle against the moral and political
crises of his time.

The Mind

In his youth, Wang Yang-ming had studied Chu Hsi's thought and
had practiced the investigation of principles. But he had not succeeded. Once he and a disciple attempted to discover the principle
of the bamboo trees. At first, the disciple gazed at them for three
days, but to no avail. Then the Master took over himself. The
record says that he sat before the trees for seven days, yet did not
discover their principle. In frustration, he gave up such investiga-
tions.

It came to him as a revelation in the middle of night, while he
was in exile, that mind is the reality of things. He leapt out of bed,
shouting: "Now for the first time I understand the teaching of the
sage. My nature [mind] is in itself sufficient. To search for principles
(*li*) in affairs and things was an error."[15] He realized that principles
do not exist outside of the mind. In fact, the mind is the spiritual
center; it is the unity of all things and gives them intelligibility:

My spirituality or consciousness is the ruler of Heaven and Earth, spirits
and things. . . . If Heaven, Earth, spirits, and things are separated from
my spirituality or consciousness, they cease to be. And if my spirituality
or consciousness is separated from them, it ceases to be also. Thus they
are all actually one body, so how can they be separated?[16]

Using flowers as an example, he said it is the mind which brings
the colors of the flowers to man. These flowers are nonexistent when
the mind is not active.[17]

Intuitional Knowledge

Wang believed that man's original mind is entirely good; he identified it with intuition. Ideally, every man can act according to his

original mind, and when he does so, his action is spontaneous and right. In actuality, man's mind is influenced by selfish desires, which hinder the functioning of its pure spontaneity. As a result, the mind is preoccupied with calculation or deliberation. Once Wang lectured on intuitional knowledge to a thief who had been caught, but the latter could not comprehend it. Wang then asked him to take off his clothes, for the weather was hot. The man proceeded to do so, until there was only a pair of pants left. When Wang asked him to remove it, the thief answered, "That does not seem to be quite right."[18] Wang then told him approvingly that what he had just said was intuitional knowledge.

It is evident that intuitive knowledge refers to the activity of the original mind. By exercising it, man restores and actualizes his original mind. Since all men possess it, every man is potentially a sage. By the steady exercise of intuitive knowledge, one will one day attain sudden enlightenment. Here, the School of Mind is parallel to Ch'an Buddhism, which says that every man is potentially a Buddha.

The Rectification of Affairs

In our discussion of Chu Hsi, we referred to the "investigation of things," which is a translation of the term *ko-wu*, mentioned in the *Great Learning*. Wang also discussed ko-wu, but he used it to mean the rectification of affairs, not the investigation of things. For Wang the word *wu* refers to conduct; it means affairs that a man carries from day to day, not an object or an event external to self. The emphasis of neo-Confucianism had shifted from Chu Hsi's investigation of external events to the examination of one's personal conduct. It is not external events, but intuitive knowledge that informs one what one should do. For instance, according to Wang, parents as object do not contain the principle of filial love; such a principle comes from the son's intuitive knowledge. "Rectification of affairs" means making one's daily activities conform to one's intuitive knowledge. Although such an interpretation of ko-wu (investigation of things) is a deviation from its original meaning, it is consistent with Wang's own philosophy. The rectification of affairs is the way to enlarge one's intuitional knowledge and thus restore one's original mind. In this pure state, when one is in unity with all things, there is no distinction between the human mind and the mind of Heaven. Hence the restoration of the original mind also means the restoration of the identity between man and Heaven.

The Unity of Knowledge and Practice

A unique aspect of Wang's thought is his emphasis on the inseparability of knowledge and practice. Although this had been discussed by the earlier Confucians, he was the first one to say that knowledge and practice are really one: the minute one sees something beautiful (knowledge), he already loves (action) it. Likewise, one shuns (action) a bad odor because he dislikes (knowledge) it. One does not have knowledge of a certain food until one tastes it. Similarly, one does not really understand filial piety or brotherly love until one practices it. He said, "No one who really has knowledge fails to put it into practice. To know and yet not to do is in fact not to know."[19]

Wang's philosophy stresses the importance of will. Whosoever uses the will to understand principles of the mind will thereby attain sagehood. By contrast, Chu Hsi's philosophy emphasized reason. Whosoever uses reason to investigate things, he said, will discover principles that will enable him to become a sage.

Influences of Neo-Confucianism

A permanent contribution of neo-Confucianism is its new interpretation of Confucian thought through the unwitting use of Taoist and Buddhist ideas, thereby broadening the base of Confucianism. Moral philosophy was fused with metaphysics. The Sung Confucians were particularly fond of the *Analects,* the *Mencius,* the *Great Learning,* and the *Doctrine of the Mean;* Chu Hsi wrote critical commentaries on each of them. After his time, they were called the Four Books. In 1313 an imperial edict of the Yüan dynasty (1260–1368) made the Four Books the basis of civil service examinations and endorsed Chu's commentaries as state interpretations. Chu also wrote commentaries on other books that similarly met with imperial approval. Students who wished to pass these examinations had to follow Chu's interpretations—a practice continued until 1905, when the government abolished the state examinations. Needless to say, six centuries' use of Chu's commentaries on the Four Books left an indelible mark on the Chinese.

Neo-Confucianism also spread to Japan, where it became indigenous. Beginning with the seventeenth century, the School of Wang Yang-ming rivaled the Chu Hsi School. The former enjoyed a special favor in Japan because of its affinity to Zen Buddhism. Some leaders of the Meiji Restoration in 1868 were followers of the Wang School.

Reactions against Neo-Confucianism

The creative phase of neo-Confucianism ended with Wang Yang-ming. Chu Hsi's rationalism, which was not followed by empirical experimentation, gradually turned into empty speculation: students parroted his words instead of studying him critically. Wang Yang-ming's intuitionism attracted dilettanti who mistook his emphasis on the inward mind to mean the uselessness of learning facts and reading books. Some even tried to justify immorality by intuition. By the end of the Ming dynasty (1368–1644), neo-Confucianism had lost its intellectual leadership.

A major force in the Ch'ing dynasty (1644–1912) was the protest against the neo-Confucians of the Sung and Ming periods. The Ch'ing Confucians developed textual criticism, but they did not investigate the texts of the neo-Confucians; instead, they studied the earlier Confucian texts written in the Han period. They believed that these works contained a Confucianism that was unadulterated by Buddhism and neo-Confucianism. Along with textual criticism, they also engaged in phonetics, philology, and historical criticism. This branch of scholarship was called the School of Han Learning. Ku Yen-wu (1613–1679) founded it; Wang Fu-chih (1619–1692) and Yen Yüan (1635–1704) developed it; and Tai Chen (1723–1777) brought it to full bloom. These men, along with others, not only investigated the humanities but also carried on research in mathematics, astronomy, and geography. Their approach was critical, inductive, and analytical. All in all, the intellectual development in China in the seventeenth and eighteenth centuries parallels the Enlightenment of the West.

The Ch'ing scholars attacked Wang Yang-ming on the ground that excessive emphasis on the mind results in introspection and leads man away from the study of concrete things. Their main criticism of Chu Hsi is the latter's dualism of Li (principle) and ch'i (material force). They conceived of reality as concrete things; there is no metaphysical realm above them. Hence there is no duality between principle and matter. The Ch'ing scholars accepted principle only as the order or arrangement within concrete things; it is immanent in and dependent on the latter. From their point of view, the contrast between the perfection of principle and the imperfection of physical nature is artificial. Yen Yüan argued this point by referring to the eye: the socket, the eyeball, and the lens are its physical nature, and vision is its principle. Now, if there is weakness in the eye's physical nature, it will certainly affect its vision. How

can one say that "the principle of this vision is to see nothing but
correct phenomena, while the socket, eyeball, and lens see incorrect
phenomena?"[20] In fact, the vision of the eye depends on its physical
nature.

The Ch'ing scholars observed astutely that the metaphysical status
of Li easily results in dogmatism, that is, the defending of one's
own beliefs in the name of Li. Tai Chen, for example, said:

The reason for this is that since the Sung dynasty there has grown up
the habit of regarding *li* as if it were a veritable object, received from
Heaven and present in the mind. The result is that those who are able
to do so regard their mere opinions as being *li*. Thus those who are
forceful, and possess the advantages of influence and position and glib
tongues, are found to have the *li* on their side, while the weak and
timorous, who are unable to debate are defeated by this same *li*.[21]

Consequently, those in positions of authority used Li to sanctify
their command and suppress the views of their subordinates, even
though the latter might be right.

Another point of attack was Chu Hsi's equation of human desire
with evil. The Ch'ing Confucians considered desires to be the basis
of both good and evil, depending on how man used them. Tai Chen
said, "Freed from selfishness, the desires all correspond to love,
propriety, and righteousness."[22] Also, "To desire to live, but at the
same time to allow other people to live as well, this is love *(jen)*."[23]
What is called the principle by Chu Hsi is actually derived from
desires, according to Tai Chen. It should be pointed out that the
word *desire* was understood differently by Chu Hsi and Tai Chen.
For Chu Hsi desire was understood in the Buddhist sense as selfishness or craving, whereas for Tai Chen desire referred to man's natural
instincts whose potentiality for good should not be negated. The
Ch'ing scholars certainly gave much higher value to man's natural
instincts than did the neo-Confucians.

It is worth noting that Jesuit missionaries were in China at the
time when the Ch'ing scholars were attacking neo-Confucianism,
and that they too were critical of the latter and were in favor of the
Confucianism of the Han period. Their introduction of Western

FIGURE 23.2 A paper horse and cart to carry the ancestral spirit to the hereafter, that
will be burned as an offering at the burial ceremony. (*Harrison Forman*)

science to China is well known. Whether or not they influenced Chinese thinkers in this period, however, remains an open question.

THE CULTIC EXPRESSION OF RELIGION IN CONFUCIANISM

In conclusion, the cultic expression of religion in Confucianism should be recapitulated in order to remind us that Confucianism, in addition to being a form of intellectual expression, has been a religion in the practical sense.

The Ancestor Cult

Confucius accepted the ancestor cult which had existed as early as the Shang dynasty (c. 1751–1112 B.C.). Although it was at first limited to the royal family, by the time of Confucius it was practiced by the Chinese in general. When the Confucian classics appeared, between 500 and 200 B.C., this cult was already well established. Confucianism emphasized family relations based on the five human relationships, particularly the filial love between parents and children. Family was the basis of ethics, and the ancestor cult was its religious expression. One cannot be understood without the other.

Formally, the ancestor cult has neither priesthood nor congregation. In practice, however, each family or clan is a congregation, and its elder is the unofficial priest. The ritual, mainly sacrifice, may take place at any time, although it is often associated with such things as birthdays, marriages, passing state examinations, and appointments to office. The ritual may take place in the household or at an ancestor temple. Food for sacrifice is put on a table in front of the ancestor shrine, where a number of wooden tablets are placed, each representing the seat of an ancestor (see Figure 23.2). The sacrifice is offered to three earlier generations; those who lived earlier than three generations ago are usually forgotten by the living. When the sacrifice is over, the offered dishes are eaten by the family as a consecrated meal. It is an occasion of family festivity.

Although the ancestor cult was universally practiced in China, there was a difference between the ways in which scholars and the commoners conceived of it: while the former considered it to be an act of reverence and an expression of propriety (li), the latter regarded it as worship. Such a difference was often stated by those (for example, Hsün Tzu of the third century B.C.) who viewed religious rituals as an aesthetic or ethical expression only. But this difference is purely academic; in practice the ancestor is a modality of the cosmos where *mysterium tremendum et fascinans* can be experienced by both scholars and commoners.

The Cult of Heaven

Heaven was originally viewed as the ancestral deity of ancient kings. Heaven and Shang Ti, the Ruler Above, were used interchangeably. The emperor was called the Son of Heaven, his duty being to carry out its Mandate. The worship of Heaven remained basically a state cult. Traditionally an emperor offered sacrifice to Heaven just before dawn on the day of the winter solstice, at the altar in the capital (see Figure 23.3). This practice was continued until the fall of the monarchy in 1912. The Altar of Heaven, T'ien Tan, a most impressive structure, used for this purpose in the Ch'ing dynasty, still stands in Peking. The worship of Heaven was led by the emperor, who was assisted by princes and cabinet officials together

FIGURE 23.3 The Altar of Heaven, Peking. Chinese emperors officiated rites at the Altar. (*Henle from Monkmeyer*)

with their retinues. In the deep silence of the cold night, the emperor read the supplication to Heaven by the light of lanterns and torches while offerings were made.

The cult of Heaven includes sacrifices to Earth and nature spirits. Since Heaven is the head of the cosmic hierarchy, it presides over both the celestial and terrestrial spirits. Thus the same sacrifice offered to Heaven is simultaneously offered to all the spirits under its domain. A portion of the emperor's written supplication in A.D. 1538 on such an occasion reads as follows:

I, the emperor of the great illustrious dynasty, have respectfully prepared this paper to inform the spirit of the sun; the spirit of the moon; the spirits of the five planets, of the constellations of the zodiac, and of all the stars in all the sky . . . the spirits of the five grand mountains . . . the spirits of the four seas; the spirits of the four great rivers; the intelligences which have duties assigned to them on earth; all the celestial spirits under heaven, the terrestrial spirits under heaven. . . .[24]

The cult of Heaven is an integral part of Confucianism; the doctrine of the Mandate of Heaven and the concept of the Son of Heaven are related to it. There has always been a tacit collaboration between the state and Confucianism. The king offered sacrifices to Heaven, to whom he was held accountable. The heads of provinces, prefectures, and districts offered periodical sacrifices to spirits of grain, rivers, hills in their own regions, in order to ensure prosperity and harmony. They performed these rituals as officials of the empire, and hence such sacrifices are related to the cult of Heaven.

Theologically, the emperor was the link between Heaven, Earth, and Man by way of his righteous and benign rule, which brought harmony between these realms. Although there is no mythology in Confucianism concerning the origin of emperors, as there is in the Shinto of Japan, and the Son of Heaven is basically an ethico-political concept, the emperor in China was considered to be the earthly agent of Heaven, and his office bore cosmic significance. The cosmic dimension of the emperor was legitimized through the bureaucracy of the state. In this sense, the imperial state was a theocratic government and the emperor was the head of both state and religion.

The Cult of Confucius

There was also a state cult of Confucius, that is, the official elevation of Confucius to the position of patron saint of scholars. From the first century A.D. on, sacrifices were offered in spring and autumn to Confucius and to other learned worthies chosen by the state at Confucian temples in various localities. These too were performed before daybreak and led by state officials. Since this cult was confined to the scholar-officials who wanted to dissociate it from popular religions, it was not considered to be a worship of Confucius as god, but rather a homage to him as the foremost teacher in China. In practice, however, the same sacrifice as was made to an ancestor or to a nature god was offered to him. Hence, in cultic practice, Confucius was a modality of the cosmos, although he symbolized the ethicointellectual tradition. Participation in the Confucian rite implies the apprehension of the cosmos through such a tradition. (See Figure 23.1.)

Conclusion

Both the cult of Heaven and the Confucian rite were sponsored by the state and were basically aristocratic in nature. Although such rites are no longer officially practiced in China, Heaven and Confucius as cultic symbols still bear vestigial power even today: patriotic parades in celebration of national holidays show traces of the cult of Heaven, and popular dramas and plays that exalt the virtue of the unselfish and condemn the evil of the selfish reflect the residual effects of the cult of Confucius. The ancestor cult was not a state religion in China; it was a popular cult deeply rooted in the Chinese soil. Although the Chinese family is undergoing rapid change today, elements of this cult can still be detected in special family events such as birthdays, weddings, funeral, and the completion of houses.

NOTES

1. Fung Yu-lan, *The Spirit of Chinese Philosophy*, trans. by E. R. Hughes (London: Kegan Paul, 1947), p. 128.
2. Fung Yu-lan, *A Short History of Chinese Philosophy* (New York: Macmillan, 1948), p. 207.

3. The Six Disciplines refer to the *Book of Songs, Book of History, Book of Rites, Book of Changes,* the *Spring and Autumn Annals,* and *Book of Music.*

4. It should be interesting to compare the cosmic picture of Han Confucianism with that of the Five Buddhas in Tibetan Buddhism (cf. p. 602).

5. Fung Yu-lan, *A History of Chinese Philosophy,* trans. by Derk Bodde (Princeton: Princeton University Press, 1959–1960), II, 31.

6. Grace E. Cairns, *Philosophies of History* (New York: Philosophical Library, 1962), pp. 171–186.

7. Fung Yu-lan, *A Short History of Chinese Philosophy,* pp. 242–243.

8. *Ibid.,* p. 285.

9. *Li* is here capitalized to distinguish it from *li,* propriety or ritual.

10. Fung Yu-lan, *A Short History of Chinese Philosophy,* p. 296.

11. Fung Yu-lan, *A History of Chinese Philosophy,* II, 567–568.

12. Fung Yu-lan, *A Short History of Chinese Philosophy,* p. 306.

13. *Ibid.,* p. 287.

14. *Ibid.,* p. 172.

15. H. G. Creel, *Chinese Thought from Confucius to Mao Tse-Tung* (Chicago: University of Chicago Press, 1953; copyright 1953 by H. G. Creel), p. 214.

16. Fung Yu-lan, *A Short History of Chinese Philosophy,* p. 309.

17. *Ibid.*

18. *Ibid.,* p. 313.

19. Creel, *op cit.,* p. 215.

20. *Ibid.,* p. 224.

21. *Ibid.,* pp. 230–231.

22. Fung Yu-lan, *A History of Chinese Philosophy,* II, 666.

23. *Ibid.,* p. 667.

24. James Legge, *The Religions of China* (London: Hodder and Stoughton, 1888), pp. 44–45.

Confucianism grew in strength during the period of the Warring States (403–221 B.C.), while other schools, among them Mohism, Legalism, and Taoism, were also arising. Although Mohism and Legalism were critical of Confucianism, they shared its emphasis on state paternalism, social solidarity, and activism. This was not the case with Taoism; it was very different in spirit from Confucianism and the other schools that we have discussed so far. Taoism preferred individualism to collectivism, nature to society, self to family, quietism to activism, simplicity to artificiality, contemplation to deliberation.

The predecessors of the Taoists were recluses who lived at the time of Confucius (551–479 B.C.). During the period of the Warring States, the number of recluses increased and their views gradually took shape. The rise of their philosophy was due in part to changes in material culture (the use of iron, asbestos, cavalry, and so on), which resulted in a loss of confidence in things of the past, and in part to the fusion of the Chou culture with life on the frontiers, where Chinese civilization was little known. Many of the early recluses, including Lao-tzu, came from a region south of the Yellow River (present-day Honan and Hunan), which had been only recently incorporated into China.

At the beginning these recluses or quietists were interested mainly in the nourishment of the ch'i, the vital spirit or life breath of man, which makes the individual physically fit and mentally adaptable. The early recluses understood Tao to mean the Way of the vital spirit.[1] The Taoists, who came out of this tradition, expanded the

FIGURE 24.1 A Taoist priest burns incense before two minor deities. (*Dimitri Kessel, Life Magazine* © *Time Inc.*)

meaning of Tao from the mysterious essence of man to the cosmic force. Both the recluses and the Taoists desired to preserve the spirit of nature (Tao), which makes man truly human. They felt that both the Confucians and the Legalists, in their different ways, were suppressing this source of nature in man: the Confucians by their efforts to make man conform to certain moral precepts and human relations; the Legalists by their efforts to subjugate man to the state. In either case, man is in danger of alienating himself from the source of life. The Taoist movement was a protest against the Confucian emphasis on reason and morality at the expense of nature and against the Legalist drive for collectivism at the expense of the individual.

LAO-TZU

Lao-tzu is believed to have been the founder of Taoism. *Lao* means old and *tzu* is an honorific title for a gentleman or master. It is most probable that Lao-tzu, or the Old Master, is not the real name of the founder of Taoism. According to Ssu-ma Ch'ien, Lao-tzu's biographer, his surname was Li and his personal name was Erh, although he was posthumously named Tan. Hence his real name was Li Erh or Li Tan. He was some fifty years older than Confucius—which would make him a man of the sixth century B.C. During his later years, he was the keeper of the archives at the Chou court. According to Ssu-ma's report, Confucius went to see Lao-tzu for advice and was told to get rid of desires and pride, to cast out his polite manners, and to live like a man who possesses nothing. Confucius, who was shocked and bewildered, later said, "Lao-tzu, whom I saw today, is indeed like a dragon!"[2] Lao-tzu realized that the Chou dynasty was declining, and decided to leave the country. At the western frontier, he was met by the pass keeper, who requested him to write down his philosophy. Lao-tzu consented and thereupon wrote over 5,000 words on the Way and its power. Then he departed and was seen no more. Presumably what he wrote was the *Tao Te Ching*.

Although our information about Lao-tzu is based on the report of his biographer, actually we have very little historical knowledge about him, nor are we certain about the authorship of the book. Problems concerning Lao-tzu's historicity and the *Tao Te Ching*'s authorship have been raised since the twelfth century A.D. At present, because of a new interest in the *Tao Te Ching*, both Western and Chinese scholars have offered such diverse views as: (1) Lao-tzu was a historical person, but not the author of the *Tao Te Ching;* (2) Lao-tzu was a legendary figure, but the author of the *Tao Te Ching* lived in the third century B.C.; and (3) Lao-tzu was a senior contemporary of Confucius, who composed the nucleus of the *Tao Te Ching.* It is clear that the book is of a composite nature, and contains the sayings of more than one person. It was compiled in the fourth or the third century B.C., with the later date being the more probable.

TAO TE CHING

The *Tao Te Ching* is a little book consisting of eighty-one chapters of verses composed in a terse, paradoxical style. These chapters are written so cryptically that one can read them through without understanding what they mean. Even someone who has mastered the classic Chinese language still has to translate the archaic words in order to arrive at some intelligible meaning. In so doing, of course, he is actually interpreting the book according to his own understanding. Since it is impossible to reach a consensus as to the exact meaning of this book, scholars have interpreted it differently. This may account for the fact that there are today more than forty English translations of the *Tao Te Ching*—making it the most translated book in the English language next to the Bible. In the discussion that follows, we will assume, for the sake of convenience and in deference to a long-established tradition, that the book contains the words of Lao-tzu.

Although the *Tao Te Ching* is a philosophical work, it does not belong to academic philosophy. Its brevity, rhythmic style, and reliance on metaphors make the book ambiguous in meaning, so that some degree of subjective interpretation is unavoidable. On the other hand, the book does contain a group of seminal, universal ideas which can be understood by men of different cultures.

Tao

Tao, the Way, is a common and central concept in Chinese thought and was used by both Confucians and Taoists, for different but compatible purposes. The Confucians emphasized Tao as the Way of man—that is, the ethical standard or truth which man should follow—whereas the Taoists emphasized it as the Way of nature. But since man for the Taoists is a part of nature, the Way of nature is also that of man. On the whole, the Confucians used Tao to emphasize what man should do for himself and society; the Taoists conceived of it as the Principle that operates in nature and society.

Tao in the *Tao Te Ching* has three distinct meanings. First, it means the Unnamable or Nonbeing *(Wu)*, the power or source that produced the Namable (1).[3] Tao is nameless because whatever can be named is either the Whole or individual things. Although the Unnamable produces both, it is neither. The priority of the Unnamable with regard to the Namable is a logical rather than a cosmological assertion, for the latter depends on the former for existence. Tao, as the nameless, is not simply a negative concept of zero; it is also positive in that the Namable comes out of it. The negative aspect of Tao refers to its indescribable quality, although it can be alluded to by such metaphors as the "mysterious female," the "valley spirit," the "infant," and "uncarved block." But these metaphors can only point to some character of Tao; they cannot define it. Tao conceals its essence from man, who is ever mystified in its presence, and in this sense, Tao is mysterious. The Unnamable is eternal, absolute, and unchanging, because it is the basis of the changeable and temporal order. Secondly, Tao means the Namable or Being *(Yu)*, which refers to the creative order (1). It is variously called the "One," "Mother," "Ancestor," and "Heaven and Earth." It is the inherent Principle in nature and society, which holds things together as a Whole. As such, it corresponds to the law of nature. In Taoism this law can be observed through cycles of movements: day and night, seasons, birth and death; the harmony between the active (Yang) and passive (Yin) forces; and particularly the movements of reversal, that is, the destiny of things to move to their opposites. For instance, day ends in night, heat ends in cold, the soft becomes hard, and so on. This phenomenon of reversal is "the movement of Tao" (40). Lao-tzu said that the Unnamable produces the Namable, which in turn produces "the Ten Thousand Creatures" (40).[4] Ontologically, the Namable depends on the Unnamable for existence; but the individual things owe their being to the Namable. They are produced through the function of the Principle in nature and society, that is, the Namable aspect of the Tao. Hence Being is the Mother of all things (25, 52, 59). Thirdly, Tao means both the Unnamable and the Namable; for they are actually inseparable. Being must continuously depend on Nonbeing for the production of myriad things. On the other hand, Nonbeing needs Being for the manifestation of Tao in the world. In the *Tao Te Ching* the meaning of Tao varies according to its context, but it invariably has one of the above meanings.

Inaction

The term *wu-wei* occurs frequently in the *Tao Te Ching*. Literally, it means "do nothing." Broadly, it means action not contrary to nature. Lao-tzu said that Tao "does nothing," yet through "doing nothing" all things are done (37). As the inherent Principle in nature, Tao simply operates in terms of cycles of movements, harmony of the active and passive forces, and law of reversal; it is without purpose, amoral, impersonal, and universal, yet it is not affected by the fate or special circumstances affecting the lives of individuals. Hence Lao-tzu said that Tao models itself after nature (*tzu-jan*) (25). It is apparent that wu-wei does not mean no action or inaction pure and simple; it means action according to nature.[5]

Although Tao appears to lack specific purposes and moral preferences, it has power (*tê*) (10, 51). This power is inherent in things that conform to nature. In Taoism nature is supreme, although it does not claim authority over things. Precisely because it does not insist on its supremacy, it outlasts man and institutions. Taoist teaching points out this power to man and warns him not to order his life contrary to nature. When man follows natural action, practicing *wu-wei,* he will also have this power.

Action contrary to nature is called *wei* (29) or *yu-wei* (38). This is a cursed term in the *Tao Te Ching*. It was used against the background of the Chinese society of the fourth and third centuries B.C., when China was in the twilight of the Warring States (403–221 B.C.) and a handful of independent states dominated the country. Legalism, advocacy of state control, militarism, and the enactment of harsh law, became the basic elements of political philosophy among these states. Confucianism, in stressing society, virtues, and propriety, gave too much importance to man. From the Taoist viewpoint both the Legalists and the Confucians were wrong, for they both emphasized schemes, institutions, and organizations. Their actions were not in accord with the Way of nature; they were committed to yu-wei. The Taoists called upon the rulers to give up their devices and return to Tao. They believed that since man is a part of nature, he is subject to it; the Legalists and Confucians, on the other hand, believed that man is the center of nature and can use it for his benefit.

Inaction in Taoism also means nonaggression or modesty. This aspect of Tao is usually expressed by metaphors. Tao is like a soft-wood tree, water, a valley, a woman, an infant, the empty space of a wheel—symbols which suggest lowliness and nonaggression, but also imply strength. Hence the softwood tree still stands while the useful trees are being cut down; gentle water forms a torrent, which ultimately buries things under it; the lowly valley is secure and becomes a shelter for men; the helpless infant has a bundle of energy and grows; a woman conquers man by her receptivity; the empty space of a wheel is the point at which the spokes are united around the hub to make the wheel run. These metaphors suggest the power of inaction; they are symbols of Tao. Nature functions quietly (it teaches by silence); yet through its inaction things are produced, accomplished, and destroyed.

Return

One of the invariable laws of nature is the return (*fu*) of every-thing to the Nonbeing (16, 28). This is the destiny (*ming*) of things. Nonbeing gives existence to Being, and Being produces individual things. But each namable thing, after completing its cycle of existence, returns to Nonbeing. We have mentioned previously that a phenomenon tends to move to its opposite pole; hence happiness ends in calamity, goodness reverts to evil, the hollow becomes filled, the high becomes low, and so forth. These phenomena of reversal are called the movements of Tao. Returning to Nonbeing is a more radical expression of this same principle.

Both reversal and return imply change as a basic principle of nature. Confucians also accepted the phenomenon of change, but they believed that morality, as an attribute of the cosmos, does not change. The Taoists believed that change characterizes whatever is namable, including moral truth, and the only thing that is perma-nent is Nonbeing.

The doctrine of return implies that Lao-tzu did not believe in the immortality of the soul; when man dies, he passes into Non-being and individuality is dissolved. To accept this destiny of man is called quiescence (16). When man can face his fate without re-sistance, he understands the secrets of Tao and hence is an enlightened person. Confucianism viewed the destiny of man as the actual fulfillment of man's moral duties, not the return to Nonbeing. From the Taoist viewpoint, the Confucian is still besieged with action, yu-wei, because he confuses Tao with moral striving.

Relativity

We have so far dealt with the ontological status of Tao: its aspect of Nonbeing and Being and its character of inaction. Our next step is to show how this view affects man and how he attempts to cope with it. As man begins to look critically at the world and himself, he finds Tao very much at work. The phenomena of change and reversal prevail everywhere; nothing is stable. What man considers to be permanent turns out to be the opposite. The permanent is but a certain pattern or habit of thinking about the world, which varies from place to place and from time to time. Even in the same region, when conditions change, the old pattern is forced to give way. What is cold climate for the people of the south would be considered warm for the inhabitants of the north; water is a constant hazard for people in the lowlands, but is precious for travelers in the desert. Similarly, standards of beauty and values are relative to time and place; as conditions change, they also change. Lao-tzu was fully aware of the relative and subjective character of knowledge and truth. What is right for one is wrong for another; what is good for one is evil for another. Judgments such as these are relative to one's personal situation and needs.

Although the phenomena of change and reversal are evident in nature and society, this does not mean that man really takes them to heart. In sober moments, he knows this truth; otherwise he resists it with all his power, particularly when it comes into conflict with his vested interests. Efforts to resist change are what Lao-tzu called action (yu-wei). This takes many forms; underlying all of them is the desire to maintain one's egoism. Hence the wealthy man works to protect and increase his fortune, and a learned man builds his security on intellectual pursuits. Most people live as though they believe that they will not die. Egoism is the basis of aggression.

Lao-tzu's philosophy of inaction does not mean that since changes are inevitable, man simply drifts along with the tides of change. Inaction in essence refers to a cultivated attitude, which involves living in tension between change and the negation of change. A Taoist recognizes the existence of things under the condition of relativity. Thus knowledge, morality, truth, all have their place in life; they are manifestations of Tao. But a Taoist, being fully aware of the instability and relativity of things, does not dare to possess them, although he makes use of them. Since a Taoist affirms the relative place of the self, he takes care of himself. But he does not insist on his own views and does not impose them upon others. He continuously negates himself in the same way as he negates other conditioned things. For him, the self is no more important than other things—which is the general meaning of negation. In particular, negation means that one has no preference for one pole over its opposite (good against evil, the beautiful against the ugly, for instance). By insisting on one pole over its opposite, he not only makes the relative an absolute, but also denies the relative value of its opposite (the ugly may be beautiful to others). Negation means that all opposites are equally negated. Hence Lao-tzu said that one who knows the white (glory) and yet keeps to the black (humiliation) is the model for the world (28).[6] The Taoist recognizes the relative values of both glory and humiliation, while holding to neither. Living in this way, he exemplifies inaction. He does not have his own personal ideas, but regards people's ideas as his own (49). This means that he understands and respects the viewpoints of others and gives them equal consideration; he will not prefer one above the others.

Lao-tzu was critical of Confucianism because it regarded knowledge and morality as eternal truths. From the Taoist viewpoint the Confucians not only elevated the relative to the absolute, but also encouraged wickedness: whenever morality is emphasized, wickedness follows. Confucianism in the fourth and third centuries B.C. stressed book learning and the practice of propriety in family and social relationships. Lao-tzu felt that the Confucians were making human precepts and laws at the expense of the law of nature; they were pursuing action instead of inaction.

Although the philosophy of inaction emphasizes the relativity of things, it is not nihilistic. When man follows Tao, he practices morality. A Taoist has three treasures: compassion, frugality (simplicity), and humility (67). Compassion entails courage, frugality produces generosity, and humility enables one to become a leader (67). Compassion (tz'u) in Taoism is similar to the jen (goodness) of Confucianism. A Taoist always helps others and will not turn his back on them (27). In fact, he even uses up his last scrap for others; yet the more he gives, the more he receives (81). On the other hand, there are differences between Taoist and Confucian morality. A Taoist practices morality in terms of inaction: while he does good deeds, he is not attached to them. A Confucian performs moral deeds because they are the fulfillment of universal precepts. Morality in Taoism is entirely a human affair; it changes with human conditions and has no metaphysical basis. In Confucianism, by contrast, morality is metaphysical; it is derived from Heaven or nature.

Government

The early Taoists emphasized quiescence and nonviolence. We would hardly expect them to have been interested in government; yet the *Tao Te Ching* devoted several chapters to government and warfare. In fact, the book was mainly addressed to rulers of the states. It should be remembered that, at the time when it was being written, other schools were also offering solutions for the problems of China. Taoism was no exception.

The fundamental principle of government is the noninterference of the ruler with the affairs of his people; he takes their feelings and opinions as his own (49). He does not impose policies upon his subjects, but lets their actions determine the policies of the state. Hence, when things are accomplished, people feel that they are the ones who have done them (17). Taoism believed in a laissez-faire government, in which the ruler is the mirror that reflects the views of the people. He performs only those things that he must do to satisfy the wishes of his people and lets them do the rest. This is called the administration of the empire by wu-wei (inaction) (57).

Government by inaction holds the view that man, who is a part of Tao, is basically good: the power of nature will make him good if there is no interference from society. Man finds wisdom in nature and is able to manage his affairs according to its principles. When the state advocates knowledge, people begin to discriminate; when it stresses morality, they act artificially; when it favors skill and profit, competition arises and robbers abound. Lao-tzu said that the things initiated by the state are impositions (19)—that is, they are external to man; they lead him away from his inner self and make him a victim of ambitions and conventions. Consequently, strife and inhumanity prevail in the country.

Lao-tzu frequently mentioned the undesirability of morality. He said that when the state banishes human kindness and discards morality, then the people will become dutiful and compassionate (19). We should bear in mind that he was not against genuine morality. In fact, he said that only the one who takes upon himself the evils of the country can be its king (78), for a ruler has to be a very worthy person. What Lao-tzu was against was the codification and enforcement of moral laws by the ruler; for such acts merely create stereotyped morality to the detriment of man's natural goodness. Lao-tzu also had the Confucian precepts in mind when he spoke against morality; for there were 3,000 rules of propriety in those days. From the Taoist viewpoint such rules create artificial conduct. In essence, the ruler should not drive people to action. He should rule a country as though he were cooking a small fish (60): when a small fish is stirred much in the frying pan, it turns into a patty!

Lao-tzu also taught that the ruler should keep the people ignorant (3, 20, 65). When people have too much knowledge, they become difficult to govern (65). Lao-tzu was not opposed to simple and basic knowledge; he would have had no quarrel with anyone who wanted to learn the secrets of nature or the basic art of human relations. What he was primarily against was book learning and the accumulation of knowledge. When one's knowledge increases, his desires also increase. He then begins to demand more and to ask for favor and privilege; he becomes proud and feels superior to others. A Taoist ruler does not want to see learned men in his country, because it is difficult to satisfy their desires. Furthermore, if they are treated as a superior group by the ruler, complaints and competition arise and there will be strife in the country. It is therefore the duty of the ruler to keep the minds of people vacuous (hsü) (3), which means to keep the people in a state of mind in which they are free from worry and desires and live in peacefulness and contentment.

Both Taoism and Legalism advocated the policy of keeping people ignorant, but they did so with fundamentally different motives. The Taoist ruler did it in order to maintain a laissez-faire state, in which individual freedom and nonaggression would prevail. The Legalist ruler kept the people ignorant so that he could use them to work for the expansion of the state.

Defensive war is necessary if it cannot be avoided (31). However, the general must halt such a war once the enemy has been defeated, and should not take advantage of his victory (30). Although Lao-tzu justified a war of defense, he approved of it only as a regrettable necessity, for war entails the slaughter of men and the destruction of earth. Whether or not a defensive war falls within the category of inaction depends on the attitude of the general. If his aims are peace and defense, and if he commands the battle with compassion and without taking delight in slaughter, it is a war of inaction, for he does not have aggressive and violent intent.[7]

Religion

The question may be raised as to whether Taoism in its early development was a religion. We consider it so for the following reasons: (1) Tao is the cosmos conceived both as the source and order of nature. As has been mentioned, religion is the apprehension of and participation in the cosmos. Although Tao is impersonal, a right relation with it enables man to live a life of modesty, simplicity, and compassion and to have mystic union with it. Early Taoism can be regarded as a religion insofar as its metaphysics and ethics have a reference to the Ultimate. (2) Lao-tzu admitted the existence of spiritual beings (shên and kuei) (39, 60), although he considered them to be simply the namable expressions of Tao; their own existence is relative and perishable, while Tao as the source of the cosmos is unnamable and eternal. Lao-tzu said that if Tao is made to rule the empire, even spiritual beings will do no harm to man (60). The implication is: If the world is ruled by Tao, it will be so harmonious that the work of spiritual beings will become useless. In both Confucianism and Taoism there is something higher than spiritual beings; in Confucianism it is the rational moral order, and in Taoism it is the mystic source of the cosmos. (3) Lao-tzu accepted the ancestor cult as a legitimate practice. In fact, he held that it is the power of Tao which makes the continuation of the ancestral sacrifice possible (54). The ancestor cult symbolizes the infinite power of Tao.

CHUANG-TZU AND NEO-TAOISM

The next best-known Taoist philosopher after Lao-tzu was Chuang-tzu or Chuang Chou (c. 369–286 B.C.), who lived in the state of Meng in the area between present-day provinces of Shantung and Honan. Little is known about his life, but his writings indicate that he lived a normal and happy one, enjoying friendship and freedom. It was reported that once he declined an offer to be prime minister of a state because he did not want to give up his leisure. Although it is difficult to decide how much of the *Chuang-tzu,* which consists of thirty-three chapters, was actually written by him, scholars generally agree that he wrote the principal part of it.

In terms of literary style, lucidity, and imagination, the *Chuang-tzu* is the best book of philosophical essays ever produced in China. Although the thought of Lao-tzu and that of Chuang-tzu were basically the same, the latter elucidated the former's ideas more fully and with more sophistication. There are also some differences in emphasis. While Lao-tzu stressed modesty and contentment, Chuang-tzu dwelt on the tranquillity of the mind and the calmness of the self. Lao-tzu pictured man as a part of nature; but Chuang-tzu was preoccupied with the fate of man—his toil, labor, and death.

Transformation

Lao-tzu spoke of return (fu), that is the dissolution of things into Nonbeing. Chuang-tzu, however, emphasized transformation (*hua*): when a thing dies, it becomes a new form. Life is a transition from one form to another. Chuang-tzu told of a Taoist who, struck with a severe disease, was about to die. With perfect calmness, this man said to a visiting friend: "Suppose my left arm is transformed into a cock. With it I should herald the dawn. Suppose my right arm is transformed into a sling. With it I should look for a dove to roast. Suppose my buttocks were transformed into wheels and my spirit into a horse, I should mount them."[8] The story is also told of another Taoist who was about to die. The members of his family were weeping, but a visiting friend told them not to disturb the man in bed because transformation was about to take place. The friend looked out of the window and said to the dying man: "Great is the Creator [Nature]. What will he make of you now? Where will he take you? Will he make you into a rat's liver? Will he make you into an insect's leg?"[9] These anecdotes are fictional of course. Chuang-tzu employed numerous imaginative and metaphorical symbols to convey his insights and beliefs. Whether a person is changed into several forms or into a single form is beside the point; what is important is his view that life involves ceaseless changes and death is not an absolute end.

The process of transformation is the function of Tao. To let oneself follow the natural process without resistance or complaint is the way of life. Chuang-tzu did not conceive of life merely in terms of one's present stance, for such a view would be narrow and atomistic. Instead he conceived of life in terms of an infinite process of transformations, which includes all things past, present, and future. It is a truly majestic view, and he had an almost ecstatic feeling for it. "If our physical bodies went through ten thousand transformations without end, how incomparable would this joy be!"[10]

Chuang-tzu's doctrine of transformation seems to imply a belief in the permanence of soul, but this is not so. Neither Confucianism nor Taoism believes that man has a substance that persists in the midst of changes. Besides, the view that soul is separable from body is alien to Chinese thought. When Chuang-tzu discussed transformation, he did not have the idea of a "soul" in mind; he simply entertained the notion of transition from one concrete body to another. There is no transmigration of soul in Taoism.

The transformation of man from one form to another is not to be understood as a cause-effect relationship. Hence the moral condition of the present man has no influence on his future forms. His next form is not the result of reward or punishment for his present life. In Chuang-tzu's thought whatever is natural is good. Since the next form of the present man will be produced by nature, it too is good, no matter how low a form it takes. The transformation of Chuang-tzu is not like the Hindu doctrine of karma. In fact, from the Taoist viewpoint, man's preference for a better life to come, or his fear of a future form of existence, would be antithetic to his living a natural life.

Identity of Opposites

In our analysis of Lao-tzu, we discussed the relativity of things. Chuang-tzu carried this concept further and elucidated the idea that, since truth or knowledge is relative to one's stance, the opposites are identical. Many examples were used to illustrate this point. Monkeys like to live in trees, whereas man would dread having to live in them. Since what is liked by monkeys is disliked by man, the like is also the dislike. Further, measured by some standard, the tip of a hair is considered large, whereas by other standards Mount T'ai (one of the five best-known mountains in China) is small. By some measurement of time, a child who dies in infancy lives long, whereas by another measurement P'eng-tsu (the Chinese Methuselah) lived for only a short time. Hence a long and a short span of time are the same. While the termination of life is called death, a new form of life begins after the cessation of the old; and thus, life and death are identical, and the beginning and the end are the same. By the same token, when a table is made of wood, it is called an act of construction; but from the viewpoint of the wood, it is an act of destruction.[11]

All the examples above illustrate the view that opposite concepts express only truths that are relative, subjective, and changeable. At this level of experience, one can never reach absolute truth. On the other hand, when one realizes the identity of the opposites, then he neither affirms the one nor denies the other. He has attained a higher point of view, the vantage point of Tao, where he transcends the distinctions of both. All finite views are relative and distinguishable. But Tao is the Infinite—that which unites distinctions into the One which is absolute and undifferentiated.[12]

Although a Taoist lives in the midst of distinctions, he has transcended them in attitude; he simply follows the course of changes without favoring one or the other. He is at heart united with Tao. Chuang-tzu personally testified to this higher point of view. When his wife died, he was grieved at first. Then he began to think that his wife had been made a woman through a process of transformations. Now she was dead and had returned to Tao, and the same process would give her a new form in the future.[13] Consoled by this thought, he grieved no more.

Immortality

Chuang-tzu's higher point of view is also a way of explaining immortality in the philosophical sense. One should not identify oneself with a relative value, whether it be wealth, knowledge, or family, for such a value does not last long. The self is also relative in that it is transitory. The way to conquer death is therefore to identify oneself with the universe as the eternal One, which has no beginning or end. When man is united with the One, then he too will be without beginning or end. The way to attain this is to forget the distinctions between things, and simply follow the course of nature. This method is called "sitting in forgetfulness" (*tso wang*); one consciously discards all the opposite ideas and does not discriminate between them, while submitting oneself to the movements of nature. Such an enlightened person is called a True Man (*chen jen*). In this state, one has abandoned conceptual knowledge; one is in pure experience or nondifferentiation, which means that he responds to things freely, without judgment or deliberately. Pure experience is not equivalent to ignorance; the man of pure experience is one who has intellectual knowledge, but deliberation negates it in order to attain a higher point of view. An ignorant man does not have intellectual knowledge in the first place. The True Man still lives in the midst of distinctions, but for him they are no longer real.

Chuang-tzu's immortality is certainly not physical; in fact, there is no room for physical immortality, because it is contrary to the course of nature. His conception of immortality is based on the belief that there is no difference between life and death, or between self and no-self. When this duality has been dissolved, all things become the One. Man is immortal in the same sense as the universe is immortal. This is a philosophical solution to the problem of death.

Allegories

In the *Chuang-tzu* there are stories of True Men who possessed magic or supernatural powers. These men could enter water without getting wet and pass through fire without being burned.[14] Their breathing was deep, and it came from their heels rather than from their throats.[15] One of them, who lived on a river island, did not eat grain, but inhaled wind and drank dew; he mounted the clouds and drove flying dragons. He possessed powers to cure diseases and ensure good harvests.[16] These are fanciful, allegorical tales of men who possess the power of Tao. The specific powers ascribed to them are simply elements of folklore which Chuang-tzu used to create a sense of the wonder of Tao.

Religious Taoism, which arose in the late third and second centuries B.C., developed a belief in the existence of immortals (*hsien*) who by practicing Taoist yoga (breath control, mind concentration, and so on) overcame death and became divine beings. These immortals lived on secluded islands and mountains and were experts in alchemy and hygiene, two major practices necessary for physical immortality in religious Taoism. Followers of this belief took over those passages in the *Chuang-tzu* that pertained to the magic powers of True Men and treated them literally. For the religious Taoists, the True Men of Chuang-tzu were immortal beings (hsien) who possessed actual supernatural powers. To the extent that these narratives were thus interpreted by later Taoists, Chuang-tzu inadvertently influenced religious Taoism.[17]

Two factors in the *Chuang-tzu* support our contention that the True Man does not mean the immortal of religious Taoism. First, Chuang-tzu accepted death as a natural phenomenon. The True Man has transcended the duality of life and death: death is no different from life. To crave deathlessness is contrary to Tao. When Chuang-tzu was about to die, his disciples wanted to give him a grand funeral. He responded by saying: "I regard heaven and earth as my coffin and outer coffin, the sun and moon as a pair of jade gifts and the constellations as my burial jewels. And the whole creation shall come to my funeral."[18] His disciples were afraid that the vulture crows would come and eat the body of the Master. Chuang-tzu answered, "Above the ground, I shall be eaten by the vultures, and underground, I shall be eaten by the ants. Why rob the one to give it to the other?"[19] It is inconceivable that with this attitude about death Chuang-tzu would accept physical immortality.

Second, while religious Taoism associated the practice of alchemy and hygiene with hsien, Chuang-tzu was critical of these activities and considered them not worth pursuing. (Evidently, such activities began to be practiced in China in the middle of the fourth century B.C.) He considered leaving the world and going to the hills to be symbols of arrogance.[20] He ridiculed those who practiced blowing and breathing with open mouths, sat like sleepy bears, and twisted their necks like birds—referring to the practice of hygiene.[21] Although Chuang-tzu did not oppose longevity, he was against the use of such techniques to attain it.

Neo-Taoism

When the Han dynasty collapsed in A.D. 220, China sank into another period of political confusion and continuing war; the country was at first divided into three kingdoms; this was followed by a series of dynasties in the north, and then another series in central and south China, until the country was reunited in the Sui dynasty (A.D. 590–618). The four centuries from A.D. 220 to

589 are called the period of Political Disunion. At this time, Confucianism receded, Taoism was revived, and Buddhism was spreading fast.

Although Taoism enjoyed the personal favor of several emperors in the Han dynasty, the public philosophy of this period was still Confucianism. But in the ensuing Political Disunion, people were afflicted by changes of dynasties and by war, and they were looking for spiritual consolation. It was at this time that philosophical Taoism was rediscovered by the intellectuals, because it helped them to look inward for strength in the face of social disruptions. The Taoism of the Wei (A.D. 220–265) and Chin (A.D. 265–420) periods was called *hsüan hsüeh* (mysterious learning); it was a new interpretation of Lao-tzu and Chuang-tzu. We call it neo-Taoism because its character was different from early Taoism in that it showed a greater interest in logic and system. Another difference is the high respect for Confucius shown by the neo-Taoists, for by this time the exalted position of the Master had been thoroughly established and Confucius was depicted as understanding Taoism even more profoundly than did Lao-tzu and Chuang-tzu.

There were two schools of neo-Taoists: the rationalists and the romantics. The difference between them, however, is chiefly a matter of emphasis. The rationalists continued the Taoist tradition of using reason to control emotions; they represented the academic side of Taoism. The romantics stressed the enjoyment of refined emotions; they represented the artistic side of Taoism.

The outstanding rationalists were Wang Pi (A.D. 226–249), who wrote the best commentary on the *Tao Te Ching,* and Ku Hsiang (d. A.D. 312), who wrote the most widely read commentary on the *Chuang-tzu.* Both gave a logical and ontological analysis of Wu (Nonbeing). Tao for Lao-tzu is primarily the Unnamable; for Chuang-tzu it is the One (Undifferentiated); for the neo-Taoists it is the negation of any specific meanings for Being. Tao can only be talked about as Wu, Nonbeing, or *Hsü,* Vacuity. None of these terms conveys a positive meaning. Since Nonbeing is the foundation of beings, all existents in the last analysis partake of vacuity, that is, the negation of their positive meanings.

Neo-Taoists were the first to discuss the relation between substance and function in Chinese thought. Substance refers to Nonbeing, and function refers to the manifestations of Nonbeing in the myriad things. Hence they are inseparable. The term *function*

RELIGIONS OF EAST ASIA

has a twofold meaning, however: as a phenomenal activity it has positive and definite meaning, but as a manifestation of the substance (Nonbeing) it negates its own meaning. All phenomenal activities in one sense are positive and definite; but in another sense they are vacuous and lack ultimate meaning. This substance-function metaphysics enabled the neo-Taoists to accept Confucian values while at the same time negating them. Confucian morals and institutions, taken by themselves, are valuable; hence the neo-Taoists also practiced virtues and took part in affairs of family and society. But when these morals and institutions are viewed as manifestations of Nonbeing, they are vacuous and hence to be negated. The neo-Taoists lived immanently and transcendently simultaneously; they participated in mundane affairs according to Confucian principles, yet at the same time they regarded these activities as vacuous. Being detached, they were not ensnared by their own activities. The neo-Taoists took the concept of Nonbeing as the final criterion of reference—all things and activities are to be negated, including the desire for negation. They considered Confucius to be the greatest sage because he had no desire for the state of "no desire." He was in vacuity in the perfect sense.

The romantic school of neo-Taoism accepted the basic tenets of the rationalists; but its main interest was to pursue *feng liu* (literally, "wind and stream")—that is, to live a life of freedom and ease without conforming to conventions. The romantics were mainly poets, painters, and men of the arts who formed fraternal groups and lived in a world of their own. A characteristic of their fraternal life was *ch'ing t'an* (pure conversations); they discussed topics of philosophical interest and avoided mundane issues. Such conversations were both intellectual and aesthetic; they often took place in natural settings, sometimes accompanied by wine drinking. What lay behind such activities was the attitude that no matter how simple the thing they were doing, it was to be done in harmony with nature.

The Taoists of this period actually prepared the way for the growth of Buddhism in China. It was these men who first became interested in the Buddhist Sutras, which had just been brought from India. Taoists and Buddhists then worked together in translating the Sutras from Sanskrit into Chinese; they were able to do this by employing categories of philosophical Taoism. It is no surprise, for instance, that the Buddhist concept of sunyata (emptiness) was translated as *Wu* (Nonbeing or Vacuity) in Chinese. The influence of neo-Taoism on Chinese Buddhism was great.

RELIGIOUS TAOISM

Philosophical Taoism, the Alchemy school for producing elixir, the Hygiene school for longevity, and the search for the Isles of the Blessed, where immortals reside and miraculous mushrooms of immortality grow, were four independent, though somewhat related Taoist movements that emerged in the fourth century B.C. These groups, which converged in the period between 221 and 120 B.C. and formed religious Taoism,[22] were with the exception of philosophical Taoism, mainly concerned with physical immortality. The alliance of philosophical Taoism with the other movements therefore needs some explanation. As has been said, there are passages in the *Chuang-tzu* that were understood by the alchemists and the hygienists as references to physical immortality. More than that, both Lao-tzu and Chuang-tzu emphasized individualism against social control—man as a child of nature in contrast to man as a member of institutions. These ideas were basic to the followers of religious Taoism. The philosophical and religious Taoists became allies because they both represented a reaction against the Confucian ideology: they were heterodox, whereas the Confucians were orthodox. Although many practices of the religious Taoists were unacceptable to the philosophical Taoists, they nevertheless joined forces because both held an individualistic, unconventional, and Dionysian attitude, as opposed to the collectivistic, conventional, and rationalistic ideology of Confucianism.

One wonders why the Chinese in this period were so interested in physical immortality. Perhaps the answer lies in the fact that they did not have a concept of a soul that survives death. In fact, the doctrine of the dichotomy of soul and body—that spirit and matter exist independently—was alien to them. For the Chinese, the body is inherently spiritual, and spirit must be an expression of a body. They could not, therefore, envisage the survival of the soul after death. The soul in Chinese thought is basically composite; it consists of *hun*, which after death ascends to Heaven although its fate is uncertain, and *p'o*, which after death descends into earth and dwells in the Yellow Spring, the Chinese Sheol, where it eventually disappears. Neither hun nor p'o is by itself a soul in the Greco-Roman sense.

It is no surprise then that the religious Taoists at this time paid so much attention to the question of immortality, for it offered them an alternative to the immortality of the soul. It is worth noting that Judaism also does not have a dominant belief in the survival of soul after death. In fact, both Judaism and religious Taoism envisage immortality in the physical sense; but the Jewish doctrine of the resurrection of the body is an eschatological event which occurs at the end of time and only through the power of God, whereas the Taoist physical immortality takes place in present life and is realized completely through human efforts.

Although these four movements constituted the ingredients of religious Taoism, they were not all accepted by its followers. Religious Taoism was an exceedingly diverse, heterogeneous, and even self-contradictory movement; it embraced kings and paupers, philosophers and illiterates, mystics and opportunists, saints and criminals. Its beliefs and practices were eclectic; they changed according to social and political conditions and differed with respect to localities. In fact, the only common denominator that held the followers together as one body was their acceptance of Lao-tzu as their spiritual leader, an honor he would definitely have rejected. In the following we show the different facets of this complex movement through a discussion of alchemy, the Hygiene school, the Taoist Church, the Taoist pantheon, and their relations with one another.

Alchemy

In the Ch'in dynasty (221–206 B.C.) there was the popular belief that the hsien (immortals) lived on the Isles of the Blessed, imaginary islands in the Eastern Sea off the China coast, where grew drugs which, if eaten by a man, would cause him to live forever. The most sought island was called P'eng-lai. Shih Huang Ti, the founder of the Ch'in dynasty, wanted to be king forever and was eager to get hold of these drugs. Magicians (fang shih) were hired at his court to help him do so. The king sent several expeditions of ships to seek P'eng-lai, some of which never returned; others did, but with empty hands. He spent his last days at the coast watching the sea, still longing for the drugs in the magic island.

The belief in the island of P'eng-lai where the hsien lived gave impetus to the rise of alchemy. The conviction was that man could become a hsien through the practice of alchemy. In 133 B.C. Li Shao-chün, a leading magician, succeeded in getting permission from Emperor Wu Ti, the best-known ruler of the Han dynasty, to practice alchemy at the court for the king's benefit. Wu Ti had previously sponsored both Confucianism and Legalism for the government; now he pursued Taoism for his own personal interest. The practice involved the transmutation of cinnabar, placed in a stove, into gold, which was believed to be an elixir. The transmuted cinnabar, however, promised longevity only; the recipient was expected to see the hsien at P'eng-lai before he could become immortal. This perhaps explains why Wu Ti never became a hsien. It was believed that a man who became a hsien still had to die; but for him death was merely a preparatory stage for the emanation of the immortal body. This process was called the "deliverance of the corpse," a phenomenon analogous to the metamorphosis of insects.

According to magician Li Shao-chün, alchemy was not merely a pharmaceutic technique; it also required sacrifice to Tsao Chün, the God of the Hearth. Although Tsao Chün was a new deity in Taoism, he was actually an old divinity—Ssu Ming, the Controller of Destinies, who had been a god of shamans in ancient China. Apparently the alchemists were impressed by Ssu Ming's power and made him the god who would bring them to their desired goal. By the third century A.D., when alchemy declined, he became the God of the Hearth, who recorded the deeds of the members of every household and reported them annually to his superior in Heaven.

As time went by, the pursuit of immortality vanished. The chief cause was probably the spread of Buddhism. The Pure Land sect, the popular Buddhism of China, became influential after the sixth century A.D. It taught about man's future life in the Pure Land, and hence the need for physical immortality was no longer imperative. After the sixth century A.D. the Taoists did not emphasize the external process of alchemy, but stressed the "interior elixir"— namely, the internal harmony between the forces of Yin and Yang in man, by which they meant the realization of man's original nature. The "interior elixir" refers to the true self, which can be discovered by means of meditation and breath control. At this point, alchemy became the practice of mental and physical exercises, similar to the enlightened practice of hygiene.

Hygiene

Although the common goal of alchemy and hygiene in their early stages was physical immortality, they differed in the means by which they tried to attain it; the former aimed at producing elixirs, while the latter dealt with methods of controlling the adept's physical and mental forces. While the alchemists relied on external materials, the hygienists used internal forces, in order to accomplish their purpose. The origins of the practice of hygiene in China go back as early as the sixth century B.C., to about the time of Confucius, when breath control was described in writings that were later known to Chuang-tzu. But hygiene did not become an influential movement until the first century A.D.

The best-known group of hygienists arose during the first century A.D. and was called the Interior Gods school. Its name was derived from the belief that gods dwell within the human body. These gods (36,000 in number), who reside in different compartments of the body, correspond to the ones who reign in various regions of the cosmos. In order to make the interior gods happy, this theology held, man must observe certain regulations and control his breathing. This school divided the body into three centers, known as the Fields of Cinnabar (tan t'ien). They were head, chest, and abdomen. Each field was occupied by one of the triadic gods (Three Ones). Thus T'ai I (Grand One) resided in the head, T'ien I (Heavenly One) in the chest, and Ti I (Earthly One) in the abdomen. In his breathing exercise, the adept was to cultivate "interior vision"—that is, to see gods inside his body, particularly T'ai I (the Grand One).

Dietary restrictions were observed because the human body was also believed to be the habitat of the Three Worms, one in each Field of Cinnabar, which were the cause of disease, decrepitude, and death. These worms lived on the five grains (rice, millet, wheat, barley, beans); hence the adept refrained from eating food containing them. The interior gods disliked wine and meat, which were also to be avoided. Moreover, solid food was not to be eaten, for it produced excrement which obstructed the circulation of breath. The most advanced adepts lived merely on berries and roots, along with their own breath and saliva. As a rule, Taoists had no prohibition against wine and meat, and this school was the one exception.

The technique of breathing was called "embryonic respiration"; this means learning to breathe as an infant does in the womb. One held one's breath as long as he could; what one inhaled thus became material for the immortal substance. If one held one's breath for 12 heartbeats, this was called a "little tour"; if one could hold one's breath for 120 heartbeats, it was called a "big tour." But the goal was to hold it for 1,000 heartbeats.[23] The adept also knew how to make the air circulate beyond his liver and kidneys to his abdomen and from there to the soles of his feet. He then guided the circulation upward to his brain through his spine, down to his chest, and up again to his throat. While doing this, he was at the same time storing up saliva in his mouth. When his breath returned to his throat, he pressed it down by means of saliva and swallowed it. The saved breath eventually formed the Mysterious Embryo— the immortal self, which replaced the old body and lived forever.

In addition to belief in gods, dietary observance, breath control, and gymnastic exercise (to keep the pores of the body unobstructed), the adept of this school also practiced good works. Beneficent deeds could influence the gods, whose favor was needed for immortality, whereas bad deeds caused the gods to reject one. As a result, the Taoists, like the Buddhists, assisted the poor and engaged in community service. It should be noted, of course, that members of the Interior Gods school were not men without means. Poor people could not afford the time to practice rigorous breath control nor could they survive on berries and roots while doing daily labor.

This school declined in the fourth century A.D. and died out two centuries later, partly as a result of the rise of other Taoist schools and partly because of the spread of popular Buddhism, which promised future life in the Pure Land. Breath control was gradually changed from holding one's breath to regulating it by meditation. Ch'an (meditation) Buddhism probably helped soften the harshness of this Taoist practice.

The Taoist Church

The Taoist Church, a movement that was contemporary with, but superseded, the Interior Gods school, also practiced hygiene. However it followed hygiene not for physical immortality but for health and longevity. This group contributed sexual knowledge to Chinese thought, an area seldom touched on by the Confucians. The church Taoists believed that the Yin and Yang forces complemented each other. Male as Yang and female as Yin could nourish each other by coition. They regarded semen as the essence of life. To preserve and increase it was the secret of longevity for man.

The way to do this was to have frequent unions with the opposite sex, but to avoid ejaculation until the very last. Since such performance required the cooperation of cosmic and divine powers, it was regarded as a religious ritual and done in a group ceremony at the temple under the supervision of priests. The ceremony was preceded by a period of fasting and took place on nights of a new or full moon. Since this ritual was dependent on factors related to the season, the weather, the phases of the moon, and other astrological considerations, it probably was not performed very often. Although it disappeared after the seventh century, sexual theory and techniques of Taoism continued to influence the masses.

The Taoist Church arose in the middle of the second century A.D. at a time when the Han dynasty was declining. Its period of vital growth paralleled the Political Disunion, when Confucianism was suffering from stagnancy and Chinese society was undergoing disruptions; it was a period marked by restlessness and the disintegration of traditional values. During these years Taoism, along with Buddhism, provided for the spiritual needs of the people. Neo-Taoism gave intellectual and artistic direction to the scholars, and the Taoist Church supplied the religious and emotional needs of the masses. We call this new development a church movement because it possessed features resembling the Christian church such as a priesthood, assembly worship, a temple, and an ecclesiastical organization. The immediate goal of the Taoist Church was faith healing, although alchemy and hygiene were also part of its program.

Two independent but similar Taoist church movements, one in the west and the other in the east, grew up simultaneously. Chang Tao-ling, a priest-magician, started a health cult in Szechwan, a province bordering Tibet, and he and his disciples treated patients. They collected five pecks of rice as a fee from every family under their care, and as a result, his group was known as the Tao of the Five Pecks of Rice. Chang Tao-ling called himself T'ien Shih (Heavenly Teacher), thereby designating both a priestly and a magical power. This title was hereditary and was held, with some interruptions, by his own descendants, who were chosen as his successors. The cult was enlarged toward the end of the second century A.D. under Chang Lu, the grandson of the founder, and the healing practice was changed to include confession of sins by imprisonment; patients were retained to think about their past lives and to record their sins, because it was believed that diseases were caused by sins.

Chang Lu forbade his followers to drink alcoholic beverages, to lie, to steal, and to debauch. For thirty years his region was virtually an independent state, ruled by a hierarchy of priests. He even had his own soldiers, who were also believers.

While Chang Lu's cult was expanding in the west, a similar movement, called the Tao of the Grand Peace, was rising in the eastern provinces under the leadership of Chang Chüeh, also a priest-magician. His organization met the needs of the time, when famines and epidemics were ravaging the region and high taxes were antagonizing the people. It offered the dispossessed a channel for their grievances and a vehicle for action. As a prerequisite for healing, followers were given the opportunity to confess their sins in public. Chang Chüeh had his own army, and in A.D. 184 eight provinces were under his control. The central government was alarmed and sent large armies to subdue the movement. It took the government many years to stamp out Chang's military force, but by 315 it was no longer a threat to the state. The eastern Taoist soldiers wore yellow kerchiefs on their heads, and their rebellion was therefore called the Yellow Turbans Revolt.

The Taoist Church movement accepted the *Tao Te Ching* as its sacred literature, even though it was interpreted in a variety of ways, and promoted Lao-tzu to divine status. During the third century the military and political powers of the Taoist Church were stripped in both the east and the west, but as a religion it continued to thrive. The priests (see Figure 24.1) who served at local temples were called *tao shih* (gentlemen of tao). A Holy Rollers type of church meeting was held in the eastern cult after the Yellow Turbans Revolt, in which participants sang, danced, and rolled on the ground to express their repentance and the desire for forgiveness.

The Taoist Church was normalized during the period of Political Disunion (A.D. 220–589). Since it had no central hierarchy, its sects in turn had no uniform ecclesiastical pattern. In general, the local abbots were heads of temples and were responsible to no higher hierarchy. There were two kinds of priests, celibate and married. The celibate priests, influenced by Buddhism, prevailed in north China. Since they were ascetics, they deplored the cultic sexual rites and emphasized spiritual religion. One important priest in the fifth century advocated reformation of the church; he stressed good works and hygiene, but his influence did not spread widely nor last long. Since then celibate priests (see Figure 24.2) have made intermittent attempts to purify Taoism. The south and west were dominated by married priests, among whom the priesthood was hereditary. These priests, who were worldly and commercialized, lived at home, although they served in the temple. The best-known sect of the married priests was that of the Chang family, whose ancestor started the Tao of the Five Pecks of Rice mentioned earlier. In 1015 the same family received an imperial gift of land located in the Dragon and Tiger Mountains in the province of Kiangsi, which was occupied by the family in succession until 1927. In 1276 the emperor officially approved the title Heavenly Teacher which had been used by the successive members of the family. Although this title was legally abolished in 1368, it is popularly retained to this day. The hereditary Heavenly Teachers were great experts in rain making, faith healing, exorcism, necromancy, and other cultic matters. Many local priests came to the Dragon and Tiger Mountains for training. Although from time to time the Chang family did receive imperial permission to hold jurisdiction over other Taoist churches, the right was only nominal, and usually they did not have ecclesiastic authority over other churches. Since the land held by the family was confiscated by the government in 1927,[24] the last Heavenly Teacher, the sixty-third, has become a pauper.

The Taoist Pantheon

When we come to the gods in Taoism, we are in fact confronting a religion of the masses. There was virtually no difference between religious Taoism and popular Chinese religion, for they shared most of the same gods. There were hundreds of divine beings in the Taoist pantheon, the product of a gradual accumulation.[25] New gods were added because of people's new needs, but the old ones were never discarded.

Some deities were the personification of metaphysical concepts or natural forces. Even after they became gods, they still conveyed a certain sense of abstraction. For instance, T'ai I (Grand One) had been used by Chuang-tzu as the Undifferentiated One, Tao; later it was worshiped as the Cosmic Person. Likewise, the god San I (Three Ones) was actually the unity of T'ai I (Grand One), T'ien I (Heavenly One), and Ti (Earthly One), the first being a meta-

FIGURE 24.2 Taoist priests in a temple courtyard in China. (*Harrison Forman*)

physical concept and the other two, natural forces. Another set of triadic gods was called the Three Pure Ones (the Precious Heavenly Lord, the Precious Spiritual Lord, and the Precious Divine Lord). Actually these three lords correspond to the three aspects of time: past, present, future.[26]

In the second century A.D. the Taoists identified Lao-tzu with Huang-ti, the mythical founder of the Chinese Empire in Taoism, who preceded the legendary kings of Confucianism, thus making the sage the founder of China, which corresponded to being the creator of the world. Lao-tzu was given the new title, Huang Lao Chün (the Lord of Huang Lao), in which "Huang" stands for Huang-ti. According to second-century Taoists, Huang Lao Chün came to the world in human form and taught man the secrets of immortality and longevity. The idea of incarnation was influenced by the Buddhist concept of Bodhisattva (Buddha-to-be), who was reborn in physical forms in order to enlighten the unsaved.

A more popular deity than Huang Lao Chün was Yüan Shih T'ien Tsun (the Lord of the Original Beginning). He was the creator of the world, and in this sense he was identical with Huang Lao Chün. But he was higher than Lao-tzu through never having been born in human form. Because of his wish for the salvation of all men, he dictated the Ling Pao (Sacred Jewel) Scriptures to gods who, in turn, transmitted them to Chang Tao-ling, the founder of the Tao of the Five Pecks of Rice. The Ling Pao Scriptures deal with rituals for invoking the gods, releasing the dead from Hell and transporting them to Heaven, and other matters relative to man's present and future welfare. These books were actually written in the fourth and fifth centuries A.D.

The most popular and influential god in Taoism was the Jade Emperor (Yü Huang), the agent of Yüan Shih T'ien Tsun, who appeared in the Tang dynasty (A.D. 618–906). He was the cosmic counterpart of the imperial king, who saw to it that natural and human spheres functioned properly. Hundreds of celestial and terrestrial gods, each holding cosmic office (for example, the Dragon King of Rain, and the God of Wealth and Happiness), worked under his tutelage—the influence of the Confucian love for bureaucracy on religious Taoism is evident here. These gods included some deified human kings (for example, Hwa T'o, the divine patron of surgeons). Tsao Chün (God of the Hearth) was a ubiquitous terrestrial deity who listened to conversations in the household and recorded the deeds of its members, which he reported to the Jade Emperor at the end of each year. The City God, who looked after the welfare of urban affairs, also enjoyed popularity.

Immortality

The belief in physical immortality had a lasting effect on Chinese mass culture. Since most of the immortals were not scholars, this belief reflects the view that people in walks of life other than that of scholar-official could also attain divinity and that there are types of ideal men other than the Confucian scholars. The belief in physical immortality implies the view that all walks of life are equal and sacred. This can be seen in the legend of the Eight Immortals (*Pa Hsien*). Among these is a woman, a patron saint of musicians, a lover of theatrical arts, a ballad singer who loves flowers, and a beggar. None of them is a learned person. The Eight Immortals have been a common topic of painting and sculpture in China, and have given the masses a sense of identity.

THE LEGACY AND FUTURE OF TAOISM

Although Taoism appears to be anti-intellectual, as seen in the repudiation of knowledge by Lao-tzu and Chuang-tzu and in the practice of magic by religious Taoists, it did contribute to the beginnings of science in China. The philosophical Taoists stressed the independence of natural laws—these laws are neutral, devoid of moral attributes and without regard for man—and they differentiated the impersonal realm of nature from the personal realm of man—scientific knowledge is derived from the former, morality from the latter. On the other hand, the early Confucians were preoccupied with man and society and viewed nature as a reflection of man. As a result, they could not have separated natural laws from moral laws.

Philosophical Taoism emphasized the observation of nature. Chuang-tzu had almost an ecstatic interest in it; he frequently cited phenomena of sun, moon, clouds, and wind, or the behavior of fishes, birds, dogs, and horses to explain the principles of nature. A later Taoist book, the *Huai Nan Tzu*, interprets wu-wei (inaction) to mean not letting personal opinions interfere with the natural trend of things and yu-wei (action) to mean doing things against natural principles, such as using fire to dry up a well.

Although the religious Taoists resorted to magic, they were nevertheless empirical. Driven by a desire for immortality and longevity, they began to experiment with herbs, roots, and flower petals in order to find drugs. The alchemists failed to produce elixir, but they did start pharmaceutics. The hygienists had an interest in anatomy and physiology, even if their understanding of the human body was erroneous. The spirit of experimental curiosity, manual work, and toolmaking was positively present in Taoism. While the Taoists did not develop scientific method and theory, they did make technological innovations and pursued the practical side of science.

Taoism in both its philosophical and religious branches is mystical. But mysticism and science are not incompatible. Mysticism advocates the wisdom of nature and is willing to subject man's reason to it; but this awareness of the limitations of human reason and this sense of wonder about the infinite power of nature are conducive to science. Joseph Needham says that there is a great similarity between the Taoist mystics in early China and the Christian mystics in the Middle Ages in this respect: they both contributed to the early development of science.[27]

A question may be raised as to the present and future of Taoism. Religious Taoism as an institution has virtually disappeared in China; in fact, it has been declining ever since the Sung dynasty (960–1279). But religious Taoism as a substratum in Chinese mass culture still remains (see Figure 24.1). Many of its themes—such as equality of rank, sympathy for the poor and the oppressed, protest against authority, erotic love, the righteous outlaw, fraternal brotherhood—have been motifs of novels, dramas, folklore, and the visual arts for centuries. Some of these ideas have been taken up by the Chinese secret societies, which are still powerful in modern China. As long as these popular ideas continue, some form of religious Taoism will survive, even if not overtly.

Philosophical Taoism has always represented the unorthodox, romantic, and passive in Chinese thought, thus complementing the orthodox, rationalistic, and active side of the Chinese mind. As metaphysics Taoism can be regarded as a mystic naturalism: it is naturalistic because Tao is the ground of nature, and it is mystic in that Tao as the source of nature is unnamable. Historically, Taoism furnished much of the substance for the development of Ch'an (Zen) Buddhism, which gave China a religious faith that is both mystic and practical, as well as very adaptable. Today, Taoism is much studied in mainland China; the trend has been to interpret the *Tao Te Ching* in terms of the Marxist categories and to remove its mystic traces.

NOTES

1. Lao Tzu, *Tao Te Ching, The Way and Its Power,* trans. by Arthur Waley (New York: Grove, 1958), p. 49.
2. From *The Way of Lao Tzu,* translated by Chan Wing-tsit, copyright © 1963 by the Bobbs-Merrill Company, Inc., reprinted by permission of The Liberal Arts Press Division of the Bobbs-Merrill Company, Inc., p. 36.
3. The number(s) in parentheses indicates the chapter(s) of the *Tao Te Ching.* For its translation, see Lao Tzu, *op. cit.,* or Chan Wing-tsit, *op. cit.*

4. Holmes Welch, *The Parting of the Way* (Boston: Beacon, 1957), p. 68.

5. Although wu-wei is close to spontaneous action, it is not identical with it. Spontaneity implies arbitrary and capricious action. But wu-wei implies conformity to natural pattern, which is not completely spontaneous.

6. Chan Wing-tsit, *op. cit.*, see footnote 3 on p. 150.

7. Welch, *op. cit.*, p. 25.

8. Chan Wing-tsit, *A Source Book in Chinese Philosophy* (Princeton: Princeton University Press, 1963), p. 197.

9. *Ibid.*

10. *Ibid.*, p. 194; *The Chuang Tzu*, 6:6, in the *Text of Taoism*, trans. by James Legge (New York: Julian, 1959), p. 291.

11. These illustrations are taken from Chapter 2 of *The Chuang Tzu*; Chan Wing-tsit, *A Source Book in Chinese Philosophy*, pp. 179–191; and *The Chuang Tzu*, pp. 224–245.

12. Tao as the One for Chuang-tzu refers to the undifferentiated, the Unnamable; whereas for Lao-tzu the One refers to the Whole, that is, the creative order, the Namable aspect of Tao.

13. Chan Wing-tsit, *A Source Book in Chinese Philosophy*, p. 209; *The Chuang Tzu*, 18:2, pp. 444–445.

14. *The Chuang Tzu*, 6:2, pp. 285–286.

15. *Ibid.*, 6:2, p. 286.

16. *Ibid.*, 1:5, pp. 218–219.

17. About the distinctions between philosophical and religious Taoism see H. G. Creel, "What Is Taoism?" *Journal of the American Oriental Society*, Vol. 76, No. 3 (1956), pp. 139–152; Welch, *op. cit.*, pp. 91–97.

18. Lao Tzu, *The Wisdom of Laotse,* trans. by Lin Yutang (New York: Random House, 1948), p. 181. Used by permission.

19. *Ibid.*

20. *The Chuang Tzu*, 15:1, p. 411.

21. *Ibid.*, 15:1, p. 412.

22. Welch, *op. cit.*, pp. 89–90.

23. *Ibid.*, p. 108.

24. *Ibid.*, p. 149.

25. A list of gods representing the religion of the Chinese masses appears in C. B. Day's *Chinese Peasant Cults* (Shanghai: Kelly and Walsh, 1940), pp. 205–217.

26. Joseph Needham, *Science and Civilization in China*, Vol. II: *History of Scientific Thought* (Cambridge: Cambridge University Press, 1956), p. 160.

27. Needham, *op. cit.*, pp. 91–92.

25 Shinto

According to a statement attributed to Prince Shōtoku (A.D. 573–621), the three major religions of Japan are comparable to the parts of a tree. Shinto is the root, Confucianism the stem and branches, and Buddhism the flowers and fruits. This analogy implies not only the inseparableness of these three traditions, but also the view that Shinto has been the foundation for Japanese Confucianism and Buddhism. The civilization of Japan began to blossom after the arrival of the continental religions: Confucianism provided Japan with ethics, law, political institutions, and an educational system; and Buddhism gave Japan its religious philosophy and metaphysics. But it was Shinto, the indigenous religion, which forced the other two religions to adapt themselves to the Japanese environment. On the other hand, Shinto also underwent changes because of the presence of Confucianism and Buddhism. The mutual influences of these three systems can be clearly seen as we unfold the development of Shinto in Japanese history.

The term *Shinto* is a combination of two Chinese words, *shin* (god) and *to* (way), meaning "the Way of the Gods." The Chinese word *shin* is an equivalent of the Japanese term *kami,* which refers to a spirit or divinity. But kami cannot be precisely defined; even Shinto theologians have not reached any agreement on its meaning. A kami is anything that possesses an unusual quality or potency and is capable of conveying the sacred; it may also refer to the quality itself in an object. Kami is definitely associated with animism; both animate (man, fox, bird) and inanimate things (tree, rock, river, mountain) can be kami. But kami implies more

FIGURE 25.1 Tōshōgū (Shrine of the Sun God of the East), Nikko, dedicated to Tokugawa Iyeyasu. (*Japan National Tourist Organization*)

than animism; ancestors, particularly heroes of the past, and emperors, both dead and living, are kami. Nor is the term confined to good spirits; demons may also be called kami.

MYTHOLOGY

Shinto, "the Way of the Gods," refers to the Way as it was described in the mythology of early Japan. The myths describe how the kami came into being, their association with the land, and their behavior toward one another. The "Way" in Shinto does not necessarily have a rational meaning, as in Confucianism, or a mystic meaning, as in Taoism. It refers primarily to the stories and events concerning the gods, which are viewed as archetypes worthy of being remembered or reenacted through rituals or other acts of community consciousness. In order to understand Shinto it is necessary to unveil its mythology. But a proper approach to these stories requires an initial understanding of the origins of the Japanese and the writing of their mythology.

It is generally accepted that the ancestors of the Japanese came from outside the archipelago of Japan. They were composed of various Asian groups, among them (1) northeast Asians, who included the people of Siberia, Manchuria, and Korea. These people brought in the practice of shamanism and a "vertical cosmology," that is, a belief in gods who descended from Heaven to mountaintops or trees;[1] (2) South Pacific people, of Melanesian origin, who practiced hunting and had a "horizontal cosmology," that is, a belief in a realm of the dead beyond the sea;[2] (3) people from south China, who brought to Japan the art of rice cultivation, the belief in a fertility deity, and the myth about marriage between a god and his sister.[3] Each of these diverse migrant groups brought its own practices, beliefs, and myths to Japan. This means that the Shinto myths are not purely indigenous; they are composites whose origins stem back to other parts of Asia and the Pacific. Since these settlers occupied different regions of Japan in the pioneering period, their beliefs must at one time have been local in character. Only after the lapse of much time, during which the diverse groups were fused, did these myths become integrated and systematized, as they are today.

The basic myths were recorded in two works, *Kojiki* (Records of Ancient Matters) and *Nihongi* (Chronicles of Japan), both written in Chinese and completed respectively in 712 and 720. They are the earliest records of Japan. It should be pointed out that by this time Japan was already united under able emperors and that Confucianism had already become the state doctrine, while Buddhism was spreading. These facts show that the Japanese myths existed as oral tradition for centuries. Perhaps written fragments existed prior to the eighth century; but since the Chinese system of writing was not introduced into Japan until the beginning of the fifth century A.D., these stories could not have been written before that time. Since both the *Kojiki* and *Nihongi* were written under the auspices of the royal court, they reflect imperial interest in the selection and emphasis of materials. By the eighth century Japanese aristocrats knew the ancient classics of China, and hence influences of Chinese thought are also discernible in these two documents. It is also worth noting that the term *Shinto* was not coined until after the arrival of Buddhism in Japan in the sixth century, when a need was felt for a proper name for Japan's own religion. It is probable that for a long time the indigenous religion of Japan was without a name.[4]

One of the three Japanese cosmogonic myths introduces a triad consisting of a creator deity, Ame-no-Minaka-nushi, and a male and a female deity, respectively called Takami-musubi and Kami-musubi. The male and female gods can also be regarded as the two components of the creator-god. It is Takami-musubi, the male deity, who orders Ninigi, a grandson of Amaterasu, the sun goddess, to descend to a mountaintop in Kyūshū in southwest Japan and establish the Japanese imperial line.[5]

Another cluster of stories centers around two celestial beings, Izanagi (He who invites) and Izanami (She who is invited). According to the *Nihongi,* they beget the Japanese archipelago, as well as mountains, rivers, herbs, trees, fire, and other objects, all of which are kami. Finally, they beget gods who rule the cosmos: Amaterasu, the sun goddess, Tsuki-yomi, the moon deity, and Susanowo, the storm god. The moon deity does not play an important role in Japanese mythology; but Amaterasu, who represents the realm of light and controls heaven and earth, and Susanowo, who is ruler of the sea and the realm of hidden things, are prominent.

According to the *Kojiki,* it was Izanagi, the male god, who produced the three rulers of the cosmos. He washed his eyes and thereby produced the sun goddess from his left eye and the moon deity from his right eye. The impetuous storm god came out of his nostrils. In the Chinese legend of P'an-ku, the cosmic giant, his left eye became the sun and his right eye became the moon.

Izanami, the female deity, is associated with the realm of the dead, the Land of Gloom, Yomotsu-kuni. The story of the divine couple ends with the death of Izanami in the dark world and Izanagi's escape from the realm of the dead. After coming out of the dark abode, Izanagi goes to a river and bathes himself. This act of washing symbolizes purification—cleansing from pollution or evil spirits—which is a basic Shinto rite. The tragic separation between this loving couple depicts death as the inevitable destiny of man and also his fear of it.

The complex myth of Amaterasu and Susanowo, sister and brother deities, reflect the primordial forces of nature. These two deities represent respectively the bright and dark forces of the world. The sister is peace-loving, gentle, and constructive; the brother is tempestuous, violent, and destructive. One suggests order, the other chaos. Together they personify these inseparable forces in man and nature. Amaterasu as the sun goddess is also a fertility deity, since agricultural products need sunlight. This aspect of her function can be seen in the story in which Susanowo destroys his sister's rice fields and pollutes the harvest rite she is preparing. In great distress, she withdraws from the world and hides herself in a cave. Consequently, darkness prevails on the earth. It is only at the urgent request of the eighty myriads of kami, made through dancing, singing, and charms, that they induce her to leave the cave. While this episode may imply a solar eclipse, Amaterasu's association with agriculture was undeniable. At the present time, two annual agricultural rites, the Festival of Prayer for the year's crops on February 4 and the Harvest Festival at midnight on November 23, are conducted at the grand shrine in Ise, a national sanctuary of Amaterasu located in the central part of Honshū, the main island of Japan.

Amaterasu is far more than an agricultural deity, however. According to the *Kojiki,* the Japanese imperial line is derived from her offspring. We are told that she gave the three treasures—sword, curved jewel, and mirror—to her grandson Ninigi, who descended from heaven to the top of Mount Takachiho in Kyūshū. Ninigi was an ancestor of the legendary Jimmu Tennō (imperial), the first emperor of Japan who is supposed to have founded the imperial dynasty in 660 B.C. The three treasures of Amaterasu became the imperial regalia.

What probably happened is that the Yamato clan, which initially worshiped Amaterasu as their ancestress, subjugated other clans and imposed their deity upon them. By the first century A.D. the Yamato chieftain began to claim himself the descendant of the sun goddess, although Japan was then still much divided. As the influence of the Yamato clan expanded, the prestige of Amaterasu increased. By the time the myth of the sun goddess was put into writing in the eighth century, Amaterasu had already become the supreme deity of Shinto.

Susanowo, because of his many misdeeds, was at last expelled from Heaven and banished to the province of Izumo in the western section of Honshū Island. Here he married a local princess and slaughtered an eight-headed serpent, in whose body he found a sword. He presented it to Amaterasu as a gift, and it became one of the imperial symbols. This story shows that Susanowo was probably the ancestral god of the clan of Izumo. At one time the Yamato and Izumo clans must have been rivals. But when the Yamato eventually subjugated Izumo, it incorporated Susanowo into the myth of Amaterasu. Today there is a shrine in Izumo dedicated to the son of Susanowo. It is the most ancient Shinto shrine in Japan.

Not only do Shinto myths give one a clue to the study of the ancient history of Japan; they also provide the Japanese with archetypes to follow and practice. Basic events in human life—such as birth, marriage, recreation, farming, construction, and death—find their cosmic counterparts in the myths. To be a Shintoist means to practice "the Way after the manner of Gods" (*Kami nagara no Michi*).[6] In the labyrinth of Shinto mythology one can discern two themes: one is cosmological and is embodied in stories that depict the primordial phenomena of nature and men in an agricultural society; the other is imperial and is contained in stories that deal with the mythological origin of the royal house of Japan. The cosmological theme provides a foundation for the communal or folk religion; the imperial theme furnishes the basis for the Japanese state.

THE CLASSIC PERIOD

Early Japan was divided by numerous clans, each of which was ruled by a chieftain. The kami was the guiding and protecting spirit of the group. Since the clan dominated its own area, its kami often served as the local god. In many cases, the deity did not have an individual name; it was simply called the kami of the region and was often associated with a holy tree, rock, mountain, or field.[7] The kami provided a cosmic reference, which enabled the people to have an experience of transcendence. Even during the third century A.D., there were still more than thirty autonomous clan regions. But the imperial clan established the Yamato dynasty at the turn of the fourth century A.D. As this dynasty began to consolidate the country, its deity, Amaterasu, gradually became a national divinity. Historical Japan as a unified country began in the seventh century. The rise of strong dynasties in China (Tang) and Korea (Silla) inspired Japan to unite for the purpose of national defense. But even after Japan was united, Shinto continued to retain its communal character, with the worship of regional gods and the exercise of religious activities around a shrine.

Shinto did not have an ecclesiastical organization until the arrival of Buddhism in the sixth century. The appointment of professional priests by the imperial court as well by as the clan rulers was inspired by the presence of Buddhist priests. Since the imperial court aimed at building a unified state, it needed all the intellectual and spiritual resources it could muster and therefore sponsored all three religions (Confucianism, Buddhism, Shinto). Both Buddhist temples and Shinto shrines were erected at the national level by the emperor and at the regional level by clan chieftains. As a result, a class of Shinto priests arose whose work included performing ceremonies on behalf of the state. Some of the priestly families were hereditary. In the Nara period (A.D. 710–794), when the imperial court was in Nara, a bureau of Shinto affairs was established by the state and Shinto traditions were recorded in the *Kojiki* and *Nihongi*. Since the time of unification, both Buddhist and Shinto priests have served as officials of the emperor and the clan leaders. It should be pointed out that Confucianism, Buddhism, and Shinto in Japan complemented one another: Confucianism regulated family relations, as well as the relation between subjects and rulers; Buddhism gave the state a metaphysics in which the emperor is viewed as the physical representation of the cosmic Buddha; Shinto gave the state a body of myths which legitimize the imperial charisma and offer the Japanese a cosmic outlook on life.

Because it was receptive to continental thought and practice, Shinto is syncretic in character. The Japanese scholars in the seventh and eighth centuries knew Han Confucianism, which emphasizes the mutuality between the emperor and the cosmos: the right rulership of the emperor enhances the harmonizing of Heaven, earth, and man, the equilibrium of the Yin-Yang forces, and the regularity of the Five Agents (wood, fire, earth, metal, and water). Such ideas were reflected in Prince Shōtoku's seventeen-article constitution of 604 and in the *Kojiki* and *Nihongi*. Confucianism offered Shinto an ethical interpretation of theocracy; Buddhism inspired Shinto to inaugurate its own ecclesiastical system and rituals.

In the Heian period (A.D. 794–1192), when the imperial court was in Heian, Buddhism blossomed in Japan; two of the most prominent Buddhist sects, Tendai (based on the Lotus Sutra) and Shingon (Esoteric Buddhism), were founded in this era. It was also a time of cultural renascence, when indigenous literature, art, architecture, and music flourished. The Japanese rulers and aristocrats considered Buddhism superior to Shinto, and Shinto continued to absorb Buddhist elements. As a result, there arose the doctrine of Ryōbu (Two-Sided) Shinto, the view that Shinto gods are the incarnations of Buddhas or Bodhisattvas. This doctrine, which was expounded by Esoteric Buddhism, was also acceptable to Shinto priests. It was inspired by the dual character of the Buddha nature in Mahayana: the absolute nature of Buddha is transcendent, but the relative nature of Buddha is immanent. Hence the kami are the manifestations of the absolute nature of Buddha. Accordingly, Amaterasu was viewed as the incarnation of Mahavairocana, Buddha of the Brilliant Light, the Supreme God of Esoteric Buddhism.

During this period Buddhist priests performed their worship in the inner sanctuaries of many Shinto shrines as well as in Buddhist temples. At a popular level, we also see the convergence between Buddhism and Shinto. For instance, Jizō, the Bodhisattva of the nether world, who delivers souls of the dead from Hell, a popular deity in China and Japan, now became the *"kami* of the road."[8] According to Shinto tradition, the latter inhabits the roadside where infants of poor families are buried and delivers them from the lower world.

Another evidence of amalgamation was the rise of the *yama-*

bushi (mountain ascetics) during this period. These people, most of them married, lived in sacred mountains and practiced asceticism. They also served as guides for those pilgrims who climbed sacred mountains as acts of merit. In addition, they were trained in divination, healing, and exorcism.

THE MEDIEVAL PERIOD

The Kamakura period (1192–1336) and the subsequent years until the end of the sixteenth century constitute the medieval period in Japan. Imperial power existed only nominally in Heian (Kyōto), while the actual power of the government fell into the hands of shōguns, or generalissimos. In order to keep the feudal government separate from the imperial court and the aristocrats, the feudal regime was established in Kamakura for more than a century; it then moved to Muromachi, a district of Kyōto, where it stayed for the remainder of the period. In addition to the transfer of political power from the court to the military rulers, medieval Japan was characterized by war among different ruling clans, the expansion of religious sects that stressed personal faith and salvation, the rise of Shinto nationalism, and an awareness of the tragic sense of life as the result of the passing of the aristocratic mode of existence and the experience of war and violence. There was a general feeling of the transience of all things, nostalgia for the past, and a stoic acceptance of a simple and rustic manner of living.

Medieval Japan saw the dissemination of Buddhist metaphysics and Confucian philosophy among wider segments of the populace. The maturation of these thoughts within the matrix of Japanese life, together with the impact of social crises, resulted in the development of religious and philosophical movements that were truly syncretic and indigenous. The Kamakura period witnessed the wide spread of Amidism (Pure Land) and the rise of Zen and Nichiren Buddhism. The military atmosphere of the time probably contributed to the emergence of the well-disciplined and strong religious personalities who headed these groups. Meanwhile, the yama-bushi were now organized into the Shugen-dō (Order of Mountain Ascetics), which maintained close association with both Buddhism and Shinto.

Shinto in this period tended to worship the kami of dominant clans whose leaders were the actual rulers of Japan. Hence Hachiman (kami of war), the ancestor god of the Minamoto clan which held the shōgunate in Kamakura, now became the manifestation of Amitabha Buddha, the Supreme Deity of Amidism. Thus, the phenomenon of Ryōbu (Two-Sided) Shinto continued to prevail. But in spite of the deep penetration of Buddhism in this period, Shinto became conscious of its ancient origin and distinctiveness and attempted to free itself from its growing subservience to Buddhism. This new gesture was due partly to Mongol invasions and partly to the intellectual maturity of Shinto leaders.

The Mongol invasions of 1274 and 1281 gave impetus to Japanese national consciousness. The stormy winds that destroyed the Mongol ships were viewed as the supernatural act of Shinto divinities, such as Amaterasu, the sun goddess, and Hachiman, the kami of war. There also arose a number of outstanding Shinto scholars who began to articulate their faith vis-à-vis rival religions. Thus, a few years later, Kitabatake, a royal supporter of the court, wrote that Japan was superior to China and India because her emperors followed an unbroken line of succession derived from a divine origin. Kitabatake also provided an ethical interpretation for the three elements of the imperial regalia: the sword symbolizes wisdom; the jewel, compassion; and the mirror, honesty.[9]

At just about the time when Kitabatake was writing on the political aspect of Shinto, a body of literature called the Five Classics of Shinto was discovered. This work deals with the history of the imperial shrine at Ise and expounds Shinto theology and ethics; it was used as the basic source of the Only (Yuiitsu) Shinto, a movement of the fifteenth century and later, which claimed that since this literature has existed from time immemorial, it is the pure Shinto teaching. Actually, this work, which had been produced in medieval Japan, was much influenced by Buddhist thought.

A chief proponent of the Only Shinto doctrine was Yoshida Kanetomo (1435–1511), a member of a leading Shinto priestly family, who wrote about the primacy of Shinto teaching. He proposed the view that Buddhas and Bodhisattvas are the manifestations of kami, who are the original gods. This is a reversal of the early doctrine of Ryōbu (Two-Sided) Shinto. But Yoshida's pure Shinto owes much to Esoteric Buddhism and the Yin-Yang school of Confucianism. His writing shows that by the fifteenth century Shinto scholars had reached intellectual maturity and that alien thoughts had become a natural expression of Shinto teaching.

THE TOKUGAWA PERIOD

Roman Catholic Christianity entered Japan prior to the Tokugawa period. The Jesuit missionary Francis Xavier arrived in 1549, and was soon followed by the Franciscans and Dominicans. Xavier adopted Dainichi (the Great Sun Buddha of Esoteric Buddhism) as the name of the Christian God,[10] which shows his interest in appropriating indigenous religious terms for the expression of Christian faith. Nagasaki, a small fishing village on the western coast, now became a Christian as well as an international trading center. It is estimated that by 1581 there were about 150,000 Christians in Japan.

But Christianity met a setback during the early days of the Tokugawa regime. This was due in part to the strong loyalty given to the foreign priests by the Japanese Christians, which was viewed as an infringement of the shōgun's prerogative, and in part to reports that made the government suspect that these foreign missionaries were engaging in subversive activities on behalf of their native countries, chiefly Spain and Portugal. Hence, in 1614 the government issued a decree banning Christianity; this was followed by waves of Christian persecution in which churches were destroyed and missionaries deported. Because of these oppressions and other grievances, a Christian insurrection arose in 1637 in Kyūshū, which was subdued by government troops at the cost of much bloodshed. The destruction of Christianity was temporarily accomplished, but some families continued to follow Christianity in secret for generations.

It should be pointed out that religious revolt was not new in Japan; Buddhist groups had taken up arms against the state earlier. What was new about the Christian revolt was its connection with a religion whose priests were European. The government had allowed the entrance of Christian missions largely because of the foreign trade for which they opened the way. But the Tokugawa authority felt that it was better to sacrifice economic benefit than to endanger national security and the position of the shōgunate. In 1638 the government closed the door to both foreign merchants and missionaries, although limited trade with the Dutch continued. This self-imposed seclusion was not removed until the middle of the nineteenth century.

Although Buddhism continued to receive governmental backing, the real religiopolitical philosophy favored by the Tokugawa regime was the neo-Confucianism of Chu Hsi (1130–1200). The primary aim of the Tokugawa rulers was the building of a centralized state on the basis of law and order; in neo-Confucianism they found ideas, such as the concepts of humanism, rationalism, harmony, and state-craft, that were suitable to the establishment of a feudal but civil state. With the enthusiastic support of Tokugawa Iyeyasu (see Figure 25.1) and through the writings of three generations of Hayashi (Ha-yashi Razan—who served as an adviser to Tokugawa Iyeyasu—his son, and his grandson), neo-Confucianism became the official school of the government. But Japanese neo-Confucianism was different from its counterpart in China. By and large, it tended to interpret the rational principle (Li) as the Way of Gods, meaning Shinto.[11] Also, neo-Confucian ethics were explained in relation to the ethics of warriors (samurai); hence military virtue was incorporated. Japanese Confucians tended to use the original neo-Confucian concepts to support the existing feudal society, and the divine origin of the imperial house.

We can see that neo-Confucianism was closely allied with Shinto and also stimulated its revival. This was partly because the Shinto precepts were reenforced by the ethical and political thinking of neo-Confucianism and partly because the historicism of Chu Hsi motivated the Japanese scholars to pursue early Japanese history, including the Shinto cosmogony. A Confucian-Shinto movement arose in this period under the leadership of Yamazaki Ansai (1618–1682), who translated the Confucian term *ching* (reverence) as meaning devotion to Shinto gods and to the emperor of Japan, thus combining the ethics of the former with the religion of the latter.

Another synthesis between Shinto and Confucianism was the Bushidō (the Way of the Warrior). In addition to including Bud-dhist elements, such as a belief in simplicity and transitoriness as the law of this world, Bushidō combined the humanistic, literary, and ethical interests of neo-Confucianism with the traditional values of the warrior class. Yamaga Sokō (1622–1685), who lived in the peaceful reign of Tokugawa was an early architect of Bushidō. Since the samurai were no longer needed for military activities, Yamaga felt that they should now devote their time to literature, art, and other humanistic disciplines. Indeed, a warrior should behave like a gentleman and should cultivate all his talents for the service of the emperor. This view of the ideal man had a pervasive influence on Japanese society. In the late Tokugawa and the Meiji periods, the government leaders possessed both military skill and intellectual acumen.

As a consequence of neo-Confucian interest in historical research, the movement of National Learning arose in the eighteenth century, with the aim of finding among the historical documents of early Japan those elements which could be regarded as truly indigenous. This movement continued throughout the Tokugawa period and became further intensified in the time of the Meiji. Long years of self-imposed isolation also contributed to such national introspection. The Shinto scholars were aware that even the earliest Japanese historical documents contained elements of Confucianism, Taoism, and Buddhism. Baffled by this problem, they turned to early Shinto hymns, prayers, and poems in search of unique Japanese qualities. Kamo Mabuchi (1697–1769), a national leader of this movement, considered an eighth-century anthology of poems, the *Man'yōshū*, (Collection of Myriad Leaves), to be an unadultered Japanese work which best represented the spirit of Japan. In these poems he saw a spontaneous, simple, honest, and masculine quality of Japanese life.

Motoori Norinaga (1730–1801), a student of Mabuchi, continued the same search. He acclaimed the *Kojiki*, the oldest annals of Japan, as the basic Shinto Scripture, and spent more than thirty years on this work, which contains the legends and genealogy of the imperial family, together with anecdotes. Although the *Kojiki* offers little substance for intellectual stimulation, Motoori discovered in it a pure and primal human sentiment, as expressed by the adoration of the sun goddess. He also contended that its two creator-deities, Takami-musubi (vitality) and Kami-musubi (fertility), were the sublimated expression of man's life impulse.[12] His purpose was to emphasize the nonrational and emotional sentiment of man, which he considered to be genuinely Japanese. The rational or ethical contents of the early Japanese writings have their origin on the continent and represent a corruption of Japanese thought. Following the same method of hermeneutics, he considered the *Tale of the Genji*, a novel of the Heian period, the best representative of Japanese concern with the sensitive aspect of human life, or *mono no aware*.[13] The latter term has become a key word in Japanese literary criticism. It should be pointed out that in spite of the efforts of Mabuchi and Motoori, their interpretations of Shinto were influenced by the *Tao Te Ching* of Taoism.

The National Learning movement took a new turn in the nineteenth century under the leadership of Hirata Atsutane (1776–1843). Unlike his predecessor Motoori, who was mainly interested in a theory of Japanese sentiment, Atsutane wanted to demonstrate the superiority of Shinto over other religions. Thus he represented a more extreme type of religious nationalism and anticipated the Shinto movement in the Meiji period. Atsutane possessed a considerable store of Western knowledge, which he had obtained through Dutch scientific books in Japanese translation; he had also learned Christian theology through books in Chinese, written by Jesuit missionaries in China. His method was to use other sources to explain the superiority of Shinto. Thus the heliocentric theory of Copernicus was invoked for the defense of sun adoration. His interpretation of Takami-musubi as the creator-god of the Shinto pantheon shows some influence of Christian theology.

THE MEIJI PERIOD

Religion in Meiji Japan should be viewed within the context of nationalism. Buddhism lost favor because the government wanted to promote Shinto for nationalistic purposes. From 1869 to 1872 Buddhism was subject to persecution. The government made efforts to eliminate the Buddhist elements from the Ryōbu (Two-Sided) Shinto that had been in existence for 1,000 years; thus Buddhist images were removed from Shinto shrines and Buddhist priests residing in these shrines were ordered to return to the laity or else to take up Shinto priesthood. At the same time, many Buddhist temples were destroyed and their lands confiscated. In 1872, however, the government changed its policy to one of forcing both the Shinto and Buddhist priests to teach a specially prepared curriculum, which was Shinto in essence. This forced Shinto-Buddhist collaboration came to an end three years later when the government again separated these two religions. After 1882 Buddhism was made a private religion; it no longer had the official sanction of the state. In spite of the government's efforts to separate Shinto from Buddhism, it was not possible to have a Shinto without certain Buddhist ingredients, since these two religions had been influencing each other for so long. Although Buddhism suffered material loss and was disestablished in the Meiji era, these reverses actually caused its revitalization. There was a spiritual awakening, evidenced in the production of Buddhist philosophical works, in lay participation, and in the Buddhist defense of the separation of church and state.

In the early Meiji period there existed two kinds of Shinto: the Shrine Shinto and the Sect Shinto. The former refers to the traditional sanctuaries, some national, but most of them communal; the latter refers to newly developed sects, comparable to Protestant denominations in America. Shrine Shinto was the custodian of traditional beliefs and practices; Sect Shinto consisted of voluntary associations with charismatic founders. The common ground between them was that both accepted the theology of kami, although a particular shrine or sect emphasized certain divinities of its own preference.

In 1882 the Meiji government separated these two bodies of Shinto; the shrines of State Shinto were called Jinja (God House), and those of the Sects were called Kyōkai (Church) or Kyōha (Sect). The function of the State Shinto shrines was to teach the national morality, while the sects and their shrines were allowed to exist as private religious denominations. The Bureau of Shrines was created in the Department of Home Affairs to supervise the state shrines, and the Bureau of Religions was created in the Department of Education to oversee the activities of Sect Shinto as well as Buddhism and Christianity. The state shrines received financial support from the local, prefectural, or national government, depending on the grade of a shrine; the Shinto sects depended on private support.

There were two motives for the government's decision to separate the two kinds of Shinto: (1) The state sought to distinguish Shinto as education from Shinto as a religion. Shinto as education consists of a body of moral beliefs and practices, including the emperor cult, which all Japanese should follow and which belongs to the jurisdiction of the state. Shinto as a religion consists of sectarian doctrines and practices, which are subject to individual differences and personal interpretations; this is a private affair and falls within the jurisdiction of sects. (2) The government wished Japan to be known as a modern nation that follows the policy of separation of church and state. Shinto as a religion was given the same status as Buddhism and Christianity (the ban against the latter was lifted in 1872).

FIGURE 25.2 Izumo Shrine, the most ancient shrine of Japan, dedicated to the son of Susanowo. (*Japan National Tourist Organization*)

Although State Shinto was officially declared a national teaching, it was in fact the state religion of Meiji Japan; it involved the observance of religious ceremonies, belief in kami, and the divine origin of the emperors. The ultimate purpose of State Shinto was to indoctrinate all Japanese with nationalism and loyalty to the imperial house.

Shinto Sects

The Shinto sects arose as popular movements in the late nineteenth century as a reaction against Buddhism and Shinto nationalism. They also represented the discontent of the lower stratum of Japanese society, especially the peasants, against the oppressions

of the late Tokugawa and early Meiji regimes. These sects emphasized spontaneous, vitalistic religion and practiced shamanistic rites and faith healing. Although the Meiji government recognized thirteen Shinto sects, there were other groups that were considered to be subsects of these thirteen. In the following we present the five types of Shinto sects and describe a representative sect for each type.[14]

OLD OR PURE SHINTO. § Three Shinto sects—Shinto Taikyō (Great Society), Shinri-kyō (Divine Truth Society), and Taisha-kyō (Great Shrine Society)—accepted the traditional Shinto pantheon and practiced the emperor cult. The Taisha-kyō was devoted particularly to the ancestor kami of the shrine in Izumo (see Figure 25.2) on the

western shores of Honshū. The Taisha-kyō was recognized as an independent sect in 1882 as the result of a theological quarrel with the imperial shrine of Ise. The kami of the Izumo shrine was believed to control fortune and agriculture and to bring happy marriages.

CONFUCIAN SHINTO. § Two Shinto sects—Shinto Shūsei Ha (Improving and Consolidating Society), Taisei-kyō (Great Accomplishment Society)—followed the synthesis between Confucianism and Shinto. The Shūsei Ha was founded in 1876 by a patriotic supporter of the imperial rule. This group believed that man receives his body from his parents and his spirit from the Creator-triad of the Shinto pantheon.[15] But these three kami were identified with Shang Ti (Ruler Above) of Confucianism.[16]

SHINTO MOUNTAIN SECTS. § Three Shinto sects—Jikkō-kyō (Practical Conduct Society), Fusō-kyō (Mount Fuji Society), and Mitake-kyō (Great Mountain Society)—were closely related to the Order of Mountain Ascetics (Shugen-dō), which represented a synthesis between Japanese folk religion and Buddhism. These mountain groups were usually associated with Mount Fuji and Mount Ontake. Fourfifths of the land of Japan is mountainous country, and it is on the mountains that the gods are supposed to dwell. The mountain sect called Mitake-kyō lived in the northern part of Honshū. This group, which owed its beginning to an oil merchant who became interested in Mount Ontake in 1873, believed in a triad of gods, the chief one being Kuni-Toko-Tachi-no-Mikoto (Earth Eternal Stand Deity), who is the first god mentioned in the *Nihongi*[17] and is the source of creation. Members of this group followed certain shamanistic practices; some served as mediums. They carried out complicated rituals of purification, one of which involved walking over burning charcoal.[18]

PURIFICATION SECTS. § Two Shinto sects—Misogi-kyō (Purification Society) and Shinshū-kyō (Divine Learning Society)—emphasized the rituals of purification that are an ancient Shinto tradition deriving from the fear of pollution. The Shinshū-kyō, which first be-

FIGURE 25.3   Meiji Shrine, Tōkyō, dedicated to Emperor Meiji. (*Japan National Tourist Organization*)

came an independent sect in 1884 although its founder had been developing its teaching for some time before, considered these rituals to be the "unspoken teaching" of the gods. The sacred teaching is inwardly communicated to the practitioner when he participates in these acts, so that a purification rite is a means of cleansing evil as well as the way to mystic experience. Ritual performances also benefit the state by ensuring good crops and national peace. Some rites of purification involve ordeals; among them are the fire-walking ceremony and the ritual of trial by hot water.[19]

Shinto Sects with a Monotheistic or Pantheistic Tendency

Three Shinto sects—Kurozumi-kyō (Society of Kurozumi, the founder), Konkō-kyō (Society of Konkō, the kami of the group), and Tenri-kyō (Divine Reason Society)—emphasized the unity between the One and the Many, with reference to gods, and also practiced faith healing. The Tenri-kyō sect was founded by a peasant woman named Nakayama Miki (1798–1887), who as a child was a devotee of Pure Land (Amidism) Buddhism. In 1838 Miki experienced a trance in which she was possessed by the true

God, Tenri (Divine Reason). During the three days of her trance she also healed the sick. Henceforth she devoted herself entirely to the teaching of the true God, accompanying it by faith healing. She sold her property for the benefit of the poor and lived in extreme poverty. She taught that diseases are due to greed, and that restoration of original purity is the way to health and happiness. Surrender to God and service to others were also emphasized. Although the Tenri-kyō was recognized as an independent Shinto sect in 1908, it began to grow in the late nineteenth century. Even before the founder's death in 1887, the Tenri-kyō was a nationwide religion; it is indeed the fastest-growing sect in Japan today. Although this sect has drawn most of its members from the peasant class, it is also interested in education and foreign missions, and before World War II it sent missionaries to countries in Asia, including China.

MODERN SHINTO

The history of Shinto from the end of the Meiji period (1868–1912) to the cessation of World War II (1945) was inseparable from Japanese military and territorial expansion. The nation at the same time developed in two seemingly opposite directions: increasing westernization in terms of industrialization and technology, and increasing ethnocentrism in terms of religion and ideology. Confucianism was promoted in the twentieth century as a rational basis for the justification of Japanese virtues in connection with her global ambition. The Way of Confucian persuasion was now identified with the imperial way of Japan,[20] and Confucianism and Shinto became close allies in this period. In fact, during the years of military invasions in China, Japanese leaders regarded Japan as the protector and disseminator of Asian civilization against the encroachment of Western materialism.

The defeat of Japan by the Allied forces in 1945 ended State Shinto in Japan, which had begun in 1882. Through a directive issued by the occupation forces in 1945, State Shinto shrines were

FIGURE 25.4   Praying at Yasukuni Shrine, near Tōkyō. The shrine was built in memory of soldiers killed in war. (*Fujihira from Monkmeyer*)

severed from government sponsorship and returned to their former status as private religious institutions. The same directive also abolished the Bureau of Shrines in the Department of Home Affairs. A New Year's Day imperial rescript was issued in 1946, rejecting the view that Japanese emperors are divine. The new Constitution of 1947 states that the emperor is a symbol of the state and of the unity of the people. Although State Shinto was disestablished, the status of shrines remains ambiguous because a people's religious beliefs cannot be changed overnight.

There are about 100,000 Shinto shrines in Japan today. The Association of Shinto Shrines, which was formed in 1946, is composed of 80,000 shrine members.[21] The elimination of State Shinto does not change the basic structure of shrines that have been in existence for centuries. During the period of the existence of State Shinto, however, the shrines were financed to a large extent by the state; today they depend on community funds and private offerings.

The heart of Shinto is a communal religion centered around a shrine, often located in a wooded area and surrounded by scenic beauty. The most sacred part of a shrine is the *honden,* the inner sanctuary which is higher than the surrounding buildings and in which the god entity (*goshintai*) dwells. The god entity may be symbolized by a mirror, a hill, a rock, a tree, or a small pole of wood or bamboo called *nusa* (or *gohei*). Offerings such as green leaves or dishes of raw food are placed in the inner sanctuary.

The regular rituals are performed by priests or priestesses in the *haiden* (worship hall), which stands in front of the inner sanctuary. This is where visitors pay homage to the divinity. One may also leave one's offerings in the treasure box. Cleanliness and silence are strictly observed. The *torii* (Shinto gate) stands at the entrance to the shrine, and as a rule, there is a long passage between the torii and the worship hall. There may in fact be a series of torii along the passage, which remind the visitor that he is now entering the sacred place.

One important function of the shrine is the holding of celebrations of such seasonal festivals as the autumn harvest and the purification rite. Although the clergy preside on these occasions, important officials or leading citizens also take part in them. There are some national shrines related to patriotism. The Meiji Jingû (Shrine) is dedicated to Emperor Meiji (see Figure 25.3), and the Yasukuni Shrine (see Figure 25.4) is dedicated to the memory of soldiers killed in war. These shrines are similar to national monuments.

When the policy of religious freedom was adopted in 1945 by the postwar government, the number of Shinto sects rapidly increased. A recent report indicates that there are now 142 Shinto sects out of a total of 379 denominations of different religions.[22] This phenomenal increase of Shinto groups was due to the separation of the splinter groups from the thirteen older sects as well as because of a need for spiritual security as a result of the oppression of war and the uncertainty of life following the national defeat. Many of these Shinto sects, together with other newly founded groups with Buddhist and Christian affiliations, are today referred to as the New Religion.

The New Religion of Japan is highly eclectic. These sects possess the common features of Japanese folk religion: shamanism, exorcism, sorcery, divination, faith healing, and the like, and are actually modern versions of the old religion. Members of these new sects are largely drawn from the lower middle-class population and have a predominance of middle-aged and older women. A basic problem that postwar Japan faces today is the disintegration of the cosmic orientation of life as well as of the traditional values. These new sects give the ordinary Japanese a sense of continuity with the past and a simple and direct moral code as a personal guide. They also offer the people a sense of belonging at a time when urbanization has gradually destroyed the traditional clan-centered life.

NOTES

1. Joseph M. Kitagawa, "Prehistoric Background of Japanese Religion," *History of Religions,* Vol. II, No. 2 (Winter, 1963), p. 309.
2. *Ibid.,* p. 308.
3. *Ibid.*
4. *Ibid.,* pp. 327–328.
5. *Ibid.,* pp. 309, 317.
6. Masaharu Anesaki, *History of Japanese Religion* (Tōkyō: Charles E. Tuttle, 1963), p. 20.
7. Joseph M. Kitagawa, *Religion in Japanese History* (New York: Columbia University Press, 1966), p. 15.
8. *Ibid.,* p. 84.
9. *Sources of Japanese Tradition,* compiled by Ryusaku Tsunoda, William Theodore de Bary, Donald Keene (New York: Columbia University Press, 1958), p. 281.
10. Kitagawa, *Religion in Japanese History,* p. 139.
11. *Ibid.,* p. 156.

12. *Sources of Japanese Tradition,* pp. 508–509.
13. *Ibid.,* p. 509.
14. Kitagawa, *Religion in Japanese Society,* pp. 215–220.
15. The creator-triad are Ame-no-Minaka-nushi (the creator), Takami-musubi (the male deity), and Kami-musubi (the female deity).
16. Kitagawa, *Religion in Japanese History,* p. 217.
17. D. C. Holtom, *The National Faith of Japan* (London: Kegan Paul, Trench, Trubner, 1938), p. 228.
18. Masaharu Anesaki, *Religious Life of the Japanese People* (Tōkyō: Society for International Cultural Relations, 1961), p. 24.
19. Holtom, *op. cit.,* p. 238.
20. Kitagawa, *Religion in Japanese History,* p. 258.
21. *Ibid.,* p. 279.
22. *Ibid.,* p. 281.

Bibliography

BUDDHISM

*Basham, A. L. *The Wonder That Was India*. New York: Evergreen, 1959.

Bharati, Agehananda. *The Tantric Tradition*. London: Rider, 1965.

Bhikshu Sangharakshita. *A Survey of Buddhism*. Bangalore: Indian Institute of World Culture, 1957.

*Briggs, William, ed. *Anthology of Zen*. New York: Evergreen, 1961.

Buddhism in Translation, by Henry C. Warren, New York: Atheneum, 1963.

Buddhist Scriptures, trans. by Edward Conze. Baltimore: Penguin, 1959.

*Burtt, Edwin A., ed. *The Teachings of the Compassionate Buddha*. New York: Mentor, 1955.

A Catena of Buddhist Scriptures from the Chinese, trans. by Samuel Beal. London: Trubner, 1871.

Ch'en, Kenneth. *Buddhism in China*. Princeton. Princeton University Press, 1964.

Conze, Edward. *Buddhist Meditation*. London: Allen and Unwin, 1956.

*————. *Buddhism: Its Essence and Development*. New York: Harper Torchbooks, 1959.

————. *Buddhist Thought in India*. London: George Allen, 1962.

*————, ed., in collaboration with I. B. Horner, D. Snellgrove, A. Waley. *Buddhist Texts through the Ages*. New York: Harper Torchbooks, 1964.

*Coomaraswamy, Ananda K. *Buddha and the Gospel of Buddhism*, rev. by Dona Luisa Coomaraswamy. New York: Harper Torchbooks, 1964.

Ekvall, Robert B. *Religious Observances in Tibet*. Chicago: University of Chicago Press, 1964.

* Indicates paperback

Eliot, Charles. *Japanese Buddhism*. New York: Barnes and Noble, 1959.

*Fung Yu-lan. *The Spirit of Chinese Philosophy,* trans. by E. R. Hughes. Boston: Beacon, 1964.

*Hamilton, Clarence H., ed. *Selections from Buddhist Literature*. Indianapolis: Bobbs-Merrill, 1952.

Hodous, Lewis. *Buddhism and Buddhists in China*. New York: Macmillan, 1924.

Humphreys, Christmas. *Buddhism*. New York: Barnes and Noble, 1962.

*————. *Zen Buddhism*. New York: Macmillan, 1963.

Johnstone, Reginald F. *Buddhist China*. London: J. Murray, 1913.

Keith, Arthur Berriedale. *Buddhist Philosophy*. Oxford: Clarendon Press, 1923.

Kitagawa, Joseph M. *Religion in Japanese History*. New York: Columbia University Press, 1966.

Lee, Shao-chang. *Popular Buddhism in China,* with translations of Ten Buddhist Poems, Thirty-two Buddhist Proverbs, Hsüan Tsang's *Essence of the Wisdom Sutra,* and Kumarajiva's *Diamond Sutra*. Shanghai: Commercial Press, 1940.

Morgan, Kenneth W., ed. *The Path of the Buddha: Buddhism Interpreted by Buddhists*. New York: Ronald, 1956.

Percheron, Maurice. *The Marvelous Life of the Buddha,* trans. by Adrienne Foulke. New York: St. Martin's, 1960.

Pratt, James B. *The Pilgrimage of Buddhism*. New York: Macmillan, 1928.

*Rahula, Walpola. *What the Buddha Taught*. New York: Evergreen, 1962.

Reichelt, Karl L. *Truth and Tradition in Chinese Buddhism,* trans. by Kathrina Van Wageenen Bugge. Shanghai: Commercial Press, 1928.

Saunders, E. Dale. *Buddhism in Japan*. Philadelphia: University of Pennsylvania Press, 1964.

Snellgrove, David L. *Buddhist Himalaya*. Oxford: Bruno Cassirer, 1957.

*Stcherbatsky, Th. *Buddhist Logic,* 2 vols. New York: Dover, 1962.

*Suzuki, D. T. *Zen Buddhism,* ed. by William Barrett. New York: Doubleday Anchor, 1956.

*————. *Essays in Zen Buddhism*. New York: Evergreen, 1961.

*————. *Outlines of Mahayana Buddhism*. New York: Schocken, 1963.

*————. *An Introduction to Zen Buddhism*. New York: Evergreen, 1964.

Takakusu, Junjiro. *The Essentials of Buddhist Philosophy,* ed. by Chan Wing-tsit and C. A. Moore. Hawaii: University of Hawaii Press, 1949.

Teachings of Tibetan Yoga, trans. by Garma C. C. Chang. New York: University Books, 1963.

Thomas, Edward J. *The History of Buddhist Thought.* New York: Barnes and Noble, 1951.

*Watts, Alan W. *The Spirit of Zen.* New York: Evergreen, 1960.

Welch, Holmes. *The Practice of Chinese Buddhism, 1900–1950.* Cambridge: Harvard University Press, 1967.

Wright, Arthur F. *Buddhism in Chinese History.* Stanford: Stanford University Press, 1959.

Yang I-fan. *Buddhism in China.* Hong Kong: Union Press, 1956.

Zen Flesh, Zen Bones: A Collection of Zen and Pre-Zen Writings, compiled by Paul Reps in collaboration with Nyogen Senzaki. New York: Doubleday Anchor, 1961.

*Zimmer, Heinrich. *Philosophies of India,* ed. by Joseph Campbell. New York: Meridian, 1956.

*————. *Myths and Symbols in Indian Art and Civilization,* ed. by Joseph Campbell. New York: Harper Torchbooks, 1962.

CONFUCIANISM

Briere, O. *Fifty Years of Chinese Philosophy: 1898–1950,* trans. by L. G. Thompson. London: Allen and Unwin, 1956.

Bruce, J. Percy. *Chu Hsi and His Masters.* London: Probsthain, 1923.

Cairns, Grace E. *Philosophies of History.* New York: Philosophical Library, 1962.

Chan Wing-tsit. *Religious Trends in Modern China.* New York: Columbia University Press, 1953.

————. *A Source Book in Chinese Philosophy.* Princeton: Princeton University Press, 1963.

Chang, Carsun. *The Development of Neo-Confucian Thought,* 2 vols. New York: Bookman Associates, 1957–1962.

Chu Hsi. *The Philosophy of Human Nature,* trans. by J. P. Bruce, London: Probsthain, 1922.

*Confucius. *The Analects of Confucius,* trans. by Arthur Waley. New York: Vintage, 1938.

Creel, Herrlee G. *The Birth of China.* New York: Ungar, 1954.

*————. *Confucius and the Chinese Way.* New York: Harper Torchbooks, 1960.

*————. *Chinese Thought: From Confucius to Mao Tse-tung.* New York: Mentor, 1960.

*Day, Clarence B. *The Philosophers of China, Classical and Contemporary.* New York: Citadel, 1962.

The Doctrine of the Mean, trans. by James Legge, *The Chinese Classics,* Vol. II. Hong Kong: University of Hong Kong Press, 1960.

Fairbank, John K., Reischauer, Edwin O., and Craig, Albert M. *A History of East Asian Civilization.* Vol II: *East Asia: The Modern Transformation.* Boston: Houghton Mifflin, 1965.

*Fung Yu-lan. *A Short History of Chinese Philosophy,* ed. by Derk Bodde. New York: Macmillan, 1948.

————. *A History of Chinese Philosophy,* 2 vols., trans. by Derk Bodde. Princeton: Princeton University Press, 1959–1960.

*————. *The Spirit of Chinese Philosophy,* trans. by E. R. Hughes. Boston: Beacon, 1964.

*Goodrich, L. Carrington. *A Short History of the Chinese People.* New York: Harper Torchbooks, 1963.

Graham, A. C. *Two Chinese Philosophers: Ch'eng Ming-tao and Ch'eng Yi-ch'uan.* London: Lund Humphries, 1958.

The Great Learning, trans. by E. R. Hughes, *The Great Learning and the Mean-in-Action.* New York: Dutton, 1943.

Han Fei Tzu. *The Complete Works of Han Fei Tzu,* 2 vols, trans. by W. K. Liao. London: Probsthain, 1960.

*————. *Basic Writings of Han Fei Tzu,* trans. by Burton Watson. New York: Columbia University Press, 1964.

Hsün Tzu. *The Works of Hsüntze,* trans. by Homer H. Dubs. London: Probsthain, 1928.

Hu Shih. *The Development of the Logical Method in Ancient China.* Shanghai: Oriental Book, 1928.

*Lao Tzu. *The Way and Its Power (Tao Te Ching),* trans. by Arthur Waley. New York: Evergreen, 1958.

Legge, James. *The Religions of China.* London: Hodder and Stoughton, 1888.

*Levenson, Joseph R. *Modern China and Its Confucian Past.* New York: Doubleday, 1964.

Lin Yutang. *The Wisdom of China and India.* New York: Random House, 1942.

Mencius. *The Works of Mencius,* trans. by James Legge, in the *Four Books.* Shanghai: Chinese Book Co., n.d.

Mo Ti. *The Ethical and Political Works of Motse,* trans. by Mei Yi-pao. London: Probsthain, 1929.

Needham, Joseph. *Science and Civilization in China.* Vol. II: *History of Scientific Thought.* Cambridge: Cambridge University Press, 1956.

Reischauer, Edwin O., and Fairbank, John K. *A History of East Asian Civilization.* Vol. I: *East Asia the Great Tradition.* Boston: Houghton Mifflin, 1960.

Shih Ching, The Book of Songs, trans. by Arthur Waley. New York: Evergreen, 1960.

Shu Ching, The Shou King, trans. by James Legge, *The Chinese Classics,* Vol. III. Hong Kong: University of Hong Kong, 1960.

Soothill, W. E. *The Three Religions of China.* Oxford: Oxford University Press, 1923.

*Waley, Arthur. *Three Ways of Thought in Ancient China.* New York: Doubleday, 1956.

Wang Yang-ming. *The Philosophy of Wang Yang-ming,* trans. by F. G. Henke. Chicago: Open Court, 1916.

Wright. Arthur, ed. *Studies in Chinese Thought.* Chicago: University of Chicago Press, 1953.

*Yang, C. K. *Religion in Chinese Society.* Berkeley: University of California Press, 1961.

TAOISM

Chan Wing-tsit. *Religious Trends in Modern China.* New York: Columbia University Press, 1953.

―――. *A Source Book in Chinese Philosophy.* Princeton: Princeton University Press, 1963.

*Chuang-tzu. *The Sayings of Chuang Chou,* trans. by James R. Ware. New York: Mentor, 1963.

Day, Clarence B. *Chinese Peasant Cults.* Shanghai: Kelly and Walsh, 1940.

*Fung Yu-lan. *A Short History of Chinese Philosophy,* ed. by Derk Bodde. New York: Macmillan, 1948.

―――. *A History of Chinese Philosophy,* 2 vols., trans. by Derk Bodde. Princeton: Princeton University Press, 1959–1960.

Lao Tzu. *The Wisdom of Laotse,* trans. by Lin Yutang. New York: Random House, 1948.

*―――. *The Way and Its Power (Tao Te Ching),* trans. by Arthur Waley. New York: Evergreen, 1958.

*―――. *Tao Te Ching,* trans. by D. C. Lau. Baltimore: Penguin, 1963.

*————. *The Way of Lao Tzu (Tao Te Ching)*, trans. by Chan Wing-tsit. Indianapolis: Bobbs-Merrill, 1963.

———— and Chuang Tzu. *The Texts of Taoism: The Tao Te Ching and the Writings of Chuang Tzu*, trans. by James Legge. New York: Julian, 1959.

Legge, James. *The Religions of China*. London: Hodder and Stoughton, 1888.

Maspero, H. *Le Taoisme*, in P. Demieville, ed., *Mélanges Posthumes sur les Religions et l'Histoire de la Chine*, Vol. II. Paris: Civilisations du Sud, 1950.

Needham, Joseph. *Science and Civilization in China*. Vol. II: *History of Scientific Thought*. Cambridge: Cambridge University Press, 1956.

Soothill, W. E. *The Three Religions of China*. Oxford: Oxford University Press, 1923.

*Weber, Max. *The Religion of China*, trans. by Hans Gerth. New York: Macmillan, 1964.

Welch, Holmes. *The Parting of the Way*. Boston: Beacon, 1957.

SHINTO

*Anesaki, Masaharu. *Religious Life of the Japanese People*. Tokyo: Society for International Cultural Relations, 1961.

————. *History of Japanese Religion*. Tokyo: Charles E. Tuttle, 1963.

Bunze, William K. *Religion in Japan*. Tokyo: Charles E. Tuttle, 1955.

Fairbank, John K., Reischauer, Edwin O., and Craig, Albert M. *A History of East Asian Civilization*. Vol. II: *East Asia: The Modern Transformation*. Boston: Houghton Mifflin, 1965.

Earhart, H. Byron. *Japanese Religion: Unity and Diversity*. Belmont, Calif.: Dickenson Publishing Co., 1969.

Hammer, Raymond. *Japan's Religious Ferment*. New York: Oxford University Press, 1962.

Holtom, D. C. *The National Faith of Japan*. London: Kegan Paul, 1938.

————. *Modern Japan and Shinto Nationalism*. Chicago: University of Chicago Press, 1943.

*Kennedy, Malcolm. *A Short History of Japan*. New York: Mentor, 1963.

Kitagawa, Joseph M. "Prehistorical Background of Japanese Religion," *History of Religions*, Vol. II, No. 2 (Winter, 1963).

Kitagawa, Joseph M. *Religion in Japanese History*. New York: Columbia University Press, 1966.

The Kojiki, trans. by Basil H. Chamberlain. Kobe: J. L. Thompson, 1932.

Nihongi, 2 vols., trans. by W. G. Aston. London: Kegan Paul, Trench and Trübner, 1956.

Reischauer, Edwin O. *Japan: Past and Present*. New York: Knopf, 1946.

———— and John K. Fairbank. *A History of East Asian Civilization*. Vol. I: *East Asia the Great Tradition*. Boston: Houghton Mifflin, 1960.

Ross, Floyd H. *Shinto: The Way of Japan*. Boston: Beacon, 1956.

The Sacred Scriptures of the Japanese, compiled by Post Wheeler. New York: Henry Schuman, 1952.

Sansom, George B. *Japan: A Short Cultural History,* New York: Appleton-Century, 1943.

————. *A History of Japan*. Stanford: Stanford University Press, 1958.

Smith, Warren W. *Confucianism in Modern Japan*. Tokyo: Hokuseido, 1959.

Sources of Japanese Tradition, compiled by Ryusaku Tsunoda, William Theodore de Bary, Donald Keene. New York: Columbia University Press, 1958.

Index